THE LITURGY OF THE MEDIEVAL CHURCH

THE LITURGY OF THE MEDIEVAL CHURCH

EDITED BY
THOMAS J. HEFFERNAN
AND
E. ANN MATTER

Published for
The Consortium for the Teaching of the Middle Ages, Inc.
by
Medieval Institute Publications

WESTERN MICHIGAN UNIVERSITY

Kalamazoo, Michigan — 2001

Library of Congress Cataloging-in-Publication Data

The liturgy of the medieval church / edited by Thomas J. Heffernan and E. Ann Matter.
p. cm.
Includes bibliographical references and index.
ISBN 1-58044-007-X (alk. paper) -- ISBN 1-58044-008-8 (pbk. : alk. paper)
1. Catholic Church--Liturgy--History. 2. Church history--Middle Ages, 600-1500. I. Heffernan, Thomas J., 1944- II. Matter, E. Ann.

BX1973 .L58 2001
264'.02'00902--dc21

2001030276

Cover photograph: The Metropolitan Museum of Art, The Cloisters Collection, 1970. (1970.324.9)

ISBN 1-58044-007-X (casebound)
1-58044-008-8 (paperbound)

Printed in the United States of America

Cover design by Linda K. Judy

in memory of C. Clifford Flanigan

and James W. McKinnon

CONTENTS

List of Figures, Tables, Maps, and Appendices

Photograph Acknowledgments

Alinari/Art Resource, N.Y. — 285, 299, 306, 319, 321, 322

The British Library — 287

Brown University Library — 448, 451, 456, 458

Carnegie Mellon Libraries — 436, 440

Foto Marburg/Art Resource, N.Y. — 297, 308

Free Library of Philadelphia — 444, 445, 446, 453

Giraudon/Art Resource, N.Y. — 274, 302, 307, 320, 324

Martin-Sabon, Arch. Phot./CNMHS, Paris — 317

The Metropolitan Museum of Art — 278, 376, 387, 393, 394, 397, 399, 403, 406, 408, 411, 413, 414, 416, 418, 419, 421, 422

The Metropolitan Museum of Art, The Cloisters Archive — 312

Pennsylvania State University, University Libraries — 438

Peter Lang AG, Bern, Switzerland — 677

The Pierpont Morgan Library — 477, 479, 484, 491, 495, 499, 504, 505, 507, 511, 512

The Pierpont Morgan Library/Art Resource, N.Y. — 400

Touring Club Italiano, Milan — 335 (2)

The University of Chicago Library — 450

Yale University Press — 276

Contributors

KATHLEEN M. ASHLEY
Professor of English
University of Southern Maine

JONATHAN BLACK
Managing Editor, Mediaeval Studies
Pontifical Institute of Mediaeval Studies, Toronto

STEPHAN BORGEHAMMAR
Docent of Practical Theology
Faculty of Theology, University of Lund

THOMAS P. CAMPBELL
Professor of English
Wabash College

DEMETRIOS J. CONSTANTELOS
Charles Cooper Townsend Sr. Distinguished Professor of History and Religion, Emeritus
Distinguished Research Scholar in Residence
Richard Stockton College of New Jersey

MARTIN R. DUDLEY
Rector, The Priory Church of St Bartholomew the Great Smithfield
City of London

† C. CLIFFORD FLANIGAN
Associate Professor of Comparative Literature
Indiana University

LAWRENCE E. FRIZZELL
Director, The Institute of Judaeo-Christian Studies
Seton Hall University

THOMAS J. HEFFERNAN
Kenneth Curry Distinguished Professor of English and Religious Studies
University of Tennessee, Knoxville

SVEN HELANDER
Docent of Practical Theology
Faculty of Theology, University of Uppsala

J. FRANK HENDERSON
Professor Emeritus
University of Alberta

GABRIELA ILNITCHI
Assistant Professor
Eastman School of Music, University of Rochester

JEANNE E. KROCHALIS
Associate Professor of English and Comparative Literature
Pennsylvania State University, New Kensington

E. ANN MATTER
R. Jean Brownlee Term Professor of Religious Studies
University of Pennsylvania

† JAMES W. MCKINNON
Richard H. Fogel Professor of Music
University of North Carolina

ELIZABETH PARKER MCLACHLAN
Associate Professor of Art History
Rutgers, The State University of New Jersey

ELIZABETH C. PARKER
Professor of Art History
Fordham University

SHERRY L. REAMES
Professor of English
University of Wisconsin, Madison

PAMELA SHEINGORN
Professor of History
Baruch College
Professor of History, Theatre and Medieval Studies
The Graduate Center, City University of New York

NANCY SPATZ
Lecturer in History
Santa Clara University

EVELYN BIRGE VITZ
Professor of French
New York University

ROGER S. WIECK
Curator, Medieval and Renaissance Manuscripts
The Pierpont Morgan Library

AMBROSE-ARISTOTLE ZOGRAPHOS
Archimadrite in Mission of the Ecumenical Patriarchate
of Constantinople and New Rome
Seoul, Korea

INTRODUCTION TO THE LITURGY OF THE MEDIEVAL CHURCH

THOMAS J. HEFFERNAN AND E. ANN MATTER

THE LITURGY is the ritualized public celebration of the faith of the Church. The word ***liturgy***[1] itself comes from the Greek λειτουργία and literally means the work ἔργον of the people λεώσ. In its original context the Greek word had a wide and diverse connotation. It was used to refer to service to the state; service to a master; to the performance of religious rituals; and could even indicate the performance of military service. It was certainly not restricted to religious ceremonial, even when used by the same author. For example, in his treatise on the nature of animals, *Concerning the Character of Animals*, Aristotle used the word to designate any type of service or work, while in his *Politics* he used it to designate public service to the gods.

It was not until the making of the ***Septuagint***, undertaken at the instigation of Ptolemy Philadelphus (ca. 285–46 B.C.), that the word seems to have begun to restrict its meaning to works and services performed for the Temple. This application continues in the New Testament, where the word designates a religious function. Moreover, there are hints that in the New Testament the word was being used even more restrictively, referring specifically to liturgical services. The author of the "Epistle to the Hebrews"

[1]Terms in bold type are defined in the Glossary (pp. 715 ff.).

limits the word's application to refer to the individual who oversees the worship service in the Lord's sanctuary. This is an important conceptual shift, as it begins to move the idea of liturgy from the participation of the people to the service itself, and to those particular individuals presumably designated by the community to lead the service.

Drawing its inspiration from the simple narratives of Christ and his disciples in the synoptic gospels—particularly the celebration of the last supper before his death—the liturgy became by the later Middle Ages the most important, ubiquitous, and, very possibly, the most elaborate public ceremonial. However, this was decidedly not the case in its beginning. There is some evidence that suggests that the word *liturgy* in the early years of the Church referred specifically to the celebration of the **Eucharist**. In the earliest comments on the liturgy from the *First Apology* of Justin Martyr (ca. 100–ca. 165), there are some indications that the baptismal service and the Eucharist ceremony, for example, were simple ceremonies celebrated by small groups in private homes, with all of the participants well known to one other. It is difficult to know with confidence what other celebrations were being performed regularly as liturgies in the early Church. However, the celebration of the Eucharist in the early centuries of the Church as seen, for example, in the *Didache* (ca. 100?), St. Ignatius' *Letter to the Church of Philadelphia* (ca. 107), and Hippolytus' *Apostolic Tradition* (ca. 170–ca. 236), seems to have received little ceremonial embellishment, aside from very brief prayers that accompanied the breaking of the bread, the blessing of the wine, and the singing of hymns.

If we leap forward a millennium, however, and examine the liturgy of the Cluniac monks—at its apogee then, with over one thousand houses—it would take the most sophisticated student to discern the original liturgies in this new elaborate ceremonial. The Cluniac liturgy was extraordinarily elaborate, very beautiful, and certain services—particularly that of the **Divine Office**—could take hours to complete.

The liturgy, since it is the work of the people, is always changing and reflecting the practices of the Church in the world. Indeed even the most sacred moments in the liturgy of the **Mass** seem to have admitted of some change. For example, if we turn to the celebration of the Eucharist and examine the **Canon of the Mass**—the consecratory and most sacred prayer of the Mass, which is said over the gifts of bread and wine—we find that while it preserves unchanged the central institutive words of Christ: "This is my body. . . . This is my blood," it has itself been modified (particularly sections of it like the "communicantes") since St. Ambrose (ca. 339–97) quoted it in his *On the Sacraments*.

Thus the simple prayers of a persecuted sect, said over offerings to their imminently expected God, would become the hallowed words ritually intoned by bishop or priest of a Church now triumphantly powerful in both the religious and civic sphere. Traditions and the accretion of innumerable details began to attach themselves to local celebrations from the outset. Tertullian, the fiery and outspoken leader of the Church of Carthage (ca. 160–ca. 225), tells of special services in the Church of Carthage at which the martyrs were honored with prayers and hymns. Tertullian's simple service for the martyrs is a long distance from the massive ***legenda sanctorum*** of the thirteenth century and the elaborate readings of the saint's Life in the **nocturns** of the **Matins** liturgy. As different communities gave expression to heart-felt emotions in their prayer life, national or regional differences arose. Writing in the eighth century, Amalarius of Metz (ca. 780–ca. 850/51) was able to compose four long books, *On the Church's Services*, which documented differences between the Roman and **Gallican** practices.

It should not surprise us to learn that liturgies emerged that allowed for the fullest expression of an individual community's prayer life. The Church has always permitted such incorporation, provided it received the sanction of the local bishop and was consonant with the normative liturgical practices of the Church. Even if we were to restrict ourselves to the study of a single liturgical use, we would notice, given sufficient time, notable changes in the liturgical ritual. For example, Andrew Hughes shows how in the thirteenth-century Ordinal of Sarum, the minor tradition of the blessing of the salt and water before Mass was done at different times in the day depending on the hallowedness of the **feast** being celebrated.[2] Someone had to take note of this minor detail and record in a suitable text that this feast was greater in the Church's calendar than the one just celebrated, and thus the salt and water had to be blessed at a different time. Imagine the accretion of thousands of such details over a millennium across the whole of Europe and you will have some idea of the astonishing complexity of the liturgy. The growth of such liturgical richness necessitated the creation of a vast support system, including a variety of liturgical offices, officers, vestments, music, architectures, and books.

Countless generations of people from every walk of life—the rich and poor, clerical and lay, military and ecclesiastical, male and female, urban and rural, literate and illiterate—worshiped during the liturgy. The liturgy was present shortly after their birth and welcomed them into the Church; it brought them the Eucharist; made them soldiers for Christ; married them; baptized their children; and was there at their death. The very time that governed their waking and sleeping was sacralized. Virtually every day in the calendar was dedicated to a saint, and innumerable local festivals were celebrated throughout Europe. Planting and harvest seasons were begun and civic leaders, including kings and queens, were inducted into their offices via liturgical celebrations. Criminals sought sanctuary in churches, and the Church demanded that every communicant confess his or her sins to a priest at least once a year in the **sacrament** of confession during the Easter season. In sum, the faithful brought their hope, aspiration, guilt, joy, and wealth to the Lord's altar.

If the liturgy is truly the people at prayer, then we should expect that these unnumbered voices would also leave a lasting legacy. They did. They gave the liturgy its very shape. While it would be disingenuous to suggest that individuals easily left their impress on the liturgy, it is nonetheless true that the countless numbers who worshiped left a legacy to later generations

---

[2]Andrew Hughes, *Medieval Manuscripts for Mass and Office: A Guide to their Organization and Terminology* (Toronto, 1982), p. 18.

through their collective participation. One of the finest modern liturgists, S. J. P. van Dijk, has said that the history of the liturgy is one of the main sources of western culture.[3] It would be difficult to imagine any of the great cities of the West without their imposing **cathedrals**—cathedrals whose very existence and shape were a direct response to liturgical innovation. Unfortunately, it is also true that the liturgy is one of the least well-known sources for western culture. The reasons why most scholars, even historians of the period, are ignorant of the evolution and contribution of the liturgy are manifold and too complex to enter into in this brief introduction. However, it is certainly true that the labyrinthian complexity of the liturgy does present a formidable barrier to most students.

Surely some of the difficulty of informing students about the nature of the liturgy has to do with the fact that the logic of the liturgy's ceremony does not derive from some certain denotative principle as one might discern, for example, in the civil ceremony of a court of law. The language of the liturgy is often discursive and non-verbal—frequently visual or musical—and, indeed, perhaps its most important features are those which speak to us through symbol rather than speech. For example, draping the statues with purple cloth in **Lent** reminds us of the penitential season and, thereby, the communicant's penitential responsibilities. Not only does the pungent sweetness of incense rising at the adoration of the Eucharist remind us that our prayers rise to God with the sweet fumes but also the very sight and smell of the billowing smoke can move us, as St. Augustine says, beyond our souls. Where is this place which is beyond the soul? What is that state like and how do we enter it? Here we encounter the area of the reception of the liturgy. Answers to these questions vary from individual to individual and are not the subject of this brief introduction. However, it is the celebration of the liturgy, if performed appropriately, which moves us from one plane of being to another. Perhaps, if we think of the liturgy as a vehicle,

---

[3]S. J. P. van Dijk, *The Myth of the Aumbry: Notes on Medieval Reservation practice and Eucharistic devotion* (London, 1957), p. 14.

a vehicle that transports us not from place to place but from one mode of being to another, we can more nearly capture the experience of transcendence. The liturgy can help move us from our familiar domestic routine to the experience of a transcendent awakening of ineffable grace present in our lives.

The liturgy, like all religious ceremony, has a closer kinship to the theater than to virtually any other public ceremonial. Yet as all who have gone to plays and to churches will immediately acknowledge, the liturgy is utterly unlike the theater. In the theater the question of the verisimilitude of the action, of the performance's relationship to life outside the proscenium, is not in doubt. No matter how moved one might be by the bravery of Antigone opposing her uncle Creon's cruelty, we never doubt that there is an actress playing a role. Therefore, we willingly suspend our disbelief for the time of the drama so that its artistry can affect us. In the liturgy, however, the worship and presence of God in the ceremony is not fictive. Participants in the ceremony are present as believers, not skeptics. Participants believe in the efficacy of the sounds, the words, the music, the sights, and the smells. They believe that such signs can assist believers as they prepare to meet with God. For today's faithful, as well as our medieval brothers and sisters, Almighty God, the creator of the universe, the God of Abraham, Isaac, Jacob and Jesus, is present and appears to them in their humble church.

The very idea of such a presence is impossible to contain within a humanist epistemology. And for some, the belief in such a presence in the liturgy represents a repudiation of humanity's struggle to emerge from the primeval ooze of superstition. It is an unsettling belief to be sure; disjunctive. Some would find arrogant the very idea of maintaining, with certainty, that God is present at this moment in the species of bread and wine. If so, it was an ideological arrogance that the entire Christian Church believed until the Reformation—and which many millions still believe. If we suspend our skepticism for a moment and try to imagine what it is like to believe that Almighty God reveals himself to his petitioners in the liturgy, we might begin to understand the importance of the liturgy. Surely one impulse stemming from such a belief would be a desire to make the ceremony worthy. The service, in order to express the ineffable, must publicly define itself as different from the world in which it is situated. Since the goal is to create a bridge between the human and the wholly Other, the liturgy must construct observances in this liminal space. The service was designed to please God and to express to all of one's senses that what was about to take place was literally, and yet simultaneously, both in and out of this world. The physical setting had to resonate with difference; it had to trumpet that this space was different from that which surrounded it.

Even in the humblest parish church, believers could rise from the ordinary to the apprehension of the supernatural through this ritual public prayer. They were able to do this even if they were the most humble of worshipers. Even illiterate farm workers were able to understand the complexity and evolution of Judaeo-Christian traditions through the liturgy. The sharp smell of the incense, so different from the repertoire of smells they would have been familiar with, coaxed a series of complex associations as it billowed up from the thurible in the half gloom of the dimly lit church. It might have reminded parishioners of the incense brought from the East by the Magi, and possibly of the angel in Revelation (Rev. 8:3–8) who, through incense, wrought thunder, lightning, and earthquakes. At the very least, it would have left them clear that these pungent odors pointed to a new order, a realm different from that in which they dwelled. Similarly, the popular image of the tree of Jesse, to take a single example from the legion of motifs done in stained glass, joined the Old and New Testaments as an unbroken revelation and spoke eloquently of the Hebraic lineage of Jesus Christ in visual metaphors. Thus, communities of believers, literate and illiterate alike, through their worship in the liturgy participated in a complex intertextual universe.

It is difficult—some would say impossible—to re-enter imaginatively the world of our medieval ancestors. Their world was different from ours in so many fundamental ways. For example, at the beginning of this new millennium, everyone throughout the world is concerned with time. Certainly in the West, while there is some interest in apocalypticism, the major interest in the millennium seems to be in the achievement itself: to have lived when it happened. Time for the medieval European was very different. For one thing, they lived in two temporal worlds, the physical and the sacred, which continually intersected. Time was not regulated by clocks. Before the twelfth century mechanical time-pieces were non-existent, and even after their appearance, they were wonders restricted to centers of great wealth, like that of the major cathedrals. Even in the most sophisticated monastic houses time keeping was a complex business, involving often complicated equipment and supervised by a brother assigned to the task. The sun still governed one's waking and one's sleeping; still dictated, as the author of Ecclesiastes (3.2) said "the time to plant and a time to pluck up that which is planted." The basics of life changed little: patterns of behavior lost in the mists of antiquity reappeared anew in the small agricultural villages, as the seasons for toil and rest made their annual appearance. Sacred time, although it had a teleological trajectory from Creation through the Incarnation to the Apocalypse, was embodied in the ever-repeating patterns of the liturgy. The weeks were punctuated with many sacred festivals great and small throughout the year recalling the great mystery of God's salvation. The changing of the seasons at the altar, from **Advent** to **Christmas** to Lent, Holy Week and the long summer and fall of Ordinary Time, were temporal signposts as deeply engraved in medieval consciousness as the time of plowing, planting and harvesting. Within this cycle of sanctifying time were the many special days dedicated to particular saints and commemorations of events in the life of Christ and the Virgin Mary. These days helped to organize medieval society for participation in major communal events such as the feasts of patrons of towns, courts, and peoples. The liturgy was also a major focus of medieval economic and artistic development, inspiring architectural, artistic, literary, and musical creations. It is impossible to imagine medieval France, as suggested above, without the great cathedrals of Paris, Chartres, Amiens, and Reims, all of which, of course, were built specifically for liturgical celebrations.

All students of the Middle Ages are familiar with these facts, yet few of us really understand the variety of cultural expressions that made up the liturgy of the medieval Church. When we come across references in vernacular literature to particular liturgies, it can often take precious time to find out what they mean. Similar difficulties emerge, for example, when we try to explain in some detail the function of the beautiful Books of Hours and the great cathedrals. Perhaps the nuances of the liturgy have always been specialized fare. However, since the Roman Catholic Church instituted massive liturgical changes after the Second Vatican Council, most notably the employment of vernacular languages in the liturgy, the medieval liturgy seems ever more remote, archaic, overly complicated, and, to some, almost incomprehensible.

This volume is intended to address that lack of understanding by providing a series of essays on various topics of the medieval liturgy. The essays are guides for teachers who are preparing classes on the Middle Ages and for advanced students who are beginning serious study of the liturgy. The essays are intended to be introductory but to provide the basic facts and the essential bibliography for further study. They approach particular problems assuming a knowledge of medieval Europe but little expertise in liturgical studies per se.

The volume begins by describing the shape of the liturgical year in monastic devotion (Borgehammar), the Divine Office and private devotion (Black), and the vast literature of the Lives of the saints and their incorporation into the liturgy, particularly that of the night office (Heffernan). Then, several particular liturgies are described, including the liturgical life of the Byzantine Empire (Constantelos) and medieval Scandinavia (Helander), Jews in the medieval liturgy (Frizzell), sacramental liturgies (Dudley), and the influential liturgy for St. Cecilia (Reames). The physical settings of the medieval liturgy are discussed in chapters on architecture (Parker, Spatz) and the actual vessels with which the liturgy was celebrated (McLachlan). The books of the liturgy are the subject of essays on liturgical manuscripts (Krochalis and Matter) and Books of Hours (Wieck), while the artistic representations of the liturgy covered here include iconography of the Greek Church (Zographos), liturgy and its influence in vernacular literature (Vitz), liturgical drama (Campbell), and music (Ilnitchi, McKinnon). The volume ends with a rumination on the liturgy as social performance, a call to consider liturgical culture as a more central part of medieval society (Flanigan, Ashley and Sheingorn).

This last essay is based on the work of C. Clifford Flanigan, a beloved colleague who was a leader in medieval liturgical studies in the United States. Although he promised to write an introduction to this volume, his untimely death made his participation in this book impossible. However, his friends and colleagues K. Ashley and P. Sheingorn have used his work for a concluding essay meant to honor his memory and open up the field, more than simply to sum up the contributions of this volume. We hope that the background provided by these lively and varied essays will illustrate the centrality of the liturgy to other areas of medieval studies.

PART ONE

THE SHAPE OF THE LITURGICAL YEAR

A MONASTIC CONCEPTION OF THE LITURGICAL YEAR

STEPHAN BORGEHAMMAR

THE LITURGICAL YEAR as we know it today is the product of centuries of development. It embraces elements from many places and periods and milieus, elements which in part have been carefully combined, and in part seem quite accidentally juxtaposed. It contains reflections of almost all facets of Christian life and faith.

The fundamental fact about the liturgical year is that it is a sanctification of time. Certain key events in the history of salvation, and certain key elements of faith, have become attached to certain dates of the calendar like gems on a bracelet. This bracelet is like a magnificent rosary. We cannot handle it without encountering those gems, each of which carries a distinct message. In this way, as the earth spins around its axis and around the sun, creating the recurrent cycle of seasons which we call a year, we learn to experience not a ceaseless progression of days and nights but a pattern of meanings. Events from the past keep returning to us, giving days and seasons character and profile, bequeathing to us an inheritance from our ancestors, and inviting us to add to that inheritance for the future. Moreover, eternal truths are mediated to us in a form we can receive, the form of temporal events.

The Development of the Liturgical Year[1]

The sanctification of time was a feature of Hebrew religion. According to the book of Exodus, it began when the people of Israel left Egypt under the leadership of Moses in order to become consolidated as a holy people of God. The Exodus was inaugurated, in fact, by a first celebration of what was to become this people's prime annual festival, Passover or **Pascha**. The origin of the feast, the people, and the faith is one. Two more festivals were part of the basic heritage: Weeks or Firstfruits, in Greek called **Pentecost** ("fifty"), since it was celebrated on the fiftieth day after Passover; and Tabernacles.[2] There was a marked contrast between these festivals of the Hebrews and the astrological conceptions of surrounding religions and of philosophy: astrology makes the seasons themselves, and the heavenly bodies which rule them, gods; Hebrew faith was directed to a God who acted *in* time from a position *beyond* time, who made the seasons his servants.

Christianity too began with Passover. As St. Paul put it: "For Christ our pasch is sacrificed."[3] The death and resurrection of Christ marked the beginning of a renewed people of God, a renewed faith, and a renewed annual festival. This festival, called Easter in English, was observed annually by Christians from the very beginning and is the center from which the Christian holy year is sanctified. Easter continued to be accompanied by Pentecost, now a celebration of the gift of the Holy Spirit whereby the creation of the church was consummated.[4]

In the first two centuries of Christianity the chief festivals, apart from Easter and Pentecost, were the local commemorations of martyrs. The reflection of the redeeming sacrifice of Christ in the martyrdom of a woman

---

[1]The following discussion is based on standard literature—see the bibliography for details.

[2]Exod. 23:14–17; Num. 28:16–29, 39; Deut. 16:1–17.

[3]1 Cor. 5:7, quoted from the Douay translation of the Latin Vulgate (New York, 1914).

[4]Acts 2.

or man who had faithfully followed him was celebrated annually at the date of her or his "heavenly birthday" [***natalis*** or *natale*]. As the martyrs participated in the work of Christ, so did their festivals participate in the spirit of Easter.

In the third and fourth centuries, the celebration of Christ's incarnation established itself as a third universal festival, celebrated on 25 December in the West, on 6 January in the East. The western celebration focused on Jesus' birth while the eastern celebration had a broader scope: the "epiphania" or manifestation of God in the person of Jesus. Most Christian churches soon adopted both celebrations, as Christmas and Epiphany respectively.

Jerusalem became an important liturgical center in the fourth century. Its celebrations naturally utilized the possibility of local re-enactment of the events narrated in the gospels, especially from **Palm Sunday** to Easter, and the liturgical drama which this generated was soon imitated by churches around the world. This is the reason why the liturgical year even today has a markedly "re-presentative" (one might even say theatrical) character between Palm Sunday and Easter, whereas at other festivals there is little or no attempt to pursue a sequence of historical events. By way of contrast we may consider Lent, the great period of preparation before Easter, which also achieved something like its present shape in the fourth century: its structure is determined by various considerations such as proper preparation for Easter (where certain Biblical forty-day fasts provided a pattern), the typology of the present life as slavery in Egypt or as a generation-long journey through the desert (followed by liberation/resurrection), and the preparation of candidates for baptism (which in the fourth century generally took place at Easter). Lent thus corresponds to no single sequence of sacred history.

On the basic common foundation of Christmas/Epiphany, Lent, Easter, and Pentecost, more or less different shapes of the liturgical year were constructed during Late Antiquity and the early Middle Ages in the various regions of Christendom: Europe, Byzantium, Georgia, Armenia, Syria, Persia, India, Egypt, Ethiopia, and North Africa. Moreover, in each of these regions there was considerable local variation. Concentrating on Europe, we find the following important elements becoming generally established prior to the Carolingians: a pre-Lenten period of fast and abstinence lasting two and a half weeks (from **Septuagesima** to Ash Wednesday), a fast before Christmas (i.e., Advent) of four to six weeks, and a number of major saints' days (see below). Due to the reforms of Charles the Great, the liturgies of most of Europe became standardized and Romanized, and this affected also the liturgical year. Ancient Roman celebrations which became universal in the West at this time include the Marian feast at New Year (interpreted as a feast of the circumcision of Jesus) and a number of days with penitential character, the **Ember days** and ***Letania maior***.[5] By the same process the Marian feasts of Nativity (8 September), Annunciation (25 March), Purification (2 February), and Assumption (15 August), which had been introduced in Rome from the East ca. 650–700, were also established in the whole of Europe.

With this, the European liturgical year received a basic shape which since has changed little. The two most dramatic revisions of this shape in subsequent times are those which were undertaken during the Reformation, especially by more radical groups, and that introduced in the Roman Catholic Church in 1970. These upheavals fall outside our scope.

---

[5]The Ember days or ***Quattuor tempora*** were twelve penitential and liturgical days, a Wednesday, Friday, and Saturday in each season. Those of summer, fall, and winter were observed in Rome from the early third century (in June, September, and December—reference was made to the fasts of the fourth, seventh, and tenth months mentioned in Zech. 8:19), while those of spring were added no later than the seventh century. They came to be fixed at the week after Pentecost, the week after ***Exaltatio crucis*** (14 September), the third week of Advent, and the first week of Lent. The *Letania maior* ("big **litany**") was observed on 25 April. Its name (which is later than its origin) contrasts it with the *Letania minor* ("small litany"): three days of penitential processions—Monday to Wednesday before Ascension Day, which is always a Thursday—which were observed in Gaul from ca. 470. *Letania minor* is an example of a non-Roman component of the liturgical year which was early established in the West. It is lumped together with *Letania maior* in the English expression "**Rogation days**."

A brief characterization of the structure of the European liturgical year during the Middle Ages must recognize four basic components:

(1) **Sunday**, the first day of every new week (the "liturgical week" will not be treated further here but is an important topic of its own).

(2) Two outstanding feasts, Christmas and Easter, with preceding fasts and succeeding after-celebrations. Easter is preceded by Lent and followed by a festive season which concludes with Pentecost. Christmas is preceded by Advent and, strictly speaking, followed only by an octave, but Epiphany, which as we noted above is originally a double of Christmas, and the historicizing celebrations of *Circumcisio* (eighth day), and ***Purificatio*** or Candlemas (fortieth day), suggest a "Christmas season" which extends until Septuagesima.

(3) Saints' days and other days of a special character (e.g., ***Corpus Christi***, **Lammas**, *Exaltatio crucis*). These were ranked according to degree of importance or festivity, and while many were celebrated universally, others were restricted to a single region or **diocese**. Some of those celebrated universally were not celebrated with the same degree of festivity everywhere.

(4) The celebrations of the local parish: the dedication day of the parish church and the day(s) of its patron saint(s).

With respect to all four components of the liturgical year, an important distinction must be made, one too often ignored in standard clerically-oriented literature: the distinction between feasts observed only by the clergy and those which were public holidays. The latter were fewer in number but more significant in some respects—for instance, as days of popular preaching. In brief, all the feasts of categories 1, 2, and 4 were holidays but only a certain number of those of category 3. In the early Middle Ages about twenty saints' days were public holidays everywhere: the days of the Apostles, the Marian feasts mentioned above, John the Baptist (24 June), Lawrence (10 August), Michael (29 September), All Saints (1 November), and Martin (11 November). Feasts were gradually added, some universal (like the Conception of Mary), most regional or diocesan, until by the end of the Middle Ages the number was about forty in most dioceses. This may sound like a lot but is far fewer than the number celebrated by the clergy. Note that the selection of days which were holidays was not determined by their degree of liturgical solemnity (***totum duplex***, ***duplex***, ***semi-duplex***, ***simplex***) but by tradition and local circumstances.[6]

Even this cursory survey of the structure and development of the liturgical year will hopefully have indicated something of its richness and complexity. It is in fact a huge, virtually unfathomable system of meanings, or rather of meaningful structures, large and small, which interact in complex and ever-changing ways. Within the large annual cycle of feasts, whose shape varies with the variable date of Easter, lives the series of Biblical texts read at Mass, the series of lessons from the Bible and the Fathers read at Matins, the fixed and variable songs and prayers of the liturgy, the weekly cycle of psalms in the Divine Office, and a host of **antiphon**s, responsories, hymns, sequences, and tropes to suit. These texts represent numerous traditions—systems—of different age: monastic and **secular**, Roman and non-Roman. To this richness must be added all the local customs, both variations in the liturgy proper (i.e., the selection of texts and melodies, the use or not of tropes, special customs, venerated objects and the like) and in para-liturgical activities (peculiar devotions, processions, markets, games).

Having said all this, it should be clear that a single, definitive interpretation of the liturgical year cannot be given. Not only does its shape vary but also, at any given time or place, its content is so large and complex that it can be described in many different, non-exclusive ways. In our rationalistic era this may seem like a drawback (and attempts have indeed been made to remedy it in various quarters), but to the medieval mind it was a pleasure and a resource. Scholars of that time delighted in exploring complex interlocking patterns and eschewed univocal interpretations. This is

---

[6]In some areas of Europe the distinction between public holidays and other feasts was expressed as *festa fori* and *festa chori*. The former were often marked with red ink in calendars.

indeed a well-known facet of their Biblical interpretation, and we need to dwell a little on that point.

Medieval Interpretation of the Bible and of Reality

Medieval interpretation of the Bible was to a large extent allegorical, which is to say that it involved a search for hidden meanings in the text. The surface or literal meaning of the Bible was perceived to cover vast depths of spiritual truths. These spiritual truths could be roughly classified into three kinds: "allegorical" in the strict sense, "moral," and "anagogical." "Allegorical" interpretation discovered phenomena in the history of redemption; periods in that history, the nature of the incarnation, events in the life of Christ, the nature of the Church and its orders, the number and meaning of the sacraments, the relationship between Jew and Gentile. "Moral" (or "tropological") interpretation discovered phenomena in the inner man: stages in the spiritual life, degrees of virtue, the compunction of fear and of love, the five spiritual senses, the seven gifts of the Spirit, and many others. "Anagogical" interpretation, finally, discovered things about heaven: it could be in the allegorical or moral mode, describing objective facts about heaven or subjective foretastes of future beatitude in the present life, and it is not always distinguishable as a separate kind of interpretation.[7]

---

[7]The fourfold interpretation of the Bible was summarized by the Dominican Augustin of Dacia in his *Rotulus pugillaris* (ca. 1260), in the following well-known hexameter verse: "Littera gesta docet, quid credas allegoria, moralis quid agas, quo tendas anagogia." The standard work on medieval exegesis is Henri de Lubac, *Exégèse médiévale, Les quatre sens de l'écriture*, 4 vols. In 3, Théologie, vols. 41, 42, 59 (Paris, 1959–64). (An English translation is in process: see *Medieval Exegesis*, trans. Mark Sebanc [Grand Rapids, Michigan]. Only vol. 1 has so far been published [1998]). See also *The Cambridge History of the Bible*, ed. G. W. H. Lampe, vol. 2: *The West, from the Fathers to the Reformation* (Cambridge, 1969), and *Bible de tous les temps*, ed. Pierre Riché and Guy Lobrichon, vol. 4: *Le Moyen Âge et la Bible* (Paris, 1984). For additional literature see André Vernet, *La Bible au Moyen Âge. Bibliographie* (Paris, 1989).

Now, it would be a mistake to consider this "allegorical interpretation" merely as a hermeneutic tool in the study of the Bible. Its very nature reveals that it was a theory not about textual interpretation but about the structure of reality. Its focus was redemption as effected in history. In this view, the axis of history is Christ. Christ sums up, in his person and in his life, the history of the human race, the history of Israel, the history of the Church, and the history of the individual Christian. Because Christ is also God, Creator of heaven and earth, of things seen and unseen, and Lord of history, there exist intricate lines of correspondence among the history of Israel, the life of Christ, the inner life of the Christian, the orders and offices of the Church, and every facet of nature and culture. Nature, indeed, is itself an intricately patterned structure, having a physical and a spiritual part with a complicated network of connections within and between them. Thus, any object of the senses can suggest profound spiritual realities.

In view of all this, it is perhaps superfluous to point out that both the seasons of the liturgical year and the texts used at different celebrations not only *could* but also *must* become the subject of allegory. Let us look at an example of this from a Benedictine sermon of the twelfth century. It concerns the three Masses which are celebrated on Christmas Day: at night, at dawn, and in the day.

The preacher begins by seizing on the aspect of light as a symbol of understanding (spiritual sight, as it were). In the three Masses, the story of God's creation is unfolded with increasing clarity. The first Mass, celebrated in the dark, treats of God as "creator," for creation *ex nihilo* is opaque to the human intellect and can only be affirmed in blind faith. The second Mass, celebrated in twilight, treats of God as "redemptor," for the knowledge of salvation has not yet reached through to all humans. The third Mass, celebrated in daylight, treats of God as "remunerator," since on the day of the general resurrection, all humans will see clearly the heavenly and eternal things. Thus far the introductory part of the sermon: note how the progression of the three Masses is made to parallel the grand progression of the whole of history, how light (in different senses) gradually dawns during both, and how all of history is subsumed under three rhyming epithets of God—*creator*, *redemptor*, *remunerator*.

The main body of the sermon offers a detailed interpretation of the texts of the third Mass. In accordance with the initial scheme, these texts are given a consistently eschatological interpretation. The text of the Introit, for instance, "Puer natus est nobis, filius datus est nobis" (Isa. 9:6), with the verse, "Cantate Domino canticum novum, quia mirabilia fecit" (Ps. 97:1 [Vulgate], 98:1 [English Bible]), seems originally to have been chosen in order to express joy at the birth of Christ. Here, however, it is applied to individual Christians in accordance with the eschatological perspective: we are born "pueri" (i.e., fearful servants) here on earth, but it is given to us to become "filii" (i.e., true sons) when we reach heaven; and there we shall sing a new song, a "novae admirationis et laudationis jubilum," in praise of him who has raised us from the dead.

Such an interpretation may undoubtedly seem contrived at first, but it is well to consider that: (1) it is not meant to obscure or delete the more natural and obvious sense of the songs, only to *supplement* it; and (2) the central theme of Christmas, the wonder of the Incarnation, is never in fact lost sight of, for there could be neither true sonship nor participation in the glory of the world to come if Christ had not been born in Bethlehem. It is most important never to underestimate medieval exegetical thought. The accusations of arbitrariness and irrelevancy which are often directed against it lose sight of the fact that the natural, grammatical meaning of Biblical texts was so obvious and so familiar—especially in learned monastic milieus—that it did not need to be commented upon. We must accept the bitter fact that medieval authors knew their Bible much better than we do, so that they could write variations on Biblical themes without even needing to state the theme first—just as we can enjoy Mozart's variations on "Twinkle, Twinkle Little Star" even if we happen to miss the first few bars in which the melody is presented.

The metaphor of medieval exegesis as artistic variations on a theme is relevant also in another way, namely its multiplicity. One and the same author can expound one and the same passage in many different ways. There is a "silva allegoriarum," a "forest of allegories," because the network of correspondences among different parts of reality is so vast and complex.[8] In consequence, the possibilities of playing variations on any given Biblical theme are almost unlimited. And since we are here speaking about an attitude to reality rather than just a strategy of textual interpretation, it is evident that the liturgy, too, is susceptible of multiple understandings. The preacher whom we just considered has written two more sermons on the Masses of Christmas Day, and here the interpretations are different: in one sermon the Masses represent the mysteries of the God-man, his divinity, his assumed humanity, and his gift of eternal life to mankind; in the other, they represent ideal ages in a person's physical and spiritual life, i.e., birth, adolescence, and adulthood. As the author himself states at the beginning of one of his sermons, "Of the three Masses which we celebrate today many and diverse understandings are possible."[9]

The Liturgical Year as Reflected in Sermons from Admont

Clearly, then, it is impossible to talk about *the* medieval view of the liturgical year. Both the structure of the year and its interpretations varied.[10]

---

[8]See de Lubac, *Exégèse médiévale*, vol. 1/1, pp. 119–28.

[9]"De tribus his missis, quas hodie celebramus, multa et diversa intelligi valeant," PL 174: 660A. All the three Christmas sermons will be found in PL 174, cols. 656–59, 659–63, and 663–65 respectively.

[10]For a comprehensive list of medieval liturgical commentaries to the time of William Duranti (ca. 1230–96) see Roger Reynolds, "Guillaume Durand parmi les théologiens médiévaux de la liturgie," in *Guillaume Durand, Évêque de Mende (v. 1230–1296). Canoniste, liturgiste et homme politique*. Actes de la Table Ronde du CNRS, Mende 24–27 mai 1990, ed. Pierre-Marie Gy (Paris, 1992), pp. 155–68; in Table I on pp. 164–68 the letter T marks commentaries which touch on the ***temporale*** of the liturgical year. Liturgical commentaries after Duranti are listed in Cyrille Vogel, *Medieval Liturgy: An Introduction to the Sources*, rev. and trans. William G. Storey and Niels Krogh Rasmussen (Washington, D.C., 1986), pp. 16 ff. For a brief introduction to the genre, see Mary M. Schaefer, "Latin Mass Commentaries from the Ninth through Twelfth Centuries: Chronology and Theology," in *Fountain of Life*, ed. Gerard Austin (Washington, D.C., 1991), pp. 35–49.

Undoubtedly there are constants, some of which we may feel we can guess at, but to map them out with any accuracy would first require extensive study of the different interpretations in their multifariousness. The rest of this essay is devoted to *one* set of interpretations of the liturgical year: that of the corpus of sermons from which we drew our examples on the interpretation of Christmas Day. These sermons, printed in Migne's *Patrologia Latina*, vol. 174, have since the eighteenth century been attributed to Godfrey (1137–65), a prominent abbot of the Benedictine monastery at Admont in Styria (a province of Austria).[11] The sermons are undoubtedly from Admont and were composed between about 1140 and 1180, but it is far from clear who was the author (or authors).[12] That need not concern us here, however, as we are simply interested in delineating a representative

---

[11]Admont and its monastery still exist. Some basic literature: Jakob Wichner, *Geschichte des Benediktiner-Stiftes Admont, vom Jahre 1466 bis auf die neuste Zeit*, 4 vols. (Graz, 1874–80); idem, "Das ehemalige Nonnenkloster O.S.B. zu Admont," [*Wissenschafftliche*] *Studien und Mittheilungen aus dem Benedictiner-Orden* 2 (1881), fasc. 1, 75–86, fasc. 2, 288–319; Klaus Arnold, "Admont und die monastische Reform des 12. Jahrhunderts," *Zeitschrift der Savigny-Stiftung für Rechtsgeschichte* 89, *Kanonistische Abteilung* 58 (1972): 350–69; and Rudolf List, *Stift Admont, 1074–1974. Festschrift zur Neunhundertjahrfeier* (Ried im Innkreis, 1974).

[12]See Johann Wilhelm Braun, "Gottfried von Admont," *Die deutsche Literatur des Mittelalters. Verfasserlexikon*, 2nd rev. ed., vol. 3 (Berlin and New York, 1981), pp. 118–23; idem, "Irimbert von Admont," *Frühmittelalterliche Studien* 7 (1973): 266–323; and Volker Honemann, "Irimbert von Admont," *Die deutsche Literatur des Mittelalters. Verfasserlexikon*, 2nd rev. ed., vol. 4 (Berlin and New York, 1983), pp. 417–19. Despite Braun's attempts to defend the traditional attribution of most Admont sermons to Gottfried, there is really no evidence to support it. Gottfried's younger brother Irimbert, who was abbot at Admont 1172–76, was a prolific author of Biblical commentaries and certainly composed at least a handful of the extant sermons—he is a more likely candidate as author of them all. However, there is evidence that the composition of sermons at Admont was sometimes a collaborative effort. One manuscript of sermons (in Latin) is known to have been written by nuns of the monastery on the basis of notes taken when Irimbert was preaching (presumably in the vernacular). Compare note 56 below. Future work on the many still unpublished sermons may bring more clarity to these issues.

monastic conception of the liturgical year. The Admont corpus of sermons is very useful for this purpose, since it is uniquely rich in references to the meaning of various Sundays and feasts, and since its spirit is that of conservative Benedictine monasticism, faithful to the mainstream of the tradition.

In the following we shall first look at the interpretation of the major liturgical seasons one by one, then we shall look briefly at the peculiar interpretation of certain sequences of Sundays during the year.[13]

Advent

Today we tend to think of the liturgical year as beginning with Advent. This is by no means a self-evident idea. In the Patristic age Advent did not even exist. Moreover, the idea of a beginning presupposes the existence of a full year replete with festivals and sequences of Sundays, something which only gradually came into being. Even today, in fact, there is no such thing as a liturgical New Year's Day. But there is a practical consideration which inevitably gives rise to the idea of a year with a specific beginning and end, namely, the need for liturgical books to begin somewhere. Liturgical books have been ordered in many different ways, but by the twelfth century it was common to begin with the first Sunday of Advent or, in

[13]Three authors have previously done interpretive work on the Admont sermons: Johannes Beumer, "Der mariologische Gehalt der Predigten Gottfrieds von Admont," *Scholastik* 35 (1960): 40–56; Ulrich Faust, "Gottfried von Admont," *Studien und Mitteilungen zur Geschichte des Benediktiner-Ordens und seiner Zweige* 75 (1964): 271–359; and Alf Härdelin, "God's Visiting. A Basic Theme in the Homilies Ascribed to Godfrey of Admont," in his *Munkarnas och mystikernas medeltid. Tjugofyra kapitel om teologi, spiritualitet och kultur* (Skellefteå, 1996), pp. 201–18; previously printed in *Cistercian Studies* 27 (1992): 23–38, in a version that was unfortunately disfigured by editorial changes and cuts. For literature on medieval preaching see Jean Longère, *La prédication médiévale* (Paris, 1983), and *Medieval Sermon Studies*, a newsletter/journal published by the International Medieval Sermon Studies Society, in particular Thomas N. Hall, "A Basic Bibliography of Medieval Sermon Studies," *Medieval Sermon Studies* 36 (Autumn 1995): 26–42.

books containing texts for the feasts of saints only, the feast of St. Andrew (30 November). And in a sense it is very appropriate to think of Advent as the beginning of the Christian year, since it strikes a note of expectation, of waiting for the arrival of the Savior, which is heard from the very beginning of sacred history.[14]

So let us begin with Advent. The Admont sermons indeed echo the note of expectation alluded to just above. In several places in sermons for 1 Advent and Christmas Eve, the earnest expectation of the Old Testament fathers for the arrival of Christ is evoked. Expectation and desire is depicted as the driving force of their lives, the mainspring behind their prophesyings and writings. Even many "perfect" people who did not prophesy in words, the preacher assures us, had their faces intent on the fulfillment of the promise, and experienced burning desire.[15] The whole period prior to the birth of Christ is characterized by waiting for liberation more than anything else, and that waiting continued after death in hell, for that was where everyone had to go before the Resurrection.[16]

Without laboring the point, the preacher suggests that for his audience, too, Advent is a time of expectation. The monk should imitate the desire and the eagerness of the Old Testament saints. But what should be the

---

[14]By the thirteenth century Advent seems generally to have been regarded as the first part of the liturgical year. See John Beleth (ca. 1115–after 1160), *Summa de ecclesiasticis officiis*, cap. 55s, Corpus Christianorum: Continuatio Mediaevalis (henceforth CCCM), vol. 41A (1976), 100–101, lines 123 ff. and 133: "Tempore aduentuum usque ad natale Domini recolit tempus reuocationis. . . . Et sic a tempore reuocationis incipit officia. . . ."

[15]PL 174: 47A: "Antiqui Patres Christi in carne praesentiam praestolantes desiderabant, ad hoc die noctuque medullitus suspirabant. . . . Et multi perfecti, qui tunc temporis erant, verbis inde non prophetabant, sed tamen nihilominus suspensos ad hanc promissionem vultus ac flagrans desiderium habebant." Compare cols. 21C, 36–37, 642, 645–46.

[16]PL 174: 651B: "Attamen tantus hic patriarcha [Abraham], sicut et caeteri, post mortem ad inferos descendens, longo tempore exspectabat ibi adventum sui Redemptoris." That the gates of Paradise were closed to all until Christ rose from the dead is a concept that pervades early and medieval Christianity.

object of his desire? After all, the "advent" of Christ to the world when he was born as a manchild in Bethlehem occurred long ago. This question takes us to the axis of Advent understanding, from which all the various interpretations radiate like spokes from a hub.

Advent means arrival, and it is part of the original Christian heritage that Christ *arrives*. Different arrivals of Christ were distinguished very early. The New Testament is full of references to a second coming of Christ, in glory. Christ himself spoke, with clear reference to himself, about a king who went away but would one day return, bringing punishment or reward to his servants (e.g., Luke 19:12–27). St. Paul speaks in many places about Christ's return in glory (e.g., 2 Thess. 1:10), and the same is of course the major theme of the Apocalypse. We are also told that the Eucharist is a declaration of the death of the Lord, "until he comes" (1 Cor. 11:26). We need not go far forward in time before we encounter the idea that Christ also arrives mystically to the individual soul. This is the basis of many expositions of the Song of Songs.[17]

When the Gospel readings for Advent were selected, starting in the sixth century,[18] the idea of the various arrivals of Christ was already a commonplace with an established symbolism. The Gospel used in most areas of Europe on 1 Advent, Matt. 21:1–9, describes the triumphant entry of Christ into Jerusalem. The mere fact that the same Gospel is used in its historical sense on Palm Sunday suggests that in Advent it is supposed to be taken symbolically—naturally enough, for the anagogical interpretation of Jerusalem appears already in the New Testament, the allegorical and moral

---

[17]Recent publications on the interpretation of the Song of Songs include: Ann W. Astell, *The Song of Songs in the Middle Ages* (Ithaca, 1990); E. Ann Matter, *The Voice of My Beloved: The Song of Songs in Western Medieval Christianity* (Philadelphia, 1990); and Denys Turner, *Eros and Allegory: Medieval Exegesis of the Song of Songs* (Kalamazoo, Mich., 1995).

[18]On the Biblical lections of Advent see Dom Th. Maertens, "L'Avent. Genèse historique de ses thèmes bibliques et doctrinaux," *Mélanges de science religieuse* 18 (1961): 47–110 (with tables of **pericopes** [the assigned reading for the service], their date, and geographical origin).

no later than Origen (ca. 185–251).[19] The Gospel on 2 Advent is concerned with the Final Judgment (Luke 21:25–33), those on 3 and 4 Advent with the function of John the Baptist as one who prepares for the arrival of the Lord (Matt. 11:2–10; John 1:19–28).[20] This is not the place to speculate about what may have been the intention of those who selected these Gospels; let us merely note that they are chiefly concerned with the second coming of Christ, and with repentance as the proper preparation for that coming, as behooves a time of fasting.

In the Admont sermons, the concept of different kinds of arrivals has been refined and extended. Basic to the preacher's thought are the arrivals at Bethlehem and at the Final Judgment.[21] The answer to the question we posed above, then, is that the monks should expectantly prepare themselves for the *second* coming of Christ, just as the Old Testament saints prepared for the *first*. Occasionally the preacher expounds this idea objectively, with reference to the unfolding of history according to the divine plan: the present time—the time of grace, or of the Gentile Church—will reach a climax when Israel repents and converts to Christ, after which the end of the world and the Final Judgment will occur.[22] But more often the second coming of Christ is seen from a subjective point of view, as the encounter which each

---

[19]For Origen's interpretations of Jerusalem see *In Jos. hom.* 21.1 (Sources Chrétiennes, vol. 71 [1960], p. 431): allegorical; *In Jos. hom.* 23.4 (ibid., p. 463): anagogical; *In Luc. hom.* 38.3–4 (Sources Chrétiennes, vol. 87 [1962], p. 445): moral.

[20]The Roman lectionary, which after the Council of Trent became the norm in the Roman Catholic Church, had a different system of lections for Advent: Luke 21:25–33 on 1 Advent; Matt. 11:2–10 on 2 Advent; John 1:19–28 on 3 Advent; and Luke 3:1–6 on 4 Advent. What the original Roman order was is disputed: see Maertens, "L'Avent," p. 78 n2.

[21]PL 174: 21C: "Desiderantissimum hoc tempus Dominici Adventus, ad quod omnes sancti ab initio suspirabant, ea de causa annue celebratur, tum ut memoriae Dominicae Nativitatis de cordibus hominum non deleatur, tum ut ad memoriam terribilis ejus adventus, qui quotidie nobis appropinquat, revocetur." Compare col. 66A–B.

[22]E.g., PL 174: 65A, 71A.

individual has with him at the moment of death. Thus in the first sermon for 1 Advent, the preacher interprets in detail Jesus' arrival in Jerusalem with reference to the dying of an individual monk. Jerusalem first stands for a congregation of monks, which Christ "approaches" as death approaches one of its members. The dying one is explained to be the ass of the Gospel story, and with that the perspective shifts so that Jerusalem stands for the heavenly Jerusalem, which the soul enters, guided by Christ and surrounded by crowds of angels and righteous men. The basic message of the sermon is the importance of contemplating and preparing for death.[23]

Advent is, then, a celebration of the past arrival of Christ and a preparation for the future one. But there is also a third aspect, the present possibility of arrivals, or "visits," of Christ to the soul. These visits are foretastes of the heavenly glory and should be the constant object of desire of the monk. Just as Advent is a period of preparing for the final encounter with Christ at death, so it should also be a period of intensified preparation for those present encounters.[24] The present encounters in turn prepare the soul for the final one by purifying it.[25]

In sum, the season of Advent can be described as an image of the present age, the age between the two arrivals of Christ. Christ *has* arrived, and Christ *will* arrive. The desire of mankind has been partially fulfilled, grace

---

[23]PL 174: 25C: "Si enim hoc modo abjectis operibus tenebrarum et induti arma lucis, in hoc, quem annuo tempore recolimus, adventu Domini animas nostras castigaverimus; in illo ultimo ejus adventu, quando e corpore evocabimur, laeti ei et expediti occurremus, atque in illa aeternae beatitudinis gloria, quae est sine defectu et miseria, recepti aeternaliter cum ipso regnabimus."

[24]On the concept of *visitatio* in the Admont sermons see Härdelin, "God's Visiting" (note 13). The concept turns up in the Advent sermons at, e.g., PL 174: 56A–B, 57C–D, 67A. Preparation is emphasized at, e.g., cols. 25C and 645C, and in connection with the Ember days of Advent at 66D.

[25]PL 174: 88C: "Huic autem haereditati Dei, quia admitti non poterimus, nisi adventus Dei visitatione a peccatis et vitiis hic emundari meruerimus. . . . "

and mercy abound, but the fullness is yet to come.[26] Christ's presence on earth is now experienced in glimpses only, as momentary arrivals or "visits" to the desiring soul. The season of Advent recalls this whole situation and enjoins on the monk a special effort to exert himself in reaching for communion with his Lord.

Christmas and Epiphany

Advent eventually issues in Christmas. Some major themes from the Christmas sermons have already been described above. In relation to Advent, of course, Christmas is the fulfillment, the celebration of the first joyous arrival of Christ. It is worth noting, though, that the themes of the Christmas sermons differ little from those of the Advent sermons. It is now of course a question of a feast, not a fast, so the *tone* of the sermons is more festive; but in contrast to the classical Christmas sermons of Leo the Great (pope 440–61), the preacher does not dwell much on the mystery of the incarnation as such but, rather, sticks with his theme of Christ's arrival to (or birth in) the heart,[27] which prepares for his final arrival at the end of time.[28] If there is anything special about the message of Christmas as compared to that of Advent, it is that the emphasis now is more on *receiving* the internal visits of Christ than on *preparing* for them. Connected with this is a stress on Christmas night as a special time for receiving answers to prayers (what the monks have not been able to obtain during the whole year they now

---

[26]PL 174: 42D.

[27]PL 174: 648B: ". . . ut ipse adveniens in cordis nostri praesepio requiescat, et sacratas noctes in nobis faciat. . . ." Compare col. 664B–D.

[28]PL 174: 661D–662B; this place includes a fine exposition of the oft-recurring theme of fear and love. Briefly, the monk's relation to God in the present life is a mixed experience of fear and love, but in heaven fear will subside and love will be perfected.

get),[29] and on Christmas communion as a receiving of the incarnate Christ.[30] The Sundays after Christmas and Epiphany are not interpreted specifically in the light of Christmas themes, and we will therefore treat them later, in our discussion of how different series of Sundays are expounded in the sermons.

The interpretation of Epiphany, on the other hand, does echo some Christmas themes, as is natural considering the close connection of the two feasts. Thus, the main theme of the first sermon for Epiphany is the birth of Christ in the hearts of the elect.[31] But apart from such monastic adaptations of Christmas themes, there is not much that goes beyond the basic traditional perception of Epiphany, namely, that the feast celebrates three "manifestations" or "apparitions" of Christ—at his birth, at his baptism, and at the wedding feast of Cana. These three events were associated with Epiphany since the fourth century and continued to be so throughout the Middle Ages, even though the gospels about Christ's baptism and the wedding in Cana had early been moved to the Octave of and the second Sunday after Epiphany respectively.[32]

---

[29]PL 174: 655C: "Quod per totum anni circulum non possunt obtinere, hac nocte obtinebunt votique sui compotes efficiuntur."

[30]PL 174: 645B: "Celebremus ergo cum devotione intima Dominicae Nativitatis solemnia, servientes Domino in laetitia, ut in hora sacrificii salutaris, cum ad percipiendum corpus immaculatum venerimus, quod de beata Virgine Spiritu sancto cooperante est sumptum, percipientibus nobis in affectu dulcedinis corpus Dominicum, astantes sancti angeli, Regis nostri internuntii dicant nobis: *Ecce Deus vester*."

[31]PL 174: 677–83; the theme is stated right at the beginning.

[32]On the unity of the three events and their secondary distribution among three different days see PL 174:683C–84A; 696D–97A; and 703C. Compare *New Catholic Encyclopedia*, s.v. "Epiphany, Feast of." In some regions the Gospel about the wedding feast at Cana was read a week later, i.e., on the second Sunday after the *octave* of Epiphany.

The Lenten Period

The sermons for Septuagesima and **Sexagesima** have no direct reference to the liturgical season, so there is no way of determining how far the interpretations of the lections were suggested by concepts about the meaning of these Sundays. Biblical interpretation in monastic circles is always a very literary affair, and interpretations suggested by some great author in the past are sometimes adopted apparently regardless of whether they suit the liturgical context or not. This is not to say that the sermons for Septuagesima and Sexagesima seem misplaced in any way, only that it is *difficult* to determine whether there is any conscious adaptation to the liturgical season in them. The same goes for many sermons in the Admont corpus.

With Lent proper, the situation is better. We are fortunate that the first sermon for the first Sunday of Lent begins with a brief exposition of the season.[33] Lent is here compared to the forty days during which Christ fasted and was tempted by the devil in the desert. Since the devil tempted Christ himself, the preacher says, he will not fail to tempt each and every human being, however innocent. This is particularly true of this season of increased spiritual effort, when he tries by every means to draw men, and especially monks, away from the love of God. But the monks should remember that they have turned their backs on the world and entered the "desert" of monastic discipline precisely in order to fight the temptations of the devil more faithfully and effectively. In this their guide is the Lord, whose example teaches them not only abstinence, but also patience, humility, and purity of heart.

In this highly significant passage, the preacher demonstrates his knowledge of the ancient monastic heritage of the Desert Fathers. Compared with the other great season of fasting, Advent, the focus is different: in Advent, asceticism was mainly a question of preparing for "visits" of the Lord, of stretching out in expectation, whereas here it is conceived as a battle with

---

[33]PL 174: 165A–C.

the forces of evil. The obverse side of desire, namely, the rejection of what is undesirable, is what Lent is mainly about. This is in keeping not only with ancient monastic tradition but also with the ancient function of Lent as a time of preparation for baptism—a preparation which once included numerous exorcisms culminating in a solemn abjuration of the devil on Easter Eve.[34]

A couple of other places in the Lenten sermons offer a more general view of the season as a time of particularly intense effort at "living as we should."[35] These passages differ little from similar ones in the Advent sermons—which is not to say that they are unimaginative. Consider the following rather pleasing parallel between ascetic striving and agriculture: the earth is plowed, seeds sown, and vines pruned for the sake of fruit. This fruit is a gift of God, created not only in view of corporal nourishment but also in view of the holy sacrament. The monk should learn from the external world, should plow his body by spiritual exercises, sow seeds of virtue, and prune away useless thoughts and evil desires, giving place instead to good desires and holy pleasures. As the lazy farmer reaps no fruit, so the negligent monk will get nothing at the paschal harvest, when he should be reaping spiritual joys. The preacher exhorts: let us work now for God that we may then rest with him and in him; let us weep now for our sins in penitence that we may then receive pardon and rejoice with Christ.[36]

To the interpretation of particular Sundays we shall return below, but we may note one curious thing here: that the preacher calls the fourth Sunday of Lent "festive" and "excellent" and "even more joyful than Easter

---

[34]A good introduction to early Christian liturgical practice is Joseph Andreas Jungmann, *The Early Liturgy, to the Time of Gregory the Great*, trans. Francis A. Brunner (Notre Dame, Ind., 1959).

[35]PL 174: 225A: "Sacrosanctum tempus hoc quadragesimale . . . sic specialis observantiae diligentia observandum est, ut qui alio tempore vivere non valemus sicut debemus, his saltem diebus per custodiam mentis et corporis Deo placere laboremus." Compare col. 254C.

[36]PL 174: 225A–D.

Day," because of the way the joys of the future life are suggested in the songs of the Mass.[37] The key to this view is the Introit, the very song which begins Mass and the first word of which gave the Sunday its Latin name: *Laetare*, rejoice. The interpretation suggests a less monolithic view of Lent than what the teaching about this season in the Rule of Benedict might lead one to expect.

The fifth Sunday of Lent introduces that season within a season—the last two weeks of Lent—which is called Passiontide.[38] At this time contemplation of the Lord's suffering and death is intensified.[39] Lent reaches a kind of climax on Palm Sunday: now the battle against the devil comes to a head, for this is the day on which Christ prepared himself finally to vanquish the enemy, leaving an example of victory and glory to emulate.[40]

In sermons for Holy Week, finally, and in particular for Good Friday, the main theme is sharing spiritually in Christ's sufferings: *com*-passion with Christ.

Easter to Pentecost

Easter Day is the greatest day of the whole year. It goes without saying that it is a celebration of the Resurrection. Like Christmas night, we are told that

---

[37]PL 174: 235D–36A: "Tota enim hodierni officii excellentia singularis et magnae cujusdam laetitiae modum, quae non habebit modum, praescribit quae ut ita dicam, in cantu suo etiam paschalis diei solemnia praecedit." Compare the similar interpretation in John Beleth, *Summa*, cap. 93b, CCCM, vol. 41A, p. 165: "Totum officium misse illius diei de letitia est."

[38]The term *tempus dominicae passionis* in PL 174 at cols. 254C, 268D, 288D, and 292C.

[39]See PL 174: 288D–89B.

[40]PL 174: 269B: "Haec est enim dies praeclara, in qua ipse, quia salus totius humani generis advenerat, ad opus nostrae redemptionis, ad superandum videlicet hostem antiquum seipsum praeparabat, suis in hoc fidelibus relinquens exemplum qualiter de adversario triumphantes gloriam adipiscantur coelestium gaudiorum."

it is a particular time for receiving God's mercy.[41] Also in another respect we return to themes familiar from the Christmas cycle: the vigils and fasts of Lent have prepared the monks to receive the "visitation" of the Lord.[42] A recurring theme during Easter week is *conversion*, i.e., turning from a worldly to a spiritual way of life (specifically to the monastic way of life); this is understood as a form of resurrection. The sermon for ***Dominica*** *in albis* (the Sunday after Easter) presents us with a continuation of that theme, the daily resurrection from the death of sinning which the "good life" involves (the phrase is "bona conversatio," meaning the life of monastic discipline which follows upon "conversio").[43]

The sermons for the following Sundays after Easter contain no notable comments on the season. The two feasts at the end of the Easter celebrations, Ascension Day and Pentecost, compensate for this lack by the highly significant interpretations which they receive.

On Ascension Day the preacher emphasizes that Christ ascended *for* us—as always, Christ himself is the pattern for the Christian life. Everything he did, he did not for himself but for us.[44] Objectively, then, Christ's ascent into heaven prepares the way there for human beings. And more than that, it completes a work whereby human nature receives an even greater dignity than it had before the Fall, for in Christ humankind is exalted even

---

[41]PL 174: 797A: "Quemadmodum dies haec pro cunctis anni diebus est celeberrima, ita facilius in ea a salvandis omnibus obtineri et impetrari divina poterit misericordia."

[42]PL 174: 796C–D: "Qui autem cunctis diebus ac noctibus sacrae hujus quadragesimae vigiliis, jejuniis multisque laboribus non cessabant insistere . . . nequaquam hos desolatos [Dominus] relinquet . . . quia etsi pro voto suo, quod petunt vel optant, non accipiunt, tamen . . . diligentibus et quaerentibus se gratiam visitationis suae non subtrahit."

[43]PL 174: 308C.

[44]PL 174: 864D.

above the angels.[45] This involves at the same time the final triumph over the devil (with whom, as we remember, battle was engaged during Lent), who is now so trod down that he dare not raise his head aginst God's elect.[46] The preacher's emphasis, however, is as always on the subjective dimension: the ascension teaches men to spurn the things of this world and turn their whole soul toward the contemplation of heavenly things.[47]

Pentecost also receives a typically monastic interpretation, for here it is said that for "spiritales," that is, monks, this day is not simply figurative like all the other feasts, "but can be celebrated in truth," that is, with a real experience of the sweetness of the Spirit. Whereas secular people celebrate Pentecost like other feasts, with games and parties and in vain clothes, tasting nothing but carnal joy, monks can feast truly spiritually, unless they too get ensnared by secular concerns.[48]

The Easter season is said to end with the Ember days after Pentecost. The interpretation of this end may also fittingly put an end to our analysis of the interpretations of the major feasts of the liturgical year. For the end of Easter, the preacher says, signals the end of temporal feasting. In this life, all feasts are intermittent, recurring only annually. But after this life, we look forward to a feast which will not end, the festive joy of eternal gladness.[49]

---

[45]PL 174: 871B: "Humanam naturam non solum post lapsum reparavit, sed etiam, quo nunquam pervenisset, si lapsa non fuisset, supra omnes videlicet choros angelorum in semetipso transvexit."

[46]PL 174: 876A–B: "Constat quod diabolo, salutis et beatitudinis nostrae inimico, propter humanae naturae in Christo exsultationem [exaltationem?] lethalis oborta sit tristitia . . . et ipse ita conculcatus est, quod nunquam amplius contra electos Dei caput elevare audet."

[47]PL 174: 865A: "Unde non immerito animus electorum spretis infimis ad superna cogitanda suspenditur."

[48]PL 174: 876C–77A.

[49]PL 174: 372B–C: "Sanctae et venerandae Paschatis hujus solemnitatis finis, qui jam instat, finem illum universae carnis non inconvenienter nobis insinuat, cui, consummatis

Interpretations of Sunday Sequences

A prominent feature of medieval thought, which seems a little peculiar to us, is the fondness for numerical sequences and patterns. The preacher from Admont displays this fondness in his interpretations of various sequences of Sundays which occur in the course of the liturgical year.[50]

The four Sundays of Advent, to begin with, are compared to the four cardinal virtues: prudence, temperance, fortitude, and justice, in this order.

---

temporalibus quae nunc agimus festis, festiva aeternae jucunditatis gaudia succedunt, quae nullo unquam fine terminari, nec aliqua adversitatis molestia in sua aliquando aeternitate poterunt perturbari." The idea of heaven as the "aeterna et semper praesentia" of the "annua" of liturgical feasts is similarly invoked in an Ascension Day sermon, col. 876B.

[50]The interpretations of Sunday sequences in Admont are somewhat reminiscent of similar schemes found in Amalarius of Metz (ca. 775–ca. 850), *Liber officialis*, vol. 2 of *Amalarii episcopi opera liturgica omnia*, ed. J. M. Hanssens, 3 vols., Studi e testi, vols. 138–40 (Vatican City, 1948–50). A tighter scheme of four liturgical seasons appears in liturgical commentaries beginning with John Beleth (*Summa*, cap. 55–6, CCCM, vol. 41A, pp. 96–103), as well as in sermons from Jacques de Vitry to the end of the Middle Ages: Larissa Taylor, *Soldiers of Christ. Preaching in Late Medieval and Reformation France* (New York, 1992), p. 17. The scheme can be summarized as follows: Septuagesima to Easter—winter—*tempus deviationis* from Adam to Moses—guilt and punishment—night—temptation and passion of Christ—life before baptism; Advent to Christmas—spring—*tempus revocationis* from Moses to Christ—doctrine and prophecy—morning—birth of Christ—baptism; Easter to Pentecost—summer—*tempus regressionis* during Christ's life on earth—happiness and joy—midday—resurrection and ascension of Christ and gift of the Holy Spirit—life after baptism; Pentecost to Advent—autumn—*tempus peregrinationis* after Christ's ascension—sorrow and struggle—evening—the Second Coming of Christ—life in heaven. The scheme is not as neat as it might seem at first: Advent is associated with spring, the present life and the life in heaven are juxtaposed for the period after Pentecost, and the liturgical season from Christmas to Septuagesima is not accommodated but said to be "partim . . . sub tempore regressionis . . . pars uero reliqua . . . sub tempore peregrinationis"; ibid., p. 103. These inconsistencies are not necessarily flaws, however. As mentioned previously, the medieval mind delighted in the interaction of meaningful structures without apparent concern for univocal order and without our modern urge to reduce phenomena to single principles.

The virtues form a progression, he says, similar to the progression of the Sundays, for just as the Sundays bring us closer and closer to Christmas, the virtues bring us closer and closer to Christ. In order to make this explicit, he explains that the final virtue of justice means "giving to each person his due" ("unicuique tribuere quod suum est"); we must acknowledge that the three previous virtues come not from ourselves but from God, so acquiring justice is simply to give God the honor for all our virtues. Justice, then, amounts to the same thing as humility, and that is the virtue "nearest to Christ."[51]

The five Sundays after Christmas, from the Sunday in the Christmas octave to the fourth after Epiphany, are likened to the five ages of Man. This theme is connected with the Christmas season by the fact that Christ became Man and, thus, also partook of the ages of Man and gave them a spiritual significance. The five ages are infancy, childhood, youth, maturity, and old age; they correspond spiritually to knowledge about God, obedience, preaching, perfect purity, and full victory over the world and heavenly glory (or, in a supplementary series, doctrine, fear of God, love of God and neighbor, exercise in good works, and perfection).[52]

A third sequence runs from Septuagesima to the fourth Sunday of Lent. This sequence contains seven Sundays and is compared to the seven gifts of the Holy Spirit as enumerated in Isa. 11:2: fear, piety, knowledge, might, counsel, understanding, and wisdom. Although there probably once existed a complete sequence of sermons based on this pattern, only the sixth—the sermon for the third Sunday of Lent—seems to be preserved.[53]

---

[51]PL 174: 82A–D: "Haec autem virtus, virtus utique humilitatis, cum proxima sit Christo, quartae huic Dominicae, quae proxima est Nativitati Christi, recte congruit, quia hominem vere Christo proximum facit."

[52]PL 174: 125–31.

[53]PL 174: 224–35; see esp. 225D–26A: "Recte ad hanc Dominicam, quae a Dominica Septuagesimae sexta est, sextum illud sancti Spiritus donum, donum utique intellectus respicit." The same sequence of seven Sundays is singled out for allegorical interpretation by Rupert of Deutz (ca. 1075–1129), *Liber de divinis officiis*, 4.2–3, CCCM, vol. 7, pp. 103–4. The

It thus is not possible to say exactly what caused the preacher to link the gifts of the Spirit to this particular series of Sundays, over and above their numerical identity.

A brief series is provided by Passiontide: the week after the ***Dominica Passionis*** (or fifth Sunday of Lent) stands for the present life, Palm Sunday for death, Holy Week for the intermediate state, and Easter for the Resurrection. Here the symbolism is worked out in detail: the first week is filled with sadness like the present life, which we live in exile from our heavenly home and in which the elect must be conformed with the sufferings of Christ; Palm Sunday, however, is celebrated with great joy and, thus, signifies death as the liberation from the fetters of the present life; then follow further days of sorrow, which symbolize either the pains of Purgatory or the sadness even of the souls in Paradise as long as they are separated from their bodies; but of course these sorrows end with Easter, the day of the Resurrection, when death is finally overcome and body and soul are reunited.[54]

For the Sundays of the Easter season, no patterned explanation is preserved in the Admont corpus. The final series is the long sequence of Sundays after Pentecost, the ***Dominicae Aestivales***. In a lengthy introduction to a set of sermons for these Sundays they are said to be twenty-four in number and divided into three ***octonaria***. The scheme is not carried out perfectly, but the plan is clear: each *octonarium* should contain an introductory sermon plus a sequence of seven. The first sequence was to cover the beatitudes and the days of creation, the second the principal virtues and the gifts of the Holy Spirit, and the third the principal vices and the prayers of the Our Father.[55]

---

reference there, however, is to the seventy years of Babylonian captivity and the seven ages of the world.

[54]PL 174: 292C–94A.

[55]Neither the introduction nor all the sermons have been printed. The introduction and twenty-three sermons are found in Admont, Stiftsbibliothek, cod. 410, fol. 11r–. In PL 174

The Consecration of Nuns

Like several other Benedictine monasteries in Bavaria and Austria in the twelfth century, Admont housed both monks and nuns. The nuns lived strictly enclosed in their convent house, but participated fully in the liturgical year. Exactly how Mass was celebrated for them is not known, but we do know that they sang the Divine Office at the same hours as the monks. Though most of the published sermons from Admont seem to address monks, it is known that the abbot or his deputy regularly preached to the nuns and that, failing this, there were nuns who were themselves able to assume this important and demanding task. It is unfortunately difficult to determine how far the nuns were encouraged to meditate on the mysteries of the liturgical year, because the original addressees of the sermons can seldom be determined, and most of the sermons which are known to have been addressed specifically to the nuns are as yet unpublished.[56]

New nuns were consecrated on set days: Epiphany, Easter, and the feasts of the Apostles. There is nothing remarkable in this, since those were normal days for conferring minor orders in the Middle Ages (major orders were conferred on the Saturdays of the Ember seasons).[57] Nevertheless, it

---

one finds sermons on the days of creation (day 1: 387, day 2: 415, day 3: 433, day 4: 440 and 449, day 5: 459 and 467, day 6: 472, day 7: 483 and 494, day 8 [= day of resurrection]: 512 [see 518A] and 521), on six of the seven gifts of the Holy Spirit (*timor*: 542, *pietas*: 549, *scientia*: 555, *fortitudo*: 564, *consilium*: 575, *intellectus*: 580), and on the first principal vice (*superbia*: 589).

[56]Sermons preached to the nuns before 1147 by Irimbert of Admont (d. 1176) are known to be preserved in Admont, Stiftsbibliothek, cod. 651. Details about the nuns may be found in Irimbert's fascinating account of a fire which devastated the monastery, printed in Bernard Pez, *Bibliotheca ascetica antiquo-nova*, 12 tomes (Ratisbonae, 1723–40), republished in 3 vols. (Farnborough, 1967), t. 8 (vol. 2), pp. 455–64. Compare note 12 above.

[57]John Beleth, *Summa*, cap. 92b, CCCM, vol. 41A, pp. 162–63, says that minor orders may be conferred on all the feasts of the Apostles and on all Sundays, major orders only on six Saturdays (i.e., the Ember Saturdays, the Saturday in the fourth week of Lent, and Easter Eve).

is interesting to note that the nuns are likened in one sermon to the assembly of the Apostles at Pentecost.[58]

Conclusion

Having considered, albeit superficially, this particular monastic understanding of the liturgical year, it is appropriate to conclude by asking how representative it is. Was the liturgical year generally understood thus in the twelfth and subsequent centuries? Or was it only Benedictines who thought this way, or only a single abbot of Admont?

To give a detailed answer is not possible, since the understanding of the liturgical year in the Middle Ages has been too little studied. A few pertinent observations can be made, however. First, it is clear that the sermons from Admont express typically *monastic* sentiments. The basic scheme of the monastic spiritual life—the movement from meditation on Scripture to prayer to contemplation (*meditatio*, *oratio*, *contemplatio*)—is always presupposed. The people addressed are men and women who have abandoned the world in order to seek God in seclusion, not laymen or secular clergy.

Second, the spiritual culture of Admont was conservative. The language of the sermons and their style of Biblical exposition is highly influenced by St. Gregory the Great (ca. 540–604). Overt references to sources are almost always to Gregory, sometimes with an apology for offering interpretations over and above his.[59] Such respect for St. Gregory was typical of Benedictine monasticism but was becoming old-fashioned in the twelfth century. A new spiritual teacher, St. Bernard of Clairvaux (1090/1–1153), was

---

[58]PL 174: 890C–D.

[59]Some references to Gregory the Great: PL 174: 55, 154, 680, 682, 807, 853, 1038; with apology: 158, 416, 713–14. Other references I have found so far include only one to St. Augustine and two to anonymous expositors. There is some unacknowledged borrowing from Hugh of St. Victor and Bernard of Clairvaux, but those passages may well have been added by somebody other than the original author.

ascendant, and with him a spirituality that emphasized the imagination and the emotions more, a spirituality with a greater potentiality for becoming truly popular. Simultaneously, the growth of schools and the establishment of universities was introducing a new literary culture that placed less emphasis on style, more on system and an abundance of sources. This new culture may be exemplified with John Beleth (see notes 14 and 50), who was roughly contemporary with the author of the Admont sermons and whose commentaries on the liturgical year were destined for a great future: William Duranti (ca. 1230–96) worked them into his *Rationale divinorum officiorum*, which remained the standard commentary on the liturgy well into the sixteenth century. It was interpretations like those of Beleth and Duranti which were regularly offered to the laity in sermons of the high and late Middle Ages. The sermons from Admont, by contrast, seem to have been used only regionally, in monasteries, for a few decades.

The interpretation of the liturgical year in the sermons from Admont may thus be presumed to be representative mainly of Benedictine houses in southern Germany and Austria in the period before 1200. This is not to say that they would have been unacceptable elsewhere. Underneath the peculiar emphases of Admont there is an understanding of the liturgical year which would have been accepted by virtually anyone anywhere in medieval Europe: The ecclesiastical year is a miniature universe. The Church plays a key role in the history of mankind, for the history of the people of Israel is replicated spiritually in the Church and in each of its members. The unifying principle is Christ, to whom the history of Israel looks forward and whose life and redemptive acts are mystically present in the Church. The present time is above all a time of preparation and expectation. The annual feasts look forward to the eternal one. Concepts such as these do not differ in essence from what was held generally throughout the Middle Ages.

But the most fruitful use of the Admont sermons may arguably be not as a key to contemporary or immediately subsequent views, but as a key to a vastly more influential past. Since Admont's was a spiritual culture in close continuity with the period in the early Middle Ages during which much of the liturgical year was shaped, its sermons should be able to help us understand the intentions of those who instituted the ancient feasts and fasts, chose their Biblical lections, and wrote prayers and songs for them—intentions still echoing in the liturgies of today.

Additional Bibliography

A useful basic introduction to the liturgical year is Rombaut van Doren, "Liturgical Year in Roman Rite," *New Catholic Encyclopedia*, vol. 8 (1967), pp. 915–19. Less history and a good deal more theory, plus a large but not exhaustive bibliography, is provided by Klaus-Peter Jörns and Karl-Heinrich Bieritz, "Kirchenjahr," *Theologische Realenzyklopädie*, vol. 18 (1989), pp. 575–99. See also J. C. J. Metford, *The Christian Year* (New York, 1991).

The early Christian period is discussed in Thomas J. Talley, *The Origins of the Liturgical Year*, 2nd emended ed. (Collegeville, Minn., 1991). See also Willy Rordorf, *Sunday: The History of the Day of Rest and Worship in the Earliest Centuries of the Christian Church*, trans. A. A. K. Graham (London, 1968).

A large liturgiological handbook is in the process of being published: *Gottesdienst der Kirche: Handbuch der Liturgiewissenschaft*, ed. Hans Bernhard Meyer et al. (Regensburg, 1984–). Parts 5 and 6 of this handbook form a subdivision concerned with liturgical time, called *Feiern im Rhythmus der Zeit* I–II, in which two volumes have been published so far: part 5 = vol. I (1983), containing Hansjörg Auf der Maur, *Herrenfeste in Woche und Jahr*; and part 6/1= vol. II/1 (1994), containing Philipp Harnoncourt, *Der Kalender*, and Hansjörg Auf der Maur, *Feste und Gedenktage der Heiligen*. See also *The Liturgy and Time*, ed. Irénée Henri Dalmais, Pierre Jounel, and Aimé-Georges Martimort, vol. 4 in *The Church at Prayer: An Introduction to the Liturgy*, new ed., ed. Aimé-Georges Martimort (Collegeville, Minn., 1986); and Klaus Gamber, *Heilige Zeiten, heiliger Raum* (Regensburg, 1989). Older works include A. Allan McArthur, *The Evolution of the Christian Year* (London, 1953), and Francis X. Weiser, *Handbook of Christian Feasts and Customs. The Year of the Lord in Liturgy and Folklore* (New York, 1958). For the "folklore" aspect compare Ronald Hutton, *The Rise and Fall of Merry England: The Ritual Year, 1400–1700* (Oxford and New York, 1994).

The classic devotional work on the liturgical year is highly erudite and repays attention: Dom Prosper Guéranger, *L'année liturgique*, continued by Lucien Fromage, 15 vols. (Paris, 1871–1901); English trans. Laurence Shepherd et al., *The Liturgical Year*, 15 vols. (Dublin and Worcester, 1883–1904; Westminster, Md., 1948–50); new French edition revised by the monks of Solesmes, 5 vols. (Tournai, 1948–52).

A quick and easy way to gather information on particular topics is to consult the following articles in the *New Catholic Encyclopedia*: "All Saints, Feast of"; "Calendar, Christian"; "Candlemas"; "Christmas and Its Cycle"; "Easter and Its Cycle"; "Epiphany, Feast of"; "Marian Feasts"; "Pentecost Cycle"; and "Pericopes." The last-mentioned article (by Emil Joseph Lengeling) is particularly good, with tables showing, e.g., Roman Epistle and Gospel lections for Sundays after Pentecost in sources of various age.

A little outdated but useful because of their fullness of information in a compressed format are the following articles in the *Dictionnaire d'archéologie chrétienne et de liturgie*: Fernand Cabrol, "Fêtes chrétiennes," vol. 5:1 (1922), 1403–52; and Henri Leclercq, "Kalendaria," vol. 8:1 (1928), 624–67.

An overview of calendars East and West is given in Nicolaus Nilles, *Kalendarium manuale utriusque ecclesiae orientalis et occidentalis*, 2 vols.,

2nd ed. (Innsbruck, 1896–97), repr. with a new introduction by Prof. J. M. Hussey (Farnborough, 1971).

The **sanctorale** is the domain of handbooks on hagiography, e.g., Jacques Dubois and Jean-Loup Lemaitre, *Sources & méthodes de l'hagiographie médiévale* (Paris, 1993). More directly relevant to liturgical studies is Pierre Jounel, "Le Sanctoral romain du 8e au 12e siècle," *La Maison-Dieu*, no. 52 (1957): 59–88.

The liturgical years of the Greek Orthodox and oriental Churches are described by Hans-Joachim Schulz, "Liturgie, Tagzeiten und Kirchenjahr des byzantinischen Ritus," in *Handbuch der Ostkirchenkunde*, new rev. ed., 3 vols., ed. Wilhelm Nyssen, Hans-Joachim Schulz, and Paul Wiertz (Düsseldorf, 1984–1997), 2:30–100 (large bibliography); compare in the same work Irénée-Henri Dalmais, "Die nichtbyzantinischen orientalischen Liturgien," 2:101–40, and Peter Plank, "Zeitrechnung und Festdatierung als ökumenisches Problem," 2:182–91.

THE DIVINE OFFICE AND PRIVATE DEVOTION IN THE LATIN WEST

JONATHAN BLACK

THROUGHOUT THE MIDDLE AGES the Divine Office served as the liturgical fulfillment of the scriptural precepts exhorting the faithful to pray at all times.[1] In the medieval liturgy, this notion of constant prayer was taken in the sense of services—consisting of psalms, chants, readings, and orations (short prayers)—observed daily at certain hours over the course of the day and night. Psalms, chants, readings, and orations were used in other parts of the liturgy in conjunction with the sacraments and rites of the Church, but in the Office these components, and their setting within the framework of the liturgical hours, were central. The Divine Office was simply prayer schematized for liturgical usage.

As it comprised no rite or action requiring officiation by the clergy, the Divine Office may be set apart from the rest of the liturgy and compared in some respects to private, nonliturgical devotion, which could also serve as a means of fulfilling the scriptural precepts for praying constantly. In fact, parts of the Office could be observed in private under certain circumstances, and material normally used in the Office could also appear together

[1]See esp. Luke 18:1; Eph. 6:18; 1 Thess. 5:17; Heb. 13:15. "Divine Office" (or simply "Office") is the traditional term for the part of the liturgy now officially designated as the "Liturgy of the Hours."

with nonliturgical, devotional texts in prayerbooks intended for private usage. Yet despite this apparent assimilation of the Office and private devotion, they remained down to modern times as separate institutions of Christian worship: the Divine Office, as part of the liturgy, assumed a canonical form and included a standard repertory of texts to be recited or chanted at fixed times of the day, normally by a community; by contrast, private devotion, for the purposes of this study, refers to a much less regimented form of prayer suited for individuals. A full account of the medieval liturgy must address not only the evolution and place of the Divine Office in the Middle Ages but also the relevant developments outside the liturgy in the area of private devotion.

The present study will outline the history of the Divine Office from early Christianity to the end of the Middle Ages with descriptions of its various forms in the Latin West, and it also will outline significant developments in private devotion as known through various types of Latin prayerbooks that have survived. Particular attention will be given to the place of the Office and private devotion in medieval life and culture as these two distinct forms of worship evolved: the classes of society affected by the Office and private devotion, the amount of time required, the interaction of the Office and private devotion with such institutions as pastoral care or education, the manner in which they were perceived by medieval authors, and the role they played in ecclesiastical reform. Attention will also be given to the importance of the Divine Office and private devotion as subjects in the study of the Middle Ages as a whole, through such fields as medieval music, art, literature, hagiography, homiletics, biblical studies, monasticism, canon law, spirituality, and social history, in addition to the field of medieval liturgy.

Daily Prayer in Early Christianity and the Origins of the Divine Office

Apart from the precepts regarding constant prayer, which—if taken at all literally—could not serve as a practical basis for public worship or even for a formal scheme of private devotion, Scriptures provided several precedents for systems of daily prayer. In the Old and New Testaments there are references to individuals praying a certain number of times each day (Daniel praying three times a day[2] and the psalmist praising God seven times a day[3]) or at specified times of the day and night (e.g., Peter praying at about the sixth hour of daylight,[4] the psalmist rising to pray at midnight and dawn,[5] and numerous instances of morning, evening, or nocturnal prayer). In the Middle Ages these references, cited collectively, served to give scriptural authority to the full set of canonical hours observed daily as the Divine Office, but these scriptural examples are in fact instances of private prayer and fundamentally different from the formal observances that marked the hours of the fully developed Office.

There are scriptural references to more formal observances twice a day—morning and evening—in which sacrifices and incense were offered or in which the Jewish priests gathered in the temple to offer thanks and praise.[6] This system of daily observances seems to have lent itself to a

---

[2]Dan. 6:10, 13; compare also the expression "evening and morning and at noon" in Ps. 54:18 (each psalm will be cited by its Vulgate number).

[3]Ps. 118:164.

[4]Acts 10:9.

[5]Ps. 118:62, 148.

[6]See esp. Exod. 29:38–42 and 30:7–8; and 1 Chron. 23:30. The description of Peter and John going to the temple for prayer at the ninth hour of daylight (Acts 3:1) may be a reference to the evening gathering—moved forward to the afternoon at that period; see C. W. Dugmore, *The Influence of the Synagogue upon the Divine Office* (London, 1944), pp. 60–65.

formal gathering of clergy and laity for public prayer every morning and evening in early Christianity as a primitive form of the Divine Office. But such gatherings are not documented until the fourth century. Earlier evidence of a gathering for prayer and lamp-lighting at the evening meal is provided by the North African author Tertullian at the end of the second century (and there is a description in the reconstructed text of the *Apostolic Tradition*, a work believed to have been written by Hippolytus of Rome in the early third century),[7] but this does not appear to have been daily.

In other contexts Tertullian and the *Apostolic Tradition* mention an entire set of hours of daily private prayer: morning, the third, sixth, and ninth hours of daylight, evening, and (according to the *Apostolic Tradition*) midnight and cock-crow.[8] Tertullian sets morning and evening prayer apart from the other hours by calling them ***legitimae orationes*** (obligatory observances prescribed by the Law of the Old Testament), but even these two hours seem to have been intended for private observance.[9]

There is a significant distinction between this form of private devotion in the first three centuries of Christianity and the forms of private devotion evident throughout the Middle Ages: in early Christianity, private prayer

---

[7]Tertullian, *Apologeticum* 39.16–18, ed. E. Dekkers, Corpus Christianorum, Series Latina [CCL] 1 (Turnhout, 1954), pp. 152–53; *Apostolic Tradition* 25, ed. Bernard Botte, *La Tradition apostolique de saint Hippolyte: Essai de reconstitution* (Münster Westfalen, 1963), pp. 64–65. See the comments on these texts, with translations, in Paul F. Bradshaw, *Daily Prayer in the Early Church: A Study of the Origin and Early Development of the Divine Office* (London, 1981), pp. 51 and 55–57.

[8]Tertullian, *De oratione* 25, ed. G. F. Diercks, CCL 1:272–73, and *De ieiunio* 10, ed. A. Reifferscheid and G. Wissowa, CCL 2 (Turnhout, 1954), pp. 1267–69; *Apostolic Tradition* 41, ed. Botte, pp. 88–97. See the discussion of these and other third-century sources, with translations, in Bradshaw, *Daily Prayer*, pp. 48–71.

[9]For this interpretation of Tertullian's expression in *De oratione* 25.5 see Juan Mateos, "The Origins of the Divine Office," *Worship* 41 (1967): 479. As Mateos concedes (ibid. at n. 6), Tertullian does make provision for people performing this private prayer in common, using psalms with refrains; see *De oratione* 27, ed. Diercks, p. 273.

served as the only type of daily prayer at set times of the day and night; in the Middle Ages, private prayer (not necessarily intended for set times) existed in addition to a communal or liturgical type of daily prayer at set times of the day and night—the Divine Office. Since monks and clergy were obliged to participate in the Divine Office throughout much of the Middle Ages, private devotion could serve either as a means for monks and clergy to supplement their obligatory observance of the Divine Office or as a form of prayer for the laity perhaps as a substitute for the Divine Office. These possibilities do not present themselves in early Christianity; private daily prayer at set hours was simply recommended for all Christians.

The fourth century marks the beginning of the Divine Office as a gathering for formal prayer at daily hours that had formerly been observed privately. The earliest evidence, largely from the East, presents two very distinct traditions: a cathedral tradition (or secular Office), consisting of gatherings of clergy and laity in the morning and evening, and a monastic tradition. The number of daily hours observed in the monastic tradition varied from one monastic center to another; the desert monks of Egypt observed just two hours (evening and night), while some urban monasteries in the fourth century included all the hours that had formerly been observed privately: morning, the third, sixth, and ninth hours of daylight (**Terce**, **Sext**, and **None**), evening, bedtime, midnight, and cock-crow.[10] What distinguishes the various monastic practices from the cathedral tradition is the nature of the hours. The morning and evening gatherings of clergy and laity in the cathedral tradition included the recitation of psalms selected for their references to the respective hours: Ps. 62 was widely used in the morning on account of its reference to vigil at daybreak in verse 2,[11] and Ps. 140 was used in the evening on account of its reference to evening sacrifice in

[10]The evidence for the various monastic traditions is assembled in Robert Taft, *The Liturgy of the Hours in East and West: The Origins of the Divine Office and Its Meaning for Today* (Collegeville, Minn., 1986), pp. 57–91.

[11]Latin Vulgate version: "Deus deus meus ad te de luce vigilo."

verse 2.[12] By contrast, in the monastic tradition the emphasis was on the quantity of psalms (for instance, twelve psalms in the evening and twelve psalms at night in Egypt); these psalms were recited consecutively, in their scriptural order, and not selected on the basis of references to the hour.[13] The monastic hours could also include a certain quantity of readings from other books of Scriptures apart from the psalms.

By the end of the fourth century, the cathedral and monastic traditions could be combined in a single locale. In Jerusalem, for instance, there was a monastic observance before dawn, after which the clergy arrived for the morning service (**Lauds**);[14] and the evening observance (**Vespers**) seems to have assumed a hybrid character, containing a monastic element—the recitation of consecutive psalms—and a cathedral element—lamp-lighting and the recitation of Ps. 140.[15]

---

[12]These morning and evening psalms are consistently mentioned in the sources cited by Taft, *Liturgy of the Hours*, pp. 33–48.

[13]Taft, *Liturgy of the Hours*, pp. 54 and 60–61. As the accounts of the early monastic Office indicate the psalm-count for the hours without specifying individual psalms or groups of psalms, it appears that these monastic traditions employed a ***psalterium currens***, whereby the monks recited the allotted number of psalms from the Book of Psalms at one hour and continued with the subsequent psalms at the next hour or on the following day without any attempt to complete the Book of Psalms in a precise period. Positive evidence for this practice is provided by the monastic rules and Office books of the following centuries; on this practice and the expression "currente semper psalterio" in the sixth-century Rule of the Master see Odilo Heiming, "Zum monastischen Offizium von Kassianus bis Kolumbanus," *Archiv für Liturgiewissenschaft* 7/1 (1961): 101–02.

[14]Some studies written in English (for instance, the recent books by Taft and Bradshaw) use the term *Matins* (or *Mattins*) to designate the morning hour traditionally known as Lauds; in other studies Matins refers to the night hour (Nocturns). Consequently, the term *Matins* will not be used in the present study.

[15]See the description of the daily observance in *Itinerarium Egeriae* 24.1–7, ed. A. Franceschini and R. Weber, CCL 175 (Turnhout, 1965), pp. 67–69; for a translation and commentary see Bradshaw, *Daily Prayer*, pp. 77–81.

Despite the somewhat complementary nature of the secular and monastic Office traditions which allowed them to be integrated within a single locale, the two traditions remained distinct, and several of the regional liturgies or rites in the Latin West during the early Middle Ages maintained both secular and monastic Office traditions. Some remarks on the Office traditions in these rites will serve to illustrate the different extents to which the Office affected the clergy, monastic communities, and laity.

The Monastic and Secular Offices in the Ancient Rites of the West

Before the reforms of the eighth and ninth centuries, which resulted in the observance of the Roman rite throughout much of the West, the Latin liturgy differed markedly from one region to the next. The Gallican, **Celtic** (or **Irish**), Old Spanish, and **Ambrosian** (or **Milanese**) rites can be distinguished from the Roman rite not only in terms of the Mass but also in terms of the Office. From this period we have few books which might have actually been used in the Office, and consequently the specific chants, readings, and prayers used in the Offices of the ancient rites are often unknown. Monastic rules from this period, however, give us at least some indication of the general form of the monastic Office in the individual rites, and in the case of the Old Spanish and Ambrosian rites, which survived past the ninth century, the early forms of the secular Office can be reconstructed to some extent on the basis of later Office books which have come down to us.

The rules for nuns and monks written by Caesarius and Aurelian of Arles in the first half of the sixth century indicate the number of hours observed each day and the number of psalms and other components in each hour; they even indicate the specific hymns sung at the individual hours.[16]

[16]Caesarius, *Regula virginum* 66–69, and *Regula monachorum* 20–22, in *Césaire d'Arles: Oeuvres monastiques*, ed. Adalbert de Vogüé and Joël Courreau, 2 vols. (Paris, 1988–94), 1:252–67 and 2:218–21; Aurelian, *Regula ad monachos* (*ordo* in PL 68: 393–96) and

They outline a full set of hours constituting the monastic Office of the Gallican rite: Nocturns (sometimes with additional vigils), morning, **Prime**, Terce, Sext, None, ***Lucernarium*** (evening), and ***Duodecima*** (to which Aurelian added a bedtime hour, **Compline**). Most of these hours have large numbers of psalms: Terce, Sext, and None had six or twelve psalms each; *Duodecima* had twelve or eighteen; Nocturns had eighteen or thirty-six; and vigils had at least eighteen (the various rules give different figures, and for some hours the number varies according to the season). Most of the hours also had antiphons (chants accompanying the psalms), hymns, readings, and ***capitella*** (litanies of psalm verses); and vigils included a series of ***missae***—groups of readings, orations, and psalmody.[17]

For the secular Office of the Gallican rite we have no detailed outlines of the sort found in the monastic rules; documents of canon law provide some indication of the obligation on the part of the clergy to attend morning and evening hours,[18] but this information does not present a clear picture of the secular Office. Nevertheless, certain references to the secular Office in the biography of Caesarius of Arles and in his own writings shed some light on the place of the Office in the social and institutional framework of southern Gaul at the beginning of the sixth century. Upon becoming **metropolitan** of Arles (before writing his monastic rules), Caesarius is said to have introduced daily Terce, Sext, and None in the **basilica** for observance by the clergy, presumably in addition to the standard morning and evening

---

Regula ad virgines (*ordo* in PL 68: 403–06). For an outline of the components of the monastic Office based on these rules see Taft, *Liturgy of the Hours*, pp. 100–110.

[17]In this context the Latin term *missa* does not refer to the Mass but simply designates a unit of Office components; the term is used to designate a different unit of Office components in the Old Spanish rite (see below).

[18]See Pierre Salmon, *The Breviary through the Centuries*, trans. Sr. David Mary (Collegeville, Minn., 1962), pp. 8 and 133–34n22.

hours, and for others who might wish to attend as a means of penance.[19] This indicates a movement to have the clergy observe hours normally associated with the monastic Office, and it also suggests the possible application of the Office for the laity as an expression of piety. Furthermore, some of the sermons written by Caesarius for vigils over the course of the year show a concern for a practical means of working the observance of cathedral hours into the daily activities of laity,[20] and the very fact that these sermons were used in the Office gives the secular Office a pastoral dimension.

This pastoral element in the secular Office may have been peculiar to the Gallican rite, since popular preaching does not appear to have been a widespread component of the secular Office in the other rites. In fact, during the subsequent evolution of the Office in the West, as the ancient Gallican rite was suppressed, provision for the participation of the laity became less apparent. On the other hand, the participation of the clergy in a full set of hours—a goal set by Caesarius of Arles at the beginning of the sixth century—would become widespread throughout the West several centuries later.

Despite the early movement in southern Gaul to increase the number of hours observed by the clergy, the full set of hours with extensive psalmody that Caesarius and Aurelian outlined in their rules must have been intended exclusively for monks and nuns. The monastic Office traditions of the Celtic and Old Spanish rites were also characterized by the excessive amount of time required over the course of the day and night for the observance of the hours. The rule for Irish monks written by Columbanus in the sixth century outlines a set of six monastic hours with a number of psalms

---

[19] *Vita Caesarii* 1.15, in *Sancti Caesarii Arelatensis Opera varia*, ed. G. Morin (Maredsous, 1942), pp. 301–02. See the discussion in Henry G. J. Beck, *The Pastoral Care of Souls in South-East France During the Sixth Century* (Rome, 1950), pp. 112–13, 119, and esp. 120–21.

[20] See Beck, *Pastoral Care of Souls*, pp. 121–23. See also Taft, *Liturgy of the Hours*, pp. 151–56, on the references to the hours in the sermons, which are edited by G. Morin in CCL 103–04 (Turnhout, 1953).

allotted to each; the number of psalms at night increases as the nights become longer in winter, so that as many as 108 psalms could be sung in the course of a single day.[21]

In Spain the onerous nature of the monastic Office can be measured by the number of hours observed each day. The rule for monks written by Isidore of Seville in the first half of the seventh century outlines a modest Office consisting of Terce, Sext, and None (with three psalms each), Vespers (with two psalms), Compline, and vigils (with three individual psalms followed by three or more groups—*missae*—of three psalms each, and with a morning observance at the end).[22] In the same century, however, Fructuosus of Braga outlined a monastic Office containing some twenty hours.[23] The hours not already seen in Isidore's rule are designated as ***horae peculiares*** and may have been suitable for private observance, but extant monastic Office books from later centuries show the actual implementation of all these hours (in fact, a total of twenty-two). Most of the hours had three psalms or psalm-sections and a hymn, but several of the night hours had nine to twelve psalms, in addition to various types of chants, orations, benedictions, and short readings.[24]

---

[21]Columbanus, *Regula monachorum* 7, in *Sancti Columbani Opera*, ed. G. S. M. Walker (Dublin, 1957), pp. 128–33, with translation; and see the analysis in Heiming, "Zum monastischen Offizium," pp. 125–31. See also Michael Curran, *The Antiphonary of Bangor and the Early Irish Monastic Liturgy* (Dublin, 1984), esp. pp. 166–68; the actual texts used in the Celtic Office may be found in *The Antiphonary of Bangor: An Early Irish Manuscript in the Ambrosian Library at Milan*, ed. F. E. Warren, 2 vols. (London, 1893–95).

[22]Isidore, *Regula monachorum* 6 (PL 83: 875–77). See the discussion, with translations and an outline of the components, in Taft, *Liturgy of the Hours*, pp. 115–19.

[23]Fructuosus, *Regula monachorum* 2–3 (PL 87: 1099–1101) and *Regula monastica communis* 10 (PL 87: 1118–19).

[24]The observance of such an extensive Office was made possible by combining some of the day hours, but hymns and other components for each of the individual hours nevertheless were included in the composite hours. For an outline of the entire monastic Office see W. S. Porter, "Early Spanish Monasticism. V," *Laudate* 12 (1934): 31–52. The texts used in the

The secular Office in the Old Spanish rite may have originally included just the usual cathedral hours (morning and evening), and a set of morning prayers in a sixth-century fragment gives us some indication of the contents of the early Office in Spain or Gaul.[25] During the subsequent centuries the secular Office must have expanded, since the later books present the traditional morning components at the end of an extensive night/morning observance, and the secular Office also included Terce, Sext, and None, at least in fasting periods such as Lent. These additions may be the result of monastic influence, as some of their components are arranged in groups known as *missae*, which are analogous to the *missae* used in the monastic Office since at least the early seventh century. But whereas the monastic *missae* are groups of three psalms (or sometimes three **canticles**—scriptural songs akin to the psalms), the *missae* in the secular Office are groups of three antiphons and orations, and although the individual antiphons and orations in the ordinary secular Office could be accompanied by the psalms on which they were based, the psalms often were divided into sections,[26] so the secular Office in Spain did not include the excessive daily psalm-counts seen in the monastic traditions mentioned above. In fact, the secular Office in Spain is noted not for the quantity of psalms, chants, readings, or orations used each day but, rather, for the enormous repertory of different chants and orations used over the course of the year. In addition to the antiphons and

---

night hours are edited by Jorge Pinell, "Las horas vigiliares del oficio monacal hispánico," in *Liturgica* 3, Scripta et documenta 17 (Montserrat, 1966), pp. 197–340.

[25]For an edition of the orations see Jorge Pinell, *Liber orationum psalmographus* (Barcelona, 1972), pp. 203–06; in the introduction, p. [85], Pinell reconstructs the form of the early Spanish Office, suggesting the context in which these orations would have been placed. See also J. A. Jungmann, *Pastoral Liturgy* (New York, 1962), pp. 127–28.

[26]On the use of the term *missa* see Jorge M. Pinell, "El oficio hispano-visigótico," *Hispania Sacra* 10 (1957): 403–04; for examples of such groups of psalm-based antiphons and orations in the ordinary (daily) secular Office see *Liber ordinum sacerdotal (Cod. Silos, Arch. monástico, 3)*, ed. José Janini (Burgos, 1981), pp. 191–98, nos. 830–35, 855–60, and 880–85.

orations already mentioned, various distinctive components were used (e.g., chants known as ***matutinaria***, ***vespertina***, ***soni***, and ***psallenda***; and major orations known as ***completuriae***), and many of these varied from day to day or from feast to feast over the course of the year, contributing to the rich repertory and festal character of the Spanish secular Office.[27]

The Ambrosian Office, observed in Milan, is known to us through late books that represent a fusion of the ancient Ambrosian Office and the Roman Office. As a result, the precise form of the indigenous Ambrosian Office is unknown, and any distinction between monastic and secular observances has been lost. Nevertheless, some distinctive features survive, such as the *lucernarium*—or evening chant—at Vespers and processions to the baptistry (with special chants and orations) at the end of the morning and evening hours.[28] It also contained features that were subsequently borrowed by other rites, most notably the hymns composed by Ambrose of Milan. Although there were long vigils with psalm-singing on certain occasions, the daily Office was not so extensive, and there is evidence that in the early Ambrosian Office just ten psalms were used a day, Monday through Friday, and on Saturdays and Sundays canticles were used instead of psalms.[29]

---

[27]For an outline of the components in the secular Office of the Old Spanish rite see Pinell, "El oficio hispano-visigótico," pp. 400–05; in *Liber orationum psalmographus*, introduction, pp. [95]–[102], Pinell distinguishes between two major traditions within the Spanish secular Office. Texts of various chants, orations, and readings for the entire year are printed in the *Breviarium Gothicum* (PL 86: 47–740), and many others are found in extant manuscripts, some of which have been edited.

[28]The principal source through which the Ambrosian Office is known is the eleventh-century *Manuale Ambrosianum*, ed. Marcus Magistretti, 2 vols. (Milan, 1904–05). For a study of the evening, morning, and other hours on the basis of this source and earlier evidence (particularly in the works of Ambrose) see Ansgar Franz, "Die Tagzeitenliturgie der Mailänder Kirche im 4. Jahrhundert: Ein Beitrag zur Geschichte des Kathedraloffiziums im Westen," *Archiv für Liturgiewissenschaft* 34 (1992): 23–83.

[29]See W. C. Bishop, *The Mozarabic and Ambrosian Rites: Four Essays in Comparative Liturgiology* (London, 1924), pp. 121–23; see also Heiming's note in Anton Baumstark and

The final Office traditions to be mentioned are the Roman and Benedictine Offices, which became the standard throughout the West in the Middle Ages and into modern times. The Roman Office is the older of the two. By the fifth century, the Roman basilicas must have had a daily Office consisting of eight hours: Nocturns (night),[30] Lauds (dawn), Prime (after sunrise), Terce (9:00), Sext (12:00), None (3:00), Vespers (toward evening), and Compline (before bedtime).[31] This full daily Office was specifically a monastic Office. The clergy in the various types of churches may have observed morning and evening hours and occasional vigils,[32] but the clergy did not regularly observe a full set of hours. Moreover, the morning and evening hours observed by the clergy may have been distinct from the monastic Lauds and Vespers: although Lauds in the Roman basilicas must have had the character of the traditional cathedral morning observance and therefore was suitable for attendance by monks and clergy, Vespers had a monastic character, with emphasis on continuous psalm recitation, and lacked the lamp-lighting or evening psalms and chants characteristic of the cathedral tradition.[33] In fact, Vespers appears to have been coordinated with Nocturns in the Roman monastic Office to allow the complete recitation of

---

Odilo Heiming, *Nocturna Laus: Typen frühchristlicher Vigilienfeier und ihr Fortleben vor allem im römischen und monastischen Ritus* (Münster Westfalen, 1957; repr. 1967), pp. 164–65n543.

[30]Nocturns refers specifically to the individual sections (one or more) that constitute the night hour sometimes known as Matins (see note 14 above), but the term *Nocturns* may be used collectively in reference to the entire hour.

[31]The observance of all the hours in Rome at this date has been established by C. Callewaert, *Sacris Erudiri* (Steenbrugge, 1940), pp. 53–168.

[32]See Salmon, *Breviary through the Centuries*, pp. 7 and 29–31.

[33]Gabriele Winkler, "Über die Kathedralvesper in den verschiedenen Riten des Ostens und Westens," *Archiv für Liturgiewissenschaft* 16 (1974): 98–100, argues that a distinctly cathedral evening service existed in Rome at an early period—before the formation of the monastic Office described here.

the Psalter over a period of time, and at least by the beginning of the sixth century this period was exactly one week.

The recitation of all 150 psalms in one week was peculiar to the Roman monastic Office. In the monastic Offices of the Gallican, Celtic, and Spanish rites, the period required to recite the psalms never was defined, although the number of psalms allotted to each hour suggests that the entire Psalter could be recited in a few days. The number of psalms allotted to each hour was smaller in the Roman monastic Office, and by the sixth century the psalms were distributed among the eight hours and among the days of the week in such a way that the Psalter was completed in seven days and repeated each week.[34]

The Roman monastic Office, with its weekly recitation of the Psalter, served as a model for the Office that St. Benedict outlined in his rule, written in the mid-sixth century.[35] Benedict retained the principle of reciting the entire Psalter each week, but he made substantial changes in the actual distribution of the 150 psalms among the hours and days, and in doing so he changed the psalm-counts of the individual hours: the Roman Office had variable psalms at some hours and fixed psalms (repeated each day) at others; by extending the use of variable psalms to most of the hours, Benedict

---

[34]According to Joseph Pascher, when the week was first used in the Roman monastic Office as the period in which the entire Psalter was completed (in the fifth century), all 150 psalms were recited at Nocturns and Vespers over the course of the week; later in the fifth century those psalms which were used also at the other hours were omitted at Nocturns and Vespers (see "Der Psalter für Laudes und Vesper im alten römischen Stundengebet," *Münchener Theologische Zeitschrift* 8 [1957]: 255–67).

[35]Benedict outlined the Office components and the psalm distribution in chapters 8–20 of his Rule; see *La règle de saint Benoît*, ed. Adalbert de Vogüé and Jean Neufville, 6 vols. (Paris, 1971–72), 2:508–39, with commentary in 5:383–588. For a table showing the components of the Benedictine Office and the distribution of psalms, together with those of the later Roman Office, see Roger E. Reynolds, "Divine Office," in *Dictionary of the Middle Ages* 4 (New York, 1984), pp. 226–28.

was able to reduce the total number of psalms used on a single day.[36] The Office that Benedict described in detail is in fact less onerous in terms of daily psalms than the Roman monastic Office and far less onerous than the monastic Office traditions in the other rites.

Thus, while retaining the set of eight hours used in Rome and the principle of a weekly Psalter, Benedict instituted for his monks at Montecassino an Office that had its own distinctive structure. The Roman Office continued to be used by monks in Rome, and during the eighth and ninth centuries it would be adopted by the clergy throughout much of the West, while the Benedictine Office became the standard for monks.

The different structures of the Roman and Benedictine Offices are evident not only in the number of psalms assigned to each hour and in the distribution of psalms over the week but also in terms of other features. At each hour Benedict made provision for a hymn; hymns are strophic compositions that were not used in Rome until the later Middle Ages, but they had been used in the Ambrosian and Gallican Offices before Benedict, and by the ninth century, when the Roman Office began to be observed outside Rome, it too included hymns.[37] Conversely, Benedict made no provision for orations, which were used in Rome,[38] but in later centuries they were included in the Benedictine Office.

---

[36]He also divided psalms into sections and counted each section in the daily allotment; in the Roman Office this had been done only in the case of the long Ps. 118, and in this case Benedict divided each of the Roman sections into two.

[37]Many of the hymns used in the various Office traditions of the West are edited in A. S. Walpole, *Early Latin Hymns* (Cambridge, 1922).

[38]Sacramentaries containing the Mass orations of the Roman rite include some orations designated specifically for the Office, e.g., the *Orationes matutinales* and *Orationes vespertinales seu matutinales* of the Gregorian Sacramentary, in *Le Sacramentaire Grégorien: Ses principales formes d'après les plus anciens manuscrits*, ed. Jean Deshusses, 3 vols. (Fribourg, 1972–82), 1: 328–34. It should be noted, however, that these orations probably were used by the clergy, perhaps on Sundays and feasts; they may not have had a place in the daily monastic Office that Benedict used as his Roman model.

Other distinctions between the Roman and Benedictine Office remained throughout the Middle Ages. One such distinction is in the use of canticles. Both the Roman and Benedictine Offices use the New Testament canticles ***Benedictus*** (Luke 1:68–79) and *Magnificat* (Luke 1:46–55) at Lauds and Vespers respectively (the Roman Office also uses ***Nunc dimittis*** [Luke 2:29–32] at Compline), and both use a variable Old Testament canticle at Lauds, but the Benedictine Office has three additional canticles at the end of Nocturns on Sundays; the Roman Office, which has a higher psalm-count on Sundays, never used these Nocturns canticles. Another distinction is in the number of readings (lessons) at Nocturns. On Sundays and major feasts the Roman Office has nine lessons, whereas the Benedictine Office has twelve. In both traditions each lesson is followed by a responsory—a chant consisting of a refrain and verse. This distinction is a particularly useful indication of the intended usage of an Office book containing readings or chants: if twelve lessons or responsories are provided for major feasts, the book must have been intended for the Benedictine Office.

Despite these quantitative or structural distinctions, the Roman and Benedictine Offices had closely related repertories of actual chants, readings, and orations. When Benedict changed the number of psalms at the hours, he also changed the number of antiphons (chants sung with the individual psalms or groups of psalms), but he apparently retained many of the antiphons that had been used in Rome. So too, books of the Benedictine and Roman Offices often share a common stock of responsories for a given feast, and the Benedictine books simply add extra responsories for a total of twelve.

In sum, after the composition of the Benedictine Rule in the sixth century, the Roman and Benedictine Offices coexisted as two distinct Office traditions with many common features. It must be stressed that the full Roman and Benedictine Offices were both monastic Offices. The Roman clergy may have observed morning and evening hours and occasional vigils, but there was no obligation on the part of the clergy to attend all eight hours daily. It now remains to be seen how the reforms of the eighth and ninth centuries not only changed the observance of the Office throughout the

West but also gave rise to new forms of private devotion that redefined the place of the Office in medieval life.

The Office and Private Devotion during the Carolingian Reforms

The suppression of the ancient Gallican rite and the official adoption of the Roman rite in the Frankish realm during the eighth and ninth centuries affected the liturgy as a whole and had far-reaching consequences in the subsequent history of the liturgy in the Latin West.[39] These Frankish reforms had a double impact on the Office, since they not only made the observance of the Office more uniform throughout the West but also brought about a significant development in the attendance of the hours. In the various rites before the reforms, a full set of daily hours was observed by monks or nuns, whereas the clergy regularly observed just two or three hours; after the reforms, the secular Office observed by the clergy included a full set of hours corresponding to those in the monastic Office.

These developments apparently began in England, with the missions of St. Boniface and the Council of Clovesho in 747, which prescribed the observance of the Roman Office. On the continent, Chrodegang of Metz instituted a full set of hours for clergy, who were to live as canons. The establishment of a canonical clergy observing a full choral Office spread under the legislation of the Frankish rulers Pepin, Charlemagne, and Louis the Pious.[40] The Office tradition imposed on the clergy through these reforms was the Office that originally had been observed by monks in the Roman basilicas. The earlier distinction between the secular Office (consisting of two or three hours) and the monastic Office (consisting of eight hours) thus

---

[39]For a summary see Cyrille Vogel, "La réforme liturgique sous Charlemagne," in *Karl der Grosse: Lebenswerk und Nachleben*, ed. Wolfgang Braunfels, 5 vols. (Düsseldorf, 1965–68), 2:231–32.

[40]On Boniface, Chrodegang, and the legislation of the Frankish rulers see Salmon, *Breviary through the Centuries*, pp. 8–10 and 134–35 nn. 24–34.

was eliminated as the clergy began to observe the formerly monastic Roman Office tradition. But at the same time, the secular/monastic distinction was reasserted by the institution of a different Office tradition in the Frankish monasteries: the Benedictine Office.[41]

As a result of these Carolingian reforms, the Roman and Benedictine Offices became the standard secular and monastic Office traditions throughout much of the West (with the notable exceptions of Spain and Milan, which retained their indigenous traditions at least in part). Within each of the two standard traditions, the basic structure of the hours and the ordinary distribution of psalms did not vary from locale to locale or change over the course of the Middle Ages. There were, however, differences between one cathedral and another and differences between one monastery and another in terms of the actual repertory of chants, readings, and orations used at the hours on the growing number of feasts and in the various seasons of the liturgical year.[42] Moreover, in the monastic Office, certain elements were appended to the eight canonical hours, and these varied considerably from locale to locale. These supererogatory elements included special groups of psalms (e.g., the seven penitential psalms, recited in addition to the usual psalms of the hours) and also some votive hours (e.g., hours for the dead, observed in addition to the canonical hours).[43]

The various developments in the Office brought about by the Carolingian reforms (the changes in Office attendance, the suppression of ancient Office traditions, and the institution of supererogatory elements) had consequences outside the liturgy, in the area of private devotion. We may now

---

[41]On the institution of the Benedictine Rule in Frankish monasteries see Josef Semmler, "Karl der Grosse und das fränkische Mönchtum," in *Karl der Grosse*, 2:255–89.

[42]For comparative tables of the chants in six secular Office books and in six monastic Office books see vols. 1 and 2 of *Corpus antiphonalium officii*, ed. R.-J. Hesbert, 6 vols. (Rome, 1963–79).

[43]See Edmund Bishop, "On the Origin of the Prymer," in *Liturgica Historica: Papers on the Liturgy and Religious Life of the Western Church* (Oxford, 1918), esp. pp. 212–19.

consider these consequences and also the relationship of private devotion to the Office in general. Only by doing so can we appreciate the importance of the Divine Office in medieval society, spirituality, and culture.

In describing the clergy's adoption of the early Roman monastic Office, with its full set of hours, and the institution of the separate Benedictine Office in the monasteries, we have not spoken of the laity. From the earliest period in the history of the Office there are references to members of the laity observing the morning and evening hours or occasional vigils, and in sixth-century Gaul, those who wished to do penance were able to observe Terce, Sext, and None (perhaps in fasting seasons), but despite the recommendations found in patristic and medieval treatises and manuals,[44] the laity could not be expected to participate in the choral observance of the full set of daily hours that the Carolingian reforms made obligatory for the canonical clergy as well as for monks and nuns. There were, however, attempts to set up analogous programs of devotion specifically for the laity. At the beginning of the ninth century, for instance, Alcuin wrote to the emperor Charlemagne, proposing a program of devotion that he could observe, one that would include private prayer at times corresponding to the hours of the Office, but without the rigid structure (e.g., psalm-count) of the Office hours.[45] Alcuin's letter, as it has come down to us, does not contain a complete outline of the proposed program, but one of the extant manuscripts containing the letter does provide some indication of what might be included in such a program: Paris, Bibliothèque nationale de France lat. 2731a, a manuscript written in the second half of the ninth century, contains an oration for each of the day hours that Alcuin mentions in the

[44]See Josef Stadlhuber, "Das Stundengebet des Laien im christlichen Altertum," *Zeitschrift für katholische Theologie* 71 (1949): 129–83.

[45]Alcuin, Ep. 304, ed. E. Dümmler, *Monumenta Germaniae Historica, Epistulae*, vol. 4 (Berlin, 1895), pp. 462–63.

letter—Prime, *Secunda*, Terce, Sext, None, Vespers, and *Duodecima*.[46] These same orations may have been used originally in the Divine Office,[47] but—as the inclusion of *Secunda* and *Duodecima* suggests—the set of orations was not originally intended for the Roman or Benedictine Office; the orations would rather have been intended for usage in a Gallican or Celtic Office tradition that included these hours. After the suppression of the Gallican and other ancient Office traditions, the orations for *Secunda* and *Duodecima* no longer would have been suited for liturgical usage, but they found a new place in private devotion and were preserved in nonliturgical prayerbooks.

Thus, just as the Divine Office was evolving into two standard forms, one exclusively for the clergy and the other exclusively for monastic orders, the production of Carolingian books of private devotion could serve as a means to extend the observance of the hours to the laity; and just as the Roman and Benedictine Offices were replacing the Office traditions of the ancient rites, prayerbooks for private usage served as a possible outlet for material from the suppressed traditions. These observations, however, must be qualified. First, the Carolingian books of private devotion were not exclusively—or even principally—for the laity. Most seem to have been used by monks as a means of supplementing their observance of the Divine Office; and those associated with the laity (e.g., the Prayerbook of Charles the Bald in the Munich Schatzkammer) were characteristically owned by the

---

[46]Paris, Bibliothèque nationale de France lat. 2731a, fols. 60r–61r. The orations are set apart from Alcuin's letter, which appears on fols. 40r–41v of the manuscript, but in an earlier ninth-century prayerbook, Paris, Bibliothèque nationale de France lat. 5596, the same set of orations (slightly rearranged, with the oration for Prime moved to the end of the series) appears just after Alcuin's letter; see André Wilmart, *Precum Libelli Quattuor Aevi Karolini* (Rome, 1940), pp. 33–36, for an edition of the letter and orations in Paris 5596.

[47]Most of these orations are found in liturgical books as early as the late eighth century; for instance, the orations for Prime, Terce, Sext, None, and Vespers in this set appear in the *Liber Sacramentorum Gellonensis*, ed. A. Dumas, CCL 159 (Turnhout, 1981), pp. 302–04, nos. 2120, 2122–24, and 2132.

nobility, for whom they may have served as deluxe possessions or tokens of the owner's piety.[48] Second, the material that originated in the Divine Office formed only a part of the contents of prayerbooks. The bulk of the Carolingian prayerbooks consists of numerous long personal prayers, often using the first-person singular, which are quite distinguishable from the short orations, using the first-person plural, found in the Divine Office or in other parts of the liturgy. Despite these qualifications, the possibility of usage by the laity and the inclusion of some liturgical material are significant features of Carolingian prayerbooks and would become more pronounced in later books of private devotion.

Perhaps the most noteworthy feature of Carolingian private devotion with respect to the Office is its function as a new expression of underlying principles in the Divine Office. Before the Carolingian reforms there was an insular tradition of prayerbooks containing personal prayers for protection, prayers of praise, prayers addressed to the saints, prayers of confession, and collections of psalm verses.[49] These features continued to be included in the prayerbooks produced on the continent during the Carolingian period, but they appeared together with new formulations that in some respects emulated the schematized psalmody and prayer of the Divine Office: units of specific psalms, series of psalm verses, and orations, somewhat reminiscent of the units of psalms, antiphons, and orations in the Old Spanish secular Office.[50] Furthermore, by the middle of the ninth century prayerbooks began to arrange the devotional material in a weekly cycle

---

[48]See Franz Xaver Haimerl, *Mittelalterliche Frömmigkeit im Spiegel der Gebetbuchliteratur Süddeutschlands* (Munich, 1952), pp. 13–14.

[49]The early insular prayerbooks are discussed in Thomas H. Bestul, "Continental Sources of Anglo-Saxon Devotional Writing," in *Sources of Anglo-Saxon Culture*, ed. Paul E. Szarmach (Kalamazoo, Mich., 1986), esp. pp. 104–12.

[50]Such units appear, for instance, in two of the prayerbooks edited by André Wilmart in *Precum Libelli Quattuor*; see esp. pp. 27–30, 76–79, 124–38.

analogous to the weekly recitation of the Psalter in the Roman and Benedictine Offices.[51] Finally, some of the devotional programs of Carolingian prayerbooks had parallels in the supererogatory elements that increasingly were being used in conjunction with the canonical hours of the Office.

The Divine Office and Private Devotion in the Later Middle Ages

The dynamic developments in the area of private devotion during the ninth century continued through the Middle Ages. In the eleventh century new types of prayer collections were compiled, many of which included groups of psalms, antiphons, and orations that took the form of small Offices,[52] and after the eleventh century an entire new genre of prayerbooks appeared, which combined the earlier material with the prayers and meditations written by St. Anselm of Canterbury and others.[53]

In the Divine Office developments were more limited, as the structure of the canonical hours underwent no substantial changes once the Roman and Benedictine Offices became the standard in the Latin West, and the developments in the repertory of chants, readings, and orations used in the full choral Offices consisted largely of provisions for the growing number of feasts in the liturgical year. But in the monastic tradition, and later in the secular tradition, there was continued growth in the number of supererogatory elements appended to the hours (e.g., Matins, Lauds, and Vespers for the dead and a full set of hours for the Virgin in addition to the ordinary and festal observance of the hours).[54]

---

[51]E.g., *Officia per ferias* (PL 101: 509–612).

[52]See Pierre Salmon, "Libelli Precum du VIIIe au XIIe siècle," in *Analecta liturgica: Extraits des Manuscrits liturgiques de la Bibliothèque Vaticane. Contribution à l'histoire de la prière chrétienne* (Vatican City, 1974), esp. pp. 130–79.

[53]E.g., *A Durham Book of Devotions*, ed. Thomas H. Bestul (Toronto, 1987).

[54]See J. B. L. Tolhurst, *The Monastic Breviary of Hyde Abbey, Winchester*, vol. 6 (London, 1942), pp. 107–30; also Bishop, "Origin of the Prymer," pp. 220–37.

There was some reaction to these constant additions to the Office; there were not only movements to eliminate the elements appended to the hours but also movements toward the curtailment of the canonical hours. Furthermore, there was a movement toward the private observance of hours instead of the full choral observance, particularly in the thirteenth century with the rise of the new orders; when the Franciscans adopted the Roman secular Office, it was modified to suit their modes of life.[55]

The private recitation of the Divine Office should not be confused with the forms of private devotion known to us through the diverse nonliturgical prayerbooks. Yet with the rise of the private recitation of the Office, the movements to curtail the canonical hours, and the prominence of the supererogatory votive hours, the observance of the Office in some respects did converge with one form of private devotion in the later Middle Ages: the use of Books of Hours. These books of private devotion suited to the laity incorporated the hours for the Virgin and other material that had originally been used in conjunction with the Office.[56] Consequently, Office-related material formerly restricted to monastic communities or the canonical clergy became accessible to a wider public.

The Impact of the Divine Office and Private Devotion in Medieval Life and Thought

In the preceding summary of the history of the Divine Office and private devotion in the Latin Middle Ages, it has been suggested that a large

[55]On the general movement toward private recitation of the Office, and opposition to this movement, see Salmon, *Breviary through the Centuries*, pp. 11–20; on the role of the Franciscans in the development of the Roman (secular) Office see S. J. P. van Dijk and J. Hazelden Walker, *The Origins of the Modern Roman Liturgy: The Liturgy of the Papal Court and the Franciscan Order in the Thirteenth Century* (Westminster, Md., 1960).

[56]The contents of more than 300 Books of Hours are described in Victor Leroquais, *Les livres d'heures manuscrits de la Bibliothèque Nationale*, 2 vols. and plates (Paris, 1927).

segment of the medieval community did not participate extensively in the Office. Occasional attendance of the evening or morning hours (particularly on Sundays) may have been a common practice on the part of the laity,[57] and the formation of lay associations in the later Middle Ages involved some observances related to the Office;[58] but as most of the information on Office attendance that can be gathered from liturgical books, canon law, historical documents, and pastoral or literary sources pertains to the clergy or religious orders, there is little evidence to suggest regular attendance of a full set of daily hours on the part of the laity. Nonliturgical books of private devotion served as a channel by which forms of worship associated with the Office could be brought to a somewhat wider public, but it is unlikely that these extended the observance of the Latin hours to a very broad spectrum of society; in the early Middle Ages many of these books were associated with monastic communities, the same communities that had been most consistently associated with the Divine Office.

For those who *were* obliged to attend the canonical hours, however, the Divine Office had an enormous impact, taking up much more time than any other part of the liturgy; and since activities throughout the entire day and night—for instance, the celebration of Mass—were organized around the canonical hours, the Office indirectly could affect even those who did not participate regularly in the observance of the hours.

The Divine Office was the subject of intellectual polemics and treatises. In the ninth century, for instance, Amalarius of Metz provided symbolic analysis of the components and actual chants of the Office while also evaluating opposing practices and introducing reforms; he was criticized for his

---

[57]See Joseph A. Jungmann, *Christian Prayer through the Centuries*, trans. John Coyne (New York, 1978), pp. 87–88; and Paul F. Bradshaw, "Whatever Happened to Daily Prayer?" *Worship* 64 (1990): 12.

[58]See Jungmann, *Christian Prayer through the Centuries*, pp. 118–20; on the commemoration of the dead in the context of the Office and its application to various social classes see Éric Palazzo, [*Histoire des livres liturgiques*] *Le Moyen Age: Des origines au XIIIe siècle* (Paris, 1993), p. 173.

interpretations and reforms.[59] The question of whether the Office should include freely composed chants (as opposed to pieces with scriptural texts) was of particular concern.[60] The Office was also a vehicle for creative expression: the early hymns of the Office, such as those composed by St. Ambrose, are important in the history of Latin poetry, as they show evidence of the transition from classical meters based on quantity to medieval rhythmic forms based on accent or number of syllables. The chanted parts of the Office involved various methods of solo or choral singing, which evolved throughout the history of the Office, and different melodic forms and types of psalm recitation used in the various ancient Offices or introduced to the Roman Office during the Carolingian reforms attest to the musical expression evident in the Divine Office.[61] Furthermore, the Office also served as a context for an entire genre of Latin literature—saints' Lives, which were read (along with Scriptures and homilies) as lessons at Nocturns.

Similarly, private devotion was the subject of patristic treatises on prayer and medieval prayer manuals,[62] and it served as a vehicle for spiritual expression evident, for instance, in the composition of Trinitarian formulas to promote orthodoxy.[63] Above all, prayerbooks served as an important context for the artistic expression of the Middle Ages. The illustrations

---

[59]Amalarius of Metz, *Liber officialis*, bk. 4, and *Liber de ordine antiphonarii*, ed. J. M. Hanssens, *Amalarii Episcopi Opera liturgica omnia*, 3 vols. (Vatican City, 1948–50), 2:401–543, 3:1–224; for criticism by Agobard and Florus of Lyon see Egon Boshof, *Erzbischof Agobard von Lyon: Leben und Werk* (Cologne, 1969), pp. 276–86.

[60]See canon 13 of the fourth council of Toledo (633), ed. José Vives, *Concilios visigóticos e hispano-romanos* (Barcelona, 1963), pp. 196–97.

[61]For summaries see Andrew Hughes, *Medieval Manuscripts for Mass and Office: A Guide to Their Organization and Terminology* (Toronto, 1982), pp. 23–33 and 111–17.

[62]E.g., Richard C. Trexler, *The Christian at Prayer: An Illustrated Prayer Manual Attributed to Peter the Chanter (d. 1197)* (Binghamton, N.Y., 1987).

[63]See Gerard Achten, *Das christliche Gebetbuch im Mittelalter: Andachts- und Stundenbücher in Handschrift und Frühdruck* (Wiesbaden, 1980), p. 9.

in deluxe manuscripts, such as the Prayerbook of Charles the Bald mentioned above, provided visual representations of a ruler theology,[64] and the numerous miniatures in Books of Hours not only included an entire series of iconographic themes but also provide us with the most familiar images of daily life in the late Middle Ages.

By way of a conclusion to this account of the Divine Office and private devotion in medieval life and thought, reference must be made to a type of book that was used both in the Divine Office and outside the liturgy in private devotion: the psalter. Psalters were, in the first place, copies of a scriptural book—the Book of Psalms—and, as such, they often would contain numerous marginal glosses (running commentary), containing interpretations of the individual psalms,[65] and any number of biblical prologues;[66] they also have a unique place in the textual history of the Bible, since numerous Latin versions of the psalms continued to be used throughout the Middle Ages—sometimes with multiple versions in a single manuscript.[67] Second, psalters served as liturgical books presenting the psalms along with other elements used in the Divine Office, such as canticles, hymns, litanies, and sometimes the antiphons sung with psalms. Finally, they served as books of private devotion, presenting the psalms with personal prayers or providing an oration for each psalm,[68] while often retaining the

[64]See Robert Deshman, "The Exalted Servant: The Ruler Theology of the Prayerbook of Charles the Bald," *Viator* 11 (1980): 385–417.

[65]On the composition and contents of some glossed psalters and on the genre to which they belong see Margaret Gibson, "Carolingian Glossed Psalters," in *The Early Medieval Bible: Its Production, Decoration and Use*, ed. Richard Gameson (Cambridge, 1994).

[66]Nearly one hundred prologues for the Book of Psalms are listed in Friedrich Stegmüller, *Repertorium biblicum medii aevi*, vol. 1 (Madrid, 1950), pp. 260–68, nos. 358–452.

[67]For a general history of the versions used in the Middle Ages see Bonifatius Fischer, *Lateinische Bibelhandschriften im frühen Mittelalter* (Freiburg, 1985), esp. pp. 407–15.

[68]Psalters containing prayers represent about half of the manuscripts listed by Pierre Salmon in "Livres de prières de l'époque carolingienne," *Revue Bénédictine* 86 (1976): 218–34 and

interpretative and liturgical elements already mentioned. In these various functions, psalters were often extensively illustrated and therefore serve as important monuments of medieval art,[69] but even those lacking decoration of any sort played a major role as educational tools, since psalters frequently were used as elementary books for learning Latin.[70] Through psalters, as books of private study, the psalms, which were the most frequently used texts of the Divine Office, were made known to members of the medieval community who seldom might have participated in the liturgical observance of the hours.

Additional Bibliography

Bériou, Nicole, Jacques Berlioz, and Jean Longère, eds. *Prier au Moyen Age: Pratiques et expériences (Ve–XVe siècles)*. Turnhout, 1991.

Martimort, Aimé Georges. "The Liturgy of the Hours." In *The Church at Prayer: An Introduction to the Liturgy*, new edition in 4 vols. Trans. Matthew J. O'Connell. Collegeville, Minn., 1986–88. 4:151–275.

Salmon, Pierre. *L'Office divin au Moyen Age: Histoire de la formation du bréviaire du IXe au XVIe siècle*. Paris, 1967.

---

90 (1980): 147–49; many are described in Victor Leroquais, *Les psautiers manuscrits latins des bibliothèques publiques de France*, 2 vols. and plates (Mâcon, 1940–41). Three series of orations for the psalms have been edited by André Wilmart and Louis Brou, *The Psalter Collects from V–VIth Century Sources* (London, 1949).

[69]Various psalter illustration schemes are discussed by Rainer Kahsnitz, *Der Werdener Psalter in Berlin, Ms. theol. lat. fol. 358: Eine Untersuchung zu Problemen mittelalterlicher Psalterillustration* (Düsseldorf, 1979).

[70]On the early use of psalms for learning see Pierre Riché, *Éducation et culture dans l'occident barbare, VIe–VIIIe siècles* (Paris, 1962), pp. 515–16. Owners of some psalters from the later Middle Ages practiced writing by repeating psalm passages in the margins.

THE LITURGY AND THE LITERATURE OF SAINTS' LIVES

THOMAS J. HEFFERNAN

THE LITURGY is the public worship of the church. The very word *liturgy* is from the Greek λειτουργία, meaning the work of the people. With few exceptions, save certain core pronouncements of Christ, the liturgy is a ritual founded on the Church's interpretation of its mission. This mission seeks nothing less than transcendence, to create a timeless interval in an appropriate space where the laity and their God can meet in community. Although it sometimes has been viewed as a ritual entrenched in the past, the truth is that the liturgy always has been a mirror of its age. Liturgy always embodies a dynamic tension between tradition and innovation, between the faith and practices of one's ancestors and the charismatic power of the spirit in the Church. The changes in the liturgy during the Middle Ages—dictated by a host of factors, such as, for example, the reinterpretation of doctrine, increases in the Church's wealth, the growth of new religious orders, and the conversion of entire communities—often led to increased liturgical complexity.

The liturgical practices of the medieval Church were beautiful, dynamic, and their ritual always was reinterpreted in light of contemporary understanding. As the medieval Church reinterpreted its liturgical ceremony, liturgists and their congregations used these occasions to embellish these ceremonies. Although it is difficult to generalize about the medieval Roman liturgy, it is fair to say that the direction of change in the medieval Church is toward more elaborate ceremonial. Two examples will suffice to indicate such liturgical change. There is an early tradition (certainly pre-eighth century) associated with ***Laetare Sunday*** (the fourth Sunday in Lent), which has the pope processing out of St. Peter's holding a beautiful red rose. The rose symbolized the imminence of Christ's resurrection at the mid-point of Lent and was intended to give sustenance to the faithful in their Lenten penitence. By the time of Pope Sixtus IV (1471–84), however, that simple garden rose had given way to a spectacular bouquet of solid golden roses set with rubies and other precious gems. One such bouquet, completed during the Pontificate of Innocent XI (1676–89), contained twenty pounds of pure gold and substantial gemstones. My second example concerns Abbot **Odo of Cluny**'s (927–42) efforts at legislating the rigorous interpretation of the Benedictine rule preached by St. **Benedict of Aniane** (ca. 750–821). This extensive program of liturgical renewal led to the creation of the most resplendent, solemn, and lengthy liturgical celebrations the Church has witnessed. The monastic Office of Matins for example, intended as a brief prayer in the middle of the night, could, following the Cluniac reform, take hours to celebrate, and frequently caused considerable difficulty amongst monks unable to remain awake throughout the service. Such elaborate celebrations required new musical compositions as varied as the prose or sequence used in the Mass, the rhythmical antiphons chanted before and after the psalms, the hymns and readings of the Divine Office, and the composition of narratives, such as the Lives of the saints.

The liturgy was to exercise the single most important influence in the composition of the saint's Life, a genre that was to become the most popular narrative composition throughout the Middle Ages. Moreover, the liturgy provided a public vehicle for the reverence of those who are, after all, Christianity's paradigm of heroism and public virtue, viz., the saints. As the liturgy grew in beauty, complexity, and importance, so too did the composition of saint's Lives intended for use in these ceremonies.[1]

---

[1]The bibliography on the liturgy and hagiography is vast. However, there has been some considerable work done on the liturgy, and the saints. The work of Carl Horstmann is an early work, chiefly concerned with the vernacular; see his *Altenglische Legenden: Neue*

This chapter is concerned first with illustrating the crucial role of the liturgy in relation to the saint's Life (the Latin ***vitae***), second with examining the evidence of this liturgical influence in these Lives, and last with showing how the liturgy has acted as a stimulus for the continued composition of the saint's Life. In particular, I shall use the Office of Matins as celebrated in a thirteenth-century English Benedictine community as a focal point for our investigation and shall explore its influence in the composition of saints' Lives.

Early Liturgical Practice

The liturgical celebrations of the early centuries of the Church are shrouded in mystery, and for the most part detailed observations regarding these divine services are unavailable to us. The earliest ***liber sacramentorum***[2]

Folge (Heilbronn, 1881). See also Cyrille Vogel, *Introduction aux sources de l'histoire du culte chrétien au moyen âge* (Spoleto, 1966); Richard W. Pfaff, *Medieval Latin Liturgy: A Select Bibliography* (Toronto, 1982); R. E. Kaske in collaboration with Arthur Gross and Michael W. Twomey, *Medieval Christian Literary Imagery: A Guide to Interpretation* (Toronto, 1988), sect. 2; Andrew Hughes, *Medieval Manuscripts for Mass and Office: A Guide to their Organization and Terminology* (Toronto, 1982); D. W. Rollason, *The Mildrith Legend: A Study in Early Medieval Hagiography in England* (Leicester, 1982); Thomas J. Heffernan, *Sacred Biography: Saints and Their Biographers in the Middle Ages* (Oxford, 1988); C. Clifford Flanigan, "The Apocalypse and the Medieval Liturgy," in *The Apocalypse in the Middle Ages*, ed. Richard K. Emmerson and Bernard McGinn (Ithaca, 1992), pp. 333–51; and Barbara Abou-El-Haj, *The Medieval Cult of Saints: Formations and Transformations* (Cambridge, 1994). There are a number of useful web sites. The University of Dayton provides one on the liturgy with a number of helpful links, www.udayton.edu/~campmin/catechesis.htm. The Bollandists provide a very good site for the study of the Lives of the saints, http://www.kbr.be/~socboll/ and see http://www.osb.org/osb/gen/topics/liturgy.

[2]The term *Liber sacramentorum* designates the book used by the priest and the bishop in the celebration of the Mass, and for the administration of the most important sacraments; compare William Smith and Samuel Cheetham, *A Dictionary of Christian Antiquities*, 2 vols.

extant is Hippolytus of Rome's (ca. 170–ca. 236) *Traditio Apostolica*,[3] a Greek work that discusses Christian ritual practices in early third-century Rome. Although detailed treatments are lacking (notably of the early Latin liturgy, through the sixth century), there are nevertheless in the writings of the early martyrs and fathers occasional observations on liturgical practice (e.g., baptism, the Mass, and community prayer). Both Justin Martyr's *First Apology*[4] (ca. 155) and St. Ambrose's (ca. 339–97) *De Mysteriis*[5] at the end of the fourth century contain observations on such important liturgical practice as the Canon of the Mass and a primitive version of the Divine Office.[6]

Two crucial sacramentaries which present liturgical practices before the liturgical reform instituted by Gregory the Great (ca. 540–604) are the so-called ***Sacramentarium Leonianum***[7] (ca. 625?) and the ***Sacramentarium Gelasianum***[8] (ca. 725). The *Sacramentarium Leonianum*, although

(London, 1875–80), 2: 1828–31. See Matter and Krochalis, "Manuscripts of the Liturgy," in this volume pp. 433–72.

[3]*The Treatise on the Apostolic Tradition of St. Hippolytus of Rome, Bishop and Martyr*, ed. and trans. Grady Dix; reissued with corrections, preface, and bibliography by Henry Chadwick (London, 1992).

[4]Justin Martyr, "The First Apology, The Second Apology," in *Writings of St. Justin Martyr*, ed. and trans. Thomas B. Falls (Washington, 1965).

[5]Ambrose, *De Mysteriis* (PL 16: 389–410).

[6]Lucien Diess, *Early Sources of the Liturgy*, ed. and trans. B. Weatherhead (London, 1967), is an immensely useful book, as it presents in summary fashion the liturgical observations of the earliest Christians. For example, Hippolytus of Rome describes a late night practice called "Nocturnal Praise," in which the memories of ". . . the men of old who bequeathed us this tradition . . ." are prayed for. This may be a precursor of the remembrance of the saints in Matins.

[7]*Sacramentarium Leonianum*, ed. Charles L. Feltoe (Cambridge, 1896).

[8]*The Gelasian Sacramentary, Liber Sacramentorum Romanae Ecclesiae*, ed. Henry A. Wilson (Oxford, 1894); see also *Sacramentarium Veronense (Leonianum) [Cod. Bibli.Capit. Veron. LXXXV (80)]* ed. Petrus Siffrin (Rome, 1958).

incomplete in its discussion of the various parts of the Mass (notably the Ordinary and the Canon of the Mass), does contain some three hundred Mass formularies, the great majority of which are for the feasts of martyrs.[9] And it is on this point that most liturgical historians are in agreement; that is, although the information concerning the ancient Latin liturgy is limited, there is ample evidence for concluding that the saints have been celebrated in the liturgy continuously, even from the earliest times. The celebration of the saints in the liturgical practices of the early Church insured their continued popularity and their increasing self-conscious development as a distinct literary genre written often for use in the public worship of the Church.

It is within the context of the liturgical service, specifically the Matins service of the Divine Office, that the saint's Life develops what becomes its characteristic style: a style that is panegyrical; that idealizes biographical details; that emphasizes the ethical message of historical events often at the expense of the literal; and, finally, that is intended to increase devotion to the saint, by proposing the saint's virtue as an example for the audience's emulation.

Following Augustine's thesis that the universe can be divided into a city of God and an earthly city, the new paradigm for the Christian citizen of the earthly city was the saint. One might view the creation of the cult of the saint as an effort on the part of the Church to substitute its view of the ideal citizen for a now largely discredited classical model. Collection of the Lives of the saints now could provide the models for behavior that in former times works such as Plutarch's biographies would have served. The Church inculcated this substitution of examples of public virtue whenever possible, but most effectively in its liturgy.

The saints were frequently invoked in the Church's most solemn liturgical moment, before and after the consecration, in the ***communicantes*** and the *nobis quoque* (the opening words of the Canon of the Mass). Yet,

---

[9]Josef A. Jungmann, *The Early Liturgy, To the Time of Gregory the Great*, trans. F. A. Brunner (Notre Dame, Ind., 1959), p. 235.

although this prominent and frequent invocation in the Mass may have contributed to the popularity of the cult of the saints amongst the communicants, the Mass does not seem to have had as significant an effect on molding the characteristics of the saint's Life as did the Divine Office.[10]

Before investigating in greater detail the specific relationship that hagiography has played in the liturgy, it must first be said that, of course, not all hagiography—even in the early centuries of the Church—was written with a liturgical end in view. A number of important and very influential Lives were written with a more deliberate literary intention than the liturgy could provide. For example, Sulpicius Severus, in his *Life of Martin of Tours*, suggests that one of the reasons for his composition is to offer a more potent alternative to the popularity of classical literature.[11]

However, from the fifth century onward, the primary motivating force behind the composition of the majority of hagiographic texts was the liturgy. Saints' Lives were used in such important liturgical ceremonies as the Mass, the Divine Office, the monastic *lectio divina* [sacred reading], priestly ordinations, and in the canonization of the saint. Canonization,

---

[10]Josef A. Jungmann, *Missarum Sollemnia: Eine Genetische Erklärung Der Römischen Messe*, 2 vols. (Wein, 1948), 2:213–25, 309–22. This is the standard work on the history and evolution of the Roman Mass. Compare Jungmann, *The Early Liturgy*, p. 181. Although not specifically concerned with the presence of prayers to the saints in the Mass, O. B. Hardison's essay, "The Mass as Sacred Drama," in his *Christian Rite and Christian Drama in the Middle Ages Essays in the Origin and Early History of Modern Drama* (Baltimore, 1965), pp. 35–79, illustrates the great importance of the ritual aspects of the liturgy. It is interesting to note, as Hardison points out, that Amalarius of Metz's (780?–850) allegorical interpretation of the Mass in his *Liber officialis*, although condemned by the Council of Quiercy in 838, was very popular with the laity, who were said to have "read them assiduously."

[11]Sulpicius Severus, *Vie de saint Martin*, ed. Jacques Fontaine, *Sources chrétiennes* 133 (Paris, 1967), pp. 250–52: "quid posteritas emolumenti tulit legendo Hectorem pugnantem aut Socraten philosophantem, cum eos non solum imitari stultitia sit, sed non acerrime etiam inpugnare dementia. . . . Vnde facturus mihi operae pretium uideor, si uitam sanctissimi uiri, exemplo aliis mox futuram, perscripsero, quo utique ad ueram sapientiam et caelestem militiam diuinamque uirtutem legentes incitabuntur."

although a phenomenon of the later Middle Ages and the increasing centralization of power in the Roman **Curia**,[12] was never controlled completely by Rome until the Council of Trent (1545–63), although a modicum of standardization existed by the twelfth century.[13]

For the greater part of the Middle Ages, the cult and veneration [***dulia*** as opposed to the veneration due to God, ***latria***] of the saints was primarily a local institution.[14] Indeed, because of this local character, inevitably there grew up a number of extra-liturgical ceremonies native to this or that specific church. The use of the saint's Life also was common in a number of generally uniform minor liturgical ceremonies, such as the recitation of a saint's litany in the prayers for the dying; in special blessings for pregnancy and successful childbirth, and in funeral rites immediately following the recitation of the ***subvenite***.[15] Thus the saints—by virtue of the prominent public place their virtually incessant liturgical celebration had wrought—occupied an immensely important place in the minds and hearts of the faithful.[16]

---

[12]Frederick W. Faber, *An Essay on Beatification, Canonization, and the Processes of the Congregation of Rites* (London, 1848), p. 121n1: "There is a question about the first solemn canonization; some say it was Leo III's canonization of St. Swibert in 804."

[13]*Canones et Decreta Sacrosancti Oecumenici Concilii Tridentini* (Lipsiae, 1876), pp. 173–76: "De Invocatione, Veneratione et Reliquiis Sanctorum, et Sacris Imaginibus"; compare Faber, *An Essay on Beatification*, pp. 74–75; and David Knowles, *Great Historical Enterprises. Problems in Monastic History* (London, 1963), p. 10.

[14]Paolo Molinari, *Saints: Their Place in the Church* (New York, 1965), pp. 128–33.

[15]Ludwig Eisenhofer and Joseph Lechner, *The Liturgy of the Roman Rite*, trans. A. J. and E. F. Peeler, ed. H. E. Winstone (London, 1961), pp. 414, 426. William Maskell, *Monumenta Ritualia Ecclesiae Anglicanae*, 2nd ed., 3 vols. (Oxford, 1882). In volume 1 Maskell gives a copious account of services in the Church, many of which use exhortation to the saints.

[16]These continual calls to prayer and song continued to become more elaborate as the traditions became fixed. Indeed, the later Cluniacs (following the ninth-century reforms of Benedict of Aniane) attempted to live in perpetual prayer, and we have examples of their extraordinary efforts in the *laus perennis* [uninterrupted psalmody] and the vigils for saints days;

The Function of the Saint's Life in the Divine Office

The Divine Office or ***Cursus***—so called in the Middle Ages because of the daily patterned repetition of the services—which commonly consisted of seven daily services called *horae* [hours], contained no indispensable religious service, nor did it follow a specific pattern ordained by Christ or sanctioned by the Scriptures (as does the Mass). It evolved over a period of several centuries and was, initially, a local liturgical service that lacked the uniformity of certain other liturgical practices.

The beginnings of the Office, although having some affinity with earlier synagogue services such as the morning and evening saying of the ***Schemá***, are to be found primarily in the "vigil," the service of preparation, which the early Church observed the night before Easter Sunday.[17] These vigils became increasingly popular in the Church and soon were part of the Saturday evening preparation for Sunday service—and also were celebrated on the eve of a martyr's anniversary feast. The earliest record of a martyr's

---

see David Knowles, *The Monastic Order in England; A History of its Development from the Times of St. Dunstan to the Fourth Lateran Council, 940–1216*, 2nd ed. (Cambridge, 1963), pp. 25–30, 149–50; Donald Attwater, *A Catholic Dictionary*, 3rd ed. (New York, 1958), p. 284. See also Jonathan Black, "The Divine Office and Private Devotion in the Latin West," above pp. 47–74.

[17]W. O. E. Oesterley, *The Jewish Background of the Christian Liturgy* (Gloucester, Mass., 1965), pp. 111–47; compare C. W. Dugmore, *The Influence of the Synagogue upon the Divine Office* (London, 1945), pp. 59–70, and Josef M. Nielen, *The Earliest Christian Liturgy*, trans. Patrick Cummins (St. Louis, Mo., 1941), pp. 204, 340–41; see also Irénée Henri Dalmais, *Introduction to the Liturgy*, trans. Roger Capel (London, 1961), p. 144: ". . . doubtless there was never a lack of ascetics and virgins to maintain the traditional rhythm of the house of prayer taken over from the Jewish tradition and to recognize the importance of the night vigil so explicitly recommended by Jews. At the beginning of the third century, the Apostolic Tradition and Origen agree . . . in recommending nocturnal prayer. Still earlier, on the evidence of Pliny the Younger, Christians were assembling at the first light of dawn on Sundays to sing hymns to Christ as to God," and see Karl Young, *The Drama of the Medieval Church*, 2 vols. (Oxford, 1933), 1:44–75.

vigil occurs in Pontius's *The Life and Passion of Saint Cyprian*, a work Harnack has called the "first Christian biography." Cyprian had been imprisoned, and Christians kept vigil outside the prison: ". . . so that the people of God should keep watch at the suffering of the priest."[18]

The vigil, which normally lasted the entire night, in the early Church was divided into three services: one in the beginning of the evening, one in the middle of the night, and one at dawn. During each of these services, prayers were said, certain psalms were sung, passages were read from the Bible (and it seems entirely reasonable to assume that passages were also read from the ***Acta Martyrum***, although there is no direct evidence of this), and a homily was preached.[19]

During this early period of the Church's existence, the prayers of the Office were celebrated publicly in the local churches. It is not until the early years of the fourth century that the monastic Office began to separate

---

[18]Pontius the Deacon, *De Vita et Passione Sancti Caecilii Cypriani* (PL 3: 1554): "Concurrebant undique versus omnes ad spectaculum, nobis pro devotione fidei gloriosum, gentilibus et dolendum. Receptum eum tamen, et in domo principis constitutum una nocte continuit custodia delicata, ita ut convivae ejus et chari in contubernio ex more fuerimus. Plebs interim tota sollicita ne per noctem aliquid sine conscientia sui fieret, ante fores principis excubabat. Concessit ei tunc divina bonitas, vero digno, *ut Dei populus etiam in sacerdotis passione vigilaret.*" *Vide* St. Ambrose's remarks on the vigil celebrated in Milan for the feasts of SS. Peter and Paul in *Liber de Virginitate* (PL 16: 313): "Nox fuit, pauciores ad vigilias convenerunt." See also Adolf von Harnack, "Das Leben Cyprians von Pontius, Die erste christliche Biographie," *Texte und Untersuchungen zur altchristlichen Literatur* 39 (1913); and see Dieter Hoster, "Die Form der frühesten lateinischen Heiligenviten von der Vita Cypriani bis zur Vita Ambrosii und ihr Heiligenideal," Ph.D. thesis (University of Cologne, 1963). Hoster argues that the work is not a *vita* or ***passio*** and goes on to suggest its similarity to late-Classical writing: "Elemente dieser Genera [*vita* und *passio*] stecken in der schrift, doch wo sind in Wahrheit die starren Grenzen dieser lebendigsten Gebrauchsliteraturen der späten Antike?," pp. 47–48.

[19]For an indication of readings of the *Lives of the Desert Fathers* in the early days of the fifth century in the daily *lectio divina* see Robert T. Meyer, "Lectio Divina in Palladius," in *Kyriakon: Festschrift Johannes Quasten*, ed. Patrick Granfield and Josef A. Jungmann, 2 vols. (Münster Westfalen, 1970), 2:583–84.

itself from the public ceremony, the only two uniquely monastic hours being Prime and Compline (the first and last hours respectively). Apart from the growth of the Office from the Easter vigil, daily, almost continuous public prayer was urged for all Christians. Tertullian exhorted the faithful to prayer and even advised set times for their prayers—hours of the day that later were incorporated in the hours of the monastic Office.[20]

However, it was not until the fifth century that the monastic Office, with its increased formality and liturgical richness, began to assume a distinctive character. It was the monastic Office and its increased use of readings that accounted, in part, for the continued composition and spread of the stories of the saints. It is to this liturgical tradition—a tradition as yet wholly within the confines of the Church and dominated by a variety of monastic rules—that the later flowering of the legends of the saints in both the late-Carolingian period and the thirteenth century (the two periods which saw the greatest production in the composition of saints' Lives) in large measure owe their origins and narrative characteristics. This is especially true for those texts used in the Office such as the **breviary** readings, as we shall see below.

The *Pilgrimage of Egeria*, composed about the year four hundred, is an early description of a pilgrimage to the Holy Land—a pilgrimage whose express purpose was to visit shrines of the saints.[21] It contains some detailed descriptions of church services then in use in Jerusalem, and specifically describes the daily and Sunday liturgies and the canonical hours. From what the nun Egeria tells us, the Office was being celebrated daily and seems to have been celebrated either on top of or in close proximity to a

---

[20]Tertullian, *Liber de Oratione* (PL 1: 1300): "De tempore vero non erit otiosa extrinsecus observatio etiam horarum quarumdam. Istarum dico communium, quae diu inter spatia signant, tertia, sexta, nona quas solemniores in Scripturis invenire est." See also Karl Baus, *From the Apostolic Community to Constantine* (New York, 1965), p. 301.

[21]Éthérie, *Journal de voyage*, ed. Hélène Pétré, *Sources chrétiennes* 21 (Paris, 1948); see also John Wilkinson, *Egeria's Travels* (London, 1971), pp. 63–69. Wilkinson's clear exposition on the structure of the services is especially helpful.

martyr's grave. The prayers began early in the morning before cock-crow [*ante pullorum cantum*] and were offered by monks and virgins consecrated to God [*monazontes et parthenae, ut hic dicunt*] in the Church of the Holy Sepulchre, where they were continued throughout the day.[22]

From the very earliest stages of monastic life then, the celebration of the Divine Office was closely associated with the cult of the saints. Josef Jungmann suggests that from the earliest period of monastic organization there was even a decided intention to have the monastery erected over the actual grave of a martyr.[23] Thus the monks could be assured that they were performing the proper veneration [*dulia*] due to the saint and, further, could be certain that their prayers would be more favorably received by God because of their proximity to his martyrs.

The Use of the Saint's Life in the Early Liturgy

"Asculta, o fili, praecepta magistri, et inclina aure cordis tui. . . ." These famous words of Benedict's have directed the thoughts of abbot and monk alike for the past fifteen hundred years.[24] The Latin monastic Office was given its first systematic formulation in St. Benedict's enlightened, practical, and compassionate *Rule of the Monks* (ca. 523–26), a rule which was influenced by the practices of the desert fathers.[25] David Knowles has pointed out that Benedict was intimately familiar with the type of eastern

---

[22]*Journal de voyage*, p. 188; chapter 24 is of special interest because of its description of the daily prayers, which bear a close resemblance to the later *horae* of the Office.

[23]Jungmann, *The Early Liturgy*, p. 281.

[24]*The Rule of St. Benedict: In Latin and English*, ed. Justin McCann (London, 1952), p. l. See also John Chapman, *St. Benedict and the Sixth Century* (London, 1929), p. 32.

[25]Benedict, it seems, consciously followed the example of St. Anthony and the desert fathers in his personal rejection of *urbanitas* in favor of *rusticitas*; see Gregory the Great, *Vita S. Benedicti* (PL 66: 126).

monasticism brought to the West by John Cassian, "whom he cites explicitly or implicitly some ninety times, a figure far outnumbering his citations or reminiscences of any other author."[26] Benedict followed what seems to have been an established pattern of daily prayer for the pious Christian.

Benedict saw the primary occupation of the monk as prayer and contemplation, which he called the work of God, "Nihil operi Dei praeponatur."[27] His monastic day was divided into three major partitions: the ***Opus Dei***, a period of community prayer of approximately four hours; the ***lectio divina*** or spiritual reading also about four hours in length; and the ***opus manum*** which usually occupied six hours of the day.[28] These broad divisions were then subdivided by a number of formal liturgical services or hours.[29] At first the number of services was divided into seven. This division was based on the psalmist's simple utterance, "Septies in die laudem dixi tibi," a phrase quoted by Benedict in Chapter sixteen of the Rule.[30]

---

[26]Knowles, *The Monastic Order in England*, pp. 11–12.

[27]*The Rule of Saint Benedict*, ed. McCann, chap. 43, 102. See Vincenz Stebler, "Die 'Horae Competentes' des benediktinischen Stundengebetes," in *Studia Anselmiana* 42 (1957): 15–24, for a discussion of the *horae* and an interpretation of Benedict's understanding of them.

[28]For the intimate relationship between monastic contemplative prayer and the "lectio divinia," See Louis Bouyer, *The Meaning of the Monastic Life* (London, 1955), especially the last three chapters, "Lectio Divina," "Opus Dei," and "The Mass." See also Louis Bouyer, *The Spirituality of the New Testament and the Fathers*, vol. 1, p. 518 of *A History of Christian Spirituality* (New York, 1963) written with J. Leclercq and F. Vandembroucke.

[29]Knowles, *The Monastic Order in England*; see his lucid discussion of the monastic *Cursus* on pp. 448–56 and his table outlining the complete horarium on pp. 714–15.

[30]*Rule of Saint Benedict*, ed. McCann, p. 60: "*Ut ait propheta: Septies in die laudem dixi tibi.* Qui septenarius sacratus numerus a nobis sie implebitur, si Matutino, Primae, Tertiae, Sextae, Nonae, Vesperae, Completoriique tempore nostrae servitutis officia persolvamus; quia de his diurnis horis dixit: *Septies in die laudem dixi tibi*"; editor's italics. See also Psalm 55 and Daniel 6:l0. Ambrose, *De Virginibus* (PL 16: 237), cites with approval the

What is less well known, however, is that these services gradually were increased to ten, and even twelve, calls to prayer. This increment in liturgical worship was marked especially in those Benedictine establishments (such as **Cluny**) which followed the ninth-century reforms instituted by Benedict of Aniane. The extent of the liturgical services observed at Cluny were so encompassing and lengthy that, as late as the mid-eleventh century, the young Anselm rejected the possibility of becoming a monk at Cluny because the rigorous observances made study virtually impossible.[31]

The continual daily round of song, prayer, and readings that comprised the hours created a uniquely monastic literature that was chiefly concerned with historical phenomena, with the Lives of the saints a prominent part of that corpus.[32] It was, moreover, a literature markedly rhetorical in its exposition and edifying in intention. And, as one could surmise, there was a growth in the production of service books of various kinds which would conveniently contain prayers and readings made necessary by the growth of this liturgy. The Lives of the saints which were composed for reading [*legenda*] during the Divine Office were collected in such volumes and called *legendarium*.[33]

The reading from the Lives of the saints in the Divine Office is attested very early, if not fully, but was not sanctioned officially in the Roman rite

---

psalmist's precept of prayer seven times daily: "Si enim propheta dicit 'Septies in die laudem dixi tibi,' qui regni erat necessitatibus occupatus; quid nos facere oportet, qui legimus: 'Vigilate et orate, ne intretis in tentationem'."

[31]Eadmer, *Vita Sancti Anselmi* (PL 158: 53).

[32]Jean Leclercq, *The Love of Learning and Desire for God: A Study of Monastic Culture*, trans. C. Misrahi (New York, 1961), pp. 190–94.

[33]Smith and Cheetham, *A Dictionary of Christian Antiquities*, 2:970, 1132–39; A. Bugnini, "Passionario," in *Enciclopedia cattolica* (Vatican City, 1954), 9:915–17: "Passionario o leggendario é la raccolta di libelli consacrati al racconto della vita, del martirio, della traslazione e dei miracoli dei santi."

until the eighth century.[34] However, Benedict did recommend in Chapter forty-two of his Rule that readings from Cassian's *Collationes* or the ***Vitas Patrum***, or something else which may edify the listeners ["aut certe aliud quod aedificet audientes"] ought to be read publicly to the assembled community.[35] It seems never to have been remarked that when Benedict refers to "aut certe aliud quod aedificet audientes" he may well have been referring to saints' Lives. Although no standard or easily identifiable single collection comparable to the *Vitas Patrum* and the *Collationes* seems to have been available at that time, there seem already to have been collections of *lectiones* for particular feast days. For example, in his direction on the performance of the night Office on saints' days (Chapter fourteen of the Rule),

---

[34]Suitbert Bäumer, *Geschichte des Breviers: Versuch einer quellenmässigen Darstellung der Entwicklung des altkirchlichen und des römischen Officiums bis auf unsere Tage* (Freiburg, 1895), p. 266: "Aus den Biographien und den Werken der heiligen Päpste Cölestin 1 (d. 432), Leo d. Gr. (d. 461), und Gelasius I (d. 496) ist zwar ersichtlich, das man beim Gottesdienste die heiligen Schriften des Alten und Neuen Testamentes und auch Werke der Väter und Martyreracten zu Rom las." B. de Gaiffier, "La lecture des actes des martyrs dans la prière liturgique en occident: a propos du passionaire hispanique," *Analecta Bollandiana*, 72 (1954): 138–42; see note 3, p.142, where Von Dobschütz comments on the practice in Rome at the time of the Council of Hippo (October, 393): "Auch in Rom wurden die Märtyrerakten an den bestimmten Tagen bei den dem betreffenden Heiligen gewidmeten Stätten verlesen: aber eben nur hier, nicht auch in anderen kirchen." See also Pope Hadrian I's letter to Charlemagne, where he discusses the readings of the passions: "Vitas enim patrum sine probabilibus actoribus minime in ecclesia leguntur. Nam ab orthodoxis titulatas et suscipiuntur et leguntur. Magis enim passiones sanctorum martyrum sacri canones censuentes, ut liceat etiam eas legi, cum anniversarii dies eorum celebrantur," in Giovanni Mansi, *Sacrorum Conciliorum Nova, et Amplissima Collectio*, 31 vols. (Florence, 1767), 1:800, "Epistola Hadriani Papae Ad Carolum Regem." Compare Horstmann, *Altenglische Legenden*, p. xiii: "Wahrscheinlich ist auch die Regelung und Vebreitung diser Lectiones den Klöstern, besonders den Benedinern, zu verdanken, welche die Bedeutung der Legende für den Gottesdienst früh erkannten; schon Cassiodor (ca. 550, Gründer eines Klosters in Bruttien) ermahnt: Vitas patrum, confessiones fidelium, passiones martyrum legite constanter."

[35]*The Rule of S. Benet, Latin and Anglo-Saxon Interlinear Version*, ed. H. Logeman, EETS o.s. 90 (London, 1888).

Benedict stipulates that only the readings from the Lives of the saints particular to that day should be read.[36] St. Augustine's comments in his sermon in honor of St. Stephen suggest that, even at that early date, the Lives of the saints were to be found in a type of liturgical volume: "Because we scarcely find the deeds of the other martyrs which we can recite at their feasts, the passim of this one is in the canonical book" [. . . *in canonico libro est*].[37]

Eisenhofer and Lechner discuss a fifth-century practice of saying the Office and note that in ". . . the public recitation of the office in religious houses . . . a passage was read daily from the martyrology." Jungmann also confirms this practice: ". . . on feasts of martyrs the readings of one or two of the *missae* [groups of assigned readings] were taken from their passion stories." However, he unfortunately does not specify precisely the time of the day at which the passion was read. In the non-Roman rites from the

---

[36]*The Rule of St Benedict*, ed. McCann, p. 58: "In Sanctorum vero festivitatibus vel omnibus sollemnitatibus, sicut diximus Dominico die agendum, ita agatur, excepto quod psalmi aut antiphonae vel lectiones ad ipsum diem pertinentes dicantur."

[37]St. Augustine, Sermo CCCXV (PL 39:1426). Compare Cassiodorus, *De Institutione Divinarum Litterarum* (PL 70: 1147): "Et ideo futurae beatitudinis memores, vitas Patrum, confessiones fidelium, passiones martyrum legite constanter (quas inter in epistula sancti Jhieronymi ad Chromatium et Heliodorum destinata procul dubio reperitis) qui per totum orbem terrarum floruere." See also Bugnini, "Passionario," 9:915–17, and Bäumer, *Geschichte des Breviers*, p. 278: "Unter den *Passiones*, *Gesta* oder *Vitae* find nicht immer die Acten der Martyrer oder authentische Biographien der heiligen zu verstehen, sondern häufig auf Grund der Acten oder anderer mehr oder minder zuverlässigen Documente angefertigte Lebens beschreibungen, die sich zuweilen mehr als poetische oder rhetorische Umhüllung und Ausschmückung eines historischen Kernes erweisen und daher nicht selten fabelhafte Zusätze erhalten. Die selben wurden in ein eigenes Buch eingetragen, *Passionale* oder *Passionarium* genannt, weil sie mit Vorzug die Leiden der Martyrer zur Darstellung brachten. Solche *Passionaria* findet man unter den Codices des 9 bis 15 Jahrhunderts in jeder grössern Bibliothek." The number of service books used in church rituals during the Middle Ages was considerable. Maskell in his *Monumenta Ritualia Ecclesiae Anglicanae*, pp. ccxxx–ccxxxiii, lists one hundred and six.

early Middle Ages there is abundant evidence of the reading of saint's Life in the Office, as B. de Gaiffier makes quite clear: "In Africa, France, Milan and in Spain, the reading of the Acts of the Saints, during the holy services, was done during the fifth century."[38]

The Saint's Life in the Office of Matins

The Matins Office provided the greatest opportunity for both the composition and dissemination of saints' Lives. This sacred canonical hour can be divided into two readily distinguishable sections: the introductory prayers, which formally introduce the service; and the nocturns. The Matins service in the medieval Church consisted of three standard forms, that is, it contained either twelve, three, or one lesson in the nocturns.[39] This variety in

---

[38]Eisenhofer and Lechner, *The Liturgy of the Roman Rite*, p. 39. There is considerable difficulty in determining if these readings from the martyrology consistently were brief announcements of the saint's anniversary or, in some situations, extended readings. An interesting example of this lengthy martyrological reading can be found in Francis Procter and Edward S. Dewick, ed. *The Martiloge in Englysshe: After the Vse of the Chirche of Salisbury and as it is redde in Syon with addicyons* (London, 1893); see St. Oswald, February 28, and St. Mary of Egypt, April 2. This text, which was translated from Latin by Richard Whytford (a brother of Syon Monastery) and printed by Wynkyn de Worde in 1526, was completed ". . . for the edificacyon of certayn religyous persones vnlerned/that dayly dyd rede the same martiloge in latyn/not vnderstandynge what they redde.," p. 1. See Josef A. Jungmann, *Pastoral Liturgy* (New York, 1962), p. 166. Jean Michel Hanssens, "Aux origines de la prière liturgique: nature et genèse de l'office des matines," *Analecta Gregoriana* 57 (1952): 87, in a discussion of the interval between the vigil and Matins, calls our attention to *Missae*: "en automne et en hiver, ils étaient séparés par un intervalle plus ou moins grand, rempli toutefois par des lectures entre coupées de prières et de chants, et nommées *missae*." See also de Gaiffier, "La lecture des actes des martyrs dans la prière liturgique en occident," p. 143.

[39]See J. B. L. Tolhurst's exhaustive discussion of the *Cursus* in his edition of *The Monastic Breviary of Hyde Abbey, Winchester Mss. Rawlinson liturg. e. 1, and Gough liturg. 8*, in the Bodleian Library, Oxford, 6 vols. (London, 1942), 6:143–237; and Hanssens, "Aux origines

the readings was dependent on the nature of the day in the liturgical calendar. Thus, if it were a Sunday, a major feast of the Church such as Easter, or the anniversary of a prominent saint, the Matins service would contain twelve lessons. If it were a lesser feast or a weekday in winter then Matins might contain as few as three lessons. The Matins which contained one lesson was essentially a modification of the service with three lessons and was shortened to make the often lengthy night Office more compatible with the shorter summer night.

The service of Matins was immediately preceded by a round of corporate prayer. The first prayers recited by the assembled monks standing in the middle of the **choir** were the ***Trinia Oratio***, which consisted of the seven penitential psalms followed by certain brief prayers. The psalms were said in three units (thus the name *Trinia Oratio*), each of which was followed by the Lord's prayer and a brief prayer called a **collect**. The first unit consisted of three psalms with accompanying prayers, and was followed by two units, each of which contained two psalms and their corresponding prayers.

The *Trinia Oratio* was then followed by the silent recitation of the fifteen **Gradual** psalms. This service is a rather later addition to Matins and

---

de La prière liturgique . . . ," p. 9: "Par le nom de Matines, nous designons l'heure de l'office canonique destinée á être célébrée à la fin de la nuit, en telle façon que sa conclusion coïncide avec l'aube." See also Young, *The Drama of the Medieval Church*, 1:47–64. Although Young gives a quite thoroughgoing schematization of the entire cursus, his model is based on twentieth-century practice. Young's commentary often does not illustrate clearly the development of the *horae* and, thus, is best supplemented with Knowles, *The Monastic Order in England*; Eisenhofer and Lechner, *The History of the Roman Rite*; Dalmais, *Introduction to the Liturgy*; and Suitbert Bäumer, *Histoire du Bréviaire*, 2 vols., trans. Réginald Biron, "État de L'office à la fin du XIIe ou au début du XIIIe siècle" (Paris, 1905), 2:47–57. For an illuminating discussion of the symbolic and typological implications of the liturgy see Jean Daniélou, *The Bible and the Liturgy* (Notre Dame, Ind., 1956), p. 17: ". . . the life of ancient Christianity was centered around worship. And worship was not considered to be a collection of rites meant to sanctify secular life. The sacraments were thought of as the essential events of Christian existence, and of existence itself, as being the prolongation of the great works of God in the Old Testament and the New."

may have been introduced by Benedict of Aniane. The psalms were divided into three groups of five, each group being followed by a prayer. The monks had taken their seats in the choir for the Gradual psalms, and thus at their completion were ready to begin the Matins service proper.

The following description is of the Matins service for twelve lessons. This is the most complete of the three forms, the other two services being essentially abbreviations of the Matins for twelve lessons. This was also the form in which the readings from the Lives of the saints first were to become an integral part of the Office. The opening of the Office was the same for all three forms of Matins and began with the versicle "Deus in adiutorium meum intende," followed by the **doxology "Gloria patri**," and concluding with either the "Alleluia" or the "Laus tibi domine."

The versicle "Domine labia mea aperies," with its response "Et os meum annunciabit laude tuam," then followed and was sung three times. Psalm 3, "Domine quid multiplicati sunt," then was said, and was followed immediately by the "Gloria patri."[40] The next psalm to be sung was 94, "Venite exultemus domino." It usually was accompanied by a brief invitatory, which was sung by the choir following the completion of set portions of the psalm **"Venite**." This first section of Matins was concluded with the singing of a hymn; the hymn normally was taken either from the **"Commune Sanctorum**" or from the season as pointed out in the "Temporale"; certain feasts had specified hymns.

The first nocturn now was begun. The Matins service contained three nocturns, all of which had the same form, except that where the first and second nocturn began with six psalms and their accompanying anthems, the third nocturn substituted three Old Testament canticles and one anthem. After the six psalms and anthems were sung, a versicle was sung by a junior monk, and its response by the entire choir. The Lord's Prayer then was said silently by the entire congregation, the abbot concluding it aloud: "Et ne nos inducas in temptationem," the monks rejoining with the response, "Sed

---

[40]The numbering of the psalms is based on the Vulgate arrangement.

libera nos a mala." This then was followed by either a versicle or ***absolutio***. The versicle was said by the abbot with the choir making the appropriate response. However, if the *absolutio* was substituted in place of the versicle, then the response was simply *amen*.

The first lesson next was read. The three nocturns contained a total of twelve lessons, that is, four lessons for each of the three nocturns. The four lessons for the first nocturn normally were drawn from the Old Testament or the exegetical comments of the Fathers, those for the second nocturn from the *vitae* of the saints, and those for the third nocturn from the gospels. However, before Pope Innocent III caused the Office to be revised (ca. 1216), there was considerable variety in the selections chosen for the lessons. A respond was sung at the conclusion of each of the twelve lessons. The fourth lesson and its respond formed the conclusion in both the first and second nocturn. However in the third nocturn the fourth lesson was followed by the entire community singing the **"Te Deum laudamus**."

The gospel for that particular day then was sung after the "Te Deum laudamus," by either the abbot or the officiating priest, and at its conclusion the community responded "**Deo gratias**." The hymn **"Te decet laus**" then was begun, normally by the same individual who had sung the gospel, and it was completed by the entire community. The abbot then sang the "**Oremus**" and the collect for the particular day, at the conclusion of which the community responded "Amen." There also was a tradition of singing the so-called "psalmi familiares," which never seems to have established itself with any permanence or regularity, and officially seems to have been practiced little in England by the late thirteenth century. The above discussion outlines the entire Matins service as celebrated in a "typical" English medieval Benedictine monastery.

The Structure of the Second Nocturn

It is the lessons of the second nocturn which gave an impetus to the increased composition of saints' Lives. Parsch has shown how the lessons of this nocturn were added specifically in the early Church (and were a continuation of the practice of reading from the martyrology on the eve of the martyr's feast) for the express purpose of reading selections from the Lives of the saints.[41]

As the liturgical structure of the second nocturn (with its detailed set prayers and hymns) was the nocturn in which the selections from the *vita* were read, and appears to have had some considerable influence on readings which were selected from the Lives, a closer examination of the lessons in that nocturn follows.

A different monk was appointed for each of the four readings which constituted this nocturn. Immediately before the reading began the appointed lector asked the abbot for a blessing. There was a considerable variety of blessings which could be given, but it is of interest to note that the greatest variety (thirteen in number) was available when the lessons were drawn from a saint's Life. The lessons were read aloud from a lectern prominently situated in the midst of the choir.[42] Each lesson concluded with the brief prayer "Tu autem, Domine, misere nobis."

A respond immediately followed each lesson. The formula of this respond was not fixed and to some extent was determined by local practice. The simplest form of this respond, however, seems to have been divided into two parts, followed by a verse, after which the second part of the respond was again sung. For example, the Feast of St. Cuthbert, in the Monastic Breviary of Hyde Abbey, gives the following typical respond, verse, respond form:

> R. Veriloquus uates cuthbertus ecclesie iussis precibus lacrimisque coactus ut ipse ante predixerat Episcopali cathedra sublimatur populisque regendis preficitur.

---

[41]Pius Parsch, *The Breviary Explained*, trans. W. Nayden and C. Hoegerl (St. Louis, Mo., 1952), p. 96.

[42]Great care seems to have been taken to ensure that the readings in a monastic house, whatever their purpose, were performed properly. See J. B. L. Tolhurst and Laurentia McLachlan ed., *The Ordinal and Customary of the Abbey of Saint Mary, York: St. John's College, Cambridge, MS. D. 27*, Henry Bradshaw Society 73, 75, 84. 3 vols. (London, 1936), 3:149.

[Cuthbert that true speaking priest of the church by orders and prayers and tears compelled, as he himself had previously stated, on the Episcopal seat is lifted up (and) is placed in charge of ruling the people.]

V. Ex secretis extrabetur latebris et perfusus genas lacrimis.
[From the secret he is drawn out from retreats, and his cheeks are bathed in tears.]

R. Episcopalis [cathedra sublimatur populisque regendis preficitur].[43]
[is lifted up . . . on the Episcopal seat [and] is placed in charge of ruling the people.]

It is worth emphasizing that this was among the simplest of the responds. The respond sometimes was divided into three parts, with the verse after the first division, followed by two responds, and with the doxology "Gloria patri" frequently sung following the last respond in each nocturn.

Tolhurst has shown that when especially prominent feasts were celebrated, such as the Feast of St. Dunstan of Worcester, the last respond in the second nocturn incorporated the entire **"Kyrie Rex Splendens"**; in addition, an elaborate prose also could be found following a respond.[44] Young also has noted the frequently complex nature of the respond in the Carolingian period, which required both a cantor and chorus for its singing.[45] Once the four lessons and their responds were concluded, the nocturn followed the same structure illustrated above; that is, the "Te Deum laudamus" was sung, followed by the gospel, the hymn "Te decet laus," the "Oremus," and the collect.

The liturgical character of the second nocturn, with its detailed set prayers and hymns, had considerable influence on the choice of readings from the saint's Life for that particular day. The exigencies of the

---

[43]Tolhurst, *The Monastic Breviary of Hyde Abbey*, III:fol. 231r.

[44]Tolhurst, *The Monastic Breviary of Hyde Abbey*, ibid, VI:189.

[45]Young, *The Drama of the Medieval Church*, 1: 54: "In the earlier Middle Ages, the singing of the responsory was more protracted than in any arrangement used today."

ceremonial aspects of this nocturn, namely, the chanting of the six psalms and antiphons, the meditative praying of the Lord's Prayer, the recitation of the versicle [or *absolutio*] and ***benedictio***, the often complex responds bracketing as they do each of the four readings, and the predominantly oral nature of the ceremony, exercised an enormous influence both on the selection of hagiographic texts actually read as the lesson and much subsequent monastic hagiographic composition.[46] For example, it seems likely that—since the four readings taken from a Life for this nocturn were separated by the respond verse arrangement noted above, as well as an often lengthy and elaborately sung prose[47] requiring both cantor and chorus—considerable attention in the composition of the readings would be paid to their length, arrangement, and overall structure, as well as to the focus given to substantive details in the saint's Life. In short, the narrative characteristics of the

---

[46]Horstmann, *Altenglische Legenden*, p. xiv: "Ihre eigentliche und herrschende Stellung erhält endlich die Legende durch die Aufnahme in die Nocturnen, wahrscheinlich durch die Benedictiner, seit dem 8. jhdt.; hier erscheint sie nicht mehr in der knappen Fassung der Martyrologien, sondern in ausgebildeter, ausgeführter Gestalt . . . sie wird der Schwerpunct des ganzen Officium und zieht Antiphonen, Responsorien und Hymnen in ihren Bereich, die nun gleichfalls das leben und die Wunder des Heiligen, wenn auch in Knapper Fassung und mehr andeutungsweise, feiern. . . . Ohne Zweifel gab gerade diese Stellung der Legende im Gottesdienst der Production von Heiligenleben einen beudentenden Anstoss; die Vitae der Heiligen, welche früher einen mehr streng historischen Zug gehabt, tragen seit dieser Zeit einen mehr erbaulichen Character, und sind voll von Wundergeschichten." Horstmann is one of the few scholars to discuss, albeit briefly, the relationship between hagiographic style and the liturgy. He errs slightly, however, when he suggests that the so-called edifying "erbaulichen" character and marvelous stories "Wundergeschichten" are more characteristic of the later developments of the genre. I have shown above how they are part of the genre at least from the fourth century and are replete in so early a text as Athanasius's *Life of St. Anthony*; see also Antonia Gransden, "Anglo-Saxon Sacred Biography," in her *Historical Writing in England*, 2 vols. (Ithaca, 1974/1982), 1:67–91. St. Stephen the Younger (see *Vita Sancti Stephani jun*; PG 100: 1081c) was reported to be able to repeat verbatim everything read at a martyr's shrine during the vigil, whether it was a passion narrative, a life-story, or a sermon from the Fathers. This may be itself a hagiographical hyperbole.

[47]Tolhurst, *The Monastic Breviary of Hyde Abbey*, VI:154, 187–90.

hagiographic readings destined for the liturgy in the Middle Ages were dictated in part by the complex structure of the second nocturn.

Before examining some examples of this hagiographic narrative read during the nocturn, it is well to note that this idea is not universally applicable, as there can be some variety in both the form and content in the hagiographic texts used in the Office, especially in the pre-Carolingian period. For example, as the reading from the saint's Life was fixed between the other assigned prayers in the nocturn, one would have assumed it to have acquired a certain normative length. Or indeed, if the readings were of such importance that this limiting was not practicable, then they might have been spread throughout the three nocturns, as Horstmann has observed.[48] However, if we examine what de Gaiffier has termed one of the most celebrated of the early lectionaries,[49] namely the Lectionary of Luxeuil, we find a reading that follows no apparent design concerning normative length or division into several shorter selections. This reading assigned for the night vigil for the feast of the Epiphany, in the Lectionary of Luxeuil is the complete text of the *Life and Passion of the Blessed Julian*.[50] It comprises thirty-nine folios (287 x 180mm) in manuscript and is continuous throughout, showing no indication by marginal rubric or otherwise of division into less lengthy sections.

---

[48]Horstmann, *Altenglische Legenden*, p. xiv: ". . . aber bald beliebt geworden, gewinnt sie an Umfang und Bedeutung und verdrängt theilweise oder völlig die anderen Lectiones aus ihrer bevorrechteten Stellung."

[49]de Gaiffier, *La lecture des actes des martyrs*, p. 149: "Il nous reste à interroger un document célèbre, le lectionnaire de Luxeuil, dont le texte a été transcrit à la fin du VIIe siècle. . . . L'importance de ce passionnaire ne devait pas être considérable à cette époque, si nous en jugeons d'après les offices des saints qui sont mentionnés dans les lectionnaires gallicans."

[50]For a critical edition of this early liturgical service book see Pierre Salmon, "Le Lectionnaire de Luxeuil," in *Collectanea Biblica Latina* (Rome, 1944): 12; for the Vita Et Passio Sancti Ac Beatissimi Iuliani see pp. 27–56; see also Salmon's discussion of this hagiographic reading, p. 27n1.

A vigil reading of such great length appears to have been most singular and must have been a tedious night's offering, even if the narrative contained the requisite repertoire of miracle stories, as we learn from Caesarius of Arles (d. 542) who comments:

> Some days earlier, on account of those who grieve or those who labor with an infirmity of the body, being filled with paternal piety, I gave counsel and in a manner I beseeched so that when either the sufferings are long or some longer readings are read, those who cannot stand, so that they might hear humbly and with silence, [might] sit with eager ears and hear the things which are read.[51]

---

[51]Caesarius of Arles, "Ammonito ut silentium in Ecclesia Praebeatur," Sermo 78, *CCSL* 103, ed. Germain Morin, 2 vols. (Turnholt, 1953), 1:323: "Ante aliquot dies propter eos qui ante sedes dolent, aut aliqua corporis inaequalitate laborant, paterna pietate sollicitus consilium dedi *et quodam modo supplicavi, ut quando aut passiones prolixae, aut certe aliquae lectiones longiores leguntur* [my italics], qui stare non possunt, humiliter et cum silentio sedentes, adtentis auribus audiant quae leguntur." This weariness during the Office continued to vex spiritual directors, as we see in the early fifteenth century Arlyngham manuscript rubrics on the readings for the first nocturn: "In Psalmody sometimes ye stand, for ye ought to be ready and strong to do good deeds; and sometimes ye sit, for ye ought to see that all your deeds be done restfully, with peace of the other, as in you. Though this be true after the spiritual meaning, yet after the letter the changing that is in GOD's service from one thing to another, is ordained to let it drive away your dulness, that ye should not wax tedious and weary, but gladly and joyfully, not in vain joy, but in joy of spiritual devotion, continue in GOD's service"; see *The Psalter, or, Seven Ordinary Hours of Prayer: According to the Use of the Illustrious and Excellent Church of Sarum*, ed. and trans. John D. Chambers (London, 1852), p. 31. Isidore of Seville also warns against overlong readings, as they can be wearisome and cause one to forget; see "Ammonito ut silentium in Ecclesia Prabeatur," cited above. See also Knowles, *The Monastic Order*, p. 471. Abbot John of Gorze (d. 962) was fond of lengthy readings in the nocturns, and once permitted the entire Book of Daniel to be read in the three lessons of the second nocturn and Ralph, Abbot of Battle (1107–24), recited the entire psalter every day. See Parsch, *The Breviary Explained*, p. 89; compare also Smith and Cheetham, *Dictionary*, 2:1747 for instances in which monks were assigned such tasks as basket weaving in order to forestall sleeping during the Office.

But it seems likely that eventually practical convenience or, we even may say, common sense, caused *lectiones* to become shorter, and of comparable length, from about the late twelfth century onwards.[52]

The *lectiones* for Matins in the fourteenth-century Aberdeen Breviary[53] (among which are included the celebrated Celtic Sts. Kentigern, Servanus, and Columba) are approximately twelve to fifteen lines each. They are self-contained, independent narratives, often beginning with the formula "Once upon a time . . ." [*Tempore autem quodam*].[54] They narrate a simple, easily grasped incident from the Life of the saint meant to illustrate his sanctity beyond a doubt. The Lives in the Aberdeen Breviary repeatedly use the first *lectio* to introduce the saint's genealogy, which may include also an instance of miraculous birth, as well as baptism; the second *lectio* often briefly depicts early childhood and intellectual prowess; *lectiones* three to eight generally are given over to enumerating deeds from the saint's life, very often of a fantastic nature; finally, the ninth *lectio* briefly indicates the piety of the saint and concludes with his death and the assurance of his salvation in Christ.

---

[52]Bäumer, *Histoire du Breviaire*, 2:50: "La même unité régnait relativement aux *Passiones* ou, *Historia Sanctorum*; . . . ou la légende fournissait les leçons des trois Nocturnes."

[53]*The Legends and Commemorative Celebrations of St. Kentigern, His Friends and Disciples*, ed. William Stevenson (Edinburgh, 1872). The editor suggests this text is a late fourteenth-century compilation.

[54]*Breviarium Aberdonense*, ed. Walter Chepman,"Sancti Servani episcopus et confessor," 2 vols. (London, 1854), 2:xv[v] July 1 lectio iii: "Tempore autem quodam in spelunca de dysert dyabolus beatum servanum variis questionibus temptavit qui divina virtute confusus abcessit et ab illo die demon ille in spelunca illa nemini apparuit qui locus usque in honore sancti servani celebris habetur: unde diabolus videns se contra sanctum virum nil prevalere posse in sibi commissis graviter in iuriam facere conatus est unde ad miserum quendam hominem intrauit qui tantum ei appetituorum tribuit quo nullo modo saturari poterit. Servanus vero pollicem in os eius posuit et diabolus territus atque horribiliter clamans liberum dimisit illum."

These narrative characteristics of the breviary readings, specifically the episodic nature of the narrative and the dominance of a single motif in each *lectio*, can be found also in the more elaborate Lives composed specifically for the nocturns. There does seem to have been some considerable borrowing by the compilers of the breviary from these Lives written for the Office.[55]

---

[55]The Roman Breviary as we have it today has undergone a great variety of change, much of it (especially the reduced hagiographic) the result of Tridentine reform. For example, many of the short lessons in which selections of certain books of Scripture were read were arrived at in the thirteenth century, when the *Breviarum Secundum Consuetudinem Romanae Curiae* was compiled. This abbreviated [*brevis*, *e*, short, brief] form of the Office was introduced during the thirteenth century, at first to satisfy the needs of the Papal Curia, who were often engaged in diplomatic travel. The Office had developed to such an extent that prior to Innocent the Third's reform it was rather unwieldy to carry the bulky text on one's travels. The success of the *Breviarum Secundum Consuetudinem Romanae Curiae*, however, was the result not of the papal bureaucrats who instigated its development but of the most ambitious religious movement within the church since the advent of monasticism, viz., the friars. The rapid growth of the friars, who traveled considerably in western Europe and parts of the East, ensured the continued popularity of the breviary; see Jungmann, *Pastoral Liturgy*, p. 170; and Bäumer, *Histoire du Breviaire*, 2:68–69: "Breviaire de la curie et des franciscains." In some early breviaries only the first words of the psalms and hymns were given, presumably because the reader was expected to know the text by heart; see *The Hereford Breviary*, ed. Walter Howard Frere, Henry Bradshaw Society vols. 26, 40, 46 (London, 1904), for an example of an early sixteenth-century English breviary. Frere's text, although based on the Rouen edition of 1505, has been collated with at least one thirteenth-century English MS. This breviary is especially interesting as it makes significant use of the *Gesta Martyrium* (Frere, p. xxxviii) in the lessons but usually assigns to these obviously fictional Lives shorter, rather compressed readings; see Frere's discussion, pp. xxxvii–xl, on the Lives of the saints in the breviary and their transmission from other sources. For a pre-Council of Trent Roman breviary see *Breviarium Romanum nouissime*, venundantur a S. Gueygnard (Lugduni, 1508). Although the Church was watchful to encourage uniformity in the main, nevertheless there are some notable exceptions with regard to the Office and the breviary. For example, one of the most idiosyncratic monastic Offices is that used at the English Bridgettine Monastery of Syon; A. Jefferies Collins, *The Bridgettine Breviary of Syon Abbey* (Worcester, 1969), shows how this order fixed twenty-one readings for the week—three lessons read daily—developed from the foundress's belief that she received them through a divine revelation.

Stubbs has edited a *Life of Saint Dunstan* (ca. early twelfth century) that was written for the nocturn lessons and clearly illustrates this use of what I shall call the liturgical *vita* in the breviary.[56] For example, in the *lectio prima* this Life reads, "And first it should be said that having been born from holy parents, he shone so that he might merit to see among the angelic choruses those taken from the world."[57] The influence of this line seems apparent in the first *lectio* of the *Hours of Saint Dunstan* found in a fifteenth-century Sarum breviary, "Blessed Dunstan born from such parents, as he should merit to see among the choruses of angels [those] having been removed from the world."[58]

This *Life of Saint Dunstan* also shows the characteristic division into discrete lessons, in this case twelve, each approximately thirty to thirty-five lines long. The first *lectio* opens with an exhortation to emulate the life of the saint and concludes with his birth.[59] *Lectiones* two to ten depict various discrete deeds of his life; his death is the central motif of *lectio* eleven, and the final lesson celebrates his memory in a panegyrical style. The *vita* concludes with the common hagiographic motif, the prayer of intercession to the saint. This is a clear example of the saint's Life being shaped—with respect to length, content, and focus—by the exigencies of the liturgical hour.

---

[56]William Stubbs, *Memorials of Saint Dunstan, Archbishop of Canterbury* (London, 1874), p. 53: "Epistola Adelardi Ad Elfegum Archipiscopum De Vita Sancti Dunstani."

[57] Stubbs, p. 54: "Ac primo dicendum quod tam sanctis parentibus ortus claruit, ut eos saeculo exemptos inter choros conspicere mereretur angelicos."

[58]*Portiforium seu Breuiarium insignis Sarisburiensis ecclesie usum: Pars hyemalis* (Paris, ca. 1518); see "Sancti Dunstani . . ." xix Maii . . . "Beatus Dunstanus talibus parentibus ortus claruit, quales saeculo exemptos inter choros conspicere mereretur angelorum." See also Stubbs, *Memorials*, pp. xxxi and 445, where he cites additional examples of this borrowing on the part of the compilers of the Sarum, York, and Hereford breviaries.

[59]Stubbs, p. 54: ". . . et sermone exhortatorio quasi scalam nobis post eum [Dunstan] tendeni erigamus."

In his letter to Archbishop Elfege, Adelard briefly enunciates those principles which guided him in the composition of the *Life of Saint Dunstan*. Adelard's comments aptly illustrate my suggestion, that liturgical *vitae* are built up deliberately from a series of separate [*distinctum*], relatively brief narrative incidents [*brevem sermonis versiculum*] brought together [*compactum*] for the purpose of edifying the listener:

> Know moreover that in that work the history of his life is not contained, but from the same life brief narrative incidents [are] so condensed and so separate, so that even in a convent of pious hearers the whole should be gone over historically and in the place of a sermon within the sacred office of the vigils it might be divided into twelve readings. . . .[60]

Another interesting example of the liturgical *vita* is the *Life of Saint Ecgwin Bishop and Confessor*.[61] This late eleventh-century/early twelfth-century prose Life is clearly written for the nocturns in Matins and, from the apparent complaints of the monks, was thought too long.[62] It is written

---

[60]Stubbs, *Memorials*, p. 53: "Scias autem in opere isto historiam vitae ejus non contineri, sed ex eadem vita quasi brevem sermonis versiculum ita compactum et ita distinctum, ut et in conventu piorum auditorum totus quasi historialiter recenseatur, et vice sermonis inter sacras vigilias in lectiones ter quaternas distinguatur."

[61]William Dunn Macray, *Chronicon Abbatiae de Evesham ad Annum 1418* (London, 1863).

[62]Macray, *Chronicon Abbatiae de Evesham*, pp. 27–28, relates that the monks asked one Marleberge (Abbot of Evesham, ca. 1229) to abbreviate Prior Dominic's prolixity: "Rogatus fui aliquando a fratribus ut vitam eximii martyris Wistani advocati nostri sine soloecismo et alio vitio, quod nundum factum fuit, stilo commendarem prolixiori; necnon et vitam sanctissimi patroni nostri beati Ecgwini episcopi, quae prolixius tractabatur, salvo per omnia historia tenore, in tantum abbreviarem ut fastidiosi auditores taedio non afficerentur, ita videlicet stilum temperans, quod utraque pro temporum qualitate natalitiorum eorundem in eisdem festivitatibus ad legendam in nocturnis vigiliis sufficeret."

in an often ornate rhetorical style and follows what can be characterized as the Antonian pattern.[63]

The Latin translation made by Evagrius of Athanasius's *Life of St. Anthony* had influenced strongly the pattern of much later hagiographic composition. Lives that display this influence usually begin with a preface in which the writer explains how he has been urged to write this Life, usually at the behest of a religious superior, even though he clearly is not capable of the task. He then follows with a humble declaration of his lack of eloquence and, perhaps, of his rustic style. The Life proper begins with the story of the birth and occasionally something of the saint's genealogy and adolescence, with attendant miracles. A series of miracles then follows, concluding with the death of the saint, which often may be rather lengthy, the writer often giving the saint a departing speech. The Life usually ends with an account of his death, and burial, and perhaps some miracles that occurred at the tomb. The Life thus was partly eulogistic and partly didactic.

The *Life of Saint Ecgwin* contains a preface in which the writer, Prior Dominic, declares his unworthiness to write about such a man as Ecgwin:

> . . . the blessed man Ecgwin for worthily describing whose deeds Homer himself, if present, would hardly suffice. So accordingly how much do I who presume to write his life [suffice]. Furthermore, [I am] placed far beneath the feet of others and powerless and unable to entrust worthily the excellence of that man to the pen.[64]

---

[63]B. P. Kurtz, "From St. Anthony to St. Guthlac: A Study in Biography," *University of California Publication in Modern Philology* 12 (1926): 103–46; also Bertram Colgrave "The Earliest Life of St. Gregory the Great, written by a Whitby Monk," in *Celt and Saxon: Studies in the Early British Border*, ed. by Kenneth Hurlstone Jackson (Cambridge, 1963), p. 127.

[64]Macray, *Chronicon Abbatiae de Evesham*, p. 2 , "Beatus vir Egcwinus, cujus actibus digne scribendis ipse vix sufficeret, si adesset, Homerus. Quantus proinde ego qui ejus vitam scribere praesumo? Longe prorsus infra pedes aliorum positus, et digne illius excellentiam stylo commendare omnino impotens atque nescius."

The language of the Life, despite the monk's protestations, remains highly rhetorical. For example, in the fourth lesson, the narrative praises Ecgwin's emulation of the example of Sts. Peter and Paul, in binding his feet with chains before setting off for Rome thus, "O bravest victor of labors, O despiser of human reproaches" [O fortissimum victorem laborum, O contemptorem humanarum exprobrationum. . .].

The twelve lessons, each approximately thirty-five lines in length and written for the lessons in the nocturns [*ad legendam in nocturnis vigilliis*] show less concern with miraculous incidents than with the events connected with the founding of Evesham monastery and Ecgwin's bishopric. The first *lectio* gives a brief account of his birth and adolescence and sets the time of the narrative: "Temporibus regum Ethelredi atque Kenredi. . . ." *Lectiones* two through ten are concerned primarily with his bishopric and the founding of Evesham Abbey; although *lectiones* four and five do tell of the miraculous recovery of the key from the stomach of the fish. Ecgwin's death-bed speech is given in the eleventh lesson, and the twelfth recounts at some length (105 lines) the miracles performed after his death.[65]

Another interesting example of the saint's Life composed for the readings during the Office is the *Office and Miracles* (ca. 1385) of Richard Rolle of Hampole. Aside from its interest to liturgists, the Office has historic importance because it is the chief source for the outline of the story

---

[65]See Macray, *Chronicon Abbatiae de Evesham*, pp. 30–31, for the *In Translatione Sancti Ecgwini*. This text, written for the liturgical celebration of the feast of the translation of the saint's relics [". . . celebremus igitur, fratres dilectissimi devotisime tanti patris translationem"], also is divided into twelve readings, each approximately eighteen lines long. Shorter and less rhetorical than the *vita* (and perhaps read in chapter following Prime), it nonetheless gives much of the substance of the lengthier *vita* composed for the lessons in the nocturns for Matins; Raine has also printed a Life of St. John Beverly also (in the Antonian tradition), which clearly shows its liturgical character: James Raine, "Lectiones De Vita Sancti Johannis Episcopi Et Confessoris," in his *The Historians of the Church of York and Its Archbishops*, 3 vols. (London, 1879), 1:511. This early twelfth-century Life is divided into eight *lectiones*, each approximately thirty-five lines in length; see also MSS Corpus Christi College Cambridge 161 and Gray's Inn 3 for collections containing other liturgical *vitae*.

of Rolle's life.[66] The *Office* opens with a brief synopsis (quoted below at length because it is one of the few extant Offices which indicate local church autonomy for someone not yet canonized) evidently written in the imminent expectation that the official Church shortly was to honor Rolle with the status of sainthood. The faithful are asked to be content for the moment with reverencing Richard the Hermit with their private prayers, until such time when they will be able to worship him in the Divine Office and at a solemn feast in his honor:

> The Office of the holy Richard hermit after he will have been canonized by the church because meanwhile it is not permitted publicly in church to sing the canonical hours or to solemnize the feast concerning him. Only a man having evidence of his outstanding sanctity and life is able to venerate him, and in his private prayers to seek succor and to commend himself to his prayers.[67]

---

[66]*The Officium and Miracula of Richard Rolle of Hampole*, ed. Reginald M. Woolley (London, 1919), p. 5. Woolley's edition is superior, being more complete than the older edition by G. G. Perry, *English Prose Treatises of Richard Rolle de Hampole*, EETS o.s. 20 (London, 1866), pp. xv–xxxiii; Perry does not include the Miracula. A more complete edition of Perry's text of 1866 was issued by the EETS in 1921, *English Prose Treatises of Richard Rolle de Hampole*, EETS o.s. 21 (London, 1921). However, it still is not as complete as Woolley's edition and contains no preface. See Hope Emily Allen, *Writings Ascribed to Richard Rolle, Hermit of Hampole* (London, 1927), pp. 51–55; Allen paraphrases each of the lectiones. Further, almost all the historical background we have concerning the prominent fourteenth-century English mystic Richard Rolle of Hampole (d. 1349) is contained in the nine *lectiones* for Matins in his Office; see Woolley, *The Officium*, p. 23: *Lectio prima* "Sanctus dei heremita ricardus in villa de Thornton iuxta Pickering Eboracensis diocesis accepit sue propagacionis originem."

[67]Woolley, *The Officium*, p. 12: "Officium de sancto Ricardo [here]mita postquam fuerit ab ecclesia canonizatus quia interim non licet publice in ecclesia cantare de eo horas canonicas uel solempnizare festum de ipso. Potest tantum homo euidenciam habens sue eximie sanctitatis et uite eum uenerari, et in oracionibus priuatis euis suffragia petere et se suis precibus commendare."

This text is of interest for a number of reasons: first, it is a complete rhymed Office (excepting the lessons),[68] composed for a locally revered individual before official canonization, which may indicate the depth of feeling attached to the liturgical celebration of local saints both in the Office and the Mass;[69] second, it contains the only extant *vita* of one of the more prominent English religious figures of the first half of the fourteenth century; third, it contains a significant amount of local history; and finally, the nine separate *lectiones* which comprise the *vita* clearly are marked to be read in the nocturns for Matins (*Ad Matutinas*, *lectio prima*, *secunda*, etc.).

This discussion of the *Office* of the hermit Richard Rolle of Hampole illustrates the point I have been making above, that the liturgy exercised a notable influence on the saint's Life, and indeed even led to the creation of a sub-genre within hagiography which we might call liturgical *vita*; that is, Lives characterized by brief, discrete lessons, dominated by a single motif very often of a miraculous nature.[70] The composition of a saint's Life for the nocturn readings in Matins reflects the exigencies of the liturgical

---

[68]For some interesting examples of the rhymed Office or *historiae* see Guido M. Dreves, "Historiae Rhythmicae Liturgische Reimofficien des Mittelalters," in *Analecta Hymnica Medii Aevi* (Leipzig, 1889): 5; see also Karl Young's valuable discussion of *historiae* in "Concerning the Origin of the Miracle Play," in *The Manly Anniversary Studies in Language and Literature* (Chicago, 1923), p. 257: "*Historia* is the name given to the whole series of antiphons and responsories for the Canonical Office, or cursus, of a single day, especially when any, or all, of these musical pieces are given metrical form or are adorned with rhyme."

[69]Christopher R. Cheney claims that the celebration of such local unofficial saints was not uncommon in medieval England; see Cheney, "Rules for the Observance of Feast-Days in Medieval England," *Bulletin of the Institute of Historical Research* 34 (1961): 122: "For many feasts were celebrated in certain regions before the cult was officially made universal. . . ."

[70]The *Miraculum* proper, *Incipiunt Miracula Beati Ricardi Heremite*, pp. 82–93, was used within the octave of the feast, as indicated by the rubrics. The miracles reported here are briefly often baldly stated, and often are mere catalogues of the saints' healing prowess, invariably beginning with the formula "Quedam mulier nomine . . .," "Quidam puer . . .," "Quidam infans . . . ," etc.

service in the structure and tone of the Life, in the selection of incidents, and in the length. The relationship between the Life of the saint and the liturgy is more properly viewed as a symbiotic one, both the narrative and the public ceremony depended on one another. For example, in the Church's efforts at sacralizing time through the designation of specific days as holy, the prospect of being able to consecrate a day to a particular saint, and preferably a well-known one, lent a human dimension to an otherwise abstract principle. The incorporation of the cult of the saints into the liturgy offered the faithful models to emulate—models that they could refashion in their own images. Further, it held out the distant prospect that if they too lived hallowed lives, and found favor with God, they might at some distant time be celebrated among the saints in the liturgy of the Church.

PART TWO

PARTICULAR LITURGIES

LITURGY AND LITURGICAL DAILY LIFE IN THE MEDIEVAL GREEK WORLD—THE BYZANTINE EMPIRE

DEMETRIOS J. CONSTANTELOS

DAILY LIFE IN THE MEDIEVAL GREEK WORLD—known also as the Byzantine Empire (A.D. 330–1453), named after the Greek colony of Byzantion founded ca. 660 B.C.—was rich with a variety of religious and non-religious festivals: liturgical feasts; and imperial and social ceremonies. The first sort of festival included not only Sunday and feastday liturgies but also baptisms, weddings, blessings of waters, and several additional religious rites. The second sort of festival included imperial triumphal processions, anniversaries, and commemorations of the founding of cities or installations of councils and the like. According to a twelfth-century list of feasts, in addition to Sundays there were sixty-six full feasts [***panegyreis***] and twenty-seven half-feasts. The present essay is concerned with the nature and significance of the first type of liturgical feast, the Eucharistic liturgy in particular, along with baptism and matrimony.

This essay is based on Greek liturgical texts, which took their final form after the eleventh century. Complete manuscripts, tracing their composition to previous centuries, have not survived. Whatever the original form might have been, it needs to be emphasized that the liturgy was central to the daily life of the medieval Greek world. I use the term *liturgy* as a comprehensive term to describe several religious rites that involved the Christian community at large, in terms of religious, social, and economic needs.

A

The liturgy epitomizes the dogma, doctrine, code of ethics, cult, community-structure, and the metaphysical or transcendent vision of the Greek or Eastern Orthodox Christian Church as it developed in the course of a millennium. Briefly, the six categories cited above have specific meaning. *Dogma* describes the accepted and codified faith of the Christian community; *doctrine* refers to theological teachings subject to development; the term *code of ethics* is used to describe the ethical imperatives, the rules of and obligations toward personal and community action; *cult* involves the ritual and symbolic movement and activity in the execution of the liturgy, such as processions, candles, signs, or **censer**; *community-structure* explains the nature of relationships among the followers of the common faith, that is the principles that bind individual believers into a living organism and structured organization—the Church. For medieval Greek Christians, *Church* meant not the clergy alone but always the totality of believers, including laity, monastics, and imperial and ecclesiastical dignitaries, whether visible on earth or invisible in heaven, the living and the dead.

As we shall see, the liturgy is more than a narrative and re-enactment of the mystery of Christ's life. Rather, the liturgy is an unfolding, an interpretation of the meaning of history, a specifically Greek Christian understanding of history, whose vision is the ultimate presence of the human person in the glory of the Transcendent God revealed in Jesus Christ. The Transcendent invites and the human responds and fulfills his quest to go beyond the surface of daily experience. The Offering of the **Chalice**, for example, Communion, points to the Transcendent and reveals to the believer that the ultimate destiny of human existence is to achieve *theosis*, an external life in the Transcendent.[1]

---

[1]See the prayers before and after Communion in *Ieratikon*, vol. 1 (Hagion Oros, 1992), pp. 183–88. Any good edition of the Three Liturgies includes these prayers, which have been attributed to several Church Fathers from the fourth to the fifteenth century, such as Basil the Great, Symeon Metaphrastes, Symeon the New Theologian.

It was this joyful, panegyric celebration of the Greek liturgy, seeking to elevate the human person above the ephemeral daily realities, that impressed the new nations of Slavs, Bulgarians, and Russians and made them adopt Greek Orthodox Christianity. A brief illustration is in order. An eleventh-century Russian source relates the impression that the Greek liturgy made on members of a Russian delegation sent to Constantinople by Prince Vladimir in the last quarter of the tenth century.[2]

We are told that the Russian Prince Vladimir was anxious to introduce a new religion to his pagan subjects. Whether for purely religious or political and economic reasons, Vladimir was in contact with Roman Catholic Germans, Islamic Bulgars, Jewish Khazars, and Greek Orthodox Christians of the Byzantine Empire. Having heard an account of the beliefs and practices of these four religions, he dispatched "good and wise men to the number of ten" to observe the worship of Muslims and western Christians, and the rites of the Greeks. Vladimir had rejected Khazarian Judaism, and no delegation to a synagogue is mentioned.

Upon their return to their own country, the Russian delegates reported on what they had observed and heard. The Greek liturgy they had experienced in the cathedral of Hagia Sophia in Constantinople impressed the Russians so much that a vivid account of it influenced Vladimir to adopt Orthodox Christianity: "The Greeks led us to the edifices where they worship their God, and we knew not whether we were in heaven or on earth," the delegates reported. "On earth there is no such splendor or such beauty, and we are at a loss to describe it. . . . We cannot forget that beauty. . . ." Neither dogma and doctrinal theology nor Christian ethics decided the adoption of Greek Christianity by the Russians. Instead, it was the liturgy celebrated by the clergy and the choirs; the chanting, as well as the hymns, the incense, the beauty of the edifice, "the pontifical services

[2]*The Russian Primary Chronicle*, ed. and trans. Samuel H. Cross and Olgerd P. Sherbowitz-Wetzor (Cambridge, Mass., 1953), pp. 110–11.

and the ministry of the deacons" that commended Orthodox Christianity to the Russians.[3]

The term *liturgy*, from the Greek *leitourgia*, means an act or work [*ergon*] performed by or for the people [*laios, laitos*]. Though it was used in Greek antiquity in a technical and political sense, later it acquired a new technical but religious meaning as service conducted for a deity. For example, in Athens, richer citizens were obligated to sponsor such public events as dramatic performances, athletic competitions, musical festivals, and religious celebrations—all called liturgies. Christianity adopted this later sense, and Greek Christianity in particular has retained this meaning throughout the centuries, to the present day.[4]

In the Byzantine era, the term was employed to emphasize the corporate character of liturgical rituals, including baptism, marriage, funeral, and other sacraments and sacramentals. The prayer life of the Greek Church was a set of corporate rituals that formed a coherent structure and addressed several spiritual and physical needs of the people, religious as well as social, noetic (involving intellectual decisions) as well as spiritual quests.

The cycle of liturgical services included not only Bible readings, the Word of God, but also iconography, the Word of God illustrated; not only readings, but also homilies; not only symbols, but also articles of art, a coordination of visible and invisible realities, the macrocosm reduced to a microcosm. A liturgy was intended to bring together the physical and the metaphysical, the created and the uncreated and, in particular, divinity and humanity. The variety of liturgical forms we find in Byzantine religious life was a synthesis of and a compromise between the rites practiced in the

---

[3]*The Russian Primary Chronicle*, ed. and trans. Cross and Sherbowitz-Wetzor, p. 111.

[4]For a comprehensive discussion of the term's meaning and evolution see Theodore W. Jennings, Jr., "Liturgy," in *The Encyclopedia of Religion*, ed.-in-chief Mircea Eliade, 16 vols. (New York, 1987), 8:580–83; Robert F. Taft, "Liturgy," in *The Oxford Dictionary of Byzantium*, ed.-in-chief Alexander P. Kazhdan, 3 vols. (New York, 1991), 2:1240–41; E. Theodorou, "Leitourgia, Theia," in *Threskeutike kai Ethike Enkyklopaideia*, vol. 8 (Athens, 1966), pp. 179–93.

cathedral of Hagia Sophia, which exerted an overwhelming influence throughout the Empire and elsewhere, and the liturgical rules of the Stoudios Monastery, a famous monastic complex in Constantinople, which had rubrics that synthesized Palestinian and Constantinopolitan liturgical practices.

B

The liturgy of the Eucharist was central to the religious life of the medieval Greek world, and it remains of paramount significance to the present day among Orthodox believers. Liturgy as worship is the core meaning of the Greek understanding of *threskeia* [religion], which etymologically means instinctive worship of the divine; a leaping up in joyful expectation to associate oneself with the transcendent, the source of creation. The Christian religion always has emphasized worship, a worship that includes two fundamental principles: *anamnesis* [remembrance], and *eucharistia* [thanksgiving]. Remembrance presupposes a faith and recognition of a Creator, a Redeemer, and a Providential God involved in the creation, evolution, and sustenance of all creation. Thanksgiving is the human person's grateful response to God's *philanthropia*, which culminated in the God-made-human event. The faithful acknowledge the "mighty and saving deeds of God" in history. The Greek Christian liturgy includes both principles, *anamnesis* and *eucharistia*, because the two are inseparable.

Furthermore, in early Christian usage the term *liturgy* meant service to God at the altar but also meant public worship and ceremonial services for the religious life of the community. Thus, even though the term ultimately was identified with the Eucharist proper, every sacramental and religious ritual could be called liturgy, including baptism, anointment, acts of charity such as *diakonia*, service to the poor, and preaching.

By the fourth century, when the Byzantine Empire came into being, liturgy had assumed a specific meaning and referred to the Sacrament [***Mysterion***] of the Eucharist, identified with the Last Supper of Christ with his disciples. Nevertheless, the large size of several volumes of hymns, services, sacraments, liturgies, and prayers—such as the ***Menaia, Oktoechos***,

Triodion, ***Pentikostarion***, ***Euchologion***, and ***Horologion***—reveal that the Greek Church had embraced the totality of life. *Menaia* are twelve liturgical books, one for each month, containing hymns and other texts for each feast-day of the month. *Oktoechos* is a liturgical hymn-book containing the hymns in eight tones of daily services of the whole year, except those of the Lent, Easter, and Pentecost seasons. *Triodion* is a hymn-book "of three odes" containing the services of the Great Lent, the forty days before Easter, and the Easter service itself. *Pentikostarion* follows the *Triodion* and includes the hymnology of the fifty days between Easter and Pentecost. The *Euchologion* is the liturgical book of the clergy, and it contains all the services and rites conducted by **deacon**s, presbyters, and bishops. The *Horologion* is a liturgical book that contains the monastic "hours" of prayers such as the Compline and the mid-night [***mesonyktikon***].

All prayers and services in these major volumes, rites at the birth of a child, the opening of schools for classes, the installation of public officials, the seeding of fields and the reaping of crops, services for forgiveness of sins and for health of body and soul, texts of sacraments and sacramental services for baptism, *chrismation* (the equivalent of confirmation in the West), marriage, and so on, provide ample evidence that liturgical life was a daily enrichment and experience for the Orthodox subjects of the Byzantine Empire. The Greek Church never made a clear distinction between sacraments [*mysteria*] and sacramentalia [***hierai akolouthiae***], that is, between the required sacraments and the minor services such as the office of the holy Baptism and the blessing of the waters on Epiphany Day. All were intended to consecrate some aspect of life and, indeed, the totality of the cosmos.[5]

The daily life of the people—whether city dwellers in large cities like Constantinople, Thessalonike, Nicaea, Ephesos, or Trapezous, or inhabitants of provincial towns and rural areas such as Corinth, Kastoria and the islands—included daily religious services and the Eucharistic Liturgy proper. The ecclesiastical calendar includes daily commemorations of

---

[5]See John Meyendorff, *Byzantine Theology: Historical Trends and Doctrinal Themes* (New York, 1974), pp. 190–91.

celestial and earthly beings, members of the Church triumphant and the Church militant, that is the Church in heaven and the Church on earth. The Church is one composed of living and dead. Angelic hosts, prophets of the old dispensation, apostles, church fathers, martyrs, saints of the desert male and female, unmercenary physicians, the ancestors of Christ on the side of his mother, other members of the congregation "who have fallen asleep in the hope of resurrection to eternal life," are commemorated as participants in the prayer life of the faithful.

For the Greek Church the liturgy was a recapitulation of the whole economy of God—God's providence and acts in history from the moment of humanity's disobedience [*parakoe*] to God's direct intervention in the person of Jesus the Christ. In the last analysis the liturgy was perceived as the mystery of God's love. Throughout the liturgy God is described as *philanthropos* [lover of the human being], *eleemon* [merciful], *oiktirmon* or *panoiktirmon* [compassionate or most compassionate], *evergetes* [benefactor], *Soter* [savior], the *monos philanthropos* [the only true lover of humankind]. It is out of love for humanity that God assumed humanity in order to save the human. "God so loved the world that he sent his only begotten son so that anyone who believes in him may not perish" (John 3:16). God's justice is mitigated by His love and compassion for his creation.

There were six major liturgies during the Byzantine era: namely the Liturgy of Iakovos [James], the Liturgy of Markos [Mark], the Liturgy of Clement, the Liturgy of St. Basil, the Liturgy of John Chrysostom, and the Liturgy of the Presanctified Gifts. Of these, the liturgy attributed to Clement had been, in fact, spuriously written in Syria and had been incorporated into the *Diatagai ton Hagion Apostolon* [Instructions of the Twelve Apostles]. It was never adopted by the Greek Church. Up to the twelfth century, the most widely used liturgy was that attributed to St. Basil of Caesarea (329–79), but after the twelfth century it was replaced by John Chrysostom's (354–407); it continued to be celebrated, but only ten times during the year. The Liturgy of the Presanctified Gifts was celebrated throughout the Great Lent, the forty-day period before Easter, except Saturdays and Sundays.

The central point of every one of these liturgies was the Eucharist, instituted by Jesus Christ at the Last Supper, commemorated on Holy Thursday to perpetuate Christ's redemptive work to secure His *koinonia* [communion] with his people and establish a *koinonia* between the faithful themselves. For this reason the liturgy was perceived as a corporate worship of God in Christ. At no time was the liturgy conducted without laypeople present. In the early Church, in fact, the liturgy was called ***synaxis***, a gathering of the faithful for Bible reading, Communion, and a meal. The spirit that dominates every act of the liturgy is the notion of God's *philanthropia* (Titus 3:4), God's attributes manifested in God's love for the creation, especially humankind. In the earthly liturgy, which manifests God's love, angelic and human hosts con-celebrate. The atmosphere created is intended to elevate the human spirit to spiritual concerns. The faithful find themselves among the spiritualized personalities of the Old and the New Testaments—apostles and martyrs, intellectual fathers of the Church, and illiterate anchorites of the desert—all depicted in abstract icons. The visible and invisible choruses of believers unite under a common mantle of eternity. In other words, the liturgy is a highly spiritual experience that brings together the created and the uncreated, those living in time and those who have entered eternity.

As already indicated, the content of the liturgy includes doctrine and ethics, implied history, and a springboard for philanthropic action, both individual and collective, hymns with passages from the Old and New Testaments, and always two *pericopes*, short passages from the New Testament, including one from one of the four gospels and one either from the book of Acts or the letters of the Apostles—but never from the book of Apocalypse, a book considered prophetic and apocalyptic. In theory at least, the liturgy was for all, and it was in the liturgy and the sharing of the same cup that the unity of the Christian community was proclaimed. Emperors and poor peasants, patriarchs and humble monks, queens and servant girls, generals and ordinary soldiers shared of the same cup. One invisible but real kingdom in heaven, one but visible kingdom on earth. Sunday liturgy especially was the supreme spiritual experience for Byzantine believers, whether in cities and towns or villages and farm communities. The text of the liturgy constitutes a mirror of Orthodox Christianity's dogmas, social ethics, and spiritual life.[6]

C

What follows is a description and an analysis of the Liturgy of St. John Chrysostom, which ultimately dominated the liturgical life of medieval Greek Christianity. It includes a sequence of readings and events that usually lasts one and one-half hours. It was enriched over the course of time and evolved to epitomize the whole realm of spirituality and to unfold the philosophy of history held by the medieval Greek world. Petition after petition, prayer after prayer, symbols and re-enactments embrace concerns for the totality of the human person's needs and reveal a deep interest for cosmic salvation.

The Liturgy of St. John is a step-by-step ascent from the material to the immaterial, from the created to the uncreated. As a mirror of Greek Orthodoxy's philosophy of history, it is an account and re-enactment of God's invasion of human history from the moment of creation, to recreation through the God-made-human event, to the *eschaton* [end of time] and the return of the cosmos to its pristine immateriality, and finally to humankind's state of *theosis*, when God will be in all and all will be in God.

The Liturgy of St. John is preceded by the ***Orthros***, a daybreak service conducted by the priest for the faithful, which serves as an introduction to the Eucharistic Liturgy and to consecrate the day to God. The *Orthros* service opens with an assertion of an undefined God, proclaiming "Blessed is our God at all times, now and always, for ever and ever." Then follows a

---

[6]See Meyendorff, *Byzantine Theology*, pp. 6–7, 29–30, esp. 115–25. On the evolution of the Byzantine liturgy see also the comprehensive chapter "How Liturgies Grow: The Evolution of the Byzantine Divine Liturgy," in *Beyond East and West: Problems in Liturgical Understanding*, ed. Robert F. Taft (Washington, D.C., 1984), pp. 167–92.

series of psalm readings: for example, Psalms 3, 37, 62, 87, 102, 142, the Magnificat, hymn singing, and the doxology. The doxology to God "the Giver of Light" completes the *Orthros* service and introduces the faithful to the liturgical service proper.

As stated above, the purpose of the Divine Liturgy is to uplift the faithful from a material to a spiritual world. Pedagogically speaking, the whole ritual is meant to be a step-by-step ascent from the earthly to the heavenly, from the visible and created to the invisible and uncreated. The following five steps summarize the parts of the liturgical service proper:

(1) *The **Prothesis***. Preparation of the gifts for the Eucharist.
(2) ***Enarxis***. The beginning of the liturgy proper, which includes petitions, antiphons, and preparatory prayers.
(3) *Liturgy of the Word*. The reading of New Testament excerpts; instructive prayers for the catechumens (people receiving instruction and preparing for baptism); and sermon.
(4) *Liturgy of the Eucharist*. ***Epiclesis*** [invocation], Communion, Thanksgiving.
(5) *Apolysis*. Dismissal.

Prothesis

The *Prothesis* is a service that prepares the gifts of wine and bread for the Eucharist. Throughout the services of both the *Orthros* and *Prothesis*, there is in general an interplay of continuity among the Old Testament, the New Testament, and the *Ekklesia* [community of believers] in history. Fidelity is affirmed with the Old Covenant, between God and old Israel, and continuity and change between the Old and the New Covenant, the Christian people and the new Israel. However, the *Prothesis* best expresses Greek Christianity's sense of history, as will become evident in the following paragraphs.

As soon as the service has begun with the recitation "Blessed is our God at all times, now and always, for ever and ever" and the priest has vested and washed his hands, he lifts up the *prosforon* [loaf of bread] and, with a lance in his right hand, proceeds to cut the central piece of the loaf called the *Amnos* [Lamb], which signifies the Body of Christ and carries the monogram:

IC XP
NI KA,

meaning Jesus Christ is always victorious. He then pours wine and a few drops of water into the chalice. While the celebrant separates the *Amnos* from the loaf and pours wine in the chalice, he recites passages from the Book of Isaiah, such as "like a lamb that is led to the slaughter and like a sheep that before its shearers is silent, so he did not open his mouth. . ." (Isa. 53:7–8). It is after this that the commemoration of the triumphant and militant Church members starts. Their significance requires that we cite here every pronouncement that the celebrant makes while he removes a particle from the loaf of bread to be consecrated.

The first particle is "in honor and memory of our most highly blessed and glorious Lady ***Theotokos*** [the Bearer of God] and ever-virgin Mary, through whose prayers do You, o Lord, receive this sacrifice upon your altar in heaven." This particle is placed at the right hand of the *Lamb-Amnos* [unconsecrated **Host**], accompanied with the words "at your right stood the Queen, dressed in an embroidered mantle of gold."

Each recitation accompanied with a particle cut from the offertory loaf reminds us that the whole Church triumphant and militant, visible and invisible, constitutes a oneness. Members of the triumphant Church are commemorated prayerfully by the living, while the living participate in a realized *eschaton*, the presence of the end of time, time and eternity copenetrated. From the angelic hosts to the celebrant priest, the people of the Community of God are united symbolically on the *diskarion*, a small round tray known as a paten which is symbolic of the whole cosmos.

The priest recites the following passages, which commemorate saints of both the Old and the New Testaments and of the Church in history:

> in honor and memory of the archangels Michael and Gabriel and of all heavenly incorporeal powers; in honor and memory of the honorable and glorious prophet and forerunner John the Baptist; of the holy and glorious prophets Moses and Aaron, Elias and Eliseos, David and Jesse, the three Young Men and Daniel the prophet, and of all the holy prophets; in honor and memory of the glorious and illustrious apostles Peter and Paul, and of all the holy apostles; in honor and memory of our holy fathers, the great hierarchs and ecumenical teachers, Basil the Great, Gregory the theologian, and John Chrysostom, three leading Greek Fathers of the fourth century; Athanasios and Cyril, patriarchs of Alexandria (fourth and fifth centuries); Nicholaos of Myra, the popular St. Nicholas, bishop of Myra in Asia Minor, and all the holy hierarchs; in honor and memory of the first martyr and archdeacon Stephen; the holy great martyrs Demetrios, George, and Theodore of Tyre, the Commander (all three military men were put to death during the great persecution of 303–11), and all male and female martyrs; of the sainted and theophoric [literally, God-bearers] fathers of ours Anthony, Euthymios, Savvas, Onoufrios, Athanasios of Athos and all male and female ascetic saints; of the saints, miracle workers and unmercenary [physicians] Kosmas and Damianos, Kyros and Ioannis, Panteleemon and Hermolaos and all the unmercenary saints; of the holy and righteous ancestors [of Christ] Joachim and Anna; of the saints . . . whose memory we observe today, and of all the saints, through whose prayers visit us, O God[7].

Having commemorated all the above, the celebrant priest removes a ninth particle in glory and memory of the saint whose liturgy is to be celebrated (attributed to either John Chrysostom or Basil the Great).

But God's family of incorporeal beings includes not only angels and saints of all kinds and backgrounds but also ordinary human beings who live either in body on earth or within the triumphant invisible Church. Thus the celebrant uses either the same or another loaf, especially baked for the liturgy, and cuts off particles commemorating the "living and the dead." Removing a particle from the loaf of bread offered, he prays thus: "Remember, Master, lover of humankind, all Orthodox bishops, our Archbishop (name), the honorable presbyters in service to Christ, all those in the priesthood and monastic communities, and all our brethren in Christ."

[7] *Ieratikon*, ed. Apostolic Deaconate of the Church of Greece (Athens, 1977), p. 58.

Upon completion of this prayer, the priest prays for individuals including parents, brothers, and sisters, the bishop who ordained him, fellow priests, and others whose names have been given to him by members of the congregation. Then he commemorates by name those whom he wishes to pray for and those for whom he has received a request from his parishioners. First he recites "in memory and forgiveness of sins of the blessed founders of the church" in which the liturgy takes place. Then he asks the philanthropic God to remember all Orthodox fathers and brethren who have fallen asleep "in the hope of resurrection to eternal life." Last, he removes a particle for himself, praying: "remember O Lord my unworthiness and forgive me for every transgression, voluntary and involuntary."

The Divine Liturgy Proper

At the completion of the *Prothesis*, the Divine Liturgy proper begins. It is divided into four interrelated sections: the *enarxis* [beginning], the Liturgy of the Word, the Liturgy of the Eucharist, and the *apolysis* [dismissal].What follows is a brief analysis of the two central sections, that is, the Liturgy of the Word and the Liturgy of the Eucharist.

The Liturgy of the Word serves as instruction and sometimes is known as the *Synaxis* [gathering of the people] or the Liturgy of the Catechumens. It was open to all believers: the faithful and those receiving instruction to join the Church. Litanies, psalmody, scriptural readings from one of the gospels and one from another book of the New Testament, and the sermon constitute the high points of the Liturgy of the Word. The liturgy starts with a confirmation of the Triune God, God one in essence but three in person: "Blessed be the Kingdom of the Father and the Son and the Holy Spirit, now and always and for ever and ever." After a series of prayers for the catechumens and then the faithful, the gospel, which has occupied the central place on the altar, yields its place to the chalice. Bible and chalice, the Word of God and the Mystery of God's presence in the Eucharist, are the two poles of the Divine Liturgy.

While the *Orthros* service, being preparatory or anticipatory, includes many readings from the Old Testament, hymns imbued with Old Testament imagery and prophetic sayings, and also the prophetic Magnificat, the Liturgy of the Word emphasizes the New Testament. The Old Testament, of course, progressively reveals that God is, but God remains the unknown God, the obscure, present in word but absent from humanity's complete religious knowledge and experience. It was the incarnation of the Logos and the descent of the Spirit that confirmed the triune nature of God as Creator, Redeemer, and Sanctifier. Accordingly, allusions to the Old Testament are not absent from the Liturgy of the Word; it includes passages from psalms and prophetic utterances, but the biblical structure of the liturgy and the bible readings depend much more on the New Testament, the fulfillment of prophecy and expectation. Nevertheless, there is a persistent antithesis in Christianity, especially in Orthodox Christianity, between the judgment and greatness of the Old Testament God and the "unfathomable philanthropia" of the New Testament God, between the *Pantokrator Theos* [Almighty God] and the *Philanthropos Theos* [God the Lover of Humankind].[8]

In the early Church and throughout the early Middle Ages, baptism was conducted before the opening of the Eucharistic Liturgy. Believers had to be baptized before they could participate in the Divine Liturgy because participation in the eucharistic meal presupposes knowledge of the faith.[9] Thus, before the distribution of the Eucharist itself, there were read several

---

[8]See Demetrios J. Constantelos, "Die biblische Struktur der Gottlichen Eucharistie" in *Die Verkündigung des Evangeliums und die Feier der Heiligen Eucharistie*, ed. Heinz Joachim Held and Klaus Schwarz, in the series *Beiheft zur Ökumenischen Rundschau*, no. 54 (Frankfurt am Main, 1989), 26–39; and Olivier Clément, "Vasikon Diagramma tes Vyzantines Latreias" in *E Leitourgia mas*, ed. Brotherhood of the Theologians of Zoe (Athens, 1963), p. 111.

[9]Even though infant baptism had been adopted as early as the Apostolic age, adult baptism remained a regular practice in the Greek Middle Ages, and it is not rare to the present day. Missionary activity and the conversion of new nations and individuals made adult catechetical instruction and baptism a continuous practice.

petitions and prayers for the catechumens. The deacon, and in the absence of a deacon the priest, calls upon the catechumens "to pray to the Lord," and he asks the faithful to join in prayer for the catechumens:

> that the Lord may have mercy on them; that the Lord instruct them in the word of truth; that He open to them the Gospel of righteousness; that he incorporates them to His holy, catholic and apostolic church; that the Lord may save them, have compassion on them, help and protect them.

In addition to the antiphonal petitions, the celebrant priest recites the following prayer:

> Lord our God, who dwells on high but who makes the lowly prosper, who sent forth your only-begotten Son and God, our Lord Jesus Christ as Savior, look upon your servants the catechumens who have turned their heads to you. In due time make them worthy to receive the baptism of regeneration for the forgiveness of their sins and their dressing up with the garment of incorruption. Unite them with your holy, catholic and apostolic church, and add them to your chosen people. That they along with us may glorify your all honorable and magnificent name, of the Father and the Son and the Holy Spirit, now and always and unto the ages of ages.

Because the catechumens are not yet an integral part of the baptized and renewed community and are, therefore, forbidden to partake of the Eucharist, they are asked at this point to depart from the service: "All catechumens, depart; catechumens, depart. All catechumens depart. Let no catechumen remain," the priest requests. The catechumens depart, but the faithful remain, not only to continue in the communion of the eucharistic service but also to pray for the catechumens, for intellectual training or learning of the faith is not enough; catechumens cannot achieve the state of preparation without the spiritual support of the faithful. Therefore, between the litany petitions and prayers for the catechumens and the ***Anaphora*** [the Offering of the Eucharist], the congregation of the faithful offers special petitions and prayers for their future brethren and also for themselves. "All we faithful, again and again in peace, let us pray to the Lord," they recite, and the Liturgy of the Eucharist is commenced.

The celebrant is conscious of his sinfulness and limitations; he feels unworthy to stand before the altar and offer the bloodless sacrifice for the faithful and for those who prepare for baptism. Thus he prays for himself:

> Accept, o God, our entreaty; make us worthy to offer You prayers and supplications and unbloody sacrifices for all your people; and by the power of your Holy Spirit strengthen us whom You have appointed to this ministry; so that at all times and places, without blame or offence, with the witness of a pure conscience, we may invoke upon You in any time and place; and that hearing us You may have mercy on us in the plenitude of your goodness.

The faithful respond approvingly and in support of their spiritual father's feelings. They participate in his spiritual agony and pray together like one organism. Their "Amen" is a voice of agreement and support. Following an exhortation that the faithful may join again and again in "peace" and pray "to the Lord," the priest offers the second prayer of the faithful. The "again and again" [*eti kai eti* . . .] is a constant reminder of man's inability to stand by himself without divine support and a reminder that the faithful need to pray incessantly [*adialeiptos*] in the words of St. Paul (1 Thess. 5:17).

The second prayer opens with:

> again, and numerous other times, we fall down before You and beg of You because You are Good and Lover of humankind [*Philanthropos*] to pay heed to our prayers; to cleanse our souls and bodies from all defilement of flesh and spirit, and grant that we may stand without guilt or condemnation before Your holy altar. Furthermore, grant, O God, to these also who pray, with progress in life, growth in faith and spiritual understanding. Give them the insight to always worship you with respect and love, and without guilt and condemnation partake of your holy mysteries and become worthy of your spiritual kingdom.

Following these two introductory prayers,[10] the liturgy proceeds in a climactic way with the singing of the cherubic hymn that calls upon the

---

[10]For this see Robert F. Taft, *The Great Entrance: A History of the Transfer of Gifts and other Preanaphoral Rites of the Liturgy of St. John Chrysostom* (Rome, 1975); Louis Bouyer, *Eucharist: Theology and Spirituality of the Eucharistic Prayer*, trans. Charles Underhill Quinn (Notre Dame, Ind., 1968), pp. 244–314; and Panagiotes Nikolaou Trempelas, *Ai Treis Leitourgiae*, 2nd ed. (Athens, 1982), pp. 173–79n49.

faithful to set aside all earthly cares that they may receive the king of all. From now on the liturgy is a "mystery," but one with transforming existential powers. The participant finds himself in a tension between the temporal and the *eschaton*, time and eternity.

While the prayers of the Divine Liturgy are saturated with biblical passages, allusions, onomatology, and imagery, they also abound in philosophical apophatic terminology. Terms describing God or Christ as *aphatos* [unutterable], *atreptos* [unchangeable], *analloiotos* [with no essential change], *anaimaktos* [bloodless], *philanthropos* [lover of the human being], *anekphrastos* [ineffable], *aperinoetos* [beyond understanding], *aoratos* [invisible], *akataleptos* [incomprehensible], *aei on* [always existing], and *osautos on* [always the same] are found seldom in the Bible but frequently in Greek classical literature and philosophy. The influence of Greek thought in the prayer life of early and, especially, Byzantine Christianity is understood when one remembers that in the Greek East there was philosophical continuity between non-Christian and Christian Hellenism and that the Eastern Church never divorced itself from its linguistic and Greek cultural heritage. It is for this reason that early Greek Christian liturgical language shows similarities with pre-Christian religious terminology. Solemn addresses referring to the deity's attributes become common in non-Christian and Christian Hellenic religious thought.[11]

---

[11]Edwin Hatch, *The Influence of Greek Ideas on Christianity* (New York, 1957), esp. pp. 292–309 and conclusion, pp. 349–53; compare Werner Jaeger, *The Theology of the Early Greek Philosophers* (Oxford, 1947), pp. 1–17; and Jaeger, *Early Christianity and Greek Paideia* (Cambridge, Mass., 1961), esp. pp. 38–46; Samuel Angus, *The Religious Quests of the Graeco-Roman World: A Study in the Historical Background of Early Christianity* (New York, 1967), esp. pp. 107–26. On the influence of Greek liturgical terminology on Christian liturgical services see Josef A. Jungmann, *The Early Liturgy, to the Time of Gregory the Great*, trans. F. H. Brunner (Notre Dame, Ind., 1959), pp. 125–26. While the Hellenic mind did not influence apostolic Christian worship, it is acknowledged that as soon as Christianity became the state religion and felt sure of itself, Christian worship was enriched with terminology and ideas that promoted the understanding of the mystery of God's incomprehensibility and yet ever-presence in the world. The hellenization and theologizing of the

The series of petitions that follow reveals the holistic concerns of the Church, asking for the sanctification of the totality of life, for peace in the world, and in the church, for a perfect day, and for forgiveness of sins and offenses. But the highlights of the Liturgy of the Eucharist are two: first, the *spiklesis*, the invocation of the Holy Spirit for the consecration of the offered gifts, the bread and the wine, into the body and the blood of the sacrificed Christ who gave his life for the many; and second, the Offering of the Chalice for Holy Communion.

The mystery (or sacrament) of the Eucharist became known as the *Anaimaktos Thysia* [Bloodless Sacrifice] and *logiki thysia* [reasonable sacrifice]. It replaced the sacrificial blood ritual ceremonies of Old Testament practice and the bloody sacrifice of other religions. The Mosaic cultic rite, described in Exod. 24:3–8, was a blood covenant. Moses built an altar at the foot of Mount Sinai and used the blood of animal sacrifice for sealing the covenant between Jehovah and Moses' tribe. Moses sprinkled half of the blood on the altar and the other half over his people, affirming that: "This is the blood of the Covenant that the Lord has made with you . . ." (Exod. 24:8), thus dramatizing the special relationship, indeed the union, between Jehovah and the Israelite people.

But

> if the blood of goats and bulls . . . sanctifies those who have been defiled so that their flesh is purified, how much more will the blood of Christ purify our conscience to worship the living God! . . . For this reason he is the mediator of a new covenant. . . (Heb. 9:13–15)

The Eucharist is the seal of the New Covenant and proclaims the special relationship, indeed the union, of Christ with the New Israel, the Christian people.

---

liturgy was a natural adaptation to its cultural and intellectual milieu. See Dom Gregory Dix, *The Shape of the Liturgy* (London, 1945), pp. 174, 202, 430–31, and esp. 740. On the subject of continuity and change in liturgical prayers see Bryan D. Spinks, *The Sanctus in the Eucharistic Prayer* (Cambridge, 1991), pp. 46–82, esp. 65–82.

It is well known that religious practice has included sacrificial and blood ritual ceremonies throughout history, to the present day. The Christian Eucharist, however, transformed the Jewish blood sacrifice into a bloodless thanksgiving offering, confirming that Christ continues his association and ever presence among his people. During his last supper with his disciples,

> Jesus took a loaf of bread, and after blessing it he broke it, gave it to the disciples, and said, "Take, eat; this is my body." Then he took a cup, and after giving thanks he gave it to them, saying, "Drink from it all of you; for this is my blood of the new covenant, which is poured out for many for the forgiveness of sins." (Matt. 26:28, Mark 14:20; Luke 22:20; see also John. 6:56)

It also must be acknowledged that the concept of "reasonable or spiritual sacrifice" was an inheritance from Greek philosophy, which had rejected the bloody sacrifice of ancient religious practices.[12]

Soon after the pronouncement of Christ's words and the consecration of the bread and the wine, the faithful are invited to partake of the bread and the wine mixed, the body and the blood of a bloodless sacrificed Christ. Before the faithful are called to come forward and receive, however, they are admonished to pray for the unity of faith and the communion of the Holy Spirit, and to command one another in love as one harmonious body in a life dedicated to God in Christ.

Thus, from the beginning which opens with the cherubic hymn, to the very end, the faithful expect to be nourished with "the bread of life" (John 6:35) and the wine, or "the blood of the new covenant" (Matt. 26:26). The word of God instructs and illuminates the faithful's mind, but the mystery of the Eucharist achieves the *koinonia*, the communion between Christ, the

---

[12]*Constitutions of the Holy Apostles*, Bk 6.23, in the series *The Writings of the Ante-Nicene Fathers*, ed. James Donaldson, vol. 7 (Grand Rapids, Mich., 1951), p. 461: "Instead of a bloody sacrifice, He has appointed that reasonable (*logiki*) and unbloody mystical (*mystiki*) one. . . ." See also Johannes Quasten, *Music and Worship in Pagan and Christian Antiquity*, trans. Boniface Ramsey (Washington, D.C., 1983), pp. 51–57.

Lamb of God "who shed His blood for the salvation of all" and the believers, as well as the union of the believers among themselves as members of one organism. The litanies and petitions, the prayers, the recitation of the creed of faith, and the Lord's Prayer are intended to create a clear and logical uplifting, a magnificent process-parade in which all are participants: kings and peasants, generals and soldiers, patriarchs and hermits, the virtuous and the sinful, infants and adolescents, middle-aged and elderly, the faint of heart and the courageous, those present and those scattered, those in error and the orthodox in faith, the hopeful and the hopeless, the healthy and the sick—all are gathered together in expectation of the manifestation of God's *philanthropia*. It is for this reason that the Liturgy of the Eucharist is considered the central moment of the Church's life and the very best manifestation of its ecclesiology, its doctrine, its major ethical teachings, and its eschatology. For some Greek Church Fathers and theologians with a more mystical bend, such as Dionysios the Areopagite, Maximos the Confessor, Nicholas Kabasilas, Symeon of Thessalonike, Gregory Palamas, the liturgy provided the opportunity for a personal, mystical, and total consummation in divinization [*theosis*] of the individual believer here on earth. Both symbol and reality, the Divine Liturgy through Scripture and sacrament, the word and the mystery and especially communion, elevates the believer to a higher state of existence where one gains a more intimate and profound communion with God, who provides the gifts, leads to the variety of services, and activates all to the common good (see also 1 Cor. 12:4–11).[13]

The concluding prayer of the Liturgy of the Eucharist, before the dismissal, summarizes that God's mystery has been completed and perfected to the extent that it is humanly possible to describe and understand. In brief, the Liturgy is a journey whose purpose, beginning and end, is the meeting of the human person with God, the invisible, incomprehensible, indescribable but ever existing and always present everywhere and filling

---

[13]Ieromonachos Gregorios, *He Theia Leitourgia*. Skholia (Athens, 1982), pp. 380–87; see also Nicholas Cabasilas, *A Commentary on the Divine Liturgy*, trans. J. M. Hussey and P. A. McNulty (London, 1966), pp. 49–50.

all things. Christ is the fulfillment of the Law and the prophets, fulfilling the whole providential plan of God the Father, who fills the hearts of people with happiness and gladness in the present *kairos* in anticipation of the joy of eternity.

D

The Divine Liturgy was but one of several religious services, rituals, and festivities which enriched the daily life and provided opportunities for socialization and fellowship of the Byzantine Church's people. For example, in addition to Sunday and daily liturgies, from as early as the fifth century, the Church of Constantinople had adopted a system called "stational services," that is, liturgies conducted in designated stations of the city. Those liturgies were preceded by a ***lite***, a procession of clergy and laity alike that took them up to a ten kilometer walk. In the early centuries, especially between the fifth and the early eighth centuries, stational services were frequent; later, they were limited to major feast days such as the Feast of the Annunciation, Palm Sunday, or the Elevation of the Holy Cross, a practice that survives to the present day in the Eastern Orthodox world. Liturgies and processions conducted in the open made the entire city or town "a liturgical space."[14]

The Divine Liturgy with its Liturgy of the Eucharist was of supreme religious importance, but participation in the Eucharist presupposed baptism. Baptism and the Eucharist were the two obligatory sacraments or mysteries of the Christian Church and, as we indicated before, from as early as the Apostolic age, the two were interrelated. Baptism preceded participation in the Liturgy and prepared the candidates to partake of the Eucharist.

Baptism, from the Greek ***baptisma***, means immersion, and it was the sacrament that admitted a believer into the Christian Church. It traces its

---

[14]See John Baldovin, *The Urban Character of Christian Worship: The Origins, Development, and Meaning of Stational Liturgy* (Rome, 1987), pp. 167–226.

origins to the teachings of Christ (Matt. 28:19; Mark 15:16) and the practice of the early Church. The main purposes of baptism were forgiveness of sin, acceptance of the gift of the Holy Spirit (Acts 2:38), initiation to a new life (Acts 2:41; Rom. 6:3; Gal. 3:17) in the Christian Church, and enlightenment (Heb. 6:4, 10:32; 1 Pet. 2:9). Theologically, baptism was described by metaphors such as dying in the baptistry in three immersions and rising to eternity in Christ (Rom. 6:2–4).

In the Byzantine Church baptism became an elaborate initiation process that included not only prayers for the catechumens but also the service of exorcisms, a proclamation of the faith, and baptism proper. Baptism was performed in a special place of the church named the baptistry. Baptism was held usually at Easter Vigil but also on other important holidays, and also on Epiphany Day, the Saturday of St. Lazarus (the day before Palm Sunday), and Pentecost. As infant baptism gained popularity, the number of adult catechumens declined, but baptismal prayers for the catechumens have survived as an integral part of the ritual.

As in the case of the Liturgy of the Eucharist, the Sacramental service of baptism is divided into two parts. The first part includes prayers of reception, exorcisms, the denunciation of Satan, and the confession of faith in the recitation of the Nicene-Constantinopolitan creed. The opening prayer of reception is first a thanksgiving for the candidate for baptism who has been found worthy to flee to the true God and take refuge under the shelter of God's protection, and furthermore is an entreaty that God will strengthen the candidate's life with faith, hope, and love, will enable him/her to walk in all of God's commandments, and will inscribe him/her in the Book of Life and unite him/her to the flock of God's inheritance.

A series of three exorcisms follows, indicating that the Byzantine Church accepted Satan as a real power, always threatening the spiritual well-being of the neophyte (newly baptized). Satan, the satanic, demons, and demonology were perceived not as the absence of good but as the presence of evil, the realization that evil is a powerful reality which cannot be overcome without God's power and help. The devil, Satan, and evil are synonyms of the enemy. The Christian God, however, is not only holy and glorious, unsearchable and indescribable, but also he is the almighty one who has dominion over death, who sits upon the angelic hosts of cherubim, who is worshiped by angels, archangels, thrones, dominions, principalities, authorities, powers, and seraphim.[15] The exorcisms of the catechumens speak not only about God's power over evil but also about God's creative dominion and providence over the creation, about a God whom Satan should fear and by whose decree the earth was established upon the waters, who made the heavens and set the boundaries of mountains and valleys, who fixed bounds to the sands of the seas and a firm path upon the stormy waters. Water, the means of cleansing and their symbol of purification is a dominant theme of the service. Rebirth comes through both the Spirit and the baptismal water (John 3:4–5; Acts 8:29–39).

Following the example of Christ, who sanctified the waters through his own baptism, the first act of baptism proper is the blessing of the baptismal waters. The source of sanctification is God, whose works are marvelous. No words are sufficient to glorify Him. The prayer for the blessing of the baptismal water is indeed an appreciation of nature, waters, and a celebration of the creation, a thanksgiving for God's providence over the visible and the invisible cosmos, the totality of creation.

Baptism became an elaborate service in Constantinople after the sixth century in the cathedral of Hagia Sophia, where the patriarch celebrated. On Holy Saturday evening he would visit the great baptistry and bless the waters. Priests and deacons would prepare the catechumens, who for nearly three years had been receiving instruction, and the patriarch himself would baptize and anoint them. Following the act of immersion three times, the neophytes were dressed in white garments and then entered the Church to receive Communion, "the medicine of immortality."[16]

---

[15]Trempelas, *Ai Treis Leitourgiae*, pp. 338–39.

[16]Ignatius, *Ephesians 20.2* in the series *Bibliotheki Ellenon Pateron*, vol. 2 (Athens, 1955). Ignatius's teaching that the Eucharist was "pharmakon athanasias, antidotos tou me apothanein, alla zen en Iesou Christo dia pantos" [a medicine of immortality, an antidote to death and perpetual life in Christ] became a standard belief in the Byzantine Church.

While we know much about religious practices in Constantinople, our sources do not provide any concrete information about baptismal services in provincial towns. It seems that after the sixth century, by which time infant baptism prevailed, the sacrament was conducted not only on Easter Vigils, the Saturday of St. Lazarus, Epiphany Day, and Pentecost but also on any ordinary Sunday. By the thirteenth century baptism could be conducted on any Saturday or Sunday but only in a church, including a private chapel. The thirteenth-century canonist Demetrios Chomatianos wrote that baptism could take place on any day of the week, at any hour, and even in any place, provided the local bishop has given permission. Nevertheless the theological principles and symbolic elements of the service remained the same everywhere with no basic changes, including the practice of Chrismation, or Confirmation.

Chrismation had replaced "the laying on of the Apostles' hands" (Acts 8:17–18), whose purpose was the imparting of the Holy Spirit's gifts (Acts 19:1–6; Heb. 6:1–6). The multiplication of neophytes and the growth of the Church made Chrismation, always an integral part of the baptismal liturgy, a necessity. It signifies the new life in Christ made possible through the gifts of the Holy Spirit. Baptism, Chrismation, and the Eucharist completed the first and obligatory circle of a believer's religious life.

E

Every day of the year included some liturgical services. Whether funerals, weddings, anointments, blessing of fields, crops, the sea, or celebrating events of Christ's life and the life of his Mother, the *Theotokos*, celebrating or commemorating the life of a saint, the average believer was in constant contact with, if not actively participating in, the daily liturgical life of the Church. Scriptural readings, music, poetry, icons, incense, colors, and vestments served not only as means for religious growth but also for knowledge, education, and socialization. Liturgical services served the needs that newspaper, radio, and television remedy today. Each day of the calendar year provided some liturgical experience.

Matrimony, or the nuptial ceremony, as a liturgical rite was an important event in the daily life of the Greek Christian empire. Even though the doctrinal basis for matrimony is found in Holy Scripture, for several centuries theologians were not unanimous as to whether it should be classified among the sacraments, and the Church defined it as such only in the later thirteenth century. For several centuries "legally married" meant married either according to civil law or according to Church canons. Eventually, only marriage according to Church rubrics and teachings was accepted as legal. It was after the twelfth century that marriage officially was pronounced an exclusive rite of the Church. Every marriage contracted outside the Church was considered uncanonical.

The wedding ceremony was preceded by the betrothal, an independent service which ultimately was linked to the marriage rite and required benediction by a priest. The exchange of marriage rings was the highlight of the betrothal event. The betrothal then was followed by the matrimonial liturgical service.

The best way to understand the Byzantine Church's position on marriage is to study its rite of matrimony. In the first prayer, after a series of petitions, we read that it is God's will that man and woman should be legally married; and that marriage should serve as a source of a life that is happy, peaceful, and blessed with longevity, mutual love, and offspring, culminating here on earth with a crown of glory. In the third prayer of the service, the celebrant, standing before the bride and groom, adds:

> O Sovereign Lord . . . join together this your servant [man's name] and this your servant [woman's name] for by you is a wife joined to her husband. Unite them in oneness of mind; crown them with wedlock into one flesh; grant to them through physical union the gain of well-favored children.

There are three important theological elements in the prayers cited here, revealing both doctrinal teaching and the place of marriage in the life of the Church. First, God's presence in a marriage ceremony indicates that the Byzantine Greek Church accepted marriage as a mystery. The sacramental aspect of marriage is emphasized throughout the service. To view marriage as a sacrament is to accept God as the originator of marriage and as the invisible but real power that unites two heterosexual beings into one unit. Second, marriage is perceived as a union of two minds aiming at the same goal of spiritual perfection. Third, marriage is understood as the physical union of two heterosexual human beings for procreative purposes and love's fulfillment.[17]

A closer analysis of the rite reveals that marriage includes three basic interrelated elements: the natural element, which leads a man and a woman into a physical union; the moral element, which guarantees their full and perpetual cohabitation until death parts them; and the religious element, which makes marriage a communion of faith and a communion of two souls who decide to follow a common road in life, a road that leads to virtue and eternal salvation. This definition of marriage corresponds to the psychosomatic nature of the human being. "For this reason a man shall leave his father and mother and be joined to his wife, and the two shall become one flesh" (Eph. 5:31). Thus, "they are no longer two but one flesh. Therefore what God has joined together, let no one separate" (Matt. 19:6).

The sacramental character of matrimony is based, of course, on other biblical testimony, explicit or implicit. The Bible states that God made the human being [*anthropos*] as a two component being, male and female. Through their union they continue the work of God through procreation. The intimate relationship of the male and female components of the human being expresses God's continuous creative work. The human shares in the creativity and omnipotence of the Creator. Marriage is not a legal contract between two individuals but is a sacred and creative union, the consummation of two human beings into the twofold being—a new "Adam-Eve" person.

From the fourth century onward, the Byzantine Church demanded that the two partners in a marriage should both be of the Christian Orthodox

---

[17]See Demetrios J. Constantelos, "Marriage in the Greek Orthodox Church," *Journal of Ecumenical Studies* 22 (1985): 21–27; Phaedon Koukoules, *Byzantinon Bios Kai Politismos*, 6 vols. (Athens, 1947–1955), 4:70–96.

faith. After the council in Trullo (A.D. 691; also called Constantinople VI), marriage with a non-Christian was forbidden; if contracted, it was declared illegal. The Church was tolerant of a marriage with schismatics such as the Roman or Latin Catholics, but it did not permit marriage with heretics. While in theory, mixed marriages with non-Christians or heretics were forbidden, in practice there were mixed marriages between Orthodox and heretics as well as between Orthodox and non-Christians, especially among members of the imperial families and the upper classes. Mixed marriages multiplied after the eleventh century, following the first Crusade, and were rather common after the thirteenth century as a result of the establishment of Latin principalities and kingdoms in the Christian East. The Byzantine Church applied the principle of ***oikonomia*** [a judgment according to circumstances and needs] to holy matrimony more frequently than to any other sacrament and ultimately accepted the validity of such mixed marriages.

The ecclesiastical ceremony, which included several symbolic acts and the reading of two pericopes from the New Testament, was followed by festivities. Thus a divine institution assumed both a religious and social significance. Socialization was an important sequence to a religious event. The festivities of royal weddings were major events for Byzantine society.[18]

F

Whether because of the agricultural nature of Byzantine Society or its perception of the relationship between the Creator and the creation, the liturgical cycle was designed so as to consecrate the church year and the whole cosmos. This becomes clear when we study certain services, such as those of Theophany [Epiphany]. For example, the first hymn of Theophany's Vespers cries out:

> Make ready, o river Jordan: for behold Christ our God draws near to be baptized by John, that He may crush with His divinity the invisible heads of the dragons

[18] Koukoules, *Byzantinon Bios*, 2:38–39, and esp. 4:119–47.

> in your waters (Ps. 73:13). Rejoice, o wilderness of Jordan: dance with grandness, o you mountains. For the eternal life has come to recall Adam. O you voice that cries in the wilderness, John the Forerunner, cry out: Prepare you all the ways of the Lord and make His path straight (Mark 1:13).

And the hymn that follows bursts out in joy:

> O earth and all things upon the earth, dance you and rejoice exceedingly. The river of joy (Septuagint, Ps. 35:9; NRSV Ps. 36:9) is baptized in the stream; He dries up the fountain of evil and pours forth divine forgiveness.[19]

The prayers recited in the service of Epiphany reveal the understanding of the Greek Church's interrelationship among the Creator, the creation, and the human being. The following, the third, prayer read by the celebrant, is more indicative of this:

> Great are you, O Lord, and marvelous are your works: no words suffice to sing the praise of your wonders. For you by your own will have brought all things out of nothingness into being, by your power you do hold together the creation, and by your providence you do govern the world. Of four elements have you compounded the creation: with four seasons have you crowned the circuit of the year. All the spiritual powers tremble before you. The sun sings your praises; the moon glorifies you; the stars supplicate before you; the light obeys you; the deeps are afraid of your presence; the fountains are your servants. You have stretched out the heavens like a curtain; you have established the earth upon the waters; you have walled about the sea with sand. You have poured forth the air that living things may breathe. The angelic powers minister to you; the choirs of archangels worship you; the many-eyed cherubim and the six-winged seraphim, standing round you and flying about you, hide their faces in fear of your unapproachable glory. You, the uncircumscribed God without beginning and beyond speech, have come upon the earth, taking the form of a servant and being made in the likeness of man. . . . At your epiphany the whole creation sang your praises. . . .[20]

---

[19]Trempelas, *Ai Treis Leitourgiae*, pp. 28–38.

[20]Trempelas, *Ai Treis Leitourgiae*, pp. 38–40.

The above is only a part of the prayer, which continues to speak of the benefits of the God-man-event for humanity—The Incarnation of the Logos-Christ. Creator, creation, spiritual and physical worlds, fall and redemption, evil and its defeat, are described in a language that people could understand and appreciate.

G

Space allotted to this essay does not permit a detailed analysis of any other liturgical service, rite, or sacrament of the more than one hundred included in the ***Mega Euchologion*** [the Great Prayerbook] of the Byzantine Greek Church. Most, if not all, were composed between the fourth and the fifteenth centuries. Some were written by distinguished theologians and hymnographers, while others were the work of unknown monks. All, however, are marked by theological orthodoxy.

The *Mega Euchologion* includes services for betrothals and marriage, repentance and confession, holy unction for the healing of body and soul, the consecration of the waters on Epiphany Day commemorating the baptism of Christ, the blessing of the waters for home and business use, brief litanies against pestilence and drought, for safe travel and ship building, for founding of schools and public institutions, for consecration of churches, and prayers for personal, community, and state needs. All these liturgies confirm that the private life of the Byzantine church was never static and that it had encompassed in its concerns the totality of human life and humanity's visible and invisible, physical and metaphysical needs.

As indicated above, the Byzantine Greek Church offered a great cycle of liturgical services that embraced the whole of life, from birth to death, from cradle to coffin, from agriculture to commerce and trade, from grade one to the opening of one's professional office. Frequently conducted services included Vespers [*esperinos*], Compline [*apodeipnon*—following supper], Nocturns [*mesonyktikon*], Matins [*orthros*] and, of course, the Liturgy or Eucharist proper. There were morning and evening prayers and the so-called "inter-hours" [*horai*] observed more by the monastic communities than the ordinary parish.[21] All these services constitute a twenty-four hour cycle of liturgical life which, although primarily a monastic practice, affected all Christians.

In addition to Sunday liturgies, the liturgical calendar included special feast days commemorating major events of the life of Christ and in the lives of his Mother, the Apostles, Church Fathers, martyrs, and other saints. The feasts of Christ were known as *Despotikai eortai* [feasts of the Master]. Easter Day was the *eorti-eorton* [feast of feasts], but there were several additional very important feasts, including the Exaltation of the Holy Cross, the Nativity of Christ, Theophany or Epiphany, Palm Sunday, the Ascension, Pentecost, and the Transfiguration. The feasts in honor of the *Theotokos* were the birth, her entry and dedication into the Temple, the Annunciation, and the *Koimesis* or Falling Asleep of the *Theotokos*. The feasts of Peter and Paul and the other Apostles, and of several major Church Fathers, such as the three hierarchs (Basil the Great, Gregory the Theologian, and John Chrysostom) received preeminence over saints of less renown.

Several other occasions provided opportunities for the faithful to participate in liturgical life. The very poetic and theologically profound service of the *Akathistos hymnos*, a series of hymns, was celebrated during the Great Lent, where the faithful were not allowed to sit. It is described as one of the masterpieces of medieval Greek poetry and one of the most difficult services to translate. It includes a theology which starts with praises addressed to Christ's Mother, the *Theotokos*, the instrument of God's appearance among men.

The Great Lent is rich in liturgical services because, in addition to regular Sunday liturgies and Sunday *katanyktikos* [penitential] vespers, it includes the Great Compline [*mega apodeipnon*], the celebration of the Liturgy of the Presanctified Gifts usually held on Wednesdays and Fridays, and the Great Canon of Bishop St. Andrew of Crete.

---

[21]For a brief but authoritative description of these terms and services see the three volumes of the *Oxford Dictionary of Byzantium*, ed. Alexander P. Kazdan (New York, 1991).

Notwithstanding the difference in length of time and poetic quality of hymns and prayers written in the course of more than ten centuries, liturgical services provided opportunities for the hearers to learn their faith, grow spiritually, and have moral truths indelibly impressed upon their minds. They served educational, social, emotional, poetic, and spiritual needs. In times of crisis, as in the last two centuries of the Byzantine Era (1204–1453), when the state was in decline and the Church remained the most stable institution, liturgical life became more intensive. Liturgical theology became more popular and new liturgical services, such as the *Paraklysis to the Theotokos*[22] [Intercessory Service addressed to the Bearer of God-Christ] were added to the yearly cycle.

H

The nature of liturgical texts in the daily life of the Byzantine Empire was didactic and their application mystically experiential; some liturgies were major events for royalties and dignitaries, but most addressed the religious needs of all. Liturgical services, however, in honor of certain saints were of social and economic significance as well. Religious festivities were accompanied by a *panegyris*—celebration which helped to integrate society and promote a holistic understanding of life. A *panegyris* has been described as a religio-economic institution, and it appeared in Christian Byzantium as early as the fifth century.[23]

The interrelationship among religious, social, and economic needs is clearly revealed in the following account by a mid-fifth-century orator who wrote of the *panegyris*, a public assembly in honor of St. Thekla,

---

[22]*Orologion to Mega*, ed. Apostolike Diakonia tes Ekklesias tes Hellados, 10th ed. (Athens, 1991), pp. 543–71.

[23]Speros Vryonis Jr., "The Panegyris of the Byzantine Saint: A Study in the Nature of a Medieval Institution, Its Origins and Fate" in *The Byzantine Saint*, ed. Sergei Hackel, Fellowship of St. Alban and St. Sergius (London, 1981), pp. 198–202.

traditionally one of St. Paul's disciples and the first woman martyr. The *panegyris* began and ended with a liturgy. In the final liturgy:

> all rushed, citizen and foreigner, man, woman, and child, governor and governed, general and soldier, leader of the mob and individual, both young and old, sailor and farmer and everyone simply who was anxious, all rushed to come together, to pray to God, to beseech the Virgin, and having partaken of the holy mysteries [i.e., the Eucharist] thus to go away blessed and as someone renewed in body and soul. Then they banqueted and set to discussing the wonders of the panegyris. One participant praised its brilliance, another the size of the crowd, yet another the harmony of the psalmody, another the duration of the vigil, and so they continued commenting on the liturgy and prayer, the shoving of the crowd, the shouting, and the quarreling. One man commented on the fact that he was inspired by a beautiful young woman that he saw during the celebration and was consumed by the thought of having his pleasure with her so that he could only offer prayers to this end. It seems also that at the dismissal of the service gifts were given by the attendants of the sanctuary to the pious [needy].[24]

Thus a liturgy was celebrated for the renewal of body and soul; it attracted crowds, dignitaries, and ordinary people; it included prayers and gossip, praises for the brilliance of the service and the knowledge of the teachers, praise for the harmony of the psalmody but also complaints about the duration of the rite; prayers for the attraction of a bride and distribution of charities to needy pious. A liturgy-panegyris involved the total human being with all his strengths and all his weaknesses. Prayer life, satisfaction of spiritual and social needs, merged at the *panegyris*. The liturgy represented the "holy" through visible means and it filled up the vacuum between the abstract spiritual and the concrete material.[25]

---

[24]Gilbert Dagron, *Vie et miracles de Sainte Thecle: Texte Grec, Traduction et Commentaire* (Brussels, 1978), p. 378; Vryonis, "The Panegyris . . . ," p. 201.

[25]For an excellent discussion of the need for a sociological understanding of the liturgy see Kieran Flanagan, *Sociology and Liturgy: Re-presentations of the Holy* (New York, 1991), esp. pp. 57–83.

Similar descriptions of the *panegyris* as a religious-social-economic phenomenon are provided by authors of the ninth, eleventh, twelfth, and later centuries. But it is to be noted that these unique celebrations were observed during the annual memories of local saints such as St. John the Theologian, St. Thekla, or St. Demetrios, not on a regular Sunday, the Lord's Day. These liturgical-social-commercial celebrations had their parallel in the ancient Greek world and indicate cultural continuity between pagan and Christian Hellenism. This relationship between the religious and so-called secular concerns is understood when we bear in mind that the Byzantine Church sought not to destroy but to transform and consecrate culture.

In conclusion, liturgy and liturgical life in the medieval Greek world had no other purpose than to sanctify the totality of the human person and his environment. Whether in private, family type, or public liturgies, lay participation was a necessary presupposition, and it was conducted in an atmosphere of music, iconography, and symbolic representations. Furthermore, for the less well-educated people, the liturgies provided a forum for learning the Church's dogmas, and for all it served as a place for social cohesion and philanthropic activity.

Additional Bibliography

Among the several translations of the Greek text of the Divine Liturgy the following are recommended:

Cabasilas, Nicholas. *A Commentary on the Divine Liturgy*. Translated by J. M. Hussey and P. A. McNulty. London, 1966.

Contos, Leonidas, translator. *The Lenten Liturgies*. Northridge, Calif., 1995. Contains the Lenten Services including the Liturgies of the Presanctified Gifts and of St. Basil the Great. The Narthex Press, under the directorship of Rev. Spencer T. Kezios, has undertaken the major task of translating all the liturgical books of the Orthodox Church. Each volume includes the daily services of every month in the original Greek followed by an English translation.

———. *The Liturgikon*. Northridge, Calif., 1993.
Includes the texts, in Greek and English, of several services, such as the Office of the Great Vespers, the Office of Orthros, the Divine Liturgy of St. John Chrysostom, and others.

Hapgood, Isabel Florence, translator. *Service Book of the Holy Orthodox–Catholic Apostolic Church*, 3rd edition. Brooklyn, N.Y., 1956.
Translated from the Old Church Slavonic and collated with the service books of the Greek Church.

Members of the faculty of the Hellenic College/Holy Cross, translators. *The Divine Liturgy of Saint John Chrysostom*. Brookline, Mass., 1985.

Mother Mary and Kallistos Ware, translators. *The Festal Menaion*. London, 1969.

———. *The Lenten Triodion*. London, 1978.

Patrinacos, N. D., translator. *The Orthodox Liturgy*. Garwood, N.J., 1976.
Includes a lengthy article about the development of the Orthodox Liturgy from the second century to the present.

Raya, Joseph and José de Vinck, editors and translators. *Byzantine Daily Worship*. Allendale, N.J., 1968.
This edition published with the approval of the Melkite–Greek Catholic patriarchate.

Helpful Studies

Constantelos, Demetrios J. "The Holy Scriptures in Greek Orthodox Worship." *The Greek Orthodox Theological Review* 12, no. 1 (1966): 7–83.

———. "Marriage in the Greek Orthodox Church." *Journal of Ecumenical Studies* 22 (1985): 21–27.

Meyendorff, John. *Byzantine Theology: Historical Trends and Doctrinal Themes*. New York, 1974.

———. "The Liturgy: A Clue to the Mind of Worldwide Orthodoxy." In *Orthodox Theology and Diakonia*. Edited by Demetrios J. Constantelos. Brookline, Mass., 1981. Pp. 79–90.

Schemann, Alexander. *Introduction to Liturgical Theology*. London, 1966.

———. "Symbols and Symbolism in the Orthodox Liturgy." In *Orthodox Theology and Diakonia*. Edited by Demetrios J. Constantelos. Brookline, Mass., 1981. Pp. 91–102.

Taft, Robert F. "How Liturgies Grow: The Evolution of the Byzantine Divine Liturgy." In *Beyond East and West: Problems in Liturgical Understanding*. Edited by Robert F. Taft. Washington, D.C., 1984. Pp. 167–92.

THE LITURGICAL PROFILE OF THE PARISH CHURCH IN MEDIEVAL SWEDEN

SVEN HELANDER

The Parish Liturgy as Phenomenon and Problem

THE WALLS OF THE MEDIEVAL PARISH CHURCH embrace the liturgical room. The purpose of this room is to house a life of worship whose focal points are altar and font. This purpose is common to all categories of churches. But in the parish church, the liturgy has its own profile: Mass and Divine Office are celebrated differently in the parish church than in the cathedral. The two rooms of cathedral and parish church each have their own specific conditions and their own "program." The parish liturgy is colored by the circumstances of the local congregation.

For the medieval priest and his parishioners the liturgy was a living experience. But the modern student, seeking a realistic conception of parish worship as it once was, has to consider mere scattered fragments of a medieval reality. We will consider these fragments and pose two questions: What characterized the medieval parish liturgy (specifically in Sweden), and what factors shaped it?

Sources

The sources for the parish liturgy are varied and of unequal value. *Liturgical prescriptions* from diocesan and other authorities are usually not difficult to situate historically, and their meaning is always clear. However, it is quite uncertain to what extent—and how—they were implemented. *Liturgical books* have been preserved both in manuscript form (codices and fragments) and in the form of early printed editions. Many manuscripts can be tied to specific parish churches, but most of their content (texts, music, prescriptions) is common stock. Thus, they give few hints about the detailed enactment of the liturgy in the parish to which they belonged. Furthermore, they tend to mirror ideals rather than actual practice. Art and literature too can throw light on liturgical custom but should be used with caution.

Previous Nordic[1] Research

Scholarly research in the Nordic countries has applied two pairs of opposed concepts to medieval liturgical tradition: uniformity vs. diversity, and cathedral rite vs. parish rite.[2] However, the relation between these two pairs

[1]The term "Nordic" refers in this essay to Iceland, Norway, Denmark, Sweden, and Finland. This is normal usage in the Nordic countries themselves.

[2]Earlier scholars, such as Edvard Rodhe and Gustaf Lindberg, do mention that certain sources come from country parishes, but they pay no attention to the parish liturgy as such. Later, the problem of liturgical uniformity and diversity was usually approached from the perspective of the diocese. The books and conditions of the parish church now came under closer consideration. Aarno Maliniemi was the first to analyze the demands for uniformity within each diocese. In the light of canon law he studied episcopal influence on the parishes, e.g., in the choice of *patroni*, relics, and motifs in works of art. He emphasized the importance of the schooling of priests (at the cathedral) and of diocesan synods, while at the same time pointing out the use of "foreign" liturgical books in the parishes: Aarno Malin[iemi], *Der Heiligenkalender Finnlands. Seine Zusammensetzung und Entwicklung* (Helsingfors, 1925), pp. 3ff. The musicologist Carl-Allan Moberg found evidence for the use of a simpler,

of concepts has not been clarified. While there is a clear connection between them, they are not identical. It is certainly true that even though the official order of the cathedral was eventually prescribed for the whole diocese, the parish churches continued to represent significant local diversity. But at the same time, diversity cannot be associated with the parish church alone: even the cathedral could accommodate—in one of its chapels—a liturgical tradition which deviated from the norm.[3] We thus need a different set of concepts in order to gain a proper understanding of the parish liturgy.

---

more limited repertory of hymns in country churches: Carl-Allan Moberg, *Die liturgischen Hymnen in Schweden. Beiträge zur Liturgie- und Musikgeschichte des Mittelalters und der Reformationszeit*, vol. 1: *Quellen und Texte* (Kopenhagen & Uppsala, 1947), p. 91 (concerning KB [see Abbreviations, p. 186], A 50 and referring to A 99 and A 100). Hilding Johansson, studying the manual of Hemsjö, found tendencies of simplification in the parish liturgy, in that the number of clergy as well as processions and song were reduced in comparison with the cathedral: Hilding Johansson, *Hemsjömanualet. En liturgi-historisk studie* (Stockholm, 1950), pp. 152 ff. (but compare the review by Eric Segelberg in *Kyrkohistorisk årsskrift* 50 [1950], 265–70); idem, *Den medeltida liturgien i Skara stift. Studier i mässa och helgonkult* (Lund, 1956), pp. 74 ff. and passim; and idem, "Skara som stiftsstad," in *Skara I: Före 1700. Staden i stiftet*, ed. Arne Sträng et al. (Skara, 1986), pp. 447 ff., 498, 504 ff. Helge Fæhn brought Norwegian material to bear on the question of uniformity. Conditions were seen to be the same as in Sweden-Finland, but he did not adduce material of explicitly parish origin: Helge Fæhn (ed. and comm.), *Fire norske messeordninger fra middelalderen* (Oslo, 1953), p. 14. Sven Helander showed that the distinction between cathedral and parish church is evident also outside the Nordic countries, and that in Swedish sources the clearest distinction between the two is found in the texts for the Easter period: Sven Helander, *Ordinarius Lincopensis c:a 1400 och dess liturgiska förebilder* (Lund, 1957), pp. 29 ff., 47 ff. and passim. See also Ulf Björkman, *Stilla veckan i gudstjänst och fromhetsliv, med särskild hänsyn till svensk medeltida tradition* (Lund, 1957), pp. 297, 308. Carl-Gösta Frithz applied the terms *conformitas—diversitas*, which he regarded as complementary forces in the development of the liturgical tradition: Carl-Gösta Frithz, *Till frågan om det s.k. Helgeandshusmissalets liturgihistoriska ställning* (Lund, 1976), pp. 136 ff.

[3]A chapel in the cathedral of Åbo owned the Danish *Missale Hafniense* [vetus] (Mainz, 1484). Malin[iemi], *Heiligenkalender*, 18.

The Diocese as a Liturgical Unit

The liturgy often reflects the hierarchical structure of the church. A higher seat of authority, such as the cathedral, can claim the status of providing a normative pattern. Conformity "upward" in the liturgical practices of the parishes was sometimes seen as a desirable expression of the unity of the church.[4]

Several levels of the ecclesiastical hierarchy were active in setting a standard. The highest—the Roman curia—did not in the Middle Ages strive for liturgical conformity in the whole church, though specific practices did receive papal authorization. References to papal decisions are occasionally found in Swedish missals.[5]

The middle level was the archbishop and provincial council. The archbishop, however, had no absolute authority over the liturgy in individual dioceses. Provincial councils did make numerous decisions for the whole province in liturgical matters, such as proclaiming specific feastdays, cults, and other forms of devotion, yet such decisions often needed to be confirmed in diocesan prescriptions in order to take effect.[6]

The diocese and its cathedral were the decisive and dominant norm for the parishes. But the creation of a diocese and the appointment of a bishop in itself did not create a common liturgy. The earliest generations of liturgical books after the missionary period in Sweden—books dating from the eleventh and twelfth centuries—had various origins, often places in

---

[4]Such ideas are often expressed in the episcopal prefaces to printed breviaries, e.g., *BSc*, *BU*. (See list of Abbreviations at end of this chapter.)

[5]An example of a papal decision quoted in several Swedish missals is the provision by Alexander II that the Alleluia should cease on the Saturday before Septuagesima.

[6]One example among many is the provincial council of Arboga 1474, which prescribed the feast of the patron saints of Sweden for the whole ecclesiastical province; it was never embraced by the southern dioceses. Sven Helander, *Ansgarskulten i Norden* (Stockholm, 1989), p. 181. For canonical regulations see idem, *Ordinarius Lincopensis*, p. 13.

England, France, or Germany. The basis for unified liturgical practice came only with the settled implementation of canon law and the establishment of secular cathedral chapters in the thirteenth century. It became a major task of the cathedral chapter to function as a liturgical corporation because of its leading role in worship at the cathedral. The continuing development of cultic practices was in the hands of the chapter. Its resources—economic and personal—also provided the means for a corresponding development of the cathedral itself, with new chantries and chapels being added for the new devotions. Architectural space and liturgy often changed in tandem.

The bishop was responsible for guiding the worship of the whole diocese—an aspect of his *potestas ordinis* according to canon law.[7] Numerous examples of episcopal initiative in liturgical matters may be found in Nordic sources. Prescriptions issued by the diocesan synod had the widest scope; new cults and saints were typically introduced in dioceses through such synodal legislation.[8] More directly effective on the local level were, of course, the actions of the bishop in consecrating churches and altars, tying them by the deposition of relics to specific saints as *patroni*. Episcopal letters of indulgence also promoted certain cults. Further examples of influence from above may be seen in the choice of motifs for the decoration of parish churches. Finally, the episcopal visitation of a parish included control of its liturgy and examination of its books.[9]

---

[7]See e.g. Göran Inger, *Das kirchliche Visitationsinstitut im mittelalterlichen Schweden* (Lund, 1961), p. 108.

[8]The feast day of St. Dominic, for example, was introduced in the archdiocese of Uppsala by Archbishop Nils Allesson, through a decree included in the acts of the diocesan synod of 1297: "Item mandamus vt presbiteri diem beati dominici de officiis celebrem habere teneantur ac festum eiusdem in dominica precedenti coram parochianis suis vt moris est de aliis festis publicent et indicent," *DS* 1187.

[9]*Synodalstatuter och andra kyrkorättsliga aktstycken från den svenska medeltidskyrkan*, ed. Jaakko Gummerus (Uppsala, 1902), p. 97; and Inger, *Das kirchliche Visitationsinstitut*, pp. 450 ff., 479, 481.

Cathedral and Parish Liturgy: The Ideal

In the ecclesiastical province of Sweden, as in other parts of Europe, diocesan authorities became progressively more insistent in their ambitions to make the order of the cathedral the norm for the parish liturgy. There existed several means of furthering the influence of the cathedral. One was the education of parish priests.

The liturgical schooling of the priest began in the cathedral school and was followed, after his reception of holy orders, by a year or two of service at the cathedral. During this time he learned large parts of the liturgy, both words and music, by heart.[10] When assigned to his parish, the young priest brought with him a solid acquaintance with the official order of the diocese.

The annual synod of all priests at the cathedral town was used for similar purposes. Announcements were made which concerned the liturgy in the year to come: changes in the roll of saints and their liturgies, the dates of movable feasts, the coordination of *temporale* and *sanctorale*, and so on. The priests were to bring back home copies of the statutes issued. At the end of the Middle Ages, such announcements began to be printed in the form of circular letters for the diocese. There is also evidence (from Norway) that priests sometimes brought liturgical books with them to synods to be checked.[11]

The acquisition of new books to the parish was another opportunity for improving conformity with the cathedral. Scribes produced new books by copying authorized exemplars, at least theoretically supervised by the

---

[10]Ragnar Askmark, *Svensk prästutbildning fram till år 1700* (Stockholm, 1943), pp. 1–16; and Åke Sandholm, *Klockarämbetet i den svenska kyrkoprovinsen under medeltiden* (Åbo, 1963), passim.

[11]Sigurd Kroon, *Det svenska prästmötet under medeltiden. Dess uppkomst och ställning i samhälle och kyrka* (Stockholm, 1948). Another constant tie with the cathedral was the annual visit to fetch holy oils: *DS* 1240; *Statuta synodalia veteris ecclesiæ Sveogothicæ*, ed. Henrik Reuterdahl (Lund, 1841), pp. 192 ff.

diocesan authorities. The books were then checked and approved by the rural deans.[12] With the advent of the printing press complete uniformity became possible. At the end of the Middle Ages, missals were printed for Uppsala, Strängnäs and Åbo. A gradual was published for Västerås. Breviaries were printed for Linköping, Strängnäs, Uppsala, Skara, and Västerås. Some additional books (psalters, manuals etc.) were also printed. The very titles—*Missale Strengnense*, *Breviarium Arosiense*—reveal that they were intended to be normative for the respective diocese.

The liturgy itself gave expression to the idea of unity. At every Mass, the prayers of the canon reminded of the links with the Church at large, the pope, and the local bishop. The missals usually contained special Masses for the bishop of the diocese, as well as the **requiem** Mass for a deceased bishop. The breviaries contained intercessions for Church and bishop in the so-called Litany of All Saints and in the ***Preces maiores***. The commemorations served to include every parish and every priest in the communion of saints, particularly the saints of one's cathedral and the patron saint of the diocese.

The calendar of the cathedral contained a number of days which emphasized the organic unity of the diocese. While the choice of such days might vary, they often included the dedication day of the cathedral, the celebration of its chief relics and that of its *patronus*, an anniversary of benefactors, or a commemoration of deceased bishops and priests. In many dioceses, every parish was made to partake in the celebration of at least some of these days.

The liturgical ideal, clearly, was conformity with the cathedral. But did reality conform to the ideal?

---

[12]Nils Alleson's statutes, *DS* 1187. Similar statutes in Åbo 1352: Reinhold Hausen, ed., *Finlands Medeltidsurkunder*, vols. 1–8 (Helsingfors, 1910–35), no. 624; Malin[iemi], *Heiligenkalender*, pp. 19–20. Care of books checked at visitation: *DS* 2229 (Linköping).

Parish Liturgy and Cathedral: The Reality

The relation between parish and cathedral liturgy may be studied in extant liturgical books from both environments. There are two possible approaches: a bibliographic one, centering on the stock of books and their origin; and a material one, centering on the liturgy itself.[13]

The Stock of Books

An ordinary parish church in a typical Swedish diocese in the Middle Ages owned some three to eight books. The *missal* with the texts of the Mass was the main book and was kept in the church. Also in the church would have been the *manual* containing various rites other than Mass (baptism, funeral etc.), and perhaps one or more books containing songs with musical notation, both for Mass (*gradual*, ***sequentionary***) and for the Divine Office (*antiphonary*, ***hymnary***). The *breviary*, which was the basic book for the Divine Office, could be owned by the church but also by the priest himself—no other liturgical book is mentioned so frequently in last wills and testaments.

Extant manuscript material—especially the fragments—allows us to conclude that the cathedral rite in time became the norm for the books owned by the parishes of each diocese. But there exists, as a parallel phenomenon, a certain amount of deviation which reveals how the cathedral occasionally failed to assert itself. For example, a parish sometimes had "wrong" books, books from a different diocese. They may have been acquired by irregular trade, donations, or from priests who had moved. Possession of such volumes probably implies actual usage.

---

[13]Parish liturgy is of course an international phenomenon. What follows applies in many respects also to other ecclesiastical provinces. See Helander, *Ordinarius Lincopensis*, pp. 48, 52; and Isak Collijn, *Redogörelse för på uppdrag af Kungl. Maj:t i Kammararkivet och Riksarkivet verkställd undersökning angående äldre arkivalieomslag* (Stockholm, 1914), p. 36.

The acquisition of new books was limited by economic constraints. Missals were normally written on parchment, and other liturgical books sometimes were too—an expensive material. Furthermore, liturgical books (the missal in particular) were used for official records about ecclesiastical property and the furniture of the vicarage, about requiem and votive Masses, about indulgences, consecrations, and visitations; they could contain notes about deaths and ownership. All these annotations tied the books to the life of the local community. For this reason they were often in use over a very long period of time. The church of Arnäs in the diocese of Uppsala, for instance, in 1492 was still using its missal from the thirteenth century.[14] During their long period of use, books were normally kept up to date by means of erasures and additions of various kinds. The last leaves of missals and breviaries can contain disordered contributions by several different hands. Eventually, however, liturgical developments in combination with wear and tear made it necessary to put aged books aside in the sacristy, where they sometimes were kept for reference.

Toleration for liturgical books with eccentric contents seems to have varied. There exist, for example, a number of manuscripts from the diocese of Linköping which carry notes to the effect that they do contain the order of that see [*secundum ordinem Lincopensem*].[15] Such notes are largely lacking from other dioceses, suggesting that interest in diocesan uniformity was less strong elsewhere. And whatever the ideal, "uniformity" never meant a total introduction of the exact order of the cathedral liturgy, either in the age of manuscripts or in that of the printed book.

---

[14]RA, Cod. fragm. mi 536: *Missale ecclesie Arnäs fragm.*, saec. XIII. A marginal note mentions the visit of archbishop Jakob Ulfsson in 1492, yet a printed missal for the diocese had been available since ca. 1484, the *MU* vetus. It seems that one reason to retain antiquated books was precisely to record local events in them.

[15]The following example, from a lectionary fragment, has not been noted in previous literature: " . . . secundum ecclesiam Lync<opensem> alia omelia . . . " HUB, Manuscript Collection, Cod. fragm. lect. 50: *Lectionarium Lincopense fragm.*, saec. XIV.

The Liturgy

The relationship between cathedral and parish liturgy can best be studied in the contents of books from each respective environment. The following two examples illustrate the matter in some detail:

EXAMPLE 1. The three days before Easter [***triduum sacrum***] and Easter Day constitute the section of the liturgical year which affords the clearest illustrations, since at this time the dramatic subject of celebration is expressed in a particularly rich liturgy. Let us first look at cathedral vs. parish rite in sources from the diocese of Linköping. Our sources provide access to the cathedral rite of Linköping ca. 1400 and ca. 1450, and to the parish liturgy ca. 1440, in a missal probably from the church of Sten. Linköping is the only Swedish diocese from which a complete cathedral rite has come down to us. The Sten parish missal has the advantages of being securely tied to the diocese and of being preserved entire. Our comparison will be limited to that part of the liturgy which figures in the missal.

TABLE: The Liturgy from Maundy Thursday to Easter Day according to preserved sources from the diocese of Linköping (the Divine Office is omitted)

Cathedral		Parish
Maundy Thursday		
1.	Washing of feet (*mandatum*).	0
2.	Sermon (in church).	0
3.	Mass.	=
	Gloria Patri, *Gloria in excelsis* and	=
	Ite missa est sung only where	= (*Ite* not mentioned)
	chrism is confected (i.e., at episcopal Mass).	=
	Mass ends with vespers.	=
	Hosts reserved for Good Friday	=
	communion ("in honesto loco").	=
	Undressing of the altars.	=

Good Friday

1.	Lections.	=
	Altar servers (“ministri altaris”)	=
	in albs, the priest in cope.	=
	Acolyte reads the texts,	=
	priest reads the prayers,	= (priest not mentioned)
	deacon orders kneeling.	= (deacon not mentioned)
	The Passion narrative (rubric only);	= (roles indicated)
	two cloths laid on the altar beforehand,	=
	at “they parted my vestments”	=
	two deacons snatch them away.	= (two acolytes)
2.	Intercessions.	=
	Priest reads the prayers,	= (priest not mentioned)
	deacon orders kneeling.	= (deacon not mentioned)
	Choir sings Amen.	=
3.	Salutation of the cross.	=
	Two priests in chasubles hold the cross.	= (two clerics, “clerici”)
	Improperia: boys answer,	= (two boys, “pueri”)
	choir continues.	=
4.	Communion.	=
	Priests carry cross to altar.	= (priest)
	Solemn procession with the sacrament	=
	by six men of different orders	= (by priest and deacon)
	(precentor and *ebdomadarius* mentioned)	0
	to the altar.	=
	Sexton spreads altar cloth.	= (not sexton)
	Our Father concluded by choir.	=
	The communion.	=
5.	“Burial” of the cross.	=
	The cross is shrouded	=
	and laid down.	=
	The sepulcher is prepared,	=
	the corporal put there.	=
	Procession with the cross to the sepulcher.	0
	The cross is deposed.	0

Easter Eve

1.	Blessing of fire and candle.	=
	Precentor, priest, levite and	= (priest, levites,
	cleric mentioned.	= other ministers)
	The hymn *Inventor rutili* sung by "two."	= (two boys)
	Deacon in dalmatia	=
	blesses the candle with *Exultet* etc.	=
2.	The prophecies.	=
	Prayers offered by priest.	= (person not mentioned)
3.	Procession with litany (rubric) and	= (text of the litany given)
	consecration of baptismal water (rubric).	= (the whole act given)
	Archaic rubric about baptismal instruction	0
	and baptism of children.	0
4.	Mass.	=
	Precentor intones *Kyrie.*	=
	While priest intones *Gloria*,	=
	the church bells are rung.	=
	Mass ends with vespers.	=

Easter Day

1.	The cross is taken from the sepulcher.	0
2.	The Easter play at the sepulcher performed	0
	by three clerics and two deacons.	0
3.	Aspersion of holy water, *Vidi aquam.*	=
4.	Procession with songs	=
	Cum rex glorie and *Salve festa dies.*	=
	At entrance into church	= ("In reditu ecclesie")
	Sedit angelus,	= + *Nolite metuere*
	at station in middle of church *Sedit angelus*,	0
	at entrance into choir *Nolite metuere*	0
	with versicle and collect.	=
5.	The Mass *Resurrexi.*	=
	0	Ends with blessing of the
	0	Easter food.
6.	After second vespers:	=
	procession to the font with	0 ("Ad fontem")
	Vidi aquam,	0
	antiphon, psalms, versicle,	0
	collect.	=

Returning procession ("In redeundo") with	0 ("In redeundo")
Christus resurgens, versicle,	0
collect.	=
Benedicamus Domino, blessing.	0

= means that the rubric/text is the same as in the cathedral sources.
0 means that the rubric/text is missing in the cathedral or parish sources.

Sources for the cathedral order: *Ordinarius Lincopensis* prior, ca. 1400 (Stockholm, Riksarkivet, Skoklostersaml., Avd. I, no. 2, in 4° [E 8899]), and *Ordinarius Lincopensis* posterior, ca. 1450 (Uppsala Universitetsbibliotek, C 428)—almost identical in the sections cited above. Source for the parish order: *Missale Lincopense*, ca. 1436–48 (Stockholm, Kungliga Biblioteket, A 97).

The table allows conclusions to be drawn on two levels. First, the overall liturgical structure is highly uniform. Indeed, it conforms to that found in sources from other countries as well. The reason for this is that the various diocesan orders in Sweden as in other parts of Europe were the inheritors of an older, common order. But second, the liturgy of the cathedral, on its journey from cathedral to country parish, has been revised in many details: certain elements have disappeared, one or two may have been added, and the number of clergy has been reduced. Let us consider the revisions one by one.

The washing of the feet in the liturgy for Maundy Thursday is omitted in the parish. On that same day a sermon is prescribed for the cathedral but not for the parish church, even though Maundy Thursday is generally considered to have been a common day of preaching.[16]

The lections for Good Friday culminate in the Passion narrative. A dramatic recitation of the latter, with a distribution of "roles" among different readers, is known from many manuscripts. In the cathedral it is axiomatic,

---

[16]Björkman, *Stilla veckan*, pp. 73 ff., 239. The sermon was certainly a regular feature of Sunday Mass, in spite of the fact that it is almost never mentioned in missals. See Sven-Erik Pernler, "Predikan ad populum under svensk medeltid. Till frågan om sockenprästernas predikoskyldighet," in *Predikohistoriska perspektiv* [FS Åke Andrén], ed. Alf Härdelin (Älvsjö, 1982), pp. 73–94.

despite the fact that our source does not contain the text itself; the parish missal marks the different roles, but it is questionable whether a proper performance could have been staged in a rural church with few clergy.[17]

Good Friday usually ended with a symbolic representation of the burial of Christ. In the church, a "sepulcher" was often set in order for this purpose.[18] A "cross" was used; a **corporal**; and possibly—in addition to the "cross" or as an alternative to it—a host [a consecrated wafer]. By "cross" was meant an image of the body of Christ, such as the corpus from a crucifix, while the corporal was the cloth on which chalice and paten rested during Mass, and where the hosts lay during consecration. In our parish source, we find the shrouding of the cross, the preparation of the sepulcher, and the deposition of the corporal in the sepulcher. But the cathedral procession with the actual deposition of the cross in the sepulcher is not mentioned in the Sten missal. It is possible that the deposition was self-evident, while the procession was superfluous due to lack of space. Neither source mentions the deposition of a host.[19]

---

[17]On the recitation see Johansson, *Den medeltida liturgien*, p. 43: "In many small churches the priest read the whole narrative alone, but could mark the different parts by different ways of reciting." See also Björkman, *Stilla veckan*, pp. 170ff. The distribution of roles is set forth in a handwritten missal, perhaps from the cathedral of Uppsala: RA, Cod. fragm. mi 115: *Missale Upsalense (eccl. metrop.?) fragm.*, saec. XV. Roles have been added by hand in some printed missals.

[18]Björkman, *Stilla veckan*, pp. 303 ff.; and Lilli Gjerløw, *Adoratio crucis. The Regularis Concordia and the Decreta Lanfranci. Manuscript Studies in the Early Medieval Church of Norway* (Oslo & Boston, 1961). Gesine & Johannes Taubert, "Mittelalterliche Kruzifixe mit schwenkbaren Armen," *Zeitschrift des Deutschen Vereins für Kunstwissenschaft* XXIII (1969): 79–121, present continental material. Anna Nilsén, *Program och funktion i senmedeltida kalkmåleri. Kyrkmålningar i Mälarlandskapen och Finland 1400–1534* (Stockholm, 1986), pp. 404ff., lists such Easter sepulchers from country churches, town churches, and cathedrals, and cites an instance of actual use. Evidence from Gotland has also been adduced: Bengt Stolt, *Medeltida teater och gotländsk kyrkokonst* (Visby, 1993).

[19]On the burial of the host see Ludwig Eisenhofer, *Handbuch der katholischen Liturgik*, 2 vols. (Freiburg im Breisgau, 1932–1933), 1:531–32; and Solange Corbin, *La déposition liturgique du Christ au Vendredi Saint. Sa place dans l'histoire des rites et du théâtre*

At the Easter vigil, the rubric concerning baptism has not been preserved in the parish missal. This is natural, since even in the cathedral it was no more than a literary relic of an obsolete practice.

The ceremony in the cathedral on Easter morning, when the cross was taken from the sepulcher, is absent from the parish. Then came the resurrection play, which enacted the three women's visit to the sepulcher and their encounter with two angels. The play (*Quem queritis*) had developed from liturgical texts and is present in Swedish sources in various redactions from the thirteenth century onward. It could hardly have been performed in the average rural church, which had but a single priest and a ***campanarius*** to act the parts; at any rate it is absent from our parish missal. It may be noted that in the influential abbey of Vadstena there was resistance to the play for Mariological reasons: there the claim was that Christ had shown himself first to his mother. The play fell into disuse in Sweden toward the end of the fifteenth century.[20]

The processions of Easter Day were simplified. The introductory procession when holy water was sprinkled on those present exists in both cathedral and parish. But the introit follows in the cathedral an ancient pattern of three stages: a beginning, a halt or station [*stacio*] in the middle of

---

religieux (analyse de documents portugais) (Paris & Lisbon, 1960). Compare the following piece of evidence from the liturgy of Good Friday in an early Swedish missal: "Communione peracta processio eodem ordine quo accesserant ad altare procedat ad locum cum corpore ubi debeat recondi . . . ," RA, Cod. fragm. mi. 128: *Missale incerti originis fragm.*, saec. XII.

[20]Toni Schmid, "Das Osterspiel in Schweden. Ein Beitrag zur Geschichte des 'Quem queritis' im Mittelalter," *Kyrkohistorisk årsskrift* 52 (1952): 1–14; and idem, "Mysteriespel," *KL* 12 (1967): 103. After the play had disappeared, its sole remnant was the Easter sequence, sung within Matins. This last phase may be found in e.g. UUB, C 354: *Breviarium Lincopense*, ca. 1441–90 (has belonged to a country church); see Helander, *Ordinarius Lincopensis*, pp. 93 ff. Many of the extant Swedish sources for the Easter play are presented, with English translation, in Audrey Ekdahl Davidson, *Holy Week and Easter Ceremonies and Dramas from Medieval Sweden* (Kalamazoo, Mich., 1990).

the church, and the entry into the **chancel**. In the parish church, though the procession is emphasized (perhaps the church yard was used), the introit could not be so pompously staged.[21]

After Vespers on Easter Day (and throughout the following week) a procession passes with psalms and prayers through the cathedral to the font [*Descendendo ad fontem canitur* . . .] and returns in the same way. "The fountain of life" is one of its themes. In the parish church, the text is abbreviated radically to one prayer for each direction. The short form suggests that the movement to the font and back is here a fiction, which is confirmed by the fact that the disuse of this ancient procession later received official legitimation, for example, by its omission being mentioned in *BL* as an alternative.

But all is not reduction in the parish. We seem to discern something of the peculiar profile of a parish church in a formula for Easter Day. Here, Mass ends with a blessing of the food to be consumed at Easter. In the cathedral books there is no mention, at least, of this custom with its popular character.[22]

There is a notable difference in personnel between cathedral and parish church. The cathedral uses priests, deacons, acolytes, and undefined clerics, as well as cantor, *ebdomadarius* (responsible for the week's Divine Office), choir and school boys (the *scholares* of the cathedral). The parish church had a single priest, who on occasion is required by the missal to be assisted by a deacon, by "levites" (clerics fulfilling the liturgical tasks of a deacon or **subdeacon**), acolytes, "clerics," and school boys as well as a choir. The parish missal here does not give the impression of realistic accommodation to local resources. All the helpers mentioned could hardly have been present

---

[21]RA, Cod. fragm. mi. 442: *Missale incerti originis (Leodiense?) fragm*., saec. XII. The manuscript has been used in a Swedish diocese. It mentions a procession "circa claustra templi" on Easter Day and during the following week.

[22]KB, A 97, *Missale Lincopense*: "*Secuntur benedicciones super cibos Primo super panes Benedic domine creaturam istam panis*" (the rest of the prayer not written out).

in a country parish. It is undoubtedly the conditions of the cathedral which still echo in the parish book, despite attempts at simplification. The liturgy as set out in the parish missal is like a suit of clothes that is too large. This makes the investigation of the actual performance of the parish liturgy rather difficult.

Fortunately there exist fragments of liturgical books, which furnish us with additional clues. A fragment from a late fourteenth-century missal, also from the diocese of Linköping, helps us get closer to the parish liturgy as it really was. It contains parts of the services for Good Friday and Easter Eve. The personnel mentioned includes priest, deacons, levite, cleric, and choir; ceremonially, the Good Friday procession to the sepulcher is lacking, just as in the Sten missal.[23] But our fragment contains "a source within the source." A long marginal note was added in the later part of the fifteenth century, occasioned by the fact that the missal did not correspond to actual conditions. The beginning reads: "In parish churches. On Good Friday, after the salutation of the cross, Mass (= communion) follows according to the following order. . . ."[24] The liturgy is then described as performed by just a priest and a choir. The shrouding of the cross is there, but the part where the sepulcher may have been mentioned is mutilated. The order for Communion contains a new rubric regarding when the priest "turns to the people" (the presence of the people is elsewhere silently presupposed). This marginal addition may reasonably be supposed to be an authoritative revision of the missal, with the purpose of providing a rite adapted to the actual conditions of a parish church.

Other fragments from other dioceses show that conditions in the parishes actually varied a great deal. Older missal fragments tend to present a large personnel, whereas more recent sources show more realistic restraint. But the dividing line is not distinct. The above-mentioned "burial" at the

---

[23]UUB, Fragm. ms. lat. 89: *Missale Lincopense fragm*. Secondary provenance: KA, Kalmar Castle 1564 (1565).

[24]"In ecclesiis parochialibus Die paracheues post deposicionem . . . ."

end of Good Friday has several variants in the fragments. It can envisage the cross only (more than once), or cross and (optionally) host, or host only. At the Easter vigil there are many instances where baptism is mentioned in the rubric without the order of baptism being inscribed. The blessing of Easter food is also mentioned in several missals.

Our investigation of parish sources thus reveals certain simplifications. Some of these are more or less common to all books and would seem to be the result of central initiative. Other simplifications have the character of individual adaptation to conditions prevailing in specific parishes. Many of the latter modifications appear to have been carried out in the second half of the fifteenth century, and there is no evidence that they were endorsed by cathedral authorities.

To conclude: the liturgy of Easter in Swedish sources chiefly reflects common tradition, but its shape in details was conditioned by the physical architectural space and the availability of "liturgical personnel." To suit the parish church, the cathedral order had to be scaled down. Reductions in the parish rite become increasingly evident in liturgical books in the course of the fifteenth century. The implication is that the liturgical books were, by and by, made to conform to what presumably was long-established practice.

EXAMPLE 2. Printed editions of liturgical books appear in the second half of the fifteenth century. These editions evidently seek to reconcile two competing concerns: uniformity and universality. The episcopal prefaces to the secular breviaries bemoan the lack of uniformity that has come to their notice, for example, during visitations. Yet it is not an authentic cathedral rite that we find in the printed books. The production of the books has entailed a certain amount of selection and sometimes considerable adaptation to the resources of the ordinary parish. At the same time the adaptation is not consistent. Now and again the cathedral environment reasserts itself.

Liturgical personnel. The orders for Mass in *MU*, *MStr*, *BL*, and *BSc* envisage a single priest. An altar server momentarily appears at the peace greeting.[25] A single priest is usually presupposed throughout the liturgical year. Exceptions include *GrAr* and *MStr*, which mention several priests for the salutation of the cross on Good Friday. A deacon serves at some feasts, as in *MU* on Ash Wednesday and Christmas night, in *BU* on Easter Eve, and in *MStr* on Christmas night, Ash Wednesday, Palm Sunday and Easter Eve. A subdeacon serves according to *MStr* on Good Friday. The cathedral *horistanus* also appears in the order for Ash Wednesday in *MStr*.

Deacon and subdeacon are not, however, likely participants in the parish liturgy. Higher orders were imparted in such quick sequence, that one passed from subdeacon to priest in half a year. Apparently some candidates were phased out on the way, but there is nothing to indicate that they were intentionally channeled into parish churches.[26]

A cantor can well be imagined in the parish church, but his presence should not be taken for granted. According to *MU* and *BU*, he sings the *Te Deum* on Christmas night, while the celebrant with servers [*cum ministris*] prepares for Mass. In *BL* cantors (in the plural!) intone the *Kyrie Eleyson* on the paschal melody [*Kirieleyson cum nota paschali*] on Easter Day. It is surely the more lavish cathedral setting we discern here. Perhaps the same goes for the three boys [*tres pueri*], who according to *BU* appear as soloists in the responsories for matins on the first Sunday of Advent. The chanting boys also appear in other places, as when in *MU* they alternate with celebrant and choir on Easter Eve. A choir often figures in the printed liturgical books (see further below under "*Who Performed the Liturgy?*").

---

[25]*BSc*: "det pacem astanti. Pax tibi frater . . . " *BL*: "Ad ministrantem dicat. Pax tecum. Et cum spiritu [tuo] . . . "

[26]Askmark, *Svensk prästutbildning*, pp. 10 ff.; Sandholm, *Klockarämbetet*, pp. 84 ff.; and Bengt Strömberg, "Ordination," *KL* 12 (1967): 657–61. Kauko Pirinen, "Diakon," *KL* 3 (1958): 51–53, notes that a priest could perform the deacon's parts in the liturgy. (He could then even carry a deacon's vestment, the dalmatica, according to Joseph Braun, *Die liturgische Gewandung im Occident und Orient, nach Ursprung und Entwicklung, Verwendung und Symbolik* [Freiburg im Breisgau, 1907], p. 258.) This, however, is not enough to explain the unsystematic indications about liturgical Offices in the sources.

Liturgical ceremonies at Easter. The printed books do not display a division of the Passion narrative into different roles. The reason for this may be difficulties of carrying out such instructions in parish churches. If so, however, the printed books show a tendency to generalize, for in some churches the requisite personnel was clearly available. Indeed, in one or two printed missals the assignment of roles has been added in handwriting.

The ceremony of extinguishing candles during the three days before Easter is connected with the Divine Office, and for that reason has not been mentioned above. It involved the successive extinguishing of twenty-four (the number has varied) candles during the antiphons of Matins-cum-Lauds. In parish churches the lack of personnel and the cost of candles make the ceremony almost unthinkable, and indeed it normally is absent from the printed books; yet it does appear in *MStr* and *BAr*.[27]

The washing of feet on Maundy Thursday is not mentioned in the printed books. To carry out the ceremonies appropriate to it in country churches would have entailed some real difficulties. The "burial" of Good Friday appears in *MStr*, *MU*, and *GrAr*. They mention that the cross is carried to the sepulcher and deposited there but say nothing of a host. Considering what was said above (at note 19), the burial of a host seems to have been unusual. To bury both a cross (or its corpus) and a host would, of course, be a duplication of symbols.

The resurrection play on Easter morning, *Quem queritis*, has disappeared from the printed books but has left a relic of its former presence in the form of the Easter sequence, *Victimæ paschali laudes*. In *BL* this is sung after the third responsory of Matins, where the play had been.

The blessing of food at Easter, which we met in several manuscripts, appears in the majority of printed breviaries. *BU* ties this act to Easter (*in pascha*), *BL* to Easter Eve, *BSc* mentions no particular day.

In the week after Easter the vesper service ends with a procession to the font (as mentioned above in regard to an earlier period). This ceremony was abandoned in time. According to *BStr*, *BSc*, and *BL* it is optional.

---

[27]On this ceremony see further Björkman, *Stilla veckan*, pp. 206 ff.

To sum up, the printed books do revise the previously current cathedral order, with regard to both personnel and ceremonies. Some of the more characteristic rites still remain, but much has been reduced in order to fit the conditions of the ordinary parish church.

The Profile of the Parish Liturgy

We have so far looked at the parish liturgy in its relation to the cathedral. We shall now look at it from the opposite perspective: its adaptation to a locality. Liturgical features unique to the particular parish bring us face to face with local reality. Certain practices could be authorized by letters of indulgence issued by the bishop. Apart from that, two days of the year ranked highly in every parish: the anniversary of the dedication of the church, and the feast of its patron(s).[28]

The dedication of the parish church, *dedicatio ecclesie*, was commemorated annually as a separate feast day. It often appears in the church's calendar as a local addition.[29]

The feast of the patron saint (which is quite distinct from the day of dedication) was important in popular tradition. An image of the patron, either sculpted, painted, or done in a glass window, could have a prominent place in the church. Nonetheless, the patron saint was seldom indicated in

---

[28]Swedish letters of indulgence are treated by Jan Liedgren, "Indulgensbrev," *KL* 7 (1962): 393–96; Carl-Gustaf Andrén, "De medeltida avlatsbreven—instrument för kyrkans verksamhet," in *Investigatio memoriae patrum: Libellus in honorem Kauko Pirinen*, ed. Pentti Laasonen et al. (Helsinki, 1975), pp. 201–21. Notes about indulgences could be entered into the missal. Examples are given by Collijn, *Redogörelse*, 21 and 23; see also Kalmar (diocese of Uppsala), parish archives: *Kalendarium Upsalense*, saec. XIV.

[29]Examples of dedication days added to calendars: *Liber ecclesiæ Vallentunensis*, ed. Toni Schmid (Stockholm, 1945); RA, Cod. fragm. kal. 30: *Kalendarium "prepositure Sollentunensis" fragm.*, ca. 1200; RA, Cod. fragm. mi. 45: *Missale Lincopense ecclesie Böda fragm.*, saec. XIV in.

any way in calendars; these usually contained his or her feast day in any case, and knowledge of the patron's identity was simply presupposed.[30] The images of other saints were, of course, also a focus for pious devotions, and the penitent could receive indulgences if these images were venerated in prescribed ways.[31]

To the profile of every parish church belonged the dedications of altars and bells, which were often consecrated to or placed under the protection of particular saints. A very tangible relation to saints was provided by the relics which were deposited in altars at their consecration.

The profile of the parish liturgy was conditioned also by the lives of the parishioners, both in earlier generations and in the present one. As for previous generations, the names of deceased benefactors were to be read out after the sermon on Sundays, as were the names of *patroni* and of the founders of the diocesan cathedral.[32] Requiem Masses and vigils for individual parishioners further contributed to the character of the local liturgy. The names of the deceased could be noted in the calendar on the days of their deaths. It is quite realistic to reckon with a number of dedicated requiem Masses in a parish church in the course of a year, even though they of course were fewer than at monasteries and cathedrals.[33]

---

[30]For examples of local feasts of the patron saint mentioned in letters of indulgence see Helander, *Ansgarskulten*, p. 116. A rare example of such a day noted in a liturgical book is KB, A 50 a, a missal from Stockholm's Helgeandshus (a hospital), where the calendar entry for 17 Jan. says, "Anthonij abbatis patroni III 1."

[31]*Kumla kyrkas räkenskapsbok 1421–1590*, ed. Jonas L:son Samzelius (Örebro, 1946), pp. 159 ff.; and *Medelpads äldre urkunder*, ed. Algot Hellbom (Sundsvall, 1972), no. 52.

[32]*Statuta synodalia*, ed. Reuterdahl, p. 171 ("Statutkompendiet" 1438–48). Similar provisions: *Synodalstatuter*, ed. Gummerus, pp. 69, 71 ff. (diocese of Skara).

[33]Many medieval Swedish testaments are extant which provide for requiem Masses for the testator. Two examples, copied into liturgical books from parish churches: HUB, Manuscript Collection, Fasc. Kalendariefragment sine numero: *Kalendarium Upsalense ecclesie Morkarla fragm.*, saec. XIII in.–med. (addition: 30 July, gift to the church by Östanus Benason and annual requiem Mass); RA, Cod. fragm. kal. sine numero: *Kalendarium Upsalense*

The lives of the present generation received expression in votive and special Masses of various kinds which could be celebrated, for example, for peace, for rain, for seafarers, for enemies, or for benefactors of the church. Texts for these Masses are always found at the end of the missal, and occasionally in a separate votive missal. Local calendars may contain set dates for votive Masses. The local pattern of dates could, however, be interrupted by central directives about votive Masses, such as a series for the days of the week.[34] Each parish thus had a relatively stable, albeit small, festal cycle of its own, which supplemented the official one of the diocese.

Parishioners were also tied by personal ties to their local church and its liturgy. This was encouraged by the authorities: letters of indulgence promote gifts for the maintenance of a certain named church, or enjoin prayers for the deceased in the graveyard.

Guilds have made a mark in varying degrees on life in the parish. With regard to church and parish, they have helped fill the need for local infrastructures. In the parish church a guild could have its own altar, and in towns its own chaplain too. Funerals, requiem Masses and vigils for deceased members were of central concern to the guild.[35]

The circumstances of the individual were furthermore mirrored in the various sacramental rites which accompanied him through life. Baptism and

---

(ecclesie Forsa?) fragm., saec. XV (RA, Removed fragments, S 5), ed. in Schmid, *Liber ecclesiae Vallentunensis*, pp. 119 ff. source V (addition: 29 Sept. Matins for Olav Biörnson, 3 Oct. two annual Masses for Olav Biörnson and his wife Birgitta Olofsdotter). Further examples in Collijn, *Redogörelse*, pp. 21 ff., 26 ff.

[34]Series of votive Masses become common in the late Middle Ages. Examples: *Synodalstatuter*, ed. Gummerus, p. 28 (diocese of Skara); Johansson, *Den medeltida liturgien*, pp. 57 ff.; Helander, *Ansgarskulten*, p. 110.

[35]Guilds which sponsored Masses include the Corpus Christi guild ("Helga Lekamens gille") in Stockholm, and the guild of St. Catherine in the parish of Björke, Gotland. See *Handlingar rörande Helga Lekamens gille i Stockholm (Acta Convivii Corporis Christi Stokholmis)*, ed. Isak Collijn, vol. 1: *Gillesboken, 1393–1487* (Stockholm, 1921); and Sven-Erik Pernler, "S:ta Katarina-gillet i Björke," *Gotländskt arkiv* 52 (1986): 67–91.

confirmation made demands on the godparents, who were required to recite publicly the Creed, the Our Father, and the Hail Mary. These catechetical pieces were to be engraved on the minds of all parishioners by recitation in the vernacular at Mass on Sundays, after the sermon. Confession entailed the exercise of another catechetical piece, the Ten Commandments, as a mirror for the examination of conscience. Marriages altered the relations of families and were thus important public events. The rites surrounding illness, death, and burial were elaborate and impressive. Altogether, these personal rituals—every year in a new mixture—contributed to the liturgical life of the parish.

The profile of the parish liturgy is thus shaped partly by what it received from the cathedral, partly by modifications dictated by local circumstance. As with all traditions, it was dynamic and developing: a distinct accent marked the liturgical "dialect" of every parish church.

The Parish Liturgy in Practice

In cathedral and monastery, the daily liturgies of Mass and Divine Office were sung by the community in the chancel. Various private Masses were celebrated in simpler format at a side altar or in a specific chapel. Collegiate churches throughout the diocese strove to attain a rich liturgy patterned on that of the cathedral.[36] The practice of the parish liturgy, in contrast, was based on local resources, which differed from one locality to another. The "average" country parish is what we will be concerned with here.

---

[36]The chapter-like institution planned for the town of Kalmar in 1430 was to follow the cathedral liturgy; see Helander, *Ordinarius Lincopensis*, p. 93. Similarly, the college of priests at the town church St. Per (=Peter) in Vadstena had to follow cathedral use as given in the *Ordinarius*: RA, parchment letter, 10 Feb. 1462; see Ingmar Milveden, "Mensuralmusik," *KL* 11 (1966): 535–47 (at pp. 541 ff.).

How Often was the Liturgy Celebrated?

The question of daily celebration of Mass in Swedish parishes has not been broached by previous research. Daily Mass was, of course, the rule in monasteries and cathedrals; both communal Mass and private Masses were celebrated there every day.[37] But the ecclesiastical province of Sweden does not seem to have issued clear provisions for practice in the parishes, and medieval material from the continent provides no uniform picture.[38]

The breviaries contain Offices for every day, whereas the missals do not provide every day of the year with its own Mass. But the Sunday Mass could be repeated during the week, and the missal moreover contained votive Masses for various concerns which could be used on days which lacked a proper.[39] Series of votive Masses—with a specific theme for each weekday—were increasingly prescribed in the later Middle Ages. Saturday was always dedicated to the Virgin Mary. Such provisions strongly suggest that daily Mass was the rule. The impression is strengthened by a regulation stating that the *campanarius* (on which more below) was to serve at all Masses, on both feast days and ordinary weekdays.[40]

---

[37]An example of double daily Masses is the choir regulation of Nils Alleson for Uppsala cathedral, 1298 (*DS* 1235–36). For the hospitals see Åke Andrén, *Högmässa och nattvardsgång i reformationstidens svenska kyrkoliv* (Stockholm, 1954), p. 38; Frithz, *Till frågan*, pp. 189 ff. In the hospital of Enköping, Mass was celebrated on all Sundays, feast days, and Fridays. Frithz remarks that this frequency "hardly deviated from that of an ordinary country church."

[38]Josef Andreas Jungmann, *Missarum sollemnia. Eine genetische Erklärung der römischen Messe*, 2 vols. (Wien, 1962), 1:303 ff. Frithz, *Till frågan*, p. 204n26, cites a diocesan statute from the Province of the Teutonic Knights: in parish churches Mass should be celebrated on Sundays, feast days, and at least three weekdays.

[39]Regulations to this effect, giving different alternatives for different seasons (Advent, Lent, etc.) may be found in UUB, C 428: *Ordinarius Lincopensis posterior*, fol. 107v.

[40]*Statuta synodalia*, ed. Reuterdahl, p. 214; and Sandholm, *Klockarämbetet*, pp. 70, 112 ff. For the Office of *campanarius* see note 61 below.

Thus, although the evidence is not unequivocal, there are grounds for regarding daily Mass as a common practice in Swedish rural churches in the later Middle Ages. But the intermittent lack of priests and the impoverished state of some parishes worked against any norm, as did the fact that sacramental wine was not always readily available in the Nordic countries.[41] For the early centuries (ca. 1000–1300) the evidence is altogether too scant to allow a firm conclusion. Furthermore, it should be noted that whatever the frequency of celebration was, on ordinary weekdays parishioners were not obliged to be present.

While the ideal was that all priests should celebrate Mass daily, a priest was in principle not allowed to celebrate more than one Mass each day.[42] The general exception was Christmas Day with its three Masses, and an exception was sometimes made also for Easter Day. The principle, however, could not always be honored. There exist statements to the effect that a priest in case of need could celebrate twice in one day.[43]

Votive Masses provided one reason for relaxing the rule of allowing only one daily Mass. As was mentioned above, votive Masses could be officially prescribed for the diocese. This included the Mass for the dead [*pro*

---

[41]A Norwegian statute 1320 prescribes more water than wine for the Mass, presumably for reasons of economy; see Fæhn, *Fire norske messeordninger*, 65. In the ecclesiastical province of Sweden the opposite was prescribed; see *Synodalstatuter*, ed. Gummerus, p. 78; and *Statuta synodalia*, p. 150 ("Statutkompendiet" 1438–48).

[42]The canon law term for multiple celebrations of Mass by one priest in one day is *binatio*; it was forbidden by Innocent III in 1212. Continental evidence in Jungmann, *Missarum Sollemnia*, 1:304. Swedish statutes could motivate the principle with reference to the priest: ". . . legitur quod felix est qui vnam missam in die poterit digne celebrare," *Synodalstatuter*, ed. Gummerus, p. 59 (diocese of Skara). Compare the following note.

[43]The quotation in the previous note from *Synodalstatuter*, ed. Gummerus, p. 59 (diocese of Skara) goes on: "Potest tamen ad idem altare vnam de tempore et aliam pro defunctis, si opus fuerit, celebrare; vel duas eciam in diuersis ecclesiis, si necessitas id exposcat." See also *Statuta synodalia*, ed. Reuterdahl, pp. 58 and 75 (diocese of Linköping).

defunctis], sometimes celebrated on a weekly basis.[44] But requiem Masses for individuals were also celebrated frequently in the parishes. Concessions were thus issued for a priest to celebrate "at the same altar," on the same day, both a regular Mass according to the liturgical year and a requiem Mass.[45] More than one requiem Mass, in fact, could be celebrated on the same day in a parish church, but only if the day was free from other celebrations;[46] no votive Mass of any kind was allowed on major feast days.[47]

The annex church, that is, a church without its own priest, was the other setting which allowed parish curates to celebrate Mass more than once in one day. Annex churches were numerous in some areas: the county of Uppland with its 123 parishes had about 50 of them.[48] But regulations about the celebration of Mass in annex churches were restrictive. There may be several reasons for this, including concern for the welfare of the priest. A priest responsible for two churches, for instance, could be required to celebrate in them on alternate Sundays.[49] In a northern parish where a single priest served three churches rather distant from each other, the archbishop laid down as a general rule that Mass in the annexes should be held every

---

[44]Requiem Mass and Office to be performed on Mondays according to "Brynolfsstatuterna," in *Synodalstatuter*, ed. Gummerus, pp. 56 ff. (diocese of Skara); similarly each week, ibid., p. 74 (diocese of Skara).

[45]*Synodalstatuter*, ed. Gummerus, p. 59 (diocese of Skara). For a similar case, probably mirroring the cathedral environment, see "Brynolfsstatuterna," in *Synodalstatuter*, ed. Gummerus, p. 57 (diocese of Skara).

[46]See note 33, the second example; the Masses on 3 October may have been moved from 29 September because it was St. Michael's day.

[47]Such a Mass was moved as a general rule; see *Synodalstatuter*, ed. Gummerus, pp. 56 ff., 74 (diocese of Skara); an example is cited in Ann Catherine Bonnier, *Kyrkorna berättar. Upplands kyrkor 1250–1350* (Uppsala, 1987), p. 252.

[48]Inger, *Das kirchliche Visitationsinstitut*, p. 505.

[49]"Item curati habentes duas ecclesias celebrent vicissim diebus dominicis," *Synodalstatuter*, ed. Gummerus, p. 30 (diocese of Linköping).

fourth week, while the celebration of Christmas, Easter, and the patron saint should alternate among the churches.[50] Good Friday is a special case: there was no consecration of the Eucharist on that day, only a distribution of pre-consecrated hosts, and a priest who celebrated in several churches on Good Friday was to receive communion once only.[51]

A snapshot of conditions in the large and sparsely populated country of Sweden is provided by a letter of 1523 from Bishop Hans Brask to the Pope, concerning the sleigh-ride of a country priest in the archdiocese of Uppsala:

> One day at the beginning of Lent, when he had celebrated Mass and also heard confession, and had eaten his lunch, he was on his way to another church in the neighbouring parish, in order, as is customary in this country, to celebrate there too. Alas, the second Mass could not be celebrated, as the priest was assaulted on the way.[52]

Prevalent conditions are further mirrored in a regulation stating that a parish priest is to have one single ***crismale*** [a vessel for holy oil] for "all his churches."[53] It should be noted, however, that annex churches need not always have been without a priest, since the archives indicate the existence of assistant priests; indeed, even country parishes without an annex sometimes had an assistant priest.[54]

---

[50]*Medelpads äldre urkunder*, no. 43. I am grateful to Dr. Birgitta Fritz for this reference.

[51]*Statuta synodalia*, ed. Reuterdahl, p. 163 ("Statutkompendiet" 1438–48); and ibid., p. 188 (diocese of Uppsala).

[52]*Röster från svensk medeltid. Latinska texter i original och översättning*, ed. Hans Aili, Olle Ferm, and Helmer Gustavson (Stockholm, 1990), pp. 38ff. The expression translated "Mass" here is *officium divinum*.

[53]*Synodalstatuter*, ed. Gummerus, p. 68 (diocese of Skara).

[54]From the diocese of Uppsala the *Miracles of St. Erik* mention an assistant *vicarius* in Närtuna, a *sacerdos* in addition to the parson in Funbo, and as employee of a nobleman *sacerdos ejusdem*; see Israel Erlandi, *Miracula S. Erici regis et martyris*, in *Scriptores rerum Svecicarum medii ævi*, ed. Erik M. Fant et al., T. II:1 (Upsaliae, 1828), pp. 278–317 (at 280–81, 290–91, 312–13).

The daily Office of the breviary (possibly sung, in accordance with antiphonary and hymnary) was obligatory for every priest and deacon. The prescribed seven times of prayer formed the backbone of his daily routine. In content the breviary was connected with the missal: the same themes, even the same words, reappeared in the divine services throughout the day. Office and Mass were also coordinated in time: Matins-cum-Lauds and Prime were to be read before the celebration of Mass.[55] The bishop was accustomed when making his visitation to enquire about how the priest practiced the Divine Office.

The Office for the dead supplemented the ordinary Office. A vigil (a word which originally meant Matins but later came to denote the whole Office for the dead) could be recited for an individual on a specific day, and could be read on other days with a general intention. There were also vigils held in connection with wakes.[56]

How was the Liturgy Performed?

Medieval liturgical books normally presuppose that worship includes a great deal of singing. But that does not mean that musical notation is always written out.

With regard to the Mass, the missals (manuscripts as well as printed books) give alternative melodies for some of the fixed texts which constitute the Mass ordinary (*Kyrie*, *Gloria*, *Credo*, *Sanctus*, *Agnus Dei*, *Ite missa est*). But usually only the beginning is given, since the melodies were known and sung by heart. The tones for the recitation of Epistle and Gospel are not given, but the various alternatives for the Preface appear often. The proper of the Mass, containing the texts unique to each day or feast—

---

[55]*Statuta synodalia*, ed. Reuterdahl, p. 75 (diocese of Linköping); ibid., p. 152 ("Statutkompendiet" 1438–48). High Mass on Sundays and feasts was usually not celebrated until after terce; compare note 73 below.

[56]Johansson, *Hemsjömanualet*, pp. 91 ff.

introit, gradual, alleluia (sometimes followed by sequence), offertory, communion—appears with its numerous melodies in most manuscripts but not in the printed missals (*MU*, *MStr*, *MAb*). The music for the proper could, when necessary, be taken from separate graduals (manuscripts and one printed book: *GrAr*) and sequentionaries.

With regard to the Divine Office, one similarly notes that the breviaries do not give the basic musical repertory (versicles, etc.), or the psalm tones; it is taken for granted that all this is known. The ***proprium officii***, in contrast, with the texts unique to each day (antiphons, responsories, hymns), is provided with music in many manuscript breviaries; but as in the case of the missals, melodies never occur in the printed books (*BU*, *BStr*, *BL*, *BAr*, *BSc*). For the celebration of the Divine Office, too, separate musical sources were available: antiphonaries and hymnaries.

Other rites were contained in the manuals, where as a rule many sections are supplied with musical notation, for instance the funeral rite and various consecrations.[57] The proportion of liturgical books with a preponderance of songs can be gauged from the corpus of preserved medieval fragments. The index of these in the Swedish National Archives notes at present (1994) 4595 separate sources, including 924 missals as against 214 graduals and 201 sequentionaries; and 2309 breviaries as against 530 antiphonaries and 46 hymnaries. The majority of these books belonged, of course, to parish churches.

We may conclude that parish churches normally owned the books required to perform all the ordinary liturgy. Priests also owned some books privately. Furthermore, the stock of liturgical books has in large measure provided for sung services. But it is a moot point whether the wealth of manuscripts containing music should be ascribed to parish initiative or to the guiding influence of cathedral *scriptoria*.

[57]The various terms used in the sources—*legere*, *dicere*, *cantare*—do not indicate significantly different modes of performance.

Who Performed the Liturgy?

As we saw above, instructions concerning personnel in the liturgical books generally overwhelmed parish resources. In the parish, services were as a rule performed by a single priest together with a server/*campanarius*. But all sources, even the most restrained, mention a choir. We shall here focus first on the priest, second on the *campanarius* and choir, and finally on the congregation.

Did the parish liturgy require more than one priest? Both liturgists and art historians have asked this question in the light of those country churches which have large chancels, choir stalls, and several altars, and which once had multiple endowments for the performance of requiem Masses. The churches of canons and rural deans seem occasionally to have had special resources. Were these institutions required to have—and were they able to support—multiple priests?[58]

The growth of pious endowments favors such an idea. Testaments providing for requiem Masses (occasionally vigils) in the testator's parish church, sometimes tied to a specific altar, became increasingly common in the late Middle Ages. An annual anniversary Mass—on the day of the testator's death—was often prescribed. Such endowments, especially in prosperous areas, would have increased considerably the number of Masses needing to be celebrated.

But two related circumstances must be kept in mind. First, the testaments frequently have the local curate in view, stating an explicit intention

---

[58]A.-C. Bonnier has recently discussed evidence from Uppland concerning the relation between church architecture, liturgy and personnel. She shows that goods could be bequeathed for requiem Masses without any sign that additional priests got employed, while there are other cases—such as the church of Vendel with its six side altars—where additional priests do seem to have been needed. See further Bonnier, *Kyrkorna berättar*, pp. 230–55; for "hundred churches" esp. pp. 249–51. On the function of choir stalls in churches on Gotland see Sven-Erik Pernler, *Gotlands medeltida kyrkoliv. Biskop och prostar: En kyrkorättslig studie* (Visby, 1977), pp. 261 ff.

to improve his income. We must assume that it was the curate himself who said the Masses stipulated in such testaments. Second, as noted above, requiem Masses formed an exception to the prohibition against multiple celebrations on the same day.

In ordinary country parishes we thus have reason to believe that the resident priest had sole responsibility for each Mass. Yet it is possible that certain more prosperous churches sometimes (if not for the ordinary liturgy) made use of more than one priest, as suggested both by the attested existence of assistant priests and by the size and equipment of these churches.

The liturgical books themselves give no hint about how many priests may have been active in any parish service. They have, generally speaking, nothing at all to say about actual local conditions, for the simple reason that they were not compiled with the practice of a specific church at a specific time in mind.[59]

Was there a Choir in the Medieval Swedish Parish Church? One's immediate response to such a question is doubt, since the practical exigencies were great. The melodies are often so advanced that their performance requires thoroughly schooled singers. Furthermore, singers needed to be literate and possessed of some liturgical education. Were such people available in the countryside?

Some evidence is offered by the churches themselves, in the form of inscriptions on sanctuary walls. They tell us where the singers stood, perhaps also something of who they were and what they sang. In four churches there are directions about the chancel as "the place for those who sing, and no others." It is the northern side of the sanctuary which is pointed out as the place for the choristers, and the inscriptions dismiss "the rustic buck" from this area.[60] These words, and other similar evidence, convey a sense

---

[59]The above-mentioned votive missals constitute an exception.

[60]An inscription in the church of Film (county of Uppland) has the characteristic wording, "Rustice buck, quis te tulit huc? Est locus illorum, qui cantant, et non aliorum." Similar

of high status for the choir. But do they mirror reality or an ideal, realized infrequently at best?

The question cannot be answered without consideration of the liturgical books. These, as we have seen, contain a great deal of music and seem to take a choir for granted. Two arguments must be weighed against each other. On the one hand, evidence seems too plentiful and widespread to be entirely without basis in fact. On the other hand, the music is so advanced that one cannot reasonably suppose a permanent choir, however small, to have existed in every parish. A sensible middle ground suggests that the office of "choir" was usually filled by the *campanarius* acting as precentor. That was the minimum level, improvements on which may have occurred in various parishes from time to time.

Let us therefore focus on *the function of the campanarius*.[61] According to a preserved regulation, his duties were as follow: he was to serve "at all Masses," had to know the Latin *confiteor* [confession of sins], and must be able to sing "his own parts" in a sung Mass, that is, on Sundays and major feasts (on ordinary weekdays Mass was said, not sung). If he was unable to do this, he had to compensate with other work. The last-mentioned regulation suggests that the capacity of a *campanarius* could leave much to be desired.[62]

---

inscriptions are to be found in the churches of Vendel (also in Uppland), Björkeberg (in Östergötland), and Runsten (in Öland). The church of Häverö (in Uppland) has a chalk painting in the corresponding position, showing a choir conducted (it seems) by the *cantor* with an open gradual on a pulpit before him. See further Nilsén, *Program och funktion*, pp. 75, 162, 241 ff.

[61]The *campanarius* (Swedish *klockare*) was the equivalent of the English parish clerk and normally not in orders. The name suggests that his chief duty was to ring the bells, but he was also supposed to act as precentor, in addition to performing various practical chores. When qualified, and especially in later centuries, he assumed the role of local school master.

[62]Sandholm, *Klockarämbetet*, pp. 93 ff. presents the sources for the statutes about the *campanarius*. See also *Statuta synodalia*, ed. Reuterdahl, pp. 209–14 (*Confiteor* mentioned 214); and Sandholm, *Klockarämbetet*, p. 70.

The *campanarius* played a central role in the development of the parish liturgy. At least in the early centuries, he could be a cleric from the cathedral town who had interrupted his schooling after having received a few of the ordinations preparatory to the priesthood.[63] Such interruptions were not uncommon. Indeed, the liturgy for the lower ordinations (below subdeacon) envisaged activity in a parish and accommodation to its practice.[64] The years spent in training Latin and song naturally made a difference. A *campanarius* with such a background could assist at Mass both as server and as precentor.[65]

In the later Middle Ages, ordained *campanarii* became less common. This conceivably meant a lowering of standards in liturgical performance. Presumably now the priest himself often had to sing or even read passages which the books allotted to a *campanarius* or precentor. From a practical point of view it is reasonable to assume that in these circumstances the priest, as far as possible, sang the Mass ordinary, even if he had to read the proper. Practice will have varied from one parish to another, and this must

---

[63]Sandholm, *Klockarämbetet*, pp. 76, 84 ff. and passim.

[64]In late medieval **pontifical**s from Lund (in the Middle Ages a Danish diocese), those in minor orders are enjoined to read "horas de sancto Spiritu, de sancta crvce, et de beata virgine precipue in festiuis diebus prout mos parrochie habet, vbi constituti fueritis": Bengt Strömberg, *Den pontifikala liturgin i Lund och Roskilde under medeltiden. En liturgihistorisk studie jämte edition av Pontificale Lundense enligt handskriften C 441 i Uppsala Universitetsbibliotek och Pontificale Roscildense enligt Medeltidshandskrift nr 43 i Lunds Universitetsbibliotek* (Lund, 1955), p. 91.

[65]The altar server can be seen from two perspectives. On the one hand, even if he is unordained, he replaces the assistant clerk (ultimately the deacon) of earlier ages; on the other, he represents the congregation. See Jungmann, *Missarum Sollemnia*, 1:302 ff. "Statutkompendiet" 1438–48 prescribes in accordance with earlier medieval practice: "Item quod sacerdos non celebret sine astante clerico vel campanario . . . ," *Statuta synodalia*, ed. Reuterdahl, p. 149. Similar provisions distinguish different tasks of the server according as he is ordained or not, see *Synodalstatuter*, ed. Gummerus, p. 59 (diocese of Skara). The alternatives are due to a development toward non-ordained *campanarii*; Sandholm, *Klockarämbetet*, pp. 87 ff. and passim.

have affected considerably the impression which the celebration of Mass made on participants in different parishes.[66]

A further factor to consider with respect to the choir is that it could on major feast days be filled out with *scholares*, that is, students from the cathedral school, making their rounds of those specified parishes where they were allowed to collect alms.[67] The medieval "choir" was thus undoubtedly a dynamic entity; but a realistic assumption is that it often was modest, to say the least.[68]

Congregational singing is one of those perennial problems. Hymnological literature tends to regard sequences and the quasi-popular "leise" [a vernacular song based on the cry of ***Kyrie eleison***] as the musical genres which were open to congregational participation. We also know that ecclesiastical authorities in the fifteenth century supported popular singing with the Sacrament after Mass. The fact remains, however, that sources from the Nordic countries never mention regular singing by the people at Mass.

But congregational participation in the liturgy was not limited to the occasional song. Some insight into lay activity at Mass is afforded by the expositions of the Mass which circulated in Swedish translation at the end of the Middle Ages. The most well-known are *Speculum missæ* and *Siælinna thrøst* ["Consolation of the Soul"]. These gave directions for how to act at various moments: genuflection during the Collect and *Kyrie*, sitting during

---

[66]A rich level would mean that both ordinary and proper were sung. This increases the possibilities of "simultaneous déroulement," i.e., that the song of the precentor and the actions of the priest carry the liturgy forward on two different planes at once. Examples: the Offertory is sung while the priest prepares paten and chalice, the Sanctus while the priest starts his silent reading of the Canon. According to Israel Erlandi, *Miracula S. Erici*, p. 280, it could be left to the discretion of the priest whether he sang or said Mass (in this case on the feast of St. Erik).

[67]Gustaf Sivgård, *Vandrande scholares. Den gamla djäknegångsseden* (Stockholm, 1965), pp. 7–37 and passim.

[68]Organs were not rare in the churches of prosperous districts in Sweden as early as the fourteenth century. In country churches the majority probably had only one stop. See Reine A. Unnerbäck & Göran Söderström, "Orgel," *KL* 12 (1967): 692–97.

the Epistle, standing with head bared during the Gospel, adoration at the **elevation** of host and chalice, genuflection during the *Agnus Dei*, making the sign of the cross at diverse points, etc. In these sources, parts of the Mass are given in translation, parts receive a symbolic interpretation.[69]

The spiritual disposition of the congregation is, from one point of view, the foundation of parish liturgy. Swedish sources occasionally allow us to catch sight of an individual. Setting aside the prayer books of nuns and the literary heritage of the learned, we may still catch the occasional glimpse of the man behind the plow and the woman at the distaff (we see them thus in contemporary art). Particularly expressive are some personal statements by and about laymen, such as the following from the miracles of St. Erik, the patron saint of Sweden: A boy on a farm in Uppland fell into a well. When they pulled him out he was completely inert. The farmer made a promise to St. Erik for him and called on God's mercy for help. On the third day, the powers of movement and reason returned to the boy. He opened his eyes, asked for a priest to confess to, and was at once completely healed.[70]

Where was the Liturgy Performed?

High Mass was performed at the high altar, as were special rites such as the consecration of ashes and of palm fronds (branches of Sallow, according to Swedish custom). While it seems natural to think of the side altars as having been used for weekday Masses—and especially the altar of St. Mary for the Marian Mass on Saturday—there are no indications about this in the liturgical books. Testaments, in contrast, do prescribe Masses at particular side altars.

---

[69] *Siælinna thrøst*, ed. Samuel Henning, 3 vols. (Uppsala, 1954–56); "Speculum missæ," ed. Robert Geete, in *Svenska kyrkobruk under medeltiden* (Stockholm, 1900); and Sven-Erik Pernler, "En mässa för folket?" in *Mässa i medeltida socken. En studiebok*, ed. Sven Helander et al. (Skellefteå, 1993), pp. 102–22.

[70] A condensed rendering of one of the miracles in *BU*, *Miracula sancti Erici*.

The Divine Office may have been performed either in church or in the parsonage. A statement about this from the early fourteenth century is found in the *Suffragium curatorum*, a digest of canon law compiled by a dean of Uppsala, Laurentius de Vaxald (Vaksala, just east of Uppsala). Although the sources of this work are not Swedish, it no doubt came to affect Swedish practice. It states that under certain conditions, one may "read the divine office alone in private, or with someone else, in church or outside."[71]

The different locations of services are reflected in the "domicile" and format of the liturgical books. The missal in principle never left the church and was carefully stored between Masses.[72] The breviary had a more handy format and could be moved around. The manual—the handbook for rites other than Mass—followed the priest in his rounds of the parish, from baptism to extreme unction and funeral.

The liturgical books relatively seldom say anything about the place for the liturgy. In some cases, however, a connection is made between Mass and Divine Office. The first Mass of Christmas night is, according to the missals, immediately followed by Lauds, "without the congregation departing." From Ash Wednesday to Easter Eve, weekday Masses were to end with Vespers.[73] Special rules for Good Friday are given in some sources: the

---

[71]UUB, C 69: Laurentius de Vaxald, *Suffragium Curatorum*, fol. 14r: "Si uero legerit horas canonicas priuatim per se, uel cum alio, in ecclesia uel extra non officiando ecclesiam, nullam irregularitatem incurrit."

[72]The missal is to be swept in a cloth of clean linen, *Statuta synodalia*, ed. Reuterdahl, p. 149 ("Statutkompendiet" 1438–48). The books of the church are not to be taken away, *Synodalstatuter*, ed. Gummerus, p. 69 (diocese of Skara).

[73]Continental sources indicate that weekday Masses in Lent were celebrated literally in the "afternoon" (i.e., after Nones), hence the appropriateness of concluding them with Vespers. On the various times for Mass celebrations see Andrew Hughes, *Medieval Manuscripts for Mass and Office: A guide to their organization and terminology* (Toronto, 1995), pp. 18 and 358n43. Compare the following statement by the German preacher Gottschalk Hollen (†1481), quoted in Rudolf Cruel, *Geschichte der deutschen Predigt im Mittelalter* (Detmold, 1879 [repr. Hildesheim, 1966]), p. 210: "Celebratur autem missa popularis in diebus dominicis et festivis hora tertia, in profestis hora sexta, in quadragesima vero hora nona . . . .

Offices during the day "are read silently in a corner of the church" or "vespers is read in private."[74] On Easter Day and during the following week, Vespers in the cathedral (and elsewhere, as a rule) is to be followed by a procession to the font—we return here to this striking ceremony discussed above. A modification was introduced in Linköping in the later part of the fifteenth century. According to this, the procession is to be carried out only "in parish churches with font; but if a font is lacking, and in private places" a briefer ceremony is used.[75] Later breviaries, both manuscript and printed, provide for this abbreviation "when the font is not visited." What that means is made explicit in *BStr*: "when vespers is not read in parish churches during Easter week."[76] Evidence from other Nordic dioceses is similar. The Danish breviary of Odense mentions as an alternative that Matins on Easter Day is not celebrated in church;[77] and an Icelandic source intimates that the breviary might be read in private only.[78]

Sed missae peculiares id est privatae possunt fieri ante horam tertiam." Presumably Scandinavian practice was the same, but no definite evidence is extant.

[74]UUB, frag. ms lat. 215: *Breviarium incerti originis (Anglicum?) fragm.*, saec. XIV (secondary provenance Krigsarkivet Areby [?] 1565). The liturgy is close to the order of Sarum. After the night Office: "In die omnes hore intra ecclesiam in uno angelo sub silentio dicantur." RA, Cod. fragm. mi 284: *Missale Suecanum (Scarense?) fragm.*, saec. XII–XIII: " . . . uespertinum officium canat unusquisque priuatim in suo loco." Similar rubrics are found in sources from abroad.

[75]*Ordinarius Lincopensis posterior*, ca. 1450. Later addition, fol. 38r: "Nota quod iste suprascriptus ordo ad uesperas per ebdomadam pasche habeatur aput ecclesias parochiales vbi fons fuerit. Sed vbi fons non fuerit siue in priuatis locis sic legatur . . ." (abbreviated rite). The addition should be interpreted as an accommodation to the varying capacities of parish churches. The older *Ordinarius Lincopensis prior* still lacks the abbreviation.

[76]*BStr*: "Item notandum quando vespere non leguntur in ecclesijs in ebdomada pasce." *BL*: "Ubi non itur ad fontem vespere istius hebdomade hoc modo dicantur." *BSc*: "Si fons non visitatur iste ordo ad vesperas seruabitur." A manuscript example is UUB, C 354: *Breviarium Lincopense*, ca. 1441–90, fol. 151v: "Quando fons non visitatur."

[77]*Breviarium Ottoniense* (Othonie, 1482), fol. 199v: "Ubi matutine non celebrantur."

[78]*Norges gamle love, 2. række*, ed. G. Authén Blom et al., vol. 2 (Christiania, 1914–1934),

More light on the practice of the Divine Office is shed by letters of indulgence which require the recipient's presence in a certain church on certain occasions. Most often it is participation at Mass which is required, but sometimes also at the Divine Office. Christmas and Easter Day, Ascension, Pentecost, the day of the patron saint and of the dedication of the church are the ones normally mentioned, but there are examples of thirty to fifty different days mentioned in the same letter—days when the Divine Office, or parts of it, may have been performed in the presence of laymen. One supposes that at such times it was sung. In most cases the Office in question would have been Vespers, but also Matins is mentioned.[79]

A word, too, about bell-ringing. The daily chiming in town and countryside is thought to have been connected with the major canonical hours, Matins-cum-Lauds, and Vespers-cum-Compline, and in particular with their final prayers to the Virgin Mary for peace. The *campanarius* was obliged by law "every evening to clapper Mary's praise." Such chiming, however, was performed also in churches where no priest was present, in other words without actual connection to the Divine Office.[80]

Several of the above issues concerning the celebration of the Divine Office receive illustration in a letter of admonition to Swedish parish clergy, probably issued from the influential Birgittine abbey of Vadstena. The letter

---

no. 286; and Helander, *Ordinarius Lincopensis*, p. 28n3.

[79]A common expression concerns presence on certain days with hearing of "missas vel/et alia diuina officia." Examples: *DS* 3766; RA, parchment letters, 21 Feb. 1444 with among others the feast of St. Ansgar. See Samzelius, *Kumla kyrkas räkenskapsbok*, pp. 158, 161; and Helander, *Ansgarskulten*, p. 114. Matins are expressly mentioned in the following example from the hospital of Enköping, quoted by Frithz, *Till frågan*, p. 204n29: "matutinas et utrasque vesperas sollempniter decantet vel decantari faciat." There are correspondences between the commonest days of indulgence and the days which normally appear in the Lutheran *Liber cantus* tradition. The selection of days in the latter follows of course principles of dogma, but may also be rooted pragmatically in medieval custom.

[80]Nils-Arvid Bringéus, *Klockringningsseden i Sverige* (Stockholm, 1958), pp. 86, 95 ff., 122–27. The duty of the *campanarius* "to ring for all tides and Masses" is included in provincial law: Sandholm, *Klockarämbetet*, pp. 131 ff. and Appendix II, p. 207.

exhorts priests to read the canonical hours in church whenever possible and above all to sing (or solemnly read) Matins and Vespers in the sanctuary on all Sundays and feasts. On these occasions, the church bells should be tolled *debito more* in order to excite the devotion of people in the vicinity. The people should be invited to attend or, if unable to come (presumably prevented by distance and weather conditions), to read set prayers at these hours as well as at the time of Mass.[81]

To sum up: there is clear evidence that canonical Offices on some occasions—major celebrations in particular—were sung publicly in the parish church. There is no evidence that such public performance was the general rule. Probably the Divine Office was read privately to a considerable extent, either in church or in the parsonage.

Summary: The Parish Liturgy as Microcosm

The parish liturgy can be described as "a liturgical microcosm." This microcosm stands in a double relation. One is its link with the diocesan cathedral and, beyond that, with the universal church, the "macrocosm." The other is its implantation in the rural culture of which the country church is a part. The parish liturgy thus joins the local congregation and its traditions to the whole body of the church.

The liturgical order in general, the "cosmos," is inherited from above and provides the parish liturgy with its structure and chief contents. "Micro," the lesser format, receives its characteristic profile from the local parish with its particular needs and resources. This binary relationship allows for a certain balancing of the prescriptions from the diocesan authorities against the traditions of the local congregation.

---

[81]UUB, C 7, fols. 182v–85r. Maria Berggren of the Department of Classics, Uppsala University, kindly provided me with a transcription of this text, which she has since published: Maria Berggren and Alf Härdelin, "Ad sacerdotes. A 'Pastoral Letter' from Vadstena. Critical Edition and Translation," *Master Golyas and Sweden. The Transformation of a Clerical Satire*, ed. Olle Ferm & Bridget Morris (Stockholm, 1997), pp. 365–406 (at p. 394–95).

With the diocesan authorities, the general concern for unity guides all liturgical dealings. In the parish, integration with existing conditions is the dominant concern. Liturgical books are sanctioned from above. In the later part of the fifteenth century, simplifications of certain rites in these books reveal that the exigencies of parish life were recognized by the diocesan authorities. But actual worship—including the actual use made of the books—still meant a supplementation from below, an adaptation to local customs and conditions which in its details always must elude us. The full implementation of both perspectives is a chimera—neither then or now is the tension between ideal and reality ever resolved.

The liturgy of the cathedral has large dimensions, discernible in texts, tangible in ceremonial. The cathedral rite is pontifical, that is, led by the bishop. It is also collective, performed by all those active in the chancel—*capitulares*, *vicarii*, *chorales*. But there is no regular lay congregation. The liturgy of the parish church is humble. It is normally served by a single priest and a *campanarius*. However, there is a lay congregation in regular attendance. The constitution and resources of this congregation affect the handling of text and rite.

The liturgy is ideally the same for both cathedral and parish, for example, the order of Uppsala. The task of the parish priest is carried out as a delegation from the bishop. At the same time, however, the difference in practice between cathedral and parish church is considerable, and each parish has its own profile, even if the missal which the bishop has approved rests on the altar.

A synthesis can be glimpsed, though fleetingly. When the bishop with his train comes from the cathedral town on a visitation, takes his seat in the parish sanctuary, and celebrates Mass—then the distance between the two sacred spaces, between cathedral and parish church, is obliterated, and their liturgical patterns converge; then the liturgical life of a country parish is revealed to be truly part of the episcopal structure of the medieval church.[82]

[82]I gratefully wish to acknowledge a grant from Dalarna University College, Sweden, towards the cost of getting this essay translated into English.

Abbreviations

General Abbreviations:

DS	*Diplomatarium Suecanum / Svenskt diplomatarium* (Stockholm, 1829–)
HUB	Helsingfors universitetsbibliotek (Helsinki University Library)
KA	Kammararkivet (Chamber Archives, Section of National Archives), Stockholm
KB	Kungliga biblioteket (Royal Library), Stockholm
KL	*Kulturhistoriskt lexikon för nordisk medeltid*, 22 vols. (Malmö 1956–78)
RA	Riksarkivet (National Archives), Stockholm
UUB	Uppsala universitetsbibliotek (Uppsala University Library)

Abbreviations of liturgical prints:

BAr	*Breviarium Arosiense* (Basilee, 1513)
BL	*Breviarium Lincopense* (Norimberge, 1493)
BSc	*Breviarium Scarense* (Norimberge, 1498)
BStr	*Breviarium Strengnense* (Holmie, 1495)
BU	*Breviarium Upsalense* (Holmie, 1496)
GrAr	*Graduale Arosiense*, ca. 1500; ed. Toni Schmid, *Graduale Arosiense impressum. Facsimiledition med efterskrift och register*, Laurentius Petri Sällskapets Urkundsserie, vol. 7 (Lund, 1959–65)
MAb	*Missale Aboense* (Lubek, 1488)
MStr	*Missale Strengnense* ([Holmie] 1487)
MU	*Missale Upsalense*, novum (Basilee, 1513) or vetus ([Holmie, ca. 1484])

JEWS AND JUDAISM IN THE MEDIEVAL LATIN LITURGY

LAWRENCE E. FRIZZELL AND J. FRANK HENDERSON

Introduction

AS THE CHRISTIAN FAITH SPREAD from the eastern Mediterranean to the rest of Europe and beyond, its adherents carried two streams of the past into the cultures they encountered. The world of the Hebrew Bible had mingled with Greco-Roman thought and culture in the wake of Alexander's conquests and the advance of the Roman Empire to the East. These influences formed the warp and woof of the fabric that supported the Christian vision of reality. The stamp of Jewish spirituality and practices imbued the Church's worship; biblical moral values, Greek philosophical perspectives, and Roman legislative genius laid the foundations for the social order.

In a far-flung Dispersion [Diaspora], Jews preceded Christians into the major cities of the Roman Empire. The Torah ["instruction," rendered as "Law" in Greek] or five Books of Moses had been translated into Greek in Alexandria during the third century B.C.E. The other parts of the Hebrew Bible, along with additional works, were translated later and became vehicles for the early Church to present the Christian message to the Greek-speaking peoples of the Mediterranean. This translation of the Bible (the Septuagint) was used in worship and became the basis for Christian rendering of God's Word into Latin. Besides providing the key to understanding the literary corpus that became the "New Testament," the Jewish

Scriptures served to prove to the pagans that Christianity possessed venerable credentials. Novelty was spurned by most cultures of that era, so the record of a heritage going back beyond Plato and Homer was crucial to the Church.

Did Jews and Christians stand together in presenting the biblical message to the world? Tragically, their common history was frequently marred by polemics and recriminations. The burdens of past misunderstandings and animosity often joined current frictions and persecutions during the Middle Ages, to foment hatred between the communities. The purpose of this study is to sketch the positive and negative dimensions in the Latin liturgy of the Church's relationship to Judaism and the Jewish people during the period prior to the sixteenth century. Seasons of the liturgical year and particular ceremonies are discussed in some detail to present the impact of the liturgy on the perception of Catholics regarding their Jewish neighbors.

The Jewish Roots of the Christian Liturgy

The long and rich spiritual heritage incorporated into the Hebrew Bible was integrated into the liturgy of the Second Temple period (538 B.C.E.– C.E. 70), first in the Temple of Jerusalem and later in houses of prayer and study known as "synagogues" throughout the land of Judah and in the Dispersion.

From its beginnings in Jerusalem, the Christian community shared the rhythms of prayer that defined Judaism: an annual cycle of feasts and fasts, a weekly day of rest and worship, and daily times of prayer. The synagogue service and its use of the Hebrew Bible provided the basis for the Christian "liturgy of the Word," although the Gospel came to replace the Torah as the most important reading. The command of Jesus to employ bread and wine from the Passover Meal for a Thanksgiving Sacrifice in his memory (Matt. 26:17–19) laid the foundation for the second part of the Eucharistic liturgy, also known as the *Mass*, a term derived from "Ite, missa est," the final formula of commissioning [*mittere, missus*] the faithful to carry God's gift into their daily lives.

Celebrating the sacraments and other prayers of the Church became the occasion for teaching aspects of God's plan for the larger community and its members as a parish or family. Symbols and words drawn from the Jewish Scriptures became part of this pedagogical process. Moreover, the psalms and canticles used in the Temple and synagogue became part of the daily and weekly rhythms of prayer, especially in the "liturgy of the hours" (the Divine Office). In the early Church, these times of prayer were modeled after the Jewish practice of praying in union with the sacrifices being offered in the Temple, but eventually the themes of these "hours" were related to the time of events during the Passion of Jesus and the descent of the Holy Spirit at Pentecost. The designation of seven "hours" for the Office came later, with reference to Ps. 118 [119]:164[1] ("Seven times a day I praise you").

At an early date both the synagogue morning prayer and the Christian Eucharist used the seraphic hymn of Isa. 6:3 ("Holy, holy, holy . . .") to celebrate the union of the liturgy on earth with its heavenly model. In the Mass this is followed by a Christian application of Ps. 117 [118]:25–26 (used in the Passover meal and in Matt. 21:42) to the return of Christ triumphant, who will lead the created world to the eschatological goal of worship.[2]

After the "institution narrative" (words of consecration), the canon of the Roman rite Mass includes a prayer linking this offering of the pure, holy, spotless victim with "the offerings of your just servant Abel" (Gen. 4:2–5), the sacrifice of Abraham our Patriarch (Gen. 22:1–14) and "that which Melchisedek, your high priest, offered to you, a holy sacrifice, a spotless victim" (Gen. 14:18–20).[3] This prayer dates back at least to the

---

[1]Following the Septuagint, St. Jerome's Vulgate numbering of the Psalms is given first, followed by the Hebrew number in brackets.

[2]"Sanctus, sanctus, sanctus Dominus Deus *Sabaoth*." The Hebrew term for "hosts, armies" was retained in the liturgy, even though the Vulgate of St. Jerome translated "dominus Deus exercituum," which means "Lord God of hosts." Evidently the early liturgy preserved the term as it did other Hebrew words, such as *Amen*, *Alleluiah*, and *Hosanna*.

[3]In the Gelasian Sacramentary (see Appendix 1) the preface for Christmas notes that a victim was always being immolated in praise of God, mentioning the just Abel, Abraham, and the

fourth century and is interesting for several reasons. For our purpose, it is noteworthy that Abraham is designated as "our Patriarch," probably adapting the phrase "Abraham our father" in the New Testament (Luke 1:73, 16:24, 16:30; Rom. 4:1, etc.).

The Liturgical Year

The Eucharistic Liturgy for Sundays, major feasts and saints' days drew heavily upon the Psalms and other parts of the Jewish Scripture for chanted texts that varied with each Mass: these came to be called the Introit, Psalm and Gradual, Offertory, and Communion. The Gallican liturgy, used in the realm of the Franks until the eighth century, included three readings in the Liturgy of the Word: one usually taken from the Jewish Scriptures, the second from the Epistles or the Acts of the Apostles, and the third from the Gospel.[4] Unfortunately, as the Roman rite became more dominant in western Europe, the practice of reading first from the Jewish Scriptures was lost for Sundays and the ordinary week days except for the seasons of Advent and Lent. These Lenten passages were selected for their Messianic implications, pointing for the Christian community to the Incarnation of Jesus and to the Paschal Mystery of his death and resurrection. The very term *Pascha* [Aramaic for the Hebrew word *Pesach* or "Passover"] shows that the Church interpreted the culminating work of Jesus in relation to the Exodus and its symbols. Mystically, the deliverance of the Hebrew people from Egyptian servitude by the blood of the lamb points to the rescue of the Church from diabolical servitude by the Passion of Christ.[5]

---

priest Melchisedek. The prayer then remarks that Christ, the true lamb and eternal priest, fulfilled these figures or types. See Bibliography at end of this chapter for editions of all the sacramentaries cited.

[4]Josef A. Jungmann, *The Mass of the Roman Rite: Its Origin and Development*, 2 vols. (New York, 1951), I:47.

[5]Compare this reflection of a very influential medieval liturgical commentary by William

1. Ember Days (Quattuor tempora, "the four seasons")

The practice of fasting on Wednesday and Friday is very ancient [*Didache*, Teaching of the Twelve Apostles 8:1], distinct from the Jewish tradition of fasting on Monday and Thursday. The Bridegroom was taken away on Friday (Mark 2:20), so this was an especially appropriate day for Christians to do penance. According to later sources, Pope St. Callistus (217–22) added a fast on Saturday for the "ember days" at the time of the grain harvest (June), the wine harvest (September), and the pressing of oil (December). These times were said to fulfill a prophetic text (Zech. 8:19 or Joel 2:19). Was this an adaptation of Jewish custom to the Italian agricultural cycle or do we have a Christian interpretation applied to pagan fasts related to the harvests? Pope St. Leo (440–61) urged that the fast of the tenth month (December) not be neglected "because its observance is taken from the Old Law" (Zech. 8:19). Perhaps because Zechariah mentioned *four* fasts, another set of ember days was added in Lent (March).

Three of the series of ember days were shaped by the important liturgical seasons—Advent, Lent, and Pentecost, respectively. Thus, on the Ember Wednesday in Advent, Isa. 2:1–5 and 7:10–15 were proclaimed; on the Friday, Isa. 11:1–5; and on the Saturday, Isa. 19:20–22, 35:1–7, 40:9–11, 42:1–9, 45:1–8, and (in some manuscripts) Dan. 3:47–51, followed by part of the hymn of the three youths (Dan. 3:52–56). The prophet Isaiah was the source of many passages in the Mass and Divine Office for Advent because, for the pious Christian, they clearly point to Jesus. The readings for the Lenten ember days are listed for the first week of Lent (Appendix 2). The

---

Durand with that of the Second Vatican Council's Declaration on Non-Christian Religions: ". . . the salvation of the Church is prefigured mystically in the exodus of God's chosen people from the land of bondage" (*Nostra Aetate* #4). Throughout, I will quote Durand, *Rationale Divinorum Officiorum* (Naples, 1859) by book, chapter, and number. See Timothy Thibodeau, "William Durand: Compilator Rationale," *Ecclesia Orans* 9 (1992): 97–113 and his "Enigmata Figurarum: Biblical Exegesis and Liturgical Exposition in Durand's Rationale," *Harvard Theological Review* 86 (1993): 65–79.

ember days of the Pentecost season had a selection from Joel (3:23–24, 26–27) on Friday; on Saturday the readings were Joel 2: 28–32, Lev. 23:9–11, 15–17, 21, Deut. 26:1–3, 7–11, Lev. 26:2–12, and Dan. 3:47–51.

The September ember days had very evocative readings, especially when we recall that this is approximately the time of the Jewish high holy days. The readings from the Jewish Scriptures for Ember Wednesday were Amos 9:13–15 (on the abundance of harvest in Messianic days) and 2 Esdras (Nehemiah) 8:1–10, which speaks of the holy day in the seventh month. Hos. 14:2–10 (on the transforming power of divine forgiveness) was read on Ember Friday, and on the Saturday the selections were Lev. 23:26–32 (concerning the day of Atonement), 23:39–43 (on the feast of booths), Mic. 7:14–20, Zech. 8:1–2, 14–19 (on the four fasts), and Daniel 3, followed by Heb. 9:2–12, which describes the Temple and its liturgy in relation to the priestly work of Jesus. Thus, both the solemn fast of Yom Kippur and the autumnal eight-day feast were background for Christian reflection on the need for penance and for gratitude to God the provider.[6]

Ember Saturdays were the customary context for ordination to minor and major orders in the medieval Church. Berno of Reichenau (d. 1048) explained that lessons from the Jewish Scriptures reminded the ordinands that they should know the Law and the Prophets, which are recapitulated in the Gospel. This benign teaching was supplemented by Berno's explanation for the choice of the ember days: Wednesday was the day when the Jews plotted to kill Christ; on Friday they carried the plan into effect; on Saturday the Apostles mourned his death.[7]

2. The Great Antiphons (17–23 December)

The climax of Vespers (evening prayer) is the Magnificat (Luke 1:46–55), the canticle of Mary, which is chanted by the standing community

---

[6]See Jean Daniélou, "Les Quatre-Temps de septembre et la fête des Tabernacles," *La Maison-Dieu* 46 (1956): 114–36.

[7]*Libellus de quibusdam rebus and missae officium pertinentibus*, PL 142: 1073–98.

as the altar is incensed. The anticipation of Christmas during the seven days before the Vigil (24 December) is celebrated by a special series of antiphons for the Magnificat. Each begins with the vocative interjection "O" followed by a title of the Messiah drawn from the Jewish scriptures. In reverse order the initials of the titles spell an acrostic ERO CRAS ["I shall be here tomorrow!"]. The series goes back at least to the eighth century and shows how the piety of the Latin Church drew upon the prophets and wisdom writers of ancient Israel, moving from creation through the history of Israel. The second title is the Hebrew term "Adonai" [Lord], known to these Christians from Jerome's Vulgate for the hymn of Judith (at 16:16). Appropriately, this substitute for the Tetragrammaton [the four letter Name YHWH revealed to Moses in Exod. 3:14–15] is used in reference to the burning bush and the gift of the Torah [*Lex*] at Mount Sinai. Themes about the Davidic Messiah from Isaiah are woven into the third and fourth antiphons, celebrating the titles Root of Jesse and Key of David. The urgent need of deliverance for the Gentiles is clear in several antiphons. The hope for the union of Jew and Gentile is expressed in the second last prayer. "O King and desire of all nations (Hag. 2:8) and chief cornerstone (Ps. 117 [118]:22), who makes the two to be one: "come and save the human being, whom you have formed from clay." Drawing upon Eph. 2:14, which sees unity flowing from the work of the Prince of Peace, the petition focuses on the redemption of all humanity, in the person of the first Adam. Christians everywhere knew the meaning of the Hebrew phrase "Emmanuel" [God is with us] from Isa. 7:14 and 8:10. The final antiphon uses this title: "O Emmanuel, our King and Lawgiver, the expectation of the peoples (Gen. 49:10) and their Savior, come to save us, O Lord our God."[8]

---

[8]See Thomas J. Knoblach, "The 'O' Antiphons," *Ephemerides Liturgicae* 106 (1992): 177–204.

3. Lent and Holy Week

a. Ash Wednesday to Spy Wednesday. The forty days of Lent constituted a penitential season patterned after the fast of Moses (Exod. 34:28) and Elijah (1 Kings 19:8) and the way that Jesus prepared for his public ministry (Matt. 4:1–11). The faithful would acknowledge their sinful condition and reflect on the mystery of Jesus' persecution and death. Why does this fast move directly to the celebration of this Paschal Mystery? The great canonist and liturgical scholar William Durand (ca. 1230–96) explained: (1) In Lent we represent the people of Israel, who spent forty years in the wilderness immediately after they celebrated the Passover. (2) The resurrection of Christ flows from his Passion, so it is reasonable that our mortification relate to the Savior's Passion. Just as he suffered for us, we must suffer with him so that we may reign with him. (3) As the children of Israel afflicted themselves and ate bitter herbs before they ate the lamb, so we must first be afflicted through the bitterness of penance so that immediately afterwards we may worthily eat the lamb of life, which is the body of Christ, in order that we may receive the mystical Paschal sacraments.[9] For Durand, the season of Lent not only commemorated the time when the children of Israel remained in the desert but also reminded people of the sojourn of Jacob and his descendants in Egypt, the seventy-year captivity in Babylon, recalled on Septuagesima Sunday, and the dispersion caused by Vespasian and Titus throughout the whole world, which Christians do not commemorate because they will never be called back from it. "The Lord has delivered me into their grip; I am unable to rise" (Lam. 1:14) is his proof-text for this prevalent Christian view of the fate befalling the Jewish people.[10] This type of prejudice, grounded on an interpretation of the Bible that can be traced back to

---

[9]Durand, *Rationale Divinorum Officiorum*, VI.32.12. On Septuagesima (the seventieth day before Easter) and the Babylonian captivity see ibid., VI.24.4. For a general survey see Roger E. Reynolds, "Holy Week," *Dictionary of the Middle Ages*, vol. 6 (1985), pp. 276–80.

[10]Durand, *Rationale Divinorum Officiorum*, VI.28.6.

the early Church in a time of intense competition with Judaism, frequently found expression in biblical commentaries, homilies, and tracts "against the Jews" [*adversus Judaeos*]. It is beyond the scope of this essay to analyze examples of preaching that reflect on Jews and Judaism. It only can be noted that the Lenten season provided the faithful with many readings from the Jewish Scriptures (see Appendix 2). Joseph and Jeremiah, who were persecuted by their family and fellow countrymen respectively, were regarded as types of Jesus in his Passion. Ideally, as many spiritual writers have noted, the faithful should have reflected on their sinfulness and the Gospel call to conversion and penance. However, for those whose Latin was limited, the proclamation of biblical passages would offer a challenge to the community only inasmuch as the preacher developed such a point in his homily. Regarding the Palm Sunday liturgy, Durand aptly remarked:

> We must rejoice concerning the fruit of his Passion, and suffer with him, because he suffered for us. We rejoice, therefore, of the love which he showed for us on the cross, and we are sad because of our sins, which are so many, on account of which the Son of God had to suffer.[11]

One would hope that preachers integrated this biblical perspective (Rom. 4:25, etc.) into their homilies! This point was emphasized in the Catechism of the Council of Trent (Article IV). Both in the liturgy and in devotions such as the sorrowful mysteries of the rosary and the stations of the cross, the piety of the faithful focused increasingly on the pain and anguish of Christ crucified. All too frequently, the Jewish complicity with the Romans was emphasized, even to the point of linking all the various malicious acts done by others with Jews. Already in the early fifth century, Augustine of Hippo noted concerning "the sacrifice of Isaac" that the ram caught by the horns in a thicket (Gen. 22:13) prefigured Jesus "crowned with Jewish thorns [*spinis Judaicis*] before he was immolated."[12] Why speak of "Jewish

---

[11]Durand, *Rationale Divinorum Officiorum*, VI.37.11.

[12]*City of God*, XVI:32, in *Corpus Christianorum, series latina* 48 (1955): 537.

thorns?" The ordeal of crown of thorns was a deed of the soldiers, not the Jewish leaders or "the crowd" (see Matt. 27:29).

Among the extensive pedagogical reflections on the Holy Week liturgy, only a limited number represent the medieval Christian's attitude toward the Jewish people. The pattern was often negative, but this was not always the case. According to the Palm Sunday Gospel (Matt. 21:1–11), Jesus sent two disciples to find a donkey and her colt. The number "two" shows that they practice the twin commandments of loving God and neighbor. The animals represent the Jewish and Gentile people whom Jesus will lead into the heavenly Jerusalem.[13] The practice of taking particular details of the text and using them for an allegorical basis for teaching important moral and doctrinal points is pervasive in the Church from early times.

On Palm Sunday the Passion narrative according to Matthew was chanted in three parts (narrator, Christ, and *turba* [the crowd; also designated as "synagogue"]); Mark and Luke were proclaimed in like manner on Tuesday and Wednesday of Holy Week. How many of the lay faithful understood the Latin of each Gospel that they heard being dramatized with considerable artistry? Especially as private devotions to the Passion of Jesus developed and the events were portrayed in painting, sculpture, and glass, everyone knew the story and associated its details with the liturgy being celebrated. Ideally, this should have provoked an attitude of penance and promoted the ideal of modeling one's life on the example of the Master. "Have among yourselves the attitude that was in Christ Jesus" is the challenge introducing the well-known call for self-emptying recorded in the Christological hymn of Philippians (2:5–11). Did the ordinary people consider that they were being represented by the fickle "crowd" and the individuals (such as Judas, Peter, high priest, servants) whose words were chanted in a high voice? That would have brought the lessons of the Gospel home to them. But the title "synagogue" in some manuscripts indicates that for people who knew this designation these groups and individuals were identified simply as "the Jews."

---

[13]Durand, *Rationale Divinorum Officiorum*, VI.67.14.

b. The Sacred Triduum. The most solemn days of the liturgical calendar are calculated from sundown, following the Jewish practice, as the Church does for Sunday as well. Thus, in early times, the Last Supper on Holy Thursday evening began the three-day commemoration of Christ's passion, death, and resurrection. The early Church's custom of an *evening* Mass to commemorate the Last Supper was lost by the tenth century. Throughout later times (until 1955) there was a Mass in the morning, so the connection with the Passover Meal was less obvious to participants in the ceremonies.[14]

i.) Good Friday. This service began with two readings (Hos. 6:1–6 and Exod. 12:1–11),

> because Christ suffered for two peoples, Gentiles and Jews, or for the salvation of body and soul. One is taken from the Law, the other from the Prophets, because Christ's Passion was foretold by the Prophets and the Law and prefigured by the Patriarchs. Figuratively, Abraham immolated the flesh of Christ when he sacrificed the ram [Gen. 22]. In a similar way, Abel did this when he offered the lamb. . . .[15]

The Passion according to John was proclaimed to move the faithful from reflecting on the Passion of Christ to that of the Church in imitation of him, as Peter said: "Christ suffered for you so that you will follow in his footsteps" (1 Pet. 1:21). "The lamb of Exod. 12:5 is the spotless body of Christ; the goat is the Church, which means us, who are sinners. Christ's Passion is his immolation; ours is celebrated in the mortification of vices."[16] At this point the scholar's proper application of the liturgy is clear.

The Good Friday liturgy preserved a series of solemn supplications [*orationes solemnes*] that were common in the worship of the early Church

---

[14]See James Monti, *The Week of Salvation: History and Traditions of Holy Week* (Huntington, 1993), pp. 101–39.

[15]Durand, *Rationale Divinorum Officiorum*, VI.77.2.

[16]Durand, *Rationale Divinorum Officiorum*, VI.77.4.

(1 Tim. 2:1–2). In contrast to the Eastern liturgies, the tradition of Rome included prayers for Jews and pagans, heretics and schismatics, and for the destruction of error. As Durand pointed out, Christ prayed for enemies and friends so the Church must pray for everyone, that Christ infuse his grace into them and turn them to faith.[17] The nine prayers followed a structure: an introduction that focused on the given category of people, a time of silent prayer while kneeling, and a collect proclaimed by the celebrant. The deacon omitted the order to kneel at the second last prayer, which was for the Jews. Durand explained that the Church bends the knee in these prayers to show humility, except for the Jews, because they genuflected in mockery before the Lord, saying: "Prophesy to us, Christ, who struck you?" (Matt. 26:67–68). So in detesting this insult, the Church does not bend the knees in praying for them, so that she might avoid deceitful works.[18] The text was chanted as follows:

> "Let us pray also for the unbelieving Jews so that our God and Lord may remove the veil from their hearts and that they would know Christ Jesus our Lord." This introduction is followed by a moment of silence. "Let us pray. Almighty, eternal God, who do not reject even Jewish unbelief from your mercy, hear our prayers which we offer to you for the blindness of this people, that having acknowledged the light of your truth, which is Christ, they may be rescued from their darkness. . . ."[19]

---

[17]Durand, *Rationale Divinorum Officiorum*, VI.77.12.

[18]Durand, *Rationale Divinorum Officiorum*, VI.77.13.

[19]The Latin "*Oremus et pro perfidis Judaeis*" is often rendered "let us pray for the perfidious Jews . . . ." John M. Oesterreicher argued that the English should read "unbelieving"; see his study "Pro perfidis Judaeis," *Theological Studies* 8 (1947): 80–96 and that of Kathryn Sullivan, "Pro perfidis Judaeis," *The Bridge* 2 (1956): 212–23. Many pertinent issues cannot be treated within the limits of this paper, but we must note recent developments. Pope John XXIII ordered that the call to kneel be inserted for the petition concerning the Jews. After the Second Vatican Council, the prayer itself was replaced by one that shows respect for the Jewish people and their faith.

Drawing on St. Paul's reflection concerning the veil worn by Moses after his experience of God on Mount Sinai (2 Cor. 3:7–18 on Exod. 34:29–35), the people formulated the prayer as a petition that Jews come to faith in Christ. The theme of blindness is derived from Matthew (15:14; 23:16, 19, 24), where the criticism of Pharisees who accepted the title "guides of the blind" (see Rom. 2:19), is generalized to all Jews of all ages after the coming of Jesus. The identification of Christ with the truth of God is especially familiar, drawn from the Fourth Gospel (John 1:9, 14:6, etc.). Within the limitations of its time, probably from prototypes in early Christian liturgy, the prayer is benign to the extent that it did not curse Jews but offers hope to them, as individuals and a community. Of course, the fact that this hope is expressed in precisely Christian terms is problematic to people sensitive to triumphalism in the Church. Durand remarked that their blindness cannot be dispelled by prayer until the plenitude of the Gentiles enters in (see Rom. 11:25–26).[20] Therefore the prayer is not to be said intensely nor with bended knee but, rather, is to be said because the time will come when the One exalted on the Cross will draw all to himself (see John 12:32–34). How many of the laity would have understood the prayer? Even fewer would have been alert to the biblical allusions. However, everyone would have sensed a negative dimension to this petition for the Jews because they did not genuflect during the time of silent prayer. The Jews were treated differently and most people would have thought immediately of the role played by some Jews in the persecution and death of Jesus.

The next part of the ceremony was a solemn procession and unveiling of the cross, held by two priests. In Rome it can be traced back to the ninth century. As the faithful venerate the cross individually, the choir would sing the **Reproaches [*Improperia*]**; the refrain to each verse, sung by the opposite sides of the choir in Greek and then in Latin is rendered: "Holy God, Holy and Mighty One, Holy Immortal One, have mercy on us." This use of Greek indicates the antiquity of the petition. Abbot Rupert of Deutz (ca. 1075–1129) linked the Reproaches to the title on the cross of Jesus, which

---

[20]Durand, *Rationale Divinorum Officiorum*, VI.77.13.

was written in Hebrew, Greek, and Latin. "There is no response in Hebrew because that people still denies its king and curses and detests that title."[21] Durand offered a different interpretation. The priest who chants while carrying the cross sings, as it were, in Hebrew, in the person of the Savior; the acolytes sing in Greek, in the person of the Greeks; and the choir responds "Sanctus, sanctus," in the person of the Latins. Thus God is praised in three languages: Hebrew which, on account of the Law, is the mother of all languages; Greek because it is the teacher; and Latin, because it is the ruler on account of the dominion of the Roman Empire and the papacy.[22]

The bilingual plea for mercy constitutes a response to the question and complaints expressed as the voice of Christ. The pattern is drawn from the prophet Micah and follows the model of the court case against a vassal accused of breaking a treaty: "O my people, what have I done to you? In what have I wearied you? Answer me. For I brought you up from the land of Egypt . . ." (Mic. 6:3–4).[23] Using the principle of typology and accepting Paul's admonition in 1 Cor. 10:6 ["These things happened to them as an example and they have been written down as a warning to us"], the early Christian community probably included itself in each indictment. The Greek refrain (in the first person plural), introduced into the Latin liturgy in the ninth or tenth century, clearly reminds the faithful approaching the cross in procession that *they* need divine mercy and forgiveness. However, the intense debate between Christians and Jews, already in the second century, is the context for twisting the impact of the sacred text. Rather than a challenge to the community hearing God's Word in the liturgical readings, most Christians dissociated themselves from the Jews. The latter were blamed in a global fashion for all the events of the Passion, including the

---

[21]*Liber de divinis officiis, Corpus Christianorum, continuatio mediaevalis* 7 (1957): 201.

[22]Durand, *Rationale Divinorum Officiorum*, VI.77.14.

[23]See Julien Harvey, *Le plaidoyer prophètique contre Israël après la rupture de l'alliance* (Paris, 1967); and James Limburg, "The root RIB and the prophetic lawsuit speeches," *Journal of Biblical Literature* 88 (1969): 291–304.

actions of the Roman soldiers (see 2 Esd. 1:4–37 and Melito of Sardis, *On the Passover*).[24] Durand summarized earlier commentators.[25] The recurring question ("my people, what have I done to you?") is attributed to Christ, and the priest—speaking in the Lord's name—addresses the Hebrews and is considered, as it were, to be speaking Hebrew. Jews had brought three accusations against Christ: that he refused to pay tribute to Caesar (Luke 23:2), that he made himself king (John 19:21), and that he declared himself to be God's Son (John 19:7). In response Christ reproached them regarding three of his benefits: liberation from Egypt, guidance in the wilderness, and entry into a good land. It is as if he said:

> You accuse me of refusing to pay taxes, but you should rather give thanks because I freed you from tribute, from slavery to Egypt. You accuse me of saying that I am king, whereas you should rather give thanks that I governed you in the desert and fed you regularly. Moreover, you accuse me of claiming to be Son of God, whereas you should rather give thanks because I led you to a land flowing with milk and honey.[26]

Through this juxtaposition of these contrasts between the Exodus experience and the trial of Jesus, people lost the sense that the historical events in the Exodus and sojourn in the wilderness have a typological value for the

---

[24]See the text with commentary by Othmar Perler, *Meliton de Sardes, Sur la Paque* (Paris: Cerf, 1966); Eric Werner, "Melito of Sardis, the first poet of deicide," *Hebrew Union College Annual* 37 (1966): 191–210; Vittorino Grossi, "Melitone di Sardi, Peri Pascha 72–99, 523–763," in *Dimensioni drammatiche della liturgia medioevale: Atti del I Convegno di studio* Viterbo, 31 Maggio, 1–2 Giugno 1976 (Rome, 1977): 203–16; and Michael Brocke, "On the Jewish origin of the 'Improperia,'" *Immanuel* 7 (Spring 1977): 44–51.

[25]Commenting on Mic. 6:3, Jerome applied this passage to Christians in their sinfulness; see *Corpus Christianorum, series latina* 76 (1969): 496. Sicardus of Cremona (1150?–1215) noted that Micah 6 is the source for the *Improperia*. He lists three accusations of Jews against Jesus, to which the Savior replies with three accusations taken from Micah (*Mitrale*, Patrologia Latina. 213:317). See his study "The Liturgy of the liberation of Jerusalem," *Medieval Studies* 52 (1990): 110–31.

[26]Durand, *Rationale Divinorum Officiorum*, VI.77.15.

Christian community (see 1 Cor. 10:1–13). The greater tragedy was a pervasive tendency of Christians to attribute the attitude of those Jewish leaders who condemned Jesus to the contemporary Jewish community at large and to all succeeding generations of Jews.

During the procession before the veneration of the cross it was unveiled in three stages. According to Durand, this was done as a sign that perverse Jews stripped the Savior; this unveiling took place in three stages to teach that Christ was mocked three times in his Passion: (1) In the courtyard of the high priest, where they blindfolded him and struck his face (Mark 14:65); this is indicated when only the top of the cross is unveiled and the face of the Crucified is not seen. (2) Before the praetorium, when the soldiers mocked him; plaiting a crown of thorns (Mark 15:17) and genuflecting, they said: "Hail, king of the Jews." This is represented when the head and face of the Crucified is unveiled. (3) When he was hanging on the cross, passersby said: "Aha! You would destroy the Temple . . ." (Mark 15:29). The veil is removed entirely from the cross to recall that Christ was naked on the cross. It also signified that all which was obscure in the Law and the Prophets was now open and manifest in the passion.[27]

The cross was unveiled after the petitions to emphasize that prayer has its effect and exemplar in the cross, because Christ prayed for both friends and enemies. Durand further explained that the right side of the cross is unveiled first because Christ crucified was adored with true faith by the Apostles and the Jewish disciples, who were on the right. The faith was proclaimed by them devoutly and was carried into the midst of the Gentiles; this is shown when the priest places the cross before the middle of the altar. Then, because Christ, now resting, watches over the Church and does so until the end of time, the cross is placed on the altar, by which the Church of the Gentiles is designated. At last, because at the end of time faith in the hearts of the Gentiles will grow cold and according to Isaiah (10:20), he will be accepted by the remnant of Israel, he will be held in common by

[27]Durand, *Rationale Divinorum Officiorum*, VI.77.17.

Jews and Gentiles. To signify this, the cross is taken down from the altar at the end of Mass and located in a common place.[28]

This passage shows how each movement in the liturgy is laden with meaning for salvation history. These explanations flow from a long tradition concerning the ceremonies of the Mass as such. Because teachers forgot early Christian roots in the Jewish practices at Passover Meal and in the Temple, Amalarius of Metz (780?–850) and others explained details in terms of the Passion of Jesus. According to their familiarity with this general tradition, the faithful would be disposed to interpret Good Friday ceremonies as Durand suggests.[29]

ii.) The Paschal Vigil. The Easter Vigil ceremony, beginning with the blessing of the Paschal candle, followed by numerous readings with chants, and the celebration of Baptism in the context of commemorating the Lord's resurrection, must have been very impressive. Jerome explained the significance of the night vigil as follows:

> The tradition of the Jews is that the Messiah [*Christus*] is to come in middle of the night as in the days of Egypt. When the Passover is celebrated the exterminator (angel of death) comes and the Lord passes over the dwellings and our doorposts are consecrated by the blood of the lamb. Thus I think the apostolic tradition persists that, on the day of the Paschal Vigil, it is not licit to dismiss the people before midnight, awaiting Christ's coming. . . .[30]

---

[28]Durand, *Rationale Divinorum Officiorum*, VI.77.18.

[29]At times the Jewish feast of Purim, with its mockery of the crucified Haman (Esther 9: 20–28), fell at a time close to Good Friday. This could have led to tensions between the Jews and the Christian community. See Cecil Roth, "The feast of Purim and the origins of the blood accusation," *Speculum* 8 (1933): 520–26. Another example of tension, this time around the fast commemorating the destruction of Jerusalem on the Ninth of Abh, has been studied by Amnon Linder, "The destruction of Jerusalem Sunday," *Sacris erudiri* 30 (1987–88): 253–92.

[30]Jerome, Commentary on Matthew in *Corpus Christianorum (series latina)* 77 (1969): 237, quoted by Amalarius. See J. M. Hanssens, *Amalarii Episcopi Opera Liturgica Omnia*, 3 vols. (Vatican City, 1948), 2:109–110.

Which passages from the Scriptures were read? Zeno, bishop of Verona for a time between 360–80, preached briefly on each reading and 62 of his sermons for the Paschal rites have survived. He spoke on Genesis 1 (creation hymn), Exodus 12 (Passover meal), 14 (crossing of the sea), Isaiah 1 (judgment of sinful Israelites), 5 (song of the vineyard), and Daniel 3 (youths in the furnace). Later there is reference to twelve readings from the Jewish Scriptures (i.e., six passages were read in Greek and then in Latin). The Gelasian Sacramentary (between 560–90) has the following readings: Gen. 1:1–2:2 (Creation), 22:1–17 (sacrifice of Isaac), Exod. 14:24–15:1, Isa. 4:1–6 (forgiveness and divine indwelling), Deut. 31:22–30 (Moses' final message), and Psalm 41. At a second stage, Isa. 54:17–55:11 (God's redemptive gifts) replaced 4:1–6, and Ezek. 37:1–14 (vision of the dry bones) was chosen instead of Deuteronomy 31.[31]

The response to each reading is a canticle from the Scriptures, followed by a prayer; the celebration of God's mercy through Christ is rooted in the divine care for Israel. The liberation of one people from Egyptian persecution prepares for the salvation of the nations through the waters of regeneration: "Grant that the fullness of the whole world may come into the children of Abraham and the dignity of Israel." The theme of this prayer is derived from St. Paul's explanation that baptism introduces the Gentiles into the family of God and of Abraham (Gal. 3:26–29). It provides a basis for the Church to exhort the faithful to a deep respect for the Jewish people in the mystery of salvation.

At the beginning of the Easter Vigil the church building is in darkness and a new fire is sparked by a rock being struck with flint. Durand explained that

> the old fire symbolized the Old Law, whose images were completed in Christ's death and therefore it must be allowed to cease, but the Holy Spirit poured upon

---

[31]G. P. James, "The Paschal Liturgy in Zeno of Verona," *Studia Patristica* 18/2 (1989): 375–79; see Bernard Botte, "Le choix des lectures de la veillée pascale," *Questions liturgiques et paroissiales* 33 (1952): 65–70.

> us from the rock, that is, from Christ, who is the cornerstone. . . . The new fire is blessed so that, like the one who is inextinguishable light, enlightening every person coming into the world, the fire guided Moses. The Paschal candle signifies the column of fire which preceded the people of Israel at night. Second, the candle signifies Christ, who enlightens us in the night of this world. . . .[32]

The *Exultet* or solemn salutation of Christ, symbolized by the Paschal candle, draws extensively from the Exodus experience but does not imply the cessation of its meaning:

> This is our Passover feast, when Christ, the true lamb, is slain, whose blood consecrates the homes of all believers. This is the night when first you saved our ancestors: you freed the people of Israel from their slavery and led them dryshod through the sea. . . .

The Jewish people do not appear prominently in other parts of the liturgical year. The New Testament readings would provide a context for homilies that might allude to the Jews. However, the study of such feasts as the Circumcision of Jesus (1 January), the Presentation and Purification (2 February), the Presentation of Mary (21 November), etc. did draw on the Jewish Scriptures and their traditions. Of course, the readings from the New Testament would provide a context for homilies that might include allusions to the Jews and their faith.

The Jewish Scriptures and Saints in the Latin Rites of Passage

The popular practice of declaring certain people to be holy (or blessed) is rooted in the ancient Jewish tradition. Thus, the elect are called "the holy people of the Most High" (Dan. 7:27). The early Church celebrated the martyrs whose deaths are recorded in 2 Macc. 6:18–7:41, especially the mother

[32]Durand, *Rationale Divinorum Officiorum*, VI.80.1, 4, and 5.

and her seven sons, whose feast is celebrated on 1 August.[33] The martyrologies include a great number of saints not mentioned in the liturgical calendar that governs the celebration of Mass and the Divine Office. In many prayers from the liturgy of baptism, marriage, ordination, sickness, death, and burial there are references to personalities and themes of the Jewish Bible.

On Holy Thursday, the oils are consecrated for the sacraments of baptism, confirmation, orders, and anointing of the sick. The precedents of anointing kings, priests and prophet (1 Kings 19:16) are mentioned in prayers, which find types of the sacraments in biblical texts.

> David foreknew by prophetic inspiration the sacraments of your grace and that our faces would be made glad with oil [Ps. 103 [104]:15]. When of old the world's sins were expiated by the flood, a dove announced that peace was restored to the earth by bearing an olive branch [Gen. 8:11] the type of gifts to come, which in these latter days has been manifested. . . .[34]

In the early Church, candidates were prepared for baptism in a series of steps and baptized during the Vigil for Easter or Pentecost. Prayers used on these occasions were included in medieval liturgical books, even though the steps of the catechumenate, moving through Lent to Baptism in the Easter Vigil, were no longer followed. The first prayer for the exorcism of male candidates evoked the God of the patriarchs:

> God of Abraham, God of Isaac, God of Jacob, God who appeared to your servant Moses upon Mount Sinai, and led the children of Israel out of the land of Egypt, sending to them the angel of your goodness to guard them day and night. . . .[35]

---

[33]See Margaret Schatkin, "The Maccabean Martyrs," *Vigiliae Christianae* 28 (1974): 97–113; Bernard Botte, "Les saints de l'Ancien Testament," *La Maison-Dieu* 52 (1957): 109–20; and F. Lurz, "Jeremia in der Liturgie der alten Kirche," *Ecclesia Orans* 9 (1992): 141–71.

[34]Gelasian Sacramentary 386–88, Gregorian Sacramentary 335. See Bibliography at end of this chapter for editions of all the sacramentaries cited.

[35]Gelasian Sacramentary 291, Gregorian Sacramentary 1071.

The prayer over women began with reference to the God of the patriarchs, "who admonished the tribes of Israel and freed Susannah from false accusation . . ." (Dan. 13).[36]

The marriage ceremony includes prayers that develop themes from the story of Eve being taken from Adam's side (Gen. 2:21–24); the nuptial blessing also asks that the bride "prove loving to her husband, like Rachel; wise, like Rebecca; long-lived and faithful, like Sarah."[37] Jerome's Latin version of Tobit influenced marriage customs in western Europe. A blessing over the couple was drawn from Tob. 7:15 (Vulgate): "May the God of Abraham, the God of Isaac and the God of Jacob be with you and join you and fill you with his blessing."[38]

The Temple liturgy and the roles of priests and Levites were important paradigms for the ordination prayers for deacons, priests, and bishops. The ceremonies for the dedication of a church also drew heavily upon the accounts about the consecration of the Temple.

When visiting the home of a sick person, the priest prayed: "God, you gave fifteen years of life to your servant Hezekiah [Ezekias in Latin, see 2 Kings 20:1–11]; likewise by your power give your servant (name) to rise from the sickbed to health."[39] The Gregorian Sacramentary reminds us that Tobit and Sarah were healed through the intercession of Raphael, whose name was known to mean healing or medicine of God.[40] These persons and Job are mentioned in other prayers for the sick.[41] Among prayers for the dying is a litany with the petition:

---

[36]Gelasian Sacramentary 295, Gregorian Sacramentary 1076.

[37]Gelasian Sacramentary 1451, Gregorian Sacramentary 838.

[38]Sarum Manual, p. 49. On the development of the Christian marriage liturgy from Jewish roots see T. Fisch and D. G. Hunter, "Echoes of the early Roman Nuptial Blessing: Ambrosiaster, De peccato Adae et Evae," *Ecclesia Orans* 11 (1994): 225–44.

[39]Gregorian Sacramentary 987, 1386.

[40]Durand, *Rationale Divinorum Officiorum*, IV.33.19.

[41]Gelasian Sacramentary 1721, Gregorian Sacramentary 980.

> Deliver, Lord, the soul of your servant as you delivered Enoch and Elijah from ordinary death, Lot from Sodom and the burning flame, Isaac from the hand of his father Abraham, Moses from the hand of Pharaoh, Job from his sufferings, David from the hand of Goliath and from King Saul, Daniel from the lions' den, the three youths from the burning furnace, Susanna from false accusation.[42]

Such prayers and the use of psalms in all key moments of the life pilgrimage give an insight into the importance of the Jewish Scriptures in the ministry of the Church.

Conclusion

The encounter over the centuries between Christians and Jews included moments of positive exchange and mutual respect for the integrity of the other faith. However, the intense debate of early centuries contributed to a set of interpretative principles that pitted "Ecclesia" against "Synagoga," in Christian exegesis of the Jewish Scriptures and the New Testament. This twisted use of the biblical message entered into the liturgy in a number of places. After the Second Vatican Council, the application of the documents on Divine Revelation, the Liturgy, and the Relation of the Church to Non-Christian Religions [*Nostra Aetate/In Our Age*] provide the foundation for reforms that endeavor to correct the bias and to foster a wholesome appreciation of the Jewish people, their faith and their heritage.

---

[42]Sacramentary of Gellone 2893; Sarum Manual, p. 118.

Appendix 1

Sacramentaries

The liturgy consists of texts that remain constant (the Ordinary) and others which vary daily. The earliest collection of liturgical texts gathered the second category of prayers. More elaborate collections became known as "sacramentaries." Those associated with Rome include first the Gelasian Sacramentary (mistakenly attributed to Pope Gelasius I, who reigned 492–496), prime example being Vatican manuscript Reginensis latinus 316 from the mid-eighth century, and the Gellone Sacramentary, later in the same century. The second Roman text is represented by the Gregorian Sacramentary, attributed to Pope Gregory I (590–604) but probably compiled some decades after his death.

See Henry Ashworth, "Sacramentaries," *New Catholic Encyclopedia* (New York, 1967), 12:792–800; and Roger E. Reynolds, "Sacramentary," *Dictionary of the Middle Ages* (New York, 1988), 10:605–06.

Appendix 2

Readings for Lenten Liturgy

	Würzburg	Murbach	MR 1570
Ash Wed.	Joel 2:12–13	Joel 2:12–13	Joel 2:12–19
Thur.		Isa. 38:1–6	Isa. 38:1–6
Fri.	Isa. 58:1–9	Isa. 58:1–9	Isa. 58:1–9
Sat.		Isa. 58:9–14	Isa. 58:1–14
WEEK 1			
Mon.	Ezek. 34:11–16	Ezek. 34:11–16	Ezek. 34:11–16
Tue.	Isa. 55:6–11	Isa. 55:6–11	Isa. 55:6–11
Wed.	Exod. 24:12–18	Exod. 24:12–18	Exod. 24:12–18
	1 Kings 19:3–8	1 Kings 19:3–8	1 Kings 19:3–8
Thur.		Ezek. 18:1–9	Ezek. 18:1–9
Fri.	Ezek. 18:20–28	Ezek. 18:20–28	Ezek. 18:20–28
Sat.		Deut. 11:22–25	Deut. 26:12–19
			Deut. 11:22–25
			Sir. 36:1–10
			Dan. 3:47–51
WEEK 2			
Mon.	Dan. 9:15–19	Dan. 9:15–19	Dan. 9:15–19
Tue.	1 Kings 17:8–16	1 Kings 17:8–16	1 Kings 17:8–16
Wed.	Esther 13:9–17	Esther 13:8–17	Esther 17:8–11, 15–17
Thur.		Jer. 17:5–10	Jer. 17:5–10
Fri.	Gen. 37:6–22	Gen. 37:6–22	Gen. 37:6–22
Sat.	Gen. 27:6–39	Gen. 27:6–39	Gen. 27:6–40
WEEK 3			
Mon.	2 Kings 5:1–15	2 Kings 5:1–15	2 Kings 5:1–15
Tue.	2 Kings 4:1–7	2 Kings 4:1–7	2 Kings 4:1–7
Wed.	Exod. 20:12–24	Exod. 20:12–24	Exod. 20:12–24
Thur.		Jer. 7:1–17	Jer. 7:1–17
Fri.	Num. 20:1–13	Num. 20:1–13	Num. 20:1–3, 6–13
Sat.	Dan. 13:1–62	Dan. 13:1–62	Dan. 13:1–9, 15–17

WEEK 4

Mon.	1 Kings 3:16–28	1 Kings 3:16–28	1 Kings 3:16–28
Tue.	Exod. 32:7–14	Exod. 32:7–14	Exod. 32:7–14
Wed.	Ezek. 36:23–28	Ezek. 36:23–28	Ezek. 36:23–28
	Isa. 1:16–19	Isa. 1:16–19	Isa. 1:16–19
Thur.		2 Kings 4:25–38	2 Kings 4:25–38
Fri.	1 Kings 17:17–24	1 Kings 17:17–24	1 Kings 17:17–24
Sat.	Isa. 49:8–15	Isa. 49:8–15	Isa. 49:8–15
	Isa. 55:1–11	Isa. 5:1–11	

WEEK 5

Mon.	Jonah 3:1–10	Jonah 3:1–10	Jonah 3:1–10
Tue.	Dan. 14:27–42	Dan. 14:27–42	Dan. 14:27–42
Wed.	Lev. 19:11–19	Lev. 19:11–19	Lev. 19:1–2, 11–19, 25
Thur.		Dan. 3:25, 34–35	Dan. 3:25, 34–35
Fri.	Jer. 17:13–18	Jer. 17:13–18	Jer. 17:13–18
Sat.	Jer. 18:18–23	Jer. 18:18–23	Jer. 18:18–23

HOLY WEEK

Mon.	Isa. 50:5–10	Isa. 50:5–10	Isa. 50:1–10
		Zech. 11:10–13; 13:6–9	
Tue.	Jer. 11:18–20	Jer. 11:18–20	Jer. 11:18–20
	Wis. 2:12–22	Wis. 2:12–22	
Wed.	Isa. 62:11–63:7	Isa. 62:11–63:7	Isa. 62:11–63:7
	Isa. 53:1–12	Isa. 53:1–12	Isa. 53:1–12
Thur.	—	—	—
Fri.		Hos. 6:1–6	Hos. 6:1–6
		Exod. 12:1–11	Exod. 12:1–11

Additional Bibliography

Editions

Sarum Manual: A. Jefferies Collins, ed. *Manuale ad usum Percelebris Ecclesie Sarisburiensis*, vol. 91. London, 1960.

Gregorian Sacramentary: Jean Deshusses, ed. *Le Sacramentaire Gregorien*. Fribourg, 1979.

Sacramentary of Gellone: A. Dumas, ed. *Liber Sacramentorum Gellonensis*. Turnnolt, 1981.

Gelasian Sacramentary: L. C. Mohlberg, L. Eizenhöfer and P. Siffrin, eds. *Liber Sacramentorum Romanae Aeclesiae Ordinis Anni Circuli*, Cod. Vat. Reg. lat 316. Rome, 1960.

Texts in Translation

Bradshaw, Paul F. *Ordination Rites of the Ancient Churches of the East and West*. Collegeville, Minn., 1990.

Dudley, Martin. "Rites for the blessing of oils and anointing: The Western Tradition." In *The Oil of Gladness: Anointing in the Christian Tradition*. Ed. Martin Dudley and Geoffrey Rowell. London, 1993.

Porter, Harry B., *The Ordination Prayers of the Ancient Western Churches*. London, 1967.

Searle, Mark, and Kenneth W. Stevenson. *Documents of the Marriage Liturgy*. Collegeville, Minn., 1992.

Whitaker, E. C. *Documents of the Baptismal Liturgy*. London.

Further Reading

Burtchaell, James T. *From Synagogue to Church: Public Services and Offices in the Earliest Christian Communities*. New York, 1992.

Chavasse, Antoine. *La Liturgie de la Ville de Rome du Ve au VIIIe siècle*. Rome, 1993.

Chydenius, Johan. *Medieval Institutions and the Old Testament*. Helsinki, 1965.

Diller, Hans-Jürgen. *The Middle English Mystery Play: A Study in Dramatic Speech and Form*. New York, 1992.

Gameson, Richard, ed. *The Early Medieval Bible: Its Production, Decoration and Use*. New York, 1994.

Grayzel, Solomon. *The Church and the Jews in the XIIIth Century*. Vol. 1, *1198–1254*. Philadelphia, 1933; New York, 1966.

———. *The Church and the Jews in the XIIIth Century*. Vol. 2, *1254–1314*. Detroit, 1989.

Harper, John. *The Forms and Orders of Western Liturgy from the Tenth to the Eighteenth Century*. Oxford, 1991.

Jasper, Ronald C. D. and G. J. Cuming. *Prayers of the Eucharist: Early and Reformed*. 3rd ed. Collegeville, Minn., 1992.

Kottje, Raymund. *Studien Zum Einfluss des Alten Testamentes auf Recht und Liturgie des fruhen Mittelalters (6–8 Jahrhundert)*. Bonn, 1964.

Monti, James. *The Week of Salvation: History and Traditions of Holy Week*. Huntington, Ind., 1993.

Nardone, Richard M. *The Story of the Christian Year*. Mahwah, 1991.

Palazzo, Eric. *Le Moyen Age: Des Origines au XIIIe Siècle*. Paris, 1993.

Riche, Pierre, and Guy Lobrichon, eds. *Le Moyen Age et la Bible*. Paris, 1984.

Rubin, Miri. *Corpus Christi: The Eucharist in Late Medieval Culture*. New York, 1991.

Schreckenberg, Heinz. *Die Christlichen Adversus-Judaeos-Texte (11–13 Jh) mit einer Ikonographie des Judenthemas bis zum 4 Laterankonzil*. Frankfurt, 1988.

———. *Die Christlichen Adversus-Judaeos-Texte und ihr Literarisches und historisches Umfeld* (1–11Jh.) Frankfurt, 1988.

Simon, Marcel. *Verus Israel: Etude sur les relations entre Chrétiens et Juifs dans l'Empire romaine*. Paris, 1964.

———. *Recherches d'Histoire Judéo-Chrétienne*. Paris, 1962.

Simonsohn, Shlomo. *The Apostolic See and the Jews*. 7 vols. plus addenda. Vols. 1–6, *Documents: 492–1555*. Toronto, 1988–91.

Spinks, Brian D. *The Sanctus in the Eucharistic Prayer*. New York, 1991.

Stow, Kenneth R. *Alienated Minority: The Jews of Medieval Latin Europe*. Cambridge, Mass., 1992.

Vogel, Cyrille. *Medieval Liturgy: An Introduction to the Sources*. Rev. and trans. William G. Storey and Niels Krogh Rasmussen. Washington, D.C., 1986.

SACRAMENTAL LITURGIES IN THE MIDDLE AGES

MARTIN R. DUDLEY

THE CAMPANILE OF FLORENCE was begun in 1336. Its architectural and decorative scheme was set out, in broad terms, by Giotto, the Italian artist declared by his contemporaries Dante, Boccaccio, and Sacchetti to be the greatest painter since antiquity. When Giotto was born, around 1267, the Dominican theologian Thomas Aquinas was Regent Master at Santa Sabina in Rome, and the Franciscan theologian Giovanni di Fidanza, known to history as Bonaventure, was Minister General of his order. The year before, Aquinas had started work on his *Summa Theologiae*.

In 1269 he returned to Paris, just as John Peckham succeeded Eustace of Arras in the Franciscan chair of theology. Aquinas finished his career as Regent of Theology in Naples, where, between September 1272 and December of the following year, he wrote those parts of the *Summa* concerned with the sacraments. He died on 7 March 1274, leaving his sacramental theology unfinished. Bonaventure died in July of the same year. In 1279, John Peckham became Archbishop of Canterbury.

As far as sacramental theology was concerned, Aquinas was the more influential theologian. Though his work was incomplete, he wrote systematically about the sacraments. In particular, he developed a theology of causality that differed significantly from Bonaventure's understanding of the sacraments as signs of God's grace and that was accepted more widely. Bonaventure and Franciscan theology, though influenced by the new Aristotelianism, represented and maintained an older tradition. Answering a question about the number of the sacraments, Aquinas quotes "some people"—a frequent method of introducing arguments in theological treatises—who regard seven as appropriate because it corresponds in a certain sense to the virtues. Bonaventure was one of those holding that the sacraments corresponded to the three theological and four cardinal virtues. This correspondence—which could be expressed in art as well as in theology—was one of the ways in which the seven sacraments were inserted into a broader moral, theological, and cultural context. Peckham, archbishop and legislator as well as theologian, had the more difficult task of promoting the use of and safeguarding the sacraments in their actual celebration in the life-cycle of medieval men and women.

The decorative scheme of the campanile of Florence, continued after Giotto's death in 1337, depicts human spiritual progress through labor, art, and the sacraments. A set of reliefs in the upper cycle represents the seven Sacraments—baptism, Eucharist, confirmation, penance, matrimony, ordination, and extreme unction. Each is depicted, within a lozenge-shaped frame, by two figures set on a platform. In the triangular space beneath the platform is an allegorical head appropriate to the sacrament. This is the first significant sacraments' cycle in Italy and dates at the earliest from the early 1340s and at the latest ten years later. The reliefs are poorly visible from the piazza but could be seen clearly from the bridge that linked the tower to the cathedral **nave**. "How fitting it was," writes art historian Marvin Trachtenberg, "to set the mysteries of the church not openly exposed to the life of the street, but huddled in shadows next to the nave of the Duomo where only the clergy who were spiritually intimate with the Sacraments might be visually so."[1] If this was the intention, then it contradicted the nature of the sacraments as defined by Aquinas and Bonaventure and enforced by Peckham, for they taught that the sacraments were intended not for the clergy but to render mankind perfect in all that pertains to the worship of God and,

[1]Marvin Trachtenberg, *The Campanile of Florence Cathedral: "Giotto's Tower"* (New York, 1971), p. 97.

further, to counteract the harmful effects of sin.[2] However, it is still possible that Trachtenberg's explanation is correct, for much in the sacramental liturgies of the Middle Ages was, indeed, contradictory.

Rogier Van der Weyden's *Seven Sacraments Altarpiece* dates from about one hundred years after the Florence reliefs. Its three panels give us an extensive and peopled church interior. The Mass is being celebrated in the middle ground of the central panel behind the scene of the Crucifixion. There a priest elevates the sacred Host at an altar replete with its own carved altarpiece. In the panel to the left—the north aisle of the painted church—the sacraments of baptism, confirmation, and confession are depicted. To the right—in the south aisle—a minister is being ordained, a couple married, and a sick man receives extreme unction. Above each celebration angels with banderoles explain the significance of the image. Van der Weyden gathers within a single picture the sort of individual images which we find in illuminated manuscripts and liturgical texts. He also places the seven sacraments within a church, indicating with merely the artistic license involved in placing a bed in the south aisle, that the sacraments are constitutive of the Church in the fullness of her life. At the same time human life, from the naked baby at the font to the naked man on his death bed, is placed in a sacramental context. The pastoral celebration of the sacraments, by holy dedicated pastors, touching each stage of the life-cycle was an ideal rarely achieved in the Middle Ages. It was, however, an ideal held up by reformers of the Church throughout the period and would be central to the Counter-Reformation model of the priest.

Theology and Rite

The sacramental rites of the Church had gone through one thousand years of development before a theology of the sacraments emerged. Washings, blessings, and anointings, initiation, ordination, and consecration, the

---

[2]Thomas Aquinas, *Summa Theologiae*, Blackfriars edition, vol. 56 (New York, 1975), 62, 5; 63, 1; 65, 1.

forgiveness of sins and the ministry to the sick and dying already existed and provided the raw material for the theologians who, in the twelfth century, created and ordered that body of teaching that we now can call sacramental theology. They sorted out and clarified the various meanings of *sacramentum* and listed those ritual actions that henceforth would be known as sacraments. The theology of the sacraments represents only one part of the picture. The theology stands in relation to the liturgical text.

The liturgical texts needed to celebrate the sacraments were contained in a number of different books. In the early Middle Ages the liturgy of the Mass was contained in a set of books used by different ministers. The Sacramentary contained the texts needed by the priest. Various types of lectionary contained the readings, and the chant books provided the texts for the *schola*. From the end of the eleventh century, the texts were gathered together to provide the priest with one volume—the plenary Missal. Rites administered by the bishop, that is, confirmation and ordination, were contained in the Pontifical. All the other sacramental rites were contained in a book that carried a number of names: ***rituale***, ***manuale***, ***agenda***.

Theologians commented upon the texts and also played a part in reshaping them. But the written text is not paramount. The performed text is the true liturgical text. The performance very often contradicted the intention of the text and nullified its effect. A constant concern of ecclesiastical legislators and reformers, from Charlemagne to the Council of Trent (1545–63), was that the sacraments be celebrated in the way intended by Christ and set down by the Church. At Lambeth in 1281, Archbishop Peckham applied himself anew to the reform of the English Church. His opening line expresses the fullness of his concern:

> The most High hath created a Medicine for the Body of Man (which was taken out of the Earth) reposited in seven Vessels, that is in the seven Sacraments of the Church, which are handled, and dispensed with little reverence and diligence, as our own eyes inform us.[3]

---

[3]Text of Peckham's Constitutions may be found in John Johnson, *A Collection of all the Ecclesiastical Laws . . . of the Church of England*, 2 vols. (London, 1720).

His Constitutions then seek to correct a large number of abuses.

This consideration of the sacramental liturgies in the Middle Ages deals with six of the seven sacraments. The one omitted is Holy Order. There were large numbers of ordinations to the seven orders of ministry taking place every year across Christendom. In a populous and wealthy diocese, Winchester, 1,000 men were ordained between 1316 and 1319, including 247 to the priesthood.[4] Ordinations took place on seven occasions in the year and were not limited to cathedrals; they were celebrated in the chapels of episcopal manors, in parish churches, and in abbeys as well, but they were not a regular feature of the life of ordinary people.

Initiation: Baptism and Confirmation

He entered then, leading the way for me
down to the first circle of the abyss.

Down there, to judge only by what I heard,
there were no wails but just the sounds of sighs
rising and trembling through the timeless air,

the sounds of sighs of untormented grief
burdening these groups, diverse and teeming,
made up of men and women and infants.

Then the good master said, "You do not ask
what sort of souls are these you see around you.
Now you should know before we go on farther,

they have not sinned. But their great worth alone
was not enough, for they did not know Baptism,
which is the gateway to the faith you follow,

---

[4]See Virginia Davis, "Rivals for Ministry? Ordinations of Secular and **Regular Clergy** in Southern England c. 1300–1500," in *The Ministry: Clerical and Lay: Papers Read at the 1988 Summer Meeting and the 1989 Winter Meeting of the Ecclesiastical History Society*, ed. W. J. Sheils and Diana Wood (Oxford, 1989), pp. 99–109.

and if they came before the birth of Christ,
they did not worship God the way one should.[5]

This is Dante's account of the *Limbus puerorum* or *infantium* on the edge of Hell, the abode of children and others who have died without baptism. He expresses the generally accepted medieval doctrine that baptism was necessary for salvation. Virgil tells the troubadour Sordello that this is his place of abode:

There is a place below where sorrow lies
in untormented gloom. Its lamentations
are not the shrieks of pain, but hopeless sighs.
There do I dwell with souls of babes whom death
bit off in their first innocence before
baptism washed them of their taint of death.[6]

It was just such a vision of limbo and its guiltless yet hopeless infants which, combined with the high infant mortality rate, shaped baptism in the later Middle Ages.

Birth was an important event in the predominantly rural European communities of the Middle Ages, but without rebirth in the water of salvation, life was merely temporal. Aquinas taught explicitly, and the Church has never denied the truth of what he said, that the baptism of infants should not be delayed, because death is always a possibility and because no other remedy is available to infants.[7] The canons and statutes of the medieval Church show an early concern for prompt and valid baptism. An anonymous ninth-century Frankish Address to the Clergy told clergymen to see that no infant

---

[5]Dante, *The Divine Comedy*, vol. 1: *Inferno*, trans. Mark Musa (New York, 1984), canto IV, 31–38.

[6]Dante, *The Divine Comedy*, vol. 2: *Purgatorio*, canto VII, 28–33; trans. in Jacques Le Goff, *The Birth of Purgatory* (Chicago, 1984), p. 336.

[7]Aquinas, *Summa Theologiae*, 3a. 68, 3.

died without baptism through their neglect.[8] It also limited baptism to the eve of Easter and Pentecost, unless there was danger of death. The priest was at least to know how "to read well the exorcisms and the prayers for making the catechumen, also for consecrating the baptismal font, and the other prayers concerning male and female, when several are to be baptized together." Before 900, Theodulph of Orleans instructed his clergy that if a sick infant was brought for baptism from another parish, the child was not to be refused the sacrament, and he warned: "should anyone refuse to grant this office upon request, and the infant should die without the grace of Baptism, the one who did not baptize him shall know that he shall render an accounting for his soul."[9] In 1126 Archbishop William de Corbeil's canons for the English Church charged that no price should be demanded for chrism, oil, or baptism, or for visiting the sick, anointing, Communion, or burial.[10] A similar canon was issued by the papal legate in 1138, adding penance and espousals to the list of free rites. Archbishop Stephen Langton reiterated these canons in 1222, saying that the sacraments are not to be denied on account of money, though there appears to be some expectation of an offering. In 1236 Archbishop Edmund Rich, who gave the English Church the requirement of changing the water in the font weekly, paid particular attention to the well-established practice of baptism of children by laymen in cases of necessity. The priest had to enquire how it was done so as to ensure its validity. Such was the likelihood of this that women "big of Child" were told to "have Water in readiness for baptizing the Child, if necessity require." The legatine constitutions of Otho, the **cardinal** legate who held a council at St. Paul's Cathedral in London in 1237, drew

---

[8]A number of bishops and theologians have been proposed as the author, from Caesarius of Arles to Rather of Verona. Translation and discussion in *Early Medieval Theology*, ed. George E. McCracken (Philadelphia, 1957), pp. 371–78.

[9]PL 105: 191–205; trans. in *Early Medieval Theology*, ed. McCracken, p. 386.

[10]Text of all English canons cited below are from Johnson, *A Collection of all the Ecclesiastical Laws. . . .*

attention to a curious misunderstanding. He pointed to the days—the eves of Easter and Pentecost—appointed by the Holy Canons for the solemn celebration of baptism because of their proximity to the great feasts, but said that he had heard of some "being imposed upon by a diabolical fraud [who] suspect danger, if the children be baptized on these days." It is nowhere explained how this irrational fear had arisen but Otho argued that it is contrary to faith and groundless because "the chief Pontiff does personally solemnize this Ministry on the days before named." Though he called for a return to baptism on these days, he also admonished the clergy to teach the laity how to baptize, in the vulgar tongue, in case of necessity. The Sarum Manual devoted a section to the teaching to be given regularly to the people, with the form given in English and Latin. The thirteenth-century archbishop John Peckham stressed that when lay people baptize in case of necessity and observe the due form, such baptism is sufficient for salvation. Further, he castigated "some foolish priests" who re-baptize in such a circumstance "which is an indignity to the sacrament." The belief that the unbaptized were unredeemed was reinforced by refusing them burial in the churchyard. Yet even if the foot of a child appearing from its mother at birth should be baptized, the child was allowed to lie in holy ground.

Despite lay baptism, the normal minister of baptism "solemnly and properly celebrated" (that is, including all the rites) was the priest who had the cure of souls, the parish priest.[11] The proper place was the parish church. Many churches used regularly for worship did not have a font. Candidates, both adults and children, were taken to a major baptismal church or to one of the detached baptisteries, such as those in Florence and Pisa, which stayed in use throughout the Middle ages. As long as the traditional times for baptism—Easter and Pentecost—were maintained, this practice persisted. It was reinforced by financial interests. No fee was charged for baptism, but offerings were made and were kept by the officiating clergy. The purification of women after childbirth frequently was performed at the

---

[11]Aquinas, *Summa Theologiae*, 3a. 67, 4.

same time as the baptism, and offerings always were made then. Monastic and collegiate churches and the greater baptismal churches, therefore, hung on to their prerogatives. The growing fear of damnation encouraged baptism within a few days of birth, and this led to the provision of fonts in all parish churches, together with instructions given to midwives to enable them to baptize immediately after birth if the need arose. The diary of the Florentine businessman Gregorio Dati, covering the period 1393–1422, contains a list of his more than twenty children. None of them was baptized by a midwife, but each was presented for baptism at the baptistery of S. Giovanni. Most of the children were baptized the day after birth; five days was the longest delay Dati recorded.[12]

The medieval rite of baptism was adapted gradually to take account of the change from adults to babies as the usual candidates for baptism. Liturgical change never involves a clean break, however, and the medieval rite that emerged from the eleventh century onwards retains remnants of older forms of Christian initiation. It was a complicated rite, and English depictions regularly show a clerk beside the priest at the font holding the rituale or manual.[13] The account given here follows the **Use** of Sarum, the liturgy of the Cathedral Church of Salisbury, which came to be the dominant English use until the Reformation. English customs, as Peckham declared in 1281, differed at many points from those of the rest of the western Church, and some of these differences will be noted. The ceremonies at the church door were all that remained of the old rite of making a catechumen.[14] After an initial enquiry about the name and sex of the child,

---

[12]*Two Memoirs of Renaissance Florence: The Diaries of Budaccorso Pitti and Gregorio Dati*, comp. Gene Brucker (New York, 1967), pp. 115–17, 126–28, 134–36.

[13]Ann Eljenholm Nichols, *Seeable Signs: The Iconography of the Seven Sacraments, 1350–1544* (Rochester, 1994), p. 200.

[14]Text of the rite from the Sarum Manual may be found in John D. C. Fisher, *Christian Initiation: Baptism in the Medieval West: A Study in the Disintegration of the Primitive Rite of Initiation* (London, 1965), pp. 158–79.

the infant was signed with the cross on forehead and breast and received the laying on of hands. Salt was exorcised and, being called the "salt of wisdom," was placed in the infant's mouth. Then came remnants of the rite of candidacy in which the child was exorcised, again with signing with the cross on the forehead and the holding of the hand on the head for the accompanying prayer of illumination. The Gospel from Matthew (19:13–15) read at this point concerns the bringing of children to Jesus, who blesses them. Immediately afterwards the priest would spit in his left hand and touch the ears and nose of the infant with saliva, using his right thumb and saying "Effeta," the word rendered in most translations as ***Ephphatha*** used by Jesus in Mark 7:34 when he restored hearing and speech to a man. The godparents next were required to repeat the Lord's Prayer, the Hail Mary, and the Apostles' Creed. The child then was blessed and taken into church. There, if the water was to be renewed "which often ought to be done because water grows stale," a rite of blessing was carried out.[15] It involved a litany of the saints, a collect, and a lengthy prayer of blessing. The prayer was accompanied by elaborate ceremonial: the water was divided in the form of a cross, the sign of the cross was made over it eight times, water was cast from the font in four directions, the priest breathed into the font three times in the form of a cross, he changed his tone of voice, he dropped wax from a candle into the water in the form of a cross, he dipped the candle in, dividing the water in the form of a cross. The "oil of unction" was poured in, again in the form of a cross, followed by chrism (the oil mixed with balsam that was consecrated solemnly by the bishop on Maundy Thursday) in the same manner, and then oil of unction and chrism together. Then came the baptism. According to the Sarum Manual, the child is carried to the font and held by the godparents. Godparents are often included in the illustrations, sometimes as onlookers, sometimes holding the child or holding a candle, touching the infant, or wrapping it. The priest holds a hand over the child and asks the name. When it is given the priest asks the child

---

[15]Fisher, *Christian Initiation*, p. 165.

by name for a three-fold renunciation of Satan; the godparents reply each time. The priest then anoints the child on the breast and between the shoulders with the oil of unction. The name is again asked and followed by a three-fold interrogation concerning the creed. The priest again asks the name of the infant and asks "What seekest thou?" The godparents reply: "Baptism." The priest asks: "Dost thou wish to be baptized?" They reply: "I wish." The Manual describes how this is done:

> *Then let the priest receive the infant sideways in his hands: and having asked his name let him baptize him with a threefold dipping invoking the Holy Trinity once saying thus*:
>
> N. I also baptize thee in the name of the Father (*and let him dip him once with his face turned towards the north and his head towards the east*) and of the Son (*and again let him dip him once with his face towards the south*) and of the Holy Ghost. Amen. (*and let him dip him the third time with his face towards the water*).
>
> *Then let the godparents receiving the infant from the hands of the priest raise him from the font.*

The child then was anointed on the head (not on the forehead) with "the chrism of salvation" and robed in a white robe, called the chrismal robe (which was to be brought back to church in due course), and then a burning candle was placed in the hand of the infant! If a bishop was present, the child was confirmed and received Communion immediately. Otherwise, the godparents were charged to ensure confirmation if the bishop came within seven miles. The parents were charged to preserve the child from fire and water and all other dangers until the age of seven years (generally counted as the age of discretion).

Although the rite was identical in essential details, there were variations from place to place. The most obvious difference is the use of the vernacular appropriate to each country and people. The Sarum interrogations are in English; those in the Würzburg Agenda—the manual for celebrating the sacraments in the diocese of Würzburg—are in German.[16] There is also a lengthy German admonition to the godparents, which cites Jesus' command to baptize at the end of Matthew's Gospel, and the godparents themselves are required to know and teach the child the Ten Commandments in addition to the Pater noster, Ave Maria, and Credo in Deum. The interrogations were to be conducted in Latin or German. There is no order for blessing the water, which again reflects a difference between England and the rest of Europe. In England, the water might be changed every week; in most of Europe water was only consecrated at Easter and Pentecost. So also the baptism itself followed a pattern common in western Europe, but not in England, from the twelfth century: water was poured three times over the child while "Ego te baptiso . . ." was said. In European illustrations the godparents sometimes are shown holding the baby while the priest pours the water over it. The two practices, of immersion and infusion, are the subject of a lengthy explanatory note in the Würzburg Agenda, which justifies either of them. The child was anointed with chrism, but no candle was given (though the picture on the title page of the Agenda shows a candle held at the font by a godparent). The Sarum Manual combines in one rite the prayers to be used for male and female children, while the Würzburg Agenda provides two rites. This is partly because the prayers actually differ somewhat in content but mostly because of the difficulty, already noted in the ninth century, which some clergy had in using the correct Latin forms when switching from masculine to feminine.

The Pontificals show the scene of Confirmation with the mitered bishop anointing a child held up by a kneeling sponsor, with a crowd of others jostling for place. Confirmation does appear to have been somewhat disordered. John Peckham observed that a very large number of those baptized neglected this sacrament, and he ruled that none should be admitted to Holy

---

[16]A fifteenth-century edition, formerly in Sion College Library, is now in Lambeth Palace Library.

Communion unless confirmed, except at the point of death.[17] It was not only parents and godparents who were neglectful but also the parish clergy in exhortation and the bishops themselves in celebration of the rite. Archbishop Reynolds of Canterbury told priests to exhort their people to carry their children to be confirmed by the bishop, not waiting for him to come to them but going to him when he is in the neighborhood. It was a short rite and did not require a full and elaborate service. After the bishop had prayed over all the children, he anointed each of them, by name, with chrism. Reynolds tells parents to take long pieces of cloth to wrap around the forehead and dry up the chrism. On the third day after, the children were taken to church. Their foreheads were washed, in the baptistery but not in the font, and the cloths were burned.[18]

The Mass

The faithful participated in the Mass in three ways: by paying the stipend for the priest to offer the Mass on their behalf or for some person—for example, a deceased relative—or intention specified by them; by being present, especially at the elevation; and by receiving Holy Communion. On payment of a stipend a priest would offer the Mass for the specific intention of the donor. This involved a change in the understanding of the Mass, which was seen no longer in its fully ecclesial context, the celebration of the people of God united with Christ, but in the context of human need, in which the Mass was offered for someone, living or departed, and the act of offering well might be limited to the priest and a server. The close connection between participation and presentation was reduced to a transaction. Nevertheless, drawing on our understanding of patronage in other

---

[17]Constitutions at Lambeth, 1281, ch. 4.

[18]Archbishop Reynolds Constitutions, 1322, ch. 2, found in Johnson, *A Collection of all the Ecclesiastical Laws. . . .*

fields—for example, the commissioning of altarpieces—we can see that the contractual agreement was seen in terms of the donors' full participation in the gift. Hence, the person paying the Mass stipend participated in the Mass whether present or not.

The faithful generally were present at Mass on Sundays and feast days, but this was probably a low Mass without singing or elaborate ceremonial. Their participation was limited to being present and to seeing the various ceremonies, culminating in the elevation of the Host. The solemn liturgy of the cathedral, collegiate, and conventual churches maintained the basic principles of a more ancient form of celebration with a diversity of ministers. The laity deliberately were excluded from these celebrations and, in greater churches, were separated from the choir by a screen. Communion was given at an altar erected outside the screen.

Holy Communion was received infrequently, but canon 21 of the Fourth Lateran Council of 1215 made it a requirement for all the faithful to receive Communion at least at Easter each year.[19] The discipline of the sacrament required the parish priest to give Communion only to those of his own parish whom he knew, having heard them himself or having some testimonial, to have made confession.[20] Only the consecrated bread was given. Peckham charges the clergy to instruct the simple that the body and blood of the Lord is given them at once under the species of bread.[21] The wine that was given after the bread was not the sacrament but was drunk "for the more easy swallowing" of the bread. The faithful were also instructed not to grind the sacrament with their teeth in case a particle should lodge between them.

---

[19]Text 9 of the canon may be found in *Enchiridion Symbolorum definitionum et declarationum de rebus fidei et morum*, ed. Heinrich Denzinger and Adolf Schönmetzer, 33rd ed. (Barcelona, 1965), p. 812.

[20]Aquinas addresses the question of whether a person should be believed if he says he has confessed to another in *Quodlibetal Questions 1 and 2*, ed. Sandra Edwards (Toronto, 1983), pp. 54–55.

[21]Constitutions at Lambeth, 1281, n. 1.

Penance

The Pontifical, the book used by the bishop for the parts of the liturgy reserved to him, frequently had illustrations that showed the way in which the rites were to be performed.[22] It contained the rites for the expulsion of penitents on Ash Wednesday and their reconciliation by the bishop on Maundy Thursday. We see them kneeling, scantily clothed and bare-footed, before the robed bishop; then, holding tapers and clothed in hair-shirts, they are led by the bishop, in cope and miter, carrying his crozier, to the church door. They are then expelled. Bishop John Grandisson's *Ordinale Exoniensis* of 1337, setting out the ceremonies to be used in Exeter cathedral, summarizes the heart of the rite in four words: *Eiectis penitentibus, claudatur ianua* [The penitents are ejected; the doors are closed].[23] On Maundy Thursday, these same penitents made individual confession to a priest and were brought back into the church in the same manner in which they were expelled. From the twelfth century onward, this was termed *paenitentia solemnis*.

The rite, as illustrated, was performed rarely in the Late Medieval period other than for the most monstrous sins. It was superseded by individual sacramental confession and by other regular forms of penance, notably pilgrimage and penitential exercises such as flagellation, walking barefoot, offering of tapers, and by some more extreme acts of public penance. The Maundy Thursday rite of reconciliation was removed from the version of the Pontifical produced in 1485 by Pius II's adopted son and secretary, Agostino Patrizzi Piccolomini, with the papal master of ceremonies, John Burchard. In other respects this version faithfully followed the late thirteenth-century Pontifical of William Durandus, Bishop of Mende.[24]

---

[22]Illustrations from a number of fifteenth-century pontificals were reproduced in W. H. Frere, *Pontifical Services: Illustrated from Miniatures of the XVth and XVIth Centuries*, 2 vols. (London, 1901). Two further volumes illustrated with woodcuts from the sixteenth century were issued by the Alcuin Club in 1907–08.

[23]*Ordinale Exon.* (London, 1909), p. 311.

[24]The rites appeared in later editions because, until the edition of Clement VIII, 1595, there

The Fourth Lateran Council, 1215, laid upon the faithful the obligations of confessing secretly all their sins to their priests at least once a year and of diligently striving to fulfill the penance imposed by the priest. Illustrations of confession found in windows and illuminated manuscripts and on fonts give us a fairly uniform picture of what confession was like. The penitent knelt on the floor or on a cushion before a seated priest who usually wore a stole over a surplice. Confessions were heard in open church, not in the confessional boxes of the Tridentine Church, but there was still a concern for secrecy and decorum. The penitent inclined toward the priest to whisper a confession. The priest's head generally was covered by a hood or almuce, so the penitent's words would go no further. When other waiting penitents are depicted, they stand some distance away. Male penitents sometimes placed their hands into those of the confessor or put them on his knees. The space between a female penitent and the priest usually was greater, and sometimes women are shown kneeling at a prie-dieu. The priest sat with his hands in his lap while hearing the confession. The priest's hand was raised or laid on the penitent's head when absolution was given.

Little was laid down in the liturgical texts concerning the form of confession, and local uses prevailed. The Würzburg *Agenda Ecclesiastica* refers the priest to another text, on the virtues and number of the sacraments, for a detailed consideration of penance and it lays down only what was absolutely necessary: that the priest should hear the penitent's confession of sin, that a penance should be given, that two prayers should be said and then absolution should be given, with the priest first laying his hands on the penitent's head and then making the sign of the cross over him or her, at the points indicated, saying: "Et ego te absolvo a peccatis tuis in nomine Pa † tris et Fi † lii et Spiritus † Sancti," which was the generally accepted form of absolution.[25]

---

was no officially authorized pontifical but a series of overlapping local uses, mostly based on Durandus; see Cyrille Vogel, *Medieval Liturgy: An Introduction to the Sources* (Washington, D.C., 1986), pp. 253–57.

[25]See the discussion of this formula by Thomas Aquinas, *Summa Theologiae*, 3a, 84, 3.

The manuals and rituals tell us nothing about what was going on during the confession, but from the seventh century onwards theologians and spiritual writers call for a full and sincere confession of sins.[26] Bede said that "sins cannot be forgiven without confession of amendment," and Alcuin, calling the priest a physician of souls, pointed out that a priest cannot reconcile someone whom he does not know to be a sinner. The festering ulcers of our crimes, he said, must be revealed to those who have been appointed in the Church of Christ to heal them. The remedies and prescriptions for these wounds were set out in penance manuals, which appear in a number of editions, and both Abelard and Hugh of St. Victor were concerned about confessors who were ignorant of the appropriate measure of exterior penance, that is the work to be done in satisfaction agreed before receiving absolution.

There are numerous stories of the use and abuse of the confessional. Friar Salimbene, a Franciscan and an inveterate thirteenth-century traveler, gave two stories of women invited and even forced to sin by priests to whom they confessed.[27] Etienne de Bourbon (ca. 1185–1261), a Dominican inquisitor, produced a collection of *exempla*, stories to be used in preaching. One of them is the story of a priest who knew a woman of his parish to be a grievous sinner, but when she came to confession she merely justified herself and refused to acknowledge her sin. He, therefore, treated her as a precious relic, a sinless woman, and shamed her into making a real confession.[28] In one story of *The Decameron*, Filomena, intent on showing that "the priesthood consists for the most part of extremely stupid men" shows

---

[26]For a fuller discussion and sources see Martin Dudley and Geoffrey Rowell, *Confession and Absolution* (Collegeville, Minn., 1990), pp. 56–68.

[27]*The Chronicle of Salimbene de Adam*, ed. Joseph L. Baird, Giuseppe Baglivi, and John Kane (Binghamton, N.Y., 1986), pp. 412–15.

[28]A. Lecoy de la Marche, *Anecdotes Historiques tirés d'Étienne de Bourbon* (Paris, 1877), p. 162; trans. in George G. Coulton, *Life in the Middle Ages*, 4 vols. in 2 (Cambridge, 1967), p. 87.

confession being used by a young woman to secure the favors of a young man.[29] In another, a jealous husband disguises himself in the robes of a priest "with a large hood that came down over his cheeks, like the ones that are often worn by priests," to hear his wife's confession.[30] Two rather different confessors are to be found in *The Canterbury Tales*. The first is a friar, "a wanton one and merry," says Chaucer, who goes on to describe him in this way:

> Highly beloved and intimate was he
> With Country folk within his boundary,
> And city dames of honor and possessions;
> For he was qualified to hear confessions,
> Or so he said, with more than priestly scope;
> He had a special licence from the Pope.
> Sweetly he heard his penitents at shrift
> With pleasant absolution for a gift.
> He was an easy man in penance-giving
> Where he could hope to make a decent living;
> It's a sure sign whenever gifts are given
> To a poor Order that a man's well shriven.
> And should he give enough he knew in verity
> The penitent repented in sincerity.
> For many a fellow is so hard of heart
> He cannot weep, for all his inward smart.
> Therefore instead of weeping and of prayer
> One should give silver for a poor Friar's care.[31]

Chaucer's account shows us that there was always a risk of some attempting to buy forgiveness, and always priests prepared to be bought. The other

---

[29]Giovanni Boccaccio, *The Decameron*, trans. G. H. McWilliam (Harmondsworth, 1972), third day, third story.

[30]Ibid., seventh day, fifth story.

[31]Geoffrey Chaucer, *The Canterbury Tales*, trans. into modern English by Nevill Coghill (Harmondsworth and New York, 1977), p. 25.

confessor may go some way to reassuring us that there was more good practice than chroniclers and story-tellers would have us believe. It was the parson "rich in holy thought and work" whose tale, the last to be told before the pilgrims reach Canterbury, is actually a prose sermon on the proper preparation for Confession and the true nature of the Seven Deadly Sins.[32]

Marriage

A sermon of San Bernardino of Siena (1380–1444) contains a story of a young man who takes a wife. On the day when she was to be taken to his house, he received Communion in the morning, and she did as well; then he led her to his house, where they held a feast and the marriage celebration. In the evening they did not consummate the marriage. They waited three days, sleeping clothed and remaining in prayer for part of the night.[33] There is no liturgy here, and whatever the celebration was it did not take place in church or even at the church door. Medieval marriage combined domestic and public ceremonies that ensured the recognition of the marriage. We can say that there were rites to be followed, linking the families and proclaiming the union, which were, for the most part, not liturgical and did not require the presence and ministry of a priest. Even when, from the eleventh century onwards, the Church made provision for a full and integrated marriage rite in which the priest took a central role, it was accepted only slowly. Archbishop Reynolds of Canterbury (1313–27) set out the conditions:

> Let Matrimony be celebrated as other sacraments with reverence in the day time, and in the face of the Church without Laughter, Sport or Scoff. Let the Priests while the Marriage is contracting, interrogate the People under pain of Excommunication by three publick Banns concerning the Immunity of the Bridegroom

---

[32]Text in *The Riverside Chaucer*, Larry D. Benson, gen. ed., 3rd ed. (Oxford, 1987), pp. 287–437.

[33]See Christopher Brooke, *The Medieval Idea of Marriage* (Oxford, 1991), pp. 29–30.

> and Bride on three Lord's-days, or Festivals distant from each other. If the Priest neglect these Banns, let him not escape the Punishment lately enacted in the General Council [three years suspension]. And let Priests often forbid such as are disposed to plight their Troth any where but in some notable place before Priests or publick Persons call'd together for this purpose under pain of Excommunication.[34]

Ecclesiastical control made greater advances in the north than it did in Italy, though four-fifths of marriage cases dealt with in the Ely consistory court, 1374–81, had been contracted privately and not publicly solemnized.[35] When there was a ceremony in England it was at the church door or in the porch, as in the case of Chaucer's Wife of Bath, who took five husbands at the church door,[36] and the enlarged porches of English churches, used as well for the preliminary rite of baptism, suggest that this was the case.[37] By the end of the fifteenth century, episcopal admonition seems to have made marriage a public act presided over by the priest. Font reliefs show the bride and groom, the priest, lay witnesses, and at least one attendant cleric, usually holding the manual.[38] *Handfasting*, the joining of the right hands, is the usual way in which marriage is presented on English fonts, on the Campanile, in Van der Weyden's altarpiece, and in the Würzburg Agenda.

The picture is rather different in Italy. A late medieval view of marriage is provided by "The Story of Romeo and Julietta," which, by way of William Painter's *The Palace of Pleasure* (1567), provided Shakespeare with the plot of "Romeo and Juliet." The story itself is centuries old but was given a fixed form by Matteo Bandello (1485–1561), a Lombard writer and

---

[34]Archbishop Reynold's Constitutions, 1322, found in Johnson, *A Collection of All the Ecclesiastical Laws. . . .*, ch. 7.

[35]Michael M. Sheehan, "The Formation and Stability of Marriage in Fourteenth-Century England: Evidence of an Ely Register," *Medieval Studies* 33 (1971): 250.

[36]*The Riverside Chaucer*, p. 30, line 459 ff.

[37]G. H. Cook, *The English Medieval Parish Church*, 3rd ed. (London, 1961), p. 189.

[38]Nichols, *Seeable Signs*, p. 275.

bishop of Agen in France, 1550–55. It certainly reflects much earlier practice. The couple is married before Friar Lawrence in his cell or in the shriving chapel, that is, the small chapel where he heard confessions. He "shut fast the door as he was wont to do," so it was not a public ceremony.[39] He first shrived them and then asked:

> Daughter, as Romeo here present hath certified me, you be agreed and contented to take him to husband, and he likewise you for his espouse and wife. Do you now still persist and continue in that mind?
>
> The lovers answered that they desired none other thing. The friar, seeing their conformed and agreeable wills, after he had discoursed somewhat upon the commendation of marriage dignity, pronounced the usual words of the Church; and she having received the ring from Romeo, they rose up before the Friar.[40]

It is incidental to this ceremony that it took place in the chapel or cell and that a friar directed it. The only part that expresses the provision in late medieval manuals is the commendation of marriage dignity. Otherwise this clandestine ceremony replaces the second part of the Italian wedding procedure, which usually took place at the house of the girl.[41] The union already had been negotiated by the families and a notary, not a priest, elicited express acquiescence from those to be married in the form required by the Church. Then the notary drew the woman's right hand toward her husband, and he placed the nuptial ring on her right ring finger. The betrothed couple was considered married after this, though there were still public signs to be given, including the move to the husband's house, before the marriage was consummated. There could be some delay in doing this. Gregorio Dati was betrothed on 31 March 1393 and gave his bride Isabetta the nuptial ring on

---

[39] "The Story of Romeo and Julietta," in *Elizabethan Love Stories*, comp. T. J. B. Spencer (Harmondsworth, 1968), pp. 62–63.

[40] *Elizabethan Love Stories*, comp. Spencer, p. 63.

[41] Christiane Klapisch-Zuber, *Women, Family and Ritual in Renaissance Italy* (Chicago, 1985), pp. 183–87.

7 April; she did not move in until 22 June.[42] In Rome, the couple would have gone to Mass and received a benediction; this was much less likely in Florence, despite the teachings and exhortations of Antoninus, Archbishop of Florence 1446–59. Christiane Klapisch-Zuber observes that the heart of the nuptial ritual lay in a place other than the Church's blessing. The Würzburg Agenda has the interrogation in German, after which the priest gives divine confirmation to the marriage the couple has contracted and declares a personal ratification, confirmation, and benediction.

The history of matrimony shows us that the medieval mind did not distinguish between the canonical and sacramental aspects of liturgies. To be contracted validly in the eyes of the Church and to enjoy the benefits of sacramental grace, a marriage had to conform to the rules laid down by general councils and in episcopal constitutions. Yet the evidence is that for much of the Middle Ages there was no wedding ceremony involving a priest and no service in church. Marriage in all social classes was considered much more as a contract between two families.

Sickness and Death

The liturgy for the sick and dying responds to three tendencies in the life of the Church. The first identifies the sick person with Christ. It is well expressed in the Rule of St. Benedict:

> Before all else and above all else, care must be taken of the sick, so that they may be served as Christ himself in very deed, for he said: "I was sick and you visited me" and "What you did for the one of these least you did for me."[43]

The second tendency comes from an attempt to reconcile divergent understandings of sickness in relation to sin and punishment. The connection

[42] *Two Memoirs of Renaissance Florence*, comp. Brucker, p. 114.

[43] *The Rule of St Benedict* 36.

between sin and sickness is found in the Old Testament, the source of much medieval liturgical practice. Though apparently denied by Jesus, it reappears in the Letter of James, in which the anointing of the sick is linked to confession of sins and the prayer of the Church for the sick is linked to forgiveness. Gregory the Great expressed a view of sickness as a divine scourge, as a disciplining of the flesh, and as a means of being united to Christ in his suffering. This view remained current throughout the Middle Ages, and the relation of sin and sickness was specifically reaffirmed by the Fourth Lateran Council of 1215. The third tendency displays a lack of confidence in any form of healing, other than miraculous means, and a recognition that death is inevitable.

The first tendency made the sick a group that required special attention. They received compassion but were also pushed to the margins of society. The rules of both Augustine and Benedict provide for an infirmarian to care for the sick. Such a specialized ministry guaranteed seriousness and efficiency but also separated the majority of the monastic community from the suffering of Christ expressed in and through the sick. This was true in the wider community as well, yet both inside and outside religious houses it continued to be recognized that Christ's words were addressed to all. Confraternities with a particular ministry to the sick and dying expressed through their para-liturgical rites (e.g., the bringing of a holy candle) this wider ministry. The combination of the second and third tendencies led to the abandonment in the eighth century of the early Church's ministry of healing and the substitution of an elaborate rite of passage for the dying.

The developed ministry to the sick, liturgical and sacramental, can be divided into five parts. First, the general visitation of the sick involving the presence of a priest and other ministers, members of the family, and possibly members of devout confraternities. Pictures that depict the sick in bed show the ministers with crucifix, candles, incense, and holy water. They also show the presence of other beings, angels or devils depending on the destination of the deceased. The rite included the penitential psalms and the litany. The second part included confession and the absolution of excommunicants who had repented. Hugh of St. Victor urged the baptized not to leave repentance to the last moment, to the death bed "when pain binds the limbs and grief oppresses the sense," but he affirmed that it is better late than never and promises that a person who does then repent truly goes forth "in firm hope with the pledge of good devotion."[44] The third part, the sacrament of extreme unction, was the last of the anointings given to Christians. Fourth came the Viaticum, the food for the journey from life to death. Finally came the watch with the dying person and the commendation of the departing soul, after which the deceased left the house.

The rites, and changes in them, can be documented from liturgical sources and also, in fact more vividly, from medieval stories, letters, and Lives of the saints. Paulinus's Life of St. Ambrose, dating from the early fifth century, has the Bishop of Milan receiving the Lord's body from Bishop Honoratus of Vercelli; he took it, swallowed it, and breathed his last.[45] This reception of the Viaticum—literally, food for the journey—seems to have been the normal pattern for several centuries. In Bede's Life of Cuthbert, written about 721, the saint received "the sacraments that lead to eternal life." This apparently meant the Lord's body and blood and not anointing. Charlemagne also received Holy Communion but was not anointed.[46] There is no anointing in the Arthurian romances of Chrétien de Troyes and the absence of anointing in accounts of the deaths of noted twelfth-century clergy is remarkable. Peter the Venerable's letter to Heloise (1142) on the death of her husband Abelard details his profession of faith, confession of sin, and reception of the Viaticum, followed by the commendation of his soul.[47] There is no recorded anointing despite the detailed

---

[44]*Hugh of St. Victor on the Christian Sacraments (De Sacramentis)*, trans. Roy J. Deferrari (Cambridge, Mass., 1951), XIV, 5; p. 412.

[45]*The Western Fathers: Being the Lives of SS. Martin of Tours, Ambrose, Augustine of Hippo, Honoratus of Arles, and Germanus of Auxerre*, ed. Frederick R. Hoare (New York and London, 1954), p. 183.

[46]Einhard and Notker the Stammerer, *Two Lives of Charlemagne* (Harmondsworth, 1969), p. 83.

[47]*The Letters of Abelard and Heloise*, trans. Betty Radice (Baltimore, 1974), p. 283.

instructions for the anointing of monks in the infirmary at Cluny in Ulrich's ***Consuetudines*** *Cluniacenses* of 1086.[48] In the 1130s Abelard himself prescribed the method for anointing nuns at the Paraclete in one of his Letters of direction addressed to Heloise.[49] Abbot Peter does say that all Abelard's brothers in religion and the whole monastic community could bear witness to the manner of his death, indicating that, in the usual monastic practice, there was a considerable gathering at the death-bed. Paintings of the death of the Virgin, of St. Benedict, of St. Francis, and of other saints, show us these death-bed scenes. In William of St. Thierry's *Vita Prima* of St. Bernard (1145–48) the saint hears the confession of a dying man, made with tears and sighs, and then gives him the sacrament, that is, the body of Christ.[50] This suggests that there was a deliberate move in the early twelfth century towards anointing as an essential part of the last rites and that it was accepted as normal practice by the end of the century. We read of St. Dominic receiving extreme unction at the Benedictine Priory of Monte-Mario in August 1221.[51]

In 1273, the Synod of Evreux decreed:

> If anyone, young or old, because of the fault, negligence, or absence of his priest dies without baptism, confession, reception of the Body of the Lord, and extreme unction, the priest so convicted is to be suspended from the celebration of the divine mysteries. . . .

An idealized version of the rites as set down for the Dominicans is given in Bernard Gui's Life of St. Thomas Aquinas (1274) in which the dying theologian calls for the Viaticum, then makes the profession of faith "as the Church discipline requires," and the next day asks to be anointed. His

---

[48]PL 149: 770–71.

[49]*The Letters of Abelard and Heloise*, pp. 215–16.

[50]These Cistercian accounts are gathered and translated by Pauline Matarasso in *The Cistercian World: Monastic Writings of the Twelfth Century* (New York, 1993).

[51]M.-H. Vicaire, *Saint Dominic and his Times* (London, 1964), p. 373.

mind, we are told, remained clear throughout the ceremony, and he answered the prayers himself. Then he joined his hands and gave back his spirit to its maker.[52]

The importance of death-bed confession is apparent in the first story from the *Decameron* (begun by 1350) in which two Florentine brothers have to resolve the problem of what to do with the notorious sinner, Ser Ciappelletto, who has fallen ill in their house. They cannot evict a dying man for fear of public opinion, but they doubt either that he would be willing to make his confession or receive the sacraments; and if he dies unconfessed, no church will receive his body. Even if he did make confession, no one would absolve him, and the result would be the same. The sick man himself resolves the problem: he deceives an old and holy friar, makes his confession, and then asks him to send "that true body of Christ which you consecrate every morning on the altar" and afterward "to receive the holy Extreme Unction, so that, having lived as a sinner, I shall die as a Christian." He receives Communion and, failing rapidly, receives the anointing and dies.

The rites found in the story from the *Decameron* appear to have been normative in the late Middle Ages. During the Black Death, the number of people dying together with the desertion of priests severely reduced the possibility of performing these rites for every baptized person. Certain exceptions were allowed (e.g., confession to a lay person, even to a woman).[53] The plague reinforced certain notions about death but also loosened the monopoly of the clergy on the rites. The full sequence continued to appear in the official texts, but sick-bed rites increasingly were performed by lay confraternities, and the inner disposition of the faithful was valued more than the rites themselves.

---

[52]Kenelm Foster, *The Life of Saint Thomas Aquinas: Biographical Documents* (Baltimore, 1959), pp. 55–56.

[53]Robert S. Gottfried, *The Black Death: Natural and Human Disaster in medieval Europe* (London, 1986), chs. 3 and 4, chronicles religious and other developments resulting from the plague.

It is a basic sacramental principle that only the living can receive a sacrament. A child born dead cannot receive baptism. Funeral rites, therefore, do not come within sacramental liturgies, though the central liturgical act was the requiem Mass offered on behalf of the dead person. As fear of damnation shaped the practice of baptism, so the fear of purgatory led to the offering of large numbers of Masses on behalf of the dead.[54] The requiem became the most common form of the Mass.[55] In this way sacramental care continued after death for as long as stipends were available to pay the priests.

Additional Bibliography

Sacraments and Iconography

Martos, Joseph. *Doors to the Sacred: A Historical Introduction to Sacraments in the Christian Church*. Garden City, 1981.

Liturgical Books

Gy, Pierre-Marie. *La Liturgie Dans L'Histoire*, Paris, 1990. See especially chapter 5, "Collectaire, rituel, processional."

Palazzo, Éric. *Histoire des Livres Liturgiques: Le Moyen Age—Des origines au XIIIe siècle*. Paris, 1993.

Wordsworth, Christopher, and Henry Littlehales. *The Old Service Books of the English Church*. London, 1904. [Despite its age, this remains a standard work, outdated only in certain details.]

---

[54]See Le Goff, *The Birth of Purgatory*, ch. 9.

[55]T. S. R. Boase, *Death in the Middle Ages: Mortality, Judgment, and Remembrance* (New York, 1972), pp. 59–69; and Philippe Ariès, *The Hour of Our Death* (New York, 1983), pp. 178–80.

Baptism and Confirmation

Davies, J. G. *The Architectural Setting of Baptism*. London, 1962. [This excellent book, which devotes fifty pages to the Middle Ages, has not yet been superseded.]

Mitchell, Nathan D. "Dissolution of the Rite of Christian Initiation." In *Made, Not Born: New Perspectives on Christian Initiation and the Catechumenate, from the Murphy Center for Liturgical Research*. Notre Dame, Ind., 1976. Pp. 50–82.

Whitaker, Edward C. *Documents of the Baptismal Liturgy*. London, 1960.

Eucharist

Jungmann, Josef A. *The Mass of the Roman Rite: Its Origins and Development (Missarum Sollemnia)*, 2 vols. New York, 1951–55. [This is the standard text on the Roman Mass before Vatican II and provides an enormous amount of detail. Translated from the German, it should only be used in the two-volume format in English.]

Rubin, Miri. *Corpus Christi: The Eucharist in Late Medieval Culture*. Cambridge, 1991. [This book swiftly has established itself as a basic text on the medieval Eucharist. Unfortunately the footnotes are inaccurate in a large number of places and should be used with caution.]

Vogel, Cyrille. "An Alienated Liturgy." *Concilium* 72 (1972): 11–25. [Vogel, one of the most distinguished medieval liturgists, here explains how the liturgy of the Mass became alienated from the people in the early Middle Ages.]

Penance

Dudley, Martin R. "The Sacrament of Penance in Catholic Teaching and Practice." In *Confession and Absolution*. Ed. Martin Dudley and Geoffrey Rowell. Collegeville, Minn., 1990. Pp. 56–91. [A concise account of the development of penance.]

Matrimony

Medieval marriage has been extensively researched in the last twenty-five years. The interests of liturgists overlap with those of the historians of marriage at just a few points, and the best study of the marriage liturgy—Stevenson's *Nuptial Blessing*—has almost nothing to say about the social context. The following, taken together, will provide an understanding of the liturgy in context.

Klapisch-Zuber, Christiane. "Zacharias, or the Ousted Father: Nuptial Rites in Tuscany between Giotto and the Council of Trent." In *Women, Family, and Ritual in Renaissance Italy*. Trans. Lydia Cochrane. Chicago, 1985.

———, ed. *A History of Women in the West*, vol. 2: *Silences of the Middle Ages*. Cambridge, Mass., 1992. See especially pp. 213–30.

Searle, Mark, and Kenneth W. Stevenson. *Documents of the Marriage Liturgy*. Collegeville, Minn., 1992.

Stevenson, Kenneth W. *Nuptial Blessing: A Study of Christian Marriage Rites*. London, 1982.

Extreme Unction

Dudley, Martin R. "Holy Joys in Store: Oils and Anointing in the Catholic Church." In *The Oil of Gladness*, ed. Martin Dudley and Geoffrey Rowell, pp. 113–33 (with bibliography). Collegeville, Minn., 1993.

THE OFFICE FOR ST. CECILIA

SHERRY L. REAMES

THE OFFICE FOR ST. CECILIA provides a good introduction to the material on saints in Western liturgical books because it is one of the earliest and most standardized offices for a non-Biblical saint. Cecilia was venerated as an early Roman martyr who founded an important church in Trastevere, and her liturgical cult in Rome goes back to at least the sixth century. Although she never became as popular a saint as Margaret of Antioch or Katherine of Alexandria, the influence of Roman tradition was sufficiently strong to ensure the observance of Cecilia's feast day (22 November) throughout the medieval West. For the sake of coherence, the present chapter will focus on examples from one region, the British Isles.

Cecilia's feast must have been well-established in Britain even before the Norman Conquest, for it appears routinely in monastic calendars written before 1100, and Aelfric retold her legend in an Anglo-Saxon homily, presumably intended for public reading on this occasion. After the Conquest some of Cecilia's relics were presented to Winchester Cathedral, and a few English churches were dedicated to her;[1] but the principal evidence for her cult in late medieval Britain is found in the Latin liturgical books that give texts for her office and in the Middle English re-tellings of her legend, including one by Chaucer, which depend directly or indirectly on the

---

[1]On the relics see Susan J. Ridyard, *The Royal Saints of Anglo-Saxon England: A Study of West Saxon and East Anglican Cults* (Cambridge, 1988), p. 23 and n43. Frances Arnold-Forster identifies four English parishes with dedications to Cecilia that seem to go back to the Middle Ages (*Studies in Church Dedications: or, England's Patron Saints*, vol. 3 [London, 1899]).

liturgical sources. Cecilia has also received considerable attention from later artists and poets; one thinks, for example, of Raphael's famous painting in Bologna and of the odes for St. Cecilia's Day by Dryden and Pope. But since the Renaissance Cecilia has been understood almost exclusively as the patron saint of musicians, a simpler and less interesting identity than she had in medieval liturgy and legend.

The liturgical office for Cecilia, like those for other saints, is found in the breviary rather than the missal. That is, it belongs to the liturgy of the hours, which was celebrated by members of the clergy and monastic orders, rather than to the Mass, which was intended for Christians at large. Although most breviaries contain texts and instructions for all the services in the daily monastic round, the day hours (Prime, Terce, Sext, and None) need not concern us. All the important texts on saints were read or sung between dusk and sunrise, at Vespers, Matins, and Lauds. Of these services Matins deserves the most attention because it was the longest and most elaborate, and ordinarily the only service that included actual readings from the Lives of saints.

The Chants

Both the chants and the lessons in the office for Cecilia were drawn primarily from the anonymous *Passio S. Caeciliae*, the standard Latin account of the saint's life and passion. As a result, the chants frequently anticipate or echo the lessons, giving special emphasis to particular phrases, images, and motifs. Ruth Steiner has described the general effect created by such sets of chants:

> In being chosen to be set to music, these passages have been singled out as themes for meditation. . . . Transformed into the texts of Gregorian chants, they have become part of a cycle: they will be committed to memory, and performed in public year after year.[2]

---

[2]Ruth Steiner, "Matins Responsories and Cycles of Illustrations of Saints' Lives," in *Diakonia: Studies in Honor of Robert T. Meyer*, ed. Thomas P. Halton and Joseph P. Williman

Although the exact sequence of chants in Cecilia's office varied somewhat in different regions and jurisdictions, the passages "singled out as themes for meditation" changed remarkably little over the centuries. The version reproduced below is the Sarum or Salisbury version, taken from the most widely used liturgy in late medieval England, Scotland, and Ireland.[3] The following abbreviations have been used: 1V and 2V = First and Second Vespers; M = Matins; L = Lauds; A = Antiphon; R = Responsory; V = Verse; E = Magnificat or Benedictus antiphon; and Inv = Invitatory.[4] The texts marked with an asterisk are borrowed from the Common service for a virgin martyr, rather than proper to Cecilia herself.

First Vespers

1VA *Triduanas a Domino poposci inducias, ut domum meam ecclesiam consecrarem* [I asked the Lord for a three-day respite, so that I might consecrate my house as a church].

1VR *Cecilia me misit* [Cecilia has sent me; see MR3 below]

*Hymn: *Virginis proles* [Offspring of the Virgin]

1VE *Virgo gloriosa semper evangelium Christi gerebat in pectore suo; non diebus neque noctibus a colloquiis divinis et oratione cessabat* [The glorious virgin always carried the gospel of Christ in her breast; both by day and by night she was constantly engaged in divine conversation and prayer].

(Washington, D.C., 1986), p. 327.

[3]The edition that follows is based on the facsimile of Cambridge University Library MS Mm.ii.9 (late 13th c.) published by W. H. Frere in *Antiphonale Sarisburiense* (London, 1901–25; rept. 1966) and two later manuscripts that give the complete office with both musical notation and lessons: London, British Library MSS Add. 52359 (early 14th c.) and Add. 32427 (middle 15th c.).

[4]These abbreviations are borrowed from Andrew Hughes, whose work underlies everything I have learned about medieval liturgical offices and the manuscripts that contain them.

Matins

*Inv *Christum venerantes Deum adoremus regem regum, qui in celis Cecilie palmam hodie dedit eternam* [Honoring Christ, let us adore God, king of kings, who on this day in heaven gave Cecilia the eternal palm.]

*Canticle: *Venite* [O come].

*Hymn: Virginis proles [Offspring of the Virgin]

First Nocturn

MA1 *Cecilia virgo Almachium exsuperabat, Tyburcium et Valerianum ad coronas vocabat* [The virgin Cecilia conquered Almachius; she summoned Tiburce and Valerian to crowns].

*Ps. 8: *Domine, Dominus noster* [O Lord our Lord]

MA2 *Expansis manibus orabat ad Dominum, ut eam eriperet de inimicis* [With outstretched hands she asked the Lord to save her from her enemies].

*Ps. 18[19][5]: *Celi enarrant* [The heavens declare]

MA3 *Cilicio Cecilia membra domabat, Deum gemitibus exorabat* [With a hairshirt Cecilia tamed her flesh; with lamentations she persuaded God].

*Ps. 23[24]: *Domini est terra* [The earth is the Lord's]

Lesson 1

MR1 *Cantantibus organis, Cecilia virgo in corde suo soli Domino decantabat, dicens: Fiat, Domine, cor meum et corpus meum immaculatum, ut non confundar* [While the musical instruments played, the virgin Cecilia sang in her heart to God alone, saying: Lord, make my heart and my body undefiled, lest I be put to shame].

V *Biduanis ac triduanis jejuniis orans, suam Domino pudicitiam commendabat. Fiat* [Fasting for two or three days at a time and always praying, she entrusted her chastity to God; then repeats prayer from MR1].

---

[5]The psalm number not in brackets is the Vulgate text.

Lesson 2

MR2 *Virgo gloriosa semper evangelium Christi gerebat in pectore; Et non diebus neque noctibus vacabat a colloquiis divinis et oratione* [same text as 1VE].

V *Cilicio Cecilia membra domabat, Deum gemitibus exorabat. Et non* [same text as MA3; then repeats second half of 1VE].

Lesson 3

MR3 *Cecilia me misit ad vos, Ut ostendatis michi sanctum Urbanum, quia ad ipsum habeo secreta que perferam* [Cecilia has sent me to you so that you will show me the holy Urban, since I have secret messages to give him].

V *Tunc Valerianus perrexit et inventis pauperibus dixit: Cecilia me misit ad vos. Ut* [Then Valerian went out and, when he found the poor people, said: Cecilia has sent me to you; then repeats rest of MR3].

Second Nocturn

MA4 *Biduanis ac triduanis jejuniis orans, suam Domino pudicitiam commendabat* [same text as in verse to MR1].

*Ps. 44[45]: Eructavit [(My heart) has uttered]

MA5 *Fiat, Domine, cor meum et corpus meum immaculatum, ut non confundar* [same text as second half of MR1].

*Ps. 45[46]: *Deus noster refugium* [God is our refuge]

MA6 *Domine Jesu Christe, seminator casti consilii, suscipe seminum fructus quos in Cecilia seminasti* [Lord Jesus Christ, sower of chaste purposes, receive the fruit of the seeds which you sowed in Cecilia].

*Ps. 86[87]: *Fundamenta* [The foundations]

Lesson 4

MR4 *Beata Cecilia dixit Tyburcio: Hodie te fateor meum esse cognatum, Quia amor Dei te fecit esse contemptorem ydolorum* [Blessed Cecilia said to Tiburce: Today I take you as my kinsman, for the love of God has made you a despiser of idols].

V *Sicut enim amor Dei fratrem tuum michi conjugem fecit, ita te michi cognatum faciet. Quia* [For just as the love of God made your brother my spouse, so He will make you my kinsman; then repeats second half of MR4]

Lesson 5

MR5 *Domine Jesu Christe, pastor bone, seminator casti consilii, suscipe seminum fructus quos in Cecilia seminasti. Cecilia famula tua quasi apes tibi argumentosa deservit* [Lord Jesus Christ, good shepherd, sower (text continues as MA6). Your ingenious handmaid Cecilia serves you as the bees do].[6]

V *Nam sponsum, quem quasi leonem ferocem accepit, ad te quasi agnum mansuetissimum destinavit. Cecilia* [For her spouse, whom she received as a fierce lion, she has sent to you as a very gentle lamb; then repeats second half of MR5].

Lesson 6

MR6 *Cilicio Cecilia membra domabat, Deum gemitibus exorabat; Almachium exsuperabat, Tyburcium et Valerianum ad coronas vocabat* [same text as MA3, followed by all but first two words of MA1].

V *Non diebus neque noctibus cessabat a colloquiis divinis et oratione. Almachium* [text as second half of 1VE, followed by all but first two words of MA1]

Third Nocturn

MA7 *Beata Cecilia dixit ad Tyburcium: Hodie te fateor meum esse cognatum, quia amor Dei te fecit esse contemptorem ydolorum* [same text as MR4].

*Ps. 95[96]: *Cantate* [O sing] i[7]

---

[6]Discussing *argumentosa* and the image of a bee as applied to Cecilia, Thomas Connolly points out the bee's traditional associations with virginity (because it was believed to reproduce asexually), the bringing of light (because it produced the wax for candles), and prophecy, wisdom, and eloquence (because honey was thought to be related to manna, the "food of angels" provided by God); see esp. part 1 of Connolly's "Legend of Saint Cecilia," *Studi musicali* 7 (1978): 20–21.

[7]I.e., the first psalm with this ***incipit***.

MA8 *Credimus Christum Filium Dei verum Deum esse, qui sibi talem elegit famulam* [We believe Christ, the son of God, is the true God, since he has chosen such a handmaid for himself].

*Ps. 96[97]: *Dominus regnavit* [The Lord has reigned]

MA9 *Nos scientes sanctum nomen, omnino negare non possumus* [We who know that name to be holy cannot deny it at all].

*Ps. 97[98]: *Cantate* [O sing] ii

Lesson 7

MR7 *Ceciliam intra cubiculum orantem invenit, et juxta eam stantem angelum Domini, Quem videns Valerianus nimio terrore correptus est* [He found Cecilia praying in the chamber and standing beside her an angel of the Lord; seeing him, Valerian was seized with great fear].

V *Angelus Domini descendit de celo, et lumen refulsit in habitaculo, Quem* [The Angel of the Lord came down from heaven, and light shone brightly in the dwelling place; then repeats MR7 from "seeing him" on].

Lesson 8

MR8 *O beata Cecilia, Que duos fratres convertisti, Almachium judicem superasti, Urbanum episcopum in vultu angelico demonstrasti* [O blessed Cecilia, who converted two brothers, overcame the judge Almachius, (and) revealed Bishop Urban with the face of an angel].

V *Beata es, virgo, et gloriosa, et benedictus sermo oris tui. Que* [Blessed and glorious are you, virgin, and blessed is the discourse of your mouth; then repeats all but first 3 words of MR8].

Lesson 9

MR9 *Dum aurora finem daret, Cecilia dixit: Eya, milites Christi, abicite opera tenebrarum et induimini arma lucis* [When dawn brought the end, Cecilia said: Come on, soldiers of Christ; cast away the works of darkness and put on the armor of light].

V *Cecilia valedicens fratribus et exhortans eos ait: Eya* [Cecilia, bidding farewell to the brothers and exhorting them, said; then repeats exhortation from MR9].

Lauds

LA1 *Cantantibus organis, Cecilia Domino decantabat, dicens: Fiat cor meum immaculatum, ut non confundar* [text as MR1].

LA2 *Est secretum, Valeriane, quod tibi volo dicere: Angelum Dei habeo amatorem, qui nimio zelo custodit corpus meum* [There is a secret, Valerian, which I want to tell you: I have an angel of God as my lover, who guards my body with extreme jealousy].

LA3 *Valerianus in cubiculo Ceciliam cum angelo orantem invenit* [Valerian found Cecilia in the chamber with an angel, praying].

LA4 **Benedico te, pater Domini mei Jesu Christi, quia per filium tuum ignis extinctus est a latere meo* [I bless you, father of my lord Jesus Christ, because the fire in my body has been quenched through your son].

LA5 *Cecilia famula tua, Domine, quasi apes tibi argumentosa deservit* [text as second sentence in MR5].

LE *Dum aurora finem daret, Cecilia exclamavit, dicens: Eya, milites Christi, abicite opera tenebrarum et induimini arma lucis* [text as MR9 except that here it is "Cecilia cried out, saying"].

Second Vespers

2VE *O beata Cecilia, que duos fratres convertisti, Almachium judicem superasti, Urbanum episcopum in vultu angelico demonstrasti* [text as MR8].

A rather unusual feature of this office is its tendency to repeat the same excerpts from the text, some of them two or three times. When the office was sung, of course, such repetitions would have created subtler and more interesting effects than they do on the page, and all the more so because the musical settings would often change. In fact, when a given passage was set as both an antiphon and a responsory, as happens again and again in this office, the two sung versions would be quite different because antiphons tended to be relatively straightforward pieces of music, generally using just one or two notes per syllable, while responsories were much more florid and elaborate, with extended melismas and the possibility of complex interplay between the response itself (sung by the choir), the verse (sung by the

Figure 1. The Sarum antiphon on "Cantantibus organis" (LA1), from BL Add. 32427.

cantor), and the partial repeat of the response (by the choir) that the form required. The point is clearly illustrated by the differences between Figure 1 and Figure 2.[8]

By comparing the texts of the chants with the legend from which they were derived, one can see which parts of the saint's life have been singled out for attention. In the Sarum Office the first Matins antiphon, the sixth and eighth Matins responsories, and the very last antiphon, at Second Vespers, give overviews of Cecilia's life that include her conversion of Tiburce and her victory over the persecutor Almachius. For the most part, however, the chants keep returning to much earlier sections of the legend. In fact, eight of the chants echo the very beginning, with its account of the saint's habitual piety, her hair shirt, and her fasts and fervent prayers before her wedding (1VE, MA3, MR1, MR2, MA4, MA5, MR6, and LA1). The second Lauds antiphon comes from her wedding-night revelation to her

---

[8]I am indebted to Denise P. Gallo for making these two transcriptions from the medieval musical notation system in BL Add. 32427.

Figure 2. The Sarum responsory on "Cantantibus organis" (MR1), from BL Add. 32427.

husband, Valerian. The third Matins responsory refers to Valerian's journey to find Pope Urban, who is to baptize him. MR5, MA6, and LA5 are excerpts from Urban's prayer of thanksgiving on this occasion, and MR7 and LA3 describe Valerian's ability to see the angel when he returns to Cecilia. By contrast, only two chants are derived from the long scene in which Valerian's brother, Tiburce, is converted: MR4 and MA7, both of which quote Cecilia's joyful reaction when Tiburce demonstrates his willingness to renounce idol-worship. And the martyrdoms of the three saints provide only five chants, none of which refers unambiguously to martyrdom. Three of these are derived from the scenes relating Cecilia's arrest, trial, and martyrdom, but one would have to know the legend well in order to recognize their original context: MA8, a tribute to the saint spoken in the legend by the officers sent to arrest her; MA9, a tiny excerpt from one of her own speeches at her trial; and the very first chant, 1VA, an excerpt from her final speech to Urban before she dies. Much clearer and more emphatic are the last Matins responsory and the Benedictus antiphon at Lauds, which repeat Cecilia's exhortation to her converts on the day of their execution, which preceded her own arrest.

If one continues the analysis by focusing on the structure of the Sarum Office as well as its chosen themes, a more coherent picture emerges. One notices that most of the chants used for First Vespers and the first nocturn of Matins are united by the theme of assiduous prayer. The only apparent exceptions are 1VA, MA1, and MR3. The second nocturn emphasizes the virgin saint's purity (MA4 and MA5) and her fruitfulness, as shown in her conversions of Tiburce and Valerian; MR6 and its verse link her fruitfulness back to prayer. The antiphons of the third nocturn can be seen as declarations of faith by Cecilia and her converts, and the responsories that follow share the themes of vision, revelation of hidden realities, and light. In short, the central theme of the office as a whole seems to be the virtues and rewards of the contemplative life. The significance of some details remains elusive, however. Displaced from its literal, narrative context to the very beginning of the Sarum Office, is 1VA inviting us to hear the words as if spoken by Christ as well as Cecilia? What symbolic meaning is implicit in the "Cecilia me misit" passage, explaining its selection as a text to be sung over and over (at MR3 and First Vespers)? What is MR7 suggesting when it revises the original sequence of events, linking Valerian's fear to his first sight of the angel in Cecilia's chamber rather than to the earlier and more mysterious supernatural messenger (the old man who suddenly appeared after Urban's prayer, catechized Valerian, and then vanished)?

Some of these questions are answered when one turns from the Sarum version of the office to the earlier versions edited by R.-J. Hesbert in the

Corpus Antiphonalium Officii.[9] Somewhat surprisingly, the manuscripts collated by Hesbert suggest that the original form of the office was not monastic (as one might have guessed from the emphasis on contemplation) but secular—designed for use in a cathedral or collegiate church. Five of the early manuscripts he chooses to exemplify the secular tradition or "cursus romain"—manuscripts dating from the ninth century to the twelfth and ascribed respectively to Compiègne, Bamberg, Ivrea, Monza, and Verona—include the office for Cecilia,[10] and they present a remarkably uniform picture: the same nine antiphons and nine responsories, in the same order, are given for Matins in all five manuscripts, and so are five of the antiphons for Lauds. Hesbert's early monastic exemplars of the office show no such uniformity; in order to complete the monastic form of the Matins service, which required thirteen antiphons and twelve responsories, the monks had to supplement the secular office with additional chants, and these were chosen and ordered quite differently in different communities.

The principal difference between the chants in the Sarum Office for Cecilia, given above, and the traditional secular office Hesbert found on the Continent is that the traditional office does more to encourage a figurative or symbolic reading of the legend. The chants used at Matins are ordered somewhat differently than they are in the Sarum Office, departing more often from a chronological or narrative sequence.[11] But the difference is shown more clearly in the verses chosen to complete some of the

---

[9]*Corpus antiphonalium officii*, ed. René-Jean Hesbert and Renatus Prévost, 6 vols. (Rome, 1963–79).

[10]Unfortunately, the eleventh-century manuscript that Hesbert chose to represent the secular tradition in northern France—and, by extension, England—is very incomplete, lacking not only the office for Cecilia but also all the offices in the Sanctorale from the beginning of Easter season to the end of the liturgical year.

[11]Using the numbers from the Sarum version, given above, the chants at Matins in the traditional secular office are ordered as follows: MA1, MA2, MA3; MR1, MR8, MR2; MA6, MA7, MA5; MR6, MR7, MR5; MA8, MA9, and a non-Sarum antiphon (quoted below in the text); MR4, MR3, MR9.

responsories. Thus, whereas the responsory "Beata Cecilia dixit" (MR4 above) is followed in the Sarum Office by the next sentence from the same speech to Tiburce, the traditional office is more imaginative, repeating part of Urban's prayer about Valerian so that Tiburce symbolically becomes the second child of Cecilia's union with God: "Suscipe, Domine, seminum fructus quos in Cecilia seminasti" [Lord, receive the fruit of the seeds which you sowed in Cecilia; compare MA6 above]. Whereas the responsory "Virgo gloriosa" (MR2 above), which commends Cecilia's example of constant prayer, is followed in the Sarum Office by a verse on her hair shirt and sighs, the traditional office links it more boldly with Cecilia's revelation to Valerian that she has an angelic lover and guardian (a text used only as LA2 in Sarum), thus reinforcing the idea that the contemplative virgin saint participates in the life of the angels.[12]

Even more interesting is the way the traditional office treats the "Cecilia me misit" passage. The responsory with this incipit (MR3 above) is used in the third nocturn, just before the climactic exhortation to Cecilia's converts, and connected with a different verse than the one in the Sarum Office. The whole responsory now reads as follows:

R *Cecilia me misit ad vos, ut ostendatis michi sanctum Urbanum, Quia ad ipsum habeo secreta que perferam* [Cecilia has sent me to you so that you will show me the holy Urban, since I have secret messages to give him].

V *Tunc Valerianus perrexit ad antistitem, et signo quod acceperat invenit sanctum Urbanum; quia* [Then Valerian went forth to the bishop, and by the sign he had been given he found the holy Urban; since I . . .].

The verse here poses more difficulty than its Sarum counterpart because it abruptly shifts from third-person to first-person discourse when it repeats the clause from the responsory, and by adding *ad antistitem* it also seems to be treating the discovery of Urban as a two-stage process—as if Valerian

[12]Thomas Connolly discusses the significance of this motif in the early images of Cecilia and other virgin saints in his *Mourning into Joy: Music, Raphael, and Saint Cecilia* (New Haven, 1994), p. 197 and its notes, pp. 325–26.

first found the bishop and only later identified him as the saint. The traditional office places further emphasis on this text by using it twice, the second time as its ninth antiphon for Matins. The final piece of the puzzle is provided by the way the traditional office completes the responsory "O beata Cecilia" (MR8 above): it uses the verse "Cecilia me misit ad vos, ut ostendatis mihi" before the repeated clause "Urbanum episcopum in vultu angelico demonstrasti," so that the reading becomes "Cecilia sent me to you so that you might show me Bishop Urban; you revealed [Bishop Urban] with the face [*or* in the appearance] of an angel." Again there is a syntactic shift, since the two second-person verbs seem to have different subjects; but the key point here is the explicitness with which the "Cecilia me misit" passage is interpreted as another text about the revelation of a hidden reality—in this case, the angelic nature of Urban. Given the prominence of this motif in the traditional office and the wording of the verse that begins "Tunc Valerianus perrexit ad antistitem," one can only conclude that the author(s) of this office understood the mysterious old man who catechizes Valerian to be a second, angelic manifestation of Urban, rather than a separate character as a more literal reading of the legend suggests. And, unlike the later author(s) who compiled the Sarum Office, they considered this strange supernatural event just as valuable a theme for meditation as the saint's imitable example of fasts and prayers.

Although many other versions of the office for Cecilia were used in medieval Britain, all the surviving ones bear a close resemblance to one or both of the versions that have already been described. In fact, the version in the Hereford liturgy is almost identical with the Sarum version. The York version follows the traditional secular office in the way it orders the chants at Matins but agrees much more frequently with the Sarum Office with regard to the verses used after the responsories. The monastic versions of Cecilia's office used in Britain, as on the Continent, can most easily be understood as elaborations of the traditional secular office. Cluny and the Cistercians attempted to ensure uniformity of practice, each adopting a single liturgy that was used in all their foundations, but most Benedictine houses evidently were free to follow whichever version of a saint's office they deemed most appropriate or convenient. The Franciscans adopted the secular form of the liturgy that was used by the Roman curia and helped to spread it all over Christendom. In the case of Cecilia, the chants in Franciscan and Roman curia breviaries are very close to the traditional secular office, with a few distinctive changes: they use the antiphon "Est secretum" at First Vespers instead of Lauds, reorder the remaining Lauds antiphons and add "Triduanas a Domino" to fill out the sequence, and change two of the responsory verses at Matins. The Dominican version of the office has more resemblances to the Sarum version—not a surprising phenomenon, since the Dominican liturgy was drawn up by a small commission that used existing liturgical books as models and included a representative from England. Although the Dominican office for Cecilia remains fairly close to the traditional secular office for both First Vespers and the order of the chants at Matins, the verses it uses after the responsories agree with those in the Sarum Office eight times out of nine.[13]

The Lessons

The lessons about saints in medieval liturgical books have received relatively little attention in modern times, but they deserve to be studied because they can tell us a good deal about the interpretation, use, and cultural importance of saints' legends in medieval society. One little-known fact about these lessons is that they were far more variable than the other texts in the office. Whereas the surviving Ordinals of the various liturgies give exact specifications for the chants, psalms, and virtually every other aspect

[13]The only exception is the verse after "Cecilia me misit," for which the Dominican office has "Cumque signo acceperitis benedictionem eius, ducite me ad sanctum antistitem." Another distinctive feature of this office is the use of the antiphon "Triduanas a Domino" for Second Vespers. An edition of the entire Dominican antiphonal from the authoritative thirteenth-century manuscript preserved in the Dominican Archives in Rome (MS Santa Sabina XIV.L.1) is now available as part of vol. 2 of Andrew Hughes, *Late Medieval Liturgical Offices: Resources for Electronic Research: Sources and Chants* (Toronto, 1996).

of the daily office, they generally say just two things about the lessons to be read at Matins: (1) the number to be drawn from each kind of source (saint's legend, Gospel, and/or homily); and (2) the *incipit* of the first lesson from each source. The looseness of the rules on this point obviously permitted a good deal of variation with regard to the length and exact content of the lessons, even those that were based on the Bible and patristic homilies; and with regard to the less authoritative material in legends it permitted wholesale abbreviation and rewriting. And that is exactly what happened.

It is worth pausing to note that readings from legends were not just a minor element in medieval breviaries. On the feast day of an important saint, at least the first two nocturns—six lessons in secular breviaries and eight in monastic ones—would ordinarily be drawn from the saint's legend, and the remaining lessons from a homily on an appropriate passage from the Gospel. Often the saint's legend occupied more than two-thirds of the lessons, especially in secular liturgies. For example, the York office for Cecilia devoted eight lessons to her legend and just one (lesson 7) to the homily. The Sarum Office devoted all nine of its lessons to the legend, as did the Franciscan and Dominican Offices.

No matter how many lessons were given over to the saint's legend, however, late medieval breviaries show a clear and widespread tendency to make those lessons shorter and shorter. The causes of this phenomenon have been much debated. To some extent it presumably reflects actual attempts to shorten the public celebrations of Matins that had to be held every night in monasteries, cathedrals, and other communities of clergy. But two other factors seem to have been more important: the growing practice of private recitation, which permitted each individual to decide how long the lessons should be; and the sheerly practical consideration that breviaries could be made much smaller, more portable, and less expensive if the lessons were cut very short. For our purposes, what matters most about this process is that it required the abbreviators to make choices, and in the process to reveal something about their own priorities and ways of reading the text. Given what we know about the way breviaries were produced, we even can be reasonably sure about the demographic make-up of the abbreviating readers in our survey: most compilers and copyists who had the necessary knowledge to make breviaries were themselves members of the clergy, employed for this task by other members of the clergy.

The easiest and most old-fashioned way of shortening a set of lessons was just to copy some excerpts from the parent text, dividing them into the desired number of lessons. In the case of Cecilia, the breviaries that use this method tend overwhelmingly to take their excerpts from the opening scenes of the legend. Fairly typical are British Library MSS Harley 4664 (ca. 1300) and Add. 43406 (late fourteenth century), both English Benedictine breviaries, which begin with the first words of the narrative and faithfully reproduce almost everything in the first two episodes; Harley breaks off near the end of Cecilia's directions to Valerian, and Additional in the middle of Urban's prayer. Although the lessons in such breviaries look fragmentary to a modern eye, that may not have been a great disadvantage to their original users. Most obviously, there was no need for full versions of the lessons in breviaries that were used in communities where Matins was publicly celebrated, since the designated lector always would read the real lessons aloud from a larger book. Verbatim excerpts, even fragmentary ones, also would serve a purpose when the exact wording of a text was considered very important. Biblical passages were treated this way in liturgical manuscripts, and excerpts from saints' legends might be deemed to deserve the same treatment if they were rich in symbols and allusions. Hence it is probably no accident that the breviaries with verbatim excerpts from the Cecilia legend tend to reproduce the same portions of the legend that were emphasized in the chants for her office: the initial description of her piety, her hair shirt and fasts and fervent prayers before her wedding, her wedding-night conversation with Valerian, his baptism, and his return to find the angel made visible. As the office was celebrated, the lessons and chants would reinforce each other, both drawing participants' attention to the inherited ideals and symbols of the contemplative life.

By the end of the Middle Ages, however, more pragmatic ideas about the lessons at Matins were competing with the traditional ones. Liturgists had discovered the advantages of making actual abridgements of hagiographical texts—omitting or changing enough words to produce an account of the saint that was both efficient and reasonably complete as a narrative. This innovation has been attributed to the thirteenth century, when the authors or reformers of various secular liturgies drew up whole lectionaries that consisted of "choir legends"—brief, self-standing accounts of the saints that were intended specifically to provide lessons of the appropriate number and length for Matins. One of the earliest and most influential choir legends of Cecilia was the version adopted by the Roman curia and the Franciscans, which begins and ends just like the *Passio* but drastically abridges some events in the middle of the narrative; this was the abridgement that Chaucer followed for the second half of his Second Nun's Tale.[14] The Dominicans produced a distinctive choir legend of their own and included it in an official lectionary, which scribes were ordered to reproduce without further omissions or changes. The best-known choir legend from England itself is the one given in the fullest early printed editions of the Sarum Breviary and reproduced in the nineteenth-century edition by Procter and Wordsworth. Yet another choir legend seems to be the source of the lessons on Cecilia in most York breviaries.[15] Despite the historical and textual importance of these choir legends, however, they represent just a small fraction of the abridgements that actually circulated in breviaries. Even among Franciscan and Dominican breviaries, where unusual efforts were made to standardize the lessons, most of the manuscripts give lessons for Cecilia that are a great deal shorter than the prescribed choir legend. Among English secular breviaries the picture is even more chaotic—and more interesting—because a large proportion of the copyists or compilers

[14]For more detail and a full text of the Franciscan/Roman curia choir legend for Cecilia see Sherry L. Reames, "A Recent Discovery Concerning the Sources of Chaucer's 'Second Nun's Tale'," *Modern Philology* 87 (1990): 337–61.

[15]In the case of the York breviary, the standard choir legend from which the shorter versions derive is evidently the version preserved in Oxford, Bodleian MS Laud Misc. 84 and York, York Minster MS Add. 69; the early printed edition reproduced by the Surtees Society is an abridgement.

of manuscripts evidently felt free to create their own abridgements, further abbreviating and rewriting the choir legends in whatever way they liked. In a sample of sixty manuscripts of the Sarum breviary and lectionary, in fact, I have found nineteen different abridgements of the legend, ranging from the choir legend (which averages about 180 words per lesson) to very efficient synopses in which the lessons are less than 1/5 as long.

Amid the rather bewildering diversity of abridged versions, one can identify several significant patterns that occur again and again in the secular breviary lessons on Cecilia. First, there seems to be a growing emphasis on the literal events of the saint's life, at the expense of the kinds of symbolic meaning that were so important to the author(s) of the chants. Consider the opening lesson in Stonyhurst College MS 40 (ca. 1400), one of the most efficient Sarum versions:

> *Beata Cecilia virgo clarissima Valerianum habebat sponsum, qui diem constituit nupciarum. Cantantibus igitur organis, Cecilia soli Deo decantabat, dicens: Fiat, Domine, cor meum et corpus meum immaculatum, ut non confundar* [The blessed and most noble virgin Cecilia had Valerian as her betrothed, and he set the day for the wedding. Then, while the musical instruments were singing, Cecilia sang to God alone, saying, "Lord, make my heart and body undefiled, lest I be put to shame"].

In comparison with both the *Passio* and the Sarum choir legend, from which it is condensed, this abridgement leaves out the initial references to Cecilia's secret faith and ceaseless prayer, her dedication to virginity, and the hair shirt and strenuous fasts with which she reinforced her appeals to God as her wedding day approached. As a result, the abridgement has much less drama to engage the reader than the fuller versions had. But the key difference is that the abridgement has preserved almost nothing to identify Cecilia as a model of the contemplative life. Although the chants in her office would still suggest the traditional themes for meditation, the abridged lessons get on with the plot.[16]

---

[16]At least twenty other Sarum manuscripts do essentially the same thing.

The pragmatic orientation of the secular breviaries is even clearer in their final lessons on this saint. In the chants for Cecilia's office, as we have seen, the most important aspects of her legend were those exemplified at the beginning; and more traditional liturgical manuscripts maintained this focus, often selecting all their lessons from the scenes leading up to Valerian's baptism and his return to meet the angel. In secular English breviaries, in contrast, it was clearly important to identify Cecilia as a martyr, and they go to some lengths to include her death in the last lesson. Their care in this regard stands out because not even the full-length version of the legend had treated Cecilia's death as a climactic event. The narrative in the *Passio* ended with the following steps: the attempt to behead Cecilia; her three-day survival, during which she continued to encourage her followers; her final arrangements for her followers and property, including her last speech to Pope Urban on these matters; his burial of her body and consecration of her house, in accord with her wish; and a closing formula that mentions the services still held in that church, down to the present day. The actual moment of the saint's death was not important enough to mention. What mattered were the arrangements before it and the ceremonies afterward, which incorporated her individual witness into the life of the Church. In the majority of English secular breviaries, in contrast, the martyr's death has become the key point. The fullest York versions include most of the steps in the original sequence but end the text with Cecilia's burial and insert this sentence after her final speech: "Ipsa vero post hec verba spiritum celo reddidit" [After these words she yielded up her spirit to heaven]. The fullest Sarum versions run as far as the burial, or even the consecration of her house, with a similar addition on her death: "Et hec dicens, reddidit spiritum" [And saying this, she yielded up her spirit]. More typically, both Sarum and non-Sarum English breviaries omit the later ceremonies, taking Cecilia's death as the logical end of the legend. And they use so many different wordings and selections of detail as to suggest that a number of different abbreviators made this decision independently.[17]

---

[17]For example, Bodl. MS Can. lit. 215, a Sarum breviary written for use in Ireland (ca. 1400), ends the narrative with the saint's care for her followers and her death: "per triduum

The new orientation of these late medieval secular breviaries also affects the way they treat supernatural events. The best example in the Cecilia legend is Valerian's encounter with the mysterious old man when he goes to Urban to be baptized. In the *Passio* the old man, described as wearing white garments and carrying a book written with golden letters, appeared so suddenly and miraculously in response to Urban's prayer that Valerian fell down before him, overcome with fear. As we have seen, the chants for the traditional office of Cecilia make a good deal of this scene, connecting the old man both with the angel in the next scene and with Urban himself. The Sarum and York choir legends both retain the details from the *Passio*, but the manuscripts with abridged lessons betray a good deal of discontent with the complexity and mysteriousness of this little episode. The simplest and most drastic solution was to leave out the old man entirely, and a remarkably large proportion of both Sarum and York manuscripts actually have adopted this solution. Although the exact wording of what is left differs from manuscript to manuscript, the account in British Library MS Stowe 12 (ca. 1325, Sarum) is quite typical:

> *Perrexit enim Valerianus ad episcopum, cui cum dixisset omnia verba Cecilie gavisus senex baptizavit eum, docensque eum omnem fidei regulam, remisit ad Ceciliam* [Valerian went forth to the bishop. When he had told him everything Cecilia said, the old man rejoiced and baptized him, taught him the whole rule of faith, and sent him back to Cecilia].[18]

---

supervixit. Puellas quas nutrivit in fide Christi confirmatas, sancto Urbano tradidit commendendas et spiritum emisit." BL Add. 32427 and Salisbury Cathedral 152, both Sarum breviaries with musical notation from western England (middle to late 15th c.), skip from the mention of her three-day survival to her death: "Et sic supervixit per triduum, et postea Domino tradidit spiritum." CUL MS Ii.4.20, a Benedictine breviary from Ely (ca. 1300), ends with wording that does not sound like the *Passio* at all but also makes room for the saint's death: "Ignem quidem superavit, sed ferro occisa est, et ita perrexit ad Dominum."

[18]Some versions are even more efficient than Stowe—for example, Douai Bibl. Mun. 167 (early 15th c., Sarum): "Tunc Cecilia misit eum ad sanctum Urbanum episcopum, qui baptizavit eum et doctum in fide remisit ad Ceciliam."

Some Sarum manuscripts take a middle course, which suggests just what they found problematic about the old man. The abridged version in Stonyhurst 40 makes the episode both simpler and more mundane by blending the old man's role with Urban's and removing most of the marvellous details:

> *Misit ergo illum Cecilia ad Urbanum episcopum ut eum baptizaret. Subito siquidem apparuit Valeriano senex quidam tenens titulum aureis litteris scriptum sic: Unus dominus, una fides, unum baptisma. Credis inquit hec, cui ait: Nichil verius credi possit sub celo, et baptizatur* [Therefore Cecilia sent him to Urban to be baptized. Further, a certain old man suddenly appeared to Valerian, carrying a book written with golden letters which said, "One Lord, one faith, one baptism." He asked, "Do you believe this?" Valerian answered, "Nothing truer can be believed beneath heaven," and was baptized.]

Several other Sarum manuscripts also retain the old man but de-emphasize the supernatural aspects of his appearance. In Edinburgh University MS 26 (ca. 1350) and Cambridge King's College MS 30 (ca. 1400), for example, there is almost nothing to distinguish him from an ordinary catechist until the end of the scene, when he vanishes.

The English secular breviaries' focus on the literal dimension of the saint's life and their apparent preference for relatively sober and edifying material, instead of the spectacular and marvelous, are borne out in their accounts of other saints.[19] These priorities also are consistent with another important pattern in the lessons about Cecilia: the attention paid to examples of saintly conduct that could be held up as models to contemporary Christians. It is significant, though not very surprising, that the secular English breviaries—i.e., those written primarily for clergy who were expected to work with the laity—seem more concerned than the monastic

---

[19]Among 48 Sarum breviary manuscripts that retell most of the Margaret legend, e.g., fully 35 (about 73%) completely omit the famous episode in which the devil appeared to her in the form of a dragon. Similarly, the dragon and other marvelous episodes in the legend of St. Sylvester tend to disappear from the retellings in secular breviaries, displaced by realistic details about the saint's career and moral virtues.

ones to provide models that conform with late medieval ideas of how laymen and -women should behave. In the case of Cecilia, as we have seen, most of them greatly de-emphasize the traditional theme of contemplation and add a new emphasis on a holy death. More significantly, they tend to omit or rewrite extensively those parts of the legend which portray her as transgressing the usual norms of womanly behavior: two scenes in which she is shown as a powerful and authoritative teacher of the faith, preaching first to Tiburce and then publicly to the officers sent to arrest her; and the dramatic trial scene in which she stands up to the persecutor, Almachius, defying his commands and scoffing at the power he claims to have. There is just enough space here to illustrate what happens to Cecilia's trial.[20]

Although Cecilia's confrontation with Almachius is the climax of the legend in some re-tellings—including the ones in the Roman/Franciscan Breviary, Chaucer's *Canterbury Tales*, the *Legenda aurea*, and most of the vernacular *Golden Legends*—most English secular breviaries go to some lengths to get around it. Copies of the York Breviary adopt the simplest solution, removing all mention of the trial; Cecilia's arrest, presumably for her relationship with the just-martyred Valerian, is immediately followed by her execution. Sarum breviaries, on the other hand, nearly always retain Almachius's enraged command that Cecilia be executed, and they attempt to provide a suitable explanation for his anger. The choir legend gives excerpts from the trial; but a surprisingly large proportion of the abridged versions avoid the whole dialogue between Cecilia and Almachius, replacing it with brief summaries which change its actual tenor. Thus Cecilia's combativeness is transformed into something more acceptable—most often, exemplary firmness of principle. In the printed Aberdeen Breviary and sixteen Sarum breviary manuscripts, Almachius grows angry and condemns her to

[20]For the scenes in which she preaches and other details omitted here, see my article "*Mouvance* and Interpretation in Late-Medieval Latin: The Legend of St. Cecilia in British Breviaries," in *Medieval Literature: Texts and Interpretation*, ed. Tim W. Machan (Binghamton, N. Y., 1991), pp. 159–89.

die just because she refuses to sacrifice ["cum sacrificare nollet" or "cum sacrificare contempneret"]. In the Scottish Sarum breviary (later fifteenth century) published under the title of its owner, the Marquess of Bute, Cecilia's only offense is to confess that she is a Christian ["cum se Christianam esse confiteretur"]. BL Stowe 12 and Longleat House 10 (both early fourteenth century, Sarum) manage to credit her with two suitably unaggressive kinds of Christian heroism—commitment to her faith and great generosity to the poor:

> *cum omnia pauperibus erogasset, cepit eam Almachius compellere ut ydolis sacrificaret, sed eam nullatenus a proposito fidei potuit dimoveri* [since she had given everything to the poor (which the persecutor wished to seize), Almachius began to force her to sacrifice to the idols, but could not budge her at all from the precept of the faith].[21]

When they replace Cecilia's combativeness with more edifying examples of Christian and womanly virtue, the English clergymen who compiled these breviaries in the fourteenth and fifteenth centuries confirm once again that they are reading the legend more literally than their predecessors did. At the same time, however, they clearly set themselves apart from all their own contemporaries who expected saints' legends to provide dramatic confrontations and other sensational kinds of entertainment. Eamon Duffy has recently argued that "no substantial gulf existed [in the late medieval English church] between the religion of the clergy and the educated élite on the one hand and that of the people at large on the other."[22] But if Duffy and other recent authorities are right about the tastes and priorities of the "people at large," they were attracted to saints' legends by exactly the kinds of

---

[21]I quote from Stowe. Longleat has different wording about the sacrifice Almachius wants her to make. A third Sarum manuscript, Liverpool Cathedral MS 37 (later 14th century), agrees with Stowe for the beginning of this passage but omits the final clause.

[22]Eamon Duffy, *The Stripping of the Altars: Traditional Religion in England, c.1400–c.1580* (New Haven, 1992), p. 2.

material that contemporary members of the clergy were removing from their breviaries. In short, these breviary lessons strongly suggest that the late medieval English Church was by no means a single, homogeneous reading community where the legends of saints were concerned. There were noticeable tensions over some issues, including the role of the miraculous, the attention paid to marvels more generally, and the perceived transgressiveness of some saints' behavior; and efforts at reform were already underway—well before the Reformation of the sixteenth century.

Additional Bibliography

British Liturgical Books: Modern Facsimiles and Reprints

Breviarium ad usum insignis ecclesie Eboracensis. Ed. Stephen W. Lawley. 2 vols. Surtees Society 71, 75. Durham, 1880–1883.

Breviarium ad usum insignis ecclesiae Sarum. Ed. Francis Procter and Christopher Wordsworth. 3 vols. Cambridge, 1879–1886.

Breviarium Bothanum; sive, Portiforium secundum usum ecclesiae cujusdam in Scotia. Ed. W. D. Macray. London, 1900.

The Hereford Breviary. Ed. Walter H. Frere and Langton E. G. Brown. 3 vols. Henry Bradshaw Society 26, 40, 46. London, 1904–1915.

The Monastic Breviary of Hyde Abbey, Winchester. Ed. John B. L. Tolhurst. Henry Bradshaw Society 69, 70, 71, 76, 78, 80. London, 1932–1942.

Other Important Sources on Liturgical Chants and Lessons

Hesbert, René-Jean. "The Sarum Antiphoner: Its Sources and Influence." *Journal of the Plainsong and Mediaeval Music Society* 3 (1980): 49–55.

Salmon, Pierre. *The Breviary through the Centuries*. Trans. Sister David Mary. Collegeville, Minn., 1962.

Stevens, John. *Words and Music in the Middle Ages: Song, Narrative, Dance, and Drama, 1050–1350* [esp. ch. 8]. Cambridge, 1986.

Van Dijk, Stephen J. P., and Joan Hazelden Walker. *The Origins of the Modern Roman Liturgy: The Liturgy of the Papal Court and the Franciscan Order in the Thirteenth Century*. Westminster, Md., 1960.

Sources Specifically on Cecilia's Cult and Legend

Connolly, Thomas. "The Legend of Saint Cecilia." *Studi musicali* 7 (1978): 3–37; 9 (1980): 3–44.

Delehaye, Hippolyte. *Étude sur le légendier romain: les saints de Novembre et de Décembre*, pp. 73–96 [commentary], 194–220 [edition of the *Passio*]. Brussels, 1936.

PART THREE

THE PHYSICAL SETTING OF THE LITURGY

ARCHITECTURE AS LITURGICAL SETTING

ELIZABETH C. PARKER

EVEN IF IT IS NOT POSSIBLE to specify the degree to which church architecture has determined the shape of the liturgy, or has been shaped by it, it is nevertheless safe to say that from early Christian times the architectural environment of a church has been used to create a dramatic setting for liturgical ritual which, in varying forms, enhances a sense of divine presence in the midst of its performance.[1] The best known church buildings of the Middle Ages are the great cathedrals of the twelfth and thirteenth centuries—Notre Dame in Paris, for example (Fig. 1). These achievements, however, were neither the beginning nor the end of a long evolution of architectural design at the service of liturgical practice. In the course of the Middle Ages, adaptations of the form and space of a building, the arrangement of church furniture, and the principal wall and altar decoration all reflect a consistent concern to assert the reality of the intersection of the past and future of ongoing church time and the present liturgical moment of the celebration of Mass. According to Pope Gregory the Great (590–604):

---

[1]See Roger E. Reynolds, "Liturgy and Monument," in *Artistic Integration in Gothic Buildings*, ed. Virginia Chieffo Raguin, Kathryn Brush, and Peter Draper (Toronto, 1995), pp. 57–68. For their help in the preparation of this essay, I want particularly to thank Madeline Caviness, William Clark, Thomas Dale, Richard Emmerson, Dorothy Glass, Richard Gyug, Elizabeth Parker McLachlan, and Evelyn Birge Vitz. Garrick Jones prepared Figs. 6 and 7.

Figure 1. Cathedral of Notre-Dame, Paris, exterior view from the southeast. Begun 1163; completed 1225–50. Photo: Giraudon/Art Resource, N.Y.

> [W]hat right believing Christian can doubt that in the very hour of the sacrifice, at the words of the Priest, the heavens be opened, and the quires of Angels are present in that mystery of Jesus Christ; that high things are accomplished with low, and earthly joined to heavenly, and that one thing is made of visible and invisible.[2]

The primary focus of this chapter is on seeing the architecture of a church, its furnishings and decoration, as a vibrant vehicle for the processional journey in sacred time through sacred space, a solemn pilgrimage, the

---

[2]*The Dialogues of Gregory the Great* 4.58, trans. P. W., ed. Edmund Gardner (London, 1911), 256, cited by O. B. Hardison, Jr., *Christian Rite and Christian Drama in the Middle Ages: Essays in the Origin and Early History of Modern Drama* (Baltimore, 1969), p. 36.

goal of which is the eucharistic celebration at the altar, to make "one thing . . . of visible and invisible." Tracking this development is difficult when reconstructions of early church plans vary widely and early liturgical texts, which also vary, not only are scarce—especially for the early period—but also allow varying presumptions of the layout of any particular church. Furthermore, some of the prime architectural examples are buildings which are no longer standing or which have been vastly altered well into the nineteenth century. Nonetheless, we need to sketch an evolving exchange between liturgical practice and architectural space that was initiated in early Christian Rome.

Immediately on the heels of the Edict of Milan in 313, which placed Christianity among those religions recognized by the Roman Empire, the emperor Constantine initiated a church building program in Rome that was followed by those at the sacred sites in Jerusalem and at his newly founded city of Constantinople. The first of these was the Basilica of the Savior at the Lateran Palace, begun in 313—with its separate baptistry dedicated to St. John begun in 315—which he determined would be the center of the Christian community in Rome.[3] Its importance was soon to be rivaled, however, by the church dedicated to the apostle and martyr St. Peter (Fig. 2), the first and most important of the bishops of Rome, a charge that had come to him directly from Christ (Matt. 16:18–19). The church that Constantine had built around the second-century tomb containing the saint's remains was replaced by the present structure begun in the early sixteenth century.

---

[3]John Baldovin, S. J., "The Urban Character of Christian Worship: The Origins, Development and Meaning of Stational Liturgy," *Orientalia Christiana Analecta* 228 (1987): 108–09; Sible de Blaauw, *Cultus et Decor: Liturgia e architettura nella Roma tardoantica e medievale: Basilica Salvatoris, Sanctae Mariae, Sancti Petri*, 2 vols. (Vatican City, 1994), 1:130. The octagonal baptistry was the project of Pope Sixtus III (432–40). Since the time of Pope Gregory the Great, the basilica also has been identified with St. John; his relics were kept there (ibid., 1:161). For the relation of the form of the baptistry to the Holy Sepulchre at Jerusalem see Richard Krautheimer, "Introduction to an Iconography of Medieval Architecture," *Journal of the Warburg and Courtauld Institutes* 5 (1942): 1–33.

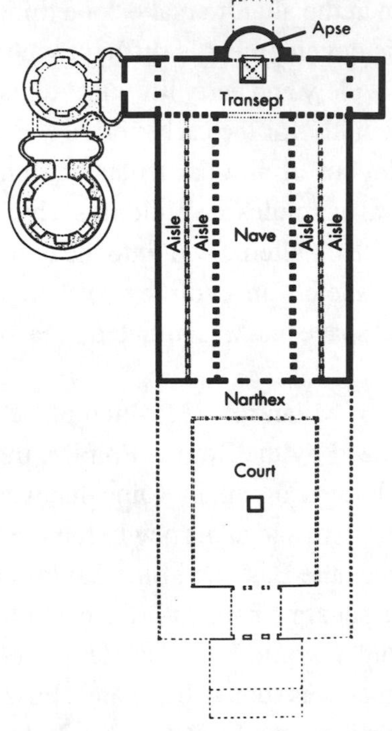

Figure 2. Plan of Old St. Peter's, Rome, as of ca. 400 (after A. Fraser; from Richard Krautheimer, *Early Christian and Byzantine Architecture* [New Haven: Yale Univ. Press, 1986], fig. 22).

The form of this and other early Christian churches is derived from secular Roman basilicas, large rectangular structures of varying design, usually with a timber roof over a central space generally on a longitudinal axis, which could be terminated by semi-circular **apse**s at one or both ends. The central area, separated by colonnades from peripheral aisles, would be lit by windows in the walls above the colonnades. These were public meeting spaces that served a variety of purposes, among them as law-courts, sanctuaries, and reception halls.[4] Old St. Peter's, too, served several functions simultaneously. Veneration of the memorial to St. Peter was an act of public penance, the primary goal of pilgrimage to Rome, and, further, its covered cemetery became a favored burial site for pilgrims as well as emperors and popes.[5] In the course of the fourth century, funerary banquets in the nave were replaced by the eucharistic celebration at the altar table, as Peter's cult increasingly was promulgated as a way to assert his memorial and his church as the symbolic center from which subsequent popes exercised their authority. Pope Leo I (440–61) established Peter's feast day on 22 February and that of Peter and

---

[4]Richard Krautheimer, *Rome: Profile of a City, 312–1308* (Princeton, 1980), p. 21.

[5]De Blaauw, *Cultus et Decor*, 2:510–13, 466 (for adjoining rotunda as mausoleum for Emperor Honorius [395–423]), and p. 469 (for burial of Pope Leo the Great in the **narthex**).

Paul on 29 June, when St. Peter's and St. Paul Outside the Walls (Fig. 3) were the ***stationes***, the places where the papal masses were held.

A stational form of liturgy was initiated by Pope Victor in 180 as a means of unifying the diverse parishes in Rome and commemorating martyr shrines in the cemeteries outside the city. By the third century the stational system incorporated the distribution of a portion of the consecrated bread to each of Rome's twelve original **titular churches**, established for the administration of baptism and penance. By the early fifth century, the more organized and elaborate papal processions extended to the new larger basilicas used on Sundays and the great feast days. Old St. Peter's was the station for the Christmas Mass, along with Santa Maria Maggiore, the church dedicated to the Virgin, and Santa Anastasia, completed by Sixtus III (432–40). St. Peter's also could serve as an alternate station for the rites of Easter and Pentecost. The primary station of the papal procession from the Lateran on Good Friday was Santa Croce in Gerusalemme, the palace church of Constantine's mother St. Helena, who is credited with the discovery of the True Cross.[6]

In the ceremonial that took place within Old St. Peter's, its long, tall nave was the processional path for the clergy, while the congregation presumably assembled in the lower, darker, double side aisles divided by colonnades. The walls of the nave were covered with images of the Old Testament on the right (north) wall and New Testament on the left (south). The papal procession was echoed in the images of prophets and saints between the **clerestory** windows and images of past popes in roundels above the columns of the nave, starting on the north wall near the image of Peter on the triumphal arch between the nave and the **transept**. This decorative program was begun in the mid-fifth century, contemporary with that

[6]De Blaauw, *Cultus et Decor*, 2:507–10; Baldovin, "The Urban Character of Christian Worship," pp. 105–48, esp. 122, for processions on alternate weeks to St. Peter's, St. Paul Outside the Walls, and Santa Maria Maggiore in the mid-eighth century.

Figure 3. Interior, St. Paul Outside the Walls, Rome. Begun 386. Etching by Giovanni Piranesi (1720–78). Photo: The Metropolitan Museum of Art, Harris Brisbane Dick Fund, 1937. [37.45.3 (47)]

of its near-twin St. Paul Outside the Walls.[7] The shrine of St. Peter, strategically located on a raised platform in the center part the transept, was the focal point of the vast interior. The **conch** of the semi-circular apse that framed the shrine and its altar originally was covered with gold **mosaic**, symbolic of heaven, as was the dome of Constantine's **baldachin**, a free-standing canopy made of four spiral columns over both the shrine and the

[7]De Blaauw, *Cultus et Decor*, 2:462 (440–461), 523 (for restorations of Pope Formosus [891–96]). For a fourth-century date of original program, see Herbert Kessler, "'Caput et speculum omnium ecclesiarum': Old St. Peter's and Church Decoration in Medieval Latium," *Italian Church Decoration of the Middle Ages and the Early Renaissance: Functions, Forms and Regional Traditions*, ed. W. Tronzo, Villa Spelman Colloquia, vol. 1 (Baltimore, 1989), pp. 119–46. See James Snyder, *Medieval Art: Painting, Sculpture, Architecture 4th to 14th century* (New York, 1989), p. 57, figs. 55, 56.

silver-covered altar before it. This structure was hung with lamps and crowned by a gold cross, reminiscent of the monumental one Constantine had erected in Jerusalem at the site of the crucifixion.[8]

The participants in the processions assembled in the square open courtyard in front of the basilica, in the center of which was a fountain surmounted by a bronze cupola. This **atrium** led to a narthex area, which opened into the sanctuary space through a central portal to the nave and two pairs of doors aligned with the aisles. The gable of the facade had an image of Christ made during the time of Pope Leo I (440–61), above the "the four living creatures" (Apoc. 5:6), winged figures carrying books, who ultimately derive from the seraphim of Isa. 6:2–3 and represent the symbols of the **evangelists**: the lion of Mark and the angel of Matthew to the left; the ox of Luke and the eagle of John to the right. They in turn hovered above four groups of adoring elders of the Apocalypse imitating the homage due an emperor at his entrance into the city. This apocalyptic image is an expression, frequent in apse and triumphal arch decoration of the Early Christian period, of the *parousia* or Second Coming of Christ not only as a future event—to occur on Easter Sunday—but also as a realized, immanent presence in liturgical, ecclesiastical time.[9] It would remain the dominant theme of the sculpture of the entrance portal of twelfth-century churches, often, but not always, on the western facade (Figs. 13, 14: center portal).[10]

---

[8]De Blaauw, *Cultus et Decor*, 2:472–79, 513–14; Krautheimer, *Rome*, pp. 26–28. See Snyder, *Medieval Art*, figs. 35, 36, for a reconstruction and the altar arrangement associated with Old St. Peter's depicted on the Pola Casket.

[9]For a discussion of this image, perhaps altered in the late seventh century by Pope Sergius I (687–701) to show Christ in the form of the Lamb of God, and its relationship to the triumphal arch of St. Paul Outside the Walls see Dale Kinney, "The Apocalypse in Early Christian Monumental Decoration," in *The Apocalypse in the Middle Ages,* ed. Richard K. Emmerson and Bernard McGinn (Ithaca, 1992), p. 204nn16–17, and figs. 18 and 19. See also Clifford Flanigan, "The Apocalypse and Medieval Liturgy," in ibid., pp. 339–42.

[10]Yves Christe, "The Apocalypse in the Monumental Art of the Eleventh through Thirteenth Centuries," in *The Apocalypse in the Middle Ages*, ed. Emmerson and McGinn, pp. 234–58.

Further embellishments were made to the fourth-century sanctuary space. Pope Pelagius II (579–90) gave an **ambo**, a structure ascended by double stairs located on the floor level of the transept area. It stood on the nave side of the silver-covered beam supported by a double row of columns that was erected by Pope Hormisdas (514–23) to close off the area, further west, reserved for the clergy. Both the ambo and the beam were based on Greek models.[11] The most substantial changes to Old St. Peter's were made at the time of Pope Gregory the Great (590–604). The altar was erected on a podium directly over St. Peter's tomb and surmounted by a new baldachin supported by four silver columns, visible through the columnar screen that separated the raised part of the transept and the apse beyond from the congregational space in the nave. The saint's remains stayed visible through an opening on the side of the shrine facing the apse, but to accommodate the flow of pilgrims, the sacred relics were made more accessible by means of two lateral staircases leading from the podium level to the lowered floor of the newly installed annular crypt. In effect, an "artificial catacomb" was created that formed a passageway, which mirrored the curve of the apse above it, to a second opening on the apse side of the tomb directly below the one above. The new arrangement also allowed for greater visibility of the **cathedra**, or **throne** of the pope (the first bishop of Rome), originally on the podium to the left of the altar. Stairs from the raised floor of the **presbyterium**, a raised area in front of the altar reserved for clergy, in the central transept area led to its new position against the center of the apse wall, where the seated pope was surrounded by bishops to the left, priests to the right, on a **synthronon**, a semicircular bench around the apse.[12] Another development of importance for later church plans occurred in the

[11] De Blaauw, *Cultus et Decor*, 2:478–87.

[12] Ibid., 2:530–34, figs. 19–24; Krautheimer, *Rome*, p. 86, fig. 70. For the continuation of the synthronon in the apse of Anglo-Saxon churches, see Sible de Blaauw, "Architecture and Liturgy in Late Antiquity and the Middle Ages, Traditions and Trends in Modern Scholarship," *Archiv für Liturgie-Wissenschaft* 33/1 (1991): 23.

eighth century with the removal from the right transept of the oratory of the Holy Cross, the site of the Good Friday ritual when Pope Symmachus resided at the Vatican and not the Lateran Palace 501–06. Devotion to the Holy Cross was transferred to the altar against the south wall of the nave, which was dedicated to the apostle-saints Simon and Jude and was designated "ante crucem" in the liturgy. It was marked by a porphyry roundel on the nave floor, by a crucifix given by Leo III (795–816), and by enlarged images of the Crucifixion and Resurrection on the nave wall above the altar as part of the restorations made to the earlier New Testament cycle after the sack of St. Peter's by the Muslims in 846.[13]

In the course of the Early Christian period the liturgy, too, underwent substantial changes. The earliest idea of the content of the services comes from a manual compiled in Greek by the Roman anti-Pope Hippolytus ca. 220. At least since the time of Pope Damasus (ca. 380), Latin has predominated in the Western liturgies. It begins with the Service of the Word, derived from Jewish sources, which includes the lections, psalms, and sermon; at the liturgy of the Eucharist that follows, only the baptized could attend.[14] Reconstructions of the actual performance of the early liturgy are

---

[13]De Blaauw, *Cultus et Decor*, 2:521–23, 543, 547n187 (for crucifix of Leo III "in medio basilicae.") See also William Tronzo, "The Prestige of St. Peter's: Observations on the Function of Monumental Narrative Cycles in Italy," in *Pictorial Narrative in Antiquity and the Middle Ages*, ed. Herbert L. Kessler and Marianna Shreve Simpson (Washington, D.C., 1985), pp. 93–112; Snyder, *Medieval Art*, fig. 56.

[14]Theodor Klauser, *A Short History of the Western Liturgy: An Account and Some Reflections*, trans. John Halliburton, 2nd ed. (New York, 1979), pp. 6–24. The prayers of the Mass said by the celebrant were contained in sacramentaries, the earliest of which date to the seventh and eighth centuries but traditionally were attributed to earlier popes: Leo (440–61), Gelasius (492–96), and Gregory (590–604). The scriptural texts to be read by lectors and deacons were found in lists appended to biblical books or, by the seventh and eighth centuries, in separate books called pericopes. The chant sung by the **schola cantorum** was also contained in a separate book, the **antiphonary**, according to tradition composed by Gregory. See further *The Church at Prayer: An Introduction to the Liturgy*, ed. Aimé G. Martimort, 4 vols. in 1 (Collegeville, Minn., 1992; new ed. of *L'Eglise en Prière*, 1963), 1:3–61, with

drawn from the descriptions in the first written ritual, Roman Ordo I, which describes in general terms the celebration of the papal Mass ca. 700. On his arrival at a stational church, the pope, accompanied by two deacons, went to the sacristy located in the narthex in the front of the church and dressed in liturgical vestments that were essentially the same as those still used today. While the pope was preparing himself, an acolyte—his hands covered with a chasuble—carried the Gospel book in procession through the nave, giving it to a sub-deacon to place on the altar. Having received the papal blessing, a procession of the *schola cantorum*—the papal choir whose founding is traditionally attributed to Pope Gregory I—would move to their places on either side of the altar, creating a sacred path through which the pope—preceded by his entourage carrying candles, crosses, and censers—would file until, having stopped to greet the clergy, to kiss the Gospel book and the altar, and to make a silent prayer, he took his seat on the cathedra in the apse. Roman Ordo I describes the reading of the Old Testament lesson from the ambo and the abridged procession to the ambo again for the Gospel reading, after which the Gospel book was the object of a kiss by all the clergy in order of rank before it was returned to its ***capsa*** and sealed for safekeeping at the end of this first part of the service (which no longer allowed for the sermon for which earlier popes were renowned). The pope, standing behind the altar and facing the congregation, presided over celebration of the Eucharist that began with the Offertory procession with its gifts of bread and wine and ended with the distribution of Communion. Smaller, titular churches, such as San Clemente (remodeled by John II, 533–35), had a long, narrow enclosure within the nave leading to the *presbyterium* with spaces in front of the sanctuary barrier defined by wing walls extending from the nave enclosure for male aristocracy, the ***senatorium***, on the right side and for the women of noble rank on the left. From

bibliography; and Josef A. Jungmann, *The Mass of the Roman Rite: Its Origins and Development (Missarum Sollemnia)*, 2 vols. (New York, 1951), 1:7–103. I owe the formulation of this note to Richard Gyug.

here the pope accepted gifts for the Offertory and distributed Communion. He communicated with upper clergy and higher officials from his throne behind the altar.[15]

Early forms of the pontifical entrance, the scripture reading, the Offertory, and Communion can be traced to pre-Constantinian times. Other customs were modeled on imperial cult ritual directly or as it was incorporated into the liturgy of the Byzantine East. Roman Ordo I includes the *Agnus Dei* in the Canon of the Mass as an antiphonal song at the preparation for Communion, at the instigation of Sergius I (689–701), who is credited with the introduction of feast of the Exaltation of the Cross on 14 September and four feasts of the Virgin to Rome's liturgical calendar.[16] Already in the fifth century Gelasius I (492–96) had introduced the intercessory prayer with the three-fold Greek *Kyrie Eleison* response into the Latin liturgy; the *Sanctus*, the angelic hymn of the eucharistic prayer, came to Rome by way of the Entrance chant in the Gallican rite—observed in western churches outside Rome—from the Eastern ***Trisagion*** used in stational processions in Constantinople.[17]

---

[15]Baldovin, "The Urban Character of Christian Worship," pp. 131–34; Klauser, *Western Liturgy*, pp. 59–72; and Thomas F. Mathews, "An Early Roman Chancel Arrangement and Its Liturgical Functions," *Rivista di Archeologia Cristiana* 38 (1962): 73–95, esp. 91–95, and fig. 1, for the separate spaces for women and men at the head of the aisles to the left and right of the sanctuary space. See the discussion of Elaine de Benedictis, "The 'Schola Cantorum' in Rome during the High Middle Ages" (Ph.D. diss., Bryn Mawr College, 1983), pp. 9–20. The left/right arrangement would remain, whether or not the apse faced east.

[16]Klauser, *Western Liturgy*, pp. 83, 89–90. Of the four feasts of the Virgin with which he is also credited, the Purification on 2 February, the Assumption on 15 August, and the Annunciation on 25 March had come to Rome earlier as a consequence of the Virgin's definition as *Theotokos*—Mother of God—at the Council of Ephesus in the 431. See further discussion by Hilda Graef, *Mary: A History of Doctrine and Devotion*, vol. 1, *From the Beginning to the Eve of the Reformation* (New York, 1963), pp. 142–43.

[17]Klauser, *Western Liturgy*, pp. 49–50, 133–34; and Baldovin, "The Urban Character," pp. 240–49. The *Trisagion* itself entered the Roman liturgy for Good Friday; see *The Oxford Dictionary of the Christian Church*, ed. F. L. Cross (London, 1966), p. 1377.

The imagery of Christ flanked by the winged evangelist symbols, perhaps first depicted in the early fifth-century apse mosaic at Santa Pudenziana in Rome (Fig. 4), reinforces the reality of the divine presence throughout the liturgy. There, an arrangement suggestive of the later synthronon in the apse of Old St. Peter's shows Christ majestically enthroned amid his apostles led by Peter and Paul, who are crowned by personifications of the Church of the Jews and of the Gentiles, respectively. This group is enclosed by an architectural setting that screens a cluster of buildings which presumably mark the sacred sites in Jerusalem. The jeweled cross on the hill of Golgotha looms into the center of the heavens with the winged evangelist symbols ranged to left and right as they were in the apocalyptic vision on the upper facade of St. Peter's basilica. It is they who sing the three-fold *Sanctus* that follows the *Vere Dignum* prayer, which is the Preface of the Mass. Text and image confirm the equivalence of the liturgy presided over by the bishop of Rome to the celestial liturgy before God in heaven.[18]

The Roman liturgy was to become the model for all western bishops to follow, just as Old St. Peter's, anomalous as it was in its own time, symbolically and actually became an important model for subsequent church builders in many respects. Charlemagne's coronation as Holy Roman Emperor by Pope Leo III in St. Peter's on Christmas Day 800 confirmed the place of the Roman church at the center of a powerful new court. It also inspired a conscious revival of the grandeur of Constantinian Rome not only at that principal pilgrimage site but also elsewhere in Europe. Rome's imprint already had been felt by Charlemagne's father, Pepin III, who had ordered that the Gallican rites be replaced by the liturgy of Gregory the Great. This had occurred around the time of Pope Stephen II's anointing of Pepin, along with his sons Charlemagne and Carloman, in 754 at St.-Denis, the abbey church that was the burial place of the Merovingian king Dagobert (d. 639).

The original basilican church dedicated to St. Denis was built in the fifth century over the tomb of the martyred third-century saint who had

[18]Krautheimer, *Rome*, pp. 40–41; Staale Sinding-Larsen, *Iconography and Ritual: A Study of Analytical Perspectives* (Oslo/Irvington-on-Hudson, N.Y., 1984), pp. 48–49.

Figure 4. Christ Enthroned in Majesty, with Saints. Apse Mosaic from Santa Pudenziana, Rome. ca. 400. Photo: Alinari/Art Resource, N.Y.

been sent to convert the people of Gaul. The earlier church was enlarged in the seventh century by Dagobert, who established the monastery under the Benedictine rule. When the church, remodeled by Abbot Fulrad, was dedicated in 775, the venerated tomb of St. Denis and his martyred companions Rusticus and Eleutherius was the centerpiece of the new crypt in the annular form of Old St. Peter's, giving similar access for the pilgrims to a central recess for the relics. The principal altar—dedicated to saints Peter and Paul—was similarly placed on the **chord of the apse** directly above.[19]

[19]Anne Walters Robertson, "Music and Liturgy at the Abbey of Saint-Denis, 567–1567: A Survey of the Primary Sources" (Ph.D. diss., Yale University, 1984), pp. 9–63; Anne Walters Robertson, *The Service-Books of the Royal Abbey of Saint-Denis: Images of Ritual and*

Charlemagne continued the liturgical reforms instituted by Pepin and undertaken by Abbot Fulrad of St.-Denis by asking Alcuin of York ca. 781 to revise and supplement the papal rituals to accommodate the broader needs of Frankish churches. Much of the credit in this endeavor belongs to Benedict of Aniane, who is best known for his reform of monastic practice, completed in 817. The Benedictine liturgy was established at St.-Denis under Abbot Hilduin (814–41).[20]

Building on the Roman base, the architectural and liturgical initiative shifted to monastic foundations in Charlemagne's domain. A prime example is the Benedictine abbey at Centula (Fig. 5), in northern France, where Charlemagne celebrated Easter in 800. Later drawings as well as a copy of a liturgical text allow for an approximate reconstruction of the original church—dedicated to St. Riquier and built by Abbot Angilbert at the end of the eighth century—and its ritual relationship to other churches within the monastic complex: the smaller, separate churches of St. Benedict and St. Mary to the south and the church dedicated to the Savior, a quasi-independent entity connected to the western end of St.-Riquier by a nave with single aisles (Fig. 6). St.-Riquier recalled the Constantinian model of Old St. Peter's, with the altar of St. Peter at the eastern border of transept, the altar of the Holy Cross in the nave, and the square atrium or "paradise" to the west of St.-Sauveur. The increase in altars dedicated to the martyr saints whose relics were enclosed in them was by now common.

Music in the Middle Ages (Oxford, 1991), pp. 4–31, 218–22. See also William W. Clark, "'The Recollection of the Past is the Promise of the Future.' Continuity and Contextuality: Saint-Denis, Merovingians, Capetians, and Paris," in *Artistic Integration in Gothic Buildings*, ed. Raguin et al., pp. 92–113, with bibliography.

[20]Klauser, *Western Liturgy*, pp. 72–75. For the role of Benedict of Aniane in writing the supplement see Cyrille Vogel, *Medieval Liturgy: An Introduction to the Sources*, rev. and trans. William G. Storey and Niels Krogh Rasmussen (Washington, D.C., 1986), pp. 5, 85–86, 101, 147–54. For Hilduin at Saint-Denis see Robertson, *The Service-Books*, pp. 25–42, 222–28.

Figure 5. View of Centula. Frontispiece of P. Petau's *De Nithardo* (1612), 603.K.10. Petau's copy from an eleventh-century manuscript. Photo: by permission of the British Library.

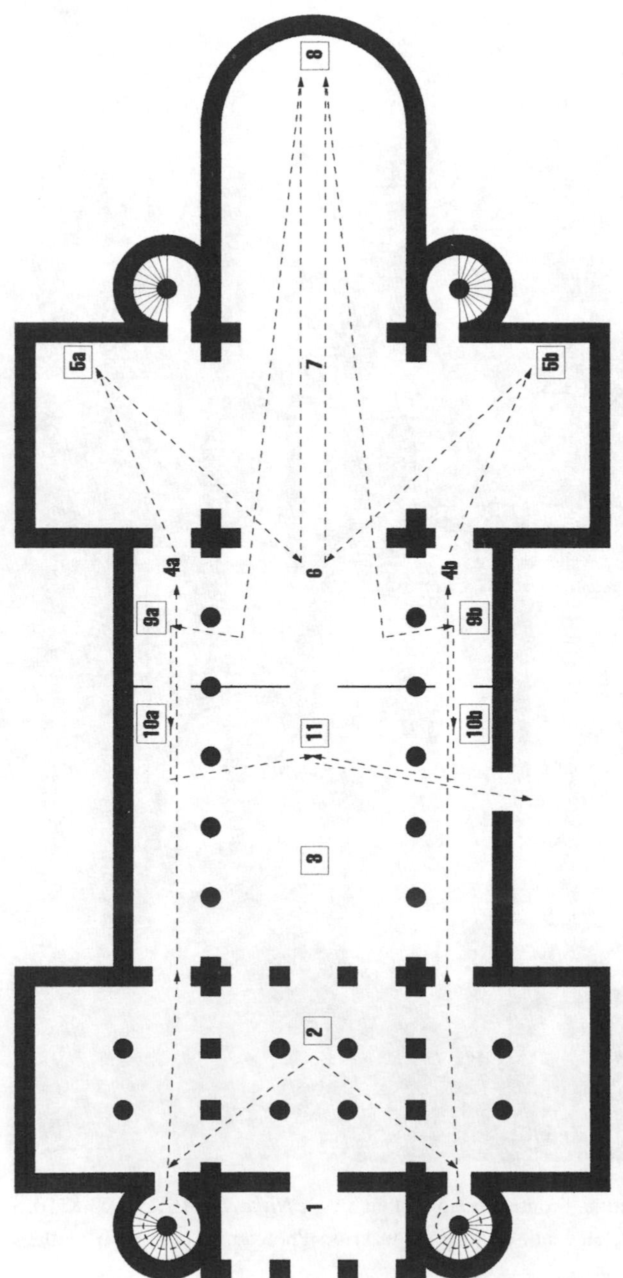

KEY. *Altars & Stations for daily prayer at St. Riquier, Centula.*
1. Nativity *station;* 2. Holy Savior *in the gallery;* 3. Saint Denis; 4a. Resurrection *station;* 4b. Ascension *station;* 5a. Saint John; 5b. Saint Martin; 6. Passion *station;* 7. Saint Peter; 8. Saint Richarius; 9a. Saint Stephen; 9b. Saint Laurence; 10a. Saint Quintin; 10b. Saint Maurice; 11. Holy Cross.

Figure 6. Plan of St.-Riquier, with routes of processions. After Taylor, figs. 12–13.

Centula differed from its model in a choir area extending east of the transept, giving the altogether smaller plan the more clear-cut shape of a Latin cross, and in having the altar of St. Riquier behind his tomb further east in the apse with two other altars in each aisle and in the north and south transept. The altar of the Cross was freestanding mid-nave, east of which was an ambo, in front of a second choir enclosure in the easternmost part of the nave. It also differs in its towered transept block to balance the design of St.-Sauveur, whose central tower appears to have been flanked by turrets over staircases leading to the gallery opening on to the nave in the upper level, which was the location of a third choir and the altar dedicated to the Savior. Directly below, on the ground floor of the western church of St.-Sauveur, an area called the "crypta sancti salvatoris" where relics of the apostles were kept, was the location of the baptismal font and the burial site of Angilbert. Towers similarly crowned the oratory over the doors dedicated to the archangels on each of the three sides of the western courtyard: that of St. Michael on the principal entrance to the west; Sts. Gabriel and Raphael to the south and north. At the same time that the triumphal apocalyptic aspect of the divine presence thus was emphasized architecturally in the new vertical thrust of the architecture, Christ's entrance into human history was reinforced horizontally by four reliefs laid out in the form of a cross that linked the two churches. Each commemorated a major feast: the Nativity was depicted over the doorway of St.-Sauveur; the Passion east of the altar of the Cross over St.-Riquier's chancel arch. This longitudinal axis was cut by the Resurrection and the Ascension over the transept arches at eastern end of the north and south aisles.[21]

The vertical extension and the attendant symbolism of the celestial realm in the upper levels of the church architecture enhanced the setting for

---

[21]Carol Heitz, *Recherches sur les rapports entre architecture et liturgie à l'époque carolingienne* (Paris, 1963), pp. 26–99; and Susan A. Rabe, *Faith, Art, and Politics at Saint-Riquier: The Symbolic Vision of Angilbert* (Philadelphia, 1995), pp. 111–37. See also Honoré Bernard, "Une Restitution nouvelle de la Basilique d'Angilbert," *Revue du Nord* 71 (1989): 307–61.

Angilbert's liturgy, which constituted a transposition of the papal stational system within the microcosm of the monastic cloister and its neighboring villages. Within the monastery—conceived of as a miniature Rome, symbolic of Augustine's vision of the City of God[22]—the solemn penitential pilgrimage of the procession was part of a more tightly organized ritual for daily services of the Divine Office as well as for major feast days. The processions would move not only from church to church but also from altar to altar within St.-Riquier. The altar of St. Savior in the upper **tribune** of St.-Sauveur was the site not only of the Easter and Christmas masses to which the lay population were invited but also of the monastic Offices of Matins and Vespers. From there the monastic community divided to descend the staircases and move down the aisles, stopping to pray at the reliefs over the aisle arches and at the transept altars before meeting in the choir in front of the Passion relief and proceeding to the altar of St. Riquier in the apse. From here the groups divided again into two choirs, making a stop at the altars in the aisles before they converged for further prayers at the altar of the Holy Cross in mid-nave and exited St.-Riquier through the south aisle door to continue the service at the church of St. Benedict. The Office of Terce (see glossary, "Divine Office") was celebrated at the round church of St. Mary, which was also the starting point of the Palm Sunday procession.[23]

Architectural and liturgical developments of the Carolingian period had a lasting impact. Of particular importance is the allegorical interpretation of

---

[22]Baldovin, "The Urban Character," pp. 250, 258. See also Rabe, *Saint Riquier*, pp. 138–47.

[23]David Parsons, "Liturgy and Architecture in the Middle Ages," The Third Deerhurst Lecture, University of Leicester, 1986 (repr. 1995), p. 7, fig. 2; see Carol Heitz, *L'architecture religieuse carolingienne: Les formes et leurs fonctions* (Paris, 1980), p. 59, fig. 39; H. M. Taylor, "Tenth-Century Church Building in England and on the Continent," in *Tenth Century Studies: Essays in Commemoration of the Millennium of the Council of Winchester and the Regularis Concordia*, ed. David Parsons (London, 1975), pp. 148–52, figs. 12–13; Edgar Lehmann, "Die Anordnung der Altare in Klosterkirche zu Centula," in *Karl der Grosse, Lebenswerk und Nachleben*, ed. Wolfgang Braunfels, 4 vols. (Dusseldorf, 1965), 3:374–83; and Rabe, *Saint-Riquier*, pp. 118–20.

the liturgy of the Roman stational Mass of Alcuin's pupil, Amalarius of Metz, written between 814 and 835.[24] Although criticized in his time, Amalarius's assignment of roles for the congregation as well as for the choir and the hierarchy of clergy who participate in the rememorative drama of the life, ministry, crucifixion, and resurrection of Christ that unfolds in the Mass, enriched by the chants and hymns that accompanied it, served as a model for later liturgies to complement the rubrics and tone of the structure of Mass established by Gregory the Great. The full length of the basilican space provides a setting for moving through sacred time: at the antiphonal Introit hymn, the chorus (representing the Old Testament prophets) announces the entrance of the bishop (representing the advent of Christ) at the head of a solemn procession (representing Christ's Entry into Jerusalem), acclaimed by the congregation (representing the Jewish people). The bishop's seating on the elevated chair on the synthronon in the center of the apse—an area associated with paradise—above and beyond the altar table where the eucharistic sacrifice takes place, represents the Ascension of Christ.[25]

Amalarius's allegorical interpretations of the gestures and movements of the celebrant and his assistants at different moments of the Mass in terms of events in Christ's life lie behind the dramatic embellishments added to the Easter liturgy of the tenth-century monastic reform movement in England and on the Continent, most fully recorded in the Winchester document of 973, the *Regularis Concordia*. To dramatize the reality of the events of the Passion, following the extended commemoration of the Crucifixion at the *Adoratio Crucis* that took place at the altar of the Cross on Good Friday, the document provides an extra-liturgical option of a solemn procession to a separate altar for the burial of the cross in a "sepulcher," the *Depositio Crucis*. The cross quietly would be removed at the midnight

---

[24]*Eclogae de ordine Romano* (814) and *Liber officialis* (821–35); see Hardison, *Christian Rite*, p. 37n6. See also David Bevington, *Medieval Drama* (Boston, 1975), pp. 3–8.

[25]Hardison, *Christian Rite*, pp. 35–79.

Elevatio Crucis, the conclusion of the Holy Saturday rites. At Easter Sunday Matins, the sepulcher without the cross was the destination of three monks dressed as the Marys, who were told by the monk portraying the angel that the Christ they seek is not there but has risen, and they are shown the empty tomb. The *Quem queritis*, also known as *Visitatio Sepulchri*, which proclaims the miracle of the Resurrection, was the first of the many liturgical dramas frequently performed on major feast days and eventually in the more elaborate play cycles of the later Middle Ages.[26] Later sepulchers were permanent fixtures in stone, sometimes in a separate chapel in the north transept, sometimes also serving as the tomb of a pious donor, which subsequent bequests would embellish. A favored location for the temporary arrangement of the sepulcher was at the altar in the tribune choir of the **westwork**, as has been argued for Winchester as well as for the tenth-century German convent church at Essen. There the altar in the western tribune choir was dedicated to St. Michael, the weigher of souls at the Last Judgment.[27]

---

[26] *Regularis Concordia: The Monastic Agreement of the Monks and Nuns of the English Nation*, ed. Thomas Symons (London, 1953), pp. 34–35. See also Hardison, *Christian Rite*, pp. 178–219, and 220–52 (for later development of the dramatic liturgy and the liturgical drama); and R. Delamare, *Le De Officiis ecclesiasticis de Jean d'Avranches, Archevêque de Rouen (1067–1079). Etude liturgique et publication du texte inédit du manuscrit H. 304 de la Bibliothèque de la Faculté de Montpellier* (Paris, 1923). For the liturgy of Holy Week and Easter see also Elizabeth C. Parker and Charles T. Little, *The Cloisters Cross: Its Art and Meaning* (New York/London, 1994), pp. 149–73.

[27] For frescos depicting the Last Judgment at Essen as well as St.-Savin-sur-Gartempe see Elizabeth Parker, *The Descent from the Cross: Its Relation to the Extra-Liturgical "Depositio" Drama* (New York, 1978), pp. 116–17. For altars to St. Michael in the western tribune see J. Vallery-Radot, "Note sur les chapelles hautes dédiées à St. Michel," *Bulletin Monumental* (1969): 453–78. For frescos in the north transept see also Thomas W. Lyman, "Theophanic Iconography and the Easter Liturgy: The Romanesque Painted Program at Saint-Sernin in Toulouse," in *Festschrift für Otto von Simson zum 65. Geburtstag*, ed. Lucius Grisebach and Konrad Renger (Frankfurt am-Main, 1977), pp. 72–93. For various locations of the Easter Sepulchre see Pamela Sheingorn, *The Easter Sepulchre in England* (Kalamazoo, Mich., 1987), pp. 23–25.

It is to St. Michael that Bishop Bernward's church in Hildesheim, Germany, is dedicated. Completed by 1032, it continues the Carolingian model with its square tower flanked by round stair turrets at both ends, the western being the more symbolically important, as at Centula. The larger western choir, reserved for the clergy and raised above the crypt, was enlarged in the twelfth century to the present size, as it was rebuilt after the church's destruction in World War II (Fig. 7). The principal altar was originally dedicated to St. Michael; an altar to each in the hierarchy of angels was housed in the two upper stories of each of the transept wings. When the principal altar was dedicated to the Savior in 1022, the year of Bernward's death, St. Michael's altar was moved to a chapel in the upper wall in the western apse. The Altar of the Savior stood on the border of the monks' choir, accessible by steps up from the nave, an arrangement reminiscent of Old St. Peter's. Bernward's tomb was in the crypt near the altar of St. Mary, which stood directly below the altar of the Savior. The altar of St. John the Baptist was the principal altar in the eastern lay choir.[28] The original location in the nave of the altar of the Cross is not known; it once stood before the eastern choir. Bernward's bronze column—modeled on the column of Trajan he saw on his trip to Rome in 1001—stood directly east of the Cross altar and supported a crucifix. A sixth-century marble column from Constantinople—perhaps, like the relic of the True Cross that Bernward possessed, a gift from Otto III—stood in front of this altar.[29] The alignment of the altars in different space levels gives a clarity to the hieratic structure of a stational

---

[28]For the arrangement at Bernward's church at Hildesheim and his earlier chapel (begun 993) for the relic of the True Cross, see Günther Bandmann, "Früh- und Hochmittelalterliche Altarordnung als Darstellung," in *Das Erste Jahrtausend: Kultur und Kunst im werdenden Abendland an Rhein und Ruhr*, 2 vols. (Dusseldorf, 1962), 2:407–10; Johannes Cramer, Werner Jacobsen, Dethard von Winterfeld, "Die Michaeliskirche," in *Bernward von Hildesheim und das Zeitalter der Ottonien*, Exhibition catalog, 2 vols. (Hildesheim, 1993), 1:369–82. *Grove Dictionary of Art*, ed. Jane Turner (New York, 1996), 14:532–35.

[29]*Bernward von Hildesheim*, 1:540–41 (Bernward's bronze column), and p. 549 (marble column).

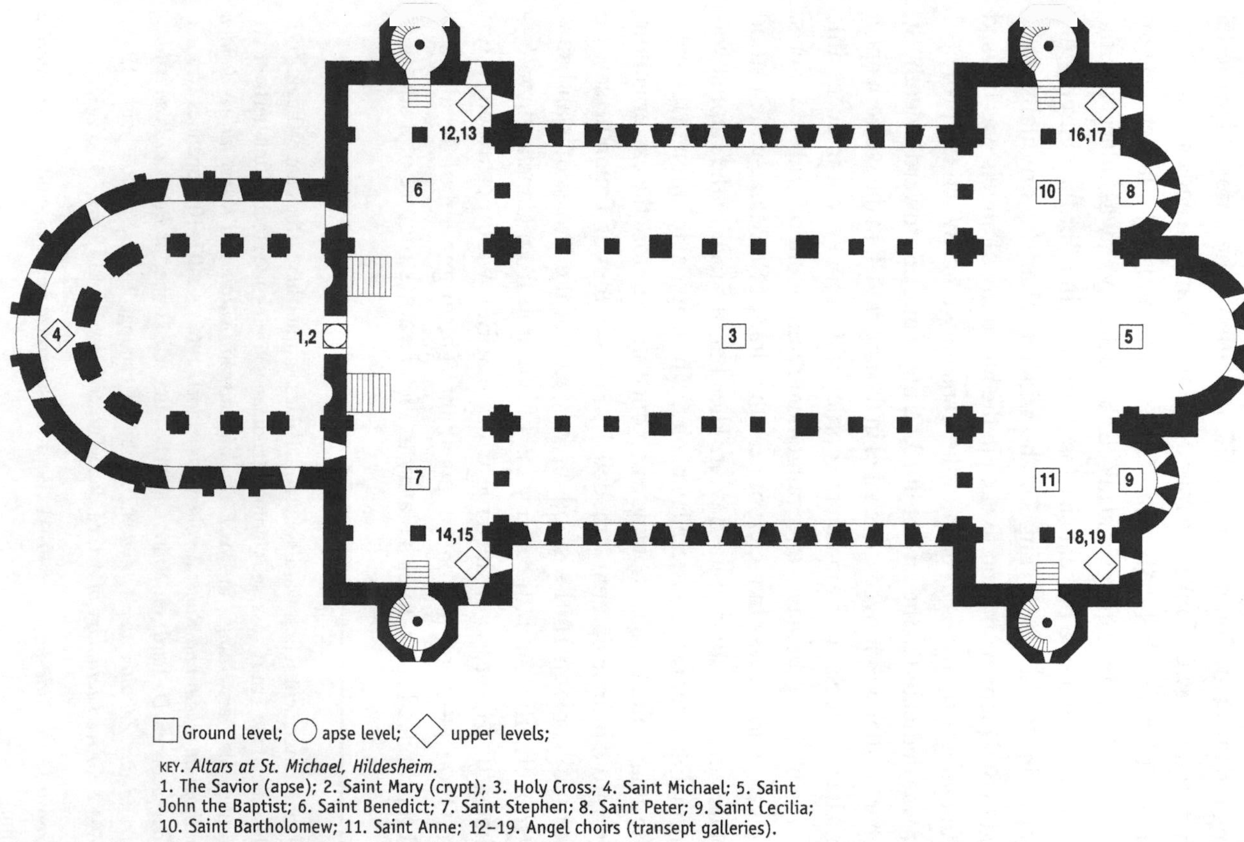

Figure 7. Abbey Church of St. Michael, Hildesheim. 1010–33. Groundplan, after Bandmann, figs. 12–13.

liturgy contained within a single church that is reinforced by the squaring of the space compartments in the nave and a rising rhythm of the two, four, and then six striped **arcade**s of the transept galleries.

St. Michael's reflects the growing cult of relics and devotional cycles to individual saints that lay behind the multiplication of altars on different levels and in an expanded crypt area. Tribunes above the nave arcades, as they are found at Winchester and elsewhere, allowed further areas for procession to altars there and for antiphonal singing of a liturgy still tied to the tenth-century monastic reform in England and the continent.[30] At this time the concept of the eucharistic celebration began to change from a communion of the redeemed of the early Roman period to the more private action of a single celebrant on behalf of a congregation, which rarely communicated even on feast days. Several church arrangements confirmed the growing isolation of the laity from the educated clergy. In cathedral spaces, the principal altar was gradually moved back toward the wall of the apse, displacing the synthronon in cathedral spaces. The clergy were relocated in facing choir stalls in front of the high altar.[31] The altar of the Cross in the nave, for the veneration of the Cross on Good Friday and other feast days and for Masses for the dead, was the principal altar serving the lay congregation.[32]

Under the new disposition of the church space, with the Offertory procession eliminated and the priest in front of the altar, his prayers inaudible, the most sacred moments of the Mass were the concern of the bishop or

---

[30]Arnold William Klukas, "'Altaria Superioria': The Function and Significance of the Tribune-Chapel in Anglo-Norman Romanesque. A Problem in the Relationship of Liturgical Requirements and Architectural Form" (Ph.D. diss., University of Pittsburgh, 1978), pp. 226–89. For a broader discussion of the nave tribune see ibid., pp. 77–95. Klukas maintains (p. 159) that the disappearance of tribunes in Anglo-Norman churches was a consequence of the greater simplicity of the liturgy that Lanfranc of Bec imposed in the mid-eleventh century. See also Peter Draper, "Architecture and Liturgy," in *Age of Chivalry: Art in Plantagenet England 1200–1400*, ed. J. J. G. Alexander and Paul Binski (London, 1987), p. 86.

[31]Jungmann, *Mass of the Roman Rite*, 1:82–84.

[32]Parker and Little, *The Cloisters Cross*, pp. 128, 138–41.

priest alone, distanced from a lay congregation that was reduced to the role of passive observer.[33] A heightened consciousness of sin that was expressed in the prayers of the celebrant reflects a shift in the emphasis of the Mass to the Consecration, on the sacrificial nature of the Crucifixion rather than the triumph of the Resurrection.[34] An increasing devotion to the Christ of the Passion, especially in Germany, France, and England, resulted in the change from the use of a gold or jeweled cross to a crucifix. A large wood image of the suffering Christ on the cross became a permanent fixture. It was mounted on a column at the altar of the Cross in mid-nave or on a beam erected over the entrance to the choir. The tenth-century cross of Archbishop Gero, which contained a relic of the True Cross, is the finest, and earliest, surviving example (Fig. 8).[35]

Various expressions of the increased dramatization of the Passion narrative in the Holy Week liturgy had been developing in the Frankish liturgy—in part to offset the more passive role to which the lay congregation was consigned in the Mass. Many of these rituals were adopted in Rome, owing chiefly to the reforming efforts of the Cluniac monastic order and of the Ottonian emperors, beginning with the Romano-German pontifical, compiled at Mainz around 950. Among the new ceremonials were the Palm Sunday procession, the Maundy Thursday foot washing, the Good Friday Reproaches and other embellishments of the Veneration of the Cross, and the Easter Vigil rites on Holy Saturday, including the blessings of the New Fire, of the paschal candle, and of the baptismal water. Fresh contact with Constantinople through Theophanu, wife of Emperor Otto II, may help

---

[33]Klauser, *Western Liturgy*, pp. 98, 101–13.

[34]Jungmann, *Mass of the Roman Rite*, 1:76–83; Hardison, *Christian Rite*, pp. 64–65.

[35]Renate Kroos, "Liturgische Quellen zum Kölner Domchor," *Kölner Domblatt* 44/45 (1979): 35–203. For the crucifix showing the triumphant Christ see the twelfth-century Spanish crucifix from The Cloisters Collection, illustrated in James J. Rorimer, *The Metropolitan Museum of Art. The Cloisters: The Building and the Collection of Mediaeval Art in Fort Tryon Park* (New York, 1951), p. 29 (illus.).

Figure 8. Cross of Archbishop Gero (detail). Painted wood, height of figure: 6'2". Ca. 970. Cathedral, Cologne. Photo: Foto Marburg/Art Resource, N.Y.

account for the inclusion of the angelic hymn of the *Gloria* as a regular feature of the Roman Mass, not just of the papal liturgy, along with the reciting of the Creed as standard practice after the reading of the Gospel, urged by the Ottonian emperor Henry II. These elements were included in the liturgical reforms initiated by Gregory VII (1073–85), who sought to impose a unity on practice north and south of the Alps.[36]

Evidence of the newer ideas introduced to Rome from northern liturgical practice can be seen in the upper church of San Clemente, built between 1110 and 1130 (Fig. 9), even as it preserved older forms relating to the earlier church and its place within the stational system of the Early Christian period. Similar to the plan of the original fourth-century church five meters below it, an atrium and porch on the eastern end precede a nave separated from unequal side aisles by two sets of five arcades on Corinthian columns. The nave is divided by a pier that marks the eastern extension of the slightly raised pavement that leads to the transverse barrier, which was surmounted by some sort of screen closing off the sanctuary space with an altar beneath a **ciborium** in the western end.[37] The chancel area is dominated by the apse mosaic depicting an image of the crucified Christ with the mourning figures of Mary and John. Above it, the hand of God extends from the canopy of heaven. Below the cross is a frieze of lambs flanking the haloed Lamb of God and directly above on top of the apse arch is the bust of Christ pantocrator flanked by the evangelist symbols. The iconographic program is a transformation of earlier programs where the triumphant jeweled cross

---

[36]A process that took several centuries to achieve: Klauser, *Western Liturgy*, pp. 76–84, 94–95; and Jungmann, *Mass of the Roman Rite*, 1:92–103. For particular rites see John Harper, *The Forms and Orders of Western Liturgy from the Tenth to the Eighteenth Century: A Historical Introduction and Guide for Students and Musicians* (New York, 1991; repr. 1994), pp. 139–50; and Karl Young, *The Drama of the Medieval Church*, 2 vols. (Oxford, 1933; repr. 1967), 1:1–43.

[37]Krautheimer, *Rome*, pp. 161–62; 182–87; and de Benedictis, "The 'Schola Cantorum' in Rome," pp. 58–71.

Figure 9. Interior view, upper church, San Clemente, Rome, ca. 1120–28. Photo: Alinari/Art Resource, N.Y.

was the center of the eucharistic image.[38] At San Clemente, Christ's cross is lined with doves and is characterized as the Tree of Life by the lavish vines that sprout from it and by the two harts at its base who drink from the Water of Life, an allusion to Psalm 41 [42] and the rivers of paradise. The imagery of the Cross as the Tree of Life was especially favored by Venantius Fortunatus (ca. 535–600) in his sixth-century hymns, which by the tenth century were a standard part of the liturgy of Good Friday and of

[38]For further discussion of San Clemente—its sources, inscription, and sacramental imagery—see Krautheimer, *Rome*, pp. 183–86; Sinding-Larson, *Iconography and Ritual*, pp. 49, 63–65, 87; and Hélène Toubert, "Le Renouveau paléochrétien à Rome au début du XIIe siècle," *Cahiers Archéologiques* 20 (1970): 99–154.

the Exaltation and Invention of the Cross. The compartment found within the body of the mosaic corpus for a relic of the True Cross is an arrangement comparable to the reliquary function of such monumental wood figures as the cross of Archibishop Gero in Cologne Cathedral (Fig. 8).[39]

Each of the low side walls of the nave enclosure at San Clemente stops one meter short of the chancel barrier, allowing for two doors in addition to the one in the center. Located in the mid-point of the south wall is the ambo and its two staircases, with a paschal candlestick—a spiral column with a Corinthian **capital**—set at its northeast corner. Directly opposite on the south wall is a **pulpit** with a single flight of stairs and two lecterns, the larger in the east and a smaller, higher one in the west. The walls are made of panels taken from the narrower enclosure of the sixth-century remodeling of the church by John II (533–35), and completed by others decorated with similar motifs. A chain of twenty-two mosaic roundels, twelve within the nave enclosure, link the entire nave space to the chancel, recalling the porphyry roundel before the altar in the nave of Old St. Peter's and at other liturgical stops.[40] The nave enclosure is commonly called the *schola cantorum*, designating the location of the papal choir that accompanied the pope when he made San Clemente a station once or twice a year. It has been argued that this space was made within the nave to accommodate the terms of the edict of Urban II in 1095, which made both the communal choral chanting of the Office of the Virgin and the Divine Office mandatory for both monastic and secular clergy. The rule of the regular canons was

[39]Henrik Shulte Nordholt, "Der Baum des Lebens: Eine Analyse des Mosaiks in der Apsiskalotte von S. Clemente in Rom," *Römische Historische Mitteilungen* 28 (1986): 17–30, esp. 25–26. My thanks to Thomas Dale for this reference. For the hymns of Venantius Fortunatus see Joseph Szövérffy, "'Crux Fidelis. . .': Prologomena to a History of the Holy Cross Hymns," *Traditio* 22 (1966): 6–12.

[40]De Benedictis, "The 'Schola Cantorum' in Rome," pp. 58–66; for the ambo's location on the south side, no matter whether the church faced east or west, see p. 103 (at San Clemente as at St. Peter's, the apse faces west). See also Dorothy Glass, *Studies on Cosmatesque Pavements* (Oxford, 1980), pp. 47, 83.

adopted at San Clemente, perhaps at the urging of Urban's successor, Paschal II (1099–1118), who came from San Clemente and enforced the new reforms. San Clemente's nave enclosure was one of the first among many, not all at stational churches for the papal liturgy, to be erected in Rome at this time.[41]

North of the Alps, the choir had long been the architectural space reserved for clergy for the reciting of the Divine Office, as at Centula and Hildesheim, for example. By the twelfth century, the eastern choir area had increased in size, the apse was surrounded by an **ambulatory** aisle with projecting chapels, and the high altar was moved further back in the apse, creating a separate clerical church space with its own transept, as at Cluny III (Fig. 10). With more services of growing complexity, the beam for the crucifix, or **rood**, at the entrance to the choir came to be replaced or supplemented by a more substantial screen. These imposing double-storied structures, such as the one at Salisbury Cathedral from the thirteenth century (Fig. 11), served as the entryway to the sanctuary space. This **pulpitum**, as it was called, was the final step in the separation of the clergy, who alone could enter the eastern choir and have access to the sacred mystery of the Eucharist at the high altar beyond the choir. As the celebrant now generally stood with his back to the community rather than facing, it was more difficult for the lay congregation even to observe the celebration at the altar of the Cross, which also had moved from its free-standing location to the western side of the pulpitum.[42] Under these circumstances the need for visual stimuli increased, and the **choir screen** often had a sculptural program to supplement and extend the images once confined to the now less visible altar frontal and the rood. The thirteenth-century choir screen at

---

[41]De Benedictis, "The 'Schola Cantorum' in Rome," pp. 136–52.

[42]Jungmann, *Mass of the Roman Rite*, 1:83–84. For architectural arrangements in Gothic England, especially Salisbury, see Draper, "Architecture and Liturgy" (note 31 above), pp. 83–91; see also Arnold Klukas, "Durham Cathedral in the Gothic Era: Liturgy, Design, Ornament," in *Artistic Integration in Gothic Buildings*, ed. Raguin et al., pp. 69–83.

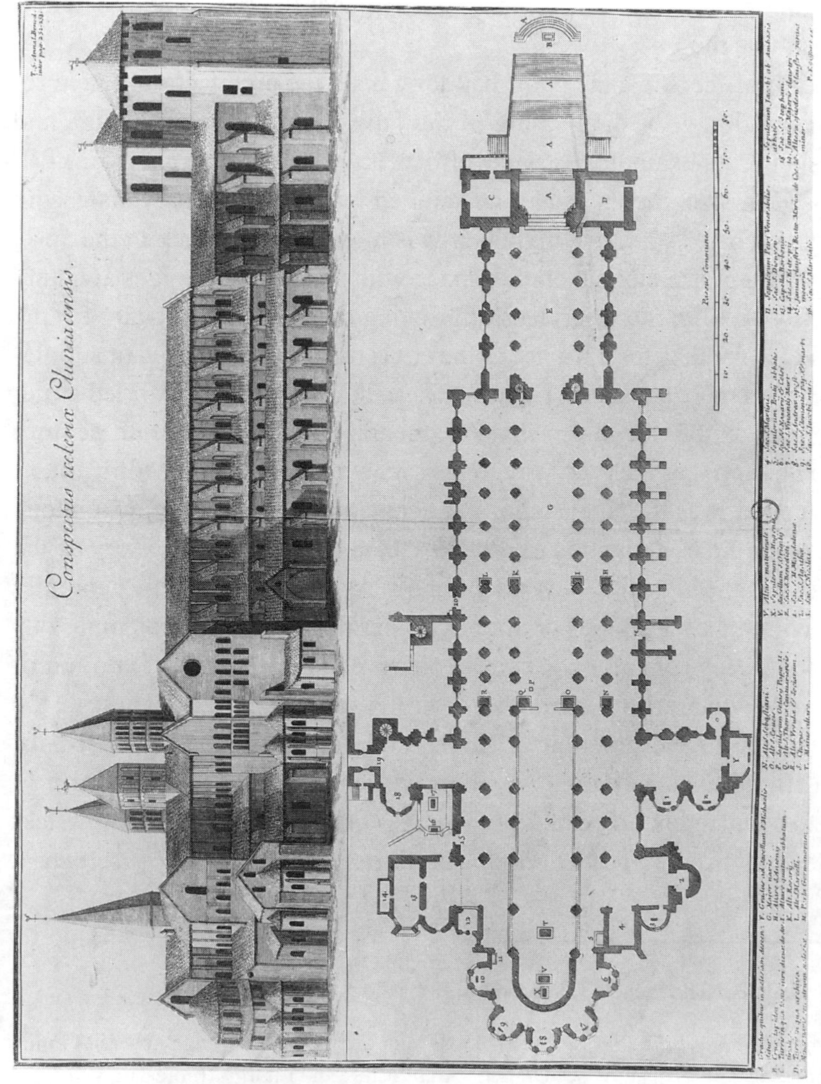

Figure 10. View and plan of Cluny III. Bibliothèque Nationale de France. Photo: Giraudon/Art Resource, N.Y.

Figure 11. Salisbury Cathedral Choirscreen. Thirteenth century (engraving by Biddlescomb from B. Winkles, *Illustrations of the Cathedral Churches of England and Wales*, 1838).

Naumburg, Germany, has an image of Christ crucified with Mary and John brought to eye level at the double doorway into the choir; a frieze of narrative scenes of the Passion runs behind the gable above, the sculptural counterparts of the extended play cycles developing at the time.[43] Indeed, by the Late Medieval period, the upper story of a rood screen could be the stage for extra-liturgical dramas, in addition to such other functions as housing the organ and the pulpit.[44] These structures, which took on a variety of forms, depending on the time they were constructed and regional traditions, were nearly all torn down in the wake of the Counter-Reformation in the sixteenth century, when the church space was unified once again.[45]

The fourteenth-century fresco in the upper church of San Francesco at Assisi depicting St. Francis inducing a vision of the Christ Child at a

---

[43]Snyder, *Medieval Art*, fig. 554. See further Willibald Sauerländer, "Integrated Fragments and the Unintegrated Whole: Scattered Examples from Reims, Strasbourg, Chartres, and Naumburg," in *Artistic Integration in Gothic Buildings*, pp. 162–64nn23–25 (for further bibliography). For the Christmas and Passion plays of the *Carmina Burana* from Benediktbeuern see Bevington, *Medieval Drama*, pp. 178–223.

[44]See Arnold Klukas, "Durham Cathedral in the Gothic Era," p. 73n15. At the feast of the Annunciation, for instance, a sculptured Angel Gabriel suspended on a wire might descend from the choir screen and appear before an image of the Virgin, placed within a curtained baldachin. In the *Officium Pastorum*, the shepherds's play performed on Christmas Day, or the *Officium Stellae,* the Visit of the Magi, performed at the feast of Epiphany just before the Offertory of the Mass, the object of their adoration and of the gifts brought by the Magi was a wooden image of the enthroned Virgin and Child set within a curtained baldachin on the altar. The lower part of the choir screen would sometimes be the location of the sepulcher for the Good Friday rites and for the enactment of the *Quem Quaeritis* Easter morning. For the Annunciation and Easter dramas at Parma see Parker, *Descent from the Cross*, pp. 184–99; for the Shepherds Play and the Magi see Barbara Lane, *The Altar and the Altarpiece: Sacramental Themes in Early Netherlandish Painting* (New York, 1984), pp. 55–57, 64. See also Sauerländer, "Integrated Fragments," fig. 2 (p. 324), for the king enthroned on the choir screen in the coronation rites at Reims Cathedral.

[45]For further discussion and bibliography see de Blaauw, "Architecture and Liturgy" (note 13 above), pp. 26–27.

Christmas Mass in Greccio locates the scene in front of an altar beneath a gabled baldachin inside the choir enclosure (Fig. 12). While singing monks and some pious laymen are gathered together within that space for this occasion, the women are clustered at the door from the nave, confirming the persistence of the custom of separating the sexes at that time. The women's view is blocked by a lectern that stands just inside the entrance to the choir. The doorway of the *pontile* or *tramezzo*, as these screens were also called in Italy, is surmounted by a painted crucifix projecting toward the nave and a pulpit to the left.[46] In the wake of the growth of the Franciscan and Dominican preaching orders, sculpted pulpits, such as that of Nicolo and Giovanni Pisano in Siena Cathedral, achieved prominence in Italy, and an iconographic cohesion more generally reserved for northern portal sculpture that has survived from the twelfth and thirteenth centuries.[47]

The earliest monumental portal sculpture is associated with the many churches built in the late eleventh and twelfth centuries that lined the pilgrimage routes leading through France to their destination at Santiago da Compostella in northwest Spain. It was especially in these churches that the apocalyptic depiction of the Second Coming—in the form of the **Christ in Majesty** with the four evangelist symbols—appeared in the **tympanum**, the semicircular area above the main entrance. On the south portal at Moissac,

---

[46]Marcia B. Hall, "The *Tramezzo* in Santa Croce, Florence, Reconstructed," *Art Bulletin* 56/3 (1973): 339; eadem, "The Italian Rood Screen: Some Implications for Liturgy and Function," in *Essays Presented to Myron P. Gilmore*, ed. Sergio Bertelli and Gloria Ramakus, 2 vols. (Florence, 1978), 2:213–18. For architectural reinforcement of the strict separation of nuns within a church space see Caroline A. Bruzelius, "Hearing is Believing: Clarissan Architecture, ca. 1213–1340," *Gesta* 31/2 (1992): 83–91; and Jeffrey F. Hamburger, "Art, Enclosure and the Cura Monialium: Prolegomena in the Guise of a Postscript," in ibid., 108–34.

[47]For the architectural response to the rise of preaching and preaching orders see Reynolds, "Liturgy and the Monument" (note 2 above), p. 63. For the original placement of the pulpit and the liturgy of Siena Cathedral see Kees van der Ploeg, *Art, Architecture, and Liturgy: Siena Cathedral in the Middle Ages* (Groningen, 1993), esp. pp. 78–81, and fig. 41.

Figure 12. Giotto di Bondone (1266–1336). St. Francis in Adoration. Upper Church, S. Francesco, Assisi. Photo: Alinari/Art Resource, N.Y.

Figure 13. Tympanum of the façade (South Portal). St.-Pierre, Moissac, ca. 1115–30. Photo: Giraudon/Art Resource, N.Y.

the image of Christ in Majesty surrounded by seraphim and smaller figures of seated elders derives from the early Christian idea of the immanence of God's triumph realized through the liturgy (Fig. 13). Old Testament prophets Isaiah and Jeremiah with Sts. Peter and Paul framing the door and the central **trumeau**, together with scenes of Christ's First Coming on the right wall of the porch, correspond to Amalarius's interpretation of the Introit of the Mass. On the left side the themes of judgment and redemption are depicted, with the image of Lazarus in the bosom of Abraham as the type of the saved sinner.[48]

[48]Snyder, *Medieval Art*, pp. 269–72, figs. 331–35; Christe, "The Apocalypse in Monumental Art" (note 11 above), pp. 254–55, and Hardison, *Christian Rite*, pp. 35–79. The Last Judgment to occur at the Second Coming is the dominant theme of the west portal at Autun. For

Figure 14. The Royal (West) Portal. Cathedral, Chartres. West portals, ca. 1145–70. Photo: Foto Marburg/Art Resource, N.Y.

The central portal of the western facade at Chartres Cathedral again shows the Christ in Majesty above seated elders (Fig. 14). The increased complexity of the mid-twelfth-century sculptural program, expanded over three portals, has been seen to reflect contemporary allegorical interpretations of the place of the sacraments in time and history that further build on the work of Amalarius of Metz and other earlier writers. A consideration of these ideas as they relate to the antiphons and tropes of the Introit of the

---

the related theme of confession and repentance central to the ritual of public penance during Lent on the south portal see Otto K. Werckmeister, "The Lintel Fragment Representing Eve from Saint-Lazare, Autun," *Journal of the Warburg and Courtauld Institutes* 35 (1972): 1–30. See also Hardison, *Christian Rite*, pp. 87–109; and Snyder, *Medieval Art*, figs. 358–60.

Mass has allowed for a new reading of the separate portals as a rich reformulation of the interaction of past, present, and future time in the bishop's entrance into the cathedral on the major feast days.[49]

The tympanum of the south portal of the western facade, devoted to Christ's First Coming, depicts a freshly envisioned sacramental image in which new prominence is given to Mary, to whom the cathedral is dedicated. The Romanesque Madonna enthroned in Majesty—the seat of divine wisdom from which Christ rules—is flanked by censing angels and placed beneath a baldachin now lost, with Christ seated on the altar of her lap. The Infancy scenes on the registers below show the incarnation of Christ, through the Child on an altar table at the Nativity directly below his presentation on the altar of the temple, both on a vertical axis with the Madonna in Majesty above.[50]

The tympanum and **lintel**s of the south portal represent the theological idea, argued since the Carolingian period, of Christ's physical presence in the bread and wine of the Eucharist. The belief in the transubstantiation of eucharistic elements at the Consecration into the body and blood of Christ

---

[49]Margot Fassler, "Liturgy and Sacred History in the Twelfth-Century Tympana at Chartres," *Art Bulletin* 75 (1993): 499–520. This interpretation involves a new interpretation of the north portal, traditionally read as an image of the Ascension (507–10). See Snyder, *Medieval Art*, pp. 365–67, figs. 471–75. See also Jungmann, *Mass of the Roman Rite*, 1:107–12.

[50]Fassler, "Liturgy and Sacred History," pp. 510–13; Adolf Katzenellenbogen, *The Sculptural Programs of Chartres Cathedral: Christ, Mary, Ecclesia* (Baltimore, 1959; repr., New York, 1964), pp. 12–15. The Madonna in Majesty, the *sedes sapientiae*—from which the image of the Virgin enthroned with her Child on Chartres' south portal evolved—can be traced back to the tenth century in the north. These wood figures had stood on an altar—or hung above it, or were mounted on a column near it—when not carried in procession or used as a focus of liturgical drama. See Ilene Forsyth, *The Throne of Wisdom: Wood Sculptures of the Madonna in Romanesque France* (Princeton, 1972); and Hans Belting, *Likeness and Presence: A History of the Image before the Era of Art*, trans. Edmund Jephcott (Chicago, 1994), p. 300.

was officially defined at the Fourth Lateran Council of 1215.[51] From that time on into the late Middle Ages, from the point of view of the lay worshipers, the public proclamation of the mystery of the transubstantiation at the Elevation of the Host at the Consecration was the virtual high point of the Mass. Alerted by the ringing of a bell, they could see the host—in ever more elaborate containers—raised up by the priest—in ever more elaborate vestments—to signal their salvation. Communion, following confession, had been affirmed by the Council in 1215 as a yearly obligation, usually at Easter, but unlimited opportunity to see the elevated host was the primary form of lay piety.[52] The intensity of eucharistic devotion spawned the new and more expressive images of Christ's suffering as well as a new liturgical feast of Corpus Christi, initiated in 1246 and of increasing importance in the later Middle Ages.[53]

The emphasis on the need for visual stimuli was further satisfied not only by art and drama but also in the pomp and spectacle of ever more elaborate processionals, for Corpus Christi and other feast days in England and on the continent. In Paris, for example, the old Roman stational system that had been adapted at Centula was imposed on routes through the city on Palm Sunday and special saints' days. Liturgical descriptions of the

---

[51]"Eucharist," *Oxford Dictionary of the Christian Church*, p. 468.

[52]For the Elevation see Jungmann, *Mass of the Roman Rite*, 1:120–22, 2:206–12, and Hardison, *Christian Rite*, pp. 64–65. See also Miri Rubin, *Corpus Christi: The Eucharist in Late Medieval Culture* (Cambridge, 1991; repr. 1992), pp. 49–63. For popular piety in the Late Medieval period see Eamon Duffy, *The Stripping of the Altars: Traditional Religion in England, c.1400–c.1580* (New Haven, 1992), pp. 95–107.

[53]Rubin, *Corpus Christi*, pp. 165–212. The fifth Thursday after Trinity Sunday (p. 174); according to William Durandus's *Rationale divinorum officiorum* (ca. 1298), the fifth Sunday (p. 178). The liturgy is attributed to Thomas Aquinas (pp. 185–96). For the evolution of devotional texts and images see James H. Marrow, *Passion Iconography in Northern European Art of the Late Middle Ages and Early Renaissance: A Study of the Transformation of Sacred metaphor into Descriptive Narrative* (Kortrijk, 1979), esp. pp. 1–27. For the range of images see Henk van Os, *The Art of Devotion in the Late Middle Ages in Europe, 1300–1500* (Princeton, 1994).

processions on Maundy Thursday and All Saints' Day locate the altars in the twelfth-century cathedral of Notre Dame and in the three adjacent churches that had served as satellites to the original Merovingian cathedral of St.-Etienne. Existing altars were enhanced and others added in the thirteenth century when new cathedral space of Notre Dame (Fig. 1) was expanded by the placement of side chapels between the buttresses of the nave and later in radiating chapels extending from the ambulatory and apse.[54]

Many important innovations of the Gothic period were incorporated in Abbot Suger's campaign begun about 1135 to renovate and enlarge the royal abbey church of St.-Denis (Fig. 15). He started with the reconceived twin-towered westwork related to the ninth-century structure that was particularly famous for the rich program of its bronze doors consecrated in 1141. Suger's self-proclaimed triumph, however, was the enlarged design of the eastern chevet, which encompassed the eighth-century choir and the eastern extension of the crypt dedicated to the Virgin made by Abbot Hilduin in the ninth century. The new upper choir was the raised stage for the richly redecorated shrine of St. Denis and his martyred companions, moved up from the crypt to a space "pervaded by wonderful and uninterrupted light

---

[54]Rebecca Baltzer, "The Geography of the Liturgy at Notre-Dame of Paris," in *Plainsong in the Age of Polyphony*, ed. Thomas Forrest Kelly (Cambridge, 1992), pp. 45–64. The Maundy Thursday procession for the washing of the altars, which took place after the main meal, began in the raised sanctuary area—the altar of the Trinity furthest east, the main altar of the Virgin, and that of St. Marcel before his shrine on a high platform between them—followed by the altar of the Magdalen in the south aisle, then up from the nave to three altars in the ambulatory, including the altar of St. Michael in the north ambulatory on a line with the martyrs' altar, then west through the nave to the church of St.-Jean-le-rond, the site of the baptismal font and altars to three other saints, then east along the north cloister to the altar of St. Denis in the church of St.-Denis-du-Pas, reentering the cathedral through the south transept and into the choir through its center door beneath the monumental cross. See also Craig M. Wright, "The Shape of the Liturgy in the Late Middle Ages," in *Music and Ceremony at Notre Dame of Paris, 500–1500* (Cambridge, 1989), pp. 98–139 and fig. II (diagram and seating plan of the choir of Notre Dame).

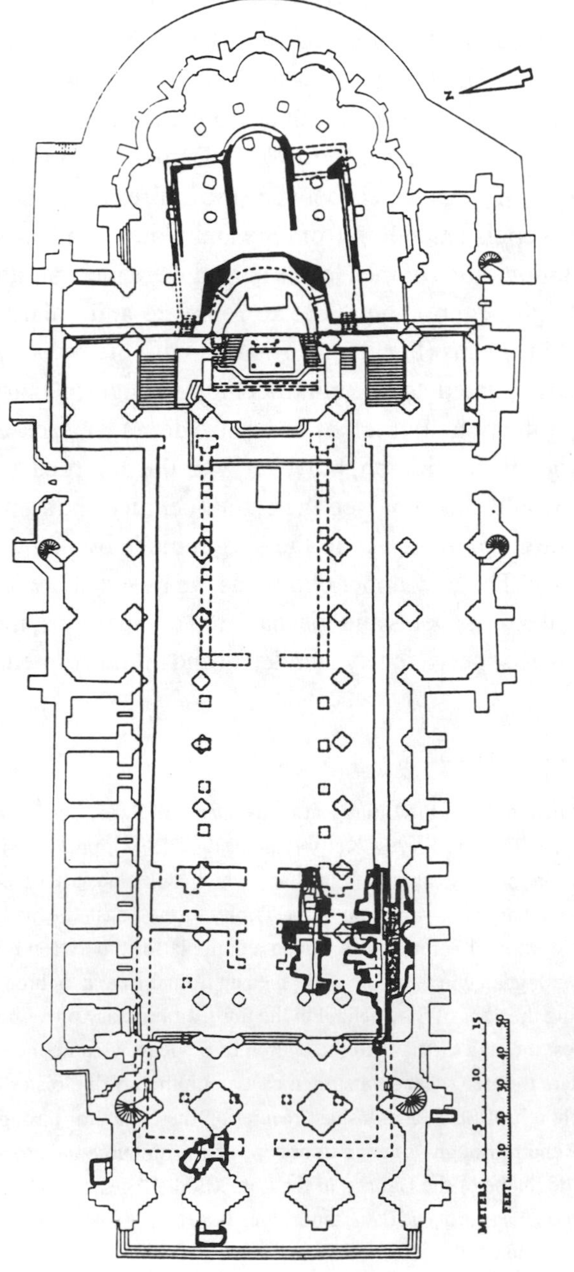

Figure 15. The plans of Fulrad's eighth-century church (775) and Hilduin's ninth-century chapel (822) superimposed on the plan of St.-Denis. (From: The Papers of Sumner McKnight Crosby, The Cloisters Archives, The Metropolitan Museum of Art).

of most luminous windows," as he put it,[55] in the radiating chapels ringing the upper choir and apse. The prominent display of the shrine in a raised area behind the high altar dedicated to the martyrs was a feature to be imitated widely in subsequent church design, for example the provisions made at Canterbury for the shrine of Thomas of Becket, martyred in 1170. Suger's arrangement left the altar to Sts. Peter and Paul at the eastern end of the lower choir, in a placement analogous to its original location (Figs. 15, 16). In other words, for all the innovation with which he is credited, Suger made a conscious effort to recall, if not actually reuse, parts of the fabric of the earlier church. Its liturgy, too, retained its earlier structure, even as liturgical embellishments were added. The new choir stood over an enlarged crypt of a similar plan of nine altars, in which the center chapel on the eastern axis on both levels was dedicated to the Virgin. The Fourth Lateran Council's reiteration of Pope Urban II's requirement of a Mass to the Virgin daily rather than only on Saturday promoted the rise of enlarged chapels dedicated to her, often in the same location as in Suger's arrangement, until they became so large as to warrant a separate space. The central chapel, originally dedicated to the Trinity, was the location of daily Masses to the Virgin in the squared east end of Salisbury Cathedral.[56]

The expression of divinity through the rich dark colors of the glass has long been associated with the liturgical allegorization of the Syrian

---

[55]*Abbot Suger on the Abbey Church of St.-Denis and Its Art Treasures*, ed. and trans. Erwin Panofsky, 2nd ed. Gerda Panofsky-Soergel (Princeton, 1979), p. 37. See also William W. Clark, "Suger's Church at Saint-Denis: The State of Research," in *Abbot Suger and Saint-Denis: A Symposium*, ed. Paula Lieber Gerson (New York, 1986), pp. 105–30 (and bibliography).

[56]For a discussion of renovation versus innovation in the architecture at St.-Denis see Eric C. Fernie, "Sugers's 'Completion' of Saint-Denis," and Clark, "Continuity and Contextuality," in *Artistic Integration in Gothic Buildings*, pp. 84–91, 92–113. For Canterbury's shrine as a copy of Saint-Denis see Jean Bony, "What Possible Sources for the Chevet at Saint-Denis?" in *Abbot Suger and Saint Denis*, ed. Gerson, pp. 132–33, fig. 5. For the **Lady chapel** see Klukas, "Durham Cathedral" (note 43 above), p. 76; for Salisbury see Draper, "Architecture and Liturgy," pp. 86–88, fig. 54.

Figure 16. View of the upper and lower choirs of St.-Denis. Viollet-le-Duc, *Dictionnaire raisonné de l'architecture française*, 3:233.

theologian Pseudo-Dionysius the Areopagite (ca. 500) to whom Abbot Hilduin had laid special claim in the liturgy of the Office of St. Denis, which he wrote for Louis the Pious. Dionysian writings were best known through the translation of John Scotus Erigena (ca. 810–ca. 870), although Hilduin had also made a translation of some of these texts and in his *vita* of St. Denis had conflated his identity with both the first-century Dionysius, the disciple of St. Paul, and the patron saint of Paris to whom the abbey church was dedicated. It is thought that interest in Dionysian ideas renewed by the contemporary commentaries of Hugh of St. Victor (ca. 1096–1141) lies behind the aesthetic of Suger's glass that imbues his choir space with a new sense of divine presence within the architecture of the heavenly Jerusalem, but it also might be seen as another form of conscious revival of the abbey's past.[57]

A further expression of transcendent radiance was Suger's great cross of gold and jewels, which once stood on its richly enameled base at the western edge of his upper choir. According to an *ordo* written 1234–36 after further amendments had been made to Suger's plan to enlarge and enhance the original church building, it would seem to be this cross which was carried by four deacons on Good Friday before the altar and tomb of the martyrs in the apse for the abbot to adore and then was placed before the main altar of Sts. Peter and Paul in the lower choir—dedicated to the Savior in Suger's time—where it was raised up high and uncovered. Members of the lay congregation (presumably male) were permitted to venerate this or another cross at the altar of the Trinity further west in the lower choir, which was the location of several tombs, including that of Charles the Bald.

---

[57]See *Abbot Suger and Saint-Denis*, ed. Gerson, especially Grover A. Zinn, Jr., "Suger, Theology, and the Pseudo-Dionysian Tradition," pp. 33–40; Neils Krogh Rasmussen, O.P., "The Liturgy at Saint-Denis: A Preliminary Study," pp. 41–48; Paula Lieber Gerson, "Suger as Iconographer: The Central Portal of the West Facade of Saint-Denis," pp. 183–98, esp. 195nn7 and 8; and Madeline Harrison Caviness, " Suger's Glass at Saint-Denis: The State of Research," pp. 257–72. See also Robertson, *The Service Books of the Royal Abbey of Saint-Denis* (note 20 above), pp. 46–49, 235–48.

For the feasts of the Invention and Exaltation of the Holy Cross, "ante crucem" was the place in the nave between the crucifix with Mary and John that at that time stood above the doorway of the choir screen and the oratory of St. Hippolytus in the north **crossing** of the transept.[58]

The dramatic possibilities of a program of stained glass as coherent as that of portal sculpture can be seen in the Gothic **retrochoir**, the area east of the monks' choir in the transept, added at the end of the twelfth century to the church of St.-Remi at Reims (Fig. 17). The architectural vision of the heavenly Jerusalem shows the eucharistic image of the crucified Christ—above a chalice and the skull of Adam—with Mary and John in the **axial** window of the choir tribune. Directly above in the axial window of the clerestory, the Virgin and Child presided over her heavenly court, originally flanked by a full contingent of single figures of apostles, prophets, and patriarchs seated above archbishops in each of the lights on either side. The clerestory of the darker Romanesque nave continued the sequence with images of Frankish kings beneath Old Testament precursors to supervise the procession that brought the new French king to Mass the day after his coronation.[59] In the more flowing space of the nave and transepts of a Gothic building, the clerestories and aisle walls were filled with glass depicting saints' lives and biblical scenes for the benefit of a lay congregation behind choirscreens that barred access to the sanctuary reserved for the clergy beyond. Above them all, the Queen of Heaven enthroned with her Child, as

---

[58]Edward B. Foley, *Paris, Bibliothèque Mazarine 526: The First Ordinary of the Royal Abbey of St.-Denis in France* (Fribourg, 1990), pp. 183–260, 382. For the change in the placement of the altar of St. Hippolytus from Suger's time see esp. pp. 225–32. Its move to the nave near the tomb of Pepin corresponds to its original location in the Carolingian westwork. For the liturgy of St.-Denis see further Anne Robertson, "The Reconstruction of the Abbey Church of St.-Denis 1231–1281: The Interplay of Music and Ceremony with Architecture and Politics," *Early Music History* 5 (1985): 187–238.

[59]For Saint-Remi see Madeline Harrison Caviness, *Sumptuous Arts at the Royal Abbeys in Reims and Braine* (Princeton, 1990), pp. 21–64.

Figure 17. Reims, Saint-Rémi. Interior of the retrochoir, angled view toward the east. Late twelfth century. Photo: © Martin-Sabon/Arch. Phot./CNMHS, Paris. Cliché MH 52893

in the St.-Remi clerestory, or at the center of a rose window, was the unifying assertion of divine presence at the Mass.[60]

In Italy mosaic continued to cast the spell that northern churches expressed in stained glass, particularly in the apse mosaic, where new prominence was given to the Virgin as evidence of the increased devotion to her. The image of the crowned Virgin enthroned with Christ beneath the canopy of heaven in the apse mosaic in Santa Maria in Trastevere in Rome depicts her coronation that is the culmination of the feast of the Assumption on 15 August (Fig. 18). Peter stands to the right of Christ, leading the donor Pope Innocent II (1130–43) and other church saints carrying the jeweled processional cross and gospel books of the papal processions when icons of the two figures met on that day.[61]

The Coronation of the Virgin is a dominant theme in the thirteenth-century Gothic churches. It is depicted in the gable of the central portal of the west facade of Reims Cathedral, above the standing figure of the crowned Virgin holding her child in the trumeau between jamb figures depicting the Annunciation and Visitation on the right and the Presentation in the Temple on the left (Fig. 19). The image of the Virgin and Child is brought to the altar itself in Giotto's *Enthroned Madonna and Child* of 1310 for the Church of the Ognissanti in Florence, where her monumental presence within a Gothic ciborium—flanked by saints and angels of the heavenly liturgy as with a commanding gaze she presents the Christ Child on the "living altar" of her lap—is a vivid visualization for the worshiper of the nature of the Eucharist (Fig. 20).[62]

---

[60]See, for example, the discussion of Chartres, in Louis Grodecki and Catherine Brisac, *Gothic Stained Glass, 1200–1300* (Ithaca, 1985).

[61]Belting, *Likeness and Presence* (note 50 above), pp. 73, 322, 327–29, figs. 196, II (the eighth-century icon); and Krautheimer, *Rome*, p. 164, fig. 121.

[62]For the Virgin as altar/altar-table see Lane, *The Altar and the Altarpiece* (note 45), pp. 16–18.

Figure 18. The Savior, Virgin Mary, various saints and other figures. Mosaic (1139). Apse. Santa-Maria in Trastevere, Rome. Photo: Alinari/Art Resource, N.Y.

In Duccio's ***Maestà*** of 1311 for the high altar of Siena Cathedral, the iconographic program is expanded around the central image of the enthroned Virgin and Child flanked by smaller standing figures of angels within a gable, which resembles the cathedral's facade (Fig. 21). A full complement of saints stand on either side, beneath half-length apostles in the arcade above and behind four kneeling patron saints, to whom the side altars are dedicated.[63] Originally the **predella** below showed Infancy scenes between figures of Old Testament prophets, and in the pinnacles above were

[63]For the *Maestà* on the high altar in relation to the four side altars see van der Ploeg, *Siena Cathedral* (note 48 above), esp. pp. 109–15. See also James H. Stubblebine, *Duccio di Buoninsegna and his School*, 2 vols. (Princeton, 1979), 1:1–62; 2:figs. 45–127.

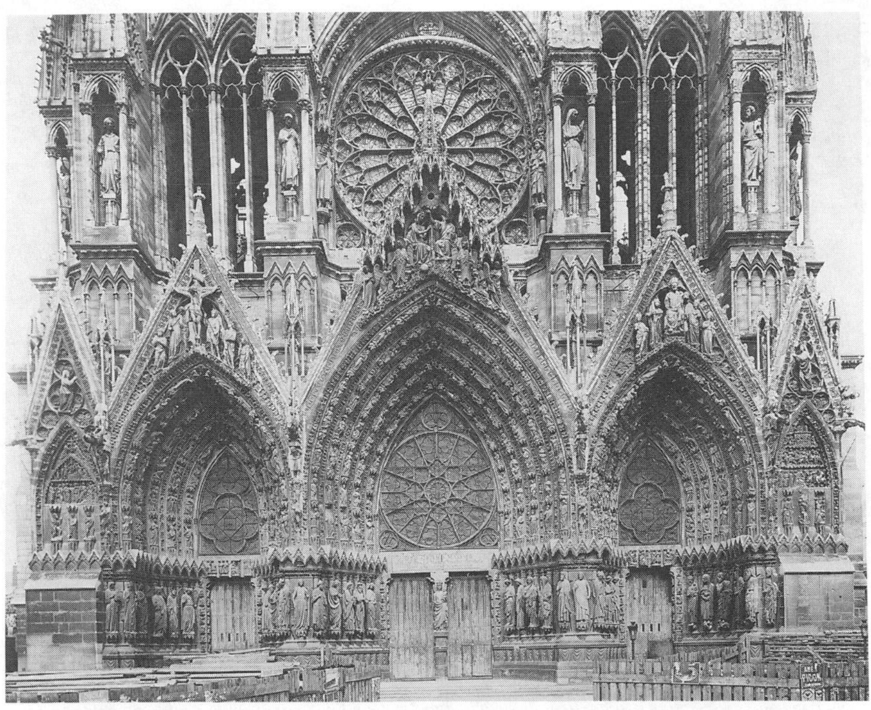

Figure 19. Portals of principal (west) façade. Cathedral, Reims. Photo: Giraudon/Art Resources, N.Y.

a sequence of scenes from the death of the Virgin to her coronation in heaven that relate to the hours of her Office. The back of the panel had forty-three scenes of the life, passion, and resurrected life of Christ that visualize the events remembered in devotions to him.[64]

---

[64]For the Offices of the Virgin and other votive cycles see Harper, *The Forms and Orders of Western Liturgy* (note 37 above), pp. 130–37; and Roger S. Wieck, *Time Sanctified: Books of Hours in Medieval Art and Life* (New York/Baltimore, 1988), pp. 60–93, for the Hours of the Virgin and of the Passion based on those in the breviary made popular through Books of Hours produced in the thirteenth through the sixteenth century. See *Meditations on the Life of Christ*, ed. Isa Ragusa and Rosalie Green (Princeton, 1961), passim, for extended material for devotions to Christ and to Mary written by the Pseudo-Bonaventura, a Franciscan friar living in Tuscany in the second half of the thirteenth century (p. xxi, n20).

Figure 20. Giotto di Bondone (1266–1336). Virgin and Child with Angels (Ognissanti Madonna). 1310. Uffizi, Florence. Photo: Alinari/Art Resource, N.Y.

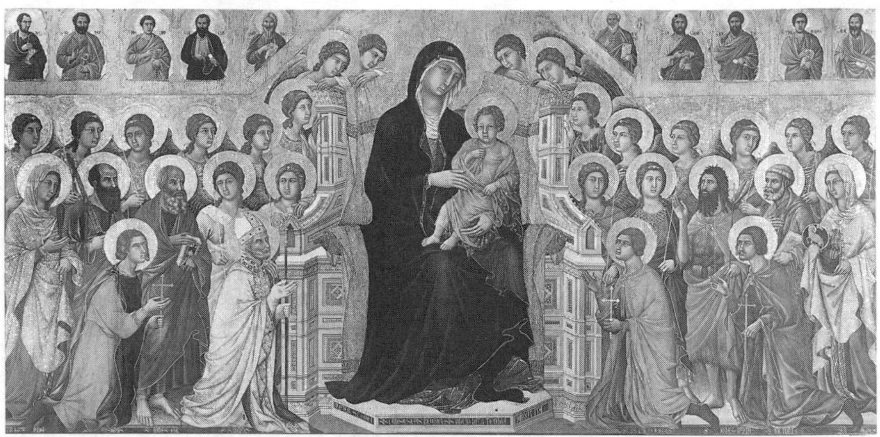

Figure 21. Duccio. Maestà. Museo dell'Opera Metropolitana, Siena. Central Panel (1308–11). Photo: Alinari/Art Resource, N.Y.

Images of a more accessible mother and her playful child become standard as the human aspect of both becomes increasingly emphasized in the Late Medieval period. In late thirteenth-century Italy, painted Romanesque icons of the timeless dignity of a rigidly frontal Virgin are transformed into the sorrowing mother, no doubt affected by newer, more expressive forms of a living presence in icons imported from Byzantium. This image of Mother and Child becomes the centerpiece of altarpieces taking the form of a triptych with scenes of Christ's life and passion in the wings that proliferated under the patronage of the new mendicant orders, particularly that of St. Francis.[65] The grieving images of Mary and John on Italian painted crosses depicting the suffering savior parallel the northern images long associated with the altar of the Cross and in Crucifixion scenes that reflect the heightened devotion to the suffering of the Virgin, especially in

[65]Belting, *Likeness and Presence*, pp. 261–86, 349–408; and Anne Derbes, *Picturing the Passion in Late Medieval Italy: Narrative Painting, Franciscan Ideologies, and the Levant* (Cambridge, 1996).

the writings of Anselm of Canterbury and Bernard of Clairvaux.[66] The Benedictine devotion to the Virgin led to the rise of the cult of the seven sorrows and joys of the Virgin and to the *planctus mariae*, the lament of the Virgin at the foot of the cross.[67] The lament appears in France and Italy in the twelfth century and flourished in the later Middle Ages, both in Latin and in the vernacular, nurtured by Franciscan spirituality and the development of Passion plays. The *planctus* expressed the idea central to the Marian devotion of the Late Medieval period: her compassion, her ability to share in the suffering of her son, gave her the role of co-redemptrix and intercessor on behalf of the believer.[68]

Perhaps nowhere is the reality of this liturgical tradition made more vividly alive to the contemporary—or even a present day—beholder than in Flemish altarpieces of the fifteenth century. Roger van der Weyden's Altarpiece of the Seven Sacraments, for example, is conceived as an architectural vision within an architectural frame (Fig. 22). The foreground of the central panel is dominated by an enormous crucifix in the nave extending high up into the vaults. At the foot of the cross on which her dying son is suspended, the Virgin faints in the arms of St. John, surrounded by mourning figures of the three Marys—Mary Magdelene, in fifteenth-century dress, the particular model for the repentant beholder. The image is a visualization of the transubstantiation that takes place at the Elevation of the Host, the

---

[66]Sandro Sticca, *The Planctus Mariae in the Dramatic Tradition of the Middle Ages*, trans. Joseph R. Berrigan (Athens, 1988), esp. pp. 1–18, 50–58. See also discussion of devotional literature and imagery in Marrow, *Passion Iconography* (note 54 above).

[67]Another innovation of Eastern origin, the Virgin's *planctus* entered the liturgy of the Veneration of the Cross on Good Friday, the earliest known example from Augsburg, Germany, in the tenth century. See Sticca, *Planctus Mariae*, pp. 31–49, for the Eastern tradition; pp. 59–70, for the Marian cult; and pp. 149–51, for the Augsburger Passionlied in Old Romansh in the Good Friday Veneration of the Cross.

[68]Sticca, *Planctus Mariae*, pp. 71–117; and Otto von Simson, "*Compassio* and *Co-Redemptio* in Roger van der Weyden's Descent from the Cross," *Art Bulletin* 35 (1953): 9–16.

Figure 22. Roger van der Weyden (1400–64). Crucifixion. Center panel from the Triptych of the Seven Sacraments (ca. 1450). Koninklijk Museum voor Schone Kunsten, Antwerp. Photo: Giraudon/Art Resource, N.Y.

liturgical moment depicted in the action of the smaller scale figure of the priest at the altar of the Cross in front of the choir screen behind them. The priest holds up the host above an altar **retable** crowned by a sculpted shrine enclosing a statue of the Virgin and Child accompanied by an angel hovering to the right.[69] The upward thrust of the arches of the nave arcade, continued by colonettes, leads the eye to the network of slender ribs in the vaults of the apse and the glass-filled areas of the **triforium** and axial clerestory windows, an expression of the unity of the heavenly realm beyond the architectural and liturgical divisions of the space below.

What is striking in a consideration of the changes to the configuration of sanctuary space in the course of the Middle Ages is that the essential form is constant. The emphasis changes from the horizontal progression in early Christian churches to the soaring vertical of the later medieval churches, from the devotion to the triumphal jeweled cross to the contemplation of the suffering Christ. The architecture and the imagery reflect the shift in emphasis in the Mass itself and in the understanding of the nature of the eucharistic celebration. Nonetheless, the basic structure of the Mass maintains a remarkable consistency, as does the basic basilican form of the groundplan to accommodate a processional movement through the church and the establishment of a hierarchy of space levels. The dominant images of church decoration—on portals, apse, choir screen, and altarpiece—have their roots in the early period. In architecture as well as the liturgy, there is a marked tendency to maintain the older tradition even as new forms elaborate them. It is thus possible to see the stational system of early Christian Rome behind the many processions for the faithful throughout the late medieval church year that transformed their own place and time and brought

---

[69]Lane, *The Altar and the Altarpiece*, pp. 82–85. The priest is similar in scale to the figures depicting the sacraments of baptism, penance, and confirmation on the left wing of the triptych; ordination, marriage, and extreme unction on the right.

them into the celestial realm of the church itself.[70] Whatever the innovations in devotional practice and in the embellishment of the setting and the church furniture it housed, they remain tied to traditions established in an earlier period and to the desire to make visible and real both the immediacy and the transcendent nature of the Mass celebration.

---

[70]In a brief overview, it is not possible to encompass the variety of medieval structures, nor to account for the regional differences that responded to varying requirements of specific patronage, politics, and local rivalries as well as to varying devotional customs and veneration of local saints. But the variety was embraced within the broad outlines sketched here.

CHURCH PORCHES AND THE LITURGY IN TWELFTH-CENTURY ROME[1]

NANCY SPATZ

CHRISTIANITY ALWAYS HAS BEEN CONNECTED INTIMATELY with architecture: its messiah was born in a stable; he preached in the temple in Jerusalem and celebrated his last meal in the upper room of a house in Jerusalem; he was interrogated in the palaces of the Roman and Jewish authorities and buried in a tomb hewn from rock; his first adherents gathered together in a room where they experienced the risen Christ and received the Holy Spirit. During the liturgical year these places and events are memorialized in Christian churches throughout the world. Through liturgy the church building itself could become a physical metaphor of Solomon's Temple in Jerusalem or of the Heavenly Jerusalem of the Apocalypse.

---

[1]The author wishes to thank the National Endowment for the Humanities and the Graduate School and Foundation of the University of Northern Colorado for their financial support for this research. She also wishes to express her deep appreciation to Dale Kinney and Birgitta Wohl, directors of the NEH 1993 Summer Seminar *Spolia: The Medieval Reuse of Antiquity* at the American Academy in Rome where work on this paper was begun; without their support and expertise this paper could not have been written. She also thanks Barbara Newman and Johannes Tripps for their helpful comments and corrections. Special thanks are due to E. Ann Matter and Thomas Heffernan who were endless sources of encouragement, practical advice, and expertise. The opinions and errors in this paper are solely the responsibility of the author.

This chapter will demonstrate some possible connections between liturgy and architecture by looking at one discrete architectural unit, the porch, added to Roman churches in the twelfth and early thirteenth centuries. How could a porch serve the needs of the parish community? And how did it complement the architecture and liturgy of the entire city? By pursuing these questions precisely limited in space and time, this chapter will suggest some possible general avenues of research for those wishing to further investigate the interface between liturgy and architecture.[2]

Statement of the Problem: Church Renovation in Rome ca. 1100–1217

An enthusiasm for remodeling churches and basilicas arose in Rome in the twelfth century. At least three forces were behind this in varying degrees: a papacy claiming more authority and prestige as a result of the Gregorian Reform and the successful resolution of the Investiture Controversy; a newly constituted college of cardinals proclaiming itself a spiritual Roman Senate, and eager to embellish its titular churches; and the general revival of culture and society in western Europe known as the Twelfth-Century Renaissance.[3] During this period many church interiors were newly

---

[2]For an excellent survey of modern scholarship on architecture and liturgy see the recent article by Sible de Blaauw, "Architecture and Liturgy in Late Antiquity and the Middle Ages: Traditions and Trends in Modern Scholarship," *Archiv für Liturgiewissenschaft* 33 (1991): 1–34.

[3]The best recent general work on Medieval Rome is Richard Krautheimer, *Rome, Profile of a City, 312–1308* (Princeton, N.J.,1980); see also his *Three Christian Capitals: Topography and Politics* (Berkeley, 1983); and *St. Peter's and Medieval Rome* (Rome, 1985). The classic historical account is Ferdinand Gregorovius, *History of the City of Rome in the Middle Ages*, written 1859–1870; trans. Mrs. Gustavus W. Hamilton, 8 vols. (London, 1894–1902; repr. New York, 1967). See also Percy Ernst Schramm, *Kaiser, Rom und Renovatio: Studien und Texte zur Geschichte des Römischen Erneuerungsgedankens vom Ende des Karolingischen Reiches bis zum Investiturstreit*, 2 vols. (Leipzig and Berlin, 1929); Robert Brentano, *Rome*

decorated with marble fragments laid in geometric patterns, known as "cosmatesque" marble work; typically, pavements, chancels, thrones, ambones, candlesticks, and lintels would receive this ornamentation.[4] This building enthusiasm also manifested itself in the appearance, for the first time, of large bell towers (*campanili*) throughout the city. Ann Priester has connected this particular building program to the laity's heightened interest in observing the prayers of the canonical hours. In her words, "belltowers served as architectural symbols for liturgical regularity and reform."[5]

Another striking element of this building campaign was the addition of front porches to churches. These porches projected from and were supported by the **facade** of the church. Usually consisting of a clay tile roof supported by wooden beams over antique column shafts and capitals, the

before Avignon: A Social History of Thirteenth-Century Rome (Berkeley,Calif.,1974, repr. 1990); Mary Stroll, *Symbols As Power: The Papacy following the Investiture Contest* (Leiden and New York, 1991); and the Festschrift for Reinhard Elze, *Rom im Höhen Mittelalter: Studien zu den Romvorstellungen und zur Rompolitik vom 10. bis zum 12. Jahrhundert*, ed. Bernhard Schimmelpfennig and Ludwig Schmugge (Sigmaringen, 1992). For the Gregorian Reform see Uta-Renate Blumenthal, *The Investiture Controversy: Church and Monarchy from the Ninth to the Twelfth Century* (rev. ed. and trans., Philadelphia, 1988). For the papacy and the college of cardinals in the twelfth century see I. S. Robinson, *The Papacy 1073–1198: Continuity and Innovation* (Cambridge and New York, 1990). The fundamental work on the Twelfth-Century Renaissance is Charles Homer Haskins, *The Renaissance of the Twelfth Century* (Cambridge, Mass., 1927); for a rebuttal see Erwin Panofsky, *Renaissance and Renascences in Western Art* (rev. ed., New York, 1972). See also the important reappraisal *Renaissance and Renewal in the Twelfth Century*, ed. Robert L. Benson and Giles Constable with Carol D. Lanham (Cambridge, Mass., 1982), especially the essay by Robert Benson about papal, communal, and imperial politics in twelfth-century Rome, "Political *Renovatio*: Two Models from Roman Antiquity," pp. 339–86.

[4]See Dorothy F. Glass, *Studies on Cosmatesque Pavements*, (Oxford, 1980); and Peter Cornelius Claussen, *Magistri Doctissimi Romani: Die Römischen Marmorkünstler des Mittelalters* (Stuttgart, 1987).

[5]Ann Edith Priester, "The Belltowers of Medieval Rome and the Architecture of Renovatio" (Ph.D. thesis, Princeton, 1990), p. 196.

Figure 1. S. Lorenzo fuori le mura, exterior of trabeated porch. Photo: Author.

porch ran along the entire facade of the church and typically was some five meters in depth. The columns were surmounted by a flat **architrave** or an arched arcade (see Figs. 1, 2, 3). Nine of these porches remain attached to church facades out of an original total of approximately twenty-seven built ca. 1100–1217: the titular churches S. Cecilia in Trastevere (St. Cecilia beyond the Tiber), S. Clemente (St. Clement), SS. Giovanni e Paolo (Sts. John and Paul), S. Lorenzo fuori le mura (=FLM) (St. Laurence outside the walls), S. Lorenzo in Lucina (St. Laurence in Lucina), S. Stefano in Monte Celio (St. Stephen on the Caelian Hill), and the ***diaconia*** S. Giorgio al Velabro (St. George in the Velabrum) and the monastic church S. Giovanni a Porta Latina (St. John at the Latin Gate) (see Table in Appendix).[6] The

[6]For S. Cecilia see Richard Krautheimer et al., *Corpus Basilicarum Christianarum Romae: The Early Christian Basilicas of Rome (IV–IX centuries)*, 5 vols. (Vatican City, 1937–77) (hereafter referred to as *Corpus*), 1:94–111; and Guglielmo Matthiae, *S. Cecilia*, Le chiese

Figure 2. S. Clemente, arcaded porch within the atrium (part of quadroporticus in atrium). Photo: Author.

diaconia S. Maria in Cosmedin (St. Mary in Cosmedin) also has an extant porch, but in a very different style; its porch, composed of arcaded brick

---

di Roma illustrate 113 (Rome, 1970). For S. Clemente see *Corpus*, 1:117–36; Joan Barclay Lloyd, *The Medieval Church and Canonry of S. Clemente in Rome* (Rome, 1989); and Leonard E. Boyle, O.P., *A Short Guide to St. Clement's, Rome* (Rome, 1989). For SS. Giovanni e Paolo see *Corpus*, 1:267–303; and Adriano Prandi, *SS. Giovanni e Paolo*, Le Chiese di Roma illustrate 38 (Rome, 1957). For S. Lorenzo FLM see *Corpus*, 2:1–144; and Guglielmo Matthiae, *S. Lorenzo fuori le mura*, Le Chiese di Roma illustrate 89 (Rome, 1966). For S. Lorenzo in Lucina see *Corpus*, 2:159–84; and Luigi Huetter, *S. Lorenzo in Lucina*, Le Chiese di Roma illustrate 27 (Rome, 1930, 1939). For S. Stefano in Monte Celio, see *Corpus*, 4:199–240. For S. Giorgio al Velabro see *Corpus*, 1:244– 65, and A. Giannettini and C. Venanzi, *S. Giorgio al Velabro*, Le Chiese di Roma illustrate 95 (Rome, 1967); the porch of S. Giorgio was destroyed by a bomb in July 1993. For S. Giovanni a Porta Latina see *Corpus*, 1:304–19; and Guglielmo Matthiae, et al., *S. Giovanni a Porta Latina e l'Oratorio di S. Giovanni in Oleo*, Le Chiese di Roma illustrate 51 (Rome, 1958).

Figure 3. S. Lorenzo fuori le mura, interior of porch. Photo: Author.

piers, is preceded by a small foreporch supported by two antique columns.[7] Cardinal churches comprising ***tituli*** (the oldest Christian places of worship in Rome) and *diaconiae* (founded later as community welfare centers) served as parish churches in Rome; their clergy ministered to the needs of the faithful and celebrated the mass for those who lived nearby.[8]

These porches are what Richard Krautheimer defines as nartheces, "... the transverse **vestibule** of a church either preceding nave and aisles as an inner narthex (**esonarthex**) or preceding the facade as an outer narthex (**exonarthex**); the exonarthex may also serve as the terminating transverse **portico** of a quadriporticus" (see **atrium** in Glossary).[9] While the familiar

---

[7]For S. Maria in Cosmedin see *Corpus*, 2:277–307; and G. B. Giovenale, *La Basilica di S. Maria in Cosmedin* (Rome, 1927).

[8]The fundamental reference work on medieval Roman churches is Krautheimer, *Corpus*; it omits churches founded after the ninth century. Christian Hülsen, *Le Chiese di Roma nel Medio Evo: cataloghi ed appunti* (Florence, 1927), summarizes the archival evidence for all the medieval churches of Rome, and includes two large detailed maps of medieval Rome. The survey by Mariano Armellini, *Le Chiese di Roma dal secolo IV al XIX*, rev. ed. Carlo Cecchelli, 2 vols. (Rome, 1942) is somewhat dated but offers brief descriptions of each church. See also *Roma cristiana*, ed. Carlo Galassi Paluzzi, 18 vols. (Bologna, 1961–67), esp. vol. 4: *Le Chiese di Roma dall'XI al XVI secolo*, ed. Vicenzo Golzio and Giuseppe Zander (Bologna, 1963). For a short but thoughtful study see Émile Mâle, *The Early Churches of Rome*, trans. David Buxton (Chicago, 1960). Claussen, *Magistri*, includes detailed information about the marble work in twelfth- and thirteenth-century Roman churches, and suggests revised dates for the renovation of some churches. A series of pamphlets of varying quality on individual Roman churches has been published in Rome since the 1920's entitled *Le Chiese di Roma illustrate*. For churches built in or near ancient monuments see Ernest Nash, *Pictorial Dictionary of Ancient Rome*, 2 vols. (New York, 1961–62). The author thanks Joseph Dyer for alerting her to a valuable new work that appeared too recently to incorporate into this study: Ferrucio Lombardi, *Roma: Le chiese scomparse: la memoria storico della città* (Rome, 1996).

[9]Richard Krautheimer, *Early Christian and Byzantine Architecture* (Baltimore, 1965; repr. 1967), p. 361. For discussions of the liturgical significance of *atria* and nartheces in late antiquity see Suzanne Spain Alexander, "Studies in Constantinian Church Architecture," *Rivista di archeologia cristiana* 47 (1971): 281–330 and 49 (1973): 33–44; and Jean-Charles

Romanesque churches in northern Europe ca. 1100 have interior nartheces or vestibules, the churches of Rome in this period tend to have external nartheces similar to those of late antique churches.[10] (See Fig. 4.) Only three churches had the full **quadriporticus** and atrium of late antiquity added in the twelfth century: the *tituli* S. Clemente and SS. Quattro Coronati (Four Crowned Saints), replacing the structures heavily damaged by the Norman raids of 1084, and S. Gregorio Magno (St. Gregory the Great), a monastic church (see Fig. 5).[11] The other churches received only the simple exo-narthex, a feature dating from antiquity and the Carolingian period.

Why did so many churches in Rome have porches added to them in this period? In the past scholars have tried to explain the appearance of these porches in either ideological or aesthetic terms. One way of understanding them is in relation to the practice of incorporating ***spolia*** into new buildings. *Spolia* means, literally, goods plundered from something or someone (compare in English, "the spoils of war"), but in relation to architecture it means

---

Picard, "L'Atrium dans les églises paléochrétiennes d'occident," in *Actes du XIe congrès international d'archéologie chrétienne*, 3 vols. (Rome, 1989), 1:505–58. More specialized studies include Guglielmo Matthiae, "Basiliche paleocristiane con ingresso a polifora," *Bolletino d'arte* n.s. 42 (1947): 107–21; and Richard Stapleford, "Constantinian Politics and the Atrium Church," in *Art and Architecture in the Service of Politics*, ed. Henry A. Millon and Linda Nochlin (Cambridge, Mass., 1978), pp. 2–19.

[10]The most comprehensive treatments of Roman church porches built in the twelfth century are by P. Pensabene and M. Pomponi, "Contributi per una ricerca sul reimpiego e il 'recupero' dell'Antico nel Medioevo 2. I portici cosmateschi a Roma," *Rivista dell'istituto nazionale d'archeologia e storia dell'arte*, s.III, 14–15 (1991–92): 305–46; and Golzio and Zander, *Le Chiese di Roma dall'XI al XVI secolo*, pp. 32–49. See also Mâle, *Early Churches*, pp. 138–39; Krautheimer, *Profile*, pp. 173–75, 325; and John Onians, *Bearers of Meaning: The Classical Orders in Antiquity, the Middle Ages, and the Renaissance* (Princeton, 1988). For the portals and westworks of northern Romanesque and Gothic churches see the important book by Peter Cornelius Claussen, *Chartres-Studien zu Vorgeschichte, Funktion und Skulptur der Vorhallen* (Wiesbaden, 1975), esp. pp. 6–13 for a discussion of their liturgical importance.

[11]For SS. Quattro Coronati see *Corpus*, 4:1–36; for S. Gregorio see *Corpus*, 1:320–26.

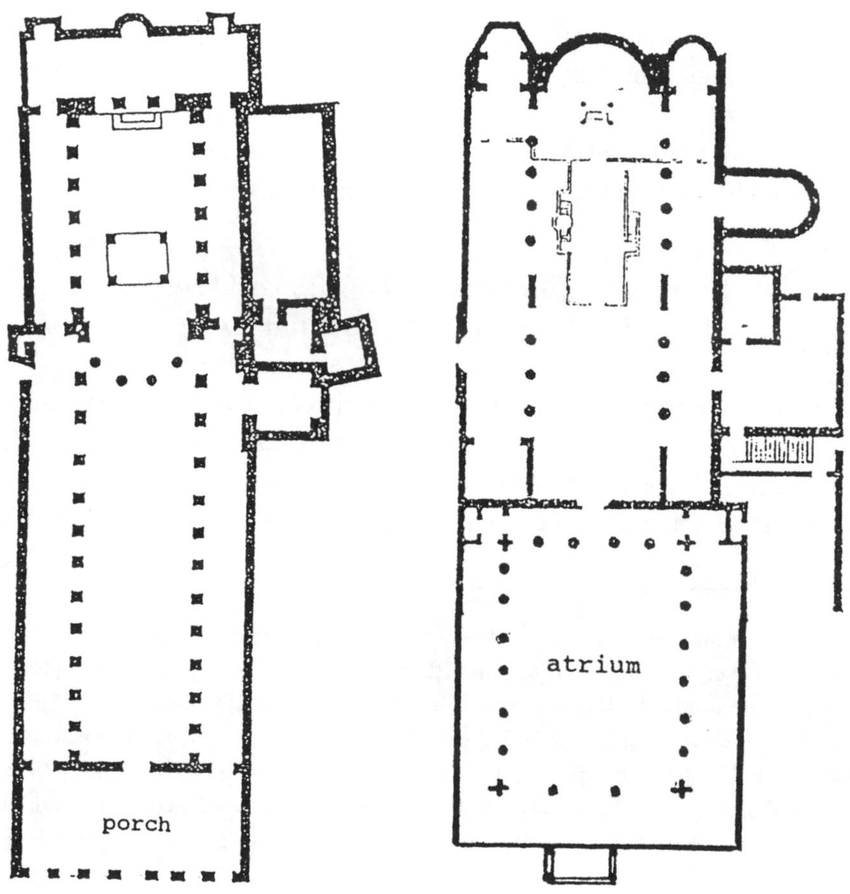

Figure 4. S. Lorenzo fuori le mura floorplan of church. Diagram after *Guida d'Italia: Roma*, 8th ed. (Milan: Touring Club Italiano, 1993). Used with permission.

Figure 5. S. Clemente floorplan of church. Diagram after *Guida d'Italia: Roma*, 8th ed. (Milan: Touring Club Italiano, 1993). Used with permission.

the reuse of antique materials. All of the column shafts and many of the capitals used in these porches date from the classical period; other capitals were carved by medieval craftsmen *ex novo* in a precise imitation of the antique.[12] Or porches can be explained as "triumphal openings," the product of the ideological building campaign of the papacy displaying its triumph over the emperors.[13] According to other scholars they are part of a classicizing trend inspired by the early Christian forms seen in the basilicas of St. Peter and St. Paul and echoed in Montecassino.[14]

Liturgical and Sacramental Functions of Porches for the Local Parish Community

The above theories treat the porches as static aesthetic monuments of art with little consideration of their actual intended functions or place in the community of worshipers. An alternative method of research is to turn to liturgy to ascertain how the porches might have been used in the twelfth

[12]For a discussion of *spolia* see Arnold Esch, "Spolien. Zur Wiederverwendung antiker Baustücke und Skulpturen im mittelalterlichen Italien," *Archiv für Kulturgeschichte* 51 (1969): 1–64; and the articles by Dale Kinney, "Spolia from the Baths of Caracalla in S. Maria in Trastevere," *Art Bulletin* 68 (1986): 379–97; "Rape or Restitution of the Past? Interpreting *Spolia*," in *The Art of Interpreting*, ed. Susan C. Scott (University Park, Penn., 1995), pp. 52–67; and "Making Mute Stones Speak: Reading Columns in S. Nicola in Carcere and S. Maria in Aracoeli," in *Architectural Studies in Memory of Richard Krautheimer*, ed. Cecil L. Striker (Mainz, 1996), pp. 83–89. Compare Pensabene and Pomponi (see note 11), "Contributi," pp. 335–46. For contemporary laws regarding *spolia* see John Phillip Lomax, "*Spolia* as Property," *Respublica litterarum* 20 (1997): 83–94.

[13]Peter Cornelius Claussen, "Renovatio Romae. Erneuerungsphasen römischer Architektur im 11. und 12. Jahrhundert," in *Rom im Höhen Mittelalter*, ed. Schimmelpfennig and Schmugge (see note 8), pp. 87–125, esp. pp. 99–122. Compare Ingo Herklotz, "Der mittelalterliche Fassadenportikus der Lateranbasilika und seine Mosaiken: Kunst und Propaganda am Ende des 12. Jahrhunderts," *Römischen Jahrbuch der Bibliotheca Hertziana* 25 (1989): 25–95, esp. pp. 33–36.

[14]See Herbert Bloch, "The New Fascination with Ancient Rome," and Ernst Kitzinger, "The Arts as Aspects of a Renaissance: Rome and Italy," in *Renaissance and Renewal*, ed. Benson et al., pp. 615–36 and 637–70 respectively. Compare Krautheimer, *Profile*, pp. 176–85.

century.[15] It must be remembered that there would be no complete uniformity in liturgical practice until after the Middle Ages: typically each bishop followed a local tradition of liturgical practices in his diocese, and instructed his priests in it.[16] Fortunately there is a sizeable amount of information about the liturgy of medieval Rome.

It is particularly rewarding to study the liturgy of Rome because it influenced the whole western Church. The Roman liturgy became predominant for five major reasons. First, from the eighth through the eleventh centuries, the Frankish and German rulers desired to institute and spread the "official Roman liturgy" to demonstrate their piety and enhance their prestige. Second, the pope and his curia were destined to spend long periods in exile from the eleventh to the fifteenth centuries due to political struggles between the papacy and the emperor, revolts of the Roman people and local nobility against papal government, and the Great Schism (1378–1417). These periods of exile helped spread Roman liturgical rites throughout France and the Empire. Third, the pope had tremendous influence over the liturgical practices of his **suffragan** bishops, who numbered about one

---

[15]In early Christianity the narthex may have been used by adults preparing for baptism [catechumens]; after attending the first half of the Mass consisting of the entrance rites, scriptural readings, and homily, they were sent outside the church to wait, possibly in the narthex or atrium. In the early middle ages infant catachumens were baptized only on Easter Vigil and Pentecost; on the Sundays previous to these feasts they would be blessed and then sent outside the church, presumably to the porch or atrium, in a ceremony called the "scrutiny." By the eleventh century babies seem to have been baptized soon after birth, and the practice of scrutinies fell into disuse. See Krautheimer, *Early Christian and Byzantine Architecture*, pp. 19, 69; Antoine Chavasse, "Le carême romain et les scrutins prébaptismaux avant le IXe siècle," *Recherches de science religieuse* 35 (1948): 325–81; and Pierre-Marie Gy, "Du Baptême pascal des petits enfants au baptême *quamprimum*," in *Haut moyen-âge: culture, éducation et société. Études offertes à Pierre Riché*, ed. Michel Sot (Nanterre, 1990), pp. 353–365.

[16]The best introduction to the different liturgies of the West is Cyrille Vogel, *Medieval Liturgy: An Introduction to the Sources*, rev. and trans. William G. Storey and Niels Krogh Rasmussen, O.P., with John K. Brooks-Leonard (Washington, D.C., 1986).

hundred in central Italy. In liturgical matters these bishops would follow the tradition of their metropolitan, the bishop of Rome. Fourth, the growing power and prestige of the papacy, buttressed by the success of the four general councils held at the Lateran in Rome in 1123, 1139, 1179, and 1215, and the triumph of the papal-sponsored First Crusade (1095–99), also helped spread the influence of the Roman liturgy.[17] Finally, the Franciscan movement was also very important in disseminating Roman liturgical practices throughout Europe in the thirteenth century.[18]

The most detailed information about the actual performance of the rites of the liturgy of the Mass—the gestures and movements of the celebrants and worshipers and their physical location in and around the church—is found in the types of liturgical books called *ordines* and pontificals.[19] While

---

[17]For the story of the spread of the Roman liturgy see Vogel, *Medieval Liturgy*, pp. 135–271. See also Michel Andrieu, *Le Pontifical romain du XII*[e] *siècle* (hereafter *Pont. XII*), introduction, pp. 1–19; this is the first volume of Andrieu, *Le Pontifical romain au moyen âge*, which also contains: 2. *Le Pontifical de la Curie romaine au XIII*[e] *siècle*; 3. *Le Pontifical de Guillaume Durand*; 4. *Tables alphabétiques* (Vatican City, 1938–40, 1941). For the liturgy of the three greatest basilicas of Rome see Sible de Blaauw, *Cultus et Decor: Liturgia e architettura nella Roma tardoantica e medievale: Basilica Salvatoris, Sanctae Mariae, Sancti Petri* (Vatican City, 1994; originally published in Dutch in 1987). For a good introductory account of the medieval papacy see Geoffrey Barraclough, *The Medieval Papacy* (New York, 1968). For the liturgy and music of medieval Rome see Joseph Dyer, "The Schola Cantorum and Its Roman Milieu in the Early Middle Ages," in *De Musica et Cantu: Studien zur Geschichte der Kirchenmusik und der Oper: Helmut Hucke zum 60. Geburtstag*, ed. Peter Cahn and Ann-Katrin Heimer (Hildesheim and New York, 1993), pp. 19–40; "Prolegomena to a History of Music and Liturgy at Rome During the Middle Ages," in *Essays on Medieval Music: In Honor of David G. Hughes*, ed. Graeme Boone (Cambridge, Mass. and London, 1995), pp. 91–119; and "Roman Singers of the Later Middle Ages," in *Cantus Planus. Papers Read at the Sixth Meeting of the International Musicological Society Study Group in Eger, Hungary, 1993* (Budapest, 1995), pp. 45–64.

[18]See Stephen Joseph Peter Van Dijk and Joan Hazelden Walker, *The Origins of the Modern Roman Liturgy: The Liturgy of the Papal Court and the Franciscan Order in the Thirteenth Century* (Westminster, Md. and London, 1960).

[19]The following description of *ordines* is from Vogel, *Medieval Liturgy*, pp. 135–224. For further details and the critical edition of fifty *ordines* see Michel Andrieu, *Les Ordines*

sacramentaries contain the necessary prayers for the chief celebrant, lectionaries contain the yearly cycle of readings from the Bible, and antiphonaries contain the texts sung by cantors, the *ordines* contain only the directions for the performance of the liturgy (see the essay in this volume by Matter and Krochalis).

Each *ordo* contained different material. They covered matters as diverse as the practice of penance, the transfer of relics, the liturgy of Holy Week and other important feasts, and the ordination of lectors, deacons, priests, and the pope. Dating from the eighth to the tenth century, the Roman *ordines* are a mixture of Roman, Frankish, and German liturgical traditions, although they purport to be the official tradition of Rome. They were popularized and widely disseminated due to the efforts of the Carolingian and German emperors and the widespread prestige of Rome as a place of pilgrimage to the tombs of the martyrs.

In the tenth century the practices outlined in many of the *ordines* were revived in Rome through the efforts of Holy Roman Emperor Otto the Great during his visits to Italy between 950 and 973. In Rome the local liturgical tradition had decayed and many ceremonies were lost ca. 850–950, a time of widespread confusion and violence. Otto and his papal appointees introduced the work known as the Mainz Pontifical or the Romano-Germanic Pontifical of the Tenth Century (hereafter RGP); through it the traditions of Rome were brought back to the city after centuries of adaptation in Germany and France.[20] The pontifical was a new type of liturgical book that first appeared in the countries north of the Alps in the ninth century. It contained both the prayers and the directions necessary for ceremonies normally reserved for the bishop, and thus is an amalgamation of the sacramentary and *ordines*. In time the pontifical would supplant collections of

---

romani du haut moyen âge, 5 vols. (Louvain, 1931, 1948–61). See also Andrieu, *Le pontifical romain au moyen âge*.

[20]For the history of the RGP see Vogel, *Medieval Liturgy*, pp. 225–247. For the text see Cyrille Vogel et al., *Le Pontifical romano-germanique du dixième siècle*, 3 vols. (Vatican City, 1963, 1972).

ordines in most dioceses. New *ordines* would continue to be written in Rome describing papal ceremonies, particularly those connected with the liturgical year; these will be discussed later in this chapter.

The RGP was immensely influential. It was composed originally at the monastery of St. Alban in Mainz, and soon other German dioceses adapted it enthusiastically as part of the *Renovatio imperii*, renewal of the empire. The political and religious endeavors of the Ottonian emperors spread it even further. This pontifical was copied widely and served as the basis for the Twelfth- and Thirteenth-Century Roman Pontificals, themselves superseded by the Pontifical of William Durandus, composed ca. 1293–1295.[21] The latter became a standard reference work for Catholic bishops presiding over the liturgy. In time the texts of rites reserved for priests were removed from the old pontificals and put into the Ritual, a separate liturgical book. The Pontifical of Durandus and several different Rituals were printed in the fifteenth century; the official standard versions of the Pontifical and the *Rituale Romanum* were published, respectively, in 1595 and 1614.[22]

The principal source for liturgy in the city of Rome in the twelfth century is the Twelfth-Century Roman Pontifical. The edition by Andrieu is based on four different manuscript versions composed ca. 1150, ca. 1073–1119, and ca. 1200. The latest exemplar, known as the Pontifical of Apamea, was transcribed in Syria and provides the best information for actual liturgical practices in the city of Rome. It relies heavily on the earlier versions of the Twelfth-Century Roman Pontifical and also on the different papal *ordines* of the twelfth century by Benedict, Albinus, and Cencius. Although it includes a description of ceremonies specific to the city of Rome, it also has general descriptions of ceremonies appropriate for any bishop in the western Church.[23]

---

[21]For the history of the Roman Pontifical see Vogel, *Medieval Liturgy*, pp. 249–56. *Le Pontifical de Guillaume Durand* was edited by Michel Andrieu as the third volume of his *Le Pontifical romain au moyen âge*.

[22]For the history of the Ritual see Vogel, *Medieval Liturgy*, pp. 257–65.

[23]*Pont. XII*, introduction, pp. 102–14.

Let us return to our initial question. Does the Twelfth-Century Roman Pontifical mention any activities taking place on the porch of a church? The words *atrium* (the open roofed forecourt of a church of which the porch may be a part) and ***porticus*** (a covered arcaded walkway) appear only a few times in the entire work. *Ordines* for the consecration of new suffragan bishops stipulate that the ceremony take place in a special Saturday evening ceremony held in the atrium of a Roman basilica.[24] An *ordo* for Holy Thursday states that the ceremony for the public penance of sinners is held in an atrium outside a church.[25] This ceremony would have traditionally taken place at the cathedral of the city, S. Giovanni in Laterano (St. John in the Lateran); however, it is unlikely that the rites of public penance were still practiced in Rome in the twelfth century.[26] The word *porticus* appears only in reference to the portico of S. Venanzio (St. Venantius) at the baptistry of the Lateran, the site of part of the Holy Saturday service.[27]

Despite the fact that there is no further mention of the word for porch in the Twelfth-Century Roman Pontifical we can conjecture about activities that took place in that space based on knowledge of the floor plan of Roman churches. Unlike northern churches, Roman medieval churches generally lack public side entrances: one enters only from the front of the church (generally oriented to the west). Therefore, anything that takes place

---

[24]*Pont. XII*, pp. 138–52, ordo X, and App. IV, pp. 291–92. According to de Blaauw, *Cultus et Decor*, pp. 605–08, 611–16, 735, episcopal consecrations took place at S. Pietro, as did the coronation of emperors; a porphory *rota* in the narthex of the medieval basilica marked a station in the coronation ceremony.

[25]*Pont. XII*, pp. 214–26, ordo XXX.A. Compare de Blaauw, *Cultus et Decor*, passim.

[26]Cyrille Vogel, "Les rites de la pénitence publique aux Xe et XIe siècles," in *Mélanges offerts à René Crozet*, ed. Pierre Gallais et Yves-Jean Riou, 2 vols. (Poitiers, 1966), 1:137–44, esp. p. 141. For a general introduction to the different rites of penance in the middle ages see Cyrille Vogel, *Le Pécheur et la pénitence au moyen-âge* (repr. Paris, 1982); and Mary C. Mansfield, *The Humiliation of Sinners: Public Penance in Thirteenth-Century France* (Ithaca, N.Y., 1994).

[27]*Pont. XII*, pp. 238–49, ordo XXXII. Compare de Blaauw, *Cultus et decor*, pp. 302–04.

immediately in front of the church doors must occur on the porch or in the open if there is no porch (see Figs. 4 and 5).

In much of medieval Europe, including parts of Italy, couples exchanged vows and were blessed in front of or on the porch of the church.[28] What evidence exists for this custom in medieval Rome? The best nonliturgical source for aristocratic marriage customs in late fourteenth-century Rome is the treatise *Li nuptiali* written shortly after 1500 by the Roman humanist Marco Antonio Altieri.[29] Altieri wrote this treatise to explain the meanings of traditional marriage practices that were being ignored and forgotten in his own day. For evidence he relied upon his own youthful

---

[28]According to Jean-Baptiste Molin and Protais Mutembe, *Le Rituel du mariage en France du XIIe au XVIe siècle*, (Paris, 1974), pp. 32–47, in England and northern France wedding Masses were preceded by the exchange of vows in front of the church, sometimes on a special porch called the wedding porch. In southern France, however, under the influence of Visigothic law, these preliminary ceremonies took place inside the church. The authors believe that this tradition of the ceremony taking place outside the church began in Normandy, but add that it is also documented in Hamburg, Hungary, Poland, and certain manuscripts of the Roman Pontifical. For French practices see also Georges Duby, *Medieval Marriage: Two Models from Twelfth-Century France* (Baltimore and London, 1991). David Herlihy, *Medieval Households* (Cambridge, Mass., 1985), pp. 13–14, writes that in late antiquity in Italy according to Roman Law the custom was to exchange vows at the door of the church. For practices in Tuscany see Christiane Klapisch-Zuber, *Women, Family, and Ritual in Renaissance Italy*, trans. Lydia G. Cochrane (Chicago and London, 1985), pp. 178–282. For medieval Italy in general see Francesco Brandileone, *Saggi sulla storia della celebrazione del matrimonio in Italia* (Milan, 1906). For other accounts of wedding ceremonies in medieval Europe see Karl Ritzer, *Le mariage dans les Églises chrétiennes du Ier au XIe siècle*, (Paris, 1970); and Kenneth W. Stevenson, *Nuptial Blessing: A Study of Christian Marriage Rites* (London, 1982, and New York, 1983). For a recent study of the iconography of wedding ceremonies in fourteenth-century Italian painting see Max Seidel, "Hochzeitsikonographie im Trecento," *Mitteilungen des Kunsthistorischen Instituts in Florenz* 38/1 (1994): 1–47.

[29]Marco Antonio Altieri, *Li nuptiali*, ed. E. Narducci (Rome, 1873); for the ceremonies described below see pp. 50–53, 66–67. Altieri's account is summarized and analyzed by Brandileone, *Saggi*, pp. 291–306; and Klapisch-Zuber, *Women, Family, and Ritual*, pp. 181–97, 247–60.

memories (he wrote it when he was about sixty) and the testimony of elderly friends and relatives.[30]

According to Altieri, the first step to marriage was the ***abboccamento***, initial marriage negotiations undertaken by the fathers or legal guardians of the couple; the two men sealed the agreement with a kiss. Next was the ***fidanze***, a solemn, public meeting of the males from the two families in a church. There they drew up an official contract of engagement including dowry arrangements and the dates for the marriage ceremonies. This arrangement was also sealed by a kiss.

After this, typically one or two weeks later, the ***arraglia*** took place. At this ceremony the couple exchanged vows in the bride's house and the groom put a ring on the bride's finger while a notary presided. An exchange of gifts and a feast for all the family followed.

The final ceremony, called the ***traductio***, could take place as long as a year after the *arraglia*. On a Sunday morning the bride would leave her parents' house on a white palfrey and ride to the church where she would meet her intended. Even though Altieri does not specify the exact location of the meeting, it most probably took place directly in front of or on the church porch. Together the bride and groom then would enter the church and sit near the altar to hear the nuptial Mass and receive a blessing from the priest. Afterwards the couple continued on to the groom's house where they began living as man and wife.

Although Altieri does not situate the exchange of vows and bestowal of the ring at the door of the church, the best liturgical source, a version of the Twelfth-Century Roman Pontifical copied in Sora, does. This manuscript, written in the beginning of the thirteenth century, contains a description of a wedding ceremony, "Incipit ordo sponsalium."[31] Sora lies about fifty-five

---

[30]For Altieri's career and writings see Klapisch-Zuber, *Women, Family, and Ritual*, pp. 247–60.

[31]The Sora ms. is described and discussed in *Pont. XII*, pp. 71–77, 93–94; text of ceremony transcribed pp. 300–02, App. VIII, "Incipit ordo sponsalium." Andrieu believes that the *ordo*

miles southeast of Rome at the edge of the papal territories in the twelfth century. According to the *Liber Censuum* the pope was the metropolitan of Sora in the twelfth century, and he consecrated new bishops there himself.[32] Given that Sora was included in the jurisdiction of the Roman Pontiff it is likely that practices there were similar to rites in Rome.

According to the Sora *ordo* the couple, their parents, the lord or legal guardian of the woman, and the maid of honor would stand outside the church [*ante fores ecclesie*] together with the celebrant, either a bishop or a priest. The celebrant formally questions the couple about degrees of consanguinity and any possible violence involved in the courtship, both impediments to a valid union, and he witnesses their vows to each other.

Then the priest blesses the ring with the sign of the cross and holy water. In addition to two other prayers he also intones this obscure verse, roughly based on Ps. 67:29–31 [Vulgate numbering]:

> God, entrust your strength. Confirm, God, this that you have done for us from your holy temple in Jerusalem. Kings will offer you gifts. Rebuke the beasts of the woods; let the council of the bulls among the cows of the people exclude those who were tempted by silver.[33]

---

of marriage represents a local tradition, and that, since Sora was close to Naples, the pontifical might reflect some practices imported by the Normans; see *Pont. XII*, p. 94. Ordo XXXVII, "Ad sponsam benedicendum," pp. 260–62, is taken from the Pontifical of Apamea; it provides no description of the preliminary wedding ceremony on the porch of the church apart from the prayers for the blessing of the ring. These prayers are very similar to those in the wedding service in the Pontifical of Sora. The Pontifical of Sora is discussed by Molin and Mutembe, *Le Rituel du mariage*, passim; compare Stevenson, *Nuptial Blessing*, pp. 72, 92, 169–70.

[32]See the remarks by Andrieu, *Pont. XII*, p. 77.

[33]*Pont. XII*, p. 300: "Manda Deus virtutem tuam. Confirma hoc Deus quod operatus es in nobis a templo sancto tuo quod est in Ierusalem. Tibi offerent reges munera. Increpa feras silvarum et concilium taurorum inter vaccas populorum, ut excludantur hi qui probati sunt argento."

This verse appears for the first time in eleventh-century Anglo-Norman rites.[34] The temple of Jerusalem mentioned in the prayer is a potent metaphor: the image of the heavenly Jerusalem, God's kingdom in heaven, is invoked, as are the great temples of Solomon and of Herod in Jerusalem. Thus this present-day event, the celebration of the wedding, is linked to the Old Testament kings and prophets, to events in Jesus' life, and to the Heavenly Jerusalem of the Apocalypse, via the image of the Holy Temple in Jerusalem, the direct spiritual and religious ancestor of the Church. The twelfth-century liturgist Honorius Augustodunensis asserts in *Gemma animae*, his commentary on the Mass, "And so our church takes its form from the temple that Solomon built."[35] Thus the building the couple stands in front of exchanging their vows symbolizes the original Temple in Jerusalem which, according to Scripture, had a deep porch along the width of its nave.[36]

After this prayer the husband slides the ring first on the thumb, then the index finger, and then the middle finger of his bride while saying "With this ring I wed you, in the name of the Father, Son, and Holy Spirit." The celebrant blesses them both, and the party goes inside the church for the Mass.[37]

Although this ceremony is documented in an *ordo* from Sora, this type of wedding liturgy taking place in front of the church and incorporating many of the same prayers probably was common in medieval Rome, too, as its later inclusion in the sixteenth- and seventeenth-century Roman Ritual shows.[38] The location of the ceremony described in the pontifical was not

---

[34]According to Molin and Mutembe, *Le Rituel du mariage*, pp. 136–38; compare Stevenson, *Nuptial Blessing*, pp. 66–67.

[35]Honorius Augustodunensis, *Gemma animae*, PL 72: 541–738, I.cxxvi, "A templo itaque quod Salomon fecit, ecclesia nostra formam accepit" (col. 585).

[36]1 Kings (Vulgate, III Rg) 6:3: "et porticus erat ante templum viginti cubitorum longitudinis iuxta mensuram latitudinis templi et habebat decem cubitos latitudinis ante faciem templi."

[37]*Pont. XII*, p. 301.

[38]See Molin and Mutembe, *Le Rituel du mariage*, pp. 73, 147.

unusual: weddings were commonly celebrated in front of churches throughout much of Italy, Florence being the notable exception.[39] Although Altieri situates the exchange of vows and the bestowal of the ring in the privacy of the bride's house, the entrance to the church and hence its porch still served as a focal point for the ceremony of the *traductio*. And it is possible that in his time non-aristocratic Romans exchanged their vows and bestowed the ring in front of the church as described in the *ordo*. In earlier times the Roman aristocracy, too, might have followed the practices in the *ordo*, since it predates Altieri's evidence about wedding ceremonies by about two hundred years.

From the eleventh century onward the Church attempted to add a religious dimension to marriage; these efforts reached fruition in the decrees concerning marriage at the Council of Trent in the sixteenth century. Thus it is not surprising to find aristocratic Roman couples attending a nuptial Mass as part of their wedding ceremonies, or a priest serving as a witness to marriage vows. But why did the *traductio* described by Altieri specify that the bride and groom should meet *in front of* the church? Why did the vows and exchange of ring described in the *ordo* from Sora take place *outside* the door of the church? The porch may have been used for the exchange of vows for a legal reason; a contract carried out in public in front of a throng of people ensured there would be numerous witnesses in case

[39] Brandileone, *Saggi*, pp. 75–78, 93n1, 90n3, 92, 95, lists statutory evidence for the location of wedding ceremonies in Gaeta (eleventh century "in porta ante ecclesiam"); Padua (from the twelfth century to 1285 "in facie ecclesie"); Cassino (1179 "in conspectu ecclesiae"); Naples (1332 "in facie ecclesiae"); Piacenza (1336 "facto sacramento ante ecclesiam"); and Aquilea (1339 "in facie ecclesiae"). Appendix II, pp. 109–13 in the same work has a transcription of an *ars notaria* composed in the fourteenth century by Leone Speluncano which records ceremonies he notarized "in facie ecclesiae" in Sperlonga. Brandileone also cites extensive evidence for weddings being celebrated in secular places with or without the presence of a priest. And he concludes (p. 95) that since councils and synods again and again reissued directives stipulating clerical involvement in weddings many people must have knowingly or unknowingly disregarded these regulations. For Florentine customs see Klapisch-Zuber, *Women, Family, and Ritual*, pp. 178–282.

the marriage was contested.[40] Likewise the ceremony of the *traductio* served to "publicize" the wedding to the entire community.[41] And perhaps these public ceremonies afforded an opportunity for anyone who might know of any legal impediments to the marriage to come forward.

Let us now turn from a personal sacramental rite of the liturgy, marriage, to a liturgical ceremony for the whole community, the consecration or dedication of a church. A major liturgical event in the life of a church's community, Honorius compares it to a marriage ceremony: "The dedication of a church is the nuptial coupling of the Church and Christ."[42] The following description comes from the Twelfth-Century Roman Pontifical and is heavily dependent on the RGP.[43]

The ceremony begins with a dramatic rite at the doors of the church. Twelve candles are lit and placed throughout the church. Everyone leaves the church except for one deacon. The bishop blesses the water and salt in front of the doors [*ante fores*] of the church while a litany, a recitative prayer invoking divine aid, is sung. Then the bishop, followed by the clergy and people, circles the church, sprinkling it with the holy water.

When he has finished this he stands in front of the entrance [*ante ostium*] and prays. Then, knocking on the lintel of the church with a cross, he recites Ps. 24:7–8: "Lift up, o gates, your lintels, reach up, you ancient portals, that the king of glory may come in!" The deacon inside responds,

---

[40]See Molin and Mutembe, *Le Rituel du mariage*, p. 33.

[41]Klapisch-Zuber, *Women, Family, and Ritual*, p. 186.

[42]Honorius, *Gemma animae*, I.cl: "Ecclesiae Dedicatio est Ecclesiae et Christi nuptialis copulatio." (col. 590) Honorius was also the author of two commentaries on the Song of Songs where this nuptial imagery is developed: *Sigillum Beatae Mariae* PL 172: 495–518; and *Expositio in Cantica Canticorum* PL 172: 347–496.

[43]*Pont. XII*, "ordo XVII. Incipit ordo ad benedicendum ecclesiam," pp. 176–95. For more information on church dedications see Vogel, *Medieval Liturgy*, pp. 180, 220–21; and Geoffrey Grimshaw Willis, *Further Essays in Early Roman Liturgy* (London, 1968), pp. 133–74.

"Who is this king of glory?" The bishop responds, "The Lord who is strong and mighty: the Lord mighty in battle." Two more times the bishop circles the church sprinkling holy water and then knocks on the church door, repeating the same psalm. The third time the bishop adds the command, "open." The deacon comes out of the church, and the bishop enters saying "Peace be to you." According to Honorius and other commentators, in this sequence the bishop represents Christ exorcizing the church of a demon, represented by the deacon.[44] But the use of Psalm 24 (Vulgate, Ps. 23) also evokes Solomon's Temple because it was originally sung by alternating choirs when the Ark representing God's presence was carried to Zion or into the temple.[45] Thus the church symbolizes once again Jerusalem, the seat of the Davidic kingdom and the place of Christ's death and resurrection.

After many elaborate rituals inside the church (strewing ashes on the floor in the shape of a cross and drawing the alphabet in it, sprinkling the altar and walls with holy water, etc.), the ritual for transferring relics begins. The bishop, clergy, and people go to the place temporarily holding the relics. After prayer they take up the relics, placed in a travel container by the priests, and carry them along with a cross, censers, and lamps, in procession to the new church singing the following:

> Walk, saints of God, go out into the city of God; a new church was built for you where the people may adore the majesty of the Lord.
>
> Rise up, saints, from your dwellings, sanctify this area, bless the people and guard us human sinners in peace.
>
> Walk, saints of God, to the destined place, prepared for you since the beginning of the world.[46]

---

[44]Honorius, *Gemma animae*, i.cli, cols. 590–91.

[45]*The New American Bible* (New York, 1970), Ps. 24, footnote.

[46]*Pont. XII*, p. 185: "Ambulate, sancti Dei, ingredimini in civitatem domini; aedificata est enim vobis ecclesia nova, ubi populus adorare debeat maiestatem domini. Surgite sancti de habitationibus vestris, loca sanctificate, plebem benedicite et nos homines peccatores in pace

The "city of God" is the actual physical city but also metaphorically is heaven, God's dwelling place. The saints are invited to repose in their destined resting place, a church, but at the same time they are presumed to be at rest with God: thus there is a conflation of the eternal with the here-and-now, Paradise within a church.

When the procession arrives at the church being dedicated, the bishop carries the relics around the church followed by the clergy. They chant the following:

> The Lord will be my God, and this stone that I have raised up for a title shall be called the house of God, and of all things that you give me I will offer tithes and peaceable sacrifices to you. I shall have returned prosperously to my father's house, of all things that he will have given to me. (compare Gen. 28:21–22)[47]

The people follow the clergy, the women and children singing "Kyrie eleison." This passage from Genesis about Jacob's vow to build an altar after he dreamed of God, and an angelic ladder serves to remind the listeners of the link between the earliest temples to God and this newly dedicated church in their midst.

After this, the bishop returns to the entrance of the church and there is silence. Then he speaks to the people about the priestly office, the tithes and offerings to the churches, and the dedication of this particular church. He announces in whose honor this church was constructed and dedicated and the names of the saints resting there. He mentions also the lord and builder of the church, and speaks about the reputation of the church and its priests.

Consecration ceremonies often would include the translation of relics and attract a great deal of popular interest and attendance. It might be thought that the consecration of a church would be an extremely rare event.

---

custodite. Ambulate, sancti Dei, ad locum destinatum, qui vobis paratus est ab origine mundi."

[47]*Pont. XII*, pp. 185–86: "Erit mihi dominus in Deum et lapis iste quem erexi in titulum vocabitur domus Dei et de universis quae dederit michi decimas et hostias pacificas offeram tibi. Si reversus fuero prospere ad domum patris mei. De omnibus quae dederit michi."

But actually, church dedications or re-dedications, the consecration of altars, and the transfer of relics occurred rather frequently in the twelfth century, due to extensive rebuilding campaigns, the generosity of wealthy or pious donors, and the friction between claimants for the papal throne. For example, the main altar of S. Lorenzo in Lucina was consecrated by the bishop of Ostia and relics of twenty-eight saints were placed beneath it in January 1112. At two separate occasions later that same year the cardinal priest Benedict "found" four and then two more saints' remains in and around Rome. These he added, presumably with additional ceremonies, to those already under the altar. During the pontificate of Gelasius II (1118–19), Benedict "discovered" another saint's body and placed it beneath the altar, necessitating another ceremony. In 1130 the anti-pope Anacletus II consecrated the church. Since all acts of this pope were annulled by the Second Lateran Council of 1139, the church needed to be re-consecrated. This was finally done by Celestine III in 1196.[48]

Roman church porches, with their elegant arcaded or **trabeated** marble columns and capitals, were a striking showcase for weddings and church dedications. Their dramatic architecture, bringing to mind the proscenium stage of ancient Roman theaters or the famous portico of Solomon's temple, drew the viewer's attention to the sacred rites unfolding therein. And in many cases the marble ornamentation of the porch's frieze and columns is stylistically and/or sacramentally connected to marble work in the interior of the church. The handsomely columniated roofed porch may have called to mind the columniated **baldacchino** or canopy commonly placed over church altars, shrines, and tombs.[49] The baldacchino functioned as an

---

[48]See Huetter, *S. Lorenzo in Lucina*, pp. 12–16. Compare *Corpus*, 2:159–84, esp. 161–62. This information about relics and dedications is found in inscriptions in the porch and in the bishop's chair.

[49]The baldacchino over the main altar, that is, the *ciborium*, of S. Croce was built in the same mid-twelfth-century remodelling project that produced its porch; see Claussen, *Magistri*, pp. 14–15. The *ciborium* of SS. Giovanni e Paolo is from the late twelfth century, probably built at the same time as its porch; see Claussen, *Magistri*, p. 95. The *ciborium* of S. Lorenzo

aedicula, a ceremonial shelter from the elements, thus emphasizing the sacredness of events unfolding beneath it, somewhat as the church porch framed and highlighted sacred rituals.[50] The small foreporch of S. Maria in Cosmedin is even somewhat in the shape of an aedicula, echoing the baldacchino over the church's main altar.[51] Many Roman churches had marble cosmatesque pavements laid in a cruciform pattern. This pattern may have been a memorialization of the distribution of ashes on the floor in the shape of a cross during the church's dedication ceremony, just as the church porch may have memorialized the opening and concluding rites of the church's consecration.[52] The porches also served as background and stage for another type of religious ceremony in Rome, the **stational liturgy**.

Porches and the Stational Liturgy of Rome

Stational liturgy is the practice of celebrating Sunday Mass and other religious holidays at particular churches ("stations") during the liturgical year. The stational liturgy, which sometimes includes processions, is presided

---

FLM was built in 1148, sixty to seventy years before the remodelling project that created the porch and greatly enlarged the basilica, necessitating the moving of the *ciborium*; Claussen, *Magistri*, pp. 16–17, 138–44. For photographs of these and other *ciboria* see the plates at the end of Claussen, *Magistri*.

[50]For the function and meaning of *aedicula* see Kent C. Bloomer and Charles W. Moore, *Body, Memory, and Architecture* (New Haven and London, 1977), pp. 5–7.

[51]S. Maria in Cosmedin's baldacchino, replaced in the fourteenth century, came from the same early twelfth-century remodelling project that produced the porch and foreporch. For photographs and description see Krautheimer, *Profile*, pp. 168–70, in addition to works mentioned above, n. 8.

[52]See Glass, *Studies on Cosmatesque Pavements*, pp. 50–51; she mentions in particular the cruciform pavements of SS. Quattro Coronati, S. Croce, and S. Clemente. Compare Irmgard Voss and Peter Cornelius Claussen, "Das Paviment von S. Clemente: Mit einer Neuen Zeichnerischen Aufnahme," *Römisches Jahrbuch der Bibliotheca Hertziana* 27/28 (1991/1992): 2–22.

over by the bishop or his representative and serves as the chief liturgical celebration of the day. There is evidence for the existence of stational liturgies in fourth-century Antioch and Jerusalem and in fifth-century Tours, Rome, and Constantinople. In the following centuries many other cities and monasteries in Germany, Gaul, and Italy developed their own stational liturgies, often in imitation of those in Rome and Jerusalem.[53]

---

[53]My definition of stational liturgy is based on the fine book by John F. Baldovin, S.J., *The Urban Character of Christian Worship: The Origins, Development, and Meaning of Stational Liturgy* (Rome, 1987), pp. 36–37. His monograph focuses on origin and nature of the stational liturgies of Jerusalem, Rome, and Constantinople. Other important works on the stational liturgy of Rome are Hartmann Grisar, *Das Missale im Lichte römischer Stadtgeschichte: Stationem, Perikopen, Gebräuche* (Freiburg, 1925); Johann Peter Kirsch, *Die Stationskirchen des Missale Romanum: mit einer Untersuchungen über Ursprung und Entwicklung der liturgischen Stationsfeier* (Freiburg, 1926); Willis, *Further Essays in Early Roman Liturgy*, pp. 1–87; Josef A. Jungmann, S.J., *The Early Liturgy to the Time of Gregory the Great*, trans. Francis A. Brunner (Notre Dame, Ind., 1959), pp. 254–77; Victor Saxer, "L'Utilisation par la liturgie de l'espace urbain et suburbain: l'example de Rome dans l'antiquité et le haut moyen âge," *Actes du XIe Congrès international d'archéologie chrétienne*, 3 vols. (Rome, 1989), 2:917–1033; Gerhard Wolf, *Salus Populi Romani: Die Geschichte Römischer Kultbilder im Mittelalter* (Weinheim, 1990); and de Blaauw, *Cultus et Decor*. For stational liturgies in other cities see Frans van de Paverd, *Zur Geschichte der Messliturgie in Antiocheia und Konstantinopel gegen Ende des vierten Jahrhunderts. Analyse der Quellen bei Johannes Chrysostomos* (Rome, 1970); Anton Baumstark, "Das Kirchenjahr in Antiochien zwischen 512 und 518," *Römische Quartalschrift* 11 (1897): 31–66; Gregory of Tours, *Historia Francorum* 10.31 in *MGH Scriptores Rerum Merovingicarum*, I (2nd ed., Berlin, 1937–51); Angelus Albert Häussling, *Mönchskonvent und Eucharistiefeier: einer Studie über die Messe in der abendländischen Klosterliturgie des frühen Mittelalters und zur Geschichte der Messhäufigkeit* (Münster, 1973); Ursmer Berlière, "Les stations liturgiques dans les anciens villes episcopales," *Revue liturgique et monastique* 5 (1919/1920): 213–16, 242–48; Luzian Pfleger, "Frühmittelalterliche Stationsgottesdienste in Strassburg," *Archiv für Elsässische Kirchengeschichte* 7 (1932): 339–50; Stephan Alexander Würdtwein, *Commentatio historico-liturgica de Stationibus ecclesiae Moguntinae* (Mainz, 1782); Theodor Klauser, "Eine Stationliste der Metzer Kirche aus dem VIII Jahrhundert," *Ephemerides liturgicae* 44 (1930): 162 ff.; Michel Andrieu, "Règlement d'Angilramne de Metz (768–91) fixant les honoraires de quelques fonctions liturgiques," *Revue des sciences religieuses* 10 (1930): 349–69; Pietro Borella, "Le stazioni ambrosiane," *Ambrosius* 9

It is generally agreed that in Rome the stational liturgy was derived from the eucharistic custom of the *fermentum*. This custom, later ascribed to Pope Miltiades (311–14), first is described in a letter from Pope Innocent I to the bishop of Gubbio in 417.[54] According to this custom, the bishop of Rome celebrated the main Sunday Mass for the faithful, and part of the bread he consecrated would be sent to priests presiding over other Sunday gatherings at the *tituli* of Rome. This custom preserved the sense of unity in the Body of Christ for all the faithful gathered under the one shepherd of the diocese, the bishop, even when the Christian population had grown to such a degree it could no longer be contained under one roof. The homilies of Gregory the Great (590–604) mention that the pope celebrated the *fermentum* at different churches in and around Rome; these form the earliest known list of liturgical stations.[55] In time the practice of ***collectae*** developed: for some feasts, particularly during Lent, the people and clergy gathered at a certain church known as the *collecta* and then continued in procession to the station where Mass was celebrated.

Judging from the number of relevant texts, the second half of the twelfth century saw an efflorescence of interest in the stational liturgy of Rome. Benedict, canon of St. Peter's, wrote a description of the stational liturgy of Rome including processional routes in his *Liber politicus* (or

---

(1933): 36–43; J. Dorn, "Stationsgottesdienste in frühmittelaltlichen Bischofstädten," in Heinrich Gietl and Georg Pfeilschifter, eds., *Festgabe für Alois Knöpfler zur Vollendung des 70. Lebensjahres* (Freiburg, 1917), pp. 43–55; Carol Heitz, *Recherches sur les rapports entre architecture et liturgie à l'époque carolingienne* (Paris, 1963); and R. Ousterhout, "The Church of Sto. Stefano: Jerusalem in Bologna," *Gesta* 19/2 (1981): 18–26.

[54]For text of letter and discussion see Willis, *Further Essays*, pp. 5–7; Baldovin, *Urban Character*, pp. 121–23; Saxer, "L'Utilisation," 2:924–30, 2:938–42; and Antoine Chavasse, "Les Grandes cadres de la célébration à Rome 'in urbe' et 'extra muros' jusqu'au VIIIe siècle," *Revue bénédictine* 96.1–2 (1986): 7–26, esp. pp. 23–25.

[55]See Baldovin, *Urban Character*, pp. 124–26; for the list of stations derived from Gregory's homilies see his App. 3, p. 285.

polyptychus) ca. 1140–43.[56] This is most probably the same Benedict who wrote a description of the antiquities of the city known as "Mirabilia urbis Romae" that would serve as a pilgrim's guide for centuries.[57] Probably around the same time Prior Bernhard of the Lateran wrote *Ordo officiorum ecclesiae Lateranensis*; although this work focuses on the services of the Lateran clergy for the liturgical year, it includes extensive descriptions of the stational liturgy of Holy Week.[58] Cardinal Albinus included a shortened version of Benedict's *ordo* along with papal budget accounts in his *Gesta pauperis scholaris* written ca. 1183–88.[59] Cencius Savelli, papal chamberlain and later Pope Honorius III, included in his *Liber censuum* composed ca. 1188–97 a description of the papal liturgy based on Albinus's account; this work is generally accepted to have been preserved in a 1254 transcription of the *Liber censuum*.[60]

---

[56]For Benedict see Paul Fabre, Louis Duchesne, and Guillaume Mollat, *Le Liber censuum de l'église romaine* (hereafter *Liber censuum*), 3 vols. (Paris, 1910–1952), introduction, 1:3–4, 105–07. The text of *Liber politicus* is found in 2:141–64.

[57]See *Liber censuum*, introduction, 1:32–35, 97–104. "Mirabilia urbis Romae," ed. Roberto Valentini and Giuseppe Zucchetti, in *Codice topografico della città di Roma*, 3 (Rome, 1946), pp. 17–65. English translation: *The Marvels of Rome*, ed. and trans. Francis Morgan Nichols, rev. 2nd ed. Eileen Gardiner (New York, 1986). For a discussion of the date, authorship, and meaning of the work see Dale Kinney, "Mirabilia urbis Romae," in *The Classics in the Middle Ages*, ed. Aldo S. Bernardo and Saul Levin (Binghamton, N.Y., 1990), pp. 207–21. Compare Gregorovius, *History of the City of Rome*, 4.2:653–65.

[58]*Ordo officiorum ecclesiae Lateranensis*, ed. Ludwig Fischer (Munich and Freising, 1916); for Holy Week services see pp. 42–91. For a discussion of this work see Van Dijk and Walker, *The Origins of the Modern Roman Liturgy*, pp. 77–80, and de Blaauw, *Cultus et Decor*, passim.

[59]Text in *Liber censuum*, 2:90–137.

[60]Text in *Liber censuum*, 1:290–316. For a recent discussion of Benedict, Cencius, and Albinus see Bernhard Schimmelpfennig, "Die Bedeutung Roms im päpstlichen Zeremoniell," in *Rom im Höhen Mittelalter*, ed. Schimmelpfennig and Schmugge, pp. 47–61. See also Vogel, *Medieval Liturgy*, pp. 136, 194–95; and Van Dijk and Walker, *The Origins of the Modern Roman Liturgy*, pp. 76–77, 104–12.

There are two other important supplemental works for the stational liturgy in the twelfth century. The eighteenth-century scholar J. Mabillon published "*Ordo XVI*, Index solemnium collectarum et stationum Sanctae Romanae Ecclesiae" based on two unidentified Vatican manuscripts in his monumental work, *Museum Italicum*. Believed to have been composed sometime after ca. 1070 and before 1200, this *ordo* reflects twelfth-century practices. It is an important document for twelfth-century stational liturgy because it contains collects and stations for days omitted in other *ordines* of the period, particularly for the period of Lent.[61] The Pontifical of Apamea contains descriptions of the stational liturgy for the Purification of the Virgin Mary, Ash Wednesday, and Holy Week. Written in the last years of the twelfth century, this pontifical is believed to have drawn upon all of the above-mentioned papal *ordines* as well as the RGP.[62]

The greatest amount of information about collects, stations, and processions for the liturgical year in the twelfth century is obtained by collating Benedict's work with Mabillon's *Ordo XVI*. According to these two works, certain holy days have particularly elaborate processions: for the Purification (2 February), Annunciation (25 March), and Nativity of Mary (8 September) the processions begin at S. Adriano (St. Hadrian) in the Roman Forum, the old public and ceremonial center of pre-Christian Rome, and end at S. Maria Maggiore (St. Mary Major), some 1.7 kms. northeast on the Esquiline Hill[63] (see map on next page). Far from being the civic center of

---

[61]Text is in Jean Mabillon, *Museum Italicum*, 2 vols. (Paris, 1689), 2:544–48, and reprinted in PL 78: 1367–72 (references will be to the PL edition). For the date of this *ordo* see Baldovin, *Urban Character*, pp. 140–41.

[62]Text in *Pont. XII*, *ordines* XXVII–XXIX, XXX.C, XXXI–XXXII, pp. 206–14, 228–49. There are two other *ordines* for Holy Thursday included in the pontifical: XXX.A and XXX.B, pp. 214–28.

[63]*Liber censuum*, 2:148, 149, 159. The distance was calculated using the itinerary of Benedict plotted on the map of medieval Rome in Hülsen, *Chiese*. For the processions involving S. Giovanni in Laterano, S. Maria Maggiore, and S. Pietro in Vaticano see de Blaauw, *Cultus et Decor*, passim.

..... Routes of major stational liturgy processions in twelfth-century Rome

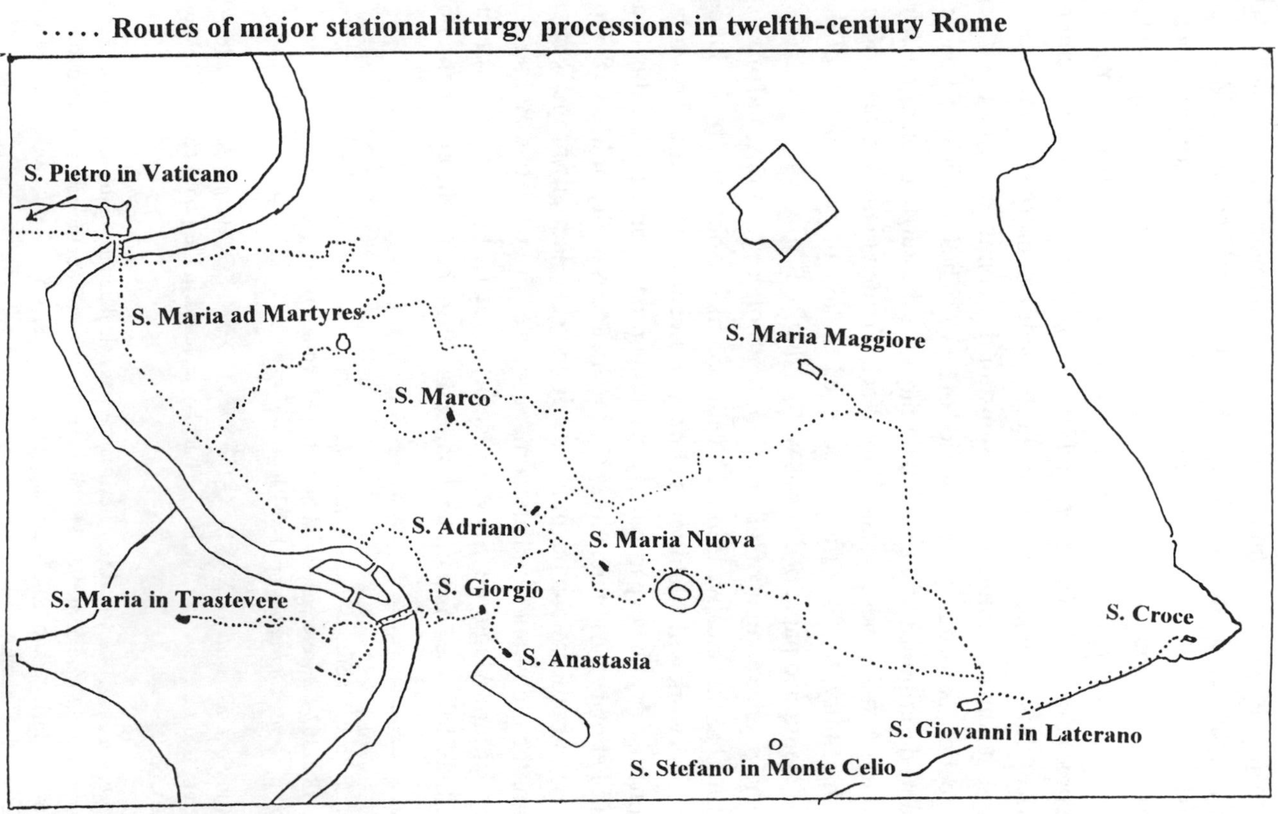

Rome, the Roman Forum in the middle ages and Renaissance was almost unpopulated except for the clergy and religious attached to the churches and monasteries there, to such a degree that it was known as Campo Vaccino, the cow pasture. For the other major Marian feast, the Assumption (15 August), the procession begins at S. Giovanni in Laterano at the far southeastern gate of the city, and passes through virtually unpopulated country to S. Adriano in the Roman Forum, and from there to S. Maria Maggiore, a total of approximately 3.9 kms.[64] On Christmas Day, according to Benedict, the first station is at S. Maria Maggiore and the second station is at S. Anastasia (St. Anastasia), a church at the northern end of the Circus Maximus, a desolate area reached by passing through the Roman Forum. The third station of the day is either back at S. Maria Maggiore (4.6 kms. total), or at S. Pietro (St. Peter, 5.6 kms. total), reached by following along the Tiber River north through the most densely populated part of Rome and then crossing at Castel Sant'Angelo to the Vatican.[65]

Two feast days entailed a procession that crossed the entire city. On Easter Monday the procession begins at S. Giovanni in Laterano at the far southeastern gate of the city, a sparsely inhabited area, and ends at S. Pietro on the Vatican Hill west of the city, passing through the densely populated heart of medieval Rome. After Mass there was a procession back to the Lateran following an alternate route, thus inscribing a circle around the entire city (11.7 kms. total). The pope and entourage take the same path on the Great Litany (25 April), with the faithful joining in halfway at the collect S. Marco (St. Mark), just north of the Capitoline Hill on the ancient Via Lata (today the Via del Corso).[66]

---

[64] *Liber censuum*, 2:158–59. For a detailed study of the Assumption procession see Wolf, *Salus Populi Romani*, pp. 37–59.

[65] *Liber censuum*, 2:144–47. Benedict says S. Maria Maggiore might be substituted for S. Pietro due to the shortness of the day and the condition of the roads, 2:145. *Ordo XVI*, col. 1367, lists only S. Pietro as the station.

[66] *Liber censuum*, 2:154–56. The itinerary of the procession from S. Giovanni to S. Pietro and back is also described by Krautheimer, *Profile*, p. 278; and Gregorovius, *History of the City*

The shortest major processions take place on Good Friday, from S. Croce in Gerusalemme (Holy Cross in Jerusalem) to S. Giovanni in Laterano (0.9 km.), on Easter, from S. Giovanni in Laterano to S. Maria Maggiore (1.6 kms.), and on the Exaltation of the Holy Cross (14 September) from S. Maria Maggiore to S. Giovanni (1.6 kms.), all in the rural area far to the east of the populated area of the city.[67] During Lent there are numerous short processions between *collectae* and stations; notable among these were processions in Trastevere and the east bank of the Tiber from the Theater of Marcellus south to the Aventine Hill, neighborhoods largely omitted in the long itineraries described above.

Out of the total of fifty-four churches mentioned in the stational liturgy, approximately nineteen were remodeled with the addition of porches ca. 1100–1217 (see Appendix). Among these were five of the greatest in the city: S. Maria Maggiore, S. Giovanni in Laterano, S. Lorenzo fuori le mura, S. Stefano in Monte Celio, and S. Croce in Gerusalemme, mentioned, respectively, fifteen, thirteen, four, three, and three times in the stational liturgy. All basilicas (except for S. Stefano), these were also among the largest churches in Rome, along with S. Pietro and S. Paolo fuori le mura (St. Paul outside the walls) (mentioned seventeen and four times in the stational liturgy) which already had porches dating from the fourth century.[68] Some of these basilicas—S. Lorenzo, S. Paolo, and S. Pietro—were

---

of Rome, 4.2:656–58. This was also the itinerary of the papal coronations described by Albinus (XI,3) and Cencius (LVIII); see *Liber censuum*, introduction, 1:106–07. Compare de Blaauw, *Cultus et Decor*, pp. 61, 285, 685, 717n187.

[67]*Liber censuum*, 2:151–54, 159.

[68]For S. Maria Maggiore see *Corpus*, 3:1–60; and de Blaauw, *Cultus et Decor*, pp. 335–447. For S. Giovanni in Laterano see *Corpus*, 5:1–92; de Blaauw, *Cultus et Decor*, pp. 109–331; de Blaauw, "The Solitary Celebration of the Supreme Pontiff. The Lateran Basilica as the New Temple in the Medieval Liturgy of Maundy Thursday," in *Omnes Circumadstantes: Contributions towards a History of the Role of the People in the Liturgy Presented to Herman Wegman...*, ed. Charles Caspers and Marc Schneiders (Kampen, 1990), pp. 120–43; and Herklotz, "Die mittelalterliche Fassadenportikus der Lateranbasilika." For S. Croce see

built outside the city because they were memorials on the sites of their namesake's graves, and Ancient Roman law required all burials be outside the city's ***pomerium*** or boundaries. The other churches are all in the eastern part of the city, sites apparently chosen by Constantine and later imperial and papal patrons in the fourth and fifth centuries in part because they were far away from the pagan religious centers of Rome, the Capitol, the Fora, and the Campus Martius, and also because there was more room for building in the green belt of Rome along the eastern walls of the city.[69]

This eastern expanse perhaps was intended to be a sort of Christian show area competing with the older pagan and civic monuments in the western and central part of the city. By the twelfth century this eastern area was very thinly populated except for small suburban communities clustering around S. Maria Maggiore and the Lateran complex, and between S. Maria Nuova (New St. Mary) on the edge of the Forum and the Colosseum.[70] Yet nine major stational processions took place in this area: perhaps for this reason a great number of the smaller churches in this little-populated area received renovations including new porches in the twelfth century. The following churches were remodeled with porches: just west and east of S. Maria Maggiore, the *tituli* S. Pudenziana (St. Pudentiana) and S. Eusebio (St. Eusebius); just north and west of S. Stefano, the *tituli* S. Clemente, SS. Quattro Coronati, SS. Giovanni e Paolo, and the monastic church S. Gregorio Magno; and far to the southwest and south of S. Stefano, the two monastic churches S. Saba (St. Saba) on the little Aventine Hill and S. Giovanni a

---

Corpus, 1:165–95. For S. Pietro see *Corpus*, 5:165–285; and de Blaauw, *Cultus et Decor*, pp. 451–756. For S. Paolo see *Corpus*, 5:93–164.

[69]Krautheimer, *Profile*, pp. 21–31, 54–58; and Krautheimer, *Three Christian Capitals*, pp. 26–40.

[70]Krautheimer, *Profile*, pp. 245, 248–49, 310–26; Krautheimer, *Three Christian Capitals*, pp. 93–121; and Krautheimer, *St. Peter's and Medieval Rome*, pp. 34–35 and fig. 18.

Porta Latina.[71] The porches of S. Stefano, S. Giovanni a Porta Latina, SS. Quattro Coronati, S. Clemente, S. Eusebio, and S. Gregorio Magno were arcaded; those of S. Maria Maggiore, S. Giovanni, S. Lorenzo fuori le mura, S. Croce in Gerusalemme, S. Saba, and SS. Giovanni e Paolo were trabeated.[72] All of these churches except for the monastic churches S. Gregorio Magno and S. Saba were mentioned in the stational liturgy.

Another important ceremonial area for the stational liturgy was the old Roman Forum. By the eighth century numerous temples and governmental buildings had been converted to churches: from west to east along the north side of the Forum, facing south into the Forum, were S. Martina (St. Martina, formerly the Secretarium Senatus, today SS. Luca e Martina), S. Adriano (formerly the Curia Julia, the Senate House), S. Lorenzo in Miranda (St. Laurence in Miranda, formerly the Temple of Antoninus Pius and Faustina), and SS. Cosma e Damiano (Sts. Cosmas and Damian, formerly the audience hall of the city prefect). Bracketing these were the *diaconia* SS. Sergio e Bacco (Sts. Sergius and Bacchus), built in the Arch of Septimius Severus, and the *diaconia* S. Maria Nuova (today S. Francesca Romana), constructed *ex novo* in the ninth century.[73] Seven major liturgical processions passed through this area. S. Adriano, S. Lorenzo in Miranda, and SS. Cosma e Damiano all had antique trabeated porches which were probably still extant

---

[71]For S. Pudenziana see *Corpus*, 3:277–302. For S. Eusebio see *Corpus*, 1:210–16. For S. Gregorio see *Corpus*, 1:320–26. For S. Saba see *Corpus*, 4:51–71.

[72]There is insufficient archaeological and archival evidence to determine the appearance of the porch of S. Pudenziana.

[73]For S. Martina see *Corpus*, 3:82–86. For S. Adriano see *Corpus*, 1:1; and Nash, *Pictorial Dictionary*, 1:301–03, "Curia Iulia." For S. Lorenzo in Miranda see Nash, *Pictorial Dictionary*, 1:26–27, "Antoninus et Faustina, Templum." For SS. Cosma e Damiano see *Corpus*, 1:137–43; and Nash, *Pictorial Dictionary*, 1:438–45, "Forum Pacis" and 2:268–69, "Romulus, divus, Templum." For SS. Sergio e Bacco see Krautheimer, *Profile*, p. 203; Golzio and Zander, *Chiese*, p. 34; and M. Bonfioli, "La diaconia dei SS. Sergio e Bacco...," *Rivista di archeologia cristiana* 50 (1974): 55 ff. For S. Maria Nova see *Corpus*, 1:220–41 (S. Francesca Romana).

in the twelfth century. SS. Sergio e Bacco and S. Maria Nuova received trabeated porches in the second half of the twelfth century. All of these churches except for S. Lorenzo in Miranda were explicitly mentioned in the stational liturgy.

The Campus Martius also figured prominently in the major stational processions of Easter Monday and the Great Litany. In this populous area S. Silvestro in Capite (St. Sylvester in Capite), S. Lorenzo in Lucina, S. Apollinare (St. Apollinaris), S. Maria in Cyro (in Aquiro), and S. Eustachio (St. Eustachius) all received porches in the twelfth century. The only church with a porch from an earlier period was S. Maria ad Martyres (St. Mary by the martyrs), formerly the Pantheon, a round temple with a rectangular trabeated porch.[74] S. Lorenzo in Lucina and S. Eustachio both were remodeled with trabeated porches, while S. Silvestro and S. Apollinare received arcaded porches.[75] Although processions passed by all of these churches only S. Lorenzo in Lucina, S. Apollinare, and S. Maria ad Martyres served as *collectae* or stations in the stational liturgy.

In the twelfth century the bulk of the population in the city of Rome lived in the bend of the Tiber and immediately across it to the south in Trastevere and to the north in the enclave surrounding the Vatican. Three of the major stational processions ended at S. Pietro. Just west of S. Pietro, the *diaconia* S. Stefano degli Abbessini (St. Stephen of the Abyssinians), omitted in the stational liturgy, probably received some sort of porch in the twelfth or thirteenth century. The two other important population areas, Trastevere and the area east of Tiber Island from the Theater of Marcellus to the old Forum Boarium, were circumscribed by stational processions eight weekdays in Lent. Three of these linked the two areas: processions from the *collecta* S. Giorgio al Velabro terminated at the stations S. Cecilia

[74]For S. Silvestre in Capite see *Corpus*, 4:148–62. For S. Apollinare see *Corpus*, 1:75. For S. Maria in Cyro see *Corpus*, 2:275–76. For S. Eustachio see *Corpus*, 1:217–18. For S. Maria ad Martyres see Nash, *Pictorial Dictionary*, 2:170–75, "Pantheon."

[75]There is insufficient archaeological and archival evidence to determine the appearance of the porch of S. Maria in Cyro.

in Trastevere, S. Maria in Trastevere (St. Mary beyond the Tiber), and S. Crisogono (St. Crysogonus). All four of these churches had trabeated porches built in the twelfth century. Two other churches serving as *collectae*, S. Angelo in Pescheria (Holy Angel in the fishmarket) and S. Anastasia, had porches from an earlier period. S. Angelo, built inside the ancient Porticus of Octavia in the eighth century, had part of the old enormous portico serving as a sort of porch or atrium; S. Anastasia had an arcaded porch probably dating from the ninth century.[76]

There are three other notable churches in this area: S. Maria in Cosmedin, S. Stefano delle Carozze (St. Stephen of the Carriages), and S. Maria ad Gradellis (St. Mary by the steps). S. Maria in Cosmedin received an arcaded brick porch in the early twelfth century. S. Stefano delle Carozze, a second century B.C. round columniated temple dedicated to Hercules Victor, was transformed into a church in the twelfth century.[77] S. Maria Secundicerii, popularly known as "ad Gradellis" for the nearby staircase descending to the Tiber, was originally a first century B.C. rectangular temple dedicated to Portunus; it was probably consecrated as a church in the ninth century.[78] The monastic church of SS. Bonifacio e Alessio (Sts. Boniface

---

[76]Mabillon, *Ordo XVI*, cols. 1367–70; and *Liber censuum*, 2:149–50. For S. Stefano degli Abbessini see *Corpus*, 4:178–98. For S. Maria in Trastevere see *Corpus*, 3:65–71; and Dale Kinney, "Santa Maria in Trastevere from its Founding to 1215" (Ph.D. thesis, New York University, 1975). For S. Crisogono see *Corpus*, 1:144–64. For S. Angelo in Pescheria see *Corpus*, 1:64–74; and Nash, *Pictorial Dictionary*, 2:254–57, "Porticus Octaviae." For S. Anastasia see *Corpus*, 1:42–61.

[77]See Nash, *Pictorial Dictionary*, 1:411–17, "Forum Boarium"; Friedrich Rakob and Wolf-Dieter Heilmeyer, *Der Rundtempel am Tiber in Rom* (Mainz, 1973); and Robert E. A. Palmer, "Cults of Hercules, Apollo Caelispex, and Fortuna in and around the Roman Cattle Market," *Journal of Roman Archaeology* 3 (1996): 234–44.

[78]In the fifteenth century the church was re-named S. Maria Egiziaca. The structure was restored as a temple in 1916 and is popularly known as the Temple of Fortuna Virilis. See Nash, *Pictorial Dictionary*, 1:411–17, "Forum Boarium"; and Antonio Maria Colini and Carlo Buzzetti, "Aedes Portuni in Portu Tiberino," *Bullettino della Commissione archeologica comunale di Roma* 91/1 (1986): 7–30, esp. p. 21.

and Alexis) on the Aventine Hill also received an arcaded narthex sometime in the twelfth century; in an unpopulated area, this church was not included in the liturgical procession linking S. Anastasia and S. Sabina (St. Sabina) on Ash Wednesday.[79]

Conclusion

From this brief survey it is clear that a great number of the churches remodeled with porches in Rome in the twelfth and early thirteenth centuries were part of the stational liturgy. Furthermore, many of these had trabeated porches, a style not before seen except in churches made from converted Roman temples and buildings such as the Pantheon and the Curia Julia. Previously, church porches were usually arcaded, a fashion made de rigueur by the influence of S. Pietro and S. Paolo fuori le mura built in the fourth and fifth centuries. Ten churches had this more traditional arcaded porch added ca. 1100–1200, a style recalling Constantinian foundations and the promotion of Christianity over paganism as the official religion of the empire. Fourteen churches are known to have received trabeated porches ca. 1118–1217, an innovation obviously inspired by ancient Roman classical architecture. Perhaps the style of trabeated porches was chosen for churches in areas where there were trabeated antique buildings such as in the Campus Martius, the Roman Forum, and the Forum Boarium, in order to give an aesthetic unity to a neighborhood. Quite likely the great basilicas of S. Lorenzo fuori le mura, S. Maria Maggiore, S. Croce in Gerusalemme, and S. Giovanni in Laterano received trabeated porches in an attempt to compete with the grandeur of the pagan monuments to the west. Their remodeled facades would give an imposing look to the otherwise desolate quarter of the city where the pope resided.[80]

---

[79]For SS. Alessio e Bonifacio see *Corpus*, 1:40–41.

[80]Compare Mâle, *Early Churches*, p. 138; Krautheimer, *Profile*, p. 325; and Herklotz, "Der mittelalterliche Fassadenportikus der Lateranbasilika."

Why this joint phenomenon of a spate of church porch remodeling and a surge of interest in the stational liturgy in the twelfth century? Both events are tied to the same factors: the growing prestige and strength of the papacy and the college of cardinals, and a widespread interest in classical culture, both pagan and Christian. The pope chose to show his dominion over the city of Rome and the entire Catholic Church through building campaigns and liturgical processions.[81] There is documentation that the papacy restored and redecorated many churches in Rome; among these papal projects was the addition of porches to perhaps as many as eight churches (see Appendix). Several times a year during stational liturgical processions the pope wore his ceremonial crown symbolizing his temporal power.[82] By doing this the pope re-inscribed his personal rule over an unruly city oftentimes dominated by hostile emperors and rebellious townspeople. The entire city of Rome became a backdrop for the spectacle of the stational liturgy led by the pope.[83] The churches with their new porches served as theatrical background, or *scaena*, incorporating shapes reminiscent of those used in ancient theater.[84]

It is clear that these porches served no single liturgical function but, rather, enhanced both private and public ceremonies. As the location of the wedding ceremony, the ornate porch highlighted the most important transition in the life of the laity, marriage. As the focal point of the opening ceremony of the consecration of churches, the porch served as a monument or

---

[81]Stroll, *Symbols of Power*, passim; and Krautheimer, *Profile*, pp. 190–97, 311–26.

[82]Benedict mentions the pope wearing his crown during processions on Christmas Day, St. Stephen's Day, Epiphany, Easter, Easter Monday, and Ascension Thursday; see *Liber censuum*, 2:146–48, 152, 154, 156. For bibliography and discussion of papal coronations see Schimmelpfennig, "Die Bedeutung Roms."

[83]See the remarks in the conclusion of Baldovin, *Urban Character*, esp. pp. 265–68; and Saxer, "L'Utilisation," pp. 983–86.

[84]Compare Onians, *Bearers of Meaning*, pp. 6–58, 94–96.

souvenir of foundation for a community and its church. And as a place and background for the stational liturgy, the porch provided a specifically Roman ecclesiastical decor for ceremonies that literally linked the entire city together by processions commemorating events in the life of the Lord Jesus Christ and his followers, the apostles and martyrs.

Appendix

TABLE: Roman Churches with New Porches ca. 1100–1217

T=***titulus***
D=*diaconia*
M=monastic
*serves as *collecta* or station in stational liturgy

Chronological Order of Dated Porches:

(all dates based on Krautheimer's *Corpus* unless otherwise noted)

*1099–1125 S. Clemente (St. Clement), arcaded quadroporticus with columns, by Anastasius, cardinal priest. T

*1099–1118 SS. Quattro Coronati (Four Crowned Saints), arcaded porticus (not extant) on facade (three arches on two columns) and on right side of atrium, by Paschal II. T

*1118–29 S. Lorenzo in Lucina (St. Laurence in Lucina), trabeated narthex with columns, probably by Benedict, cardinal priest. T

1120s S. Maria in Cosmedin (St. Mary in Cosmedin), arcaded brick narthex with small foreporch with two columns, by Alfano, papal chamberlain. D

*1123–30 S. Crisogono (St. Crysogonus), trabeated narthex with columns (not extant), by John of Crema, cardinal priest. T

*1130–43 S. Maria in Trastevere (St. Mary beyond the Tiber), trabeated narthex with columns (not extant), by Pope Innocent II. T

*ca. 1130–43 S. Stefano in Monte Celio (St. Stephen on the Caelian Hill), arcaded narthex with columns, perhaps by Innocent II who repaired it. T

*ca. 1144–45 S. Croce in Gerusalemme (Holy Cross in Jerusalem), trabeated narthex with columns (not extant), perhaps by Lucius II who restored it. T

*1145–53 S. Maria Maggiore (St. Mary Major), trabeated narthex with columns (not extant), by Pope Eugenius III Patriarchal Basilica.

*1161 S. Maria Nuova (New St. Mary), trabeated porch with columns (not extant), by Eugenius III. D

*ca. 1180[85] SS. Giovanni e Paolo (Sts. John and Paul), trabeated narthex with columns, by John, cardinal priest. T

*ca. 1188–98[86] S. Giovanni in Laterano (St. John in the Lateran), trabeated narthex with columns (not extant), perhaps by Clement III or Celestine III Cathedral.

*1187–98, SS. Sergio e Bacco (Sts. Sergius and Bacchus), trabeated narthex with columns (not extant), by Lothario dei Conti di Segni, cardinal priest (later Pope Innocent III). D

*ca. 1191, S. Giovanni a Porta Latina (St. John at the Latin Gate), arcaded narthex with columns. M

ca. 1196 S. Eustachio (St. Eustachius), trabeated narthex with columns (not extant). D

*ca. 1199[87] S. Giorgio al Velabro (St. George in the Velabrum), trabeated narthex with columns (heavily damaged July 1993), by Prior Stephen of Stella. D

ca. 1205[88] S. Saba (St. Saba), trabeated narthex with columns (columns not extant), probably by Abbot John. M

*ca. 1210 S. Pudenziana (St. Pudentiana), narthex (not extant), probably by Peter Sassonis, cardinal priest. T

---

[85]Claussen, *Magistri*, p. 32, suggests this later date based on stylistic and documentary evidence; traditionally dated to 1154–59.

[86]Claussen, *Magistri*, p. 26, and Herklotz, "Der mittelalterliche Fassadenportikus," p. 37, suggest this later date based on stylistic evidence.

[87]Pensabene, "Contributi," p. 307, suggests this date; *Corpus*, 1:247–48, suggests first half of thirteenth century.

[88]Claussen, *Magistri*, p. 75, suggests this later date based on stylistic evidence; traditionally dated to ca. 1145.

*ca. 1217 S. Lorenzo fuori le mura (St. Laurence outside the walls), trabeated narthex with columns, project probably begun earlier by Cardinal-Chancellor Cencio Savelli and completed after he became Honorius III. T

Alphabetical Order of Porches without Specific Dates

*S. Apollinare (St. Apollinaris), narthex with three arches (not extant), twelfth or thirteenth century. T

SS. Bonifacio e Alessio (Sts. Boniface and Alexis), arcaded narthex with columns (not extant), twelfth century. M

*S. Cecilia in Trastevere (St. Cecilia beyond the Tiber), trabeated narthex with columns, probably second half of the twelfth century.[89] T

*S. Eusebio (St. Eusebius), arcaded narthex with pillars (not extant), possibly twelfth century. T

S. Gregorio Magno (St. Gregory the Great), probably an arcaded quadroporticus with columns (not extant), twelfth century. M

S. Maria in Cyro (in Aquiro) (St. Mary in Aquiro), narthex (not extant), twelfth century. D

S. Silvestro in Capite (St. Sylvester in Capite), arcaded narthex with columns (not extant), possibly ca. 1200. D

S. Stefano degli Abbessini (St. Stephen of the Abyssinians), narthex (not extant) possibly added in twelfth or thirteenth century (could possibly be ninth century). D

---

[89]Claussen, *Magistri*, p. 26, suggests this period based on stylistic evidence.

LITURGICAL VESSELS AND IMPLEMENTS

ELIZABETH PARKER MCLACHLAN

Introduction[1]

IN THE SERVICE OF THE EUCHARIST, liturgical vessels were essential. One could, under some circumstances, conduct the various ceremonies of the Christian liturgy without a sheltering architecture,[2] but it was impossible to celebrate the Mass, in particular, without the consecrated service vessels for the wine and bread of the Eucharist. Other containers, such as those for water or the sacramental oils, and additional accessory objects also were

---

[1]I am grateful to a number of colleagues and students for information and suggestions: particularly my co-author in this volume Elizabeth C. Parker, and others mentioned in relevant footnotes. I am also indebted to Charles T. Little and Christine Brennan of the Medieval Department of the Metropolitan Museum of Art for their help and for the loan of photographs, and to Mary Dougherty of the Metropolitan Museum's Photographic Department for her patient assistance, as also to Stephanie Leone of Art Resource. Both the Metropolitan Museum and the Morgan Library have generously waived reproduction fees for this volume. Figures 1–6, 8–16 are reproduced by permission of the Metropolitan Museum of Art; Fig. 7, by permission of the Pierpont Morgan Library. Figures 1–6, 8–18, All Rights Reserved, The Metropolitan Museum of Art.

[2]Provisions for celebration of the Eucharist, when conditions dictated, in as yet unconsecrated spaces or in the open air, do exist, although generally originally limited or local in application. See for example the ruling of Hincmar of Reims on this subject cited and discussed in Joseph Braun, *Der christliche Altar in seiner geschichtlichen Entwicklung*, 2 vols. (Munich, 1924), 1:72 ff.; hereafter Braun, *Altar*.

important and requisite. These implements, often wrongly regarded in modern times as "minor arts," were in fact of major significance in the liturgical functioning—and the aesthetic and symbolic impact—of the medieval church. In the Middle Ages they were accorded the respect their importance merited, and by the High Middle Ages they were invested with additional layers of symbolic meaning, as recounted in the late thirteenth-century *Rationale divinorum officiorum* of William Durandus, Bishop of Mende.[3] Their materials also, particularly the gold and precious stones, carried symbolic value: they evoked the description in the Apocalypse of the Heavenly Jerusalem, "built of pure gold, like to clear glass" (Rev. 21:18), and its twelve foundations set with precious stones: jasper, sapphire, chalcedony, emerald, sardonyx, chrysolite, beryl, jacinth and amethyst, and its gates of pearl (Rev. 21:19–21).[4] Marie-Madeleine Gauthier, discussing the

---

[3]Durandus, William or Guillelmus, Bishop of Mende 1285–1296, *Rationale Divinorum Officiorum I–IV*, ed. Anselmus Davril and Timothy M. Thibodeau (Turnholt, 1995), hereafter Durandus, *Rationale*, 1995 ed. An English translation of Book I exists: John Mason Neale and Benjamin Webb, *The Symbolism of Churches and Church Ornaments: A Translation of the First Book of the Rationale Divinorum Officiorum written by William Durandus* . . . , 3rd ed. (London, 1906), hereafter Neale and Webb, *Symbolism*. Such interpretations appeared already centuries earlier: that of Germanos, Byzantine patriarch active in the first third of the 8th century, recapitulates what by then was a very old tradition; see Victor Heinrich Elbern, "Altar Implements and Liturgical Objects," in *Age of Spirituality: Late Antique and Early Christian Art, Third to Seventh Century*, ed. Kurt Weitzmann (exhibition catalogue, New York: Metropolitan Museum of Art, 1979), hereafter *Age of Spirituality*, ed. Weitzmann. See also Victor Heinrich Elbern, "Liturgisches Gerät des Frühmittelalters als Symbolträger," *Simboli e simbologia nell' alto medioevo, Settimane Stud. Centro Italiano di Studi sull' Alto Medioevo* (Spoleto, 1976), pp. 348–86; and Joseph Sauer, *Symbolik des Kirchengebäudes und seiner Ausstattung in der Auffasung des Mittelalters, mit Berücksichtigung von Honorius Augustodunensis Sicardus und Durandus* (Münster/Westfalen, 1964), esp. pp. 155–215. Amalarius of Metz in *De ecclesiasticis officiis*, first completed in 821, also contributed substantially to the tradition of symbolic interpretation: see O. B. Hardison, Jr., *Christian Rite and Christian Drama in the Middle Ages* (Baltimore, 1965), passim, and J. M. Hanssens, *Amalarii episcopi opera liturgica omnia*, 3 vols. (Vatican City, 1948–50).

[4]For the symbolism accorded to gemstones in the Middle Ages see also the medieval

role of gold in the medieval church, refers to its luster, malleability, and ductility: it was the "perfect metal," which took on added symbolism when given to the Church:

> removed from economic circulation, gold was the offering *par excellence* with which to honor God: metal without fault, it came to guarantee totally abstract values—political prestige, moral authority, social dedication. During these centuries gold was not the instrument, but the tangible sign, of power.[5]

The prestige of fine metalworking also is reflected in accounts of the life of St. Eligius or Eloi (d. ca. 660), Bishop of Noyon but also a goldsmith and the patron saint of metalworkers, who was credited with the manufacture, among other items, of a splendid golden chalice of cloisonné set with enamels or precious stones, now known only from a seventeenth-century engraving.[6] (It is perhaps worth noting that this preeminence of metalsmiths was acknowledged even in antiquity: Hephaistos the metalsmith was the only craftsman-god in the Greek pantheon.)

Such opulent materials for liturgical equipment came into use primarily from the fourth century. The Edict of Milan (A.D. 313), in which the Emperor Constantine declared official toleration of Christianity, inspired an "immediate enrichment of the liturgy," and with it an assimilation of Christian ritual to that of the imperial court and of pagan cults.[7] From that time, liturgical utensils, which in Palaeochristian times probably often were made of relatively modest, everyday materials—even originally secular vessels

---

Lapidaries, treatises on the properties of gems, as discussed by Joan Evans, *Magical Jewels of the Middle Ages and Renaissance* (Oxford, 1922, repr. New York, 1976).

[5]Marie-Madeleine Gauthier, "L'or et l'église au moyen âge," *Revue de l'art* 26 (1971): 64 (trans. McLachlan).

[6]*La Neustrie. Les pays au nord de la Loire de Dagobert à Charles le Chauve (VIIe–IXe siècles)*, ed. Patrick Périn and Laure-Charlotte Feffer (exhibition catalogue, Rouen, 1985), pp. 286–88.

[7]Anon., "Art et liturgie," *Revue de l'art* 24 (1974): 4 (trans. McLachlan).

co-opted and blessed for eucharistic employ—were crafted whenever possible of the most precious and durable materials available, to reflect both the sacrality of their function and contents and, very frequently, the high rank and generosity of their donors. From as early as the reign of Constantine, records survive of lavish imperial gifts of such vessels, together with other adornments for the churches of Rome.[8] Even those of more austere views, opposed to lavish expenditure that might divert funds from the care of the poor and the sick, such as the Cistercian St. Bernard of Clairvaux, acknowledged that the surfaces actually in contact with the elements of the Eucharist—notably the bowl of the communion chalice—should be only of the purest and finest materials—gold or silver.[9] And the prevalent view appears to have been that of Abbot Suger of St.-Denis, as summarized by Erwin Panofsky in the introduction to his translation of Suger's accounts of his accomplishments:

> Nothing, he [Suger] thought, would be a graver sin of omission than to withhold from the service of God and His saints what He had empowered nature to supply and man to perfect: vessels of gold or precious stone adorned with pearls and gems, golden candelabra and altar panels, sculpture and stained glass, mosaic and enamel work, lustrous vestments and tapestries.[10]

Although the vast majority of these sumptuous and sacred objects have not survived, enough have come down to us to give a good idea of their preciousness and beauty. They survive today in some historic church and

---

[8]A major source is the *Liber Pontificalis*: see *The Book of Pontiffs* (Liber Pontificalis): *The Ancient Biographies of the First Ninety Roman Bishops to AD 715*, ed. and trans. Raymond David (Liverpool, 1989). Excerpts are also published in Caecilia Davis-Weyer, *Early Medieval Art 300–1150: Sources and documents* (Englewood Cliffs, N.J., 1971), pp. 11–13, 34–35; in Joseph Braun, *Das christliche Altargerät in seinem Sein und in seiner Entwicklung* (Munich, 1932), hereafter known as Braun, *Altergerät*; and in Braun, *Altar*.

[9]For the materials of chalices see Braun, *Altergerät*, pp. 18–19 and passim.

[10]Erwin Panofsky, *Abbot Suger on the Abbey Church of St.-Denis and its Art Treasures*, 2nd ed., with Gerda Panofsky-Soergel (Princeton, 1979), pp. 13–14.

cathedral treasuries, such as those of St. Mark's in Venice, or the cathedrals of Sens, Aachen, and Cologne;[11] in the treasuries of monasteries, especially those which were the sites of medieval pilgrimages, such as Santo Domingo de Silos and Ste. Foy de Conques;[12] and in modern museum collections such as those in the Metropolitan Museum of Art in New York,[13] or the Victoria and Albert Museum[14] and the British Museum in London,[15] the

---

[11]For Aachen see Ernst Günther Grimme, *Der Aachener Domschatz. Aachener Kunstblätter*, Bd. 42: 2nd, enl. ed. (Düsseldorf, 1973); for Cologne see Walter Schulten, *Der Kölner Domschatz* (Cologne, 1979); for Sens see Eugène Chartraire, *Inventaire du trésor de l'église primatiale et métropolitaine de Sens* (Sens and Paris, 1897), and selections in *Les Trésors des églises de France*, ed. Jean Taralon (exhibition catalogue, Paris, 1965), hereafter *Trésors des églises*; and for San Marco see David Buckton et al., *The Treasury of San Marco, Venice* (exhibition catalogue, New York, 1984), hereafter *Treasury of San Marco*.

[12]For Santo Domingo de Silos see Eugène Roulin, *L'Ancien trésor de l'Abbaye de Silos* (Paris, 1901); some individual works are discussed, with bibliography, in the exhibition catalogue, *The Art of Medieval Spain, A.D. 500–1200* (New York, 1993), hereafter *Art of Medieval Spain*; see also works on individual media such as enamel, and general works on the history of Spanish medieval art. I am grateful to Elizabeth del Alamo for information on the Silos treasury. For Saint Foy de Conques see *Trésors des églises*, cat. nos. 532–54 *bis*; also Marie-Madeleine Gauthier, "Le trésor de Conques," in Georges Gaillard, *Rouergue roman* (La-Pierre-qui-Vire, 1963), pp. 98–133.

[13]See, for example, Margaret English Frazer, *Medieval Church Treasuries*, *The Metropolitan Museum of Art Bulletin* 43 (Winter 1985/6), and Charles T. Little and Timothy Husband, *Europe in the Middle Ages* (New York, 1987), as well as numerous other publications and exhibition catalogues.

[14]See *The Medieval Treasury: The Art of the Middle Ages in the Victoria and Albert Museum*, ed. Paul Williamson (London, 1986), as well as other specialized catalogues and exhibition catalogues.

[15]See, for example, Neil Stratford, *Catalogue of Medieval Enamels in the British Museum*, vol. 2, *Northern Romanesque Enamel* (London, 1993); vol. 1, David Buckton on early medieval enamels, is forthcoming. There are many other, earlier catalogues that include treasury items in the British Museum's collections.

Cluny Museum in Paris,[16] and many others throughout Europe. In addition, scholars and curators have reconstituted, in exhibitions and catalogues, such once-great but now-dispersed liturgical treasures as that of St.-Denis, scattered at the time of the French Revolution,[17] or the Guelph Treasure, now located primarily in museum collections in Berlin and Cleveland.[18]

When not displayed on or near the altar—a phenomenon more widespread in the later than in the earlier Middle Ages—these precious objects were stored in a secure place such as the sacristy, a room adjacent to the sanctuary reserved for this purpose and for the vesting of the clergy before the liturgy. Even in the medieval period, this treasure-room with its cupboards had something of the quality of a museum, and this element of display is reflected also in the later engravings of the treasure of St.-Denis as it appeared in the early eighteenth century.[19]

The survival of liturgical objects today in museums and private collections, however—and even perhaps in the museum-like context of many modern church treasury installations—tends to introduce a dangerous factor

---

[16]Jean-Pierre Caillet, *L'antiquité classique, le haut moyen âge et Byzance au musée de Cluny* (Paris, 1985); also Alain Erlande-Brandenburg, Pierre-Yves Le Pogam, and Dany Sandron, *Musée national du Moyen Age, Thermes de Cluny: Guide to the Collections* (Paris, 1993); and numerous other publications.

[17]See, for example, the exhibition catalogue, *Le Trésor de Saint-Denis* (Paris, 1991), hereafter *Trésor de Saint-Denis,* with exhaustive earlier bibliography. Recent works in English include Sumner McKnight Crosby et al., *The Royal Abbey of Saint-Denis in the Time of Abbot Suger [1122–1151]* (exhibition catalogue, New York, 1981), hereafter *Royal Abbey of Saint-Denis*; and essays by Danielle Gaborit-Chopin and William D. Wixom in *Abbot Suger and Saint-Denis: A Symposium*, ed. Paula Lieber Gerson (New York, 1986), pp. 282–304; as well as Panofsky, *Abbot Suger.*

[18]Dietrich Kötsche, *Der Welfenschatz im Berliner Kunstgewerbemuseum* (Berlin: Staatliche Museen Preussischer Kulturbesitz Kunsgewerbemuseum, 1973), and Patrick M. De Winter, *The Sacral Treasure of the Guelphs* (Bloomington, Ind., 1985).

[19]Dom Michel Félibien, *Histoire de l'abbaye royale de Saint-Denys en France* (Paris, 1706), pls. 1–5, reproduced in *Trésor de Saint-Denis*, pp. 31–35.

of isolation: divorced from their actual context of *use in the liturgy*, they are in danger of losing the numinous quality of their symbolism and function, and of becoming mere *objets d'art* inseparable from those made for pure pleasure and display. "In entering into the *'musée imaginaire'* they have lost their essential character as sacred objects . . . the incomparable quality of authenticity linked to objects which survive *in situ* . . . their absolute character as instruments of religious ceremonial . . ."[20] This tendency can be counteracted to some degree, however, by reconstructions based on records of actual use such as Edward Foley's inventory of the treasures of St.-Denis, derived from the abbey's *liber ordinarius* of 1234, which provided texts and instructions for its liturgical ceremonies.[21] The vision of these objects as functioning in a sacred world also can be restored, in part, by contemporary narratives and images, such as paintings of the lives and miracles of saints, for example the Flemish painting of the Consecration of St. Augustine in the Cloisters collection (Fig. 1),[22] or manuscript illuminations of liturgical ceremonies, such as the initials of the ninth-century Drogo Sacramentary[23] or the miniature in the Gospels of Uta of Niedermünster of ca. 1020 showing Bishop Erhard celebrating Mass at an altar on which are placed a set of implements—among which can be recognized the

---

[20]Anon, "Art et liturgie," (note 7 above), p. 4.

[21]Edward Foley, "The Treasury of St.-Denis According to the Inventory of 1234," *Revue bénédictine* 105 (1995): 167–99.

[22]See Frazer, *Medieval Church Treasuries*, figs. 20 and 30, pp. 24–25 and 30, for discussion of this painting and of the mosaic of Justinian in San Vitale with its depiction of liturgical objects; and the several examples of the use of altar crosses in Elizabeth C. Parker and Charles T. Little, *The Cloisters Cross: Its Art and Meaning* (New York, 1994), pp. 119–48. Joseph Braun, in *Altargerät* and *Altar* (notes 2 and 8, above) also makes frequent reference to informative images in pictorial media.

[23]Wilhelm Koehler, *Drogo-Sakramentar: manuscrit Latin 9428, Bibliothèque nationale Paris*, Codices selecti, 2 vols. (Graz, 1974); and idem, *Die karolingischen Miniaturen*, vol. 3 (Berlin, 1960), pp. 143–62 and pls. 76–91.

Figure 1. Master of St. Augustine, *Consecration of St. Augustine as Bishop*. Flemish, ca. 1490. Oil on wood. New York: The Metropolitan Museum of Art, The Cloisters Collection, 1961. (61.199)

portable altar-ciborium of Arnulf, made in northern France ca. 870 and today in the Residenz-Schatzkammer in Munich.[24]

Literary records, in chronicles and devotional literature such as the accounts of the saints' lives and miracles, offer additional evidence that sometimes brings these objects alive in a most vivid manner. There is, for example, the story in Gerald of Wales's *Gemma Ecclesiastica* concerning a statue of the Virgin on an altar in Canterbury which, when the sanctity of her church was threatened by a cleric who attempted to rape a pious maiden in front of the altar, stood up, seized a nearby candlestick, and belabored the priest with it, thus saving the girl's virtue and preventing the desecration of the church.[25] This edifying tale informs us that—at least in twelfth-century England—it was not only customary for cult statues, such as that of the Virgin and Child, to rest permanently on the altar but also for candlesticks to be left on it even between services.

In addition to actual surviving pieces and pictorial and anecdotal depictions, numerous inventories survive—sometimes a succession covering several centuries of the history of a single treasury.[26] Their range encompasses

---

[24]Parker and Little, *The Cloisters Cross*, pp. 143–45; see also *Regensburger Buchmalerei: von frühkarolingischer Zeit bis zum Ausgang des Mittelalters. Ausstellung der Bayerische Staatsbibliothek München und der Museen der Stadt Regensburg* (exhibition catalogue, Munich, 1987), cat. 17 for color reproduction and bibliography.

[25]*Giraldi cambrensis gemma ecclesiastica, distinctio I, cap. 34*, cited in Otto Lehmann-Brockhaus, *Lateinische Schriftquellen zur Kunst in England, Wales und Schottland vom Jahre 901 bis zum Jahre 1307*, 5 vols. (Munich, 1955–60), vol. 3, §5863; translation in John J. Hagen, *Gerald of Wales, The Jewel of the Church: A Translation of* Gemma Ecclesiastica *by Giraldus Cambrensis* (Leiden, 1979), p. 82.

[26]In addition to the material for St. Denis cited above, see also *Mittelalterliche Schatzverzeichnisse*, ed. Bernhard Bischoff, vol. 1 (Munich, 1967); Otto Lehmann-Brockhaus, *Schriftquellen zur Kunstgeschichte des 11. und 12. Jahrhunderts für Deutschland, Lothringen und Italien*, 2 vols. (Berlin, 1938); idem, *Lateinische Schriftquellen* (note 25 above). There are also many publications of individual inventories, for example, *Inventories of Christchurch, Canterbury, with historical and topographical introductions and illustrative documents*, ed. John Wickham Legg and William H. St. John Hope (London, 1902); Alexandre Vidier, *Le*

the equipment and treasures of cathedrals, abbeys, and royal or ducal palace chapels. Among the most revealing are the lists of ecclesiastical treasures collected and delivered to Henry VIII of England at the time of the Dissolution of the Monasteries in 1536–40. From these we learn, for example, that the objects removed from the treasury of Canterbury Cathedral alone filled twenty-four carts when transported to London to be melted down in the royal mint. Some of this loot constituted, to be sure, the ornamentation of the shrine of Thomas Becket, the national martyr-saint; but much of it also would have consisted of chalices, **paten**s, and other liturgical vessels.[27]

Most such inventories are not as informative as we today might wish them to be: descriptions are generally limited to formulae such as "of the most splendid workmanship," or "weighing *x pounds* of gold [or silver]"; but they nonetheless do provide some idea of the quality and quantity of precious materials typically employed for these objects, and of the large numbers of them held in major treasuries. A few descriptive records, such as the *Liber de Rebus in Administratione sua Gestis* and the *Libellus Alter de Consecratione Ecclesiae Sancti Dionysii* of Suger, abbot of St.-Denis, the shrine of the patron saint of France and burial-place of her kings, are more detailed, and so vividly evocative of the precise appearance of specific vessels that scholars have been able to identify many of the surviving pieces.[28]

The commissioning and presentation of such objects was a major form of patronage in the Middle Ages, practiced not only by royalty, nobility, and the clerical elite but also by more humble donors. Such donations served, of course, not only to demonstrate religious devotion but also to display wealth, power, and authority; as such, they often were commemorated

---

Trésor de la Sainte-Chapelle, inventaires et documents (Paris, 1911), or Georg Kentenich, "Ein Verzeichnis des Trierer Domschatzes aus dem Jahre 1429," *Triererisches Archiv* 24/25 (1916): 228–32.

[27]C. Eveleigh Woodruff and William Danks, *Memorials of the Cathedral & Priory of Christ in Canterbury* (London, 1912), cited by Williamson, *The Medieval Treasury*, p. 14.

[28]Panofsky, *Abbot Suger*; *Royal Abbey of Saint-Denis*; *Trésor de Saint-Denis*.

by inscriptions on the objects themselves, and for that reason a number of the liturgical objects surviving today have preserved not only their original provenance-associations but also the names of those who commissioned and gave them to favored churches and abbeys. Occasionally, too, in spite of the prevalent anonymity of medieval craftsmen, the name of the artisan in charge of their manufacture survives in an inscription or the inventory notice of an identifiable work.[29] The twelfth-century German Benedictine monk who wrote, under the *nom-de-plume* of Theophilus, the treatise *De diversis artibus*, has been most persuasively identified by scholars as the metalworker Roger of Helmarshausen, creator of two portable altars today in Paderborn, one in the cathedral and the other in the Church of St. Francis.[30] Even the more modest pieces of liturgical equipment found in poorer parish churches probably were most frequently given to them by local donors, either lay or ecclesiastic. Adolf Reinle lists the objects essential to any church and observes that even the simplest basic equipment would have been beyond the means of most congregations: much of it must have been donated or paid for, in country parishes, by local monastic or noble patrons and, in towns, by merchants and aristocrats, brotherhoods and guilds, as well as by the upper echelons of the local ecclesiastical elite.[31]

---

[29]For example, Hugo d'Oignies, 13th-century goldsmith to whose hand a number of altar-crosses have been attributed: see *Rhin-Meuse: art et civilisation 800–1400* (exhibition catalogue, Cologne and Brussels, 1972, hereafter *Rhin-Meuse*), cat. M8; or Master Alpais of Limoges, who made and signed a magnificent ciborium now in the Louvre: *Enamels of Limoges 1100–1350* (exhibition catalogue, New York: Metropolitan Museum of Art, 1996, hereafter *Limoges*), cat. 69, pp. 246–49, with earlier bibliography.

[30]Charles Reginald Dodwell, ed. and trans. *Theophilus: De Diversis Artibus* (London, 1961), esp. pp. xxxiii–xliv; also *Theophilus on Divers Arts: The foremost medieval treatise on painting, glassmaking and metalwork*, ed. and trans. John G. Hawthorne and Cyril Stanley Smith (New York, 1979), esp. pp. xv–xvii; see also *Ornamenta Ecclesiae: Kunst und Künstler der Romanik*, 3 vols. (exhibition catalogue, Cologne, 1985, hereafter *Ornamenta Ecclesiae*), esp. 1:117–384.

[31]Adolf Reinle, *Die Ausstattung deutscher Kirchen im Mittelalter: eine Einführung* (Darmstadt, 1988), p. 2.

Actual liturgical objects owned by members of the clergy sometimes were buried with them as identifying insignia, thus preserving the identity of provenance and patron;[32] more frequently, replicas, made of baser metals such as lead—or even of terra cotta and summarily silvered or gilded—were substituted.[33] Even these, however, when recovered from their burial places, provide relatively firmly dated and localized examples of fashions in shape and, occasionally, ornament.

The Essential Liturgical Vessels

The institution of the Eucharist, the commemorative re-enactment of the Last Supper and of Christ's sacrificial death on the cross, in which according to Christian dogma the symbolic wine and bread are miraculously transubstantiated into the actual blood and body of the Savior, is described in the synoptic gospels, for example Matt. 26:26–28: Christ and his apostles were at supper in the upper room of a house in Jerusalem, celebrating the Hebrew Passover.

> And whilst they were at supper, Jesus took the bread and blessed and broke and gave to his disciples and said: Take ye and eat. This is my body. And, taking the chalice, he gave thanks and gave to them, saying: Drink ye all of this. For this is my blood of the New Testament, which shall be shed for many unto remission of sins.[34]

---

[32]For example, the chalice and paten found, together with episcopal ring and two pins, in the tomb of Archbishop Hubert Walter of Canterbury (d. 1205): see *English Romanesque Art 1066–1200*, ed. George Zarnecki et al. (exhibition catalogue, London, 1984), cat. 324a–f; see also Neil Stratford, Pamela Tudor-Craig, and Anna Maria Muthesius, "Archbishop Hubert Walter's Tomb and its Furnishings," in *Medieval Art and Architecture at Canterbury before 1220* (Leeds, 1982), pp. 20–26.

[33]Victor H. Elbern, *Der eucharistische Kelch im frühen Mittelalter* (Berlin, 1964), pp. 44–57. See also F. Van Molle, "Notes sur quelques calices furéraires du XIe siècle en France et en Belgique," *Les Monuments historiques de la France* 12/1–2 (1966): 113–19.

[34]See also: Mark 14:22–24; Luke 22:17–20; in John 6:51–59. Christ, teaching in the synagogue at Capernaum, presents his body and blood as food bestowing everlasting life; in

The Cup derives added symbolic significance from Christ's prayer in Gethsemane before his betrayal, "Father, if thou wilt, remove this chalice from me . . ." (Luke 22:42), thus representing his suffering on the cross.[35]

In earliest Christian times, the bread and wine of the Eucharist were not accorded extraordinary reverence, but as the Middle Ages progressed, and the belief in transubstantiation developed, they were held in increasing awe. The two elements, wine and bread, in Christian doctrine, became, once consecrated, the actual blood and flesh of Christ, and as such were worthy—even demanding—of the purest and most precious materials for their service, as well as the most careful protection against desecration by spillage or pollution.

While they developed from basically utilitarian containers in the earliest period of Christianity to precious vessels suitably honoring and glorifying the body and blood of Christ in the High Middle Ages, the chalice, paten, and other objects used in the liturgy also tended to reflect and copy the forms and styles current at any period in vessels of secular use. In a number of cases also, precious secular objects, particularly items of great antiquity or of exotic materials, were converted for use as liturgical vessels. Particularly popular were those made of semi-precious stones such as rock crystal, sardonyx, or agate, which survive in both simple and richly carved forms, adapted to Eucharistic use by the addition of rims and linings, feet, and handles of gold or silver, enamels, and gems.[36] The antiquity, radiance, and

---

1 Cor. 11:23–28, Paul describes the commemorative meal and its significance. For all citations of Scripture I have used the Douay translation of the Latin Vulgate.

[35]This is vividly embodied in a series of English 12th-century miniatures, beginning with that in the St. Albans Psalter of ca. 1123 (Hildesheim, St. Godehard), p. 39: see Otto Pächt, Charles Reginald Dodwell and Francis Wormald, *The St. Albans Psalter (Albani Psalter)* (London, 1960), pl. 25b and p. 89.

[36]In addition to the numerous examples in the treasury of San Marco in Venice (*Treasury of San Marco*), surviving examples include the 11th-century Chalice of Urraca in the treasury of León Cathedral, with both cup and foot of sardonyx (*Art of Medieval Spain*, cat. 118) and the Chalice of Abbot Suger from Saint-Denis, now in the National Gallery of Art in

durability of such re-used stones, either as the body of a chalice or other vessel or as carved cameos and intaglios set into the metal matrix of rim or foot, lent them great aesthetic value in the medieval view of beauty.[37]

I. Chalice[38]

Central, and most necessary, to the service of the Mass were the chalice and paten, the cup and plate for the communion wine and bread. Of these, the chalice was the more essential: the bread could be held in the hand or simply placed upon table or altar; but the liquid wine must, by its nature, be contained in a cup or jug. Thus, the chalice, the "cup" which Christ urged his apostles to take and drink from, is the first and most important of liturgical vessels.

Many different materials were used for early chalices:[39] in some cases, we know of their popularity because of later regulations forbidding their use on grounds of fragility or impurity. Thus, although glass chalices are known

---

Washington, one of several surviving liturgical vessels thus adapted (*Trésor de Saint-Denis*, cat. 28; *Royal Abbey of Saint-Denis*, cat. 25). The "Cup of the Ptolemies," a two-handled sardonyx cantharus carved with scenes of preparation for a Dionysiac rite, was similarly mounted: *Trésor de Saint-Denis*, cat. 11.

[37]See William S. Heckscher, "Relics of Pagan Antiquity in Medieval Settings," *Journal of the Warburg Institute* 1 (1937–38): 204–20; also Jean Taralon, *Treasures of the Churches of France* (London, 1966), pp. 26–28.

[38]A useful summary of the history and symbolism of the chalice is found in Heidi Roehrig Kaufmann et al., *Eucharistic Vessels of the Middle Ages* (exhibition catalogue, Cambridge, Mass., 1975), hereafter *Eucharistic Vessels*, pp. 23–31. See also *Dictionary of Art*, s.v. "Chalice," with further bibliography, and Elbern, *Der eucharistische Kelch im frühen Mittelalter* (note 33 above). Still the most exhaustive treatment is that of Braun, *Altargerät*, pp. 17 ff.

[39]Braun, *Altargerät*, pp. 30–51; also Durandus, *Rationale*, 1995 ed., I, §44, 45 (trans. in Neale and Webb, *Symbolism*, pp. 63–64).

from records and a few fragments,[40] they soon were forbidden because of the possibility of breakage and the resultant spillage of the eucharistic wine. Horn and ivory, similarly, were prohibited early because they, as animal products, were believed to contain blood themselves, which threatened to pollute the blood of Christ contained within them, while wood was disqualified because it would absorb the blood of Christ.[41] One ivory chalice does survive, however, from the Carolingian era, indicating that a certain latitude was practiced, even if frowned upon by the Church.[42] By far the most popular materials were gold and silver: ideally, the interior of the chalice bowl was lined with gold or at least was gilded. Even St. Bernard, as noted earlier, allowed that the cup of the chalice must be lined at least with gold or silver. In the more lavish chalices, the exterior might be adorned with precious and semi-precious gems, enamel inlays, or applied metal ornament such as filigree or an open-work outer cage; images, ornamental designs, and inscriptions might also be engraved into it, and possibly filled with contrasting sulfur-and-metal paste, *niello*, to make them more visible. Figural images typically refer directly to, or symbolize, the Eucharist and the salvific sacrifice of Christ it re-enacts.

---

[40]See examples in *Age of Spirituality*, ed. Weitzmann, cat. 545. Elbern, "Altar Implements and Liturgical Objects," p. 593, suggests that these may have been souvenirs from the Chapel of the Cup on the Mount of Golgotha in Jerusalem, rather than actual Communion chalices, a view expressed earlier also by Braun, though the latter also cites, with qualifications, documentary evidence for glass and crystal examples (*Altargerät*, pp. 35–50).

[41]*Eucharistic Vessels*, p. 23 and again Braun, *Altargerät*, pp. 17ff., for exhaustive discussion of documentary evidence for chalices in these materials.

[42]The Lebuinus Chalice, in the Archiepiscopal Museum in Utrecht: an early 9th-century ivory chalice now in a 14th-century silver setting that includes a cup-lining: see *Karl der Grosse: Werk und Wirkung* (exhibition catalogue, Aachen, 1965, hereafter *Karl der Grosse*), cat. 533, with earlier bibliography; also Elbern, *Der eucharistische Kelch im frühen Mittelalter*, pp. 19–21, 124–32, and Peter Lasko, *Ars Sacra 800–1200* (2nd ed., New Haven, 1994), ill. 15.

Chalices were made in various sizes. Very small ones served individual clergy and accompanied them on their travels: one such, found at Gourdon in France, survives from the sixth century, together with a rectangular plate variously identified as a paten or portable altar, exquisitely fabricated of gold with colored inlays. In shape it echoes the antique ***kantharos***, a two-handled cup with flaring lip, fluted bowl, and tapering base.[43] That the same form was used also for larger chalices is suggested by that offered to Abraham by Melchisedek (in an action seen as an Old Testament "type" of the Eucharist) in the fifth-century mosaic of their encounter in Santa Maria Maggiore in Rome.[44] For much of the earlier part of the Middle Ages, it was common to find chalices in at least two sizes: the smaller, or ***calix sanctus*** or *minor*, sufficed for the use of individuals or small groups, while the larger types served a variety of functions: the "community chalice," the ***calix offerendae***, received the offerings of wine brought by the community and offered in procession at the altar; the *scyphus* or ***calix consecrationis***, an immense vessel placed on the high altar, held the wine blessed by the pope or bishop before distribution; and the ***calix ministerialis*** contained the mixture of water and consecrated wine to be administered to the entire congregation present at such major feasts as Easter Sunday.[45] Such a large

---

[43]Now in Paris, Bibliothèque nationale de France, Cabinet des Médailles: *Karl der Grosse* (note 41 above), cat. 216. See also Helmut Roth, *Kunst der Völkerwanderungszeitr* (Frankfurt am Main, 1979), ill. 234b. The Gourdon chalice is 7.5 cm. tall; an even smaller example is the golden chalice from the tomb of Archbishop Poppo von Babenberg, only 4.6 cm. high, now in the Cathedral Treasury in Trier; see *Schatzkunst Trier* (Trier, 1984), cat. 21. The material and signs of wear suggest that this chalice may have been used during the Bishop's lifetime: Braun (*Altar*, 1:438) suggests that the set may have belonged originally to the portable altar/reliquary of St. Andrew's sandal-strap in the Trier treasury and have been appropriated by or for Poppo. The pristine condition and elaborately decorated lip of another Trier miniature, that of Archbishop Ruotbert from the mid-10th century, in contrast, indicate that it was made especially as a grave treasure; see *Schatzkunst Trier*, cat. 20.

[44]André Grabar, *The Golden Age of Justinian* (New York, 1967), ill. 155. On the two-handled form see also Braun, *Altargerät*, pp. 53–67.

[45]For nomenclature and sizes see the discussion in Braun, *Altargerät*, pp. 19–30.

chalice, in gold set with emeralds and pearls, is shown being borne by Empress Theodora in procession, as if for presentation to the church of San Vitale in Ravenna, in the famous mosaic panel in the presbytery of that church; of this type, too, are the two eighth- or early ninth-century Irish chalices from Ardagh and Derrynaflan. Although these have a smaller capacity than that held by Theodora, they are generous in size and their swelling bowls imply an ample quantity of wine and water.[46] The large bowl and low foot, probably joined by a rounded knob or knop, of Theodora's chalice are echoed in one of the most splendid of surviving Early Christian examples, the sixth-century Antioch Chalice in the Metropolitan Museum in New York.[47] This magnificent cup, clearly intended for the liturgy, is over seven inches high and consists of a simple silver inner cup enclosed in an openwork silver cage-like overlay, inlaid with gold and depicting inhabited vine-scrolls among which are set the seated figures of the teaching Christ and his apostles. The tall, generously curved bowl rests on a knop above a low, spreading foot, smaller in diameter than the cup it supports: the center of gravity is low, typical of early chalice shapes.

Beginning in about the ninth century, liturgical reforms increasingly separated the congregation from the clergy and increasingly invested the Eucharist with awesome mystery. The growing reverence with which the consecrated elements were regarded led to a great dread of spilling or profaning the communion wine, and by the thirteenth century it was common practice to administer the sacrament in one element only, the bread or wafer, to the community of the faithful. Only the celebrants, in that case, partook of the wine, and so a smaller chalice was all that was needed. Thus,

---

[46]See Susan Youngs, ed., *'The Work of Angels': Masterpieces of Celtic Metalwork, 6th–9th Centuries AD* (exhibition catalogue, London, 1989): the Derrynaflan chalice is cat. 124 and is illustrated together with the Ardagh Chalice in a color plate on p. 160. See also *The Derrynaflan Hoard, 1: A Preliminary Account*, ed. Michael Ryan (Dublin, 1983), pp. 3–15, and Michael Ryan, *Early Irish Communion Vessels: Church Treasures of the Golden Age* (Dublin, 1985).

[47]*Age of Spirituality*, ed. Weitzmann, cat. 542.

from the later Middle Ages, we find few if any *calices offerendae* or *ministeriales*, and a standard chalice of medium size becomes the norm. Around the ninth century, the deep bowl of the Early Christian chalice, while still vertically oval in shape, typically diminishes in capacity and becomes more slender, while the base, still separated from it by a rounded knop, grows taller and more conical: examples such as the well-known chalice of Duke Tassilo of Bavaria, given by him to the monastery of Kremsmünster between his marriage in 768/9 and his deposition in 788, and bearing an inscription in which he is named as donor, display equality of proportion between bowl and foot.[48] This balance is continued in chalices of the eleventh, twelfth, and thirteenth centuries, but the bowl loses depth and the general proportions are squatter and broader, as in an example of ca. 1235 from the convent of St. Trudpert in Germany, now in the Metropolitan Museum (Fig. 2).[49] Theophilus describes a similar shape in his instructions for making chalices in *De Diversis Artibus*.[50] In the later Middle Ages, chalices again grow taller and more slender, and the bowl becomes smaller and shallower in relation to the base, which often displays exaggerated height; the stem of such chalices is often also extended as an additional vertical element above and below the knop. It is probable that such exaggerated height resulted from the desire to enhance the visibility of the chalice from a distance, inspired by the new importance placed on the viewing of the consecrated elements by the faithful, even when they did not partake of them. Numerous late medieval examples of such tall chalices survive, often embellished with scenes in translucent enamel or with embossed or

---

[48]Kremsmünster, Abbey Treasury: see *Karl der Grosse*, cat. 548; more recently, Lasko, *Ars Sacra*, ill. 1 and *Lexikon der Kunst*, s.v. "Tassilokelch."

[49]Frazer, *Medieval Church Treasuries*, fig. 2, p. 9, and *The Year 1200: A Centennial Exhibition at the Metropolitan Museum of Art*, ed. Konrad Hoffmann (New York, 1970; hereafter *The Year 1200*), cat. 125.

[50]Book III, §26–43: Dodwell, *Theophilus*, op. cit., pp. 75–94; Hawthorne and Smith, *Theophilus on Divers Arts*, op. cit., pp. 99–117, with diagrams.

Figure 2. Chalice and matching paten from monastery of St. Trudpert, Germany. German (Freiburg im Breisgau), ca. 1235. Silver with gilding, niello, gems. New York: The Metropolitan Museum of Art, The Cloisters Collection, 1947. (47.101.26 and 47.101.27)

engraved decoration; a typical feature of these also is the ornamental articulation of the foot—and sometimes also of the cup—with lobes or radiating segments. Paired handles, common in the Early Medieval period, become rarer and disappear in the later Middle Ages.[51]

---

[51]Examples include chalices in *Eucharistic Vessels*, pp. 29–30 and cat. 1–4; *Trésors des Églises de France*, cat. 216; and the "Zafiro" chalice of ca. 1490 in the Treasury of the Cathedral of Monza; for the last-named see Augusto Merati, *Il Tesoro del Duomo di Monza* (2nd ed., Monza, 1969), p. 67. On the presence or absence of handles see Braun, *Altargerät*, pp. 53–137.

II. The Paten[52]

Almost as central as the chalice to the celebration of the Eucharist was the paten, the plate on which the bread was placed for consecration and distribution. Unlike the chalice, however, it is not specifically mentioned in scriptural accounts and thus never achieves the same symbolic significance. In the early Church, and for a longer period in the East than in the West, the eucharistic bread consisted of large home-baked loaves, brought by the faithful as offerings to the church and divided and distributed by the celebrant. These would have required large serving-platters or chargers: possibly the broad, shallow bowl held by the Emperor Justinian in the pendant panel to Theodora's in San Vitale in Ravenna represents such a piece. Silver plates and *missoria* or large, slightly dished platters from the eastern Roman Empire, dating largely from the fourth to seventh centuries, although made for secular courtly use, give some idea of the size and magnificent decoration of early pieces.[53] Several silver patens clearly made for liturgical use survive from the sixth and seventh centuries: while most are decorated simply with symbolic elements such as the ***Chi Rho*** symbol and vine-scroll borders,[54] two of these (the Riha and Stuma patens, in Dumbarton Oaks and Istanbul) bear depictions of the *Communion of the Apostles*, in which Christ himself administers both elements to his disciples in a composition that

---

[52]See the useful essay by Elaine K. Bryson Siegel, "Patens," in *Eucharistic Vessels*, pp. 36–41; also *Dictionary of Art,* s.v. "Paten"; Braun, *Altargerät*, pp. 197–246; and Elbern, *Der eucharistische Kelch*, pp. 132–47.

[53]For example, the silver plate with Heracles and the Nemean Lion in the Cabinet des Médailles, Bibliothèque Nationale de France, Paris (*Age of Spirituality*, ed. Weitzmann, cat. 139); the David Plates from Cyprus (*Age of Spirituality*, cat. 425–433), and many others.

[54]For example, the plate of Paternus, in the Hermitage Museum in Leningrad: *Age of Spirituality,* ed. Weitzmann, cat. 546. Many simpler examples survive as well: see, for example, Erica Cruikshank Dodd, *Byzantine Silver Treasures* (Bern, 1974), ills. 19–25, pls. XII, XIII.

merges commemoration of the historical Last Supper with depiction of the liturgical celebration of the Eucharist.[55]

Like chalices, patens survive in a wide range of sizes; and like domestic serving-dishes, they could be made of a variety of materials;[56] while these were less stringently regulated by the Church than were the materials for chalices, from the early tenth century onward a succession of rulings prescribed gold or silver, with pewter allowed only for poor congregations.[57] One early limestone paten or paten-mold (mid-eighth century) survives from Germigny-des-Prés, in fragmentary form, but sufficient to indicate a composition consisting of a circle of roundels containing busts of angels, surrounding a larger medallion with the half-length figure of Christ.[58] Such rich ornamentation of patens as that on the Riha, Stuma and Germigny examples was relatively rare in the Early Medieval period; but a number survive from the High and Late Middle Ages with elaborate and complex imagery designed to complement that of the chalices with which they form sets (Fig. 2).[59] Typically, the paten was placed on top of the chalice for the procession to the altar, and had a central depression, usually circular or

---

[55]*Age of Spirituality*, ed. Weitzmann, cat. 547 (the Riha paten) and fig. 82, p. 593 (the Stuma paten).

[56]An antique serpentine dish with inlaid golden dolphins, converted for use as a paten by the addition of a gem-set golden rim in the court workshops of Charles the Bald, now in the Louvre, probably formed a pendant in the treasury of Saint-Denis to the chalice made from the "cup of the Ptolemies": *Trésor de Saint-Denis*, cat. 12; Lasko, *Ars Sacra*, ill. 72.

[57]*Eucharistic Vessels*, p. 38; Braun, *Altargerät*, pp. 203–06. The humblest material on record is straw: the 5th-century bishop Exuperius of Toulouse is said to have sold the church silver and replaced it with glass chalices and straw patens: Braun, *Altargerät*, p. 356.

[58]Orléans, Musée historique et archéologique de l'Orléanais: *La Neustrie*, cat. 21, with earlier bibliography. See also Elbern, *Der eucharistische Kelch im frühen Mittelalter*, p. 136.

[59]For example, the St. Trudpert paten, mentioned above: see Frazer, *Medieval Church Treasuries*, p. 2; and *The Year 1200*, cat. 125.

lobed,[60] of a diameter roughly equal to that of the bowl of the chalice, while the encircling broader rim allowed it to rest on the chalice lip. A major change in format and size came with the substitution of the wafer of the Host for the original large loaf, beginning in the eleventh century.[61] As the bowls of chalices became smaller, so too did the diameter of the patens made as companion pieces. Toward the end of the Middle Ages patens tended to become more utilitarian and much less richly decorated.

The ecclesiastical treasure discovered in 1980 on the site of the ruins of the Irish monastery of Derrynaflan included not only a large and richly decorated paten[62] but also a separate paten stand, a shallow metal cylinder of copper-alloy decorated with stamped silver panels and enamel-inlaid bronze plaques. Pins projecting from its upper edge fit into holes in the lower surface of the paten, holding the two pieces in alignment.[63] The large size of this paten perhaps reflects the elaborate and symbolic arrangement of multiple fragments of the Host—up to sixty-five particles for Easter, Christmas, and Pentecost—as stipulated in the late eighth-century Irish Stowe Missal.[64]

---

[60]While Braun (*Altargerät*, p. 213) attaches little significance to the lobed form, Elbern (*Der eucharistische Kelch*, pp. 138–43) notes that the varying number of lobes may have varying symbolic value; it is also perhaps worth noting their resemblance to the scalloped border popular on the surface of altar tables, especially in southern France.

[61]Joseph A. Jungmann, *The Mass of the Roman Rite: Its Origins and Development (Missarium Sollemnia)*, trans. Francis A. Brunner (New York, 1951–55; repr. Westminster, Md., 1986), 2:33–34.

[62]Diameter 35.6–36.8 cm., or roughly 14 inches. Youngs, *'The Work of Angels'*, cat. 125a; Michael Ryan, *The Derrynaflan Hoard* (Dublin, 1983), pp. 17–30; and idem, *Early Irish Communion Vessels*, pp. 19–20.

[63]On paten stands in general, see brief mentions in *Eucharistic Vessels*, p. 39 and Braun, *Altargerät*, p. 209; the Derrynaflan paten stand is cat. 125b in Youngs, *'The Work of Angels'*. See also *The Derrynaflan Hoard*, pp. 17–30, where it is discussed together with the paten, and Ryan, *Early Irish Communion Vessels*, p. 20.

[64]*The Stowe Missal: MS D. II.3 in the Library of the Royal Irish Academy, Dublin*, ed. and trans. George F. Warner (London, 1906, 1915; repr. Woodbridge, Suffolk, 1989), pp. 41–42.

Accessory Vessels and Containers

1. Ewers, cruets, and aquamanilia

In the Gospel narratives of the Crucifixion, the soldier's spear-thrust into Christ's side releases a stream of blood and water (John 19:34); this, together no doubt with the antique custom of mixing water with wine for drinking (also a part of Jewish ritual),[65] led to the custom of mixing water with the consecrated wine: a very small amount of consecrated wine, in fact, could render a large amount of water sacred. From very early, these minglings of water and wine are interpreted as symbolizing the inseparability of the faithful from Christ, and the duality of Christ's two natures, divine and human.[66] ***Amulae***, the jugs in which offerings of wine were brought by the faithful, should also be noted: it is possible that some of the vessels richly decorated with Christian imagery but impossible to identify from context or other factors specifically as liturgical vessels, may belong to this category.[67]

To pour the wine and water, **ewers** and jugs similar to domestic utensils of parallel function were used: many, even, may have been co-opted from originally secular use. A number of fine early ewers survive, in contexts or with inscriptions or images that suggest a connection with liturgical

---

Diagrams of these patterns of confraction are provided in Kristopher Dowling, *Celtic Missal: The Liturgy and Diverse Services from the Lorrha ("Stowe") Missal* (Akron, Ohio, 1996). See also Ryan, *Early Irish Communion Vessels*, p. 7; and Dom Fernand Cabrol, in *Dictionnaire d'archéologie chrétienne et de liturgie*, hereafter *DACL*, vol. 5, pt. 2 (Paris, 1923), cols. 2112–15, s.v. "Fractio panis."

[65]Kaufmann et al., *Eucharistic Vessels*, pp. 57–58; see also Dom Gregory Dix, *The Shape of the Liturgy*, 2nd ed. (London, 1945), p. 57.

[66]Jungmann, *Mass of the Roman Rite*, 2:38–41.

[67]Braun, *Altargerät*, pp. 415–16; see also Elbern, "Altar Implements and Liturgical Objects," p. 593.

functions (Fig. 3):[68] a unique early Frankish example, made ca. 500, of a wooden core covered in sheets of bronze stamped with Christological scenes, clearly betrays, by its beaked spout and ample handle, the combination of utilitarian form and Christian imagery.[69] By about 1000, specific mention is made of pairs of vessels, probably matching in form, for the wine and water:[70] this format became standard by the twelfth century (Fig. 1), and still survives, frequently with the distinguishing labels "*aqua*" and "*vinum*," or simply *a* and *v*. A number of medieval examples are preserved in museums and church treasuries, a good example being the elegant Late Gothic cruets from Lübeck in the Metropolitan Museum[71] (Fig. 4). A single cruet in The Cloisters, of typical Limoges manufacture in bronze with *champlevé* enamel decoration,[72] exemplifies a common class of accessory

---

[68]Three slender flagon-shaped vessels in repoussé (embossed) silver with biblical scenes or images of the apostles, in Edinburgh, the Metropolitan Museum, and the British Museum, date to the 4th or 5th century and could perhaps have been ewers or *amulae*, but there is some doubt as to their actual function, and they may even have been secular domestic utensils in Christian households: see *Age of Spirituality*, ed. Weitzmann, cat. 389, 400; and Little and Husband, *Europe in the Middle Ages*, no. 25, p. 35. Note also the 6th-century silver ewer with dedication inscription in Baltimore, part of the Hamah treasure of liturgical objects: *Age of Spirituality*, ed. Weitzmann, cat. 535.

[69]St. Germain en Laye, Musée des Antiquités nationales: see Jean Hubert, Jean Porcher, and W. F. Volbach, *Europe of the Invasions* (New York, 1969), p. 260 and ill. 287. Also René Joffroy, *Le Cimetière de Lavoye (Meuse), Nécropole Mérovingienne* (Paris, 1974) and Roth, *Kunst der Völkerwanderungszeit* (note 43 above), no. 236. Found in the grave of a Frankish chieftain, this piece was most probably intended for private use, but its scenes include the transformation of wine to water at the Marriage at Cana, a miracle associated with the Eucharist. While Joffroy considers the jug to have been looted by the pagan occupant of tomb 319 from a Gallo-Roman church, Roth suggests that is was used at his baptism.

[70]Braun, *Altargerät*, pp. 414–40; also Kaufmann et al., *Eucharistic Vessels*, pp. 57–61.

[71]Frazer, *Medieval Church Treasuries*, pp. 10–11; this pair is also discussed in Kaufmann et al., *Eucharistic Vessels*, cat. 6, pp. 63–64 and fig. 6.

[72]"Raised field" enamel, in which the enamel, in paste or granular state, is placed in grooves or hollows carved into a metal plate and then fired. See *Dictionary of Art*, s.v. "enamel"; also Marian Campbell, *An Introduction to Medieval Enamels* (London, 1983).

Figure 3. Ewer from Vrap (Armenia), with inscription on neck indicating its use as container for holy water and monograms identifying a donor. Byzantine, seventh–eighth century. Silver, partly gilded. New York: The Metropolitan Museum of Art, Gift of J. Pierpont Morgan, 1917. (17.190.1704)

Figure 4. Pair of cruets for wine and water by Hans Plate, Lübeck. German, 1518. Silver, partly gilded. New York: The Metropolitan Museum of Art, The Friedsam Collection, Bequest of Michael Friedsam, 1931. (32.100.219)

liturgical vessels produced in that important metalworking and enameling area.[73] Bronze and brass, while too base for chalice or paten, were eminently practical for use in secondary liturgical objects, being both economical and, when inlaid with colorful enamels, splendid and highly decorative. Typically, Abbot Suger adapted several antique stone vessels as cruets and ewers for the treasury of St.-Denis, among them the famous porphyry eagle vase described in his *De Administratione*[74] and the crystal vase [the *justa*] given by Eleanor of Aquitaine as a wedding gift to Louis VII, who in turn presented it to St.-Denis.[75]

Water jugs, ***aquamanilia***, were used to pour water for washing, and in the later Middle Ages often were made of bronze cast in fanciful shapes of beasts and humans, which appear to have been used in home and church alike.[76] The water for ritual cleansing was poured into ***gemellia***, twin shallow basins with drainage spouts affixed to, or just below, their rims. Examples in bronze and Limoges enamel survive.[77]

---

[73]Frazer, *Medieval Church Treasuries*, pp. 10–11; *Limoges*, cat. 136; another, from Saint-Denis, is *Limoges*, cat. 137.

[74]Panofsky, *Abbot Suger*, pp. 78, 222; and *Trésor de Saint-Denis*, cat. 31. See also Danielle Gaborit-Chopin, "Suger's Liturgical Vessels," in *Abbot Suger and Saint Denis*, ed. Gerson (note 17 above), figs.5–7, pp. 285–86. All three vessels are now in the Louvre.

[75]Panofsky, *Abbot Suger,* pp. 78, 220; *Trésor de Saint-Denis*, cat. 27; and Gaborit-Chopin, "Suger's Liturgical Vessels," figs. 14–17, p. 289. Another cruet, of sardonyx, is probably that mentioned immediately after the *justa* in *De Administratione*: Panofsky, *Abbot Suger*, pp. 79, 221; *Trésor de Saint-Denis*, cat. 29; and Gaborit-Chopin, "Suger's Liturgical Vessels," figs. 12, 13, p. 289.

[76]*Dictionary of Art*, s.v. "Aquamanile"; see also Braun, *Altargerät*, pp. 531–51.

[77]Braun, *Altargerät*, pp. 531–51; for examples typical of the form, though with secular imagery, see *Limoges*, cat. 125, 126, 131, 132. It is possible that, as in the case of aquamanilia, gemellia with secular decoration were also used for liturgical cleansing: see also Ursula E. McCracken, *Liturgical Objects in the Walters Art Gallery* (Baltimore, 1967), ill. 15.

II. Containers for the Reserved Host

Any consecrated wine remaining after the Mass was to be drunk by the priest, in order that it not be spilt or desecrated in any way during the clearing up and cleaning of the sacred vessels. It became common practice, however, to preserve the remnants of the consecrated Host for the Communion of the Sick and similar purposes.[78] The Reserved Host was most commonly kept in a **pyx** or **pyxis**, or the larger ciborium, but might also be preserved in its symbolically figural variant, the eucharistic dove, in a cupboard-like tabernacle or, in the later Middle Ages, in a **monstrance**.

1. Pyx or Pyxis.[79] The term refers simply to a "box," which might be of any size, shape, or material; in the early Christian period, pyxides appear most often to have been made of ivory, their cylindrical shape and frequently large dimensions[80] reflecting not only the size and shape of available elephant tusks but also the considerable bulk of the early communion loaves and their remnants. Ivory pyxides survive in considerable number from the third to the sixth century, most carved with biblical scenes referring to their Christian use and specifically to their Eucharistic function (Fig. 5) or, in the case of depictions of Christ's healing miracles, to their

---

[78]See Frank L. Cross, ed., *The Oxford Dictionary of the Christian Church* (3rd, rev. ed., ed. E. A. Livingstone, Oxford, 1997, hereafter *ODCC*), s.v. "Reservation."

[79]For a good general introduction see the essay "Pyxes and Ciboria" by Thomas DaCosta Kaufmann in Kaufmann et al., *Eucharistic Vessels*, pp. 65–71. Braun (*Altargerät*, pp. 280–347), discusses all containers under the rubric "Ziborium."

[80]The largest are the great Berlin pyxis, 14.6 cm. in diameter: Wolfgang F. Volbach, *Elfenbeinarbeiten der Spätantike und des frühen Mittelalters* (Mainz, 1976), cat. 161; and a 6th-century pyxis in a private collection, also 14.6 cm. in diameter: *The Carver's Art: Medieval Sculpture in Ivory, Bone, and Horn*, ed. Archer St. Clair and Elizabeth Parker McLachlan (exhibition catalogue, Jane Voorhees Zimmerli Art Museum, Rutgers University, New Brunswick, N.J., 1989), cat. 15. Most surviving examples are smaller, some closer to half that diameter.

Figure 5. Pyxis with Miracle of the Loaves and Fishes, from San Pedro de la Rua, Estella (Spain). Byzantine, sixth century. Ivory with wooden additions and gilded copper fittings. New York: The Metropolitan Museum of Art, Gift of J. Pierpont Morgan, 1917. (17.190.34)

function in the Communion of the Sick.[81] Others preserved in church treasuries bear secular and even pagân scenes, indicating that they originally were fabricated for general use and later co-opted for the service of the church.[82] Pyxides might be made of a wide variety of materials: though

---

[81]See, for example, *Age of Spirituality*, ed. Weitzmann, cat. 405, 418, 421, 436, 447, 449, 514, 518–20; also Frazer, *Medieval Church Treasuries*, p. 11.

[82]The best known of these is probably the 4th-century pyxis with Orpheus charming the animals, in the treasury of San Columbano in Bobbio: see Volbach, *Elfenarbeiten der Spätantike*, cat. 91; another, from the 5th or 6th century, with a lion hunt, is preserved in the treasury of Sens Cathedral: ibid., cat. 102, and a second Orpheus pyxis, formerly in the

there was a general agreement that they should be of materials worthy of their contents, no Church ruling actually named preferences.[83] In the later Middle Ages they were generally of metal, and their cylindrical shape and smaller dimensions reflected those of the Host wafer that replaced the earlier loaf.[84] Most common are the twelfth- and thirteenth-century examples of Limoges enamelwork, small cylinders with conical lids, usually adorned with floral ornament and sacred monograms or other symbols.[85]

2. Eucharistic Dove.[86] Pyxides might be placed on the altar or within it, or suspended from the canopy above it.[87] A variant which evoked the presence and power of the Host, and through it of the Holy Spirit at work in the world, was the Eucharistic Dove: a metal—usually Limoges champlevé enamel—figurine of lifelike shape and size, sometimes with hinged wings, and with a lidded cavity in its back in which the Host was placed. Suspended on chains above the altar, the Eucharistic Dove was a permanent symbol and reminder of the Holy Spirit's effective presence in the world (Fig. 6).[88]

---

treasury of the church of St. Julien in Brioude, is now in the Bargello Museum in Florence: ibid., cat. 92.

[83]On materials used for pyxides, see Braun, *Altargerät*, pp. 291–98.

[84]The wafer began to replace the loaf in the 11th century; see Jungmann, *Mass of the Roman Rite*, 2:33–34. The typical diameter of a 13th-century Limoges pyxis is between 6.5 and 7 cm.

[85]*Limoges*, cat. 74, 128, 129, 138, 139.

[86]See Braun, *Altargerät*, pp. 319–23.

[87]For pyxides of all types suspended above the altar, see Braun, *Altar*, 2:599–623.

[88]Frazer, *Medieval Church Treasuries*, pp. 11–12; *Limoges*, cat. 105, 106; *The Year 1200*, cat. 166.

Figure 6. Eucharistic dove. French, early thirteenth century. Limoges champlevé enamel on gilded copper. New York: The Metropolitan Museum of Art, Gift of J. Pierpont Morgan, 1917. (17.190.344)

3. Ciborium.[89] To contain a quantity of consecrated Hosts for distribution to large numbers of communicants, for example on Easter Sunday, a larger container, later called the *ciborium*, was developed; the best surviving examples date to the twelfth and thirteenth centuries. The name is variously derived from the Greek *kiborion*, the seed-pod of the Egyptian lotus, or the Latin *cibus*, food. Typically the ciborium mimics the shape of the chalice, raised on a rounded knop and conical foot, with a swelling bowl

[89]Braun, *Altargerät*, pp. 280–347.

Figure 7. The Morgan or Malmesbury Ciborium. English, ca. 1160–70. Champlevé enamel on gilded copper. The Pierpont Morgan Library/Art Resource, N.Y.

and close-fitting domed lid terminating in an elaborate finial. Three superb twelfth-century English examples survive in various states of completeness, adorned with champlevé enamel roundels depicting scenes from the Old and New Testaments with Eucharistic references (Fig. 7);[90] ciboria were also produced in the Limoges workshops in France, and a particularly fine example of these is attributed by its inscription to the hand of the Paris metalworker, Master Alpais.[91]

---

[90] *English Romanesque Art*, ed. Zarnecki, cat. 278–80; see also Neil Stratford, "Three English Romanesque Enamelled Ciboria," *The Burlington Magazine*, 126, no. 973 (April 1984): 204–16.

[91] *Limoges*, cat. 69.

4. Tabernacle. When kept on or near the altar, the reserved Host in its container might be placed in a shrine-like cupboard known as a tabernacle, from the Latin *tabernaculum* [tent].[92] Originally this would have been a fairly simple structure, as represented by two early thirteenth-century Limoges examples with tent-like pyramidal lids.[93] Two slightly later Limoges tabernacles, one in the Metropolitan Museum,[94] the other in the treasury of Chartres Cathedral,[95] are more elaborate: their gabled front leaves open like those of a triptych to reveal a shallow stage-like interior with bronze-relief scenes of the Passion. Later the tabernacle became more monumental, as the wall-cupboards of the Renaissance or the freestanding architectural, tower-like *Sakramentshäuser* of the German Gothic demonstrate.[96]

5. Monstrance.[97] Following the proclamation of the dogma of transubstantiation at the fourth Lateran Council in 1215, the number of Eucharistic miracles recorded increased dramatically.[98] Great importance was placed upon the viewing of the consecrated Host by the worshiper, and miraculous effects were attributed to the mere sight of it: a glimpse of the elevated Host

---

[92]*ODCC*, s.v. "Reservation" and "Tabernacle"; *Lexikon der Kunst*, s.v. "Tabernakel."

[93]*Limoges*, cat. 70.

[94]*Limoges*, cat. 98. See also Frazer, *Medieval Church Treasuries*, pp. 11–12; and Little and Husband, *Europe in the Middle Ages*, no. 79, pp. 88–89.

[95]Taralon, *Treasures of the Churches of France*, pp. 147–49, 280.

[96]Lexikon der Kunst, s.v. "Sakramentshaus"; also Braun, *Altar*, 2:588. Possibly the best-known is that sculpted by Adam Krafft for the Lorenzkirche in Nuremberg in 1493–95.

[97]Braun, *Altargerät*, pp. 348–411.

[98]Peter Browe, *Die Eucharistischen Wunder des Mittelalters* (Breslau, 1938; repr. Rome, 1967), esp. pp. 93 ff.

at morning Mass, for example, was believed to protect one from harm during the entire ensuing day, and could convert unbelievers on the spot.[99] Such beliefs, together with the institution in 1246 of the feast of Corpus Christi, and in particular the growth of the associated public processions in which the Host was carried through the streets, stimulated the development of *monstrances* or *ostensoria*: containers that would both protect the Host and, as the names suggest, display it for veneration.[100] Typically these consist of a tall foot like those of contemporary chalices, surmounted by a glass or crystal tube or two-sided circular window, within which the wafer of the Host rests in a crescent-moon-shaped holder. This window is framed and surrounded by elaborate metalwork decoration, often in the shape of towering Gothic architectural pinnacles in delicate metal openwork, inhabited by the figures of saints, and by biblical scenes (Fig. 8). Such monstrances were particularly popular in the fifteenth and sixteenth centuries,[101] and paralleled "transparent reliquaries" in which the bones of saints were similarly displayed for veneration.[102]

---

[99]Miri Rubin, *Corpus Christi: The Eucharist in Late Medieval Culture* (Cambridge, 1991), esp. pp. 243–71, 288–94. On the conversion of heathens who viewed the Eucharist see, for example, Leah Sinanoglou, The Christ Child as Sacrifice: A Medieval Tradition and the Corpus Christi Plays," *Speculum* 43 (1973): 491–510.

[100]See Rubin, *Corpus Christi*, pp. 290–91.

[101]Lotte Perpeet-Frech, *Die gotischen Monstranzen im Rheinland* (Düsseldorf, 1964), also provides a good general introduction on pp. 9–28. Their popularity in the Rhineland and the Moselle area is well illustrated by the numerous examples surviving in, for example, Aachen and Trier.

[102]The treatment of the Eucharist as a relic is noted by Patrick J. Geary, *Furta Sacra: Thefts of Relics in the Central Middle Ages* (Princeton, 1978), pp. 29–30, 39–40.

Figure 8. Gothic Monstrance. Flemish or German, late fifteenth–early sixteenth century, silver gilt. New York: The Metropolitan Museum of Art, The Michael Friedsam Collection, 1931. (32.100.226)

Accessory Liturgical Implements

Additional objects, though not essential for the storage and administration of the elements of the Eucharist, nonetheless played important roles in the performance of the liturgy and similarly served also as vehicles for symbolism and patronage.

1. Spoons, ladles and strainers[103]

These were used for various purposes, such as removing pieces of the Host from pyx or ciborium,[104] adding consecrated wine to the chalice,[105] or transferring incense from boat to censer (see below). Straniers were used to remove impurities from wine or water before consecration. Numerous spoons survive with inscriptions or other decorations that seem to imply their use in the liturgy; most of these, however, apparently were intended for domestic use.[106] Together with chalice, paten, and paten stand, the Derrynaflan treasure included a long-handled tin-bronze ladle set with rock crystal and ornamental enamels, its bowl bisected by a decoratively pierced wall that adapts it as a strainer, making a doubly-useful hybrid form.[107]

---

[103]Braun, *Altargerät*, on "Eucharistisches Löffel" or "Kelchlöffelchen," pp. 265–79; on spoons in general, pp. 444–47; on strainers, pp. 448–54.

[104]In the Eastern rite only; see Braun, *Altargerät*, pp. 265–79.

[105]Braun, *Altargerät*, pp. 444–47.

[106]Braun (*Altargerät*, pp. 266–67) warns that most surviving spoons, even those engraved with specifically Christian inscriptions or symbols, were made for secular rather than liturgical use. A ladle, strainer and spoon found as part of the Hamah treasure of liturgical objects probably, however, from their find-context, were used in the liturgy: see *Age of Spirituality*, cat. 537–39.

[107]Youngs, *'The Work of Angels'*, cat. 126; *The Derrynaflan Hoard*, pp. 31–34. For strainers, see also Braun, *Altargerät*, pp. 448–54. Just as the Hamah ladle noted above can be assumed

II. *Fistula*[108]

High and late medieval concern for the protection of the wine from spilling led to the use of a tubular metal straw, or ***fistula***, by the communicant or by the celebrant who must empty the leftover consecrated wine from the chalice: although these were probably not universally used, a few survive. They were often made in pairs, as in the case of those from St. Trudpert's monastery in Germany, now in the Metropolitan Museum (Fig. 9),[109] and often have decorative wing- or flange-like handles.

III. *Flabellum*[110]

The ***flabellum*** or liturgical fan (also known in Greek as *rhipidion*) originally was wielded by the sub-deacon to protect the Eucharist from pollution by flies, hairs, or other debris; eventually, it appears to have become purely symbolic rather than functional and probably was in evidence only in very ceremonial and luxuriously-equipped rituals. Its use and appearance recall the fans waved over rulers and potentates in antiquity and, thus, carried over these honorific connotations to the Eucharist, the embodiment of Divine rulership. Originally, such fans were made of peacock-feathers: an example may be seen in the miniature of the Healing of King Hezekiah in

---

from its find-context to have been used in the liturgy, a 6th-century silver sieve set with garnets, now in the Cluny Museum in Paris, may be assumed from its engraved inscription, naming St. Aubin or Albinus, bishop of Angers 529–ca. 550, to have been made for liturgical use: see Erlande-Brandenburg et al., *Musée national du Moyen Age, Thermes de Cluny*, cat. 75, p. 73.

[108]Braun, *Altargerät*, pp. 247–65.

[109]Frazer, *Medieval Church Treasuries*, p. 2; *The Year 1200*, cat. 125. Braun (*Altargerät*, pp. 247–65) lists other examples.

[110]Elbern, "Altar Implements and Liturgical Objects," pp. 593–94; and Braun, *Altargerät*, pp. 642–60.

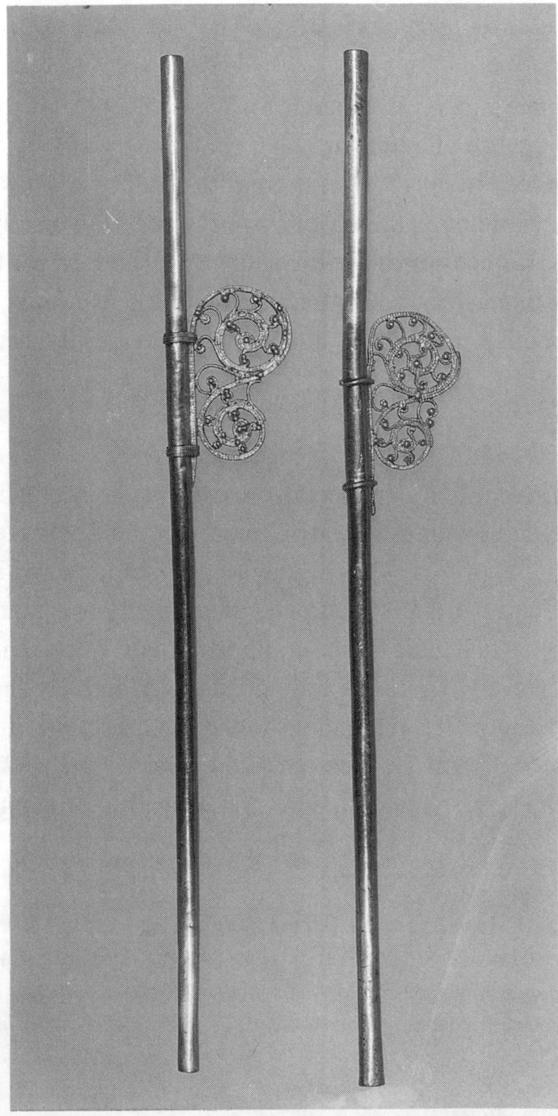

Figure 9. Pair of fistulae, part of a set including the chalice and paten from St. Trudpert's monastery (fig. 2). German (Freiburg im Breisgau), ca. 1235. Silver, gilded. New York: The Metropolitan Museum of Art, The Cloisters Collection, 1947. (47.101.28,.29)

the tenth-century Paris Psalter.[111] Actual peacock-feather fans still appear in later medieval inventories,[112] but as early as the sixth century more durable versions were being produced in precious materials: two superb sixth-century Byzantine examples survive in silver, engraved with peacock-feathers and biblical images such as tetramorphic seraphim with eye-set wings, described in the vision of the prophet Ezekiel as guarding the throne of God in heaven.[113] A remarkable Carolingian survival is the mid-ninth-century flabellum of Tournus, its handle and fan-box made of ivory carved with animals and pastoral scenes reminiscent of the illustrations of Roman bucolic poetry, and the head consisting of a collapsible pleated vellum roundel painted with foliate ornament and the figures of saints.[114] Later examples of openwork metal, set with stones and enamel plaques, survive, notably a twelfth-century German pair now in Leningrad and New York with central cavities for relics (Fig. 10).[115]

---

[111]Paris, Bibliothèque nationale de France, MS gr. 139, fol. 446v; see Anthony Cutler, *The Aristocratic Psalters in Byzantium* (Paris, 1984), fig. 258, p. 205.

[112]Braun, *Altargerät*, p. 656.

[113]Ezek. 1:5–28; see Elbern, "Altar Implements and Liturgical Objects," pp. 593–94 and *Age of Spirituality*, ed. Weitzmann, cat. 553.

[114]See Lorenz E. A. Eitner, *Flabellum of Tournus* (New York, 1944); *La Neustrie*, cat. 121; Danielle Gaborit-Chopin, *Ivoires du Moyen Age* (Fribourg, 1978), ills. 66–69. That this is an ancient form is demonstrated by an image of a Roman example in secular use illustrated in George Henderson, *From Durrow to Kells: The Insular Gospel-Books 660–800* (London, 1987), ill. 172, p. 119. That it continues into the Gothic period is attested by illustrations in liturgical manuscripts, for example the 13th-century Jumièges Missal, Rouen, Bibliothèque Municipale MS 199, fol. 152r (Dom Victor Leroquais, *Les Sacramentaires et les missels manuscrits des bibliothèques publiques de France*, Paris, 1924, pl. XLVII), and the Missal of St.-Corneille de Compiègne, also 13th-century, Paris, Bibliothèque nationale de France, MS lat. 17,318, fol. 173r (Leroquais, *Les Sacramentaires et les missels*, pl. LI).

[115]*The Year 1200*, cat. 118; Frazer, *Medieval Church Treasuries*, p. 20; Little and Husband, *Europe in the Middle Ages*, no. 39, pp. 46–47.

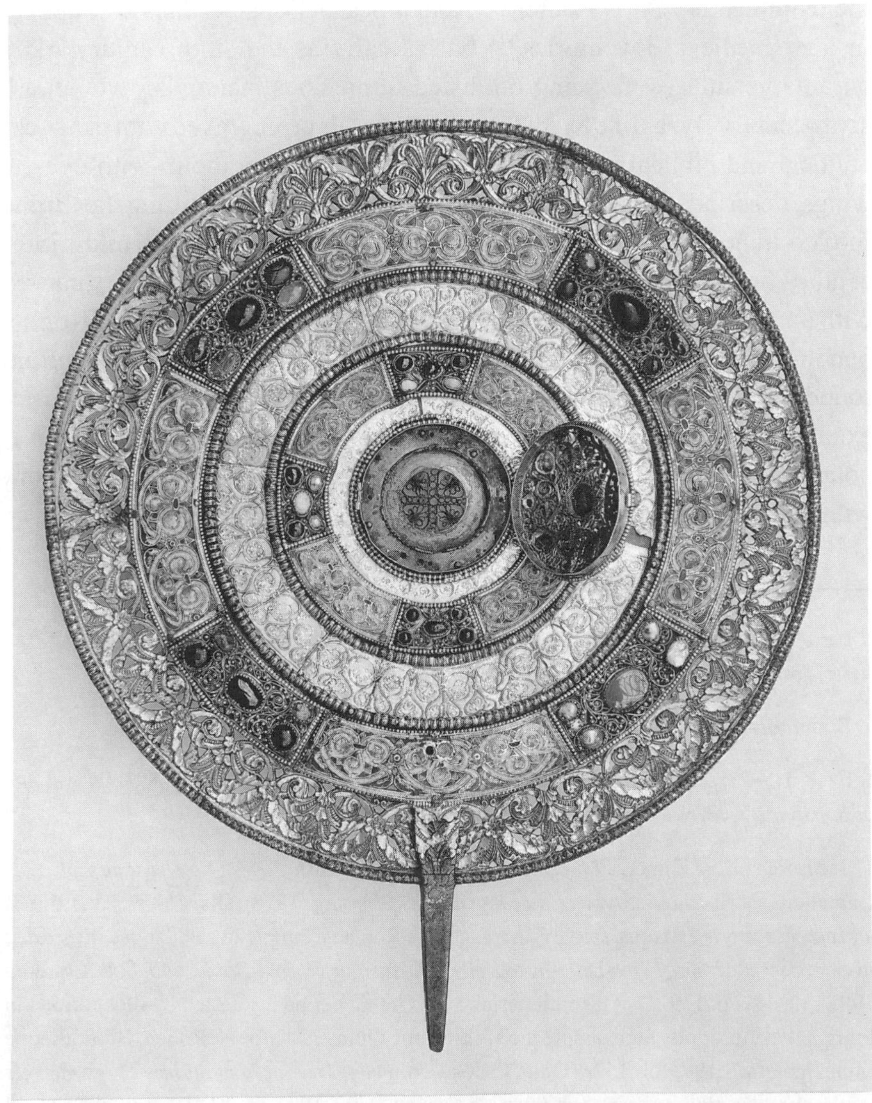

Figure 10. Flabellum, with door open to show cavity for relics. German (Rhenish, possibly Cologne), late twelfth century. Champlevé enamel on gilt bronze with silver, gems and glass. New York: The Metropolitan Museum of Art, The Cloisters Collection, 1947. (47.101.32)

IV. Censer or *thuribulum*[116]

The burning of incense is known from antiquity and would have been known to the early Christians from both Roman and Jewish rites. Originally associated with funerary ritual, it came also to be used in conjunction with sacrifices burnt on altars.[117] In Christian practice these associations continued: in the early years of the Church its use was forbidden, precisely because of its pagan associations, though it may have been used for purely practical purposes such as the cloaking of noxious orders.[118] By the Constantinian period the use of incense in the liturgy became standard in both East and West: censers and spices for incense are listed among Constantine's gifts to the churches of Rome in the *Liber Pontificalis*.[119] The censing of the altar and of the eucharistic Elements recalled both the purifying use of incense in funeral rites and the symbolic sacrifice of Christ.[120] The Gospel-book and sacred images were also censed, and censers were carried by deacons in procession before bishops as they entered or left a church.[121]

---

[116]Braun, *Altargerät*, pp. 598–632. See also Alec Bain Tonnochy, "The Censer in the Middle Ages," *Journal of the British Archaeological Association*, 3rd ser., 2 (1937): 47–62; and *Dictionary of Art*, s.v. "Censer" and *Lexikon der Kunst*, s.v. "Rauchfass," with extensive recent bibliography.

[117]Edward Godfrey Cuthbert Frederic Atchley, *A History of the Use of Incense in Divine Worship* (London, 1909). I am grateful to Lisa Victoria Ciresi for this reference and for other information on censing in the liturgy.

[118]Braun, *Altargerät*, p. 110.

[119]*Liber Pontificalis*, ed. David (note 8 above), pp. 14–26.

[120]Censers figure prominently in the early iconography of the Resurrection of Christ, represented by the scene of the Holy Women at the Tomb, and one can to some degree trace the development of censer design through these images. Early examples include late 6th-century ampullas in Monza and Washington, and a miniature in the Rabula Codex of AD 584 in Florence: see Gertrud Schiller, *Ikonographie der christlichen Kunst*, vol. 3: *Die Auferstehung und Erhöhung Christi* (Gütersloh, 1986), figs. 5, 6, 7.

[121]Braun, *Altargerät*, p. 600. Atchley, *A History of the Use of Incense*, has much to say on

Early Christian and Early Medieval censers were traditional and basically utilitarian in form: an open bowl with a low base or foot, usually of bronze but sometimes of silver, ornamented with cast or engraved portrait-busts and simple biblical scenes and suspended by chains, usually three in number, from a ring: one such is carried by a deacon in the Justinian mosaic in San Vitale.[122] In the later medieval West, however, the form of the censer became more elaborate: the foot grew somewhat higher and a lid, pierced with holes, often keyhole-shaped, to allow air to enter and smoke to escape, was added, with the suspension chains passing through rings in both lid and bowl. Frequently the lids took on symmetrically gabled and pinnacled architectural form, symbolizing the Temple of Solomon and the Old Testament sacrificial rites that prefigured the Crucifixion and the Eucharist, but possibly also the Heavenly Jerusalem to which Christians ultimately aspired (Fig. 11).[123] Other Old Testament personages and events interpreted as foreshadowing key events in Christian history might also be depicted.[124]

---

the subject of the liturgical use of incense, but very little, on pp. 318–24, on the actual form or development of the censer.

[122]*Age of Spirituality*, ed. Weitzmann, cat. 562, 563, 564. Illustrations of the Justinian mosaic panel are ubiquitous: e.g., Frazer, *Medieval Church Treasuries*, p. 30.

[123]Marie-Thérèse Gousset, "Un aspect du symbolisme des encensoirs romans: la Jérusalem céleste," *Cahiers archéologiques* 30 (1982): 81–106. She assigns most Romanesque examples to Rhenish or Mosan workshops and suggests that the Byzantine "Anastasius reliquary" in Aachen, probably brought back from crusade in the early 12th century—actually a censer or lantern of a type referred to as "Sion" or "Little Jerusalem"—may have been influential in the formation of the type. See also André Grabar, "Le Reliquaire byzantin de la cathédrale d'Aix-la-Chapelle," in *Karolingische und Ottonische Kunst: Werden, Wesen, Wirkung*, Kunstgeschichtliches Institut der Johannes Gutenberg-Universität in Mainz (Wiesbaden, 1957), pp. 282–97; and *Ornamenta Ecclesiae*, vol. 3, cat. H 12.

[124]As for example on the Gozbert censer in Trier: see *Rhin-Meuse*, cat. H1, and Hiltrud Westermann-Angerhausen, "Zwei romanischen Thuribula im Trierer Domschatz und Überlegungen zu Theophilus und dem Gozbert-Rauchfass," *Zeitschrift für Kunstwissenschaft* 42 (1988): 45–60. Another example, attributed to the Mosan metalworker Rainer of Huy, is suitably adorned with figures of the three youths in the fiery furnace and their angel protector (Lasko, *Ars Sacra*, ill. 243).

Figure 11. Lid from an "architectural" censer. Mid-twelfth century, from the Meuse area. Gilt bronze. New York: The Metropolitan Museum of Art, The Cloisters Collection, 1979. (1979.285)

Elaborate architectural censers survive from the Romanesque and Gothic periods (Figs. 1, 11); simpler versions were produced by the enameling workshops of the Limoges area (Fig. 12).[125] And although no censers survive that can be identified positively as having belonged to the treasury of St.-Denis, the censer is the single artifact most frequently noted in the St.-Denis ordinary of 1234: mention of a single one occurs fifty-six times, and of a pair sixty-three times, indicating the frequency of their use.[126]

V. Incense-boat or *navicula*[127]

Containers for the granular incense were a necessary accompaniment to the censer. In the Early Christian and Early Medieval periods, incense-containers were simply small boxes, resembling pyxides or reliquaries: surviving examples cannot usually be identified with any certainty as to their function. In the later Middle Ages, however, these took the form of a pointed-oval, footed dish with a two-part lid, hinged at the center and opening at each tapering end, often with a curving handle. This shape facilitated the pouring of incense grains into the bowl of the censer, and suggested the name of "boat" (Figs. 1, 13).[128]

---

[125]See, for example, Frazer, *Medieval Church Treasuries*, p. 21 (a simple Limoges example) and p. 22 (a very fine Gothic silver censer).

[126]Foley, "The Treasury of St.-Denis" (note 21 above), pp. 193–94.

[127]Braun, *Altargerät*, pp. 632–42. On pp. 637–38, Braun discusses the earliest forms of incense-container, drawing on nomenclature and evidence in other visual media, as surviving examples are difficult to distinguish from other small containers.

[128]Braun, *Altargerät*, pp. 538–642. The "navicula" proper begins in the 12th century and becomes increasingly popular in the 13th and subsequent centuries, as evidenced by inventories and surviving examples; see, e.g., Frazer, *Church Treasuries*, p. 21; see also Foley, "The Treasury of St.-Denis" (note 21 above), p. 195.

Figure 12. Censer. French, thirteenth century. Limoges champlevé enamel on gilded copper. New York: The Metropolitan Museum of Art, The Cloisters Collection, 1950. (50.7.3 ab)

Figure 13. **Navicula**, or incense boat. French, thirteenth century. Limoges champlevé enamel on gilded copper. New York: The Metropolitan Museum of Art, Gift of J. Pierpont Morgan, 1917. (17.190.126)

VI. *Situla* or Holy-Water bucket, and sprinkler or *aspergillum* [Fig. 1][129]

From as early as the ninth century, it was customary for the priest to "asperse" or sprinkle holy water on both altar and worshipers, and similar ritual cleansing was enacted over the dead, in coffin or grave. For this purpose, the ***situla*** or small bucket, a form known from antiquity, was adopted; it might be made of metal, such as bronze, or wood, as in the case of the early Hiberno-Saxon Clonard bucket, which has a core of yew-wood overlaid with sheets of copper-alloy openwork.[130] It is not known for certain

[129]Braun, *Altargerät*, pp. 581–98; also *Lexikon der Kunst*, s.v. "Weihwasserbecken."

[130]Youngs, *'The Work of Angels'*, cat. 119, 120.

whether this or other similar Insular buckets actually had an ecclesiastical function, but later examples, notably three sumptuous ivory Ottonian situlas, one probably made for the coronation of Emperor Henry II and now in the Aachen Cathedral treasury, a second in Milan, and a third, the "Basilewsky situla" today in the Victoria and Albert Museum, were clearly, from their provenance and carved decoration, made for liturgical use.[131] Like the Basilewsky *situla*, a fourth tenth-century ivory bucket now in the Metropolitan Museum, from the German church at Kranenburg, is covered with carved scenes from the passion of Christ (Fig. 14).[132]

The basic instrument for sprinkling holy water from a *situla* was a sprig of hyssop, referring to Ps. 50:9, "Thou shalt sprinkle me with hyssop and I shall be cleansed . . .," and, according to Durandus, symbolizing the humility of Christ.[133] A more luxurious and efficient delivery system was the metal ***aspergillum***, a sprinkler with handle and hollow head pierced with holes, which filled with water when dipped in the *situla* and could then release its contents when shaken. Metal handles with fiber brush-attachments were also used (Fig. 1).

VII. Processional and Altar Crosses[134]

Crosses of wood, covered with precious metals and set with gems, were carried by clerics in procession to the altar: in the mosaic panel of

---

[131]Adolf Goldschmidt, *Die Elfenbeinskulpturen aus der Zeit der karolingischen und sächsischen Kaiser, VIII.–XI. Jahrhundert*, 4 vols. (Berlin, 1915–26; repr. 1969–75), vol. 2: the Aachen situla is cat. 22, the Milan situla, cat. 1; the Basilewsky situla, cat. 3. See also Ernst Günther Grimme, *Der Aachener Domschatz* (note 11 above), cat. 26 and John Beckwith, *The Basilewsky Situla* (London, 1963).

[132]Goldschmidt, *Elfenbeinskulpturen*, 2:71; Frazer, *Medieval Church Treasuries*, p. 23; and Little and Husband, *Europe in the Middle Ages*, no. 39, pp. 46–47.

[133]Durandus, *Rationale*, 1995 ed., I, ch. VII, §20.

[134]See Parker and Little, *The Cloisters Cross*, ch. 3, on function and history. Also Braun, *Altargerät*, pp. 466–92; and *Dictionary of Art*, s.v. "Cross, III, portable."

Figure 14. Situla or holy water bucket, from Church of Saints Peter and Paul at Kranenburg (Germany). German (Lower Rhine), tenth–eleventh century. Ivory with gilt bronze fittings, glass inlays. New York, The Metropolitan Museum of Art, Gift of J. Pierpont Morgan, 1917. (17.190.45)

Justinian's procession in San Vitale mentioned earlier, Archbishop Maximian carries just such a processional cross, and a number of early examples survive, such as the cross of Justin II in the Vatican,[135] the *Cruz de los Angeles* and the *Cruz de la Victoria*, of the ninth and tenth centuries respectively, in the treasury of Oviedo Cathedral,[136] or the four splendid crosses of the tenth and eleventh centuries in the treasury of Essen Minster.[137] Processional crosses would be inserted into a long carrying-staff by means of a metal tang, often an integral part of the cross; there is evidence from the ninth century that the cross, upon arrival at the altar, might be removed from its staff and inserted into a holder attached to, or adjacent to, the altar. By the eleventh century crosses appear to have been placed on the altar itself, though the first official acknowledgment of this practice dates to the early thirteenth.[138] Evidence for the growth of this practice from the twelfth century onward is provided also by a number of cross-feet, usually in cast bronze (Fig. 15), with images frequently referring to the Passion:[139] one of the best known is the twelfth-century cross base from the Norman

---

[135]Christa Belting-Ihm, "Das Justinuskreuz in der Schatzkammer der Peterskirche zu Rom: Bericht über die Untersuchung des Römisch-Germanischen Zentralmuseums zu Mainz," *Jahrbuch des Römisch-Germanischen Zentralmuseums Mainz* 12 (1965) (Mainz, 1967), pp. 142–66; and André Grabar, *The Golden Age of Justinian* (note 44 above), ill. 359 (reverse).

[136]Pedro de Palol Salellas and Max Hirmer, *Early Medieval Art in Spain* (London, 1967), pp. 42–43, 473–74, pls. VII, VIII, ills. 37–39; and *Art of Medieval Spain* (note 12 above), cat. 72.

[137]Victor Heinrich Elbern, *Das Erste Jahrtausend. Kultur und Kunst im werdenden Abendland an Rhein und Ruhr*, vol. 1, pt. 2 (Düsseldorf, 1962), ills. 376–79; and Lasko, *Ars Sacra*, ills. 135–37, 140, 188.

[138]Parker and Little, *The Cloisters Cross*, pp. 120–21; and Durandus, *Rationale*, 1995 ed. I, ch. III, §31.

[139]Peter Springer, *Kreuzfüsse, Ikonographie und Typologie eines hochmittelalterlichen Gerätes* (Berlin, 1981).

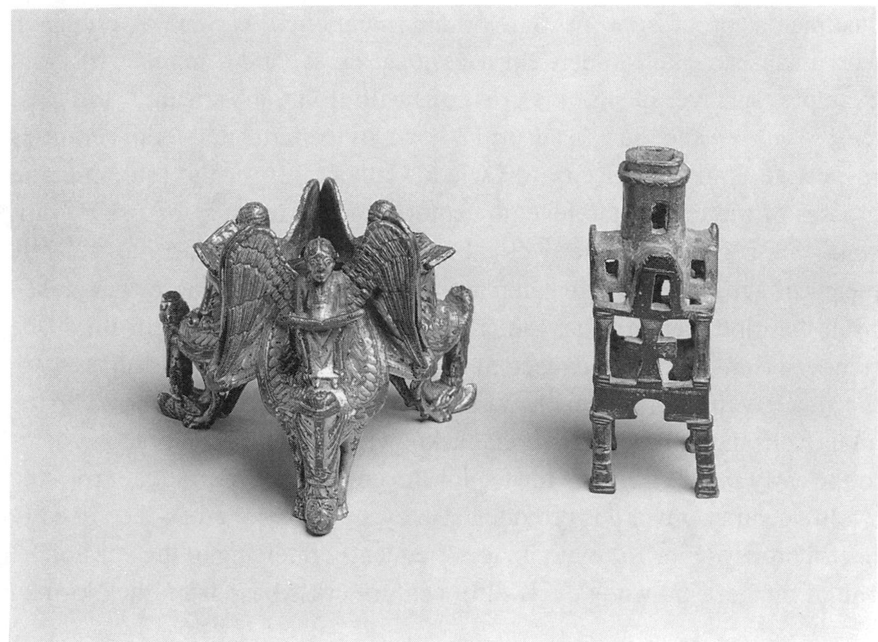

Figure 15. Two cross-feet, (L) Meuse area, 1150–75, gilt bronze. (R) Byzantine (possibly Istanbul), eleventh–twelfth century?, bronze. Both New York: The Metropolitan Museum of Art, Gift of Mrs. Charles F. Griffiths, 1962. (62.10.8)

abbey of St.-Bertin, made in a Mosan atelier by a workman from the circle of Godefroid de Huy and bearing champlevé enamel depictions of Old Testament scenes interpreted as "types" or forerunners of the Cross and Crucifixion.[140] The "Cloisters Cross" in New York (Fig. 16), elaborately carved from walrus ivory, made in the twelfth century, is a fine example of the genre in the High Middle Ages;[141] two Spanish silver processional crosses in the Metropolitan Museum of Art demonstrate the continuity of

[140]*Rhin-Meuse*, cat. G17; see also the related crosses with similar Old Testament "types" of the Crucifixion such as that in the British Museum: Stratford, *Catalogue of Medieval Enamels*, vol. 2 (note 15 above), cat. 4.

[141]Parker and Little, *The Cloisters Cross* (note 22 above).

Figure 16. The Cloisters Cross, front, English, Bury St. Edmunds?, late twelfth century. Walrus ivory with traces of polychromy. New York: The Metropolitan Museum of Art, The Cloisters Collection, 1963. (63.12 recto)

the genre (Fig. 17).[142] In the High and Late Middle Ages, such crosses usually bore a figure of the dead Christ, the *corpus*, which might be detachable: cross and corpus played special roles in liturgical celebrations on Good Friday and Easter Sunday.[143]

VIII. Pax

The **pax, pax brede, *osculatorium***, or pax tablet was a late addition to the equipment of the liturgy, possibly introduced under Franciscan influence. It is first documented in England and was used only in the West.[144] Its use derived from the prayer and kiss of peace enjoined by St. Peter—"Salute one another with a holy kiss" (1 Pet. 5:14)—and it was used to deliver the Kiss of Peace from the celebrant to the other clerics and the lay congregation. In form it is a small plaque which can be oval, rectangular, or of other ornamental shape, with a devotional image, for example Christ in Majesty or the Crucifixion, and can be quite elaborate in material and workmanship. A number of surviving pax tablets appear to be objects—or parts of objects—originally created for another purpose or function and adapted, often by means of a metal mounting and handle on the back, to their later use (Fig. 18).[145]

---

[142]Frazer, *Medieval Church Treasuries*, pp. 32–33. For the earlier example, see also *Art of Medieval Spain*, cat. 130.

[143]Elizabeth C. Parker, *The Descent from the Cross. Its Relation to the extra-Liturgical "Depositio" Drama* (New York, 1978). Also Parker and Little, *The Cloisters Cross*, pp. 149–73.

[144]*ODCC*, s.v. "Pax Brede"; Braun, *Altargerät*, pp. 557–72.

[145]The pax of Duke Oros or Ursus of ca. 900 in Cividale was probably a book-cover plaque: see Goldschmidt, *Elfenbeinskulpturen*, vol. 1, cat. 166, and Magnus Backes and Regine Dölling, *Art of the Dark Ages* (New York, 1969), p. 242. A pax in the treasury of San Isidoro in Léon is a pointed-oval plaque from an ivory shrine, fitted with a metal frame and handle: see *Art of Medieval Spain*, cat. 113. For late medieval and early 16th-century pax tablets see Peter Ludwig and Ernst Günther Grimme, *Grosses Kunst aus tausend Jahren. Kirchenschätze aus dem Bistum Aachen* (*Aachener Kunstblätter*, 36, 1968), cat. 45, 69, 75.

Figure 17. Processional Cross with corpus, Spanish, from church of San Salvador de Fuentes (Asturias), twelfth century. Silver, partly gilded, with filigree, gems, crystal. New York: The Metropolitan Museum of Art, Gift of J. Pierpont Morgan, 1917. (17.190.1406)

Figure 18. Pax tablet, possibly originally part of a devotional diptych or other piece, South German, ca. 1360–70, adapted in the seventeenth century as pax. Ivory with later silver-gilt frame. New York: The Metropolitan Museum of Art, The Cloisters Collection, 1970. (1970.324.9)

IX. Chrismatory or Chrismal[146]

Containers for the holy oils, also known as ***olearea***, were important not only for transport but for protection, since the oils were consecrated by the bishop only once annually, at the Chrismal Mass on Maundy Thursday, and precautions had to be taken to ensure their availability for the entire year.[147] There were three distinct holy oils: that of the catechumens, that of the sick, and chrism, a mixture of oil and balsam which gives its name to the container and which was used to anoint those undergoing the sacraments of baptism, confirmation, and ordination into Holy Orders, and also in the consecration of rulers, of churches, and of holy objects such as altars and chalices.[148] Typically a **chrismatory** is a rectangular box of metal or other material, such as wood or ivory, with fitments inside to hold the phials of oil upright and secure. Some fine examples in Limoges enamel survive,[149] and a fifteenth-century silver example in the Metropolitan Museum expresses its protective function in form and ornament evoking a fortified castle, with feet in the shape of guardian lions.[150] A single crystal receptacle, with silver mounts and enamel images of John the Baptist and the *Noli me Tangere*, now in the Boston Museum of Fine Arts, may have contained the oil of the catechumens: it is the sole survivor of a hypothetical set of three.[151]

---

[146]Frazer, *Medieval Church Treasuries*, fig. 19 and p. 26. Curiously, Braun, *Altargerät*, does not discuss olearea.

[147]Ludwig Eisenhofer and Joseph Lechner, *The Mass of the Roman Rite*, trans. A. J. and E. F. Peeler, ed. H. E. Winstone (Freiburg im Breisgau, 1961), pp. 195–96.

[148]*ODCC* s.v. "Chrism."

[149]*Limoges*, cat. 71 and 73, the former with rack inside showing holes for the 3 phials.

[150]Frazer, *Medieval Church Treasuries*, p. 25.

[151]Hanns Swarzenski and Nancy Netzer, *Catalogue of Medieval Objects in the Museum of Fine Arts, Boston. Enamels and Glass* (Boston, 1986), cat. 39.

X. Lamps and Candlesticks[152]

Christ declared, "I am the Light of the World" (John 8:12), and light took on mystical importance in Christian doctrine. This is nowhere better shown than in the writings of Abbot Suger of St.-Denis, in which Neo-Platonic philosophy combines with devotional zeal to glorify light and color, particularly as exemplified by precious stones and stained glass windows.[153] Artificial light was necessary for the frequent night-time services, notably the canonical hours celebrated by monks but also the vigils of the great feasts of the Church, and from the earliest records of imperial gifts, lamps and candelabra figure prominently in church inventories.[154] These followed contemporary secular styles very closely: in the case of altar candlesticks especially it is often difficult to tell whether a medieval example was intended for church or domestic use, unless the ornament is explicitly religious as, for example, on the gilded bell-metal Gloucester candlestick, in which climbing figures and inscribed bands spell out the soul's arduous climb toward the light of salvation.[155] The monumental paschal candlestick, in contrast, really a piece of church furniture rather than a liturgical accessory, was situated on the north side of the sanctuary and held the large candle lit by the deacon

---

[152]Elbern, "Altar Implements and Liturgical Objects," p. 594; and Braun, *Altargerät*, pp. 492–530.

[153]Panofsky, *Abbot Suger*, passim.

[154]*Liber Pontificalis*, passim. Atchley, *A History of the Use of Incense* (note 117 above), pp. 324–27, discusses the *number* of candlesticks placed on the altar and its increase over time.

[155]Zarnecki, *English Romanesque Art*, cat. 247, with earlier bibliography; Alan Borg, "The Gloucester Candlestick," in *Medieval Art and Architecture at Gloucester and Tewkesbury*, ([London], 1985), pp. 84–92 and pls. XIV–XV; Lasko, *Ars Sacra*, ills. 199, 300; see also the pair of candlesticks of Bishop Bernward of Hildesheim, discussed in Lasko, *Ars Sacra*, ills. 153–54, with fullest discussion in Rudolf Wesenberg, *Bernwardinische Plastik: zur Ottonischen Kunst unter Bischof Bernward von Hildesheim* (Berlin, 1955), pp. 21–28 and pls. 123–38.

from the new fire on Holy Saturday morning as the first return of light to the church after its extinction on Good Friday, thereby symbolizing the Resurrection of Christ. In Italy paschal candlesticks are usually carved of stone and often attached to the pulpit or choir enclosure, while in other European areas they were normally of cast bronze, and free-standing.[156]

Coronas, the crown- or wheel-shaped chandeliers set with candle-lanterns or prickets, against which St. Bernard inveighed,[157] survive in Aachen, Hildesheim, and Gross-Comburg; the combination of the basic circular shape, resembling a medieval town wall, and the tower-like lanterns, encouraged symbolic interpretation as the Heavenly Jerusalem, a visual metaphor reinforced by inscriptions.[158]

XI. Liturgical Comb[159]

A comb was used ceremonially during the vesting of the celebrant before the Mass to prevent the pollution of the eucharistic Elements by falling hair,

---

[156]For a good general discussion of paschal candlesticks see *Lexikon der Kunst*, s.v. "Osterleuchter." See also *Enciclopedia dell'arte medievale*, s.v. "Candelabro." I am also grateful to Judith Totaro for information on this subject.

[157]"Hence the church is adorned with gemmed crowns of light—nay, with lustres like cartwheels, girt all round with lamps, but no less brilliant with the precious stones that stud them. Moreover we see candelabra standing like trees of massive bronze, fashioned with marvellous subtlety of art, and glistening no less brightly with gems than with the lights they carry. What, think you, is the purpose of all this? . . ." Bernard of Clairvaux, *Apologia to William of St. Thierry*, as translated in Caecilia Davis-Weyer, *Early Medieval Art, 300–1150 sources and documents* (Toronto, 1986) (note 8 above), p. 169.

[158]For a good general discussion of the three surviving examples see *Lexikon der Kunst*, s.v. "Lichtkrone."

[159]See *Dictionary of Art*, s.v. "Comb, liturgical," with earlier literature. Still useful is Henry John Feasey, "The Use of the Comb in Church Ceremonies," *Antiquary* 32 (1896): 312–16, as is Henri Leclerq, "Peigne," in *DACL* 13/2, cols. 2932–2959, with some discussion of their use in cols. 2934–35. Frazer, *Medieval Treasuries*, pp. 23–25, discusses briefly the "liturgical" role of the comb.

lice, or dander, and also in connection with the anointing of clerics and rulers (Fig. 1: the comb, together with a pair of cruets, is placed on a book held by an acolyte at the right of the scene). There are records of combs with ecclesiastical connections as early as the tenth century, though their use is not mentioned in actual liturgical texts until fairly late.[160] Some sources suggest that the ritual combing of the hair was a survival from pagan times, symbolizing the priest's purification from demons and other evils,[161] an interpretation possibly borne out by a Frankish tombstone showing a dead warrior combing the hair on one side of his head while a dragon attacks the other.[162] **Liturgical comb**s were similar in shape and material to those produced for secular use; but while bone was common in less luxurious domestic examples, most surviving "liturgical" combs are made of ivory and decorated with carving and inlays; unlike many domestic combs, they are usually carved from a single piece. Their form varies, but frequently they have double rows of teeth of contrasting thickness and some are of extraordinarily large size.[163] Some, like the ninth-century comb of Heribert in Cologne, have decoration indicating their religious function.[164] Like chalice and paten, liturgical combs were frequently the personal property of

---

[160]Leclercq, "Peigne," lists mentions of gifts of combs, and cites passages in late liturgical texts, but observes that Durandus, writing in the late 13th century, is apparently the first to mention a specifically liturgical comb. I am indebted also to email discussion by Sarah Larratt Keefer and Kendra Adema which indicates the absence of any mention of combs in early Anglo-Saxon liturgical texts.

[161]See Durandus, *Rationale*, 1995 ed., IV, §1–4, ch. 3, pp. 259–62.

[162]Hubert, Porcher, and Volbach, *Europe of the Invasions* (note 69 above), ill. 295.

[163]For example, Frazer, *Medieval Church Treasuries*, ill. 19, a comb twelve inches tall. One this size must have been designed as much for its visual impact as for its practical use.

[164]Goldschmidt, *Elfenbeinskulpturen*, 1:97; and *Ornamenta Ecclesiae*, vol. 2, cat. E92. The recto of the comb bears an image of the Crucifixion. That of Gauzelin (see below, note 165) displays doves perched in vines emerging from a chalice, while that in the Metropolitan Museum, cited above, has a version of the "Tree of Life" with animals.

high clerics and were buried with them, as in the case of the comb of St. Cuthbert; a more elaborate example is the ivory comb of St. Gauzelin of Toul (d. 962), found in his tomb together with his chalice and paten.[165]

Space does not allow extensive discussion of other categories of liturgical accessories, such as vestments (Fig. 1) and the textiles used for curtains, eucharistic veils, and altar hangings;[166] insignia such as the crozier, the symbolic shepherd's crook of a bishop or abbot;[167] or monumental church furniture such as the bishop's throne or *cathedra*,[168] and the altar-canopy (also, and confusingly, known as a *ciborium*).[169] These too were of major importance to the celebration of the liturgy, and were frequently made of the most luxurious and splendid materials; these too were vehicles of patronage and sometimes expressions of personal ambition for power or salvation.

---

[165]Goldschmidt, *Elfenbeinskulpturen*, 1:101; and Backes and Dölling, *Dark Ages* (note 145 above), p. 225.

[166]See Joseph Braun, *Die liturgische Gewandung im Occident und Orient nach Ursprung und Entwicklung, Verwendung und Symbolik* (Freiburg im Breisgau, 1907); Cyril Pocknee, *Liturgical Vesture, its Origins and Development* (London, 1960); Jane Hayward, "Sacred Vestments as they developed in the Middle Ages," *Metropolitan Museum of Art Bulletin* 29 (1971): 299–309; Donya Schimansky, "The Study of Medieval Ecclesiastical Costumes: A Bibliography," *Metropolitan Museum of Art Bulletin* 29 (1971): 313–17, with useful glossary; Janet Mayo, *A History of Ecclesiastical Dress* (London, 1984); and *Dictionary of Art*, s.v. "Vestments, ecclesiastical." There are many excellent examples in exhibition catalogues such as *Ornamenta Ecclesiae*, or Christa C. Mayer-Thurman, *Raiment for the Lord's Service: A Thousand Years of Western Vestments* (exhibition catalogue, Chicago, 1975). Joseph Braun, *Die Liturgiscehn Paramente in Gegenwart und Vergangenheit: ein Handbuch der Paramentik* (2nd, rev. ed., Freiburg-im-Breisgau, 1924), discusses altar-hangings and other liturgical textiles in addition to vestments.

[167]See Frazer, *Medieval Church Treasuries*, pp. 34, 36–37; croziers and other insignia are frequently discussed in studies of vestments, and in dictionaries and encyclopedias.

[168]See, for example, *Dictionary of Art*, s.v. "Throne, II, Europe, 1. before c.1500 (I) Ecclesiastical"; also *Enciclopedia dell'arte medievale*, s.v. "cattedra" for discussion of monumental Italian examples, and *Lexikon der Kunst*, s.v. "Bischofsstuhl."

[169]This and other altar accessories are discussed in Braun, *Altar*.

One item which cannot be passed over, however, is the altar itself. Beginning in the earliest Christian period as a simple movable table, a slab or *mensa* on legs, it developed after the Peace of the Church in 313 into a monumental, fixed structure, often with a cavity for major relics; its size increased as the Middle Ages progressed. Much has been written about the forms and development of the Christian altar;[170] and we shall limit our treatment here to a brief discussion of its smaller form, the portable altar or "portatile," more closely related in scale, form and material to other liturgical implements.[171] These are documented as early as the Carolingian period[172] but the oldest surviving example is the one found in the tomb of St. Cuthbert at Durham, consisting of an inscribed oak board of the seventh century, encased in silver as a relic of the saint in the eighth.[173] Portable altars proliferated in the ninth to twelfth centuries in particular: the requisite components came to be a piece of precious or semi-precious stone, consecrated as the *mensa* proper, and set into a wooden base which could be either a slab or a box, with or without feet and opening at top or bottom. This in turn frequently was decorated with sheets of gold or silver, gems or enamels, often bearing imagery relevant to the altar's Eucharistic function. Relics normally were inserted into the portable altar as they were in its monumental counterpart, and when the portable altar or portatile took the form of a box it might serve as container for miniature Communion vessels: the tenth-century reliquary of the sandal strap of St. Andrew in Trier, which is most notable for its gold-encased and jeweled sculpture of the apostle's foot, is actually a chest-shaped portable altar. A small *mensa* of millefiori

---

[170]Braun, *Altar*; Cyril E. Pocknee, *The Christian Altar in History and Today* (London, 1963); *Dictionary of Art*, s.v. "Altar," and countless additional bibliography.

[171]Braun, *Altar*, pp. 71–100, 419–89; see also *Dictionary of Art*, s.v. "Altar, §3(ii): 'Western European, to c. 1550: Portable'."

[172]See note 2 above for Hincmar's ruling on their use.

[173]*The Making of England: Anglo-Saxon Art and Culture AD 600–900*, ed. Leslie Webster and Janet Backhouse (exhibition catalogue, London, 1991), cat. 99.

glass is set into the top of the supporting box, which once may have held also the miniature golden chalice and paten later placed in the grave of Archbishop Poppo.[174] Such complex forms are unusual, however. The simple slab or box is the standard form from Carolingian to Gothic times: an excellent example of a Romanesque enamel-decorated portable altar with champlevé enamel images illustrating the Salvation story and its Old Testament prophetic "types" is that made in the mid-twelfth century for Abbot Wibald of Stavelot, now in Brussels.[175] At least as much was lavished on these objects in the way of precious materials, consummate craftsmanship, and iconographic ingenuity, as on any of the other vessels and implements we have surveyed, and they survive in significant numbers.

In sum, then, liturgical vessels and other accessories not only were essential to the service of the Eucharist: they also, by virtue of their intrinsic material value and brilliant colors, rendered it suitably magnificent; and by the symbolism of their imagery and inscriptions, added depth to the meaning of its ceremonies. Their association with specific donors and owners adds to our knowledge of the patterns of piety and patronage among medieval ecclesiastics and laymen alike, and on occasion adds the poignant illusion of personal contact with these long-dead benefactors, making us vividly aware of their hopes of earning eternal blessedness. As the craftsman-monk Theophilus repeatedly makes clear, their manufacture as well as their actual use in the liturgy constituted a form of worship.[176]

---

[174]For the foot reliquary see *Schatzkunst Trier*, cat. 23, also Lasko, *Ars Sacra*, pl. 132. For the possibility that it contained Poppo's chalice and paten, see note 43 above.

[175]Lasko, *Ars Sacra*, ill. 269, *Rhin-Meuse*, cat. G13.

[176]Theophilus, *De Diversis Artibus*, (note 30 above), passim, especially in the introductions to the separate books, e.g., book III, on metalwork.

PART FOUR

THE LITURGY AND BOOKS

MANUSCRIPTS OF THE LITURGY

JEANNE E. KROCHALIS AND E. ANN MATTER

IN ANCIENT CHRISTIANITY, the climax of the liturgy, the eucharistic celebration, was esoteric; that is, it was witnessed by the baptized only. Children and catechumens, those who had begun instruction but were not yet initiated, were sent out of the service after the reading of the Gospel. The term *Mass*, used throughout the Middle Ages to describe the eucharistic celebration, comes from the words spoken at this moment of sending out the uninitiated: "Ite, missa est." Because of the secret nature of the rites, Christian liturgies were not written down much before the middle of the fourth century. Although a few famous liturgical manuscripts remain from the seventh and eighth centuries, most of the extant medieval service books date from the ninth century or later.

The liturgy of the medieval Church in western Europe evolved slowly, developing into a number of regional rites, such as the Ambrosian (in Milan), the **Mozarabic** (in Spain), the **Sarum** (from Salisbury, the Late Medieval English rite), and the Old **Roman** Rite. A few of these ancient rites still are used in Roman Catholic services today, for example, the Ambrosian liturgy celebrated in the diocese of Milan. The Rite of Rome, nevertheless, gradually became standard for most of western Europe. This phenomenon was helped greatly by movements of political consolidation in which various popes and emperors either shared or vied for power, and often used theological and liturgical reforms as a unifying tool. The Carolingian Reforms of the church, overseen by Charlemagne and his heirs in the late eighth and ninth centuries, and the eleventh-century movement sparked by Pope Gregory IX, known as the Gregorian Reforms, are the most successful examples of the role liturgy played in the building of western European empires. Despite these reforms, however, there was still great variety in liturgical practice throughout the Middle Ages: monastic orders had their own liturgies, and countries and dioceses their own rites centering around local saints and customs. This makes a study of medieval liturgy a patchwork of variations of times and places.

The early medieval manuscripts of the medieval liturgy are generally divided into a number of books, not gathered together into a Missal for the Mass and a Breviary for the Office as became, and remains, the case. From the ninth century onward, liturgical practices and changes are well-documented by extant manuscripts. Thus, it frequently is possible to date and place even a fragmentary medieval liturgical manuscript, given some knowledge of its contents. It is beyond the scope of this essay to survey the great variety of local and particular medieval liturgies; rather, we aim to introduce the various types of liturgical manuscripts, from various centuries of the Middle Ages, with which medievalists in a variety of disciplines must deal.

From the twelfth century on, the increasing sophistication of medieval liturgical music, and the increasing number of saints whose feasts were celebrated, meant that church services became more elaborate, requiring more separate volumes with specialized functions to perform. The economic circumstances of religious institutions dictated how elaborately these books could be produced. The enormous and richly painted Antiphonals of Fra Angelico (ca. 1400–55) and his successors, still on display at the Dominican house of San Marco in Florence, represent the highest artistic level of liturgical books. In contrast, a Missal or a Psalter produced for a relatively modest parish might have no ornamentation at all. As was the case with all medieval books, liturgical books were considered very precious and were kept carefully in monastic houses, cathedral chapters, and individual homes. The more elaborate the book, the less frequently it would be used in liturgical services. In fact, liturgical books which were used regularly tended to wear out more quickly; because of this, we probably have extant a larger proportion of the richly decorated, deluxe editions than we do of the everyday books of the liturgy.

We intend this essay to serve as a convenient guide to particular liturgical manuscripts that might be mentioned in a literary or historical work, or seen in medieval art. What follows is in two parts: an alphabetical list of the major medieval Latin manuscripts in which liturgical texts are found, and a bibliography. The bibliography first lists some general books about the western liturgy, and then gives examples of specific studies, critical editions, facsimile editions, and English translations of each type of liturgical book. In addition to editions and facsimiles of medieval liturgical manuscripts, we have included some reprintings of early modern printed liturgical books, since they often reproduced Late Medieval manuscripts. This list is by no means exhaustive (in some cases we found no relevant specialized literature at all), but it tries to show the richness and diversity of medieval liturgical books available in twenty-first-century libraries. There are a great many more liturgical books of the Middle Ages and Early Modern period published by the Henry Bradshaw Society, which began publishing editions and facsimiles of liturgical books in 1890. A few hours spent among the volumes of the Henry Bradshaw Society would be very rewarding for those who wish to know more about the variety of medieval liturgical manuscripts.

We also have included a number of plates of pages from medieval liturgical books in order to show what they actually did look like. All photographs are of liturgical manuscripts now in North American libraries—it is not necessary to make a pilgrimage to the great libraries of Europe to see a medieval liturgical manuscript! We recommend that the description, bibliography, and photograph of each type of liturgical manuscript be consulted together and in reference to one another.

Manuscripts of the Liturgy

Antiphonal or Antiphonary [*Antiphonale or Antiphonarium*]; Figure 1. An Antiphonal originally contained texts and music for the antiphons or short prayers sung before each Psalm during the Mass [*Antiphonarium Missarum*

ure igni congruo. accincti ut sint
ppetim. luxu remoto pessimo.
Ut quiq; horas noctium. nunc
concinendo rumpimus. donis bte
patrie. ditemur omnes affatim.
Pra pater pyssime.
Quia mirabilia. Euouae. Alleluia.
Cantate domino
Canticum nouũ:
Quia mirabilia
fecit.
Saluauit sibi
dextera eius: et
brachium sanc-
tum eius.
Notum fecit dñs salutare suu;:
in conspectu gentium reuelauit
iusticiam suam.

Figure 1. Antiphonal-Hymnal-Psalter. Carnegie Mellon University, Pittsburgh, Penn. MS 7. Fifteenth century, Italy. Melody for the antiphon; text of Ps. 97. The illustration shows a group of Dominican friars singing from a large Antiphonal. Courtesy of Special Collections, Carnegie Mellon Libraries, Pittsburgh, Penn. Photograph © J. Krochalis.

or *Graduale*] or the Divine Office [*Antiphonarium Officii*], and occasionally repeated at later parts of the service. Antiphonals eventually came to contain only the sung portions of the Office, and to contain music and text for all sung parts of the Breviary, including hymns, responsories, versicles, Psalms, and the "Te Deum." For texts, but not music, see the collection of R. J. Hesbert. (See also Gradual).

Benedictional [*Benedictionale*]. A Benedictional is a volume containing blessings (*benedictio*, blessing) and short services of prayer. As well as the standard services said in a church, Benedictionals sometimes also listed prayers and litanies said outside the church buildings, such as blessing for vines, fields, and crops. A modern example of this sort of prayer is grace before meals. Several early Benedictionals have been printed and/or published in facsimile. The tenth-century manuscript of the Benedictional of Aethelwold is now in the Public Library of Rouen, France; it combines a collection of episcopal blessings over the people with materials characteristics of a Pontifical. (In practice, Benedictional texts were frequently included in Rituals and Pontificals, see below.)

Book of Hours [*Horae*]; Figure 2. Strictly speaking, a book of extra-liturgical Psalms and prayers for lay use, the Book of Hours was the most common book of private prayer of the later Middle Ages. The lay custom of praying the Hours ultimately derives from the monastic Office, adapted for devotional life in the world. Although the texts can vary greatly, Books of Hours are often divided into the Hours of the Virgin, the Hours of the Holy Spirit, the Hours of the Holy Cross, Devotions for the Dead, and petitional prayers to particular saints.

There is great regional variation among Books of Hours, especially in the prayers to local saints; this makes them among the easiest of medieval books to place and date. Sometimes case endings of Latin prayers make it possible to tell that a certain Book of Hours was intended for use by a woman or a group of women. John Harthan, *Books of Hours and Their Owners*, gives an overview of how to date and place a Book of Hours manuscript. Books of Hours frequently were illustrated richly. Many of

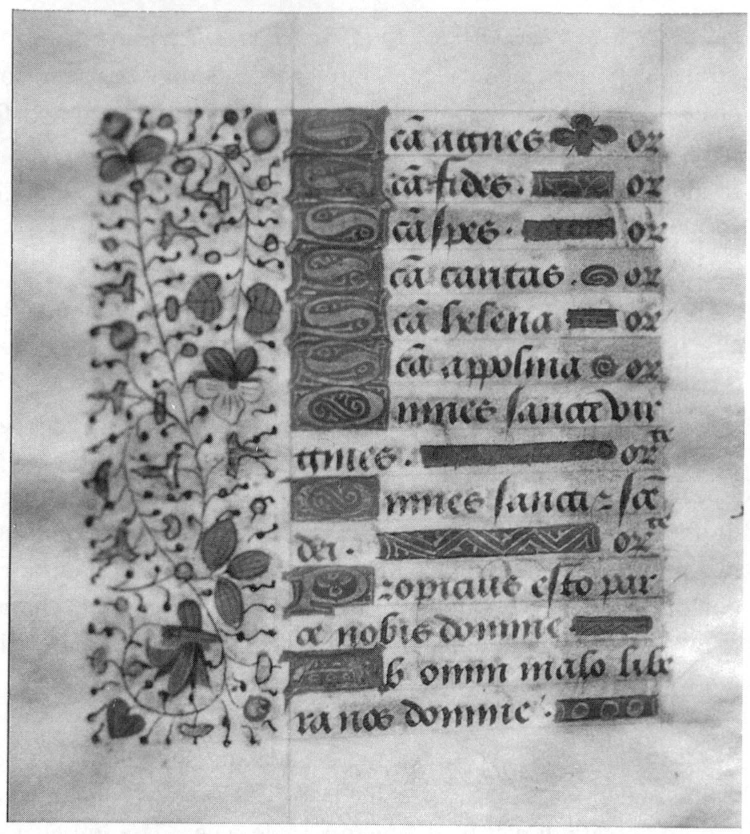

Figure 2. Book of Hours, Litany. Pennsylvania State University Rare Books Room, University Park, Penn. MS PSV-MED-5. Leaf. Fifteenth century, France. Invocations of Virgins: Agnes, Faith, Hope, Charity, Helen, Appollonia, all holy virgins, and all holy saints, male and female. The concluding prayer translates as: "Be favorable, spare us O Lord: Free us from all evil." Courtesy Rare Books Room, Pennsylvania State University. Photograph © J. Krochalis.

the most famous of these painted manuscripts, such as the *Belles heures* and the *Tres riches heurs* of Jean, Duke of Berry, have been printed in facsimile. Books of Hours are among the most common medieval manuscripts in American libraries.

Breviary [*Breviarium*]. This is the essential monastic book for the recitation of the prayers at the eight canonical hours prescribed in the *Rule* of St. Benedict: Matins (the Night Office, actually said very early in the morning, before daybreak); Lauds (at daybreak); Prime ("the first hour," six A.M.); Terce ("the third hour," nine A.M.); Sext ("the sixth hour," noon); None ("the ninth hour, three P.M.); Vespers (at sundown); and Compline (before retiring for the night). The services for each canonical hour were composed of antiphons, Psalms, hymns, canticles, and lections or readings from the Old Testament, New Testament, or Lives of the saint whose feast was being celebrated.

Cathedral clergy, who were priests in the world rather than cloistered monks or nuns, also used Breviaries, but, given the more secular nature of their duties, they tended to have fewer readings. For example, in medieval monastic communities, major feasts would have twelve lections in Matins, whereas cathedral clergy never said more than nine. Cathedral communities were also more apt to combine offices such as Matins and Lauds, or Vespers and Compline, thus saying only one early morning or one evening office. The Mendicant orders (Franciscans and Dominicans) also adapted the monastic Breviary to their religious profession in the world.

Like many liturgical manuscripts, Breviaries often were tied to a particular religious order or location by feasts of patrons or church dedications. Breviaries were among the earliest printed books; several facsimiles have reproduced the early modern compilations made for specific persons. Books of Hours also frequently contain Calendars, see below.

Calendar [*Calendarium*]; Figure 3. Calendars are lists of feasts kept by any particular church, diocese, or religious order; they usually occur as parts of other books, most commonly Books of Hours, Breviaries, or Missals, often as a preface. Calendars also indicate the relative liturgical solemnity of a given feast. The far left column of a Calendar usually records days of the week using not names but the first seven letters of the alphabet, *a* through *g*, so that the Calendar could be reused every year. The next column lists days of the month, the third the names of the saints or feasts commemorated

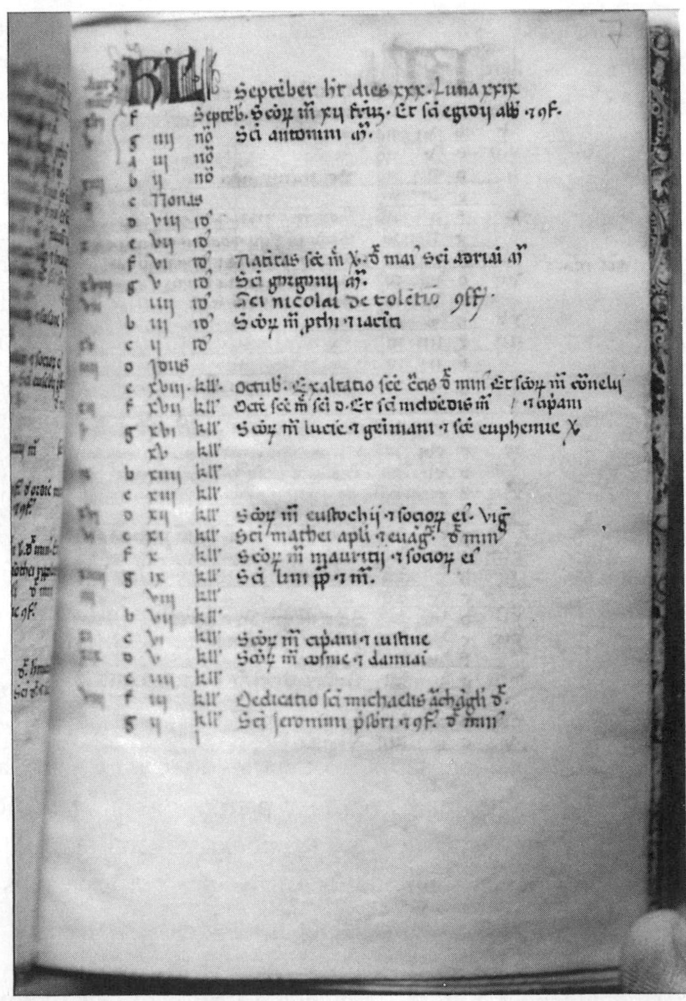

Figure 3. Calendar. Carnegie Mellon University, Pittsburgh, Penn. MS 7. Fifteenth century, Italy. September, including the feast of St. Nicholas of Tolentino, who died in 1305 and was canonized in 1446. Other saints include the early martyr Antoninus, September 2; the Nativity of the Virgin and St. Adrian, Martyr, September 8; St. Gorgonius, Bishop, September 9; Protus and Iacinthus, September 10; the Exaltation of the Holy Cross, September 14. Courtesy of Special Collections, Carnegie Mellon University Libraries, Pittsburgh, Penn. Photograph © J. Krochalis.

(such as feasts of the Blessed Virgin Mary). The liturgical Calendar records seasons such as Advent and Lent, and feasts of saints. Major feasts often are written in red ink, which can aid in localizing a particular manuscript. Many Calendars also indicate changes of zodiac sign, and illustrated Calendars sometimes contain zodiac pictures. Calendars tend to be slim volumes; Francis Wormald has edited twenty different English Calendars of ninth- and tenth-century England in one volume. A religious community also frequently would add to its calendar new feasts and, sometimes, deaths of patrons and members of the community. Sometimes the number of lections for a particular feast will be indicated in a Calendar. (See Martyrology.)

Collects [*Collectarium*]. A Collect contains collections of the short prayers used at the Mass, such as Introits, sometimes Graduals, Offertories, Communions, and Post-Communions. Unlike a Gradual, a Collectarium does not necessarily include music. Collects were intended for the use of the priests, not the cantors or choirs. Several early medieval Collects from England have been printed.

Communal [*Communale*]. This is the first of two parts of a Missal or Breviary, containing the prayers and readings for the liturgical seasons, beginning in Advent, and continuing through Christmas, Epiphany, Lent, Eastertide, and ordinary Time, but not those for feasts of saints. (See Sanctoral.)

Consuetudinal [*Consuetudinalis*]; Figure 4. This book contained the customs [*consuetudo*, custom] of a religious community. It frequently included descriptions of particular processions and elaborate services, such as the Christmas and Easter Vigils, feast of the patron saint of a given church, and the visit of a bishop. (See Ordinal.)

Epistolary [*Epistolarium*]. The Epistolary contains New Testament Epistle readings for Mass. These usually were arranged in the order of the liturgical year, although there are also medieval manuscripts of New Testament Epistles with marginal rubrics and/or preface charts to indicate liturgical use.

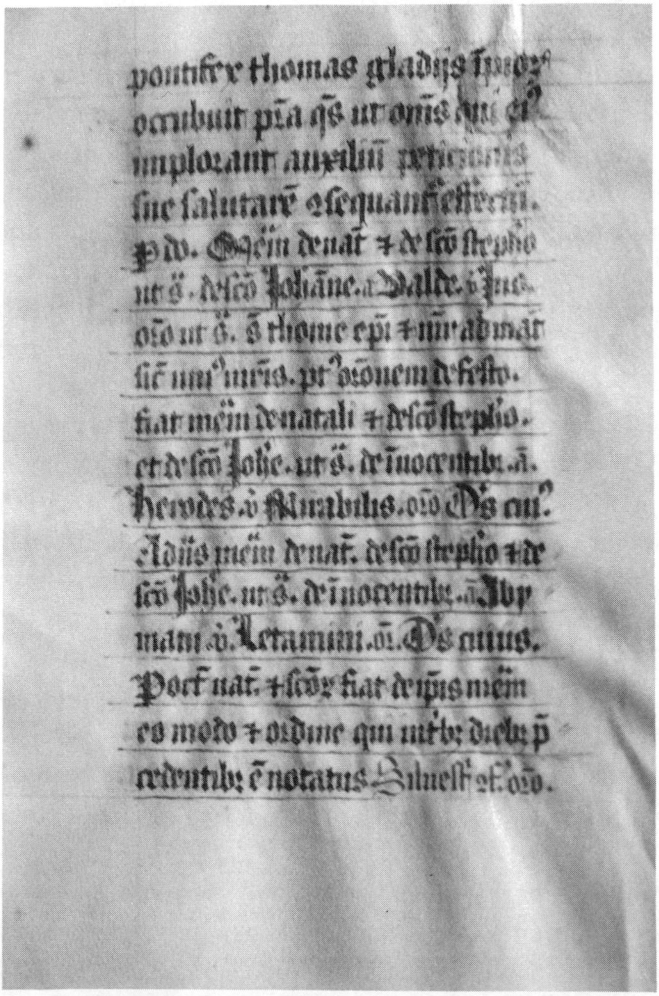

Figure 4. Consuetudinal or Ordinal. Collection of Jeanne Krochalis, State College, Penn. Fifteenth century, France. The underlined section gives instructions for commemorating the Nativity, St. Stephen (December 26), and St. John Evangelist (December 27) on the feast of St. Thomas Becket (December 29), followed by orations for Thomas, John, and the Innocents (December 28). Complete texts of antiphons and prayers are not included. Photograph © J. Krochalis.

Some Epistolaries contain only Sunday readings; others include readings for every day. Epistolaries were sometimes combined with an Evangelary to form a Lectionary.

Evangelary [*Evangelarium*]; Figure 5. The Evangelary contains Gospel [*Evangelium*, Gospel] readings for Mass in the order of the liturgical year, or in the order of the canonical New Testament (Matthew, Mark, Luke, John), but prefaced by a chart that gave the order of the Gospel readings throughout the year. Some Evangelaries contain only Sunday readings; others include readings for every day. Evangelaries often were combined with Epistolaries to form a Lectionary. Evangelaries often were richly decorated and are among the most famous extant medieval books, such as the Book of Kells and the Lindisfarne Gospels.

Gradual [*Graduale*, ancient: *Gradale*]; Figures 6, 7. A Gradual is so-called because it contained the Gradual prayer, the prayer recited by the cantor, originally from the steps [*gradus*] of the ambo, as the priest ascended the steps [*gradus*] of the altar to say Mass. The texts in the Gradual were sung by lectors, cantors, and choir. Graduals sometimes also contained other short, sung prayers, such as Introits, Tracts, Alleluias, Offertories, and Post-Communions. The contents of a Gradual depended on the custom of the particular church or community with regard to which prayers were sung rather than said. Medieval Graduals available in facsimile or modern editions include the tenth-century Gradual of Notker of St. Gall, Switzerland, an eleventh-century Gradual from the Church of St. Cecilia in the Trastevere section of Rome, and a thirteenth-century Gradual from Salisbury, England.

Homiliary [*Homiliarium*]. A Homiliary is a collection of short sermons [homilies] on biblical themes, especially those collected from Patristic and Early Medieval writers, which were used as lections in the monastic Office. The custom of such arrangements is as old as the sixth century; the most important medieval Homiliary is the late eighth-century collection prepared for Charlemagne by the Italian scholar Paul the Deacon. Homiliaries can be

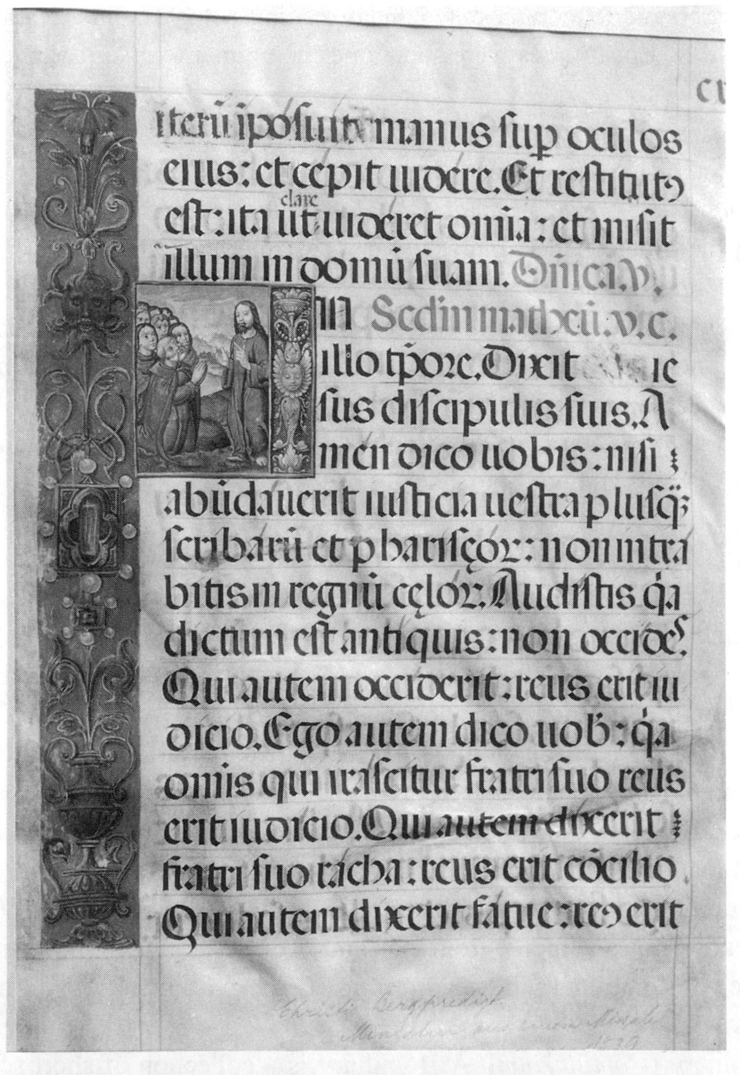
iterũ iposuit manus sup oculos
eius: et cepit uidere. Et restitut9
clare
est: ita ut uideret omia: et misit
illum in domũ suam. Dñica .v.
Scdm matheũ .v. c.
illo tpore. Dixit ie-
sus discipulis suis. A-
men dico uobis: nisi a-
bũdauerit iusticia uestra plusq̃
scribarũ et phariseor: non intra
bitis in regnũ celor. Audistis q̃a
dictum est antiquis: non occides.
Qui autem occiderit: reus erit iu
dicio. Ego autem dico uob: q̃a
omis qui irascitur fratri suo reus
erit iudicio. Qui autem dixerit
fratri suo racha: reus erit cõcilio.
Qui autem dixerit fatue: reus erit

Figure 5. Evangelary. Philadelphia Free Library, Philadelphia, Penn. MS Lewis M49:4. Leaf. Fifteenth century, Italy. The conclusion of the Gospel for the Fourth Sunday after Pentecost, Mark 8:24–26, and the beginning of the Gospel for the Fifth Sunday after Pentecost, Matthew 5:19–22. The miniature shows Jesus talking to the apostles. Courtesy of the Rare Book Department, The Free Library of Philadelphia. Photograph © J. Krochalis.

Figure 6. Gradual. Philadelphia Free Library, Philadelphia. Penn. MS Lewis M64:12. Late fourteenth century, Bohemia. The end of the Vigil for Pentecost, and the beginning of the Feast of Pentecost. Four-line square notation. Courtesy of the Rare Book Department, The Free Library of Philadelphia. Photograph © J. Krochalis.

Figure 7. Gradual. Philadelphia Free Library, Philadelphia, Penn. MS Lewis M72:9. Leaf. Fifteenth century, Italy. Note the instructions just above the picture for finding other texts used for the feast of an apostle: the Response *Justus ut palma*; the office *Gloria et honore*; the Communion *Magna est Gloria*; with page numbers. Courtesy of the Rare Book Department, The Free Library of Philadelphia. Photograph © J. Krochalis.

arranged either by author or by the order of the liturgical year; they imply liturgical use. Medieval homilies differed from sermons in that they were always on a biblical subject, in Latin, and intended for liturgical use, whereas sermons were often on non-biblical subjects (saints' lives, sins), and in the vernaculars. Nevertheless, especially after the twelfth century, the two words *homily* and *sermon* came to be used interchangeably in medieval manuscripts and library catalogues. Homiliaries often were richly bound and illustrated. (See Sermons.)

Hymnal [*Hymnarium*]; Figure 8. Hymns are poetic compositions set to music in praise of God, the Virgin Mary, or the saints, sung in the Divine Office, Mass, and sometimes in other liturgical services, such as processions. Hymnals usually contain both text and music. Hymns to God and to the Virgin tend to be grouped thematically; those for the seasons (Advent, Lent) and the saints usually follow the liturgical calendar. As hymns were consistently the most variable part of the medieval liturgy, hymnals show great variety. Texts for most medieval hymns are gathered in the multi-volume set of the *Analecta Hymnica*. For the hymns sung throughout the year on weekdays, and for specific feasts such as Advent, Christmas, Lent and Easter (which were fairly standard), see the *Canterbury Hymnal*.

Lectionary [*Lectionarium*, *Comes*, *Liber Comitis*, from *comes*, companion; also *Legenda*]. Lectionaries contain either: (1) the Epistle and Gospel readings for Mass arranged in the order of the liturgical year; or (2) the readings read at Matins for each nocturn or group of Psalms. Sometimes New Testaments or Bibles contain lection lists on the flyleaves, indicating how the book could be used liturgically by someone who did not own a separate Lectionary. Modern editions of medieval Lectionaries include the tenth-century Lectionary of Bishop Lambert of Maastricht, Holland, and a Dutch Lectionary printed around 1500. (See Epistolary and Evangelary.)

Legendary [*Legendarium*]. Legendaries are collections of Lives of the saints, arranged according to the order of the liturgical calendar, used for

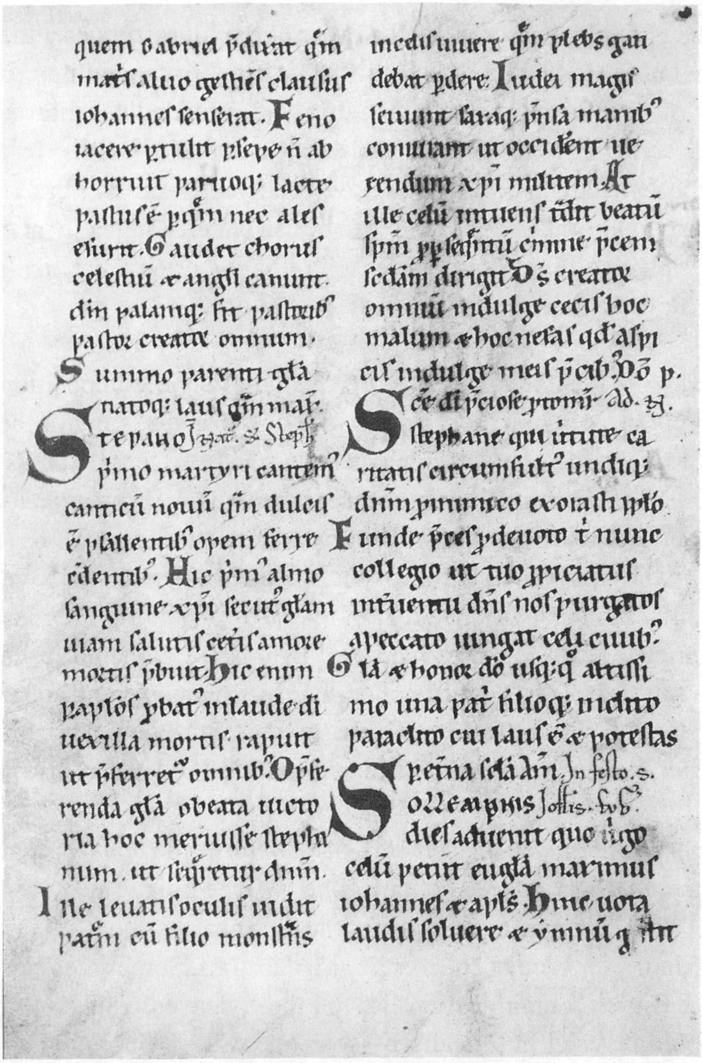

Figure 8. Hymnal. Brown University Library, Providence, R.I., Annmary Brown Memorial. MS 4.1. Thirteenth century, Germany or Austria. Hymnal with no music, though the text is punctuated for verse. The end of a Christmas hymn, followed by hymns for St. Stephen (December 26) and St. John the Evangelist (December 27). Courtesy of Brown University Library.

lections on feasts of saints. The most widely known of Late Medieval Legendaries was the *Golden Legend* [*Legenda Aurea*] compiled by Jacobus de Voragine ca. 1260. The prologue to this work describes the four complementary periods of the world, a human life, and the liturgical year: the time of deviation, the time of renewal, the time of reconciliation, and the time of pilgrimage. Even though the world and the human life begin with the time of deviation, Jacobus says, the Church begins the year with renewal; therefore the first saint in his Legendary is St. Andrew, whose feast day, November 30, was at the beginning of the Advent Season. Most Legendaries followed this pattern; in this they differ from some modern dictionaries of saints, which are arranged in alphabetical order. Religious communities also may have had smaller supplementary Legendaries for local saints. (See also Martyrology, Necrology, and Passional.)

Martyrology [*Martyrologium*]; Figure 9. Originally, Martyrologies contained the Lives of Christians who had died for the faith, with brief descriptions of their martyrdoms. The names in Martyrologies were usually arranged in the order of the liturgical year. The entry for the day was read in the monastic Chapter House after Prime; longer readings from the Legendary or from saints' Lives were part of the Divine Office. Brief Martyrologies survive from the fourth and fifth centuries—one is attributed to Jerome. Other Martyrologies are attributed to Gregory the Great (sixth century), Bede (eighth century), Hrabanus Maurus, and Usuard (both ninth century). Usuard's Martyrology is the basis of the standard modern Roman Martyrology, which includes all feasts generally celebrated throughout the Roman Catholic Church. Religious orders also still have their own Martyrologies, commemorating martyrs and saints in their own orders. (See also Calendar, Legendary, Necrology, and Passional.)

Missal [*Missale*]; Figure 10. The Missal, the book of the Mass [*Missa*], developed in the Late Middle Ages from the union of a number of separate service books (Sacramentary, Antiphonal, Gradual). This development reflects the increasing prominence of the celebration of Low Mass, where

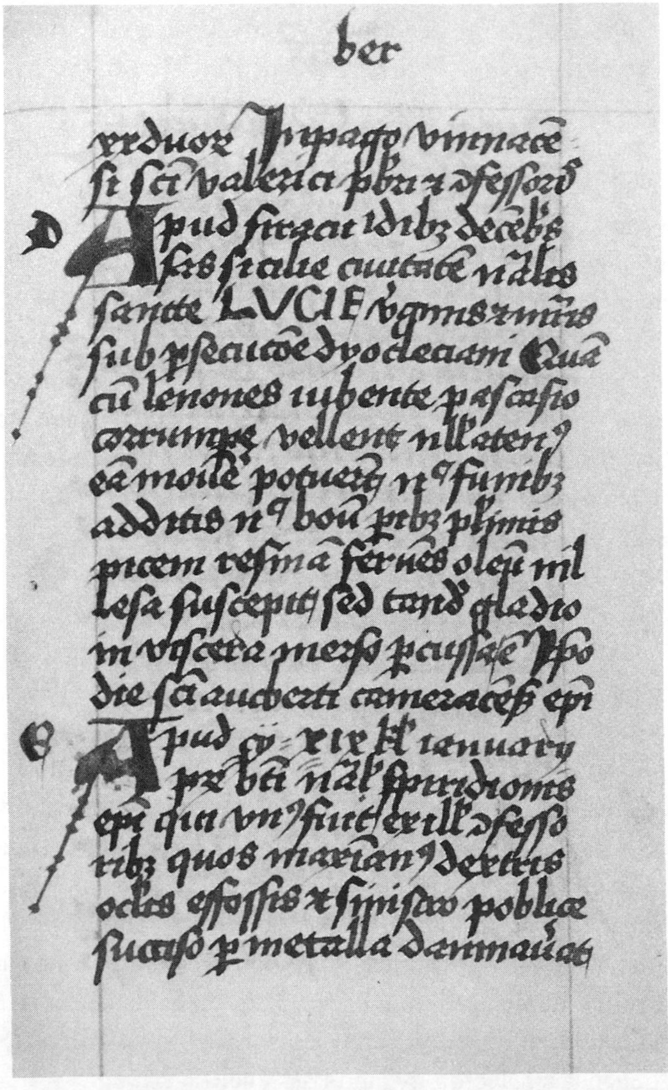

Figure 9. Martyrology of Usuard. University of Chicago, Regenstein Library, Chicago, Ill. MS Lat. 116, fol. 2. Fifteenth century, Germany. The end of the account of the martyrdom of St. Valericus (December 12), and texts for St. Lucy (December 13) and Spiridion (December 14). Courtesy of the University of Chicago Library.

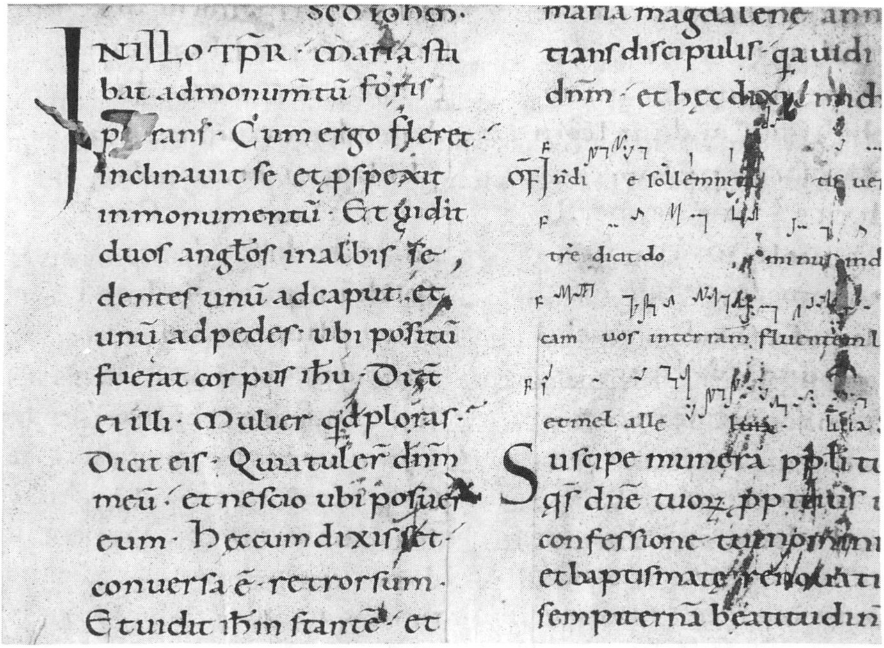

Figure 10. Missal, with neumes. Brown University Library, Providence, R.I., Annmary Brown Memorial. 1491. F7. Leaf. Pastedown in a collection of sermons: F. De Maioranis, *Sermones ab adventu cum quadragesimali*, Venice 1491–92 (Goff, M-92). Eleventh century, Italy. Gospel and Offertory, with neumes, for the Wednesday after Easter. Courtesy of Brown University Library.

the celebrant, rather than the choir, carried the burden of the liturgical responses. At the high peak of its development, the Missal contained all of the texts needed for the priest saying Mass, and the responses of the clergy or congregation, for the entire liturgical year. Missals usually began with the Ordinary (the unchanging parts) of the Mass, followed by variable prayers, arranged in the order of the liturgical calendar. Missals contained little or no music. While small, portable Missals tended to be simple, altar Missals from rich cathedrals could be sumptuously decorated and illuminated. Late Medieval Missals contain rubrics for the celebration of special Masses at the beginning. At the end of Missals are found Votive Masses for special concerns and occasions, such as for a dead spouse, for those in peril on the sea, or for the dedication of a church. Almost every medieval diocese and religious order had its own special prayers added to the Ordinary of the Mass. These are useful for dating and localizing Missals. There are modern editions or facsimiles of Missals from many areas of medieval Europe.

Necrology [*Necrologium*]. A Necrology is a list of deceased members or patrons of a religious community, arranged according to the date of death in the order of the liturgical calendar, to be used in commemoration on the Mass of that day, and sometimes in a special votive Mass for all patrons and benefactors. Up to the eleventh century, the Necrology was placed on the altar at Mass; later, the commemoration moved to the Chapter instead of the Choir. Like Calendars, Necrologies usually were not separate volumes but would be attached to a book in daily use such as a Missal, or Breviary, or the Rule or Consuetudinal of the order. Necrologies are interesting to scholars of the social world of the Middle Ages. (See also Calendar, Legendary, Martyrology, and Passional.)

Ordinary [*Ordo*, *Ordines Romani*, *Ordinalis*, *Ordinarium Missae*]; Figure 11. The Ordinary was the book a religious institution employed to organize its use of all other liturgical books. Arranged in the order of the liturgical calendar, it listed the services for every day and the books and ceremonies necessary for carrying them out. Like Missals and Brevaries, Ordinaries usually had a two-part organization: ceremonies appropriate to liturgical seasons (Advent, Lent) were described first; feasts of saints in the order of the liturgical calendar followed. The Roman Ordinals of the High Middle Ages are available in a modern edition. (See Consuetudinal.)

Passional [*Passionale or Passionarius*]. This was another name for a Martyrology, so called from the passions or sufferings of the saints who died for the faith. The thirteenth-century Passional of Bartolomeo da Trento (Northern Italy) recently has been published.

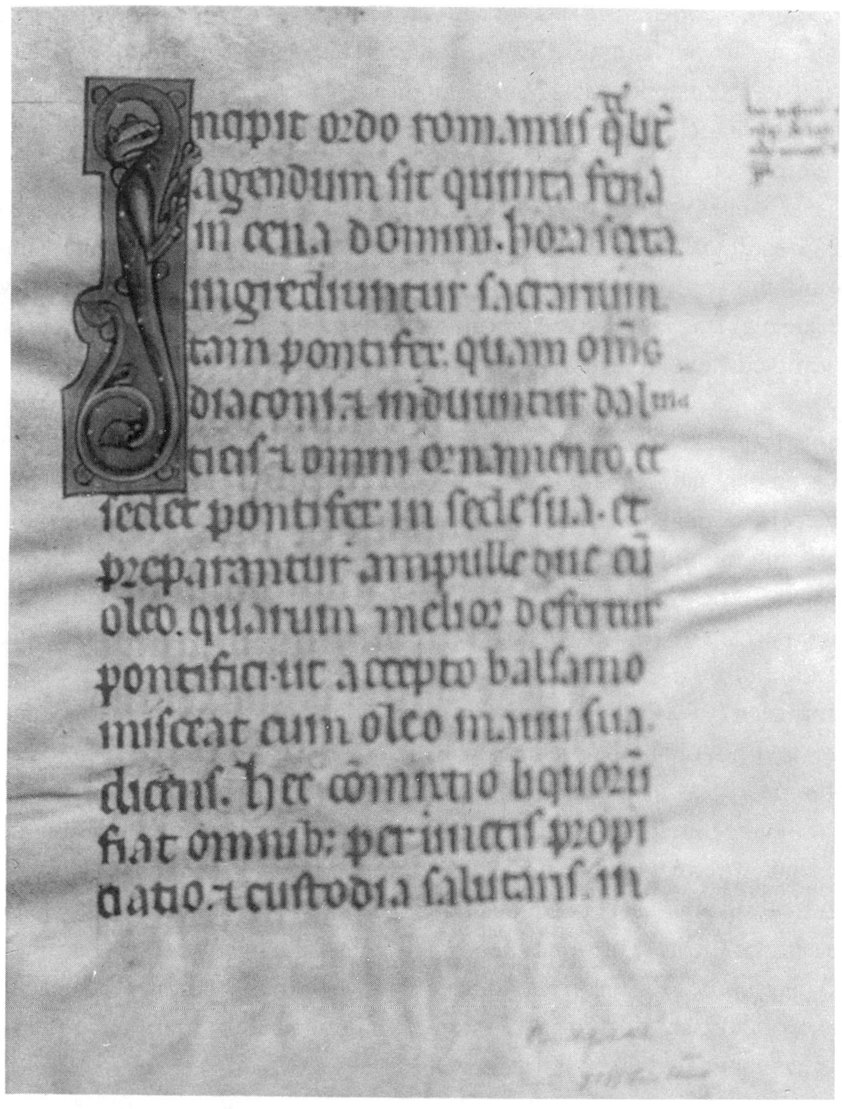

Figure 11. Ordinary. Philadelphia Free Library, Philadelphia, Penn. MS Lewis M8:12. Leaf. Thirteenth century, Italy. The beginning of the Roman Ordo for Holy Thursday, the fifth ferial day in Holy Week, the Last Supper, or *cena Domini*. The bishop enters, with all the deacons in their robes; he sits. Courtesy of the Rare Book Department, The Free Library of Philadelphia. Photograph © J. Krochalis.

Penitential [*Liber Penitentialis*]. A Penitential was a guide for the priest in defining sins and imposing appropriate penances. Penitentials were not, strictly speaking, liturgical books, but they did play a role in the developing ritual of penance. Penitentials exist from the sixth century; many were compiled in the British Isles. The usual method of organization of a Penitential was by sin, following the list of the Seven Deadly Sins given by Gregory the Great in his *Cura Pastoralis*. Penitentials have been of great interest to twentieth-century scholars who see them as a mirror of medieval society. Because of this interest, there is an extensive literature on Penitentials, including editions, translations, and selected studies.

Pontifical [*Pontificale*]. A Pontifical was a book that contained the special rites, such as Confirmation and Holy Orders, celebrated by a bishop. Modern ecclesiastical usage restricts the term *pontiff* to the Supreme Pontiff, the Pope, but in the Middle Ages the term could mean any bishop. By the end of the Middle Ages (Clement VIII, d. 1605) Pontificals were divided into three parts. The first part contained the ceremonies and sacraments that could only be performed by a bishop. For example, only a bishop could administer Holy Orders or Confirmation, bless an abbot or abbess, consecrate a virgin or another bishop, or crown a king or queen. The second part contained blessings, such as the consecration of a church or a cemetery, altar linens, or reliquaries. The third part contained rituals necessitating the presence of a bishop, such as excommunication and the reconciliation of heretics and sinners, expulsion and reconciliation of penitents during Lent, blessing of the holy oils on Maundy Thursday, the inauguration of synods, and ceremonies for the journeys of prelates and the reception of kings and queens. There have been modern studies of Pontificals from Italy, Germany, and England.

Processional [*Processionale*]. A Processional contained all the texts and music for use during processions, both inside and outside the church, such as processions from a cathedral to a parish church on the feast of its patron, and processions for blessings of fields and crops. Other liturgical books often indicated these texts without giving complete text and music; the processional was developed to fill this gap. Of necessity, such a volume had to be portable, so Processionals tend to be large (so that several singers could see the page at once) but thin enough to be carried long distances. Two Late Medieval Florentine Processionals have been printed.

Proper of the Saints. See Sanctoral.

Psalter [*Psalterium*]; Figure 12. Psalters contain all 150 Psalms in numerical order. Some copies included both versions of the Psalms translated by Jerome, on facing pages. There are also extant Psalters of early medieval localized Psalm versions, such as the Mozarabic Psalter. Since the entire Psalter was recited every week in the course of the Divine Office, and medieval religious were expected to know the entire Psalter by heart, monks, nuns, friars, and cathedral canons frequently had a Psalter separate from the Breviary. In the thirteenth century, Psalters also became popular among the more literate laity. These small volumes often are decorated with miniatures and grotesques. A number of medieval Psalters from different centuries and places have been reproduced in facsimile.

Responsorial [*Responsorium*, *Liber Responsialis*, *Liber Responsorialis*]. The Responsorial contained texts and music for all the responses of the Divine Office and the Mass, arranged according to the liturgical calendar.

Ritual [*Rituale*]. A Ritual contains the liturgical texts not included in the Missal and Breviary necessary for the administration of sacraments and blessings by a priest. It is one of the latest and least uniform of liturgical books, emerging as a discrete book after the Pontifical, not before the fourteenth century. Included are processional rites of purification and of Palm Sunday, prayers for the dead and for the churching of women, and rituals for Rogation Days. There is significant overlap between the contents of a Ritual and the contents of Pontificals, Benedictionals, and Missals. Medieval rituals from Italy and Switzerland have been edited and published.

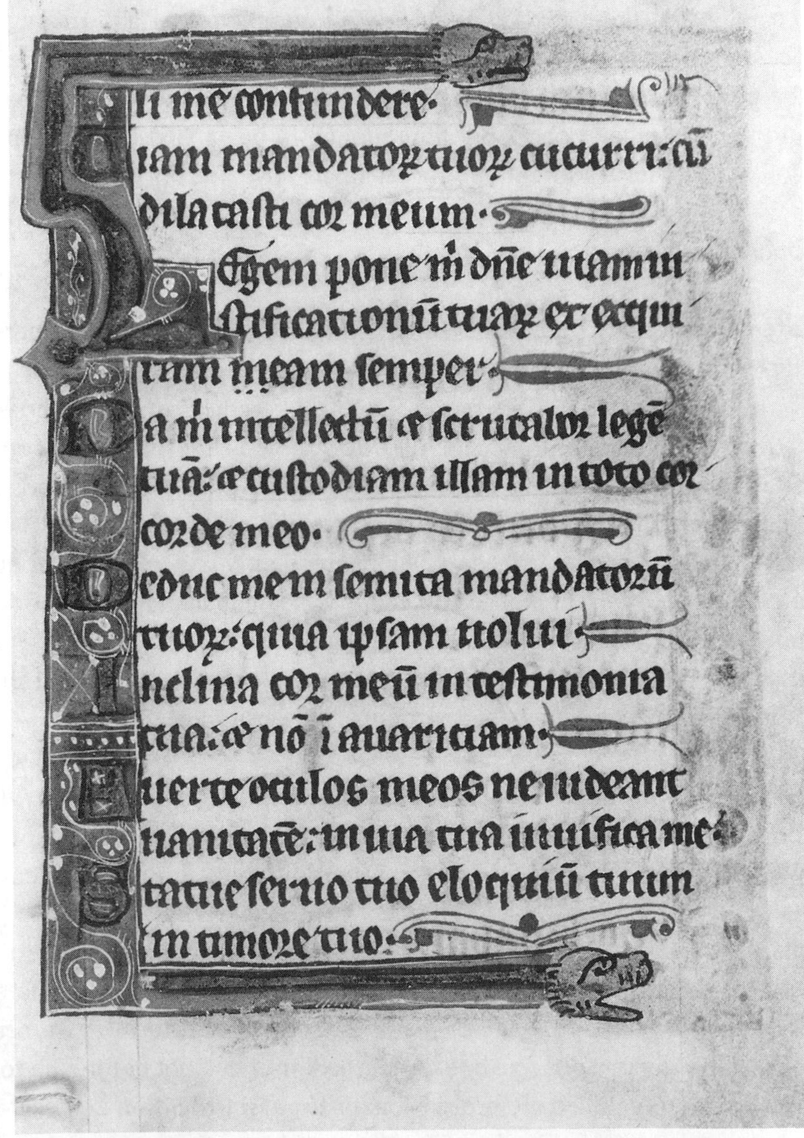
li me confundere.
Viam mandatorum tuorum cucurri: cum
dilatasti cor meum.
Legem pone mihi domine viam iu-
stificationum tuarum: et exqui-
ram meam semper.
Da mihi intellectum et scrutabor legem
tuam: et custodiam illam in toto cor
corde meo.
Deduc me in semita mandatorum
tuorum: quia ipsam volui.
Inclina cor meum in testimonia
tua: et non in avaritiam.
Averte oculos meos ne videant
vanitatem: in via tua vivifica me.
Statue servo tuo eloquium tuum
in timore tuo.

Figure 12. Psalter. Brown University Library, Providence, R.I., MS Koopman 1200? C.3. Fourteenth century, France or England. Psalm 118, verses 31–38. Note that the scribe has corrected *meam* to *eam* in line 6 by placing dots under the *m*. Courtesy of Brown University Library.

Sacramentary [*Sacramentarium*]; Figure 13. The oldest of the composite liturgical books, books designed specifically for liturgical services, the Sacramentary was the central liturgical book of the ninth to the twelfth centuries. It was essentially intended for the celebrant and included no Lessons, Introits, Graduals, Offertories but only Collects, Prefaces, and the Canon of the Mass. The oldest version is the Leonine Sacramentary, extant in one manuscript of seventh-century Verona. This is not, strictly speaking, a true Sacramentary, but it is the oldest surviving book of Mass prayers of the Roman Rite; its attribution to Pope Leo I (d. 461) has been disputed. The two main versions of the Middle Ages were the Gelasian Sacramentary (mid-eighth century, the oldest surviving Roman Sacramentary) and the Gregorian Sacramentary. The Gregorian Sacramentary is traditionally ascribed to Gregory the Great (d. 604), but the earliest known copy is the "Hadrianum," sent from Pope Hadrian to Charlemagne about 790. Local versions of the Sacramentary also existed. In addition to rituals for the performance of the sacraments, Sacramentaries contained the Common of the Mass and the shorter prayers for the Proper of the Mass, although not usually the Epistles or the Gospels. From the twelfth century on, Sacramentaries tended to be replaced by Missals and Rituals.

Sanctoral [*Sanctorale*]. The Sanctorale was the second of two parts of a Missal or Breviary, containing the prayers and readings for the feasts of saints throughout the liturgical year beginning with the Feast of St. Andrew, 30 November, but not those for the liturgical seasons of Advent, Lent, and ordinary Time. (See Temporal.)

Sermons [*Sermones*]. Sermon collections were produced throughout the Middle Ages. The term *sermon* was used interchangeably with *homily* for collections of the preaching of the Church Fathers (for example, Augustine, John Chrysostom, Gregory the Great, Leo the Great) and for preachings of later writers such as Aelfric (in Old English) and Bernard of Clairvaux (in Latin). Technically, however, *sermon* is a much broader term than *homily*, including preaching performed outside of liturgical services and in the

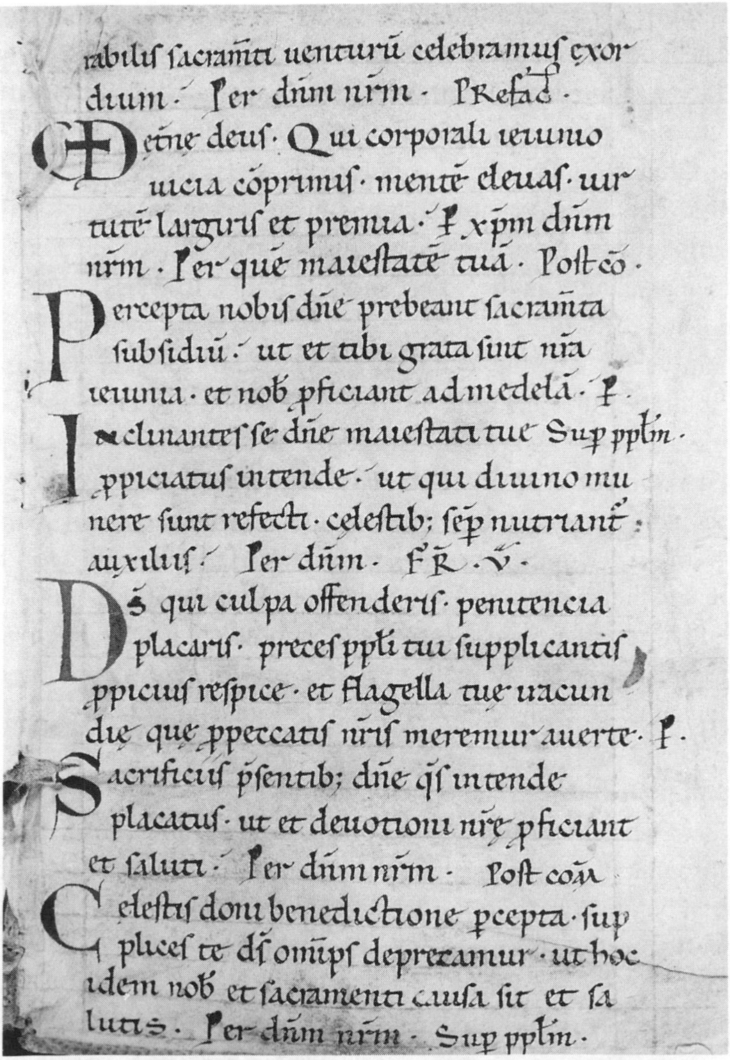

Figure 13. Sacramentary. Brown University Library, Providence, R.I., Annmary Brown Memorial. MS 313. Leaf. Eleventh century, Italy. Pastedown in P. Haedus, *Anterotica, sive de Amoris generibus*, Treviso, 1493 (Goff H-2). Communion, Post Communion, and prayer over the people for Ash Wednesday, and the Thursday and Friday—the fourth and fifth ferial days—after Ash Wednesday. Courtesy of Brown University Library.

vernacular. The rise of the Mendicant orders (the Franciscans and Dominicans) in the thirteenth century is related to the increasing prominence of preaching to the laity. Sermon collections could include the works of several authors, or of only one. Some collections covered not the entire church year but only a part of it, such as Lent or Advent, or a particular cycle of saints. Some sermon collections are on biblical texts but apparently were meant to be read or studied rather than delivered aloud; the most famous of this type of sermon are the twelfth-century sermons of the Song of Songs by Cistercians such as Bernard of Clairvaux.

Temporal [*Temporale*]. The Temporal is the first of a two-part liturgical book; it must be used in conjunction with the Sanctoral. Temporals included prayers and readings for the seasons of the liturgical year (Advent, Christmas, Lent, Holy Week, Easter, Pentecost) but not the prayers and readings for celebrations of the feasts of individual saints. (See Sanctoral.)

Troper [*Troparium*]. From at least the ninth century on, the custom of elaborating on the alleluia or other musical texts spread throughout the medieval church. These elaborations, called "tropes," were words set to music which usually began from a melisma and could grow to a length of several lines. Troping allowed theological commentary on the words of the Mass just recited; they sometimes went on in detail about the virtues of a particular saint. While any liturgical text could be troped, the elaboration on the alleluia verse of the Mass (sung before the Gospel) led especially to separate musical compositions with accompanying verses known as Sequences, sometimes called Prosae. Sequences, which were sung at major feasts, were further troped, until the Council of Trent (1545–63) forbade all troping of liturgical texts and preserved only five Sequences: "Victimae Pascali Laudes" for Easter; "Veni, Sancti Spiritus" for Pentecost; "Lauda Sion, Salvatorem" for Corpus Christi; "Dies Irae" for the Requiem Mass; and "Stabat Mater" for the feasts of the Virgin. Medieval Tropers, a number of which are available in modern editions, show great variation in feasts chosen and musical compositions provided.

References

Attwater, Donald. *The Penguin Dictionary of Saints*. Harmondsworth, 1965.

Benedict of Nursia. *The Rule of Saint Benedict*. Trans. Anthony C. Meisel and M. L. del Mastro. New York, 1975.

Butler, Alban. *Lives of the Saints*. Ed. Herbert Thurston and Donald Attwater. New York, 1956.

Cabrol, Fernand. *Liturgical Prayer, its History and Spirit*. New York, 1922.

Gushee, Marion S. "The Polyphonic Music of the Medieval Monastery, Cathedral, and University." In *Antiquity and the Middle Ages: From Ancient Greece to the 15th Century*. Ed. James McKinnon. Englewood Cliffs, N.J., 1991. Pp. 143–69.

Harper, John. *The Forms and Orders of Western Liturgy from the Tenth to the Eighteenth Century: A Historical Introduction and Guide for Students and Musicians*. Oxford, 1991.

Hughes, Andrew. *Medieval Manuscripts for Mass and Office: A Guide to their Organization and Terminology*. Toronto, 1982.

Huglo, Michel. *Les livres de chant liturgique*. Turnhout, 1988.

Kaske, R. E. *Medieval Christian Literary Imagery: A Guide to Interpretation*. Toronto, 1988. (Chapter 2, "The Liturgy," Chapter 3, "Hymns," Chapter 4, "Sermons.")

McKinnon, James. "The Emergence of Gregorian Chant in the Carolingian Era." In *Antiquity and the Middle Ages: From Ancient Greece to the 15th Century*. Ed. James Mc Kinnon. Englewood Cliffs, N.J., 1991. Pp. 88–119.

McKitterick, Rosamond. *The Frankish Church and the Carolingian Reforms, 789–895*. London, 1977.

The New Grove Dictionary of Music and Musicians. London and Washington, D.C., 1980. (Articles: Paul Frederick Cutter, "Responsory"; Michel Huglo, "Antiphoner," "Gradual," "Processional"; Ruth Steiner, "Divine Office," "Gregorian Chant"; Ruth Steiner et al., "Mass. I. Liturgy and Chant")

The Ancient Liturgies of the Gallican Church. Ed. John Mason Neale. New York, 1970.

Pfaff, Richard W. *Medieval Latin Liturgy: A Select Bibliography*. Toronto, 1982.

Swete, Henry Barclay *Church Services and Service Books before the Reformation*. London, 1896; rpt. 1914.

Taft, Robert. *The Liturgy of the Hours in the East and West: The Origins of the Divine Office and its Meaning for Today*. Collegeville, Minn., 1986.

Van Dijk, Stephen Joseph Peter, and J. Hazelden Walker. *The Origins of the Modern Roman Liturgy: The Liturgy of the Papal Court and the Franciscan Order in the Thirteenth Century*. Westminster, Md., 1960.

Vogel, Cyrille, *Medieval Liturgy: An Introduction to the Sources*. Trans. William G. Storey and Niels K. Rasmussen. Washington, D.C., 1986.

Bibliography on Specific Liturgical Books and Facsimiles of Medieval Liturgical Manuscripts

Antiphonals

Antiphonale Missarum Sextuplex. Ed. René-Jean Hesbert. Rome, 1967.

Corpus Antiphonalium Officii. Ed. René-Jean Hesbert. 6 vols. Rome, 1963–79.

Hood, William. *Fra Angelico: San Marco, Florence*. New York, 1995.

Benedictionals

The Benedictionals of Freising. Ed. Robert Amiet, with additional material by Christophe Hohler and Bernard J. Wigan. London, 1974. (Munich, Bayerische Staatsbibliothek, Cod. lat. 6430. A Gallican Benedictional from eighth/ninth century Germany.)

The Benedictional of John Longlonde, Bishop of Lincoln. Ed. Reginald Maxwell Woolley. London, 1927. (British Museum MS Add. 21974. The Benedictional of a fifteenth-century Bishop of Lincoln and Chancellor of Oxford.)

The Benedictional of St. Ethelwold. Ed. Francis Wormald. New York, 1959.

Deshman, Robert. *The Benedictional of Aethelwold*. Princeton, 1995. (Benedictional of Aethelwold, Bishop of Winchester, ca. 908–84.)

Books of Hours

The Belles Heures of Jean, Duke of Berry. The Cloisters, the Metropolitan Museum of Art. Introduction by Millard Meiss; Commentaries by Millard Meiss and Elizabeth H. Beatson. New York, 1974. (One of several sumptuous manuscripts made for the most famous patron of the arts of the fourteenth century.)

Backhouse, Janet. *Books of Hours*. London, 1985.

Book of Hours. Illuminations by Simon Marmion; Introduction and commentaries by James Thorpe. San Marino, Calif., 1976.

Donovan, Claire. *The De Brailes Hours: Shaping the Book of Hours in Thirteenth-Century Oxford*. London, 1991.

Facsimiles of Horae de Beata Maria Virgine, from English Mss. of the Eleventh century. Ed. Edward S. Dewick. London, 1902.

Grassi, Giovannino de'. *The Visconti Hours, National Library, Florence*. Ed. Millard Meiss and Edith W. Kirsch. New York, 1972. (The Book of Hours of the Visconti family of Milan by Giovannino de' Grassi, ca. 1340–98.)

Guia general das Horas del-rei D. Duarte. Lisbon, 1971. (Book of Hours of Duarte, King of Portugal, 1391–1438.)

Harthan, John P. *Books of Hours and Their Owners*. London, 1977.

The Hastings Hours: A 15th-century Flemish Book of Hours Made for William, Lord Hastings, now in the British Library, London. Ed. D. H. Turner. New York, 1983.

The Hours of Mary of Burgundy: Codex Vindobonensis 1857, Vienna, Österreichische Nationalbibliothek. Commentary by Eric Inglis. London, 1995. (Book of Hours of Mary of Burgundy, 1457–1482.)

Pucelle, Jean, *The Hours of Jeanne d'Evreux, Queen of France, at the Cloisters, the Metropolitan Museum of Art*. New York, 1957. (Jean Pucelle, fl. 1320, originator of the famous "Pucelle style" of miniatures, featuring the use of architectural space.)

The Très Riches Heures of Jean, Duke of Berry, Musée Condé, Chantilly. Introduction by Jean Longnon and Raymond Cazelles; Preface by Millard Meiss. New York, 1969.

Watson, Rowan. *The Playfair Hours: A Late Fifteenth Century Illuminated Manuscript from Rouen (V&A, L.475–1918)*. London, 1984.

Wieck, Roger S. *Time Sanctified: The Book of Hours in Medieval Art and Life*. New York, 1988.

Breviary

Breviarium caeremoniarum monasterii Mellicensis. Ed. Joachim F. Angerer. Siegburg, 1987. (The Breviary of the Austrian Abbey of Melk, on the Danube River.)

Breviarium Romanum a Francisco Cardinali Quignonio. Ed. John Wickham Legg. Cambridge, 1888; rpt. 1970. (An early modern printed Breviary from Venice.)

The Colbertine Breviary, Edited from the Copy in the British Museum (C.35.f.21.). Ed. T. R. Gambier-Parry. London, 1912–13. (A private prayer book based on medieval liturgical breviaries, compiled for J. B. Colbert and printed ca. 1675.)

The Hereford Breviary. Ed. Walter H. Frere and Langton E. G. Brown. 3 vols. Vol. 1: *Psalterium*, *Commune Sanctorum*, *Temporale*; Vol. 2: *Sanctorale*; Vol. 3: *Collector*, *Ordinal*. London, 1903, 1911, 1915. (A facsimile of the edition printed in Rouen in 1503 from thirteenth- and fifteenth-century manuscripts from Hereford, England.)

Calendar

Wormald, Francis. *English Kalendars Before A.D. 1100*. London, 1934. (Twenty Calendars from ninth- /tenth-century England.)

Collects

The Durham Collectar. Ed. Alicia Corrêa. London, 1992. (Ninth/tenth century.)

The Leofric Collectar (Harl. ms. 2961) With an Appendix Containing a Litany and Prayers from Harl. ms. 863. Ed. Edward S. Dewick. 2 vols. London, 1914–1921. (An eleventh-century Collect from Exeter.)

Rituale Ecclesiae Dunelmensis. Ed. Uno Lindelöf. Durham and London, 1927. (Collect from tenth-century North England with interlinear glosses in Old English.)

Epistolary

Het Epistolarium van Leningrad. Ed. Cebus C. de Bruin. Leiden, 1974. (A Dutch Epistolary to 1500, selections.)

Evangelary

Backhouse, Janet. *The Lindisfarne Gospels: A Masterpiece of Book Painting*. San Francisco, 1995. (A Gospel book written and richly illustrated in north-eastern England at the end of the seventh century.)

The Book of Kells: Reproductions from the Manuscript in Trinity College, Dublin. Ed. Françoise Henry. New York, 1974. (A richly illustrated Gospel Book from Ireland, ca. 800.)

Das Goldene Evangelienbuch von Echternach: Eine Prunkhandschrift des 11. Jahrhunderts. Ed. Rainer Kahsnitz, Ursula Mende, and Elizabeth Rücker. Frankfurt am Main, 1982). (Eleventh-century Germany.)

Millar, Eric George. *The Lindisfarne Gospels: Three Plates in Colour and Thirty-Six in Monochrome from Cotton ms. Nero D. IV in the British Museum With pages from Two Related Manuscripts*. London, 1923.

Sullivan, Edward. *The Book of Kells: described by Sir Edward Sullivan and Illustrated with Twenty-Four Plates in Colours*. London, 1933; rpt. London, 1986.

Gradual

Codex 121 Einsiedeln: Graduale und Sequenzen Notkers von St. Gallen. Ed. Odo Lang. Weinheim, 1991. (Tenth-century Gradual attributed to Notker of St. Gall.)

Das Graduale von *Santa Cecilia in Trastevere: Cod. Bodmer 74*. Ed. Max Lütolf. Cologny-Genève, 1987. (A Gradual dated 1071 from the church of Santa Cecilia, Rome.)

Graduale Sarisburiense: A Reproduction in Facsimile of a Manuscript of the Thirteenth Century: With a Dissertation and Historical Index Illustrating its Development from the Gregorian Antiphonale Missarum. Ed. Walter Howard Frere. London, 1894; rpt. Farnborough, 1966. (A thirteenth-century Gradual from Salisbury: MS British Library. Additional 12194.)

Homiliary

Grégoire, Réginald. *Les homéliares du moyen âge*. Rome, 1966.

———. *Homéliares liturgiques médiévaux: Analyse de manuscrits*. Spoleto, 1980.

Wiegand, Friedrich Ludwig Leonhard. *Das Homiliarium Karls des Grossen auf seine ursprungliche Gestalt hin untersucht*. 1897; rpt. Aalen, 1972. (Homilary of Paul the Deacon, ca. 720–99 prepared for Charlemagne.)

Hymnal

Analecta Hymnica Medii Aevi. Ed. Guido M. Dreves and Clemens Blume. 55 vols. Leipzig, 1886–1922.

Analecta Hymnica Medii Aevi. Ed.Guido M. Dreves, Dorothea Baumann, and Max Lütolf. 2 vols. Bern, 1978.

The Canterbury Hymnal: Edited from British Library MS. Additional 37517. Ed. Gernot R. Wieland. Toronto, 1982.

Hymnarium oscense: S. XI. 2 vols. Zaragoza, 1987. (MS Catedral de Huesca. 1, from the eleventh-century Cathedral of Huesca, Spain.)

Lectionary

Het Amsterdamse lectionarium (Lectionarium Amstelodamense). Ed. C. C. de Bruin. Leiden, 1970. (Dutch printed lectionary containing materials to 1500.)

Lectionarium Sancti Lamberti Leodiensis, tempore Stephani Episcopi paratum (901–920) codex Bruxellensis 14650–59. Ed. François Masai and Léon Gilissen. Amsterdam, 1963. (Tenth-century lectionary of Bishop Lambert of Maastricht, d. 708.)

Legendary

Jacobus de Voragine. *The Golden Legend: Readings on the Saints*. Trans. William G. Ryan. 2 vols. Princeton, 1993.

Martyrology

Das altenglische Martyrologium. Ed. Günter Kotzor. Introduction by Helmut Gneuss. 2 vols. Munich, 1981.

Hausmann, Regina. *Das Martyrologium von Marcigny-sur-Loire: Edition einer Quelle zur cluniacensischen Heiligenverehrung am Ende des elften Jahrhunderts*. Freiburg, 1984. (Eleventh-century Cluniac martyrology.)

Le martyrologe d'Usuard. Ed. Jacques Dubois. Brussels, 1965. (The most widely circulated Martyrology of the Middle Ages, the basis for the modern Roman Martyrology, attributed to Usuard, d. 876/7.)

An Old English Martyrology. Ed. George Herzfeld. London, 1900.

Rabani Mauri Martyrologium. Ed. John McCulloh. Turnhout, 1979. (Martyrology of ninth-century abbot, Hrabanus Maurus.)

Missal

The Bobbio Missal. Ed. André Wilmart, E. A. Lowe, and H. A. Wilson. 3 vols. London, 1924; rpt. London, 1991. (A Missal from the monastery of Bobbio, North Italy, mingling Gallican, Mozarabic, and Milanese Rites.)

Missale ad usum Ecclesie Westmonasteriensis. Ed. John Wickham Legg. 3 vols. London, 1891–1897. (The Missal of Westminster, England, from the fourteenth/fifteenth centuries.)

Missale Basileense saec. XI: (Codex Gressly). 2 vols. Freiburg, 1994. (A Swiss Missal from the eleventh century.)

Missale ragusinum: The Missal of Dubrovnik. Ed. Richard Francis Gyug. Toronto,1990. (Oxford, Bodleian Library, Canon. liturg. 342. A thirteenth-century Missal from Dubrovnik.)

Missale romanum Mediolani, 1474. Ed. Robert Lippe. 2 vols. London, 1899–1907. (Reprint of what is believed to be the first printed edition of the Roman missal).

Necrology

Necrologium Aquileiense. Ed. Cesare Scalon. Udine, 1982. (A twelfth-/thirteenth-century Necrology from north Italy.)

Das Necrologium des Cluniacenser-Priorates Münchenwiler (Villers-les-Moines. Ed. Gustav Schnürer. Fribourg, 1909. (A late eleventh-century Necrology from Switzerland.)

Ordinary

Ordinaire de l'église Notre-Dame Cathédrale d'Amiens par Raoul de Rouvray (1291). Ed. Georges Durand. Amiens/Paris, 1934.

The Ordinal of the Papal Court from Innocent III to Boniface VIII and Related Documents. Ed. Stephen J. P. Van Dijk and Joan Hazelden Walker. Fribourg, 1975. (Thirteenth-century papal Ordinals.)

Les ordines romani du haut moyen age. Ed. Michel Andrieu. 5 vols. Louvain, 1960–1965.

Sources of the Modern Roman Liturgy: The Ordinals by Haymo of Faversham and Related Documents (1243–1307). Ed. Stephen J. P. Van Dijk. Leiden, 1963.

Passional

Bartolomeo da Trento. *Passionale de sanctis*. Ed. Domenico Gobbi. Trent, 1990. (Passional from an Italian manuscript dated 1236 in the Stift Klosterneuburg, Austria.)

Penitentials

Alanus de Insulis. *Liber poenitentialis*. Ed. Jean Longère. Louvain, 1965. (Penitential of Alan of Lille, French Cistercian, later Dominican, d. 1202.)

Bezler, Francis. *Les pénitentiels espagnols: contribution à l'étude de la civilisation de l'Espagne chrétienne du haut Moyen Age*. Münster, 1994. (A study of Penitentials from late medieval Spain.)

Frantzen, Allen J. *The Literature of Penance in Anglo-Saxon England*. New Brunswick, N.J., 1983.

Haggenmüller, Reinhold. *Die Überlieferung der Beda und Egbert zugeschriebenen Bussbücher*. Frankfurt am Main and New York, 1991. (A study of the Penitentials of the early medieval English authors Bede and Egbert.)

Kottje, Raymund. *Die Bussbucher Halitgars von Cambrai und des Hrabanus Maurus: ihre Uberlieferung und ihre Quellen*. Berlin and New York, 1980. (A study of two Carolingian Penitentials.)

McNeill, John T., and Helena M. Gamer. *Medieval Handbooks of Penance: A Translation of the Principal Libri Poenitentiales and Selections from Related Documents*. New York, 1933; rpt. 1965. (The standard English translation.)

Das Paenitentiale Vallicellianum I: ein oberitalienischer Zweig der frühmittelalterlichen kontinentalen Bussbücher. Ed. Günter Hägele. Sigmaringen, 1984. (A Penitential from early medieval North Italy.)

Petrus Pictaviensis. *Summa de confessione: Compilatio praesens*. Ed. Jean Longère. Turnhout, 1980. (Penitential of Peter of Poitiers, Canon of Saint-Victor, Paris, d. after 1216.)

Trois sommes de pénitence de la première moitié du XIIIe *siècle: la "Summula Magistri Conradi" les sommes "Quia non pigris" et "Decime dande sunt."* Ed. Jean Pierre Renard. Louvain-la-Neuve, 1989. (Three thirteenth-century Penitentials.)

Pontifical

Andrieu, Michel. *Pontifical Romain au Moyen-Age*. 4 vols.Vatican City, 1938–41. (The Pontificals of Rome: vol. 86: c. 12 [twelfth century?], vol. 87: c.13 [thirteenth century?], vol. 88: the Pontifical of Guillame Durand, vol. 99: indices.)

Two Anglo-Saxon Pontificals: The Egbert and Sidney Sussex Pontificals. Ed. H. M. J. Banting. London, 1989.

Pontificale Lanaletense. (Bibliothèque de la ville de Rouen A.27. cat. 368). Ed. Gilbert H. Doble. London: Harrison and Sons, 1937. (A tenth-century Pontifical formerly in use at St. Germans, Cornwall.)

Processional

Cattin, Giulio. *Un processionale fiorentino per la settimana santa : studio liturgico-musicale sul Ms. 21 dell'Opera di S. Maria del Fiore.* Bologna, 1975. (A Processional from the Cathedral of Florence, fifteenth century.)

Il processionale benedettino della Badia di Sant'Andrea della Castagna. Milan, 1992. (A fifteenth-century manuscript of Badia di Sant'Andrea della Castagna. 81, a Benedictine house.)

Psalter

Cutler, Anthony. *The Aristocratic Psalters of Byzantium.* Paris, 1984.

Psalterium-hymnarium Arborense: il manoscritto P. XIII della Cattedrale di Oristano (secolo XIV–XV). Ed. Giampaolo Mele. Rome, 1994. (A late medieval century Psalter from the Cathedral of Oristano, Italy.)

Psalterium aureum Sancti Galli: mittelalterliche Psalterillustration im Kloster St. Gallen. Ed. Christoph Eggenberger. Sigmaringen, 1987. (A richly decorated Carolingian Psalter from the Abbey of St. Gall, Switzerland.)

The Mozarabic Psalter. Ed. Julius Parnell Gilson. London, 1905. (MS British Museum, Add. 30,851, the eleventh-century Psalter of the Abbey of St. Sebastian of Silos, Spain.)

The Salisbury Psalter. Ed. Celia Sisam and Kenneth Sisam. EETS 242. London and New York, 1959. (Edited from Salisbury Cathedral MS 150.)

The Stowe Psalter. Ed. Andrew C. Kimmens. Toronto and Buffalo, 1979. (A tenth/eleventh-century English Psalter glossed in Old English.)

Vintr, Josef. *Die älteste tschechische Psalterübersetzung*. Vienna, 1986. (A fourteenth-century Czech Psalter.)

Ritual

Ein Rituale in beneventanischer Schrift. Ed. Ambros Odermatt. Fribourg, 1980. (Rome, Bibliotheca Vallicelliana, Cod. C 32, a Central Italian Ritual from the end of the eleventh century.)

Das Rheinauer Rituale. Ed. Gebhard Hürlimann. Fribourg, 1959. (Zurich Rh 114, an early twelfth-century Ritual from Switzerland.)

Sacramentary

Sacramentarium Fuldense saeculi X. Ed. Gregor Richter and Albert Schönfelder. Farnborough, Hampshire, 1980. (Cod. theol. 231 Universitätsbibliothek, Göttingen, a tenth-century Sacramentary from the Abbey of Fulda, Saxony.)

Liber Sacramentorum Romanae Eclesiae ordinis anni circuli (Sacramentarium Gelasianum. Ed. Leo Eisenhöfer and Petrus Siffrin. s 4. Rome, 1981. (The Gelasian Sacramentary, mid eighth-century.)

Liber sacramentorum Gellonensis. Ed. Antoine Dumas. 2 vols. Turnhout, 1981. (The Gellonian Sacramentary, from Italy, ca. 790.)

Le sacramentaire grégorien: ses principales formes d'après les plus anciens manuscrits. Ed. Jean Deshusses. 3 vols. Fribourg, 1971. (Gregorian Sacramentary, earliest form ca. 790.)

Sacramentarium Gregorianum. Das Stationsmessbuch des Papstes Gregor. Ed. W. Gamber. 2 vols. Regensburg, 1966–1967.

Sacramentarium Veronense. Ed. Leo Cunibert Mohlberg. 3rd ed. Ed. Leo Eizenhöfer. Rome, 1978. (Verona, Cod. Bibl. Capit. Veron. LXXXV 80, early seventh century = "Leonine" Sacramentary.)

Sermons

De l'homélie au sermon: histoire de la prédication médiévale: Actes du V Colloque internationale de Louvain-la-Neuve (9–11 juillet 1992). Ed. Jaqueline Hamesse and Xavier Hermand, Ed. Louvain-la-Neuve, 1993.

Anthony of Padua. *Seek First his Kingdom: An Anthology of the Sermons of the Saint.* Ed. Livio Poloniato. Padua, 1988. (Sermons of the Dominican Saint and preacher Anthony of Padua, 1195–1231.)

Caesarius of Arles. *Sermons.* Trans. Mary Magdeleine Mueller. 3 vols. New York, 1956–1973. (Sermons of Caesarius of Arles, ca. 470–542, an important transmitter of Augustine.)

Bernard of Clairvaux. *Sermons for the Summer Season: Liturgical Sermons from Rogationtide and Pentecost.* Trans. Beverly Mayne Kienzle and James Jarzembowski. Kalamazoo, Mich., 1991. (Bernard of Clairvaux, Saint and Cistercian Abbot, 1090/91–1153.)

———. *Sermons on Conversion.* Trans. Marie-Bernard Saïd. Kalamazoo, Mich., 1981.

———. *On the Song of Songs* 4 vols. Trans. Killian Walsh (vols. 1–2), Irene Edmonds (vols. 3–4). Kalamazoo, Mich., 1976–80.

John of Ford. *Sermons on the Final Verses of the Song of Songs.* Trans. Wendy Mary Beckett. 7 vols. Kalamazoo, Mich., 1977–1984. (A continuation of the Song of Songs sermons of Bernard of Clairvaux by John, Abbot of Ford, twelfth century.)

Troper

Le prosaire de la Sainte-Chapelle (vers 1250). Ed. René-Jean Hesbert. Macon, 1952. (Troper from the Royal Chapel of Paris, thirteenth century.)

The Winchester Troper: From Manuscripts of the Xth and XIth Centuries. Ed. Walter H. Frere. London, 1894.

THE BOOK OF HOURS

ROGER S. WIECK

Introduction

FOR THREE HUNDRED YEARS the Book of Hours was the bestseller of the Late Middle Ages and the Renaissance. From the mid-thirteenth to the mid-sixteenth century, more Books of Hours were commissioned and produced, bought and sold, bequeathed and inherited, printed and reprinted than any other text, including the Bible.

The main reason for this popularity lies in the book's contents. The Book of Hours is a prayer book that contains, as its heart, the Little Office of the Blessed Virgin Mary, that is, the **Hours of the Virgin**. (For this reason the Latin term for the book is *Horae*, Hours.) The Hours of the Virgin are a sequence of prayers to the Mother of God that, ideally, were recited throughout the course of the day, Hour by Hour. Other prayers usually found in *Horae* helped round out the spiritual needs of Late Medieval and Renaissance men and women. The **Penitential Psalms**, for example, were recited to help one resist the Seven Deadly Sins. The **Office of the Dead** was prayed to reduce the time spent by one's friends and relatives in purgatory.

The Book of Hours played a key role in the Late Medieval and Renaissance cult of the Virgin. Marian devotion placed the Mother of God in the pivotal role as intercessor between man and God. As our spiritual mother, Mary would hear our petitions, take mercy on our plight, and plead our case to her Son who, surely, could not deny his own mother anything. In a Europe dominated by cathedrals dedicated to Notre Dame, the Hours of the Virgin were deemed Our Lady's favorite prayers, the quickest way to her heart.

The Hours of the Virgin are at least as old as the ninth century; they may have been developed by Benedict of Aniane (ca. 750–821) as part of a monastic movement that could not pray often enough. To the Divine Office, the daily (including nightly) round of prayers the medieval Church required of her ordained (priests, monks, and nuns), were added the Hours of the Virgin. By the mid-eleventh century, they were an established Church practice. By the late twelfth century, the Hours were also found in Psalters, the prayer books containing all 150 Psalms, a Calendar, and among other prayers, usually the Litany and the Office of the Dead. By the early thirteenth century, an era of increased literacy, both Psalters and the combined Psalter-Hours were used by not only the clergy but also the laity. By the mid-thirteenth century, however, laypeople began commissioning their prayer books *without* the cumbersome Psalter, but with the other parts, such as the Calendar, Hours of the Virgin, Litany, and Office of the Dead, intact. Thus, the Book of Hours as we know it was born. By the late fourteenth century, the typical Book of Hours consisted of a Calendar, Gospel Lessons, Hours of the Virgin, **Hours of the Holy Cross**, **Hours of the Holy Spirit**, the two Marian prayers called the "**Obsecro te**" and the "**O intemerata**," the Penitential Psalms and Litany, the Office of the Dead, and a group of about a dozen **Suffrages**; any number of accessory prayers complemented these essential texts.

Books of Hours were easy, even enjoyable, to use. The core text, the Hours of the Virgin, remained basically the same every day. The only variable was the three Psalms that constitute the nocturn of the first Hour, Matins. (The three Psalms changed depending on the day of the week: Psalms[1] 8, 18, and 23 are read on Sundays, Mondays, and Thursdays; Psalms 44, 45, and 86 on Tuesdays and Fridays; and Psalms 95, 96, and 97 on Wednesdays and Saturdays; in addition, some *Horae* contain minor textual variations for the Advent and Christmas seasons, but this is more the exception than the rule.) The contents of the remaining Hours, Lauds

[1]The numbering of the Psalms follows the Vulgate version of the Bible.

through Compline, did not change at all. And the other parts of the typical Book of Hours were also unchanging: Gospel Lessons, Hours of the Cross and of the Holy Spirit, Penitential Psalms, and so forth. One was certainly encouraged to pray the Hours of the Virgin (and, time permitting, the Hours of the Cross and of the Holy Spirit) and the Office of the Dead on a daily basis. The other common texts offered variation, as did the numerous accessory prayers that owners freely included in their *Horae*.

A Book of Hours printed in 1538 in Rouen for English export by Nicholas le Roux for François Regnault contains an introductory section called "The Preface and the Manner to Live Well" (spelling modernized). Its instructions reveal how a Book of Hours was used:

> First rise up at six of the clock in the morning in all seasons and in your rising do as follows. Thank Our Lord of rest that he gave you that night, commend you to God, Blessed Lady Saint Mary, and to that saint which is feasted that day. . . . When you have arrayed yourself in your chamber or lodging, [say] Matins, Prime, and Hours if you may. Then go to the church . . . , and abide in the church the space of a low mass, while there you shall think and thank God for his benefits. . . . When you are come from the church, take heed to your household or occupation till dinner time. . . . Then take your refection or meal reasonably, without excess or over much. . . . Rest you after dinner an hour or half an hour as you think best. . . . As touching your service, say unto Terce before dinner, and make an end of all before supper. And when you may, say Dirige [Office of the Dead] and Commendations for all Christian souls, at the least way on the Holy Days and, if you have leisure, say them on other days, at the least with three lessons. . . . (The Pierpont Morgan Library, New York, PML 19585, fols. C6r–C8r)

Until around 1400, Books of Hours were entirely in Latin. Around this time, some French appeared in *Horae* made in France, but it was not a significant amount (Calendars, some rubrics, and a few accessory prayers might be in the vernacular). The same can be said about the extent of English in Books of Hours made in England or made for use there. The only major role played by a vernacular language in *Horae* history is with Dutch manuscripts. Geert Grote (d. 1384) translated the standard *Horae* texts into Dutch as part of the *Devotio moderna*, the Late Medieval reforming movement that encouraged pious reading in the vernacular. This translation achieved great success, and in the fifteenth and sixteenth centuries, Books of Hours produced in the northern Netherlands were almost always in Dutch. Disregarding this latter phenomenon, however, Books of Hours are books of Latin. How much did the lay reader understand? Probably more than we might initially think. Speakers of French and Italian, of course, had an easy ear for the language. Plus, the great armature for the Book of Hours is Psalms. A total of thirty-seven Psalms form the Hours of the Virgin; these did not change. Nor did the seven of the Penitential Psalms or the twenty-two in the Office of the Dead. Other biblical excerpts—the Gospel Lessons, the Passion according to John, and the readings from the Book of Job (in the Office of the Dead)—would become equally familiar over time. Much of the remaining Latin is in rhymed verse, such as the "**Stabat Mater**" and "**Salve sancta facies**," or as with the Suffrages, it is rather simple "Church" Latin.

Most literate people had some working knowledge of Latin, and they knew basic prayers—"Ave Maria" [Hail Mary], "Pater noster" [Our Father], "Credo" [Apostles' Creed], and "**Confiteor**" [Act of Confession]—by heart. As children they learned to read from Books of Hours (Fig. 1). In England, Books of Hours were called "primers," a term that eventually came to mean the book from which a child first learned to read and pray; the word derives from the Hour of Prime.

Another reason Books of Hours were so popular was because of the people who used them: the laity. In a kind of bibliophilic jealousy, laypeople during this period sought for themselves a book that paralleled the use and function of the Breviary, the book containing the Divine Office that the clergy prayed from daily. In an age when rood screens blocked all but the most fleeting views of the Mass, when squints were pierced into walls in an effort to offer some glimpse of the elevated Eucharist, when, in other words, the laity's access to God was very much controlled and limited by others than themselves, Books of Hours bestowed direct, democratic, and potentially uninterrupted access to God, the Virgin Mary, and the saints.

How people felt about their Books of Hours is reflected in the varied marks of ownership—sometimes proud, sometimes personal—that they had

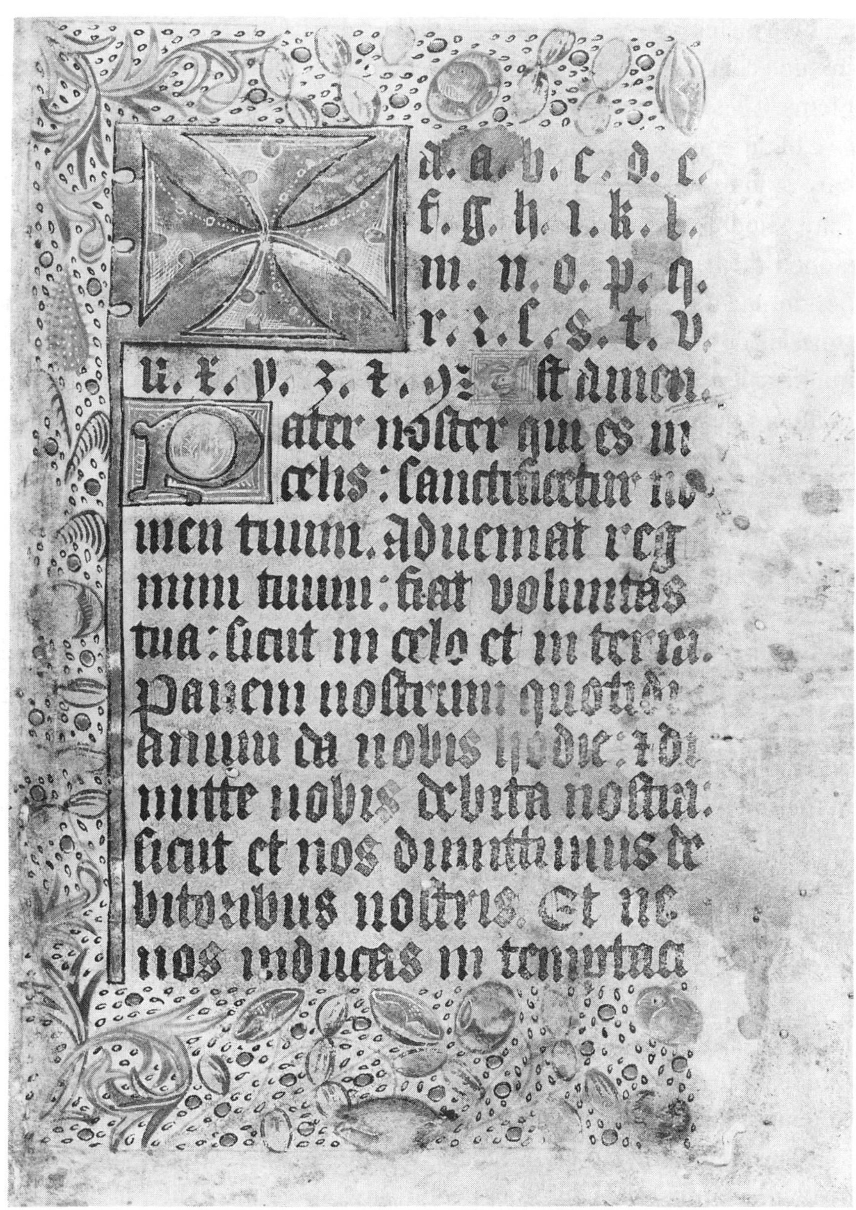

a. a. b. c. d. e.
f. g. h. i. k. l.
m. n. o. p. q.
r. ꝛ. ſ. s. t. v.
u. x. y. z. ⁊. ꝯ. Est amen.
Pater noster qui es in
celis: sanctificetur no
men tuum. Adueniat reg
num tuum: fiat voluntas
tua: sicut in celo et in terra.
Panem nostrum quotidi
anum da nobis hodie. Et di
mitte nobis debita nostra:
sicut et nos dimittimus de
bitoribus nostris. Et ne
nos inducas in temptaci

Figure 1. ABC, Pater noster, from an Hours for Sarum use. England, Winchester? 1490s (The Pierpont Morgan Library, New York. MS M.487, fol. 1r).

painted on their pages. Portraits abound (Fig. 2). Other marks of ownership include coats of arms, initials and monograms, mottoes, and personal emblems. These elements are used singly or in all combinations imaginable.

In the course of their three-hundred-year history, Books of Hours offer case studies covering all the possibilities of how men and women of the Late Middle Ages and Renaissance acquired their books. People commissioned them, received them as gifts (brides especially), inherited them, bought them new or secondhand from booksellers, borrowed them, sometimes made them themselves, and indeed even stole them. The range in their quality—from a specially illuminated manuscript with hundreds of pictures to a poor man's unillustrated *Horae* printed on paper—speaks not only of deep or shallow pockets but also of a vast audience with a shared mind-set. By the late fifteenth century, when printing opened *Horae* ownership to a whole new category of customers, nearly any literate soul, even on the slimmest income, could buy one.

A great part—really the greater part—of this lay audience was female, and women played a key role in the patronage of Books of Hours throughout their entire history. In the first hundred and fifty years, this patronage was essential, and it was due to women that the genre took off. Women, it was thought by their male clerical advisers, needed the pictures to help them in their piety. The images were, literally, visual aids.

This, finally, leads one to consider the pictures, for therein, too, lies much significance for the continual popularity and success of Books of Hours. As well liked now via Christmas cards as they were then, the pictures in any Book of Hours were often the only form of art possessed by its owner. Even to the wealthy, who could commission paintings and tapestries for their castle or chapel walls, miniatures in Books of Hours were a continuous source of aesthetic pleasure. One did not *need* more than one Book of Hours, but those who could afford to sometimes owned several.

The pictures in Books of Hours, whether manuscript or printed, were, of course, versions of subjects people saw at church. The main text, the Hours of the Virgin, was marked by a series of pictures illustrating either Christ's Infancy or his Passion. The events relating Christ's birth or his

Figure 2. Miracle of St. Hubert and Pierre de Bosredont Hunting, by Guillaume Hugueniot, from the Hours of Pierre de Bosredont, for Rome use. France, Langres, ca. 1465 (The Pierpont Morgan Library, New York. MS G.55, fols. 124v–125r).

death were the same to be seen in the multiple panels of an altarpiece. A Book of Hours mirrored the high points of the Church's liturgical year in pictorial form. Suffrages were illustrated by images of saints who were also seen at church. Books of Hours linked church and home. The entire celestial court, God and his cosmos, could be held within the palms of one's hands and taken home. Used there, the Book of Hours transformed one's chamber into a chapel.

In addition to aesthetic pleasure, these pictures had two additional functions. On a practical level, they indicated where the major texts began: they were bookmarks (Books of Hours, manuscript or printed, originally were neither foliated nor paginated). Second, as they marked certain texts, they also embodied them. They provided the themes upon which to meditate.

The usual themes for the standard texts of the Book of Hours can be summarized thus:

TEXT	IMAGE
Calendar	Labors
	Zodiac
Gospel Lessons	John on Patmos
	Luke
	Matthew
	Mark
Hours of the Virgin	
Infancy cycle	
Matins	Annunciation
Lauds	Visitation
Prime	Nativity
Terce	Annunciation to the Shepherds
Sext	Adoration of the Magi
None	Presentation
Vespers	Flight into Egypt or Massacre of the Innocents
Compline	Coronation of the Virgin
Passion cycle	
Matins	Agony
Lauds	Betrayal
Prime	Christ before Pilate
Terce	Flagellation
Sext	Christ Carrying the Cross
None	Crucifixion
Vespers	Deposition
Compline	Entombment
Hours of the Cross	Crucifixion
Hours of the Holy Spirit	Pentecost
"Obsecro te"	Virgin and Child

"O intemerata"	Lamentation
Penitential Psalms	David in Penance or Bathsheba at Her Bath or Christ Enthroned or Last Judgment
Office of the Dead	Praying the Office of the Dead or Burial or Last Judgment or Job on the Dungheap or Raising of Lazarus or Lazarus and Dives or Death Personified or Three Living and Three Dead

The history of Books of Hours is also the history of Late Medieval and Renaissance manuscript illumination. This history includes illustrious artists who worked on both panel and vellum. From the fourteenth century, for example, one thinks of the Master of the Parement de Narbonne (probably Jean d'Orléans) and, from the fifteenth century, Jan van Eyck, Bartélemy van Eyck (related by art but not blood), Simon Marmion, and the three famous Jeans—Fouquet, Poyet, and Bourdichon. French artists who specialized in illumination and who are famous for their pictures in Books of Hours include the Boucicaut Master and his followers (such as the Master of the Harvard Hannibal), the Bedford Master, Jean Colombe, and Maître François. Flemish illuminators include the Master of Guillebert de Mets, the Master of the Ghent Privileges, the Masters of the Gold Scrolls, Willem Vrelant, the Master of the Dresden Prayer Book, Simon Bening, and the Master of Charles V. The greatest of all Dutch manuscripts is a Book of Hours, painted by the eponymous Master of the Hours of Catherine of Cleves. And when Giulio Clovio completed the Farnese Hours in 1546, after nine years of work, the result was a manuscript that so dazzled Vasari that the author felt compelled to describe all of its miniatures in the second edition of his *Lives of the Painters*; Vasari called the manuscript one of the "marvels of Rome."

When Books of Hours came to be printed, beginning in the 1480s, their pictures ensured their meteoric success. Between 1480 and 1600 there were some 1,775 different *Horae* editions printed. This success was due in part to the cycles of border vignettes with which the printers embellished their products. This was a selling point, and they knew it; printers often boasted about the pictures on their title pages. As the following selective list indicates, the cycles' range of subjects (in addition to the standard ones given above in the chart) is quite extraordinary: lives of Christ and the Virgin, saints and evangelists, the Dance of Death, the trials of Job, children's games, heroines, sibyls, the Fifteen Signs of the Second Coming, the story of Joseph, the Seven Sacraments, the Seven Virtues, the Seven Vices, the Triumphs of Caesar, the story of Tobias, the Miracles of Our Lady, the story of Judith, the Destruction of Jerusalem, and, finally, the Apocalypse.

Books of Hours are one of the most instructive vehicles for understanding the relationship of liturgy to everyday men and women of the late Middle Ages and Renaissance. Ironically, the collection of prayers represented by the typical Book of Hours was never officially sanctioned nor controlled by the Church herself. This irony means, however, that the texts and their accompanying pictures are a true, uncensored, mirror of how the Church's liturgy was perceived and practiced by the unordained masses.

Calendar

Calendars, at the front of all Books of Hours, had the same function in the Middle Ages as calendars today: they tell one what day it is. They do this, however, not by enumerating the days of the month but by citing the feast that was celebrated on that particular day. Today, when we speak of St. Valentine's Day, St. Patrick's Day, or Halloween, we know we are referring to 14 February, 17 March, and 31 October. This is the medieval way of telling time.

The feasts listed in Calendars are mostly saints' days, that is, commemorations of those particular days on which, tradition customarily has it, the saints were martyred (their "birthdays" into heaven). Other feasts commemorate important events in the lives of Christ and the Virgin. In addition to Christmas Eve and Christmas, Calendars celebrate Christ's **Circumcision** (1 January) and the **Epiphany** (6 January). The Virgin's feasts include her **Conception** (8 December) and **Birth** (8 September), the **Annunciation** (25 March) and Visitation (2 July), the **Purification of the Virgin in the Temple** (2 February; as in Fig. 3), and her **Assumption** into Heaven (15 August). No Calendars include the events of Christ's Passion, his Resurrection, or his Ascension, or Pentecost. These were **moveable feasts** whose dates depend upon that of Easter, the celebration of which changed every year. Thus, Calendars in Books of Hours (like those in the Church's official liturgical service books) are perpetual calendars since they can be used from one year to the next.

Some feasts are more important than others, and their relative importance, or grading, is indicated. Most feasts are in black ink, whereas the more important ones appear in red (hence our term ***red-letter*** **day**, meaning a major event; in Figure 3, for example, the Feast of St. Ignatius on 1 February is in black while the Purification on the 2nd is in red). Some Calendars have triple gradations, with the most important holy days in gold, the less solemn in red, and the least in black. These genuinely **triple-graded Calendars** are not to be confused with those deluxe ones from around 1400 whose highly decorative layouts simply alternate their feasts in red and blue, but with the more important ones in gold.

Many Calendars from the thirteenth to the early fifteenth centuries include a number of blank spaces (as in Fig. 3). These represent the ferial days, that is, days within the middle of the week on which the feast of a saint was not celebrated. Liturgically this meant that the Mass for that particular day related to the season (from 2 January to 5, for example, the Mass of the Circumcision was said on ferial days). Calendars of the later fifteenth and sixteenth centuries, on the other hand, tend to be composites, with a saint's feast supplied for every day. While visually appealing, to the medieval eye, such Calendars were of little practical use.

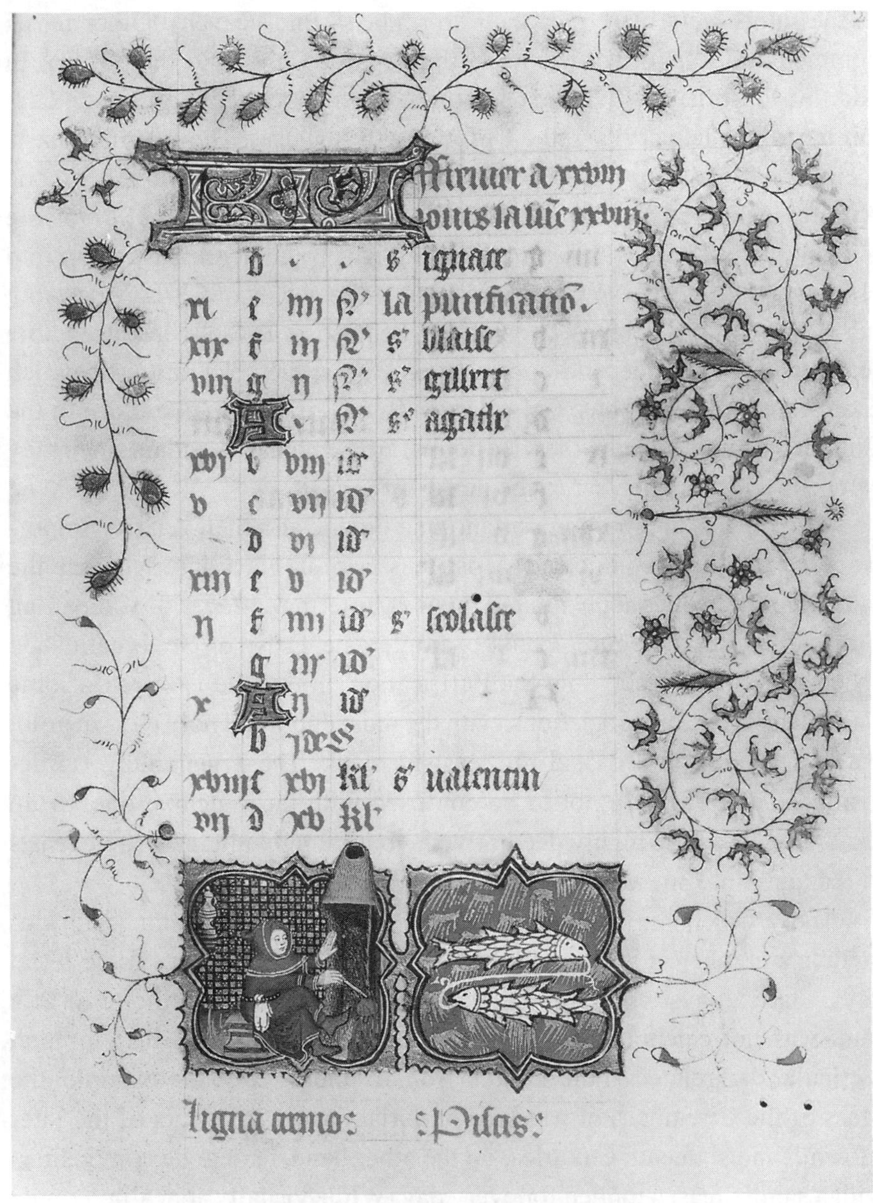

Figure 3. February, from an Hours for Rome use. Northern France, early fifteenth century (The Pierpont Morgan Library, New York. MS M.264, fol. 2r).

While most of the feasts mentioned so far have been universal (celebrated by the Church as a whole), Calendars in Books of Hours, like those in Missals or Breviaries, also include feasts of a more local interest. These help determine the Calendar's "use," that is, the place where the manuscript was intended to be prayed. Local festivals can indicate the country, region, city, parish, or in a few rare instances, the particular church in which a Book of Hours was to be used. Paris Calendars, for example, always highlight the feasts of Sts. Geneviève, patroness of the city (3 January), and Denis, patron saint of France, whose place of martyrdom, Montmartre, is named after that occurrence (9 September). Calendars for Reims list Sts. Gervasius (19 June), Martialis (3 July), and the sixth-century bishop of the city, Romanus (23 October), as red-letter days. A feast celebrating the transfer (or sometimes theft) of a saint's relics from one site to another (called a translation) is also a good indicator for local use. Rouen Calendars celebrate the translations of Sts. Audoenus, to whom a magnificent fourteenth-century church is dedicated (5 May), Eligius (25 May), and a general feast of all the city's translations (3 December).

The use of a Calendar can be helpful (but one must be careful) in determining where the Book of Hours was actually made. Paris Calendars almost always mean "made in Paris" since, with its productive workshops, the French capital had no need to import manuscripts made elsewhere. Most Dutch Books of Hours, too, were made locally. But many *Horae* with English Calendars were manufactured in Flanders or France, both of which exported many manuscripts to England. Books of Hours with Spanish Calendars, too, often were made in Belgium. The situation continued with printed *Horae* but is less confusing since their colophons or title pages often give, in addition to the manuscript's use, the name and city of the printer.

In addition to feast days, *Horae* Calendars contain other information. At the far left in most is a column of Roman numerals running from from *i* to *xix* (the series is not consecutive, however, and there are gaps). These are the Golden Numbers, which indicate the appearances of new moons and, counting ahead fourteen days, full moons throughout the year. Adjacent to the Golden Numbers are repeating series of letters running *A* through *G*. These are the Dominical Letters, so called because they help one find Sundays (and, of course, all the other days of the week) throughout the year. Each year this Sunday Letter changed, moving backward. In leap years it changed a second time (on 25 February); thus, feasts, which in non-leap years fell on subsequent days, now "leaped" to two days apart.

This esoteric information was important to medieval Christians. With it they could determine the date of Easter, the Church's most important feast, in any given year. Easter was celebrated on the Sunday following the first full moon that falls on or after the vernal equinox (the spring day when day and night are the same length); should the full moon occur on a Sunday, Easter is then pushed to the following Sunday. The varying occurrence, from one year to the next, of that first full moon and the occasional pushed Sunday account for the widely disparate dates for medieval (and modern) Easters.

Finally, many Calendars, especially those from the thirteenth to the mid-fifteenth century, include the ancient Roman calendrical system. In this most confusing of all systems, each month had but three fixed points: Kalends (always the first day of the month and whence we derive our term calendar), Ides (the middle of the month, either the thirteenth or fifteenth), and Nones (the ninth day before the Ides, counting inclusively; it fell on the fifth or seventh of the month). All the days in between were counted backward from these three fixed points. Thus St. Valentine's Day was not 14 February according to Roman time, but *xvi Kalends Martii*, or the sixteenth day before the Kalends of March (Fig. 3).

Medieval time was Roman time. It followed the reformed but still imperfect system instituted by Julius Caesar. By the thirteenth century, it was noticeably out of sync with reality, and by the late Middle Ages, full moons were not appearing until ten days after the Calendars said they were supposed to. Easter was moving on into summer. Pope Gregory XIII (papacy, 1572–85) reformed the Julian calendar and, adding ten days (4 October in 1582 was followed by 15 October) and other fine tunings, instituted in 1583 the Gregorian calendar we still use today.

When illustrated—which is only about half the time—Calendars contain representations of the signs of the zodiac and labors of the months. While the Calendar miniatures of the ***Très Riches Heures*** of Jean, duc de Berry, are among the most famous of all illuminations, they are also something of a freak, for Calendar illustrations are normally small or half-page miniatures or marginal vignettes. The traditional assignment to the months of the zodiacal signs and the labors (and a few leisures), which follow the rural peasant activities dictated by seasons, are:

MONTH	ZODIAC	LABOR
January	Aquarius (Water Carrier)	Feasting
February	Pisces (Fish)	Keeping Warm
March	Aries (Ram)	Pruning
April	Taurus (Bull)	Picking Flowers
May	Gemini (Twins)	Hawking
June	Cancer (Crab)	Mowing
July	Leo (Lion)	Reaping
August	Virgo (Virgin)	Threshing
September	Libra (Balance)	Treading Grapes
October	Scorpio (Scorpion)	Sowing
November	Sagittarius (Archer)	Thrashing for Acorns
December	Capricorn (Goat)	Slaughtering a Pig

While Calendar illustrations were traditionally small, through the course of the fifteenth century artists and their patrons took an increasing interest in these secular elements, and they indeed began to grow. Simon Bening (1483/84–1561), the last great Flemish illuminator, capitalized on the taste for large Calendar miniatures; he made them full-page. Ironically, Bening was stimulated by the singular Book of Hours just mentioned, the *Très Riches Heures,* which the artist saw when it was in the library of Margaret of Austria in Malines.

Gospel Lessons

Following the Calendar the first text proper in a Book of Hours is a series of Gospel Lessons by the four evangelists. Although not always found in *Horae* of the thirteenth and fourteenth centuries, by the fifteenth these Lessons had become a regular feature.

The first reading, from John (1:1–14), is a kind of preamble for the entire Book of Hours: "In principio erat Verbum . . ." [In the beginning was the Word . . .]. The Word of God, existing from eternity, becomes the revealer of the Father and the light of men. The text emphasizes the eternal generation of the Word, who is Christ, mankind's need of redemption, and God's willingness to provide it. The passage continues, alluding to the witness of John the Baptist, mankind's rejection of Christ, and Christians as the new children of God, and ends with the Incarnation. Luke's Lesson (1:26–38) describes the Annunciation: "Missus est Angelus Gabriel . . ." [The angel Gabriel was sent from God . . .]. Gabriel addresses the Virgin: "Ave gratia plena . . ." [Hail, full of grace, the Lord is with thee: blessed art thou among women], the salutation that would become the first part of the Hail Mary. Luke's account ends with the Virgin's acceptance of God's will. The reading from Matthew (2:1–12), after mentioning the birth of Christ, launches into the story of the Three Magi: "Cum natus esset Jesus . . ." [When Jesus was born . . .]. The passage relates the Magi's interview before Herod, their worship of Christ, their gifts, and, finally, their return home. Mark's Lesson (16:14–20), "Recumbentibus undecim discipulis . . ." [Jesus appeared to the eleven as they were at table . . .], relates Christ's appearance to the apostles after the Resurrection, his command to preach salvation throughout the world, his granting miraculous powers to them, and, finally, his Ascension.

Except for Christ's Passion, these excerpts touch on the major events from the life of the Savior. Two of them, indeed, dwell especially on the Christmas story, those events from Christ's Infancy that were so dear to medieval people. These readings, however, were not arbitrarily chosen from the New Testament for insertion into *Horae*. They are the Gospel Lessons read at Mass on four of the Church's major feasts: Christmas Day, 25 December (John's reading is from the main Mass of the day); the Annunciation on 25 March (Luke); Epiphany, 6 January (Matthew); and the Ascension, a movable feast whose date depended upon that of Easter (Mark). Each Book of Hours thus contained, in a way, the essence of the Church's liturgical year, encapsulated in these four readings. Earlier the Book of Hours was described as a kind of lay Breviary; with these Gospel Lessons, the Book of Hours also steals a small but important group of texts from the Missal. The Lessons in a Book of Hours, however, are not arranged in *liturgical* order. Their sequence has been altered so that their composite narrative relates the events in their proper *chronological* order: God's divine plan (John); the Annunciation and Incarnation (Luke); Christ's Nativity and his manifestation to the world (Matthew);and Christ's sending his apostles on their missionary way and his Ascension (Mark).

By the Late Middle Ages, these particular passages had acquired a special, almost magical position in the lay mind. As Eamon Duffy has related, priests were hired to recite them as protection against harm or damage to one's house. In England they sometimes were read aloud during annual processions that blessed the parish in the hope of scattering demons and ensuring the fertility of the fields. John's Lesson, one of the most numinous texts of this period, was used at the blessing of bread at the Offertory of Sunday Mass and was the final Gospel recited by the priest at the end of each Mass (after the "Ite missa est" [Go, the Mass is ended]). Pope Clement V (papacy, 1305–14) issued an indulgence of one year and forty days to those who, while listening to the last Gospel, kissed something—a book, a sacred object, or even their thumbnail—at the words, "Verbum caro factum est" [The Word was made flesh]. Such osculation mirrored the reverential genuflection by the priest reading these words at the end of Mass. Inscribed on a strip of vellum and hung around the neck, this sacred text was thought to ward off evil; ailing cattle could be cured by this charm if dangled from their horns.

Christ's Passion was the one important part of the Savior's life not covered by the four Lessons. This *lacuna* was clearly felt by the owners of Books of Hours, with the result that the story of the Passion was often included in *Horae* in the form of an extra reading taken from John (18:1–19:42). This is the haunting eyewitness account by the one apostle who remained at the foot of the cross, along with Mary, during the Crucifixion. It was John's version of the Passion with which people were most familiar: this account was read or chanted on Good Friday. John's Passion, something of an optional text in manuscript *Horae*, became standard in printed editions. In the latter, it is almost always found right after the customary four Lessons.

In a tradition that can be traced back to classical antiquity via Carolingian Gospel Books, each of the four Gospel Lessons usually had a portrait of its author as a frontispiece (Fig. 4). The evangelists are usually accompanied by their symbols: John's eagle, Luke's ox, Matthew's angel, and Mark's lion. John, whose text appears first, is normally shown on the isle of his exile, Patmos. The other three evangelists are usually shown as authors/scribes. Some *Horae*, instead of author portraits, depict scenes from the evangelists' lives. The most popular of these is John Boiled in Oil, the (ultimately unsuccessful) torture put to him by Emperor Domitian. Luke is sometimes shown painting a portrait of the Virgin, which tradition has it he executed from life.

In addition to evangelist portraits and scenes from their lives, miniatures for the Gospel Lessons sometimes (albeit rarely) depict events described or alluded to in the texts themselves. A French Book of Hours illuminated around 1465 by the Master of Jacques de Luxembourg (Pierpont Morgan Library, MS M.1003), for example, features the Last Supper for John, God Sending Forth the Christ Child to the Virgin Annunciate for Luke, the Journey of the Magi for Matthew, and the Ascension for Mark. John's Passion, the "fifth" Lesson, was often illustrated by one of the opening events of the Passion: Christ's Agony in the Garden, Betrayal, or the "Ego sum" (when Christ's response, "I am the one," to the soldiers who sought him made them fall to the ground in amazement).

Figure 4. Matthew, by the Master of the Ango Hours, from an Hours for Orléans use. France, Rouen, datable to 1525 (The Pierpont Morgan Library, New York. MS M.61, fol. 17r).

Hours of the Virgin

Traditionally the Hours of the Virgin follow the Gospel Lessons. There are eight separate Hours: Matins, Lauds, Prime, Terce, Sext, None, Vespers, and Compline. Each Hour consists mostly of Psalms, plus varying combinations of hymns, prayers, and lessons, to which innumerable short ejaculations (antiphons, versicles, and responses) are generously sprinkled. Mimicking canonical devotion, these eight Hours were ideally prayed throughout the course of the day: Matins and Lauds were said together at night or upon rising, Prime (first hour) around 6 A.M., Terce (third hour) at 9 A.M., Sext (sixth hour) around noon, None (ninth hour) at 3 P.M., Vespers (evensong) in early evening, and Compline before retiring.

Part of the attraction of the Hours of the Virgin for the laity is their constancy. The same basic Hours were prayed day in, day out. This sameness was clearly a comfort. Repeated on a daily basis from childhood to old age, the Hours of the Virgin became a familiar, steadfast friend. Variety could be had by adding, mixing, or substituting the Hours of the Cross and the Hours of the Holy Spirit or, indeed, any of the multiple ancillary prayers.

While the Psalms of the Old Testament form the core of the Hours of the Virgin, they do not, of course, mention the Virgin Mary. One of the great beauties of the Hours is how the Psalms throughout are given a second level of reading, a mystical interpretation. The theme of Psalm (Ps.) 8 (the first of the first nocturn) is the glory of God as shown in nature and in man:

> **Ps.** O Lord our Lord: how admirable is thy name in the whole earth! For thy magnificence is elevated above the heavens. Out of the mouths of infants and of sucklings thou hast perfected praise. . . . What is man that thou art mindful of him? . . . Thou hast made him a little less than the angels. . . .

Through the antiphons that begin and end, as a kind of frame, each Psalm, its themes are applied to the Mother of God. "Blessed art thou" is said before the Psalm; like a musical motif whose opening notes are enough to recall its entirety, the opening antiphon was only a short phrase. "Blessed art thou amongst women, and blessed is the fruit of thy womb" is the closing antiphon, said at the completion of Psalm 8. Thus, the theme of the Psalm—the glory of God made manifest in both nature and man—is expanded through the theme of the antiphons, the miracle of the Incarnation. Not only is man worthy of salvation but also this salvation is also brought about through the Virgin Mary, a member of the human race. The nocturn continues with Psalm 18:

> **Ps.** The heavens show forth the glory of God: and the firmament declareth the work of his hands. . . . The justices of the Lord are right, rejoicing hearts: the commandment of the Lord is lightsome, enlightening the eyes. . . .

The Psalm's theme is the splendor of the physical and moral orders of the universe. The short form of the antiphon recited at the beginning of the Psalm, "Even as choice myrrh," is expanded to its complete form at the end, "Even as choice myrrh, thou hast yielded an odor of sweetness, O holy Mother of God." The phrase compares Divine Wisdom to the choicest myrrh and, by extension, to the Virgin Mary. Psalm 23 is the third and last Psalm of the nocturn:

> **Ps.** . . . Lift up your gates, O ye princes, and be ye lifted up, O eternal gates: and the King of Glory shall enter in. Who is this King of Glory? The Lord of hosts, he is the King of Glory.

After the conquest of the Promised Land, the Ark of the Covenant was kept in various places until David's accession; he transferred it to his capital, Jerusalem. Tradition holds that David wrote Psalm 23 to celebrate this joyous occasion; it praises the majesty of the Lord and his glorious entrance into his shrine. "Before the couch," the opening antiphon, is expanded to "Before the couch of this Virgin sing to us often sweet songs with solemnity," recited at the end. The antiphon exhorts us to sing praises before the Virgin who, receiving Christ at the Incarnation, is the new Ark of the Covenant.

After the three Psalms there follow the nocturn's three lessons, whose teachings reiterate themes introduced by the Psalms and expanded by their antiphons. The three readings speak of Eternal Wisdom and its dwelling place on earth. Mystically interpreted, Eternal Wisdom is taken to be the Incarnate Christ. The Hours also apply these texts to the Virgin. Responses recited after the lessons, like the Psalms' Antiphons, guide the reader in these interpretations.

Like Calendars, the Hours of the Virgin will be for a specific "use." Use is reflected in textual variations that go back to the ancient monastic traditions of different locales. The variations most easily detected are in the Hours of Prime and None, in particular, the ***capitulum*** [a short reading near the end of the Hour] and the antiphon immediately preceding it. Thus, for Rome use, Prime's capitulum is "Que est ista . . ." [Who is she . . .] and its antiphon "Assumpta est Maria . . ." [Mary is taken up . . .]. None's capitulum is "In plateis . . ." [In the streets . . .] and its antiphon "Pulchra es . . ." [Thou art beautiful . . .].

Composed at least by the ninth century, the Hours of the Virgin had consoled the ordained for hundreds of years before they became the center of lay devotion in the mid-thirteenth century. By the mid-sixteenth century, the decline of the Hours of the Virgin began. The Council of Trent (1545–63), as evident in the Council's ensuing catechism, emphasized prayer directly to God. The manuscripts are no longer commissioned; the printed editions peter out. In 1568 Pope Pius V removed the general obligation on the part of the clergy to say the Hours of the Virgin as part of their Divine Office (although Breviaries, even till the twentieth century, continued to contain them). In the 1960s, the Second Vatican Council revised the Breviary and, quashing a tradition extending back over a thousand years, entirely eliminated the Hours of the Virgin from the Church's new official prayer book, *The Liturgy of the Hours*. The Hours of the Virgin are no more.

In most *Horae* the Hours of the Virgin are illustrated by the awe-inspiring events in the Virgin's life surrounding the Infancy of Christ (see above chart): Annunciation (Fig. 5) through the Flight into Egypt. Many cycles end, however, with the Coronation of the Virgin, Mary's reward, in a way, for her role in God's plan. Accompanying or substituting for the

Figure 5. Annunciation, by Jean Poyet, from the so-called Hours of Henry VIII, for Rome use. France, Tours, ca. 1500 (The Pierpont Morgan Library, New York. MS H.8, fol. 30v).

traditional Infancy cycle is sometimes a series of illustrations of Christ's Passion. And then there are some Hours that begin with an Annunciation, but break into a Passion cycle at Lauds that continues through the rest of the Hours. Finally, some rare Hours of the Virgin are illustrated not with the Christian anti-type but with the Old Testament or pagan type. The use of typology, popularized in the fifteenth century by the ***Speculum humanae salvationis*** and the ***Biblia pauperum,*** led to the frequent insertion of a picture of Augustus and the Tiburtine Sibyl (also called the Vision of the *Ara coeli*) at Lauds in printed *Horae*.

Hours of the Cross and Hours of the Holy Spirit

The Hours of the Cross and Hours of the Holy Spirit are much shorter than those of the Virgin. The canonical sequencing is the same, Matins through Compline, except there is no Lauds. These two additional Hours, one after the other, often follow the Hours of the Virgin. Sometimes, however, there occur in *Horae* what are called mixed Hours. In these cases, the individual Hours are integrated within the Hours of the Virgin. Thus, Matins of the Cross and Matins of the Holy Spirit are found right after Matins and Lauds of the Virgin; Prime of the Cross and Prime of the Holy Spirit after Prime of the Virgin; Terce of the Cross and Terce of the Holy Spirit after Terce of the Virgin; and so forth.

Each of the Hours of the Cross consists of two pairs of versicles and responses, a "Gloria Patri" followed by an antiphon, a short hymn followed by a versicle and a response, and a prayer; there are no Psalms. The structure and contents of each of the remaining Hours (Prime through Compline) is the same except for the hymn, which is, in each Hour, a different stanza from a devotional poem whose verses form meditations on sequential moments of Christ's Passion. Matins's hymn speaks of Christ's betrayal and arrest; Prime speaks of Christ before Pilate; Terce, Christ's crowning with thorns; Sext, the Crucifixion; None, Christ's death; Vespers, the Deposition; and Compline, the Entombment.

The Hours of the Holy Spirit follow the same structure as those of the Cross. The hymns of the Hours touch upon different themes relating to the attributes of the Holy Spirit or the role he played or will play in the history of mankind's redemption. Matins discusses the Incarnation; Prime, Redemption through Christ's Passion; Terce, Pentecost; Sext, the Apostles' proselytization; None, the qualities of the Holy Spirit; Vespers, the Holy Spirit as Protector; and Compline, the Last Judgment.

Sometimes the Hours of the Cross and those of the Holy Spirit are full Offices. As such, they are equal in length to and their structure parallels the Hours of the Virgin: they include Lauds; all Hours contain Psalms; and Matins has lessons. These longer Offices appear in manuscripts less frequently than the shorter Hours, and in printed *Horae* they hardly appear at all.

The subject for the single miniature that traditionally marks the Hours of the Cross is a Crucifixion. When the Hours are the longer Office, they often have a miniature at each Hour (the iconography is akin to the Passion series for the Hours of the Virgin). The traditional miniature for the Hours of the Holy Spirit is a Pentecost. When these Hours are the longer Office, they might have a set of eight pictures whose themes relate to various manifestations of the Holy Spirit; these will always include a Baptism of Christ and Pentecost, and often scenes of Peter or Paul preaching or baptizing.

"Obsecro te" and "O intemerata"

Two special prayers to the Virgin appear in nearly all fifteenth- and sixteenth-century Books of Hours. They are known by their incipits [opening words]: "Obsecro te" [I beseech you] and "O intemerata" [O immaculate Virgin]. Written in the first person singular, the prayers address the Virgin directly in especially plaintive, urgent tones. They are among the most moving of all *Horae* prayers and encapsulate the essence of Late Medieval spirituality.

The "Obsecro te" has four main sections. It opens by addressing the Virgin, reciting a list of her qualities, especially those emphasizing her tenderness; the prayer then invokes Mary's help by reminding her of the joyful role she played in the Incarnation; it then moves on to the Virgin's sorrows and the role she played in Christ's Passion; and, finally, the prayer's petition for aid appears. The petition ends with its most moving request: "And at the end of my life show me your face, and reveal to me the day and hour of my death. . . ." The slightly shorter "O intemerata" has a similar tone and structure. It, however, asks both Mary and St. John, as witnesses to the Crucifixion and thus through their special relationship to the crucified Christ, to "be, at every hour and every moment of my life, inside and outside me, my steadfast guardians and pious intercessors before God . . . , for you can obtain whatever you ask from God without delay." This last phrase is crucial. The goal was to secure the aid of intercessors to plead his or her case before a God who was more just than merciful. The Virgin and St. John, with hearts more forgiving than a righteous God's, would certainly pity the sinner. And surely God would not deny a petition from the only two people who did not fail him at the foot of the cross.

Since the first part of the "Obsecro te" emphasizes the Virgin's joy during Christ's Infancy, the prayer is frequently illustrated with a Virgin and Child, often entertained by musical angels (Fig. 6). Since the prayer is in the first person singular, the miniature was also a popular place for owners to insert their portraits. Very often, a triangular series of glances illustrates the nature of the intercession. The patron looks to Mary, who then glances toward and caresses her son; Christ, encouraged by his mother, looks at the owner and bestows the sought-for blessing. Since the main theme of the "O intemerata" is the faithfulness of the Virgin and John at the Crucifixion, a Lamentation (the great low point in Mary and John's witness) often illustrates this prayer.

Penitential Psalms and Litany

The Seven Penitential Psalms usually follow the Hours of the Cross and the Hours of the Holy Spirit. Medieval tradition ascribed the authorship of these

Figure 6. Madonna Enthroned, with Patron, by Maître François, from an Hours for Paris use. France, Paris, ca. 1470 (The Pierpont Morgan Library, New York. MS M.73, fol 13r).

seven Psalms (6, 31, 37, 50, 101, 129, and 142) to King David, who composed them as penance for his grievous sins. These transgressions included adultery with Bathsheba and the murder of her husband, Uriah. In another occurrence of sin, David offends God out of pride by commanding a census of Israel and Judah. As punishment, David is sent a choice of famine, war, or pestilence. After plague ravages Israel, David's penance appeases the avenging God.

These particular seven Psalms have a long history associated with atonement. It is thought that at least by the third century they had formed part of Jewish liturgy. In the Christian tradition, they were certainly known by the sixth century, when the Roman author and monk Cassiodorus referred to them as a sevenfold means of obtaining forgiveness. Pope Innocent III (papacy, 1198–1216) ordered their liturgical recitation during Lent. Since the number of these Psalms and the Deadly Sins was the same, the two became linked, and the Penitential Psalms were recited to ask for forgiveness for the dead. Like the Office of the Dead, the Psalms were thought especially efficacious in reducing the time the departed had to spend in purgatory. But the Psalms were also recited to benefit the living, as a means of avoiding these sins in the first place. These seven sins—pride, covetousness, lust, envy, gluttony, anger, and sloth—had the ability to land one in hell for all time. This is why they were called Deadly or Mortal.

The Penitential Psalms always are followed by the Litany. The Litany was a hypnotic enumeration of saints whom one asked to pray for us. The list begins with "Kyrie eleison, **Christe eleison**, Kyrie eleison" [Lord, have mercy; Christ, have mercy; Lord, have mercy], a shortened form of the nine-part "Kyrie" recited by the priest at the beginning of every Mass. Christ, God the Father, the Holy Spirit, and the Trinity are then invoked. Following these preliminary petitions is the Litany proper. Each invocation to the saint is followed by "Ora [*orate* in the plural] pro nobis" [Pray for us]:

Holy Mother of God—pray for us.
St. Michael—pray for us.
St. Raphael—pray for us.

All ye holy angels and archangels—pray for us.
All ye holy orders of blessed spirits—pray for us.
St. John the Baptist—pray for us.

The Virgin, as we see, heads the list, followed by archangels, angels, other celestial spirits, and John the Baptist (our future intercessor at the Last Judgment). Next come the apostles, male martyrs, confessors (male non-martyr saints), female virgin martyrs, and, finally, widows.

The Litany continues with a series of petitions called the "Ab's" [*Froms*], "Per's" [*Throughs*], and "Ut's" [*Thats*]. For example:

From lightning and tempest—O Lord, deliver us.
From the scourge of earthquake—O Lord, deliver us . . .
Through the mystery of thy holy Incarnation—O Lord, deliver us.
Through thy coming—O Lord, deliver us . . .
That thou render eternal blessings to our benefactors—We beseech thee, hear us.
That thou vouchsafe to give and preserve the fruits of the earth—We beseech thee, hear us . . .

The most common subject for the single miniature marking the Penitential Psalms is the elderly David kneeling in prayer, seeking God's forgiveness. The king is usually shown isolated, alone in the landscape to which he withdrew in his penance. Often he kneels in a kind of valley or trench, a reference to the cave to which he retired or to the opening line of the sixth Penitential Psalm, "Out of the depths have I cried unto thee." Fifteenth-century Italian *Horae* often show, instead of the elderly penitent king, the young David, triumphant after his victory over Goliath. Other *Horae*, especially late fifteenth- and sixteenth-century French, use an image not of the sinner but of the sin: Bathsheba at Her Bath. A picture of Judgment Day provided a continual reminder of the forthcoming reckoning, when good deeds will be weighed against sins, and an inducement to praying the Penitential Psalms as a means of warding off temptation. This subject, universally preferred for these Psalms in thirteenth- and fourteenth-century *Horae*, fell out of favor in much of Europe by the fifteenth (when images of David gained ground). The Last Judgment remained prevalent, however, in Dutch and Flemish Books of Hours. Although there are exceptions, Litanies in Books of Hours are hardly ever illustrated.

Accessory Texts

Books of Hours are like automobiles. While they consist of certain prayers without which they cannot properly function as—nor properly be called—Books of Hours, there was a nearly inexhaustible array of ancillary prayers that people, depending on their piety and their pocketbook, felt free to add. Medieval people personalized their prayer books the way modern people accessorize their cars (and for some of the same reasons).

One of the most frequently encountered accessory prayers is the Joys of the Virgin (fifteen is the usual number, although five, seven, and nine also appear); they celebrate the happy moments in Mary's life from the Annunciation to her Assumption into Heaven. There is also a group of prayers whose number of components is fixed at the same mystical, magical digit: Seven Requests to Our Lord, Seven Prayers of St. Gregory, Seven Verses of St. Bernard, and the Seven Last Words of Our Lord. Extra Hours (that is, in addition to those of the Virgin, Cross, and Holy Spirit) also appear. Favorites include the Hours of St. Catherine, the Hours of John the Baptist, and the Weekday Hours (Sunday Hours of the Trinity; Monday, of the Dead; Tuesday, of the Holy Spirit; and so forth). These ancillary Hours are usually short, structured like those of the Cross and the Holy Spirit.

Since Books of Hours were used in church as well as at home, many contained Masses, that is, the actual prayers recited by the priest at the altar or sung by the choir. These Masses usually contain those texts that changed from feast to feast: **Introit**, Collect, **Epistle**, and so forth. But often these Masses include some of the unchanging parts of the service: "Confiteor," "Kyrie," Apostles' Creed, "**Sanctus**," and so forth. The Saturday Mass of the Virgin is the most popular of all the Masses. Even more numerous than actual Masses in Books of Hours, however, are the many quasi-liturgical prayers with such rubrics as, "Upon entering church," "When taking holy water," "At the Elevation," "After the Elevation," "Upon receiving Communion," and so forth. Of these, the most popular were prayers recited at the Elevation. The desire to see the host raised by the celebrant moments after its consecration was felt zealously in this period; in an era of infrequent (normally once a year) Communion, seeing the transubstantiated host was second only to receiving it.

Other popular prayers include the "Stabat Mater" (whose emotional intensity, rhythm, and rhymes make it quite memorable); the "Salve sancta facies" (a prayer to the holy face of Christ that frequently was accompanied by generous indulgences); and petitions to one's **guardian angel**.

Sometimes these accessory prayers get pictures, and sometimes they do not. The Joys of the Virgin usually get, as might be expected, a miniature of a Virgin and Child; the Requests to Our Lord, an image of Christ as Judge; the Prayers of St. Gregory, a Mass of St. Gregory; the Verses of St. Bernard, a St. Bernard in His Study; and the Last Words of Our Lord, a Crucifixion or Resurrection. Extra Hours, when illustrated, often have a miniature of the logical theme or saint. The Saturday Mass of the Virgin was often an excuse for yet another picture of the Virgin and Child. The "Stabat Mater" is usually marked with an image of the **Pietà**; the "Salve sancta facies" with a **Vera Icon** (Fig. 7); and prayers to guardian angels with portraits of kneeling owners (Fig. 8).

Suffrages

Saints were the protectors of medieval people, their helpers in childbirth, their guardians during travel, their nurse in toothache, their doctor in plague. If the Virgin was the person to whom one addressed the all-important petition for eternal salvation, it was from the saints that one sought more basic, or temporal, kinds of help. While Mary became, as the Mother of God, almost a goddess herself, saints always retained more of their humanity and thus their approachability. The saints whom medieval people saw painted onto altarpieces, stained into glass, sculpted from stone,

Figure 7. Vera Icon, by the Master of Jean Chevron, from an Hours for Rome use. Belgium, Bruges, ca. 1450 (The Pierpont Morgan Library, New York. MS M.421, fol. 13v).

Figure 8. Man Praying to His Guardian Angel, by Willem Vrelant, from an Hours for Rome use. Belgium, Bruges, ca. 1460 (The Pierpont Morgan Library, New York. MS M.387, fol. 71v).

woven in tapestries, and stitched upon liturgical vestments were the same saints whose special invocations were to be found in one's own Book of Hours. They could be taken home, held in the hand, called upon at any time.

A typical Book of Hours contained a dozen or so Suffrages. They usually appear at the end of the volume, but some *Horae* include them after Lauds of the Hours of the Virgin, in imitation of monastic practice. Their order (as with Litanies) reflects celestial hierarchy. God or the three Persons of the Trinity (who, of course, are not saints) always begin the Suffrages, followed by the Virgin, the archangel Michael, and John the Baptist (the last two prominently positioned because of their importance as judge and intercessor, respectively, at the Last Judgment). The apostles appear next, followed by male martyrs and confessors. Female saints come next, virgin martyrs first.

Each Suffrage is composed of four elements: three ejaculations—antiphon, versicle, response—followed by a longer prayer [*oratio*]. The first three elements constitute a string of praises. As for the prayer, its first half recounts (albeit briefly) an episode from the saint's life or touches on some important aspect of the saint's holiness; the second half of the prayer is always a petition for aid from God through the saint's intercession. The mixture of these four elements mirrors the arrangement found in Breviaries, and, indeed, many of the elements that compose a given Suffrage are quotations or extractions from the Divine Office. Some Suffrages, too, draw from Missals, quoting the Collect, which was particular for that Mass, that follows the "Gloria." Since the prayers in both Breviaries and Missals change from feast to feast, their petitions to specific saints made them a logical quarry for the popular versions that appear in *Horae* as Suffrages. A translation of a typical Suffrage follows:

> **A.** Nicholas, friend of God, when invested with the episcopal insignia, showed himself a friend to all. **V.** Pray for us, O most blessed father Nicholas. **R.** That we may be made worthy of the promises of Christ. **Or.** O God, you adorned the pious blessed Bishop Nicholas with countless miracles; grant, we beseech you, that through his merits and prayers, we may be delivered from the flames of hell. Through Jesus Christ Our Lord. (The Pierpont Morgan Library, MS M.26, fol. 238r–v; France, Langres? ca. 1485–90; see Fig. 9)

Figure 9. St. Nicholas Resuscitating the Three Youths, from an Hours for Rome use. France, Langres? ca. 1485–90 (The Pierpont Morgan Library, New York. MS M.26, fol. 238r).

Suffrages are not always illustrated. In some manuscripts the prayers receive no pictures; in others, a few favorite saints are given illustrations while those to whom the owner obviously felt less devoted are not. Some Books of Hours have scores of Suffrage miniatures; others might treat them with a few historiated initials. The typical fifteenth-century *Horae* will have about a dozen large Suffrage miniatures. The saints are often shown standing, their attributes in hand, or are depicted in one of the more dramatic moments of their lives (often their deaths). Figure 9 is typical. It depicts the legend of Nicholas and the mutilated boys. According to tradition, an unscrupulous innkeeper had killed and dismembered three youths, storing their mangled bodies in a pickling tub as food for his guests; Nicholas was able to bring the boys back to life simply by making the sign of the cross over the barrel.

Office of the Dead

The Office of the Dead was in the back of every Book of Hours the way death itself was always at the back of the medieval mind. While most prayers in a Book of Hours are quasi-liturgical (reflecting but not wholly equaling official Church practice), the Office of the Dead in Books of Hours is exactly the same Office found in the Breviaries and Antiphonaries.

It perhaps is easier to understand the function of this prayer by recalling its old name, Office *for* the Dead. It was the cause of considerable anguish for medieval people to think of the potentially long periods of time their relatives would spend in the painful fires of purgatory. The ideal Christian death took place at home, in bed, the believer having confessed, been forgiven, and having just received Last Communion and extreme unction. Such a death cleansed the soul and permitted immediate entry into heaven. As was its nature, however, death often caught its victims unprepared. It was assumed that most people's entry into heaven would be detoured by a stay in purgatory, a delay projected to last, judging from medieval indulgences, potentially thousands of years. Along with the funding of funerary Masses, praying the Office was considered the most efficacious means of reducing the fiery price of paradise. This aid was essential, because only the living could help the dead.

The Office of the Dead consists of the three Hours of Vespers, Matins, and Lauds. Ideally, Vespers was prayed in church over the coffin the evening before the Requiem Mass. It was recited or chanted by monks hired for that purpose by the deceased's family or confraternity. Matins and Lauds were then prayed, again by paid monks, on the morning of the funeral itself. The word *dirge*, today meaning a mournful hymn used at funerals, comes from the opening Latin antiphon for Matins, "Dirige, Domine, Deus meus . . ." [Direct, O Lord, my God, my steps in your sight]; in the Middle Ages the word *dirge* commonly referred to the Matins/Lauds portion of the Office of the Dead. While monks recited it from Breviaries or chanted it from Antiphonaries, the laity would say their Office from Books of Hours. Funerals, however, were not the only time the Office was prayed. The tradition that required the ordained to recite the Office on a daily basis also encouraged the laity to pray it at home as often as possible. (The Office is not to be confused with the funeral Mass or the rite of burial. These quite different texts are found in two service books used by the priest, the Missal and the Ritual, respectively.)

Like other Offices, this one is composed mostly of Psalms, which, in this case, have been chosen for the comfort offered to the dead. The more remarkable component of the Office, however, is a moving series of readings from the Book of Job that make up the nine lessons for Matins. The trials endured by Job become an allegory for one's time on earth—or in purgatory. Thus the "I" of the readings ceases to be Job, ceases even to be the person reading the Office and, instead, becomes the voice of the dead man himself, crying for help. Pity and mercy are continually asked for, but through a veil of near despair.

Like the Hours of the Virgin, the Office of the Dead, too, has a "use." Here, it is a function of the different responses that immediately follow each of the nine lessons in Matins. In the use for Paris, for example, the first response is "Qui Lazarum . . ." [Thou didst raise Lazarus . . .], the second "Credo quod . . ." [I believe that . . .], and so forth.

With rare exceptions, a single miniature illustrates the Office of the Dead. The two most common subjects are Monks Praying the Office of the Dead (Fig. 10) or a Burial. These, however, are but two episodes from the medieval funeral, the entirety of which can be pieced together from Office of the Dead illustrations with remarkable archeological accuracy. Assembled as a series, these miniatures unfold the events, scene by scene, in an almost cinematic manner. The depicted events include the Deathbed (Fig. 11); Preparation of the Corpse for Burial (including washing it, sewing it into a shroud, and placing it into a wood coffin); Funeral Procession from Home to Church; Praying of the Office of the Dead (recited or chanted; Fig. 10); Requiem Mass; Distribution of Alms or Bread to the Poor (their prayers for the deceased were thought especially efficacious); Absolution (blessing of the coffin immediately following the Requiem Mass); Burial within the Church (very rare); Procession from Church to Graveyard; Preparations for Burial; and, finally, Burial itself (Fig. 11, bottom left).

These miniatures are rich in detail—catafalques and candles, bones and bells, graves and grievers, coffins and charnels—and reveal much to the attentive eye about medieval rituals. In addition to the visible, miniatures of Deathbeds and Burials often include the unseen metaphysical Battle for the Soul, in which the deceased's guardian angel fights off a demon for possession of the released soul. And some pictures (especially Requiem Masses) include images of the desired salvific effect of all these services, the Soul Released from Purgatory.

The iconography for the Office of the Dead is extremely rich and varied. Other common illustrations include the Last Judgment (popular in the earlier history of *Horae*, but continuing into the fifteenth century in Flemish manuscripts), Raising of Lazarus, Parable of Dives and Lazarus (the Feast of Dives or Dives in Hell), Three Living and Three Dead, Job on the Dungheap, and various types of Death Personified. A few manuscripts show hell itself; but this is quite rare. Hell is hardly ever depicted in Books of Hours: the thought was too much for the medieval mind to bear.

Figure 10. Chanting the Office of the Dead, from an Hours for Rome use. Central France, ca. 1470 (The Pierpont Morgan Library, New York. MS M.159, fol. 104r).

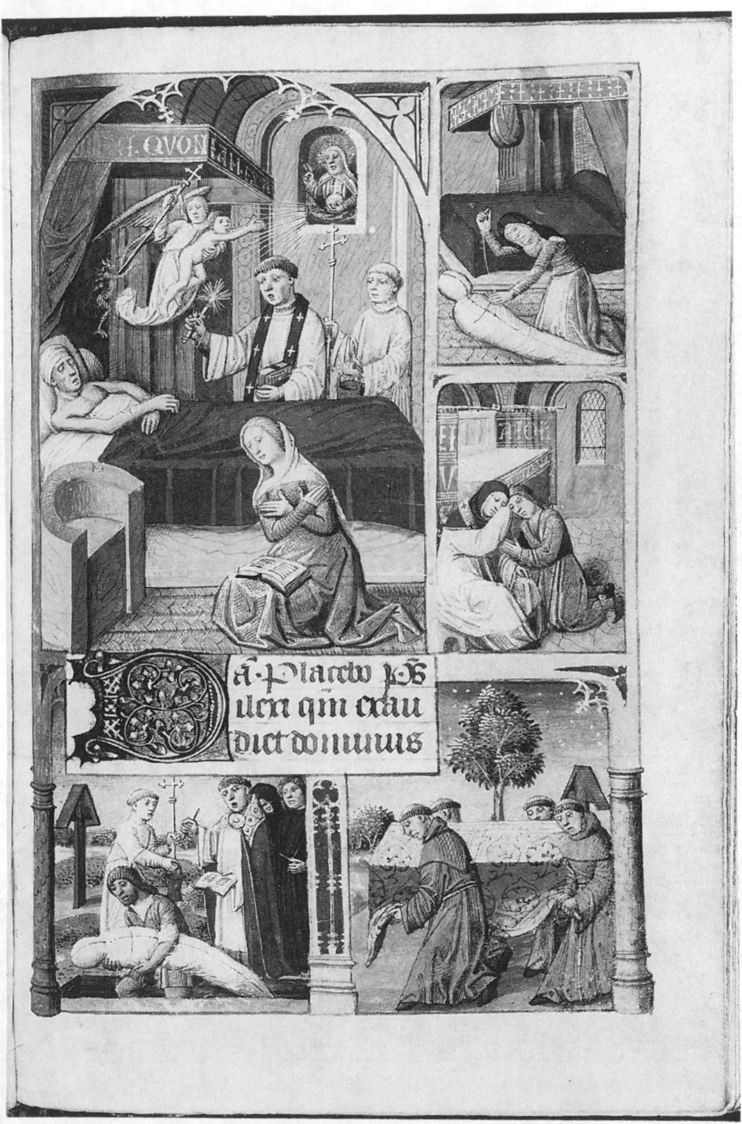

Figure 11. Last Rites, with border vignettes of the sewing of the man's corpse into a shroud, a family member confessing, a funeral procession, and burial, by the Chief Associate of Maître François, from an Hours for Paris use. France, Paris, ca. 1485–90 (The Pierpont Morgan Library, New York. MS M.231, fol. 137r).

References

The first book to consult on Books of Hours remains Victor Leroquais, *Les livres d'heures manuscrits de la Bibliothèque nationale*, Paris, 1927. Sources on the subject in English include John Harthan, *The Book of Hours, with a Historical Survey and Commentary*, New York, 1977; Robert Calkins's Chapter 8, "The Book of Hours," in his *Illuminated Books of the Middle Ages*, Ithaca, 1983; Janet Backhouse, *Books of Hours*, London, 1985; Christopher de Hamel's Chapter 6, "Books for Everybody," in his *A History of Illuminated Manuscripts*, London, 1986 (and a second edition with many different illustrations, 1994); and my two publications: *Time Sanctified: The Book of Hours in Medieval Art and Life*, New York, 1988, and *Painted Prayers: The Book of Hours in Medieval and Renaissance Art*, New York, 1997.

Time Sanctified should be consulted for its full bibliography on art history, social history, and prayer (including citations useful in determining the "use" of a Book of Hours). My *Painted Prayers* lists those helpful publications on Books of Hours that have appeared since 1988. Most significant of these are: Charles Sterling, *La peinture médiévale à Paris, 1300–1500*, 2 vols., Paris, 1987 and 1990; Henri L. M. Defoer, et al., *The Golden Age of Dutch Manuscript Painting*, New York, 1990; Claire Donovan, *The de Brailes Hours: Shaping the Book of Hours in Thirteenth-Century Oxford*, London, 1991; Eamon Duffy's section, "Prayers and Spells," in his *Stripping of the Altars: Traditional Religion in England, c. 1400–c. 1580*, New Haven, 1992; François Avril and Nicole Reynaud, *Les manuscrits à peintures en France, 1440–1520*, Paris, 1993; Knud Ottosen, *The Responsories and Versicles of the Latin Office of the Dead*, Aarhus, 1993; Jonathan J. G. Alexander, ed., *The Painted Page: Italian Renaissance Book Illumination, 1450–1550*, Munich, 1994; Roger S. Wieck, "The Death Desired: Books of Hours and the Medieval Funeral," *Death and Dying in the Middle Ages*, Edelgard E. DuBruck and Barbara I. Gusick, eds., New York, 1999, 431–76; and Virginia Reinburg, *Practices of Prayer in Late Medieval and Reformation France,* Princeton, forthcoming.

PART FIVE

LITURGY AND THE ARTS

ICONOGRAPHY IN THE LITURGICAL LIFE OF THE MEDIEVAL GREEK CHURCH[1]

AMBROSE-ARISTOTLE ZOGRAPHOS

Prologue

The use of **icons**[2] in the liturgical life of the Christian Church was

---

[1]My heartfelt thanks and deep appreciation go to Professor of Art History Dr. Slobodan Ćurčić at Princeton University, to Professor Dr. Constantine Cavarnos, and to Professor Rev. Dr. Demetrios J. Constantelos who read this essay and made critical comments and helpful recommendations for its improvement.

[2]See St. John of Damascus, *On the Divine Images, Three Apologies Against Those Who Attack the Divine Images*, trans. David Anderson (Crestwood, N.Y., 1980), p. 19: "Since we are speaking of images and worship, let us analyze the exact meaning of each. An image is of like character with its prototype, but with a certain difference. It is not like its archetype in every way"; Leonid Ouspensky, *Theology of the Icon*, trans. Anthony Gythiel, vol. 1 (Crestwood, N.Y., 1992), p. 35: "The word *icon* derives from the Greek word *eikon*, meaning *image* or *portrait*. When the Christian image was being created in Byzantium, this term was used for all representations of Christ, the Virgin, a saint, an angel or an event from sacred history, whether this image was painted or sculpted, mobile or monumental, and whatever the technique used. Now this term is used by preference to designate portable works of painting, sculpture, mosaic, and the like . . . when we speak of icons, we will have in mind all sacred images, whether they are paintings on boards, frescoes, mosaics or sculptures"; George Galavaris, *The Icon in the Life of the Church: Doctrine, Liturgy, Devotion*

introduced as early as the fourth century, if not earlier.[3] Iconography became an integral part of the worship of the Greek-speaking Church of the Middle Ages, the so-called **Byzantine** era. Byzantine iconography has gained much appreciation in recent years because it tends not only to please aesthetically or to satisfy scientific curiosity by studying the past's masterpieces, but also because of its content, its thought-world, its theology and its long standing philosophy of history.[4]

The use of icons in the liturgical life of the Church was adopted in order to teach through pictorial illustration the biblical, ecclesiological, christological, and pneumatological teachings of the Church as those teachings were defined and formulated by Ecumenical Synods.[5] The purpose of this essay is to discuss the dogmatic and liturgical character of iconography and its role in the daily life of the Greek-speaking Church in the Middle Ages (330–1453). After a brief historical review, serving as an introduction to the subject, we shall attempt to analyze the liturgical as well as the doctrinal character of Byzantine iconography and to indicate the special place which the Greek Orthodox Church has assigned to icons.

(Leiden, 1981), p. 3: "Based on Neo-Platonic theories, the icon is thought basically a mystery, a vehicle of divine power and grace, a means of God's knowledge. It is not merely a symbol of the archetype, but the represented becomes present through the icon."

[3]Leonid Ouspensky and Vladimir Lossky, *The Meaning of Icons*, trans. G. E. H. Palmer and E. Kadloubovsky (Crestwood, N.Y., 1982), p. 25.

[4]See the excellent monograph on this subject by Moshe Barasch, *Icon: Studies in the History of an Idea* (New York and London, 1992). See also Constantine Kalokyris, *The Essence of Orthodox Iconography* (Brookline, Mass., 1971).

[5]See Karl Joseph Head, *A History of the Councils of the Church, from the Original Documents*, trans. H. N. Oxenham, vol. 5 (New York, 1972); Daniel J. Sahas, *Icon and Logos: Sources in Eighth-Century Iconoclasm* (Toronto, 1986), pp. 5–9.

Icons in Christian Worship

The well-known commandment of the Decalogue, "You shall not make for yourself an idol, whether in the form of anything that is in heaven above, or that is on earth beneath" (Exod. 20:4), and the Church's opposition to idolatry served as impediments to the use of icons in the early Church, whether icons of Christ, the *Theotokos* [the Mother of Christ], or the Saints.[6]

Nevertheless, the early Church did make use of descriptive art, in pictures or sculptures, from as early as the time of the catacombs, in order to help the faithful understand the teachings of the new faith.[7] Many decorative as well as symbolic representations of the Christian faith have been found in the catacombs, such as those of the *Cross*, the *fish*, the *bread*, the *dove*, the *peacock*, the *deer*, the *vineyard*, the *lamb* and the *anchor*. However, besides these impersonal symbols, there were others that had a personal image, such as the *Praying Woman* and the *Good Shepherd*. The Church borrowed many of these symbols from the Hellenic and Roman world. But, as it happened with other aspects of culture borrowed from the Greco-Roman world, art forms too were adopted by Christianity and were given a spiritual character, in order to serve the needs of Christian worship and education.

---

[6]Hans Campenhausen, *Tradition and Life in the Church*, trans. A. V. Littledale (Philadelphia, 1968), pp. 171–200.

[7]For more about early Christian art see Rice D. Talbot, *The Beginnings of Christian Art* (London, 1957); John Beckwith, *Early Christian and Byzantine Art* (Harmondsworth, 1979); Paul Finney, "Gnosticism and the Origins of Early Christian Art," paper presented at the meeting of the North American Patristic Society, 1978; André Grabar, *Early Christian Art. From the Rise of Christianity to the Death of Theodosius* (New York, 1968); Norman H. Baynes, *Byzantine Studies and Other Essays* (London, 1955), pp. 226–239; Ernst Kitzinger, "The Cult of Images in the Age Before Iconoclasm," *Dumbarton Oaks Papers* 8 (1954): 85–150; idem, *Byzantine Art in the Making. Main Lines of Stylistic Development in Mediterranean Art. 3rd–7th Century* (Cambridge, Mass., 1980); Constantine Cavarnos, *Orthodox Iconography* (Belmont, Mass., 1992); and Barasch, *Icon: Studies*, pp. 95–182.

Eusebius of Caesarea (d. 339/340) relates that he himself had once seen in the ancient Greek city of Paneada, Caesarea of Philippi, the statue of Christ with his hands stretched out towards the bleeding woman of the Gospels.[8] Furthermore, he adds that in his time the faithful made use of icons, depicting not only Christ himself but also the Apostles Peter and Paul. Iconography began spreading slowly but steadily in the early years of Christianity, expanding to many cities and provinces during the fourth and fifth centuries. By the seventh century its use in the Christian worship had been firmly established.

As already indicated, from an early age the Church did not hesitate to use many different forms of art, including music, poetry, painting, and architecture in the service of its mission in the world. At times when various heresies attacked the Christian doctrines, the Church used iconography as a pulpit for the multitudes, instructing them to understand difficult theological ideas. An icon, of course, is something abstract and voiceless. However, it speaks in its own special way. It illustrates the contents of the Bible through colors; it demonstrates in a vivid manner the existential and heroic life of the Church in history; and it illuminates the contents of the holy Liturgy. The Church is "an earthly heaven, where the Almighty God dwells and strolls."[9] The faithful who enter a Church are taught the doctrines of the faith in a simple and descriptive way.

---

[8]Eusebius of Caesarea, *Ecclesiastical History*, book 7, ch. 18 (in the series of *A Select Library of Nicene and Post-Nicene Fathers of the Christian Church*, 2nd ser. (Grand Rapids, Mich., 1976), vol. 1, p. 304: "It has remained to our day, so that we ourselves also saw it when we were staying in the city. Nor is it strange that those Gentiles who were blessed by our Savior of old should do such things, since we have also learned that the likenesses of His apostles Peter and Paul, and of Christ Himself, are preserved in paintings, for it is likely that the ancients were accustomed, according to the habits of the Gentiles, to pay this kind of honor indiscriminately to those regarded by them as saviors." See also St. John of Damascus, *Logos Apodeicticos peri ton Agion kai Septon Eiconon*, PG 95: 316A; and Bonifatius P. Kotter, ed., *Die Schriften des Johannes von Damaskos*, 4 vols. (Berlin, 1969–1981).

[9]Germanus, Patriarch of Constantinople, *Ecclesiastike Istoria*, PG 98: 384–85. See also John of Damascus, *Logos Apodeicticos*, PG 95: 325C–28B.

Following the edict of Milan in 313,[10] and especially the official proclamation of Christianity as the state religion of the Roman Empire in 391, iconography turns from *symbolic* representation and becomes *historical* confirmation. The representation of Christ and his earthly life, as well as those of the *Theotokos*, the saints, and the martyrs of the Christian faith became an integral part of the history of Greek Christianity in icons. Later, after the defeat of the Iconoclastic movement and the official adoption of the icons by the 843 Council—known as the *Triumph of Orthodoxy* (Fig. 1)—iconography becomes *dogmatic,* that is, the aim of its contents was to proclaim and interpret dogmatic truths. Following the official restoration of icons, the interiors of numerous churches were painted in a certain order and not arbitrarily, as was the case before. This particular order was defined by the Church through relevant decisions of the Seventh Ecumenical Council in 787,[11] but it prevailed after the Council of 843, which contributed to the formation of three main iconographic cycles, used in all Byzantine churches. These three cycles are the *dogmatic*, the *liturgical,* and the *historical* (or festive).[12]

During the era of the Macedonian and Komnenian dynasties of the Byzantine era (843–1180), along with the continued interest of monasticism and the cultivation of hymnography, iconography was enriched with new ideas and new themes, such as the iconographic representation of the ***Akathist Hymn***[13] and scenes from the **Apocryphal gospels**. Later, during the

---

[10]Eusebius of Caesarea, *Ecclesiastical History*, pp. 8, 9–10, 17. Compare Alexander A. Vasiliev, *History of the Byzantine Empire (324–1453)*, vol. 1 (Madison, Wis., 1952), pp. 50–52.

[11]For an English translation of the Definition of the Seventh Ecumenical Council see Sahas, *Icon and Logos*.

[12]George A. Soteriou, "Oi Eikonographikoi Kykloi tou Byzantinou Naou," *Nea Estia* 58, no. 683 (1955): 406–15.

[13]A special service dedicated to the *Theotokos* and sung on Fridays during the Great Lent, before Easter.

Figure 1. The Restoration of the Holy Icons. Mt. Athos, Greece, twentieth century. Photo: Author.

Palaeologian era (1261–1453), Byzantine iconography reached the peak of its evolution by producing various and more complex representations, such as the receiving of Holy Communion by the Apostles, and the depiction of the Church Fathers in the holy altar.

During the second half of the thirteenth century emerged the so-called *Macedonian school* of iconography, as it was first named by G. Millet,[14] which had its roots in the preceding period of Byzantine iconography. This school was a continuation of Hellenistic art. It is characterized by its realism, its freedom of expression, and its lively depiction of movement. The illuminated faces with the use of green shades and the oversized bodies were mainly used on wall paintings. The *Macedonian school* expressed the spirit of the aristocracy, it reached its height in the thirteenth and fourteenth centuries, and by the end of the sixteenth it no longer existed. A primary representative and pioneer of that school was Manuel Panselinos of Thessalonica (ca. 1300).

Another artistic movement expressing a different spirit was the *Cretan school*. It appeared in the first half of the fourteenth century and generally adopted the style of Byzantine painting prior to the thirteenth century. The forms were ascetic, pious, and humble; the hands and legs were thin and tall, the body movements limited; and the earthly colors darker. In this school the realistic element was less prevalent. The *Cretan school* of iconography prevailed after the fall of Constantinople (1453) because it better expressed the ascetic ideal of Orthodox spirituality. The greatest and most important representative of this school was Theophanes the Cretan (sixteenth century).[15] In brief, there were five interrelated and yet different periods of iconography in the liturgical life of the Byzantine Church and the historical evolution of its art: (1) From the beginning to the eighth century;

---

[14]Gabriel Millet, *Recherches sur l'iconographie de l'évangile* (Paris, 1916).

[15]Manolis Chatzidakes, *Ho Kpetikos Zografos Theofanes. He teleutaia fase tes tehnes tou stis toihografies tes Hieras Mores Stauroniketa* (Mt. Athos, 1968); Cavarnos, *Orthodox Iconography*, p. 20.

(2) the Iconoclastic period (726–843); (3) the era of the Macedonian Dynasty, from the second half of the ninth to the end of the eleventh century; (4) the period of the Komnenian and Palaeologian Dynasties, from the twelfth century to the fall of Constantinople (A.D. 1453); and (5) the period from the fall of Constantinople to the present.[16]

The Dogmatic Cycle of Byzantine Iconography

Throughout the Byzantine era (A.D. 330–1453), the Greek Church taught the faithful not only through catechism, hymnography, and the pulpit but also through the symbolic and mystical language of iconography. As already indicated, from as early as the fourth century Church Fathers acknowledged the value of iconography. In his homily on the martyrdom of St. Theodore, St. Gregory of Nyssa writes:

> A painter colored the flowers of art depicting in icons the Martyr's prizes, the pleas, the sufferings, the beastly faces of the tyrants, the fires, the seven-time heated furnace, the blessed ending of the athlete, the crown-giving Christ. . . . He knows a speechless writing on the wall having voice and speaking and also being beneficial.[17]

Later, St. John of Damascus (d. ca. 749; Fig. 2) wrote that "what the book is to the literate, the image is to the illiterate. Just as words speak to the ear, so the image speaks to the sight; it brings us understanding."[18] The icon served as a kind of non-verbal language through which the dogmatic teachings of the Church were as vividly expressed as in speech. Iconography

---

[16]Compare Constantine Kalokyres, *He Zografike tes Orthodoxias* (Thessalonica, 1972), p. 38.

[17]St. Gregory of Nyssa, *Engomion eis ton megan martyra Theodoron*, PG: 46, 737D (translation is mine).

[18]St. John of Damascus, *On the Divine Images*, p. 25. See also St. Nilus, *Epistole 61*, PG 79: 577–80; and Barasch, *Icon: Studies*, pp. 185–253.

Figure 2. St. John of Damascus. Mt. Athos, Greece, twentieth century. Photo: Author.

became a theology seen by the eye and read through the use of shapes and colors, making incomprehensible dogmatic truths comprehensible.

The official position of the Church concerning the use of icons in public worship and private prayer was ultimately determined by the iconoclastic crisis.[19] The foundations had been laid by the Sixth Ecumenical Council (681) through its 82nd Canon, which justified the use of icons within the Church.[20]

The Iconoclastic disputes, which started in A.D. 726 and officially ended in 843, lasted for nearly 120 years except for a thirty-year interval (787–815). During this critical period, especially between 726 and 787, the Church struggled to defend the didactic and aesthetic character of icons and reiterate the Christological decisions of previous Councils. Denial of iconography was seen as denial of the doctrine of Incarnation. It has been observed that the struggle for the icons "constitutes the completion of the Christological controversy of the fifth century and the integration of the decision made by the Council of Chalcedon (451) concerning the terms of

[19]For more on the Iconoclastic controversy see Vasilios Stefanides, *Ekklesiastike Historia* (Athens, 1948), pp. 231–40; Dionysios Zakythinos, *He Byzantine Autokratoria* (Athens, 1969), pp. 151–62; George Ostrogorsky, *History of the Byzantine State* (New Brunswick, N.J., 1969), pp. 147–209; E. J. Martin, *A History of the Iconoclastic Controversy* (New York, 1930); Kitzinger, "The Cult of Images," pp. 83–150; Alisa Bank, "The Emperor Cult and the Origins of the Iconoclastic Controversy," *Byzantion* 43 (1973): 13–29; George Florovsky, "Origen, Eusebius and the Iconoclastic Controversy," *Church History* 19 (1950): 77–96; *Iconoclasm*, papers given at the Ninth Spring Symposium of Byzantine Studies, University of Birmingham, March 1975 (Birmingham, 1977); Gerhart B. Ladner, "Origin and Significance of the Byzantine Iconoclastic Controversy," *Mediaeval Studies* 2 (1940): 127–49; and Peter Brown, "A Dark-Age Crisis: Aspects of the Iconoclastic Controversy," *English Historical Review* 346 (1973): 1–34.

[20]Giovanni Domenico Mansi, ed., *Sacrorum conciliorum nova et amplissima collectio*, vol. 11 (Florence, 1759–1798), pp. 977–80; see also PG 95, 320D–321A.

the incarnation of God."[21] The icon with the representation of the incarnate Logos bears witness to the fact that God became truly human.

> Based on the decision of the Fourth Ecumenical Council of Chalcedon (451), iconography depicts the two natures of Christ, the divine and the human, unconfusedly united to eternity. Although in human eyes an icon represents the historical Christ, in the eyes of the faithful, Christ in the icon is the transfigured Christ, whom the eyes of his chosen disciples saw on the Mount of Transfiguration. The fullness in which the earthly Christ is offered helps the faithful to see not only the Christ of history in abstract art form but also the invisible Christ.[22]

The Iconoclastic controversy of the eighth century caused serious problems for the Church and society. Numerous iconophiles [defenders of iconography] were imprisoned, exiled, deposed, and tortured for defending the use of holy icons, including Theophanes the Confessor (ca. 760–817), St. Stephen the Younger (ca. 713–64), St. Theodore the Studite (759–826),[23] the brothers Theodore (ca. 775–between 841 and 844), and Theophanes the Graptoi (ca. 778–845). Icons were removed from the churches and numerous more were destroyed while new forms of art were adopted for the decoration of churches. Paintings depicting images were replaced with pictures of nature such as trees, flowers, birds, and other naturalistic subjects. Iconoclasm did much damage to the fabric of the church, but it also made some positive contributions. Excesses in the use of icons were pointed

---

[21]Panagiotes Chrestou, "Oi Eikones kai he Orthodoxia," *Gregorios ho Palamas* 740 (Nov–Dec. 1991), p. 904. See also Florovsky, "Origen, Eusebius," pp. 77–96. For more about the Council of Chalcedon see Leo Donald Davis, *The First Seven Ecumenical Councils* (Wilmington, Del., 1987), pp. 170–206.

[22]Chrestou, "Oi Eikones," p. 910. Barasch, *Icon: Studies*, p. 219: "John of Damascus . . . , believes that the central function of the icon is to make us see something of the invisible, to overcome our limitations."

[23]See St. Theodore the Studite, *On the Holy Icons*, trans. Catharine P. Roth, (Crestwood, N.Y., 1981). For more information about St. Theodore the Studite and his contribution to the theology of icons see Barasch, *Icon: Studies*, pp. 254–89.

out, and the Church assumed a more aggressive role in catechism and instruction. Ignorance had led people to worship rather than venerate or honor the persons depicted on the icons. Excessive practices of veneration revealed a kind of subconscious idolatry and superstition. The iconoclastic imperial policy of Emperors Leo III (717–41)[24] and, especially, Constantine V (741–75)[25] forced thousands of monks to flee to the West, mostly to southern Italy and Sicily, where many Greeks had lived for generations. These monks thus were able to transfer the Byzantine style of iconography to the western parts of the Empire. While iconographic art was under persecution in Byzantium, it was spreading rapidly throughout the western Empire. Another beneficial effect of the Iconoclastic era was that the Church was forced to provide a clear definition of the theology of icons[26] through the Seventh Ecumenical Council of A.D. 787. For a definition of the meaning, the didactic and doctrinal justification of icons in Liturgy and private worship, the Synod relied on the teachings of the Fathers and the experience of the Church in history. Icons, the Fathers taught, are to be used in churches and honored with the same relative veneration shown to other

---

[24]Stephen Gero, *Byzantine Iconoclasm During the Reign of Leo III; With Particular Attention to the Oriental Sources*, Corpus Scriptorium Christianorum Orientalium Subsidia 41 (Louvain, 1973); Constance Head, "Who was the Real Leo the Isaurian?" *Byzantion* 41 (1971): 105–08; Charles Diehl, "Leo III and His Isaurian Dynasty (717–802)," in *The Cambridge Mediaeval History*, vol. 4 (Cambridge, 1927), pp. 1–26; and Milton Anastos, "Leo III's Edict against the Images in the Year 726–27 and Italo-Byzantine Relations between 726 and 730," *Byzantinische Forschungen* 3 (1968): 5–41.

[25]Stephen Gero, *Byzantine Iconoclasm During the Reign of Constantine V; With Particular Attention to the Oriental Sources*, Corpus Scriptorum Christianorum Orientalium Subsidia 52 (Louvain, 1977).

[26]On the theology of the icon see Ouspensky, *Theology of the Icon* ; Paul Evdokimov, *L'Art de l'Icone: Théologie de la Beauté* (Paris, 1970); Leslie W. Barnard, "The Theology of Images," in *Iconoclasm*: Papers Given at the Ninth Spring Symposium of Byzantine Studies (Birmingham, 1977), pp. 7–13; Kallistos Ware, "The Theology of the Icon. A Short Anthology," *Eastern Churches Review* 8 (1976): 3–10.

material symbols, such as "the precious and life-giving Cross" and the Book of Gospels.[27] St. Basil the Great was quite explicit, stating unambiguously that "the honor given to the icon passes on to the prototype."[28] The Council of 787 ascribed honorary veneration to icons because the true worship belongs only to God, and it stressed that "the more the representations are seen, the more those who see them will move on to remembrance and desire of the prototype."[29] Two didactic purposes of iconography were pointed out: *remembrance* and *imitation.* The faithful through the medium of the icon were able to preserve in memory the image and the example of the depicted person, and were able to arouse within themselves through the power of the icon the desire to imitate the depicted person's life.

It needs to be emphasized that iconography expressed and taught dogmatic truths of the Church. In many churches, Christ was depicted on the gate of the inner narthex as the Teacher, holding an open Holy Gospel bearing such passages as "I am the gate" or "I am the light of the world" (John 12:35 and 46) or "I am the way and the truth and the life" (John 14:6). For instance, both of these depictions appear in the churches of Hagia Sophia in Constantinople (ninth century; Fig. 3), and St. Loukas the Steiriotes in central Greece (eleventh century). The representation of Christ that welcomes the faithful on the gate of the narthex of many churches has a sweet, approachable gaze, full of love, which manifests the dogmatic truth that the

---

[27]Mansi, *Sacrorum conciliorum,* 13:377–80: "... and to these should be given due salutation and honorable reverence (*timitike proskynesis*), not indeed that true worship of faith which pertains alone to the divine nature; but to these, as to the figure of the precious and life-giving Cross and to the Book of the Gospels and to other holy objects, incense and lights may be offered according to ancient pious custom. For the honor which is paid to the image passes on to that which the image represents, and he who reveres the image reveres in it the subject represented. . . ."

[28]St. Basil the Great, *Peri tou Hagiou Pneumatos*, PG 32: 149G.

[29]Mansi, *Sacrorum conciliorum,* 13:377–80.

Figure 3. Mosaic over the entrance of the western door of Hagia Sophia. Constantinople, ninth century. Photo: Author.

incarnate Logos, because of His infinite love for man, "emptied Himself" (Phil. 2:7) and became the "Gate" (John 10:7) and the "Way" (John 14:6) of salvation.

In the interior dome of a church, the magnificent icon of the ***Pantocrator*** "clothed with honor and majesty" (Ps.104:1) dominates (Fig. 4). The dome is a "symbol of heaven" that descended to meet the earth, and the Pantocrator Christ is both "the Father and the Son," thus expressing the doctrine of *homoousios,* that Christ is consubstantial with the Father. The Byzantine Pantocrator reveals the kingly majesty of the Creator, the expression of the active goodness of the Savior, and the severity of the impartial judge. In other words, while the Pantocrator icon manifests God's *philanthropia,*[30] the Redeemer's utmost *love*, which prompted the incarnation in order to save the human situation, it also proclaims God's divine *justice* for

[30]For *philanthropia* as an attribute of Christ in iconography see Demetrios J. Constantelos, "A Note on 'Christos Philanthropos' in Byzantine Iconography," *Byzantion* 45/1 (1976): 9–12.

Figure 4. Christ Pantocrator. Mosaic, Constantinople, early sixteenth century. Photo: Author.

which he will return in glory. The Pantocrator then is both the preexistent Logos and God incarnate, the Christ as the head of the visible Church, and the Christ who will draw all, visible and invisible, to Himself.

Since the incarnation of the Logos, the son of God, was foretold by the prophets of the Old Testament, icons of prophets surround the Pantocrator along with heavenly powers set in an hierarchical order. In the four triangles on which the dome rests, there are the representations of the four Evangelists who proclaimed the Gospel.

The doctrine that the Mother of Christ is "truly *Theotokos*" was issued by the Third Ecumenical Council of Ephesus (431). It found iconographic

Figure 5. The *Theotokos* as Playtera, fresco by Photes Kontoglou. Church of the Kapnikarea, Athens, Greece ca. 1950. Photo: Author.

expression after the iconoclastic controversy, when the icon of ***Platytera*** was introduced and placed on the upper part of the wall behind the holy Table (Fig. 5). The *Theotokos* icon is called *Platytera* because she contained in Her womb "The one Whom the universe cannot contain," and reveals the mystery of the Incarnation. Patriarch Germanus of the eighth century explains: "We draw the icon of Christ's Mother, the Holy Theotokos, to proclaim that she contained in her womb the invisible God Almighty, Who holds the Universe in His hand, and gave birth to Him."[31]

The *Theotokos* is usually depicted holding the Christ-Child. The *Theotokos* is surrounded by the two Archangels. She is also shown in a position of praying for the Church. Standing alone between heaven and earth, she represents the unity which was accomplished through her Son. For the

[31]PG 98: 157C.

faithful, the *Theotokos* is "the heavenly ladder through which God descended, and man ascended," the "mediator," "who united the heaven and earth."[32] The doctrine of the first and second Coming of the Lord is expressed in the representation known as "Preparation," showing the empty Throne of Judgment, and the instruments of the Savior's Passion, on the top part of the apse in the Altar.

"God became man, that we may be deified,"[33] taught St. Athanasius the Great (295–373) along with other Church Fathers. The earthly life of saints reflects the glory of a deified humanity, while icons project humanity's participation in God's divine life and God's uncreated light, including the whole creation.

> A holy icon not only depicts an historical event or a particular person among many others, but it further shows us the depicted person's eternal appearance, revealing the dogmatic teaching (teaching which has been defined by an Ecumenical Council and cannot be changed) about the place they hold in the ladder of the salutary events of divine Economy.[34]

While the representation of Christ and His Mother expresses the great mystery of divine Economy, the saints teach sanctity and provide the examples of people who have achieved salvation. Hagiography "does not render an external form of the saints, but it depicts the spiritual and incorruptible character of those who dwell in the heavenly Kingdom."[35] Saints and martyrs are now "citizens of heaven," and for this reason they are represented in an idealistic and symbolic manner. This depiction is intended to direct our thoughts from a world of corruption and inspire us to seek that blessed reality which exists outside the boundaries of this world. Icons of saints are

---

[32]*Akathistos Hymnos* (Athens, 1987), pp. 321–32.

[33]Athanasius the Great, *Peri Enanthropeseos*, PG 25: 192B.

[34]Leonid Ouspensky, *He Eikona*, trans. Photes Kontoglou (Athens, 1991), p. 46.

[35]Photes Kontoglou, "Hagiagraphia," in *Threskeutike kai Ethike Egkuklopaideia*, vol. 1 (Athens, 1962), p. 250 (translation is mine).

reminders that our "corruptible [nature] must put on incorruption and this mortal must put on immortality" (1 Cor. 15:53). When looking at the icon of a saint, male or female, we look at the position and the significance he or she possesses within the Church. This explains why the faces of Christ, the *Theotokos* and the saints are *always* depicted in a frontal manner (Fig. 6). As St. Macarius the Egyptian (ca. 300–90) writes: the Saints are "full of eyes,"[36] meaning that they are transparent, susceptible to divine Grace and energy. The faithful see the face of a saint as a whole and never break it into its constituent parts. The transverse depiction is used only for persons who have not acquired sainthood, such as the shepherds and wise men in an icon of the Nativity, the face of Judas or the devil's in the Last Supper. These icons signify an absence and a lack of communion with the beholder.

Looking at someone means I look at my own self and, therefore, I am in communion. That is why an icon is a means of communion between the faithful and the person depicted. Through the visible we experience the invisible. The view of Christ in pictorial representation leads the worshiper to the invisible Christ; seeing the charismatic faces of Saints in icons leads to communion with them. Even the depictions of material or objects from nature (mountains, trees, animals, buildings, flowers) do not direct one's thoughts towards a materialistic view of life. The beholder of icons is bathed in the spiritual light of the saints depicted and participates in the holiness they are in. Daily life in the Byzantine era had been enriched with iconography because its aim was more than aesthetic; mainly it was to serve as a channel for grace. The icon was intended to diminish the sense of opposition between this and the world to come; it proclaimed in a pictorial way the reality of a triumphant celestial Church with the militant Church on earth in communion with one another.

It has been pointed out that the contents of iconography in the medieval Greek Church corresponded to its theology. It introduced the redeeming work of the Lord Jesus Christ and the birth and growth of the "new creation" (2 Cor. 5:17). The spirituality of an icon projects "the new heavens

[36]Macarius the Egyptian, *Homiliae Pneumatikai*, no 33, PG 34: 741.

Figure 6. The Twelve Apostles, by Photes Kontoglou. Monastery of St. Anargyroi, Vassaras-Laconias, Greece, 1956. Photo: Author.

and the new earth" (2 Peter 3:13), the expectation that virtue and holiness will prevail. The icon is a world reborn and recreated through divine grace, where the Almighty God's eternal light illumines all.[37]

Furthermore the dogmatic character of Byzantine iconography is expressed through the artist's technique. The hagiographer, for example, renders the image in an abstract manner in order to emphasize the "works of the right hand of the most High" (Ps. 77:10), that is, to illustrate that the saints have undergone a profound transfiguration, both physically and spiritually, through their communion with God. Even if the artist had met the saint in person when he was alive, he would not have depicted him with his natural features. The faces and the bodies of the saints depicted in Byzantine icons look unnatural, disproportionate, and sometimes without any charm or beauty because the emphasis is on the spiritual beauty of an icon. The viewer is directed by these alien shapes and images to the ontology they represent. Behind, if I may use this word, those *strange* images, there hides a deep theological meaning. In order to be able to *read* a Byzantine icon, one needs to know its *language*. Photes Kontoglou, a great authority, expresses this idea in paraphrase as follows: The language of iconography is like the language of the New Testament; simple, consistent, direct, and without any vain embellishments. Every line, every shape and color holds a specific meaning and serves a specific purpose (Fig. 7). The eyes, for example, are usually drawn big and lively to show the inner intensity of the soul. The deep, staring eyes are intended to echo the gospel, "my eyes have seen thy salvation" (Luke 2:30). We can see such use of biblical typologies in virtually every instance of the depiction. For example, biblical verses underline even the depiction of certain icon's big ears, because the saint "has heard the mystery of divine Economy,"[38] and admonishes the faithful to be ready to receive the divine message. The nose, on the other hand, is

---

[37]Compare Kalokyres, *He Zografike*, p. 128.

[38]*Katavasiai* of the Elevation of the Holy Cross, Ode Four, *Menaion of September* (Athens, 1970), pp. 178–79.

Figure 7. St. Nicholas, fresco by Manuel Panselinos. Church of Protaton, Mt. Athos, Greece, 1290. Photo: Author.

Figure 8. Jesus Christ, by Theophanes the Cretan. Monastery of Stavronikita, Mt. Athos, Greece, sixteenth century. Photo: Author.

extremely huge and narrow, because it smells "a breath of spiritual fragrance" (Eph. 5:2). The small mouth, too, is an expression of spirituality since it symbolizes the mortification of the flesh [*apatheia*], that is the ascetic ideal according to which human beings should be satisfied with the daily necessities and not be greedy. Instead they should look for the riches of the heavenly kingdom. In the same symbolic manner are also depicted the hands, the feet, the lighted circle round the head (the halo), the garments' colors, and even the background. Christ's inner gown, for example, is dark red, to remind us that he assumed human flesh and blood, while his external garment is light blue, symbolizing his divine nature, since blue is the color of the heavens (Fig. 8). The *Theotokos*' inner garment is, however, blue, a symbol of the heavenly nature to which she was joined, and her outer one red, symbolizing a human but royal nature (Fig. 9). The saints are usually dressed in the same manner with the *Theotokos*. The background of an icon is typically gold, which for the Byzantines symbolized the uncreated light that the saints experienced in heaven where they dwelled, in a state of *theosis,* a state in which every thing is different, purified, incorporeal, and transfigured because it is in God.

Furthermore, through the use of exaggeration, excess, and disfigurement of natural features, the iconographer expresses the supernatural element. Byzantine iconography, however, although it displaces the realistic element, does so for theological reasons. Since Christ and the saints participated in both worlds, iconography therefore stresses the subjection of matter to the spirit and the assimilation of material elements by the spiritual power.

The sacraments are another very important element of medieval Greek iconography and underscore the theological meaning implicit in the art. The icon of Christ's baptism, for example (Fig. 10), teaches the faithful the doctrine about the sacrament of baptism. Let me illustrate: the three persons of the Holy Trinity are depicted in a perpendicular direction, from the top to the bottom of the icon: the Father is seen blessing with His hand; the Holy Spirit has taken the form of a "dove" (Matt. 3:16), and the Son is in the water.

Figure 9. The *Theotokos*, by Theophanes the Cretan. Monastery of Stavronikita, Mt. Athos, Greece, sixteenth century. Photo: Author.

Figure 10. The Baptism of Christ, by Theophanes the Cretan. Monastery of the Great Lavra, Mt. Athos, Greece, sixteenth century. Photo: Author.

When one sees this icon and hears the hymn "at your baptism in the Jordan River, O Christ, the worship due to the Holy Trinity was made manifest,"[39] one has an excellent oral-aural perception of the mystery of the Holy Trinity. Jesus is depicted naked in his baptism in the river Jordan, unlike virtually all medieval Western depictions, which depict Christ clothed wearing a gown. Christ is depicted standing at the river's bank, on a rock, and the Baptizer pours water onto Christ's head. He is naked because the liturgical verse says he "emptied Himself voluntarily in order to clothe Adam's nakedness."[40] John the Baptist baptizes the Savior in the Jordan river, "touching the Lord's head" so that the faithful too may run to touch the Lord. The icon of Jesus Christ as a teacher in the entrance of a church and as the Pantocrator on the dome, as well as the depiction of the *Theotokos* in the concha of the altar, signify the *dogmatic* cycle of the medieval Greek Church and project the spiritual orientation of Byzantine iconography.[41]

The dogmatic cycle binds together the faithful who are gathered in worship and helps them understand the meaning of the Church, as the visible body of an invisible Christ, its head. The faithful are counted together with the prophets, the apostles, the martyrs, the fathers, and all the saints of the Church, and thus achieve communion and obtain the experience of sainthood.

---

[39]The Apolytikion of Epiphany Service, *Menaion of January* (Athens, 1970), p. 139.

[40]The Vespers of Epiphany, ibid.

[41]It is beyond the scope of the present essay to present an analysis of the third iconographic cycle, known as the *Historical* or *Festive.* The Church lives the fact of salvation through history. This cycle includes facts and images of religious history and of the great festive days of the ecclesiastical year. They are depicted in the four arcades of the Byzantine style church, on the narthex and on the side walls. Here the meaning of "ypomnesis" (remembrance) applies, i.e. the participation in the fact of salvation through history. Thus, the icons which refer to the historical events of Christ's presence on earth, such as His Nativity, Baptism, Crucifixion, Resurrection, Ascension and the Pentecost are all included in this cycle. There are also scenes from the life of the *Theotokos*, of the hierarchs, saints, and martyrs.

The Liturgical Cycle of Byzantine Iconography

It has been implied that an icon is more than a religious picture—it is above all a *liturgical art.* For this reason it is impossible to interpret it without examining it in relationship to worship. With the term *liturgical art,* we mean that Byzantine iconography aims at helping the faithful to comprehend and in a deeper way experience in liturgy the central sacrament of the Eucharist.[42] Liturgical iconography makes visible the mystical elements that take place in the worship. Through its physical representation it helps worshipers experience the mystery of Divine Economy, which consists of God becoming human to save humanity, a doctrine of fundamental significance in Orthodox Christian worship. Since the Eucharist is a mystery, iconography, too, speaks the language of the mystery. It illustrates and speaks to the hearts of the faithful through symbols, shapes, and forms, surpassing material reality, transferring the worshiper to the world of the spirit. Just as in the liturgy the participating faithful in a *mystical* way represent the angelic Cherubim,[43] so too the icons manifest the presence of invisible but real members of the Church.

As I indicated before, the liturgical character of Byzantine iconography can be traced back to the early years of Christianity. The art in the catacombs, for example, included several symbols such as the *fish,* whose Greek name ΙΧΘΥΣ stands for Jesus Christ God's Son Savior, identified with the sacrifice of Holy Eucharist. Another icon symbolic of the Eucharistic bread is the multiplication of the loaves of bread and fish as related by the Gospel of Matthew (14:17). The *lamb,* too, is the "slain Lamb," "the Lamb of God which takes away the sin of the world" (Rev. 5:6; John 1:29). Christ,

---

[42]Stephen Gero, "The Eucharistic Doctrine of the Byzantine Iconoclasts and Its Sources," *Byzantinische Zeitschrift* 68 (1975): 4–22.

[43]See the *Cherubic Hymn*, from the Divine Liturgy of St. John Chrysostom, *Hieratikon* (Athens, 1977), p. 118.

through the Holy Eucharist, replaced the Lamb of the Jewish Passover and became for all of us "the new Passover."[44] In the holy altar of some churches, as for example in the church of the Monastery at Mount Sinai,[45] which represents the heavenly altar, we see icons of Old Testament personalities, such as the sacrifice of Abraham, the three children in the furnace, and the prophet Daniel—all symbols of the Eucharistic sacrifice.

From the beginning of the Christian era, Jesus Christ was the true minister of the Church's sacraments. Icons accordingly depict him in a frontal position, holding his right hand raised as in a blessing manner while holding the Gospel with his left hand. This iconographic depiction quickly became popular all over the Greek Christian world (Fig. 11).

In later centuries, during the Macedonian and Komnenian eras in particular, an attempt was made to make the sacrament of Holy Eucharist more clearly understood by placing an icon of the *Holy Liturgy* in the back of the holy table of the altar. Christ is depicted as the *High Priest*, offering his Body [*He Metadosis*] and Blood [*He Metalepsis*] to the apostles, who approach him in fear and trembling. This representation is known as *E Koinonia ton Apostolon* [The Communion of the Apostles] (Figs. 12 and 13). Every time the priest performs the bloodless sacrifice, he repeats[46] the liturgical act performed in heaven by the high priest Jesus Christ. The icon includes angels, dressed in deacon's vestments, carrying with fear and awe the holy gifts to the high priest—the Lord. Once again we have to emphasize that this type of iconography serves not a decorative purpose but a

---

[44]See also Sticheron of Easter Sunday, *Pentikostarion* (Athens, FOS, not dated), p.5. See also 1 Cor. 5:7.

[45]See Kurt Weitzmann, *The Monastery of St. Catherine at Mount Sinai. The Icons from the Sixth to the Tenth Century* (Princeton, 1976).

[46]Relevant to this is a poster found in the arch of the holy altar of the Monastery of Great Lavra at Mount Athos that says: "Seeing the altar of the Lord's Table, stand trembling before it, o man, and look down; Christ is sacrificed every day herein and the whole order of the holy angels worship him liturgically in fear."

Figure 11. Jesus Christ. Monastery of St. Catherine at Mount Sinai, first half of the sixth century (encaustic technique). Photo: Author.

Figure 12. The Communion of the Apostles. Greek Orthodox Archdiocese of America, 1996. Photo: Author.

Figure 13. *He Metalepsis*. Monastery of the Holy Transfiguration, Meteora, Greece, sixteenth century. Photo: Author.

strictly liturgical one. It aims to elevate and assist the worshiper to live experientially the sacrament of the Holy Eucharist. Seeing the highly spiritual images of the representations of the divine liturgy one is overcome by the feeling that truly "the powers of heaven minister with us in an invisible manner" as the hymn of the Great Entrance proclaims.[47]

Another iconic representation of the Eucharist dating from the twelfth century is the icon of the slain lamb of the *diskarion* [paten]. This liturgical icon is called the ***Melismos*** [dismembering] and depicts the Lord as an infant on the paten. A distinctive detail of this depiction is the very verb tense used, which calls Christ not the "one sacrificed" but the "sacrificing," thereby revealing that he is always being sacrificed, just as it is expressed in the divine liturgy with the phrase "broken and distributed is the Lamb of God . . . ." Iconography and liturgical time reenact divine events in the present *kairos* [time]. This is fully confirmed by the Church's hymnography, an additional means to involve the faithful in liturgical worship. During the Palaeologian era hagiographers painted icons of leading Church Fathers, holding in their hands liturgical scrolls inscribed with prayers and biblical sayings (Fig. 14).

In brief, the liturgical cycle we have described is the result of the relationship between the icon and the liturgical worship of the Church. The icon's pictorial language summarizes in a mystical manner the liturgical tradition of the Church. Byzantine hagiographers were anonymous liturgical instruments in the service of God's glory and God's elect people.

Conclusion

Byzantine iconography—whether private or collective—served doctrinal, liturgical, ethical, and eschatological needs of the faithful. Icons, hymns, the liturgy proper became gates of entrance from the temporal to the eternal,

---

[47]See the *Cherubic Hymn*, from the Divine Liturgy of the Presanctified Gifts, *Hieratikon* (Athens, 1977), p. 214.

Figure 14. St James, St. John Chrysostom, St. Basil the Great, and St. Gregory the Theologian. Fresco from the Church of St. Nicholas Orphanos, Thessalonica, Greece, fourteenth century. Photo: Author.

from an imperfect world to the perfect kingdom of God. More than aesthetic satisfaction, iconography epitomized the theology of the Church's sacraments and teachings. The Greek Church used the "word of God" (the Scriptures) in written form but also the "word of God" illustrated through icons and symbols. The Greek Church preached the word of Scripture, and at the same time, illustrated Scripture's word through icons and symbols. Thus the Greek Church involved more than just the rational soul and the senses; it involved the whole person, or human being, in its prayer life and teaching.

Perhaps there is no better way to conclude this essay than by turning back to St. John of Damascus, whose views were adopted by the seventh Ecumenical Council (A.D. 787) and who left a memorable statement illustrating the theological importance of the icon. In his effort to explain and defend the importance of the incarnation of Christ dogma, St. John wrote:

> It is impossible to make an icon of God the incorporeal, the invisible the immaterial and uncircumscribed, who has no form and is beyond comprehension: for how can that which is not seen be depicted? But while no one has ever seen God, yet the only-begotten Son, who is in the bosom of the Father, has made this unseen God manifest . . . (John 1:18).
>
> I do not venerate creation rather such as I am, who without abasement and degradation has come down into creation, in order to glorify my nature and make it a partaker of the divine nature. Together with the divine King I venerate the royal robe of his body. . . . And so with confidence I make an icon of the invisible God, not in so far as he is invisible but in so far as he became visible for our sakes by partaking in flesh and blood. I do not make an icon of the invisible Godhead, but I make an icon of the visible flesh of God. . . .
>
> Of old, the incorporeal and invisible God was not depicted at all; but now, since God has appeared in flesh and dwelt among men, I make an icon of God in so far as he has become visible. I do not venerate matter but I venerate the Creator of matter, who for my sake has become material, who has been pleased to dwell in matter and has through matter effected my salvation. I shall not cease to venerate matter, for it was through matter that my salvation came to pass. . . . Do not insult matter for it is not without honor; nothing is without honor that God has made. . . . Israel of old did not see God, but we "with unveiled faces behold as in a mirror the glory of the Lord" (2 Cor. 3:18).[48]

The teachings of the Seventh Ecumenical Council were reiterated by the Council of Constantinople in 843 and emphasized that icons are not to be worshiped but only to be venerated, and the veneration paid to the icon passes on to the prototype. The decree reads as follows:

> We preserve unchanged all the traditions of the Church, whether handed down to us in written or unwritten form. Of these traditions, one is the painting of icons. The pictorial image in iconography and the verbal narrative in the Gospels are in agreement with one another, and both alike emphasize that the Incarnation of God the Word is genuine and not illusory. . . .

---

[48]John of Damascus, *On Icons*, ed. Bonifatius Kotter, *Die Schriften des Johannes von Damaskos,* 7 vols. (Berlin–New York, 1969–88), 3:143.

> We therefore declare that, together with the emblem of the precious and life-giving Cross, it is legitimate for holy icons, whether painted or made from mosaic or from any other appropriate material, to be displayed in churches, on sacred vessels and vestments, on walls and panels, in houses and streets. In these icons there may be depicted our Lord and God and Savior Jesus Christ, our most pure Lady the holy Mother of God, the honored angels, and all saints and holy men. The more often we see such icons, the more we are led to recall with love the persons depicted. To these icons should be given reverence and veneration, but not the worship of faith that is due only to the divine nature. They may be honored with incense and candles, as is done with the emblem of the precious and life-giving Cross and the Holy Gospels. . . . This is the faith of the Apostles, this is the faith of the Fathers, this is the faith of the Orthodox, this faith has made firm the whole world.[49]

The teachings of the Scriptures, as they were explained by Church Fathers and Ecumenical Councils, in words and icons, in liturgy and liturgical services, in religious art and architecture, were intended to involve the whole human person, and determined the nature of religious life in the Greek Middle Ages. The essence of the liturgical life, the place of icons in Christian worship, and the spiritual outlook of the Byzantine era, are valid to the present day in much of the Eastern Orthodox Christian world.

---

[49]Mansi, *Sacrorum conciliorum.,* 13, 377B–E, 397C.

THE LITURGY AND VERNACULAR LITERATURE[1]

EVELYN BIRGE VITZ

THE CHRISTIAN LITURGY resonates in many and complex ways in the vernacular literature of the western Middle Ages. It is echoed, quoted and alluded to, translated, honored, and imitated, used in jokes and occasionally derided. "Official" liturgies such as the Mass and Offices, with texts in Latin, are cited and referred to in a wide variety of texts and genres throughout the Medieval period. Liturgical themes are developed, gestures referred to, vessels and vestments depicted, music and chant evoked. The liturgical day, from Matins to Vespers and Compline, and the liturgical year, with its many feasts and penitential moments, provide the backdrop to many medieval vernacular literary works. The panorama offered by the liturgy often expanded the vision of poets, turning their gaze from the here and now to heaven, hell, and eternity.[2]

---

[1]I am deeply grateful to the many friends and colleagues who at one point or another generously shared with me their knowledge of works and issues, or read over drafts: Margaret Bent, William Calin, John Freccero, William Mahrt, Siobhan Marshall, Giuseppe Mazzotta, Antonella Puca, Robert Raymo, Edward Roesner, Gordon Whatley, and Michel Zink. I also thank Richard Emmerson and Russell Peck of the TEAMS editorial board, and Thomas Heffernan and E. Ann Matter, the editors of this volume, for their valuable suggestions.

[2]It is perhaps useful to note here briefly a few of the alternate ways in which I could have organized this essay. It would, for example, have been possible—and interesting—to think in terms of a *typology* of texts marked by the liturgy. This approach might, however, have made for rather dry reading, and have made it difficult both to see historical change and to

This essay first briefly discusses the manner in which the terms *liturgy* and *vernacular literature* are used and the relationship between the two. It then moves on to provide examples of how vernacular literature throughout the Middle Ages reflected liturgical themes. First focusing on Early English vernacular texts, we discuss Old English and Early French literature as well as saints' Lives, songs, and parodies. Moving on to the thirteenth century, we consider French romances such as *The Quest of the Holy Grail* and *The Romance of the Rose*. Fourteenth-century examples include Dante's *Divine Comedy* and Chaucer's *The Canterbury Tales*, while fifteenth-century examples include François Villon's *Lais* and *Testament* and the influence of Books of Hours.

The Relationship between Liturgy and Literature

Even in its most official modes, the liturgy was by no means a simple entity. Different regions and orders had distinctive liturgies; all services have a complex historical development;[3] and, perhaps most important, everywhere we will see assorted official and unofficial accretions to original patterns. Much of the time, therefore, we will be adopting a loose definition of liturgy. (It is perhaps all the more appropriate to be latitudinarian in our

---

appreciate the richness of particular works. Alternatively, I might have organized these pages in terms of liturgical time or of liturgical poetry. Each of these two approaches, however, would have narrowed the frame of reference substantially. The solution that I have opted for is an essay that tries at least to suggest the wide range of kinds of allusions to and uses of the liturgy in medieval works, with a special focus on important genres and works. One final note on my general approach: I have tended to exclude works that were more or less pure translations and/or glosses of liturgical texts, or of books of the Bible such as the Psalter, as consideration of such texts would have made an already-long article longer still. I do, however, discuss a few such compositions in my pages on lyric poetry.

[3]Among the valuable works on these important topics are those of Archdale A. King, especially *Liturgies of the Religious Orders* (London, 1955), *Liturgies of the Primatial Sees* (Milwaukee, 1957), and *Liturgies of the Past* (London, 1959). See also Pierre Batiffol, *History of the Roman Breviary*, trans. Atwell M. Y. Baylay from third French ed. (London, 1912).

definition of the word *liturgy*, as this term was not used during the medieval period itself.) I will follow the example of the French liturgiologist A. G. Martimort, and will define liturgy simply—broadly—as "the church at prayer"[4] in unofficial as well as official modes, in "vulgar" tongues as well as in Latin, in private as well as public modes. We will find vast reservoirs of devotional and prayerful hymns and other texts that can be thought of as semi- or para-liturgical: as constituting a vast unofficial penumbra to the official liturgy, and as accompanying many actions such as pilgrimages, devotions, and litanies to the saints and to the Blessed Virgin Mary,[5] the veneration and translation of relics, penitential meditations, and the like.[6] Poets and writers also imitated liturgical language, created imaginary liturgies, and constructed liturgical plots that move from alienation and supplication to acceptance and communion.

Two basic points are worth making before we proceed. Vernacular literature had, in two respects, a special relationship to the liturgy. First, precisely because literature is an art based on the conjoining of words and ideas, medieval literature—in the vernacular as in Latin[7]—drew on the great verbal and conceptual beauty of the liturgy, and of sacred Scripture which

---

[4]*The Church at Prayer: An Introduction to the Liturgy,* ed. A. G. Martimort et al., trans. from *L'Église en prière*, rev. ed. by Matthew J. O'Connell, 4 vols. (Collegeville, Minn., 1986). See also the second (untranslated) edition: *L'Église en prière* (Paris, 1961).

[5]For the history of devotion to the Virgin see Hilda Graef, *Mary: A History of Doctrine and Devotion*, 2 vols. (New York, 1963).

[6]See, for example, Keith Val Sinclair, *French Devotional Texts of the Middle Ages: A Bibliographical Manuscript Guide* (Westport, Conn., 1979); *First Supplement* (1982); *Second Supplement* (1988); and *Prières en ancien français: nouvelles références, renseignements complémentaires, indications bibliographiques, corrections et tables des articles du Répertoire de Sonet* (Hamden, Conn., 1978). For the Late Medieval period in France see Pierre Rézeau, *Les prières aux saints en français à la fin du Moyen Age*, 2 vols. (Geneva, 1982–83); and *Répertoire d'incipit des prières françaises à la fin du Moyen Age: Addenda et corrigenda aux répertoires de Sonet et Sinclair* (Geneva, 1986).

[7]The same would, of course, be true of Greek, but our focus is on western Europe.

stands behind it.[8] Jean Leclercq put it eloquently when he spoke of the "poem of the liturgy," meaning that the liturgy was itself a vast and complex poem.[9]

Second, literature had quite a different relationship to the liturgy than did the other arts. The medieval visual arts (to take a prime example) were to a remarkable degree religious and liturgical; they were created largely by and for the Church. Painting and book-production required powerful patronage, as these arts are costly to produce: parchment is expensive, as are ink, colored paints and gold leaf, and the labor of scribes. But talk is cheap. True, poets and entertainers—*trouvères*, *jongleurs*, and minstrels, bards,[10] etc.—wished to be rewarded for their labors. But the raw materials of song and story-telling, namely, words and melody, are free. It is true, of course, that many vernacular compositions were produced by clerks or by poets with some measure of clerical formation and were ultimately written down in manuscripts—which brings in scribes, parchment, and the like—but such was not reliably the case. In short, the patronage system had a structurally different relation to vernacular literature (both oral and written) than it did to the visual arts, or to architecture. Moreover, the control exercised by the Church over "vulgar" songs and stories was obviously weaker than over works for which it was the direct patron. In this context, it becomes all the more striking how strongly medieval vernacular literature is influenced by the liturgy. It is not always pious, to be sure, but it speaks through the linguistic and conceptual purview of the liturgy. And poets and audiences alike appear to recognize the need to lift the mind and heart to God—as well as the deep human resistance to doing so.

---

[8]We will return to Scriptural issues at the close of this article. Very useful articles on the impact of the Bible—and therefore, though indirectly, of the liturgy—on literature can be found in *A Dictionary of Biblical Tradition in English Literature*, gen. ed., David Lyle Jeffrey (Grand Rapids, Mich., 1992); many articles go well beyond purely English concerns.

[9]Jean Leclercq, *The Love of Learning and the Desire for God: A Study of Monastic Culture*, 3rd ed. (New York, 1982), pp. 236 ff.

[10]These are but a few of the many names for poets and performers in the medieval period.

Early Vernacular Literature and Ongoing Liturgical Themes and Preoccupations of the Medieval Period

Old English Literature[11]

Much of Old English literature is religious.[12] Some works are narrative, retelling stories from Scripture or from thc Lives of the saints; others have an apocalyptic streak, Doomsday being frequently and alarmingly imagined and described; many are in part catechetical, explaining fundamental doctrines of Christian theology to the laity, and generally are homiletic as well: they preach to the audience, encouraging or exhorting them to live according to the teachings of Christ. In some cases, a Christian dimension may be

---

[11]On Old English literature in general see *A New Critical History of Old English Literature,* ed. Stanley B. Greenfield and Daniel G. Calder (New York, 1986); also *The Cambridge Companion to Old English Literature,* ed. Malcolm Godden and Michael Lapidge (Cambridge, 1991). See also Stanley B. Greenfield, *A Bibliography of Publications on Old English Literature to the End of 1972: Using the Collections of E. E. Ericson, Stanley B. Greenfield and Fred C. Robinson* (Toronto, 1980). The *Old English Newsletter* is a valuable source of scholarly material on Old English literature, with many articles and bibliographies on religious issues. On the importance of the liturgy in Old English works see also Milton McC. Gatch: "Old English Literature and the Liturgy," *Anglo-Saxon England* 6 (1977): 237–47. A volume containing various essays of interest for medieval English literature is *The Popular Literature of Medieval England,* ed. Thomas Heffernan (Knoxville, 1985). It is worth noting that Old English literature was different from the Romance tradition in two important respects. First, it began to be written down very early—substantially earlier than the Romance languages. Second, since English (like all the Germanic languages, and unlike the Romance vernaculars) is fundamentally different from Latin, liturgical, biblical, and other Latin texts had to be translated or explained to be comprehensible by the unlettered faithful.

[12]The same is true of all the emerging vernaculars. For example, for the Italian tradition see Ernesto Monaci, *Crestomazia italiana dei primi secoli: Con prospetto grammaticale e glossario* (Rome, 1955). For the German tradition see Albert Fuchs, *Les débuts de la littérature allemande* (Paris, 1952); and Maurice O'C. Walshe, *Medieval German Literature: A Survey*, book 1 (Cambridge, Mass., 1962).

superimposed onto an older work of pagan, typically heroic, inspiration, as in the case of *Beowulf.*[13] But many important works are rooted strongly in the liturgy. Caedmon and Cynewulf are used here as two brief examples from among many.

Caedmon is one of the very earliest medieval vernacular singers of whom history (in the person of the Venerable Bede) speaks by name.[14] A non-literate lay-brother at a religious house at Whitby in the seventh century, Caedmon was said to have received the gift of poetry from God, and to have been inspired to compose sacred songs.[15] While many surviving Old English poems are described as "Caedmonian" (anonymous works do tend to get ascribed to great names), only the following fragment—a song of praise to the Creator—can be ascribed with certainty to this fascinating but shadowy figure:

> Now must we praise the Guardian of heaven,
> The power and conception of the Lord,
> And all His works, as He, eternal Lord,
> Father of glory, started every wonder.
> First He created heaven as a roof,
> The holy Maker, for the sons of men.
> Then the eternal Keeper of mankind
> Furnished the earth below, the land for men
> Almighty God and everlasting Lord.[16]

---

[13]See, for example, Fred C. Robinson, "Beowulf," in *The Cambridge Companion to Old English Literature*, ed. Godden and Lapidge, pp. 142–59.

[14]Bede [the Venerable], *Ecclesiastical History of the English People, with Bede's Letter to Egbert and Cuthbert's Letter on the Death of Bede*, trans. Leo Sherley-Price, rev. R. E. Latham, trans. of the minor works, new introduction and notes by David H. Farmer (London, 1990), IV:xxiv, pp. 248–51.

[15]The relation of these songs to the official liturgy is unclear and, though the lines quoted below are often titled "Caedmon's Hymn," Bede refers to such compositions only as "songs."

[16]*A Choice of Anglo-Saxon Verse, selected, with an introduction and a parallel verse translation*, comp. Richard Hamer (London, 1970), pp. 122–23. See also S. A. J. Bradley, *Anglo-*

Among the many works sometimes attributed to the great ninth-century poet Cynewulf is a poem which scholars call "Christ I."[17] This poem consists largely of a lyric and typological elaboration of the antiphons sung at Vespers during the season of Advent. (Antiphons were originally chants sung as introductions to psalms;[18] some eventually took on autonomous devotional status as independent or "votive" antiphons[19] while continuing to be called antiphons.) Advent had specially appointed antiphons, called the **great "O's,"** of which the seven "greater" (original) antiphons were: O Eternal Wisdom; O Lord and Ruler of the House of David; O Root of Jesse; O Key of David; O Rising Brightness; O King and Desire of All Nations; and O Emmanuel.[20] "Christ I" draws on almost all these antiphons,

---

Saxon Poetry: An Anthology of Old English poems in prose translation: With introduction and headnotes (London, 1982), p. 4. Many of the poems formerly ascribed to Caedmon are given by Bradley under the heading "Junius 11" (referring to a manuscript in which they are found), pp. 7–86.

[17]This is the first part of a triptych on the Advent, Ascension, and Second Coming of Christ. Many scholars today consider only the second part—"Christ II"—to be the work of Cynewulf himself (it is signed with his runic signature). The exact shape of the Cynewulfian corpus is still debated. See, e.g., Daniel G. Calder, *Cynewulf* (Boston, 1981); he discusses the role of the liturgy in the works most commonly ascribed to Cynewulf. See also Earl R. Anderson, *Cynewulf: Structure, Style, and Theme in His Poetry* (Rutherford, N.J., 1983). Also Charles W. Kennedy, *The Earliest English Poetry: A Critical Survey of the Poetry Written before the Norman Conquest, with Illustrative Translations* (London, 1943), pp. 198–267; esp. 235–60. On "Christ I" see Robert B. Burlin, *The Old English Advent: A Typological Commentary* (New Haven, 1968).

[18]They were called "antiphons" because the psalms or canticles that they introduced or followed were sung "antiphonally," i.e., by two choirs (or groups of singers) answering each other, singing "against" each other.

[19]They might be called "anthems," a word derived from *antiphons*.

[20]See Kennedy, *Earliest English Poetry*, pp. 235–36. The Advent hymn, familiar to many, entitled "O Come, O Come Emmanuel" [Veni, veni, Emmanuel] is drawn from the "great O's."

as well as on some of the "lesser" (or optional) Advent antiphons. One of these "O" antiphons with its poetic amplification reads:

> O key of David and sceptre of the house of Israel, you who open and no one closes: you who close and no one opens; come and lead out of the prison-house the captive who sits in darkness and the shadow of death.
>
> O Judge and just King, you who guard the locks and lay open life and the blessed ways on high, and to another deny the lovely longed-for road if his attainment does not suffice: out of necessity indeed we speak these words and entreat him who created man not be slow . . . [slight damage to the only manuscript] . . . the cause of those fraught with care, for we sit sorrowing in prison. We look forward to the sun, when the Lord of life will disclose to us the light, and become to us in a source of security and enfole our feeble consciousness in glory. . . .[21]

"Christ I" also contains amplifications of antiphons for the Feasts of the Circumcision, Epiphany, and Trinity, and from the Common Preface to the Sanctus of the Mass.[22] Thus, this poem combines liturgical echoes from several moments of the Christian year into what might be called a meta-liturgical—or meta-calendrical—development. Cynewulfian poems certainly drew on audience familiarity with a broad liturgical context, evoking the religious emotions—and liturgical melodies[23]—associated not merely with Advent but with various moments of the liturgical year.[24]

---

[21]See Bradley, *Anglo-Saxon Poetry*, pp. 203–16; quotation from pp. 205–06.

[22]See Bradley, *Anglo-Saxon Poetry*, p. 204.

[23]The Advent antiphons to which the poet alludes were all sung to the same basic melody, specific to this season and to these particular antiphons. See Andrew Hughes, *Medieval Manuscripts for Mass and Office: A guide to their Organization and Terminology* (Toronto, 1982), p. 73. These liturgical elements are embedded as well in theological themes drawn from the Bible and from homilies from the Fathers of the Church, especially St. Gregory the Great.

[24]The poems attributed with virtual certainty to Cynewulf himself also have a liturgical cast. Structurally and thematically, they may draw on the litanies of the saints, as in the case of *The Fates of the Apostles*. And all Cynewulf's poems are linked to the feasts of the church

Early French Literature[25]

As in Old English—and the other emerging Romance vernaculars as well—many of the earliest surviving French texts are para-liturgical.[26] Most works from the late tenth and eleventh centuries are hymns; tropes—verbal embellishments added to words of the liturgy; or **sequences**—textual and melodic amplifications of the melisma upon the final *a* of "**Alleluia**!" and which only gradually became separate pieces. One example[27] from many is the eleventh-century play ***Sponsus***, a dramatic trope on the parable of the Wise and Foolish virgins, composed in a blend of Latin, northern French, and Occitan, found in a manuscript in the monastery of St. Martial at Limoges.[28]

---

year: 16 February (*Juliana*); 3 May (*Elene* and the elevation of the cross); Ascension (*Christ II*); and November (*The Fates*). See Calder, *Cynewulf*, esp. pp. 24, 36.

[25]Among the most valuable general introductions to French medieval literature, including its religious and liturgical themes, are Paul Zumthor's still-classic *Histoire littéraire de la France médiévale, VI–XIVe siècles* (Paris, 1954); Michel Zink, "L'Eglise et les lettres," in *Précis de littérature française du Moyen Age*, ed. Daniel Poirion (Paris, 1983), pp. 35–58; and Michael Zink, *Littérature française du Moyen Age* (Paris, 1992); and the multi-volumed, multi-authored *Grundriss der Romanischen Literaturen des Mittelalters* (Heidelberg, 1968–88). A recent general history of French literature with a number of relevant articles is *A New History of French Literature*, ed. Denis Hollier (Cambridge, Mass., 1989).

[26]See Maurice Delbouille, "Tradition latine et naissance des littératures romanes," in *Grundriss der Romanischen Literaturen des Mittelalters*, vol. 1/1 (Heidelberg, 1972), pp. 3–56; also Zumthor, *Histoire littéraire*, passim.

[27]We will see further examples in later sections on saints' Lives and on the lyric.

[28]Many poetic and musical tropes are connected with this important monastery, and with the region of Aquitaine. This work was edited by Karl Young in *The Drama of the Medieval Church*, 2 vols. (Oxford, 1933), 2:362–64; it has also been edited more recently by Lucien-Paul Thomas, *Le Sponsus; mystère des vierges sages et des vierges folles, suivi des trois poèmes limousins et farcis* (Paris, 1951).

Among the early works (from the late-eleventh century on) in French and Anglo-Norman[29] are numerous "chansons de geste," sung epics devoted to the deeds of great heroes, generally of the Carolingian period. These songs commonly contain many religious themes and have a strong Christian emphasis, and at least some of them appear to have been performed along pilgrimage routes or as part of the devotional activity at the shrines of the saints. In these poems (and many other vernacular epics as well), specific references to the liturgy generally fall into a small number of categories.[30] First, there are references to the celebration of the Eucharist and the Offices (especially to Vespers), and to funeral Masses and other burial rituals. Second, many *chansons de geste*, and vast quantities of other works as well, begin or end, or sometimes both, with prayer—at least in some manuscripts that contain them. A few examples: The twelfth-century *Chariot of Nîmes* [*Le charroi de Nîmes*], quite a funny and not an especially pious story, begins with "Listen, Lords, may God, the glorious king of majesty, increase your virtuous prowess" [Oiez, seignor, Deus vos croisse bonté, / Li glorieux, li rois de majesté; lines 1–2], and ends with King Louis "Ador[ing] God and his mother Mary."[31] *Doon of Maience* [*Doon de Maience*][32] ends with: "May God give us all everlasting life!" (line 11,505). In some cases, one function of these prayerful closures—one might call them "tags"—was probably to make the jongleurs who performed the songs appear

[29]Anglo-Norman works are those composed in the French language in England, after the Norman Conquest.

[30]See J. L. Roland Bélanger, *Damedieus: The Religious Context of the Loherain Cycle, Viewed Against Other Early French Epics* (Geneva, 1975). I am indebted to his work at various points in this discussion. See also CUER MA, Université de Provence, *La prière au Moyen Age: Littérature et civilisation* (Aix-en-Provence, 1981).

[31]*Le charroi de Nîmes: chanson de geste du XIIe siècle*, ed. Joseph Louis Perrier (Paris, 1968).

[32]M. A. Peÿ, *Doon de Maience* (1859; rpt. Nendelm, Liechtenstein, 1966).

respectable.[33] But the prayer also draws attention to a shared conviction that the poets, performers, audiences, and even the characters in the story (which is typically given as "true") ultimately share a same "plot" and are called to the same destiny.

A few epics close with official liturgical formulas: the Occitan (or Old Provençal) *Song of Girart of Roussillon* [*Chanson de Girart de Roussillon*],[34] a strongly religious work, ends with "Tu autem Domine" [But you, Lord], the opening phrase of a liturgical formula with which Matins lessons end.[35] It may be that such a closure reflects original connections between the *chanson de geste* and the liturgy, especially the commemoration of saints.[36] It is also possible that the "Tu Autem" ending is simply a way of associating a pious song with the liturgy. Thus, for example, its singing might have ended late at night. Matins, celebrated in the earliest hours of the new day, is in an important sense a night Office, and the nobles present might have been pleased to think of this song as prayerful in some "official" sense. There was some singing of epic songs during the vigils before knightly dubbing ceremonies; in light of its somewhat anti-war mentality and the very strong role it accords to women, this particular song would, however, seem an odd choice.[37] In any event, the prayer here surely provides food for thought: a reminder to listeners to think about what they have

---

[33]Churchmen with some regularity condemned *joculatores* for their vile gestures and general turpitude.

[34]*La chanson de Girart de Roussillon*, ed. Micheline de Combarieu du Grès and Gérard Gouiran (Paris, 1993), line 10,001.

[35]See Hughes, *Medieval Manuscripts*, pp. xxxiv, 60.

[36]See Jacques Chailley, *L'école musicale de St.-Martial de Limoges, jusqu'à la fin du XIe siècle* (Paris, 1960), pp. 352–60: "Saint Martial et l'origine des chansons de geste."

[37]The phrase *Tu autem, Domine* sometimes meant "Enough!" (as it were, "Time to wrap it up—to end the service!"). See Albert Henry, "Encore le 'Tu Autem'," *Bulletin Du Cange* 14 (1939): 107–11, esp. 110–11. But in this case, such a possibility seems unlikely: this is a strongly devout work.

heard, and to keep the poet or *jongleur* in their prayers as they bring the day to its close and prepare to start a new one.

Characters in the French epics often pray. The hero, either before fighting or as he dies on the battlefield, may recite a creed in which he articulates his faith as a Christian and asks God either to rescue him from death, or to save him from hell. These creeds, which are common in *chansons de geste* (some works contain more than one), are not in Latin, nor are they very close to any official Christian Creed. They are more a profession of faith *cum* short summary of biblical salvation miracles. For example, one of two creeds in *The Coronation of Louis* [*Le couronnement de Louis*; twelfth century] begins with God's creation of Adam and Eve; it speaks of Christ's Incarnation through the Virgin, his Nativity, his Crucifixion and Resurrection, and the Harrowing of hell—all close to the substance of the liturgical creeds. But this lengthy prayer also mentions Cain's murder of Abel, Noah and the ark, St. Anastasia (a midwife healed at the Nativity), the death of the Innocents, various scenes from Christ's life, Simon the leper and Mary Magdalene, Longinus, and Nicodemus and Joseph of Arimathea. It closes with a prayer for God's protection.[38] That such creeds reflect and constitute some sort of vernacular imitation or adaptation of official "credos" can hardly be doubted.

Finally, epic heroes, as they die on the battlefield, frequently carry out liturgical gestures and actions. Many of these behaviors are of course rooted in sacramentality, and we cannot always draw a sharp distinction between liturgy and sacrament. (Liturgy can be defined as adoration, praise, and prayer. The seven sacraments[39] are sacred rites, signs of God's presence, channels of divine grace. The Mass, in which Christians (1) worship and give thanks to God, and (2) receive the sacrament of Holy Communion,

---

[38]In *Guillaume d'Orange: Four Twelfth-Century Epics*, ed. Joan M. Ferrante (New York, 1974), lines 695–789, pp. 83–85.

[39]The seven are Baptism, Confession, Holy Communion, Confirmation, Holy Orders, Marriage, and Extreme Unction. See Elizabeth Rogers, *Peter Lombard and the Sacramental System* (Merrick, N.Y., 1976), esp. pp. 71–72.

thus partakes of both.) Some gestures by our epic heroes are also deeply feudal in nature, as when the dying Roland raises his glove to God, thereby symbolically handing back to God the responsibilities that had been entrusted to him. What is striking is that warriors frequently behave in a physically religious manner, using gestures from the eucharistic liturgy. Aside from being absolved and taking communion before the battle, dying warriors commonly strike their breast, a penitential action that already had been for many centuries part of the Mass: this important gesture accompanied the words of the "Confiteor" (or public confession of sin: "I confess": "Mea culpa, mea culpa, mea maxima culpa": My sin, my sin, my very great sin).[40] A few epics, such as *Garin of Lorraine* [*Garin le lorain*] and *Raoul of Cambrai* [*Raoul de Cambrai*], both dating from the late twelfth century, show the dying hero taking communion on three blades of grass. This gesture reflects the desire to die in God's friendship, so marked among epic heroes, as well as the belief that, *in extremis*, and in the absence of a priest, it was appropriate for a Christian to make this sort of spiritual communion.[41]

Works from other branches of the medieval story-telling tradition, such as romance, tend to be less markedly religious than epics. In some stories, such as Béroul's *Tristan*—a late twelfth-century work hardly renowned for its piety!—the only liturgical references are to swearing on relics. (The swearing on relics was often an elaborate religious ceremony in medieval

[40]See Josef A. Jungmann, *The Mass of the Roman Rite: Its Origins and Development*, 2 vols., trans. Francis A. Brunner (Westminster, Md., 1986; German rev. ed., 1951–55), 1:303. For other contexts in which the Confiteor is recited see Ludwig Eisenhofer and Joseph Lechner, *The Liturgy of the Roman Rite*, trans. A. J. and E. F. Peeler, ed. H. E. Winstone (New York, 1961), pp. 83–84.

[41]Sometimes a single blade of grass is divided in three; the "three" probably refers to the breaking of the Host into three parts in the Mass. On this curious symbolic viaticum see Bélanger, *Damedieus*, pp. 114–16; J. D. M. Ford, "'To Bite the Dust' and Symbolical Lay Communion," *PMLA* 20/2 (1905): 197–230; and George Hamilton, "The Sources of the Symbolical Lay Communion," *Romanic Review* 4/2 (1913): 221–42. Examples of this practice occur throughout the Medieval period, and similar examples are found in German and Italian literature; in some cases, what is taken as communion is earth rather than grass.

practice.[42]) It should be noted, however, that though characters frequently deceive others in such contexts, through careful wording of their oaths, they generally are careful not actually to lie to *God* when swearing on holy objects: when Iseut swears that only her husband King Mark and the poor beggar who just carried her piggy-back across the swamp have "come between her thighs," she has, precisely, arranged for Tristan to be there, playing the role of that beggar. In the romances of Chrétien de Troyes (late twelfth century), the male protagonist may well attend Mass in the morning before departing on his adventures. This narrative detail seldom is expanded upon, but attendance at Mass can perhaps best be understood as attesting to the character's identity as a Christian hero.

From the twelfth century on—in epics, romances (such as Chrétien's *Yvain*), and other works as well—we find references to women reading and praying the Psalter. Indeed, women seem to have had a special relationship to this book of the Bible, both as a focus of prayer (it was translated into the vernacular early) and as a primer for learning and for teaching children to read.

Romances often are anchored in some way in the liturgical year: the action may begin at Pentecost (less often, Easter or another liturgical season), and appropriate themes are sometimes emphasized. Examples come from English (and other literatures) as well as from France: *Sir Gawain and the Green Knight* is clearly in this tradition; it begins during Christmas festivities, and Gawain finds Bertilak's castle only after praying to be permitted to hear Mass on Christmas Eve of the following year; it might be argued that this is a poem for the long Christmas season, though indeed it shows involvement in the entire Christian year.[43]

---

[42]On relics and their importance see *Catholic Encyclopedia*, ed. Charles G. Herbermann, et al., vol. 12 (New York, 1912), pp. 34–38. See also Rosalind and Christopher Brooke, *Popular Religion in the Middle Ages: Western Europe, 1000–1300* (London, 1984), pp. 130 ff.

[43]See Robert J. Blanch, "Religion and Law in *Sir Gawain and the Green Knight*," in *Approaches to Teaching Sir Gawain and the Green Knight*, ed. Miriam Youngerman Miller and Jane Chance (New York, 1986), pp. 93–101.

Romances occasionally end, like epics, with prayer of a more or less strongly marked liturgical character. This tendency, perhaps particularly marked in English literature, continues throughout the Medieval period, and the fourteenth-century *Stanzaic Morte Arthur* ends as follows:

> Of Launcelot du Lake tell I no more,
> But thus beleve these ermites seven.
> And yet is Arthur buried there,
> And Queen Gaynor, as I you neven,
> With monkes that are right of lore;
> They rede and sing with milde steven:
> "Jesu, that suffred woundes sore,
> Graunt us all the bliss of heven!"
> **Amen.**[44]

Sometimes these liturgical closures seem to be a feature of the manuscript rather than of the romance (or other work) itself: the scribe may have added the prayer at the end of the text copied or of the manuscript compilation as a whole. But in any event, we find, throughout the course of the Medieval period, the belief that a literary work, like a human life, should at least *close* piously. (We will see this in the case of Chaucer's *Canterbury Tales*.) Many works, like medieval men and women themselves, end up literally or figuratively in the cloister.

Saints' Lives

Lives of the saints constitute a special case in that they frequently were translated from Latin and were sung or read regularly during religious services, especially at Matins, and read during meals in monasteries and nunneries. Some Lives are "sequences"; such is apparently the origin of the

---

[44]*King Arthur's Death: The Middle English* Stanzaic Morte Arthur *and* Alliterative Morte Arthure, ed. Larry D. Benson, rev. Edward E. Foster (Kalamazoo, Mich., 1994), p. 123.

beautiful, brief (29-line) ninth-century "Sequence of Saint Eulalie" and of the tenth century poetic French *Life of Saint Léger* [*Vie de Saint Léger*].[45]

In some saints' Lives the liturgy plays an important thematic role. In the early twelfth-century Old French *Voyage of St. Brendan* [*Le Voyage saint Brendan*, translated and adapted from Latin, with an Irish origin], the saint's great voyage to the "Island of the Blessed" is powerfully structured by the liturgical year: the major feasts commemorating the life of Christ—Christmas, Easter, Pentecost—are celebrated faithfully by the monks on their boat. The voyage has a circular quality; twice Brendan and his companions celebrate Easter on the back of a whale, which arrives providentially to serve as dining surface. The monks come upon Judas Iscariot, suffering on a small island in the midst of the sea; his punishments vary according to the days of the week and the liturgical season: all day Sunday, during the Christmas season, on feasts of Mary, and at Easter and Pentecost the demons torture him somewhat less, in honor of the Blessed Virgin and the Trinity.[46]

Some saints' stories contain scenes in which the holy person is shown praying or celebrating the liturgy, and either is surrounded by angels who carry the prayers to heaven or receives a heavenly vision. *The Little Flowers of Saint Francis* [*Fioretti*], written in Italian in the late fourteenth century, contains several such passages.[47] In one, Francis, in St. Peter's in Rome with Brother Masseo, prays with great devotion and many tears "to possess the treasure of Holy Poverty"; the Holy Apostles Peter and Paul appear to him, embrace him, and grant his prayer.[48] It is interesting to note that it is

---

[45]See *Chrestomatie de la littérature en ancien français*, 5th ed., ed. Albert Henry, 2 vols. (Bern, 1970), 1: 2–3, 9–10.

[46]Benedeit, *The Anglo-Norman Voyage of St. Brendan*, ed. Ian Short and Brian Merrilees (Manchester, 1979), lines 1300 ff.

[47]Marion A. Habig, *St. Francis of Assisi: Writings and Early Biographies: English Omnibus of the sources for the Life of St. Francis*, 3rd rev. ed., including *A New Fioretti* by John R. H. Moorman (Chicago, 1973).

[48]See Habig, *St. Francis*, #13, esp. pp. 1329–30. In a similar story, a boy who follows Francis at night when he goes out hears many voices and finds the saint at prayer and in

not during the Mass that such visions occur—Francis was not a priest and therefore could not celebrate Mass—nor even during official liturgical prayer such as the Offices; rather, they happen during personal prayer, of which Francis may be considered an unofficial patron.

We also find echoes of the Offices of the saints and other liturgies in vernacular works composed in honor of holy men and women. The Middle English poem devoted to Saint Erkenwald[49] (ca. 1380–90) offers a case in point:[50] it is influenced strongly by readings from the Latin Office and *vita* of the saint, who was classified among the "confessor bishops" in the Common of Saints. Thus we hear echo of the Vespers chant for such figures: "Ecce sacerdos magnus qui in diebus suis placuit Deo et inventus est justus" [Behold the great priest who in the days of his life pleased God and was found just; drawn from Ecclesiasticus 44 and 45]. There are other significant liturgical echoes here as well: if the feast of St. Erkenwald was 30 April, the major feast of the "Inventio S. Crucis" [the Invention, or Finding, of the Holy Cross, by St. Helena] was 3 May, within the octave of Erkenwald's feast, and there are many parallels in the English life with themes and lections—that is, liturgical readings—from the two feasts.

---

conversation with Christ, the Blessed Virgin, St. John the Baptist, St. John the Evangelist, and a "great throng of angels"; Habig, #17, pp. 1338–39.

[49]Erkenwald, †693, was a bishop of London and the most important saint of London during the Middle Ages. Founder of the monasteries of Chertsey and Barking (of which his sister St. Ethelburga was abbess), he was famed for his holy life. After his death, his relics were contested and were translated more than once. See, e.g., David Hugh Farmer, *The Oxford Dictionary of Saints*, 3rd ed. (Oxford, 1992), pp. 160–61.

[50]My remarks here are drawn from Gordon Whatley's valuable article, "The Middle English *St. Erkenwald* and its Liturgical Context," in *Mediaevalia* 8 (1982): 277–306. Whatley is one of the few to have explored carefully the relations between the Lives of the saints and the liturgies (often complex and varying significantly from place to place) devoted to them. On such services see, e.g., Andrew Hughes, *Late Medieval Liturgical Offices: Resources for Electronic Research: Texts* (Toronto, 1994). Another such study, of an Old English text, is: Peter Lucas, "Easter, the Death of St. Guthlac and the Liturgy for Holy Saturday in Felix's *Vita* and the Old English *Guthlac B*," in *Medium Aevum* 61 (1992): 1–16.

(Similarities include a central conflict between the saint—Helen, Erkenwald—and a powerful unbeliever; and the importance of relics and of baptism.) *St. Erkenwald*, like the feasts whose themes it reflects, is a strongly ecclesiastical work, celebrating the power of the sacraments, the clergy, and the liturgy.

Vernacular Lyric

Many of the earliest surviving songs in the vernaculars are para-liturgical—and indeed the French word "**trover**," which gave rise to the terms for poets *troubadours* and *trouvères*, may come from the Latin word *tropare*: to compose verbal and musical embellishments in and for the liturgy.

Thousands of medieval religious lyrics survive from the Medieval period.[51] Many are liturgical in the broad sense of worship: praise of God the Father, the Son, or the Holy Ghost, or of the Trinity. Here is a pair of examples, taken from the scores provided by Carleton Brown in his

---

[51]As there are so many medieval pious songs, of many different types, I will restrict my consideration here to those with a distinctly liturgical character. But I refer the interested reader to the many anthologies of medieval religious poetry. For English literature they are particularly abundant: see the anthologies of Carleton Brown, *Religious Lyrics of the XIVth Century* (Oxford, 1924), *English Lyrics of the XIIIth Century* (Oxford, 1932), and *Religious Lyrics of the XVth Century* (Oxford, 1939); also *The Oxford Book of Medieval English Verse*, ed. Celia Sisam (1970; rev. ed., Oxford, 1973). For French, aside from the volumes cited below, see *Recueil de chansons pieuses du XIIIe siècle*, ed. Edward Järnström and Arthur Långfors, 2 vols. (Helsinki, 1927). For the Spanish tradition see *The Penguin Book of Spanish Verse,* ed. and trans. J. M. Cohen [dual-language edition], 2nd ed. (London, 1960); and *Ten Centuries of Spanish Poetry: An Anthology in English Verse with Original Texts, From the XIth Century to the Generation of 1898*, ed. Eleanor L. Turnbull, intro., with introductions by Pedro Salinas (Baltimore, 1955). On the medieval religious lyric in general see the valuable work by Rosemary Woolf, *The English Religious Lyric in the Middle Ages* (Oxford, 1968), and by Patrick S. Diehl, *The Medieval European Religious Lyric* (Berkeley, 1985).

invaluable editions of Middle English lyrics:[52] A thirteenth-century poetic prayer to Christ begins:

Swete ihesu, king of blisse,
Min herte loue, min herte lisse,
Þou art swete mid I-wisse—
Wo is him þat þe shal misse.[53]

Here are the opening lines of a fifteenth-century poem to the Trinity:

O radiant luminar of light eterminable,
Celestiall father, potenciall god of myght,
Of heyven & erthe, o lorde incomparable,
Of all perfeccions essenciall most parfight!
O maker of mankynd thow formed day & nyȝt,
    Whose power imperiall commprehendithe every place;
My hert, my mynde & all my holl delite
    Ys, after this lyf, to se thy glorious face. . . .[54]

Countless songs in every vernacular,[55] as in Latin, praise the Virgin, especially from the late twelfth and thirteenth centuries. A Spanish poem by Juan Ruiz, Archpriest of Hita (1283–1350), "Cantica de Loores de Santa Maria," begins:

Thou Flower of flowers! I'll follow thee,
And sing thy praise unweariedly:

---

[52] *Religious Lyrics of the XIVth Century,* ed. Brown; *English Lyrics of the XIIIth Century*, ed. Brown; and *Religious Lyrics of the XVth Century*, ed. Brown. For bibliography on Middle English literature outside of the lyric see my discussion of Chaucer below (pp. 598–606).

[53] *English Lyrics of the XIIIth Century*, ed. Brown, pp. 91–92.

[54] *Religious Lyrics of the XVth Century*, ed. Brown, pp. 80–81.

[55] On the medieval English tradition see especially Woolf, *English Religious Lyric*, pp. 274–308.

Best of the best! O, may I ne'er
From thy pure service flee!

Lady, to thee I turn my eyes,
On thee my trusting hope relies;
O let thy spirit, smiling here,
Chase my anxieties![56]

A recent anthology of medieval Anglo-Norman lyrics[57] offers seven poems in honor of the Virgin whose titles suggest the variety of themes she inspired: “To the Mother of Jesus”; “Glorious Queen”; “Maiden Mother Mild”; “Mary, for Your Child”; “Litany Prayer to the Virgin.” Two poetic amplifications of the “Ave Maria” show the influence of the rosary and related devotions, like the “Joys of the Virgin,” on the lyric.[58] An Italian “lauda” (or song of praise) begins:

Heavenly light of great splendor,
in you, o sweet love, is endless consolation.
Hail queen, devoted maiden
star of the sea that is never concealed,
divine light, gracious virtue,
lady most fair in the image of God. . . .[59]

---

[56]*Ten Centuries of Spanish Poetry*, ed. Turnbull, pp. 36–39; trans. Henry Wadsworth Longfellow.

[57]*The Anglo-Norman Lyric: An Anthology*, ed. and trans. David L. Jeffrey and Brian J. Levy (Toronto, 1990), pp. 33–48.

[58]See also the Brown anthologies, cited in note 51 above. Christine de Pisan, to whom we will return, also composed prayers to the Virgin and a poem on the Joys of the Virgin. See *The Writings of Christine de Pizan,* ed. and trans. Charity Cannon Willard (New York, 1994).

[59]*The Laude in the Middle Ages*, ed. and trans. Vincenzo Traversa (New York, 1994), pp. 58–59. See also Jacopone da Todi, *The Lauds*, trans. Serge and Elizabeth Hughes (New York, 1982).

Many Marian songs and stories commemorate the Virgin's miracles. Spanish King Alfonso X the "Wise" (1221–84) produced a vast, beautifully illuminated work, called the *Cantigas de Santa Maria*, which he wanted performed in church, to honor the Virgin's mercy and countless miracles. Alfonso sang:

> And I desire to sing the praise
> of the Virgin, the Mother of Our Lord,
> Holy Mary, who is the best
> thing that He created; and therefore I
> wish to be evermore her troubadour,
> and I beseech her to desire me for her
>
> Troubadour and to wish my singing
> to receive, because in it I wish to reveal
> the miracles which she wrought. . . . (Prologue B, vv. 15–23)[60]

Many religious songs in the vernacular translate Latin liturgical hymns or prayers.[61] Franciscan Friar William Herebert (†1333) composed over a dozen,[62] one of which is a translation of a famous hymn in honor of the Cross "**Vexilla Regis prodeunt**," composed by Venantius Fortunatus for the reception of a relic of the True Cross, and traditionally sung during Passiontide, especially on Good Friday.[63] (As we shall see, Dante echoes this same hymn, to very different effect!) Herebert's translation begins:

---

[60]John Esten Keller, *Alfonso X, El Sabio* (New York, 1967), p. 65.

[61]See also, for example, #22 in *English Lyrics of the XIIIth Century*, ed. Brown; #37, #44, #45, #89, #92, #98, #99 in *Religious Lyrics of the XIVth Century,* ed. Brown; and many poems in *Religious Lyrics of the XVth Century*, ed. Brown.

[62]See *Religious Lyrics of the XIVth Century*, ed. Brown.

[63]Frederick J. E. Raby, *The Oxford Book of Medieval Latin Verse* (Oxford, 1959), p. 460. See Matthew Britt, *The Hymns of the Breviary and Missal* (New York, 1924), pp. 123–26. My thanks to William Mahrt here, and at numerous other points, for his helpful comments.

Ðe kynges baneres beth forth y-lad
Ðe rode tokne is nou to-sprad,
Whar he Þat wrouth hauet al monkunne,
An-honged was uor oure sunne.[64]

Many religious lyrics are a combination of words or phrases from the liturgy with a vernacular amplification. One might indeed think of them as the vernacular equivalent of Latin "tropes."[65] Especially numerous (as the Anglo-Norman examples suggested) are poetic developments based on the "Ave Maria" and other prayers and anthems to the Virgin. An interesting example is a fifteenth-century expansion of the "**Salve Regina**,"[66] which begins:

Salue	Hayl! oure patron & lady of erthe,
Regina	qwhene of heuen & emprys of helle,
Mater	Moder of al blis Þu art, Þe ferth,
Misericordie	Of mercy & grace Þe secunde welle.
Vita	lyfe come of Þe, as Þe sownde of a bell. . .[67]

Some poems are essentially poetic "glosses," or explanations, of a Latin text. A fifteenth-century English poem on the Nativity—the Incarnation—constitutes over the course of its seven stanzas a commentary on its Latin refrain: "Verbum caro factum est" [The word was made flesh].[68]

There are some curious blends of languages and genres. A French poem begins: "The other day, in the month of May, / *Regis eterni munere*" [Gifts

---

[64]*Religious Lyrics of the XIVth Century*, ed. Brown, p. 15.

[65]As noted earlier, a trope is a verbal (or musical) embellishment added to words from the liturgy.

[66]I will explain later what the "Salve Regina" is; this is just the first of many references to this important Marian antiphon.

[67]*Religious Lyrics of the XVth Century,* #26, ed. Brown, p. 45.

[68]Ibid., #78, pp. 114–15.

of the eternal king], and brings together into a curious but effective poetic unity a wide range of words from Latin prayers and hymns—"Veni creator spiritus" [Come, Creator Spirit], "Mater misericordie" [Mother of Mercy], and others—with a pastourelle-type narrative in which the lover-knight meets not an ordinary shepherdess but the Virgin Mary and discovers her enduring love.[69] Few poems perhaps achieve as high a level of conceptual coherence as this one, but many others are also "macaronic"[70] blends of Latin liturgical lines with vernacular (and worldly) thoughts.

Some lyrics relate to special liturgies, as those for the dead[71] and the dying. We see this in the poetry of Charles d'Orléans, who combines allegorized private grief with liturgical ceremony in a poem that begins: "I made the funeral service for my lady / in the Church of Love, / and the service for her soul / was sung by Sad Thought. . . ."[72] Some lyrics relate to the religious experience of pilgrimage[73] (pilgrimages were often rich in particular litanies and liturgies).

A great many songs celebrate particular moments or themes of the Christian year. The English tradition is particularly rich in Christmas songs and carols.[74] One fifteenth-century carol begins, cheerily and with little liturgical solemnity—there are many such—"Fare wel Advent! Cristemas

---

[69]*Chansons pieuses*, ed. Järnström and Långfors, 2:168–73.

[70]"Macaronic" means a mixture of two languages, of which one is generally Latin.

[71]See, for example, Frank Allen Patterson, *The Middle English Penitential Lyric: A Study and Collection of Early Religious Verse* (New York, 1966), esp. pp. 23–24.

[72]Charles d'Orléans, *Ballades et rondeaux*, ed. and trans. [into modern French] Jean-Claude Mühlthaler (Paris, 1992), pp. 212–15; my translation. We will see a far more profound and extensive involvement in liturgies for the dead in the poetry of François Villon, toward the end of this chapter.

[73]A Spanish poem expressing the singer's desire to go on pilgrimage in honor of the Virgin is given by Cohen in *The Penguin Book of Spanish Verse*, pp. 20–21.

[74]Here again, see the volumes edited by Brown, note 51 above.

is cum; / Fare wel fro us, both all and sum."[75] Many others are more devout, like the fifteenth-century song that begins:

> In Bedlam Þys bryd of life
> Is born of marye, maydyn and wyf;
> he is boÞe god & man I-schryf. Nowel nowel
> Thys prince of pees xal secyn al stryf,
> & wone wyth vs perpetuel.[76]

Many other seasons of the liturgical year are commemorated as well:[77] Epiphany; the Annunciation; the Passion; Easter; Pentecost; and many feasts of the Virgin and the saints.

We should note, however, that a song that is appropriate for Christmas might also be viewed—sung or read—as a meditation on the Nativity, or the Incarnation, or on the life of the Virgin. A song in praise of the Cross[78] might be traditionally linked to Good Friday, but it might also be used for one of the feasts in honor of the Cross, or any time during Lent, or indeed any Friday (as Friday always commemorates the Crucifixion).

Some vernacular songs, especially from the thirteenth century on, have a strong penitential character[79] and thus would be most appropriate during Lent. But many Italian "laude" provide further examples of the complex relationship between penitence and the official liturgy. These songs arose in Italy around 1250 to 1350. During this period of war and plague, wandering groups of generally lay penitents called ***disciplinati*** began to go

---

[75]Sisam, *Oxford Book of Medieval English Verse*, pp. 504–06; the poet is a certain James Ryman.

[76]*Religious Lyrics of the XVth Century*, #76, ed. Brown, pp. 111–12.

[77]Ibid., passim.

[78]Such as "In adoration of the Cross," in *The Anglo-Norman Lyric,* ed. and trans Jeffrey and Levy, pp. 68–69.

[79]On the English tradition see in particular Patterson, *The Middle English Penitential Lyric*, pp. 18–28.

about flagellating themselves and singing vernacular "spiritual songs" [***laude spirituali***]. Many such songs speak of sin, death, and judgment. One *lauda* by the thirteenth-century poet Jacopone da Todi, Lauda XXI, begins: "O merciful Christ, pardon my sin, for I am so deep in it that I cannot flee."[80] (Some *laude*, however, emphasize Marian themes, as we saw earlier, and themes of grace and divine love.)

Liturgical Parodies

From the Medieval period come many liturgical parodies and jokes. Some are simply charming plays on the complex relations between human and divine love: A Spanish ballad called "The Mass of Love" [La Misa de Amor][81] tells how, on St. John's Day, ladies and their gallants went to hear High Mass. One lady was so extraordinarily beautiful that a singer lost his place in the creed, the priest who read the lesson became confused, and the acolytes, instead of singing "amen, amen," sang "amor, amor."

Examples with a sharper edge include the anonymous French[82] "Usurer's Credo" and his "Patenostre." (The ***Pater Noster***—Our Father—like the Apostles' Creed, was part of the official liturgy, pronounced publicly during Mass. It was also, of course, fundamental to the private devotions of all Christians.) In the "Patenostre," each stanza begins with a short phrase from the "Our Father" in Latin, and is followed by—the poem is "farced" or stuffed with—the usurer's thoughts in the vernacular which give voice to his ambition to be the richest man who ever lent out money, his envy of the

---

[80]*Lauda XXI*: George T. Peck, *The Fool of God, Jacopone da Todi* (Tuscaloosa, Ala.,1980), p. 72. See also Jacopone da Todi, *The Lauds*.

[81]*Ten Centuries of Spanish Poetry*, ed. Turnbull, p. 101.

[82]See Eero Ilvonen, *Parodies de thèmes pieux dans la poésie française du moyen âge: Pater – Credo – Ave Maria – Laetabundus: Textes critiques précédes d'une introduction* (1914; rpt. Geneva, 1975); also Jean Subrenat, "Quatre Paternostres parodiques," in *La Prière au Moyen-Age: Littérature et civilisation* (Aix-en-Provence, 1981), pp. 515–47.

Jews whose usurious practices are unrestricted, and his hostility to his neighbors. To some degree, this poem is certainly a satire of the money-lender: of his selfishness and lack of true prayerfulness. But this usurer may also be a symbol of fallen man: are not all the sons of Adam greedy? Are not all our prayers filled—farced—with our petty and sinful concerns; thus, "fallen"? We will see many more instances, especially a bit later in the Middle Ages, of this "poetic of contrasts" (already visible in the "macaronic" poetry referred to earlier), and which was so fundamental to medieval art and culture.

The *Romance of Renart the Fox* [*Le Roman de Renart*], in several of its many branches dating from the twelfth and thirteenth centuries, presents parodies of the liturgy which reveal a detailed knowledge of—and sometimes a harsh humor concerning—the Office of the Dead, services to honor the saints, and ecclesiastical matters in general, on the part of its (typically) clerical authors.

When should liturgical parodies be thought of as "harmless," as flowing from nothing more than an easy familiarity with the liturgy, or an awareness of the contrast between the high aspirations of the liturgy and human frailty? And when are they truly blasphemous, involving rejection of God and mockery of those who believe in him? There can probably be no hard-and-fast answer to this question: tone is tricky and intentions are rarely certain. But it is hard to avoid the impression that certain passages of, say, the *Renart* are close indeed to blasphemy. For example, in Branch VII, renowned for the harshness of its treatment of religion, at one point the fox, fleeing from angry monks whose chickens he has eaten, finds a haystack in the middle of a field:

> There the fox made a nest for himself; but he went a little way off in order to relieve himself before bedding down. Arching his tail, he gave seven farts, one after the other. "Let this first one be for my father, the next for my mother's soul, the third for my benefactors and all gluttonous ruffians, the fourth for the chickens whose bones I've gnawed, the fifth for the peasant who stacked this hay, the sixth as a love-token for my dear love Lady Hersent, and the seventh for Isengrin, to whom may God grant a bad morning tomorrow and a nasty shock when he gets

> up! May he come to a terrible end, for he's someone I hate! I hope he never sees another day like today, but may he suffer the hangman's rope without anybody being able to save him! . . ."[83]

At the end of this branch Renart, unrepentant sinner that he is, eats his confessor during confession.

Thirteenth-Century Texts

Canon 21, "Omnis utriusque," of the Fourth Lateran Council of 1215 made yearly confession compulsory for all Christians. (Previously, most people confessed their sins only on their deathbed; men, before going into battle.) This decree, strongly supported by bishops and other churchmen, gave rise to a great and long-lasting wave of works, some narrowly catechetical but others powerfully inventive. Much of this literature concerns frequent reception of the sacraments, foregrounding themes of sorrow for sin, confession and penance, vice and virtue.[84] But the liturgy too often is involved in these new developments—especially, no doubt, because Lateran IV also officially defined the Catholic doctrine of Transubstantiation (the process by which bread and wine are transformed into the Body and Blood of Jesus Christ in the Eucharist).

The Quest of the Holy Grail

Perhaps the work in which these and many other important thirteenth-century developments are exemplified most powerfully is the anonymous

---

[83]*The Romance of Reynard the Fox*, trans. D. D. R. Owen (Oxford, 1994), p. 133; see also Owen's comments on this branch, p. xviii.

[84]See, for example, Evelyn Birge Vitz, "1215: November: The Fourth Lateran Council Prescribes that Adult Christians Confess at Least Once a Year," in *A New History of French Literature*, ed. Denis Hollier (Cambridge, 1989), pp. 82–88.

French romance *The Quest of the Holy Grail* [*La queste del Saint Graal*] (ca. 1225).[85] It indeed would be difficult to find a work more densely packed with liturgical and sacramental themes.[86] This is a curious book, an uneasy blend of romance traditions with Christian themes,[87] perhaps with **Cistercian** influence.[88] The quest for holiness, mystical visions, and spiritual perfection is combined with chivalric adventures. To all this we add yet another major element: a fascination with biblical-style writing and biblical exegesis, including typology and allegory: the laity are being taught to think hermeneutically, to "decode" material reality spiritually and morally.

The *Quest* devotes considerable attention, and several scenes, to the Eucharist. The liturgies represented are not "real" or "ordinary" but highly extraordinary. We first see the **Grail** not in the Mass but at a dinner at the

---

[85]Pauline Matarasso, trans., *The Quest of the Holy Grail* (London, 1969). References will be to page numbers in this edition.

[86]The *Quest* bears eloquent witness to the new preoccupation with the sacrament of Confession: only after confession and penance can Guinevere's lover Lancelot be part of the Grail quest. Gawain—previously by most reckonings the greatest knight in the world—is completely excluded from the quest in part because he cannot be bothered to confess.

[87]Chrétien de Troyes had already displayed similar interest in *Perceval or the Romance of the Grail*, with its curious liturgical procession and its fascination with a "holy grail"; much of this may well be Celtic—or even imaginary—rather than, strictly speaking, Christian.

[88]On this issue, see, e.g., the introduction and notes in Matarasso's *Quest*, and her *The Redemption of Chivalry: A Study of the Queste del Saint Graal* (Geneva, 1979). Some recent scholars are dubious about the Cistercianism of this work; see, for example, Kathryn M. Talarico, "Romancing the Grail: Fictionalized Theology in the *Queste del Saint Graal*," in *Arthurian Literature and Christianity: Notes from the Twentieth Century*, ed. Peter Meister (New York, 1999). See also Nancy F. Regalado, "'La chevalerie celestiel': Spiritual Transformations of Secular Romance in *La Queste del Saint Graal*," in *Romance: Generic Transformation from Chrétien de Troyes to Cervantes*, ed. Kevin Brownlee and Marina Scordilis Brownlee (Hanover and London, 1985), pp. 91–113. In any event, the liturgical themes of the *Quest* are not among those centrally at issue in this scholarly debate. On religious/liturgical issues in the *Quest* see also Muriel Whitaker, "Christian Iconography in *The Quest of the Holy Grail*," *Mosaic* 12/2 (Winter 1979): 11–19.

Round Table, where (in a scene reminiscent of the descent of the Holy Spirit on the Apostles in Acts 2) all present suddenly were "illuminated by the grace of the Holy Ghost" (p. 43). Then:

> . . . the Holy Grail appeared, covered with a cloth of white samite; and yet no mortal hand was seen to bear it. It entered through the great door, and at once the palace was filled with fragrance as though all the spices of the earth had been spilled abroad. It circled the hall along the great tables and each place was furnished in its wake with the food its occupants desired. When all were served, the Holy Grail vanished, they knew not how nor whither. . . . (pp. 43–44)

This and other scenes show a marked fascination for liturgical processions, gestures, vessels, and other objects, colors, and odors. But rather than using actual liturgical vessels and calling them by their proper names (such as paten or chalice), the focus is on a "holy vessel"—the Grail—containing the host, which is identified by the voice of God as "the platter in which Jesus Christ partook of the **paschal lamb** with His disciples."[89] At the end of the romance the grail returns to heaven, and will never be seen again on earth.

This work does not so much represent or quote from the Mass itself as attempt to show, in several scenes, what is "truly" happening in the Eucharist. (The pure in heart alone can see these things; others are blind to, and even sleep through, the miracle of the Eucharist.) At one point, Lancelot enters a chamber that is flooded with light; he looks around the room and sees the "Holy Vessel" standing on a silver table.

> . . . And all around were ministering angels, some swinging silver censers, others holding lighted candles, crosses and other altar furnishings, each and every one intent upon some service. Before the Holy Vessel was an aged man in priestly vestments, engaged to all appearances in the consecration of the mass. When he came to elevate the host, Lancelot thought he saw, above his outstretched hands, three men, two of whom were placing the youngest in the hands of the priest who raised him aloft as though he were showing him to the people. (p. 262)

[89]*Quest*, pp. 275–76.

We see here a representation of the presence of the entire Trinity in the Eucharist, occurring at the moment of the elevation of the host, and the offering of the Son by the Father and the Holy Spirit.

Such scenes foreground eucharistic themes. The concept of the Real Presence (that is, of the living Christ in the Eucharist) receives strong emphasis, though no technical theological terms are used. In the passage just quoted, the Real Presence is shown by the participation of the entire Trinity in the eucharistic sacrifice, with the Father and the Holy Ghost offering up the Son; in another passage (pp. 275–76), the crucified Christ rises, naked and bleeding, from the Holy Vessel and, eclipsing the priest, speaks directly to the knights.

However extraordinary these liturgies, this romance reflects important phenomena historically associated with the rise of lay piety. Josef Jungmann has noted that during the thirteenth century devout members of the laity became so interested in the doctrines underlying the Eucharist—and, in particular, so riveted by the gesture of the elevation of the host and by the action of gazing on the consecrated host—that they went from church to church to witness the elevation.[90]

Le Roman de la Rose

The *Romance of the Rose* [*Le Roman de la Rose*]—begun by Guillaume de Lorris around 1240 but left apparently unfinished, and completed (massively so) by Jean de Meung ca. 1280—exercised tremendous influence on subsequent medieval literature; its mark is felt even on works more clearly religious in inspiration because of the central role it accords to allegorical personifications and dream vision, and to the recognition that erotic love, however at odds it may be with ordinary Christian morality, is religious in

---

[90]Jungmann, *Mass of the Roman Rite*, 1:121. On the general theme of the Eucharistic host as something to be seen, rather than tasted, see Ann Eljenholm Nichols, "The Bread of Heaven: Foretaste or Foresight?" in *The Iconography of Heaven*, ed. Clifford Davidson (Kalamazoo, Mich., 1994), pp. 40–68.

nature and structure: lovers follow the commandments of the God of Love, worship as devotees at Love's shrine, and seek to enter Love's Paradise; erotic love can thus be said to be a serious parody of religious devotion.[91] *The Rose* contributed significantly to a tradition of liturgical parodies. One such work is a curious allegorical fantasy liturgy, a Mass whose various moments are enumerated and described as sung by birds: this is the *Mass of the Birds* [*La Messe des oiseaux*] by the early fourteenth-century French minstrel Jean de Condé.[92] Another work in which the religious and liturgical implications of the *Rose* are drawn out especially clearly is an elegant fifteenth-century English poem called *The Lover's Mass*[93]: the various moments of the Mass—the **Introibo**, Introit, Confiteor, Misereatur, Kyrie, **Gloria**, etc.[94]—

---

[91]On this issue see Sylvia Huot, *The Romance of the Rose and its Medieval Readers: Interpretation, reception, manuscript transmission* (Cambridge, 1993), esp. pp. 298–300; also John V. Fleming, *The Roman de la Rose: A Study in Allegory and Iconography* (Princeton, 1969), esp. pp. 205–06. See also Evelyn Birge Vitz, "Inside/Outside: Guillaume's *Roman de la Rose* and Medieval Selfhood," in her *Medieval Narrative and Modern Narratology: Subjects and Objects of Desire* (New York, 1989), pp. 64–95.

[92]Jean de Condé, *La messe des oiseaux et le Dit des jacobins et des fremeneurs*, ed. Jacques Ribard (Geneva and Paris, 1970). This variegated work is in part a satire of the mendicant orders of Franciscans and Dominicans. On this work see Huot, *Romance of the Rose*, pp. 313–14; also Pierre-Yves Badel, *Roman de la Rose au XIVe siècle: Étude de la réception de l'œuvre* (Geneva, 1980), pp. 117–23.

[93]See Douglas Gray, ed., *The Oxford Book of Late Medieval Verse and Prose* (Oxford, 1988), pp. 80–84.

[94]The Introibo [I will enter] is one of the introductory prayers at the foot of the altar; the Introit is the equivalent of the "Entrance Antiphon" in today's Mass; the Confiteor [I Confess . . .] is the public confession of sin; the Misereatur refers to the prayer which begins "May Almighty God have mercy on us . . ."; the Kyrie is "Lord, have mercy . . ."; and the Gloria is "Glory to God in the highest . . ." For discussion of these terms, and their historical development see Jungmann, *Mass of the Roman Rite*, passim. For a useful guide to these and other liturgical terms see John Harper, *The Forms and Orders of Western Liturgy from the Tenth to the Eighteenth Century: A Historical Introduction and Guide for Students and Musicians* (Oxford, 1991).

are transformed into declarations of carnal desire and worship of the "god Cupide."

From the thirteenth century on, we frequently encounter strong contrasts not merely between Latin (especially liturgical formulas) and the vernacular (sometimes several vernaculars) but also between the sacred and the profane, and the serious and the parodic. A fifteenth-century Middle English poem called "Jolly Jankin" can provide a case in point. It begins on the word "Kyrie" [Lord], associated with "aleyson"—which, it soon becomes clear, is a pun on the woman's name Alison.[95] The refrain for the seven stanzas is "Kyriéleyson" [Lord have mercy]. The voice of the poem is that of a young girl (Alison, clearly) who went to church on "Yole day" and heard Jolly Jankin (obviously a pretty clerk) sing the liturgy in his "merry tone." She was much taken with his ability to "crak notes" (sing in short notes), especially in the "Sanctus"—and with his charm. The last stanza goes:

Benedicamus Domino
Crist fro shame me shilde!
Deo gracias therto —
Alas, I go with childe!
Kyriéleyson[96]

Many different elements are brought into strong juxtaposition here and in other similar works: Latin and Middle English, the sacredness of liturgical prayer and the merry eroticism of the secular, as well as contrasts between male and female, narrative and lyric, and comic and serious. The tone of this work is unclear. Are we to laugh, perhaps a bit nervously, at the girl's shame? Is the poem supposed to be funny, or moving? Is the girl's predicament yet another symbol of fallen humanity, suffering from the results of sin and deeply in need of God's mercy?

---

[95]As we will see, Chaucer also uses this pun: Alison/Eleison.

[96]Sisam, *Oxford Book of Medieval English Verse*, pp. 445–46.

The **motet** offers further examples of medieval contrastive poetics, often with a liturgical component.[97] A motet is a polyphonic composition combining two or three distinct melodies and texts. Some motets have strong unity: all the texts may be in Latin and on a sacred theme. But it is also common to find marked divergencies in language (Latin and the vernacular), inspiration, tone, and so on. For example, one motet—"Aucun vont— Amor qui cor—Kyrie"[98]—is constructed as follows: The top (or Triplum) voice sings a rather sprightly French song, which complains about those who complain about love: loving loyally is wonderful! The middle voice (or Duplum) sings a much slower—fewer words, fewer notes—Latin text which reflects on the power of "carnalis affectio," noting that the more one loves ephemeral things, the less God is loved. The lowest voice (or Tenor) simply repeats the words "Kyrie eleison!" [Lord have mercy!], using the appropriate liturgical melody for this text.[99] Is the contrast between these divergent "messages" to be understood as resolved by an ironic interpretation of the Triplum? Or should we allow these divergencies of attitude toward love to stand?

Fourteenth-Century Texts

The fourteenth century is particularly rich (especially in Italy and England) in works that focus central attention on liturgical themes and that handle the

[97]This is not surprising as motets were originally polyphonic amplifications of liturgical texts, often produced in a cathedral environment. See, for example, Richard Crocker on the motet in *The Early Middle Ages to 1300*, vol. 2 of *The New Oxford History of Music*, 2nd ed., ed. Richard Crocker and David Hiley (Oxford, 1990), esp. pp. 632 ff.

[98]The title indicates the opening words of each of the different parts or voices.

[99]In *Anthology of Medieval Music,* ed. Richard H. Hoppin (New York, 1978), #54, p. 112. On the interplay between the secular and the sacred in the motet see Sylvia Huot, *Allegorical Play in the Old French motet: The Sacred and the Profane in Thirteenth-Century Polyphony* (Stanford, 1997).

liturgy in complex, highly *literary* ways—by which term I mean that these texts show a strongly self-conscious involvement in "intertextuality," in issues of written authority, in originality, and the like.

The Divine Comedy

In the *Divine Comedy* [*La Commedia*][100] by Dante (1265–1321), the liturgy plays an unquestionably important role. If, as a recent critic has said, "The history of Dante criticism across the centuries . . . has shown a steady awareness that the *Divine Comedy* ought to be read as the encyclopedic, all-inclusive, poetic reservoir of shared memories and languages . . . ,"[101] the liturgy contributed significantly *to* that emotionally and conceptually powerful "reservoir."

The *Inferno* is, not surprisingly, largely devoid of echoes of or references to the liturgy—though subtle details (especially in Canto XXI, lines 112–14[102]) make it clear that Dante presents his journey through hell as beginning on Maundy Thursday and ending on Holy Saturday of the year 1300. In hell, God and his mother are not praised, nor do sinners repent. Dante himself is not yet repentant: when the fearful pilgrim, upon first encountering Virgil early in the *Inferno* wails: "'*Miserere* di me', gridai a lui" ["Have mercy on me" were the words I cried; 1, line 65; pp. 4–5] he is begging not forgiveness from *God* but, rather, ordinary pity; he addresses

---

[100]Translations are taken from the three-volume dual-language edition of *The Divine Comedy*, trans. and with introductions by Allen Mandelbaum: *Inferno*, notes by Allen Mandelbaum and Gabriel Marruzzo with Laury Magnus (New York, 1980); *Purgatorio*, notes by Laury Magnus et al. (New York. 1982); *Paradiso*, notes by Anthony Oldcorn and Daniel Feldman, with Giuseppe Di Scipio (New York, 1984). References will be given to volume (1, 2, 3), line number, and page in the Mandelbaum edition.

[101]See Giuseppe Mazzotta, "Why Did Dante Write the *Comedy*? Why and How Do We Read It? The Poet and the Critics," in *Dante Now: Current Trends in Dante Studies*, ed. Theodore J. Cachey, Jr. (Notre Dame, 1995), pp. 63–79, quotation from p. 73.

[102]See the notes by Mandelbaum, Marruzzo, and Magnus, 1:375–76.

Virgil as "whatever you may be."[103] That mockery of the liturgy is, however, fairly rare in the *Inferno* may be attributed to several factors: Few devils speak. The people with whom Dante talks are not demonic but still poignantly human; while they are unrepentant sinners, they do not *hate* God. (Of course, it must be said that Dante speaks with few people in the lower circles of hell.) Finally, even in the *Inferno*, God's will is shown to reign: even hell belongs to God. (We saw this in the *Voyage of St. Brendan* as well.)

There are, however, a few moments where we see liturgical inversion and mockery. In *Inferno*, Canto XXI, demons scream sarcastically to sinners hunched over as if in prayer that "the Sacred Face has no place here" (1, line 48; p. 189). (This is, doubly, an in-joke: we are among barreters from the town of Lucca whose most sacred possession was an image of Christ. The picture was black like ebony. But here it is apparently not faces we are seeing but filthy backsides. In every sense, then, we have in this passage the inversion and mockery of holy things.) In fact, all the ugly vocal sounds of hell—the hoarse whispering, the shouting and moaning, the cacophonous wailing, the "savage lamentations"[104]—can be understood as inversions of the beautiful sounds of liturgical song whose fullest and purest expression is to be found not on earth but in heaven.

In the story of the traitor Ugolino (Canto XXXIII), we may well have the strangest inversion of a liturgical theme. Ugolino tells Dante how he was imprisoned with his four sons in a tower and brought to the edge of starvation. At one point he bit his hands in anguish. His sons:

> immediately rose and told me: "Father,
> it would be far less painful for us if

---

[103]See Robert Hollander, "Dante's Use of the Fiftieth Psalm (A Note on *Purg*. XXX, 84)", in *Studies in Dante* (Ravenna, 1980), pp. 107–13, quotation from p. 111. As Hollander notes, this is the first of several important references to the great **"Miserere" psalm**, to which we will return repeatedly; but here Dante is not yet asking for God's forgiveness.

[104]In *Purgatorio*, Canto XII, the pilgrim thus describes the horrible sounds of hell, by contrast with the beautiful music being sung by the penitent souls; 2, line 114; p. 109.

> you ate of us; for you clothed us in this
> sad flesh—it is for you to strip it off." (1, lines 60–63; p. 303)

Ugolino refused, and watched three of his children die of hunger before his eyes. Then, he says, "fasting had more force than grief" (1, line 75; p. 106). Does Ugolino simply mean that he himself died of hunger—or rather that he *ate* the remaining child, before dying himself? His loving sons had offered their bodies to him, their father, to eat, but for him actually to eat the flesh of his son perhaps is to be understood as a monstrous—a hellish—perversion of the eucharistic sacrifice and meal.[105] While not universally accepted,[106] this interpretation is supported by the fact that, before telling Dante who he was, Ugolino was (in the previous canto) chewing on the skull of one of his enemies; upon completion of his terrible story, "again he gripped the sad skull in his teeth / which, like a dog's, were strong down to the bone" (1, lines 77–78; p. 305). Though we may well pity him—as we do so many other sinners here!—Ugolino is a cannibal.[107]

The final canto of the *Inferno* opens with a spoken reference[108] by Virgil to a hymn by Venantius Fortunatus: "Vexilla regis prodeunt"[109] whose first stanza means "The banners of the king come forth, the mystery of the Cross shines forth, where He in flesh, who made our flesh, hangs upon the

---

[105]See, for example, Piero Boitani, "Inferno XXXIII," in *Cambridge Readings in Dante's Comedy*, ed. Kenelm Foster and Patrick Boyde (Cambridge, 1981), pp. 70–89, quotation from p. 83.

[106]See Jorge Luis Borges's brief but interesting discussion of this issue in "The False Problem of Ugolino," in *Critical Essays on Dante*, ed. Giuseppe Mazzotta (Boston, 1991), pp. 185–87.

[107]More generally on eucharistic inversion in this passage see John Freccero's chapter on "Bestial Sign and Bread of Angels: *Inferno* 32 and 33," in his *Dante: The Poetics of Conversion* (Cambridge, Mass., 1986); rpt. in *Dante's Divine Comedy,* ed. Harold Bloom (New York, 1987), pp. 121–34.

[108]There is no liturgical *song* in hell!

[109]This hymn was referred to earlier, in the context of vernacular lyric translations.

gibbet." But Dante transforms this line by the addition of a final word: "Vexilla regis prodeunt inferni." With these words, Virgil prepares Dante for the sight of Satan, the king of hell, who aspired to be God and now, ironically, is punished on his "cross" forever in the lowest part of hell.[110] The irony of this quotation is particularly, if subtly, striking since the attentive reader[111] knows this to be Holy Saturday, the day after Christ's crucifixion and the day of his descent into hell.

The *Purgatorio* is extremely rich in liturgical references.[112] The central fact is that Dante combines here liturgies of penitence with those of rejoicing, but it is the latter that dominate and set the basic tone: Dante arrives on the shore of the mountain of purgatory just before dawn on Easter Day—the day of the triumph of Christ over death and sin[113]—and there are many references to the Paschal liturgies. At the entrance to purgatory, in Canto II, he meets a band of repentant sinners:

---

[110]On this passage see the illuminating discussion of Charles Singleton in *Commedia: Elements of Structure* (Cambridge, Mass., 1965), esp. pp. 37–39.

[111]See note 102 above.

[112]Marcia Colish lists the liturgical and scriptural references in the *Purgatorio* and the *Paradiso*, and discusses them briefly, in her *The Mirror of Language: A Study in the Medieval Theory of Knowledge*, rev. ed. (Lincoln, 1983), pp. 283–84nn426, 427. For a useful general study of the liturgy in Dante see John C. Barnes, "Vestiges of the Liturgy in Dante's Verse," in *Dante and the Middle Ages: Literary and Historical Essays*, ed. John C. Barnes and Cormac Ó Cuilleanáin (Dublin, 1995), pp. 231–70. See also Olaf Graf, *Die "Divina Comedia" als Zeugnis des Glaubens: Dante und die Liturgie* (Freiburg, 1965). Extremely valuable general studies of liturgy in the *Purgatorio* are: Erminia Ardissino, "I Canti liturgici nel *Purgatorio* Dantesco," *Dante Studies* 108 (1990): 39–45; Louis M. La Favia, '. . . Chè Quivi Per Canti . . .' (*Purg.*, XII, 113), Dante's Programmatic Use of Psalms and Hymns in the *Purgatorio*," *Studies in Iconography* 10 (1984–86): 53–65; and Dunstan J. Tucker, "*In exitu Israel de Aegypto*: The *Divine Comedy* in the Light of the Easter Liturgy," *The American Benedictine Review* 11 (1960): 53–65.

[113]On the importance of the day of Easter—and indeed of the hours of the Crucifixion and of the Resurrection—in Dante's poetry, see Charles S. Singleton, "The Vistas in Retrospect," in *Dante's Divine Comedy*, ed. Bloom, pp. 57–76, esp. pp. 72, 75.

> "*In exitu Isräel de Egypto*,"
> with what is written after of that psalm,
> all of those spirits sang as with one voice. (2, lines 46–48; p. 15)

"**In exitu Israel**" is an antiphon taken from Psalm 113, which here is being sung in harmony: "with one voice." This antiphon was used in prayers and masses for the dead, perhaps as early as the seventh century.[114] This psalm is also traditionally the only one to be sung according to what is called the *tonus peregrinus*[115] or "pilgrim's tone": its reciting melody has a strange and mournful "wandering" quality.[116]

But this psalm, understood typologically as referring both to the exodus of the Jews and to Christ's resurrection,[117] was also an important part of the liturgy of Easter,[118] and thus serves as a symbol of hope that moves those in purgatory. (By contrast, those in hell had been advised to "abandon hope"). This psalm is, then, at once about exile—which has been shown to be one of the central themes of the *Divine Comedy*[119]—and about deliverance: the progressive return to the Promised Land.

---

[114]See Pierre-Marie Gy, "La mort du chrétien," in *L'Eglise en prière*, ed. Martimort, pp. 618–30, esp. p. 625. This psalm (like all the psalms) was also used on a weekly basis: at the end of Sunday Vespers.

[115]Hughes, *Medieval Manuscripts*, p. 112.

[116]See Eric Werner, *The Sacred Bridge: The Interdependence of Liturgy and Music in Synagogue and Church during the First Millennium* (London and New York, 1963), p. 419; the "tonus peregrinus" is apparently derived from ancient practices of Jewish psalmody.

[117]See Jeffrey T. Schnapp, "Introduction to *Purgatorio*" in *The Cambridge Companion to Dante*, ed. Rachel Jacoff (Cambridge, 1993), pp. 192–207; p. 205n8.

[118]See Tucker, "*In Exitu Israel* . . ." See also Werner, *Sacred Bridge*, p. 158.

[119]As Mazzotta has put it: "Exile for the poet . . . is not merely a perspective from which he acknowledges the storms brooding over history and nostalgically relives the pastoral order of the city. It is also the very condition of the text, its most profound metaphor"; Giuseppe Mazzotta, *Dante, Poet of the Desert: History and Allegory in the Divine Comedy* (Princeton, 1979) p. 145. See also Charles S. Singleton, "In exitu Israel," in *Dante: A Collection of Critical Essays*, ed. John Freccero (Englewood Cliffs, N.J., 1965), pp. 102–21.

Dante thus combines here sorrowful and penitential themes with joyful, triumphant themes. His use of this psalm is particularly interesting because he amplified on its meaning at some length in the "Letter to Can Grande," where (for example) he said that it symbolized anagogically "the passage of the blessed soul from the slavery of this corruption to the freedom of eternal glory."[120]

In Canto V we hear the "Miserere" Psalm (Have mercy; Psalm 50) being sung antiphonally (by two alternating sets of voices or choirs):

> Meanwhile, along the slope, crossing our road
> slightly ahead of us, people approached,
> singing the *Miserere* verse by verse.
> When they became aware that I allowed
> no path for rays of light to cross my body,
> they changed their song into a long, hoarse "Oh!" (2, lines 22–7; p. 39)

These repentant sinners thus are chanting one of the traditional "Penitential Psalms,"[121] which were especially important during Lent (as in all penitential contexts)—though the "Miserere" was also sung as the first psalm of Lauds every weekday, except during the Easter season; this was, then, an extremely important and familiar psalm. Again in Canto XXIII, words from Psalm 50 are being wept and sung by penitents (2, lines 10–11; p. 211)—though Dante reverses the order of the words of the Psalm, from "Domine, labia mea aperies" [Vulgate: Lord, open thou my lips . . .] to "Labia mea, Domine." We will see more such instances of the freedom with which Dante quotes the liturgy.

Canto VII introduces praise of Mary, which will remain an ongoing theme throughout the *Commedia*. Here, souls at rest at the end of the day

---

[120]"Dante's Letter to Can Grande" in *Essays on Dante*, ed. Mark Musa, trans. Hancy Howe (Bloomington, Ind., 1964), pp. 32–47, quotation from p. 37.

[121]On the Penitential Psalms see, e.g., the sections on "Penance and Reconciliation," "Prayer for the Sick and Sacramental Anointing," and "Christian Death" in Martimort et al., *The Church at Prayer*, vol. 3: *Sacraments*. See also other volumes of this work.

are singing "Salve regina" [Hail, Holy Queen; 2, lines 82–83; p. 63]. These are the first words of one of the four great Marian independent or votive antiphons. (The other independent antiphons in honor of the Blessed Virgin are "**Alma redemptoris mater**" [Gracious mother of the redeemer] on which more below; "**Regina caeli**" [Queen of heaven]; and "Ave regina caelorum" [Hail, queen of the heavens].)[122] "Salve regina" often was sung at the close of Vespers or Compline, as it is here; indeed, this entire passage recapitulates major elements of a Compline service.[123] While Dante quotes here only the first words, or "incipit," of the "Salve regina," the context in which it is mentioned expands this text by referring to other parts of the antiphon in which sinners plead for the intercession of the "Mother of Mercy," speaking of themselves as "mourning and weeping in this vale of tears"—and it is precisely in a valley that penitent sinners are singing this antiphon.

In Canto VIII—it is now sunset of Easter day—a soul in ante-purgatory is singing "Te lucis ante" [To Thee before the ending of the day], the great hymn for Sunday at Compline:

> He joined his palms and, lifting them, he fixed
> all his attention on the east, as if
> to say to God: "I care for nothing else."
> "*Te lucis ante*: issued from his lips . . ." (2, lines 10–13; p. 69)

As with "In exitu Israel" and the "Salve regina," Dante is not interested only in the opening words but also evokes the rest of the hymn, in which the faithful pray for God's care throughout the night and his protection against disturbing dreams and the Evil One.[124] The penitent soul sang, says Dante:

---

[122]Hughes, *Medieval Manuscripts*, p. 33.

[123]See Andew McCracken, "'*In Omnibus Viis Tuis*': Compline in the Valley of the Rulers (*Purg*. VII–VIII)," *Dante Studies* 111 (1993): 119–29.

[124]See *Poésie latine chrétienne du Moyen Age, IIIe–XVe siècle,* ed. Henry Spitzmuller (Bruges, 1971), pp. 1144–45.

> with such devotion and with notes so sweet
> that I was moved to move beyond my mind.
> And then the other spirits followed him —
> devoutly, gently—through all of that hymn,
> their eyes intent on the supernal spheres. (2, lines 14–18; p. 69)

As the song ended, two angels, bearing flaming swords, came to guard the souls against the serpent which was soon to appear.

While the Marian antiphons each had a single and familiar melody, "Te lucis ante" had several different musical settings (virtually all of a devout and gentle character).[125] Thus, Dante sometimes evokes a powerfully familiar liturgical melody, while at other times, as here, it is the words and their liturgical meaning that receive primary attention.

Dante prepares to enter purgatory proper in Canto IX. Like the other repentant sinners present, he has the letter *P* (for "Peccatum"; mortal sin) inscribed seven times on his forehead by an angel. As the door to purgatory is opened for him with a resounding noise, "I seemed to hear, inside, in words that mingled / with gentle music, 'Te Deum laudamus'" (2, lines 140–41; p. 83). These words (We praise you, Lord . . .) begin a familiar hymn sung in a number of liturgical contexts: it was sung at great feasts;[126] it was also regularly sung at the end of Matins—but *not* during Lent. Thus, in this night between Easter Day and Easter Monday, we see—hear!—the dramatic liturgical reintroduction of the "Te Deum." In purgatory, repentant sinners learn to praise and thank God.

Dante does some unusual things with scriptural and liturgical elements. In Cantos X–XII, he can be said to "rewrite" the Lord's Prayer.[127] The progressive effacement of the *P*s on Dante's forehead in the *Purgatorio* is accompanied by the sweet singing of the appropriate Beatitudes, taken from

---

[125]See *Anthology of Medieval Music*, ed. Hoppin, p. 112.

[126]Ibid., p. 100.

[127]See Teodolinda Barolini, *The Undivine Comedy: Detheologizing Dante* (Princeton, 1992), p. 155.

the Gospel of Matthew 5 but not part of any official liturgy.[128] For example, in Canto XII he hears the singing of "Beati pauperes spiritu" [Blessed are the poor in spirit] as he feels himself relieved of the weight, and cleansed of the *P* of Pride.

Much of the singing, we have seen, is being done in unison; voices are blended. Such is also the case in Canto XX, where Dante hears everyone ["tutti"] crying out "Gloria in excelsis Deo" (line 136); the very mountain trembles with their shout: the souls are all rejoicing together at the completion of the penance of one soul.[129] Liturgy, thus, provides for the expression of common striving, common worship[130]—as opposed to the solitary (and often only semi-human) voices in hell.

If, as we have seen, Dante sometimes expands the text of the *incipit*, he also on occasion restricts the text to a particular set of words: in Canto XXX, angel voices sing "In te, Domine, speravi" [In you, Lord, have I hoped; from Psalm 31]—but, Dante says, they did not go beyond the words "pedes meos" [my feet, in verse 9; 2, lines 83–84; p. 283]. Why this restriction, this particular emphasis?[131]

Dante tells, in Canto XXXI, how he was immersed in the River Lethe by Matilda:

---

[128]One source, however, might be the communion antiphon for All Saints' Day, which includes three of the Beatitudes. My thanks again here to William Mahrt.

[129]See Colish, *Mirror*, p. 325.

[130]Ibid., p. 325.

[131]See John Freccero, "Adam's Stand, *Purg.* XXX, 82–84," *Romance Notes*, 2/2 (1961): 115–18. Freccero explains that, according to the Scholastics, not until Adam received sanctifying grace could he move his feet: "stare poterat, pedes movere non poterat" (p. 117). "There were therefore two distinct stages in the creation of Adam: he was first created, able to stand firmly, and then given the grace to move toward God" (p. 118). Robert Hollander proposes an alternate view, in "Dante's Use of the Fiftieth Psalm," pp. 107–13. According to Hollander, the angels stop after verse 9 because the rest of that psalm addresses the theme of repentance, and "the moment for Dante's repentance still lies before him" (p. 112).

> When I was near the blessed shore, I heard
> "*Asperges me*" so sweetly sung that I
> cannot remember or, much less, transcribe it.
> The lovely woman opened wide her arms;
> she clasped my head, and then she thrust me under
> to that point where I had to swallow water. (2, lines 97–102; p. 291)

Here again, Dante is using, in a highly appropriate fashion, a traditional liturgical chant: "Asperges me, Domine . . ." [Wash me, Lord . . .] is an antiphon drawn from Psalm 50, which accompanies the aspersion—the sprinkling of the church and the faithful by holy water, one of the preparatory rites of the Mass, associated with the cleansing of the soul.[132]

In the final scene of the *Purgatorio* (Canto XXXIII, lines 43 ff.), Beatrice delivers a ringing but enigmatic prophesy in which she speaks of a figure, identified only by the initials DXV, who will come forth from God to slay "the thieving whore" and the "giant." This mysterious "DXV" has received many interpretations, but one of the most likely—and most relevant to us[133]—proposes that the initials are an expansion, and a thematically significant reversal, of the first letters of the preface to the Mass, quoted earlier in this essay: "Vere dignum . . .": "Truly it is right and just to praise the Lord." In the tradition of biblical and liturgical commentary, the letters D and V came (for complex reasons relating in part to the shapes of the letters themselves) to stand for and sum up the two natures of Christ—the "V" referring to the human, the "D" to the divine; the two letters became a combined monogram, joined by a cross at the center:

[132]Hughes, *Medieval Manuscripts*, p. 34; for the meaning of "aspersion" see Jungmann, *Mass of the Roman Rite*, vol. 1, esp. p. 270.

[133]See R. E. Kaske, "Dante's DXV," in *Dante: A Collection of Critical Essays*, ed. Freccero, pp. 122–40. In this discussion, I am simplifying and schematizing Kaske's subtle and complex analysis (of which indeed a longer and more detailed version had originally appeared in *Traditio* XVII (1961) under the title: "Dante's 'DXV' and 'Veltro'," pp. 185–254.

The cross and letter X reliably referred to Christ, as they still do today. (In liturgical books, this monogram often served as an abbreviation for part or all of the preface of the Mass.) Within such a tradition, Dante's apocalyptic passage would mean allegorically that at the Second Coming the divine nature, the *D*, will shine forth *first*, whereas at Christ's birth—his first coming into the world—the humanity, or *V*, was initially visible. The letter *X* makes explicit what was implicit in the cross-bar of the original monogram: it is in the person of Christ that divinity and humanity meet. (The "giant" refers to the Antichrist, his whore to corruption in the Church—inversions of the Church as the Bride of Christ.)

And *Paradiso*? Here, of course, are no penitential psalms, no weeping. Liturgically speaking, there are *only* expressions of joy and praise of the Godhead and the Blessed Virgin. Beatrice interrupted her heavenly alleluias (so Virgil declared in *Inferno*, Canto XII) to come down to intercede for Dante: "For she who gave me this new task was one / who had just come from singing halleluiah" (1, lines 88–89; p. 109). In Canto VIII, Dante says that the sound of the **hosanna**s he heard was such that he has never since been without the desire to hear it again. Canto XXVIII speaks as well of the hosannas in heaven.

In Canto XXIV the court of heaven resounds throughout its spheres with "Te Deum laudamus," in the melody in which they sing it there: "'Dio laudamo' / ne la melode che là su si canta"[134] (3, lines 113–14; pp. 220–21). In this interesting passage, the text is certainly familiar, and Dante had already spoken of hearing it sung in purgatory. But here he seems to be suggesting that in heaven the "Te Deum" is sung to a different tune than on earth. The issue of melody arises again: in Canto XXVIII, Dante hears "hosanna" being sung simultaneously to three distinct melodies by different orders of angels.

As in purgatory, many of the hymns are Marian. In Canto XXIII, where the Triumph of Christ is manifest, Dante sees white fires, spirits of the blessed:

---

[134] *Paradiso*, trans. Mandelbaum, pp. 220–21; lines 113–14.

And like an infant who, when it has taken
its milk, extends its arms out to its mother,
its feeling kindling into outward flame,
each of those blessed splendors stretched its peak
upward, so that the deep affection each
possessed for Mary was made plain to me.
Then they remained within my sight, singing
"*Regina caeli*" with such tenderness
that my delight in that has never left me. (3, lines 121–29; p. 211)

As we noted earlier, the "Regina caeli," sung here with such tenderness and such love for Mary the mother of all, is one of the great Marian antiphons—the one particularly associated with the Easter season; its melody was familiar to all Christians.

Generally, Dante presents liturgical song as providing the harmonic and the spiritual backdrop of paradise. Liturgy is what is going on in heaven—as in purgatory—when Dante is not there. Many cantos make it clear that people interrupt their hymns and anthems—and their wheeling motion through the heavens which corresponds to the circular movement of the spheres—to speak with him. But it is interesting to note that what does *not* seem to be taking place in heaven is the sacrifice of Mass itself or Holy Communion. While the liturgy in its broad definitions of praise and adoration is eternal, the sacraments—among them the Eucharist—were understood to belong to a transitory system.[135] The sacraments are signs and channels of divine grace,[136] helpful to those who bear the wounds of sin, but unnecessary to those who live in God's presence; they will pass away entirely once Christ has returned and God is seen face to face by the redeemed. To the extent that Dante and other poets aimed at suggesting

---

[135]On this issue, see, e.g., Sister Mary Vincent Hillmann, *The Pearl, Mediaeval Text with a Literal Translation and Interpretation* (Notre Dame, 1967); Note to line 1064, pp. 105–06.

[136]Thomas Aquinas defined the sacraments as signs and as causes of grace. *Summa Theologiae*, 5 vols. (Westminster, Md., 1981), 3:60.1 ff.

eternity in their images of paradise, they appear to have shied away from the sacraments, focusing instead on eternal hymns of joy and union, often taken from the Offices such as Matins.

Dante does a number of innovative things with the liturgy in the *Paradiso*. One concerns the Psalms. All the Psalms, of course, belonged to the liturgy. The Psalter was indeed at the very heart of monastic liturgy, and in monastic settings it was sung every week in its entirety. (It has been said that the very purpose of the Offices *is* the recitation of the Psalms.[137]) Dante has quoted the Psalms repeatedly in their traditional liturgical context. But here he plucks out a single line from the Psalms, using it appositely:[138] in Canto XXV, where Dante is being questioned on hope by St. James, an invisible choir sings just verse 11 from Psalm 9—"Let them hope in you":

> At first, as soon as I had finished speaking,
> "*Sperent in te*" was was heard above us, all
> the circling garlands answering this call. (3, lines 97–99; p. 229)

Canto XIV may pose a liturgical riddle: Dante says that he heard a song containing the words "'Resurgi' e 'Vinci'" ["Rise" and "Conquer"; line 125] but that he did not recognize the hymn. By this liturgical periphrasis, he may be inviting his audience to try to identify which hymn it was. But what is more likely is that Dante is presenting this hymn as sung only in heaven by the blessed—and unknown on earth.

Dante on occasion makes up "liturgical" songs: Canto VII of *Paradiso*—the second heaven—opens on words being sung by Justinian and his companions:

> Osanna, sanctus Deus sabaòth,
> superillustrans claritate tua
> felices ignes horum malacòth . . . (3, lines 1–3; pp. 56–57)

---

[137]Hughes, *Medieval Manuscripts*, p. 50.

[138]This is similar to what he did with the Beatitudes in *Purgatorio*, but whereas the Beatitudes are major scriptural texts, his choice of line from the Psalms is more unusual.

(These words mean: Hosanna, holy God of hosts, superabundantly illuminating with your brightness the blessed fires of these realms.) Despite the recourse to Latin and Hebrew,[139] and despite the liturgical feel of this passage (in the first line, Dante has indeed reorganized words from the "Sanctus" of the Mass), this is not a traditional hymn. Rather, we are to understand that this sacred song, unfamiliar to men and women on earth, is sung by the saints in heaven.

At more than one point we hear liturgical chant in the vulgar tongue: for example, in Canto XXVII, all paradise is singing, in Italian, "Al Padre, al Figlio, a lo Spirito Santo . . . gloria!" [To the Father, to the Son and to the Holy Spirit . . . glory![140]; 3, lines 1–2; pp. 242–43]. Thus, in heaven, hymns or praise are not in Latin alone but also in the vernacular. But *De vulgari eloquentia* is, precisely, a defense of the dignity of the Italian language.[141]

In Canto X the Office of Matins is presented as the Church, the "Bride of God," singing a dawnsong to her Bridegroom when she awakes and "encouraging his love" (3, lines 140–42; p. 91).[142] This is an unusual way of thinking of this Office, but it is certainly consistent with Dante's theological emphasis on love. After all, the *Divine Comedy* closes with a final evocation of "l'amor che move il sole e l'altre stelle" [the Love that moves the sun and the other stars; 3, line 145; p. 303].

---

[139]The Hebrew is in fact slightly incorrect; Dante did not know Hebrew.

[140]Similarly, in Canto XXVI, heavenly voices in heaven are singing "Santo, santo, santo" (3, line 69; pp. 236–37).

[141]For example, though Latin was the language of the Catholic liturgy, Hebrew was, it was believed, the original human language, which God had invented for Adam. Thus, the exalted status of Latin was only relative. See Dante Alighieri, *De Vulgari Eloquentia, Dante's Book of Exile*, trans. Marianne Shapiro (Lincoln, Nebr., 1991), 1:vi.

[142]I have heard John Freccero lecture eloquently on this theme.

The Canterbury Tales

The Canterbury Tales[143] of Chaucer (1340–1400) speaks of Christians at prayer—and *not* much at prayer!—in a pilgrimage setting: on the road to Canterbury.[144] In various of the tales, clerical figures intone phrases from the liturgy. In The Miller's Tale—hardly a pious story—we are told that the handsome clerk Nicholas knew well of "deerne [secret] love" and "solas" [pleasure],[145] and that he loved to sing:[146] he had a "myrie throat" (line 3218; p. 68) and a:

> . . . gay sautrie,
> On which he made a-nyghtes melodie
> So swetely that all the chambre rong;
> And *Angelus ad virginem* he song (lines 3213–16, p. 68)

---

[143]Bibliographical indications specific to Chaucer will be provided below. For general studies of Middle English literature with an interest in religious and liturgical themes see George Kane, *Middle English Literature: A Critical Study of the Romances, the Religious Lyrics, Piers Plowman* (Westport, Conn., 1979); see also J. A. W. Bennett, *Oxford History of English Literature*, vol. 1: *Middle English Literature*, ed. and completed by Douglas Gray (Oxford, 1986). See also Raymond St.-Jacques, "Middle English Literature and the Liturgy: Recent Research and Future Possibilities," *Mosaic* 12/2 (Winter 1979): 1–10. A valuable recent study is Henry Ansgar Kelly, "Sacraments, Sacramentals, and Lay Piety in Chaucer's England," *The Chaucer Review* 28/1 (1993): 5–22.

[144]For useful bibliographical references to the *Canterbury Tales* [hereafter *CT*] see the two following editions: *The Complete Poetry and Prose of Geoffrey Chaucer*, ed. John H. Fisher, 2nd ed. (New York, 1989), esp. p. 992, "Pilgrimage motif"; pp. 1003–04, "The Prioress and her Tale"; and p. 1006, "The Second Nun and Her Tale"; and *The Riverside Chaucer*, 3rd ed., Larry D. Benson, gen. ed. (Boston, 1987), bibliography to *CT*, pp. 795 ff. Both of these editions also have helpful notes. See also Beverly Boyd, *Chaucer and the Liturgy* (Philadelphia, 1967).

[145]*The Riverside Chaucer*, line 3200; p. 68. All quotations are taken from this edition, and references will be given to pages and line numbers in that edition.

[146]The seductive power of the "cantor" is virtually a comic and satirical "topos."

This reference to the Angelic Salutation as part of Nicholas's varied musical repertory[147] is not an isolated detail. Rather, it prefigures a sustained pattern of parodic parallels between, on the one hand, the Annunciation by the angel Gabriel to the Virgin, and the love between the Heavenly Bridegroom and the Beloved, as expressed in the "Song of Songs," and, on the other, Nicholas's declaration of passion to, and his seduction of, a married woman significantly named "Alison,"[148] and with an aging carpenter as her husband.[149]

The prologue to the "Lyf of Seint Cecile,"[150] told by the Second Nun, is filled with echoes of familiar liturgical chants, including the "Salve Regina"; a famous hymn by Venantius Fortunatus (beginning "Quem terra, pontus, aethera . . ."); and the Responsory for the Annunciation, "Gaude Maria." It is also full of reminiscences of the last two cantos of Dante's *Paradiso*, especially to St. Bernard's prayer to the Virgin in Canto XXXIII.[151]

This is, then, one of the very first English works to show the influence of the *Divine Comedy*.[152]

---

[147]On this song see E. J. Dobson and F. L. Harrison, *Medieval English Songs* (New York, 1979), pp. 176–83.

[148]As we noted in "Jolly Jankin," this woman's name is a parody of the liturgical word "Eleison."

[149]Thus, of course, is Mary's husband Joseph represented in the Gospels, in medieval art, and in the Late Medieval mystery plays. See, e.g., Peter Brown's chapter on "The Miller's Tale" in his *Chaucer at Work: The Making of the Canterbury Tales* (London and New York, 1994), pp. 81–101, for a discussion of religious parody—especially that of mystery plays—and the blend of the sacred and the profane in this tale, and for a useful bibliography on these issues.

[150]See esp. lines 29–84; pp. 262–63.

[151]See esp. lines 16–18 of that canto. See Paul M. Clogan, "The Figural Style and Meaning of The Second Nun's Prologue and Tale," *Medievalia et Humanistica*, n.s., 3 (1972): 213–40; also Carleton Brown, "The Prologue of Chaucer's *Lyf of Seint Cecile*," *Modern Philology* 9 (1911): 1–16.

[152]On Chaucer's debt to Dante see Howard Schless, *Chaucer and Dante: A Revaluation* (Norman, Okla., 1984).

But the tale that deals the most extensively with liturgical themes is The Prioress's Tale. This is a story full of pathos,[153] about a little Christian boy, a widow's son, in a great city of Asia, who had a deep devotion to Christ's mother: whenever he saw her image, he would kneel and say an "Ave Maria" before continuing on his way. One day, as he sat in school at his primer, he heard older boys learning the "Alma redemptoris" [Gracious mother of the redeemer], one of the great Marian antiphons discussed earlier. He loved it and learned it, though as a child he did not completely understand the Latin words; he sang it constantly—indeed he could not *stop* singing it. The devil urged some Jews to put an end to his singing as an affront to their law; they had him murdered and thrown into a latrine. His anxious mother looked for him everywhere to no avail, until Jesus called her to the pit where her son's body had been thrown:

> O grete God, that parfournest thy laude
> By mouth of innocentz, lo heere thy myght!
> This gemme of chastite, this emeraude,
> And eek of martirdom the ruby bright,
> Ther he with throte ykorven lay upright,
> He *Alma redemptoris* gan to synge,
> So loude that al the place gan to ringe. (lines 607–13; p. 211)

The child's body is borne, still singing, to the nearest abbey, where after a high Mass the abbot asks the child why he continues to sing:

> "My throte is kut unto my nekke-boon,"
> Seyde this child, "and as by way of kynde
> I sholde have dyed, ye, longe tyme agon.
> But Jesu Crist, as ye in bookes fynde,
> Wil that his glorye laste and be in mynde;
> And for the worshipe of his Mooder deere
> Yet may I synge *O Alma* loude and cleere. . . . (lines 649–55; p. 212)

---

[153]See Robert Worth Frank, Jr. "*The Canterbury Tales* III: Pathos" in *The Cambridge Chaucer Companion*, ed. Piero Boitani and Jill Mann (Cambridge, 1986), pp. 143–59.

He says that, "This welle of mercy, Cristes mooder sweete" (line 656) came to him as he was dying and bade him to keep on singing this anthem until she came to fetch him—for she promised that she would not forsake him. She then laid a "grain" (frequently interpreted as referring to the Eucharistic host) upon his tongue. When the abbot took the grain from the boy's tongue, he "yaf up the goost ful softely" (line 772; p. 212). They enclosed his "litel body sweete" in a "tombe of marbul stones cleere" (line 681; p. 212). The tale ends with a request for intercession to "yonge Hugh of Lincoln, slain also / With cursed Jews" (line 685):

> Pray eek for us, we synful folk unstable,
> That of his mercy God so merciable
> On us his grete mercy multiplye,
> For reverence of his mooder Marie. Amen. (lines 687–90; p. 212)

We have here a story of a child's intense love of Christ's mother—a love nourished, even inspired, by the Marian anthem which he sings with great feeling, though he does not fully understand the words. This is indeed a story *about* the liturgy, and about the seductive power of the music of the liturgy. The traditional melody of the "Alma redemptoris mater" is, truly, achingly beautiful, as it rises through seven introductory notes, then falls again most of the way back down before continuing. And as this was (as we have seen) one of the great Marian anthems,[154] with a fixed melody, this tune would unquestionably have been familiar to medieval audiences—which means that the story would most likely have evoked not just a liturgical text but also a beloved *song* for listeners and readers.

This is also the story of a liturgical miracle, for just as the child could not stop singing Mary's praises in life, he cannot stop in death: he goes on singing even with his throat cut. (Mary came to him as he died and bade him sing—and go *on* singing—her anthem).

---

[154]This was, indeed, apparently the most popular of the antiphons in honor of the Blessed Virgin during the Middle Ages. See Richard H. Hoppin, *Medieval Music* (New York, 1978), p. 104.

The Prioress's Tale is a strange but moving story, one rooted in passion for liturgy, a passion which was increasingly available to the laity as it had long been to the clergy. Indeed, one of the major sources of its prologue is "The Little Office of the Blessed Virgin,"[155] widely attractive to laymen and women.

But we cannot simply leave matters there: this tale, like many others in the *Canterbury Tales*, presents serious problems of interpretation. In particular, modern readers are understandably disturbed by the hatred of the "cursed Jews" expressed here.[156] That such a tale was damaging to Christian-Jewish relations is difficult to doubt. Such considerations, along with other controversies raised by contemporary approaches,[157] tend to undermine—even to deconstruct—the piety expressed in the tale.

Chaucer's original audience, as well, was invited to think twice about this tale—or at least to think of it in relation to its teller, the Prioress, a somewhat ambiguous character (as are they all).[158] Of the Prioress, we are told in the Prologue that she had a smile "ful symple and coy" (line 119; p. 25), and that she sang the divine service very well, intoning it in her nose in a manner "ful semely" (line 123; p. 25). She spoke good (though not Parisian) French. She had elegant manners at table and elsewhere. She was "so charitable and so pitous" (line 143; p. 25) that she would weep if she

[155]See Florence H. Ridley's notes to this tale in *The Riverside Chaucer*, pp. 913–16. The Little Office of the Virgin developed from the Saturday Office of the Virgin in the breviary.

[156]On this issue, and on other controversies surrounding this tale see, e.g., Ridley's commentary in *The Riverside Chaucer*, esp. pp. 913–14. While there is an abundance of scholarship on the nature and implications of the hostility to the Jews expressed here, this issue is not, I believe, truly central to our concerns.

[157]See, for example, Gail Berkeley Sherman, "Saints, Nuns, and Speech in the *Canterbury Tales*," in *Images of Sainthood in Medieval Europe*, ed. Renate Blumenfeld-Kosinski and Timea Szell (Ithaca, 1991), pp. 136–60.

[158]The jury is, however, still out—or has perhaps reconvened—on the Prioress, among others. See, e.g., Henry Ansgar Kelly, "A Neo-Revisionist Look at Chaucer's Nuns," in *The Chaucer Review* 31/2 (1996): 115–32; esp. pp. 126–28.

saw a mouse caught in a trap. On her arm she wore a rosary of coral beads, with *Amor vincit omnia* [Love conquers all] on a brooch. Is this worldly Latin inscription to be understood as expressing the message of St. John's Gospel or, rather, as suggestive of worldly *amours*? And is that mouse over which she weeps *just* a mouse (many a child has shed tears over the death of small creatures)? Or is this little rodent, as it often was in the Middle Ages, a symbol of sin?—which would make her compassion a metaphor for the weakness of her moral grasp.

In any event, the Prioress's tale expresses her character, tastes, and values, as described by Chaucer: this is the story of a sweet child who loves Mary and loves to sing the liturgy, told by a sweet, somewhat affected, perhaps rather childish nun who also loves to sing the liturgy, who prides herself on her ability to sing it well—and who, like many medieval nuns, may not fully have understood the Latin words she sang. But just as the tale is, in the modern meaning of the word, a "reflection" of the teller, so too the tale may be set up as a *speculum* in the medieval sense of the word "mirror": it may tell us what Chaucer imagines his Prioress as wanting to be, that to which she aspires: innocence, a childlike faith, pure devotion and compassion. And, indeed, as well as drawing on Marian antiphons and on the Little Office of Our Lady, the prologue to this tale echoes the Introit of the Mass of the Holy Innocents (the Feast of Childermas): "Ex ore infantium" [From the mouths of babes . . .].[159] The Prioress begins her tale with this prayer:

> O Lord, oure Lord, thy name how merveillous
> Is in this large world ysprad—quod she —
> For noght oonly thy laude precious

---

[159]See Ridley's notes in *Riverside Chaucer*; also Marie Padgett Hamilton, "Echoes of Childermas in the Tale of the Prioress," *Modern Language Review* 34/1 (January 1939): 1–8; and J. C. Wenk, "On the Sources of *The Prioress's Tale*," *Mediaeval Studies* 17 (1955): 214–19. See also Boyd, *Chaucer and the Liturgy*. "From the mouths of babes" is also echoed in line 608 (p. 211), quoted earlier.

> Parfourned is by men of dignitee,
> But by the mouth of children thy bountee
> Parfourned is, for on the brest soukynge
> Sometyme shewen they thyn heriynge. (lines 453–59; p. 209)

Her story perhaps may give a new dimension and clarity to her previously ambiguous motto: "Love conquers all."

The Canterbury Tales is in an important sense an unfinished work: the pilgrims never actually get to Canterbury or back, and only 24 of the originally promised 120 stories are told. But there is closure, namely, The Parson's Prologue and Tale, and Chaucer's Retraction. The Parson refuses to tell an ordinary story, saying "Thou getest fable noon ytold for me." Following St. Paul, he disapproves of those "that tellen fables and swich wrecchednesse . . ." (lines 31–34; p. 577). He proposes something quite different:

> I wol yow telle a myrie tale in prose
> To knytte up al this feeste and make an ende.
> And Jhesu, for his grace, wit me sende
> To shewe yow the wey, in this viage
> Of thilke parfit glorious pilgrymage
> That highte Jerusalem celestial. (lines 46–51; p. 287).

Thus he brings in—at long last, it must be said; it is late in the day, and in the book!—the theme of pilgrimage as a journey of the soul. The Parson thus proposes to shift the meaning of the narrative frame from a jolly trip toward Canterbury into a pilgrimage—merry in a very different sense—toward the heavenly Jerusalem. Thus the Parson introduces, retroactively, to the work as a whole and to the tales themselves, a dimension at once allegorical and liturgical (pilgrimage being an expression of the Church at prayer). His "merry tale" is in fact a lengthy treatise on the seven deadly sins and their remedies. It is followed by the Retraction in which Chaucer repents of and revokes all his sinful works, and all the sin in all his works. He thanks:

> . . . oure Lord Jhesu Crist and his blisful Mooder, and alle the seintes of hevene, / bisekynge hem that they from hennes forth until my lyves end sende me grace to biwayle my giltes and to studie to the salvacioun of my soule, and graunte me grace of verray penitence, confessioun, and satisfaccioun to doon in this present lyf, / thurgh the benigne grace of hym that is kyng of kynges and preest over alle preestes, that boghte us with the precious blood of his herte, / so that I may been oon of hem at the day of doom that shulle be saved. *Qui cum patre et Spiritu Sancto vivis et regnas Deus per omnia saecula. Amen*. (p. 328)

The final words of this prayer—"Qui cum patre . . ." are the formulaic doxology which concludes all collects[160] addressed to Christ. This is, then a firmly liturgical closure.

The problem, of course, is how we are to interpret the pious, liturgical conclusion to *The Canterbury Tales*,[161] which is apparently a deeply worldly work. This is not a matter that we can undertake to resolve here,[162] but a few points might profitably be made. Chaucer has given to a worthy priest the penultimate word in his work—indeed virtually the very last word, since the poet's Retraction is not clearly separated discursively from the Parson's Tale-Sermon; the one flows into the other, unless dammed by rubrication or page layout. Is Chaucer revising and revoking the earlier covenant he had established among, and with, his pilgrims—the new goal being the heavenly banquet rather than the free dinner at Harry Bailly's Inn? It must be said that the ending of the work has not reliably been attended to by readers. Or

---

[160]Collects—short liturgical prayers which sum up the prayers of the congregation—are made up of an invocation, petition, and conclusion. They are recited in the Mass before the Epistle, and toward the end of the Office.

[161]This work was composed in fits and starts over twenty years, but it nonetheless exists as a whole, with some measure of conceptual unity.

[162]For an up-to-date introduction to the problems raised by the theme of pilgrimage, by The Parson's Tale, and by Chaucer's Retraction see the bibliographical notes in the Fisher edition of Chaucer, esp. p. 986 (Philosophy, Religion); p. 992 (Pilgrimage Motif); and pp. 1007–08 (The Parson's Tale, and The Retraction). See also the notes and commentary in *The Riverside Chaucer*.

even by some editors: indeed, today even fairly substantial anthologies of Chaucer's work tend to abridge and mutilate the Parson's discourse,[163] which is arguably fundamental to Chaucer's final intentions, and to the meaning of the work as a whole; shorter collections may leave it out altogether. The parson's "tale" is, to be sure, a good deal less fun than the stories. (It has even been called long and boring, and there is some truth to the charge.) In any case, book editors—like the rest of us, and certainly like the Canterbury pilgrims themselves—are often sinful, worldly creatures.

Insofar as one takes the closure seriously, and not simply as a bow to convention, it puts the readers in a hermeneutical bind. Are we, like the narrator and the pilgrims, to ride and read along cheerily—and then repent, once we have read what the Parson and the perhaps aging and penitent Chaucer have to say?[164] Is this then a story of sin and—at the end of book and life, penitence: his, theirs, ours? Or are we to read the Parson's and Chaucer's words back *onto* the tales? Are we even to reread, to learn to read, with such considerations in mind? Chaucer's use of liturgical (and other religious) themes is complex and ambiguous; probably ambivalent as well.

Fifteenth Century Texts

François Villon's *Lais* and *Testament*

François Villon (1431–63?) was yet another poet hardly famed for his religious devotion! And yet the liturgy and prayer play a highly important role in his *Legacy* [*Lais*], his *Testament*, and his various short poems. While Villon's poetry is filled with sarcasm and vulgarity, the many liturgical

[163]E.g., E. Talbot Donaldson's edition of *Chaucer's Poetry: An Anthology for the Modern Reader* (Glenview, Ill., 1975).

[164]There is some evidence that Chaucer was, indeed, repentant at the end of his life. See Siegfried Wenzel's notes on the Retraction in *The Riverside Chaucer*, p. 965.

references in his poetry are not dissolved by the acid bath that surrounds them but are an expression of his powerfully eschatological preoccupations: he is centrally concerned with death, judgment, heaven, and hell.[165]

The references in Villon's work to liturgy and prayer fall roughly into four groups: liturgical "frames," and prayers for the dead, for the dying, and for the living. Villon both begins and ends his two mock wills with liturgical frames. He opens the testating sections of both works with liturgical formulas, heavily ironized in the case of the *Testament*, where he says:

> In the name of God eternal Father
> And of the son born of virgin
> God co-eternal with the Father
> And with the Holy Ghost
> Who saved those Adam made die
> And sets them all about heaven . . .
> It's no small thing really to believe
> Dead people are made into little gods.[166] (lines 793–800; p. 77)

Villon ends his *Legacy* (lines 273 ff.) with a long and rather garbled reference to the evening "Angelus," a famous prayer in honor of the Annunciation. He ends the *Testament* (starting from about line 1804) with extensive references to Requiem Masses and other liturgies for the dead.

---

[165]On the liturgy in Villon see Vitz, "'Bourde jus mise'?: Villon, the Liturgy, and Prayer," in *The Drama of the Text: Proceedings of the Oxford Conference on François Villon*, ed. Michael Freeman and Jane H. M. Taylor (Amsterdam, 1999), pp. 170–94. See also Rupert T. Pickens, "Villon on the Road to Paris: Contexts and Intertexts of *Huitain* XIII of the *Testament*," in *Conjunctures: Medieval Studies in Honor of Douglas Kelly*, ed. Keith Busby and Norris J. Lacy (Amsterdam, 1994), pp. 425–54. On Villon and the Office of the Dead see Barbara Nelson Sargent-Baur's *Brothers of Dragons: Job Dolens and François Villon* (New York, 1990).

[166]Quotations from Villon will be taken from dual-language edition of *The Poems of François Villon*, trans. Galway Kinnell, new ed. (Hanover, 1982). In one spot below, marked with an asterisk, I take issue with Kinnell's translation and substitute my own.

Villon prays frequently for the dead, including his father and many of his former friends, whom he evokes fondly and poignantly. He asks:

> Where are the happy young men
> I hung out with in the old days
> Who sang so well and spoke so well
> So excellent in word and deed?
> Some are stiffened in death
> And of those there's nothing left
> May they find rest in paradise
> And God save the ones who remain. (lines 225–32; p. 41)

None of these prayers, many of which draw on liturgical formulas, appear to be particularly contaminated by irony or sarcasm.

Villon's most moving prayer for the dead is no doubt the ballad in which dead men hanging from a gibbet speak to the living, asking for their prayers, and to God, asking for his mercy. It begins:

> Brother humains who live on after us
> Don't let your hearts harden against us
> For if you have pity on wretches like us
> More likely God will show mercy to you
> You see us five, six, hanging here
> As for the flesh we loved too well
> A while ago it was eaten and has rotten away
> And we the bones turn to ashes and dust
> Let no one make us the butt of jokes
> But pray God that he absolve us all. (lines 1–10; p. 209)

Villon prays for the dying. He wrote one of his most famous poems in his *Testament*, the "Ballad to Our Lady," for his mother to use as a prayer to the Blessed Virgin; in it he presents his mother as an old woman preparing to die—anxious about hell, hoping to go to heaven. This great poem, filled with traditional Marian formulas, begins:

> Lady of heaven, regent of earth
> Empress over the swamps of Hell
> Welcome me your humble Christian
> Let me be counted among your elect
> Even though I'm without any worth
> My lady and mistress your merits
> Are greater by far than my sinfulness
> And without them no soul could deserve
> Or enter heaven, I'm not acting
> In this faith I want to live and die. (lines 873–82; p. 81)

Villon presents himself, as well, as a man touched by the hand of death: one ballad (often called the "Epistle to his friends") begins "Have pity, have pity on me / You at least my friends . . ." (lines 1–2; p. 191). Those lines are a translation of the beginning of Job 19:21, "Miseremini mei, miseremini mei, saltem vos, amici mei," which was one of the lessons of the Office of the Dead.[167]

Villon presents himself as a dying (virtually a dead) man, whose body is already disintegrating: his hair is gone, he is weak and can only stammer. He will soon die—and be judged. His "Quatrain," in particular, can be read in this light:

> I am François which is my cross
> Born in Paris near Pontoise
> From six feet* of rope my neck
> Will learn the weight of my ass.

Villon is about to be "weighed"; that rope evokes the scales of judgment.

Finally, Villon prays for the living—but in his poetry, the living are seen as dying, as sinners approaching death and judgment. As he says in the *Legacy*: "Life is uncertain for humans / And there's no way-station after you die" (lines 61–62; p. 7). He warns his friends repeatedly to live wisely and avoid the gibbet: "There's no three-penny game / Where the body's at

---

[167]See Sargent-Baur, *Brothers*, pp. 70–82.

stake and perhaps the soul" (lines 1676–77; p. 133); "And for the love of God remember / A time will come when you'll die" (lines 1726–27; p.135). We are, then, perpetually sliding toward eschatology, toward the Last Things. When Villon speaks about his worst enemy, a certain Bishop Thibaut d'Aussigny, he curses him, praying that he be damned (see especially the *Testament*, lines 4 ff.)—though Villon occasionally attempts to forgive the loathsome bishop, as the Gospel demands.

His poems are, then, full of traditional liturgical prayers, and references to and echoes of the Office of the Dead and Requiem Masses. While Villon's poetry is frequently scatological, nonetheless he draws consistently on the liturgy to articulate powerfully eschatological preoccupations.

Vernacular Theatre and Books of Hours

Two of the most striking general developments of the close of the Medieval period as they relate to liturgical matters are mostly beyond the purview of this essay; both are dealt with in other chapters of this volume. The first is the extraordinary burgeoning of vernacular theatre, generally with at least a semi-liturgical function, strongly rooted in the liturgical year, and commonly dealing with liturgical themes. The second is the remarkable rise of Books of Hours and other para-liturgical works such as prayer books and manuals, vernacular psalters, and the like for the laity; this development is clearly an adaptation of older, official liturgies to a new lay audience.[168]

We will think of Late Medieval theatre in terms of its use of liturgical themes. In *Mankind*,[169] a morality play, we see a battle for man's soul.

---

[168]Most of the Books of Hours are in Latin; typically, only a few prayers if any are given in the vernacular; other para-liturgical volumes may be largely or entirely in the vernacular. On late medieval French devotional literature, see Geneviève Hasenohr, "La littérature religieuse," in *Grundriss der Romanischen Literaturen des Mittelalters*, vol. 8/1 (Heidelberg, 1988), pp. 266–305.

[169]*Medieval Drama,* ed. David Bevington (Boston, 1975), pp. 901–38.

Shown as a tiller of the soil, Mankind struggles to be a faithful Christian. He kneels in the field, holding his rosary beads, and begins his work (as did Villon) with "In nomine Patris et Filii et Spiritus Sancti" [In the name of the Father and the Son and the Holy Spirit]. But the work is hard, and the devil Titivillus—self-described as the "dominantium dominus" [lord of lords—or lord of those who dominate; line 475; p. 920]—torments Mankind, placing a board in the ground so that he cannot till the soil. He also is surrounded by bad companions. "Nowadays" (one of various characters representing the latest moral fashions, and clearly a scoundrel) leads Mankind, and the audience, in the singing of an obscene parody of a Christmas carol. He also gets Mankind to follow him in a litany of promises (reminiscent of the baptismal liturgy[170]), one of which goes as follows:

> NOWADAYS: On Sundays, on the morow erly betime,
> Ye shall with us to the all[e]-house erly to go dine[e]
> A[nd] forbere masse and matens, [h]owres and prime.
> "I will," sey ye.
> MANKIND: I will, ser. (lines 710–14, p. 929)

Mankind thus is tempted strongly by Nowadays and his ilk to stop attending church services. Another scoundrel, "New-Guise," says that, to avoid disaster, they must all learn by heart their "neck verse." This was the fiftieth Psalm—the "Miserere," one of the penitential Psalms—whose recitation allowed a man to claim right of clergy and avoid being hanged. (Members of the clergy were exempt from capital punishment.) In short: general derision of liturgy and sacred discourse. Fortunately, Mercy—whose somewhat pompous "aureate" speech the demons also mock—intercedes for Mankind both in Latin, with words drawn from the Bible and the liturgy, and in vernacular prayers, especially to the Virgin. Mankind is saved, and the play ends: "Amen!"

---

[170]The faithful repeat a litany containing the "baptismal promises": Priest: "Do you renounce Satan. . . ?" Faithful: "I do. . . ."

Books of Hours[171] and other para-liturgical works we will consider not so much in themselves but rather as forming part of a vast movement to bring the orderliness of fixed prayers, set in liturgical contexts, to men and perhaps especially women of the laity; from this same impulse come vernacular psalters. Books of Hours have, granted, a freedom and a variability—as well as some measure of recourse to the vernacular—not generally found in the breviary on which they were primarily modeled. But, along with individual tastes and concerns, they reflect aspirations to liturgical order and official status: to what we today might call "liturgicality."

In such developments we also see again how the life of prayer was related to the rise of literacy—to the use of the Book of Hours and the Psalter as primers, in which children learned to read. We may also think in this context of the many images of Mary teaching the little Jesus to read in a prayerful context, and of Mary learning to read with her mother St. Anne.[172]

The liturgical impulse takes another form in the vernacular "**Dance of Death**," which is structurally a litany: one after another, the human "estates" are called to the dance. We also can see a parody of a litany in the fifteenth-century French *Fifteen Joys of Marriage*,[173] modeled on the Joys of Mary, which traditionally numbered fifteen.[174] Here, antiphrastically, the fifteen sorrows that men find in marriage are described, each ending with a ritual closure: "And thus he finished his days in misery."

---

[171]For a valuable introduction to Books of Hours see Roger S. Wieck, *Time Sanctified: The Book of Hours in Medieval Art and Life* (New York, 1988) and his essay in this volume, pp. 473–513.

[172]See, for example, Michael T. Clanchy, *From Memory to Written Record: England 1066–1307*, 2nd ed. (Oxford, 1993), e.g., p. 110. At the International Congress on Medieval Studies at Kalamazoo, Michigan, in May 1995, Clanchy also gave a lecture, which bore in part on this issue, entitled: "Scivias: Reading without Learning, Learning without Reading."

[173]*Les XV Joies de Mariage,* ed. Jean Rychner (Geneva and Paris, 1963).

[174]Lists of five and seven Joys are also found. Many lyrics were inspired by the Joys.

The literary aspiration to liturgicality can be seen in the innumerable Late Medieval vernacular prayers,[175] some of which we saw earlier, whose devotional character is tied to the liturgical year and to liturgical themes. It is also visible in vernacular meditations such as that on patience which Christine de Pisan (1364–1429?) composed, in part translating it from Latin, especially for women; she set her meditation within the framework of "Hours of Contemplation on the Passion of Our Lord."[176]

Marian devotion was fundamental to the Book of Hours: the "Little Office of the Blessed Virgin Mary" was generally its core.[177] Some earlier vernacular songs and prayers in honor of the Virgin that were originally isolated works or part of other poetic units found their way into Books of Hours. One interesting example is the "prayer of Theophilus"[178] by Gautier de Coinci—French monk, poet, and musician—of the early thirteenth century. Gautier's long and beautiful "orison" [prayer], which begins "Resplendent jewel, glorious queen, / Gate of paradise, gracious virgin . . .",[179] is found in five surviving French Books of Hours, where it is typically one

---

[175]See Sinclair, *French Devotional Text*, with its *First Supplement* and *Second Supplement*; see also Sinclair, *Prières en ancien français*; and Rézeau, *Les prières aux saints en français* and *Répertoire d'incipits des prières françaises*.

[176]This work has never been edited, but excerpts can be found in *The Writings of Christine de Pizan*, ed. and trans. Charity Cannon Willard (New York, 1994).

[177]See, for example, Janet Backhouse, *Books of Hours* (London, 1985) p. 3.

[178]Theophilus was a cleric who sold his soul for worldly success, but whom Mary rescued in a dramatic confrontation with the devil. His story was extremely popular, and he had an official feast day, February 4.

[179]Gautier de Coinci, Les Miracles de Nostre Dame, ed. Frederic Koenig, vol. 4 (Geneva, 1970), II Priere #37, p. 580. The poem in its original form begins:

Gemme resplendissanz, roïne glorïeuse,
Porte de paradis, pucele gracïeuse,
Dame seur toutes autres plaisanz et deliteuse,
Daingne oïr ma prière de t'oreille piteuse.

of the closing prayers of the volume.[180] Thus, it serves to reconnect the read and spoken liturgy of the Book of Hours with older traditions of sacred song.

Conclusion

We can now draw out some of the most important phenomena and historical developments that we have examined in these pages, and review the treatments the liturgy has received.

(1) Some authors and works, such as medieval epics and the *Quest of the Holy Grail*, focus exclusively on the eucharistic liturgy, while others, for example, Dante, are concerned with a wider range of liturgical services. Aside from the Mass, the most commonly cited services are the Offices of Matins and Vespers, the Office of the Dead, and the Little Office of the Virgin.

(2) Vernacular works reflect the rising importance of the Blessed Virgin, in the many references to more or less officially liturgical devotions and litanies to her.

(3) Different aspects of liturgy can receive emphasis. These include: *gestures* (again, the epics and the *Grail* are prime examples); *vessels* (the *Grail* and other Grail legends are far-and-away the best examples); *processions* (the *Grail* and many a semi-liturgical, semi-literary medieval procession); *theology* (the *Grail*, Dante, *Piers Plowman*); *words* (many works, from Cynewulf's to Dante's); *music* (Cynewulf; Dante; Chaucer's The Prioress's Tale), and *liturgical structures* (penitential prayers and meditations, literary litanies, and Books of Hours).

(4) As concerns the words of the liturgy: such fundamental liturgical words as *Amen*, *Alleluia*, and *Hosanna* receive perhaps the most

---

[180]This poem is also found in a vernacular psalter, a prayer book, a prayer manual, a breviary, and a sermon handbook, where it plays a similar role. See Kathryn A. Duys, *Books Shaped by Song: Early Literary Literacy in the "Miracles de Notre Dame" of Gautier de Coinci*, Ph.D. dissertation, New York University, 1997; chap. 1.

frequent emphasis and are quoted frequently. Also commonly cited are short lines and the opening words from important prayers, such as *Kyrie* and *Pater noster* from the Mass, and prayers drawn from devotion to the Virgin, such as the "Ave Maria." Liturgical hymns such as "Te Deum" and the four great Marian antiphons are also very frequently quoted. Many lines from the Psalter are quoted in all liturgies, but perhaps the single most commonly cited Psalm is the fiftieth—"Miserere mei Deus" (one of the "Penitential Psalms").

(5) Some works are simply "hedged" or "fringed" with prayer: this is often the case with romances and other strongly secular stories. Other works, such as *The Quest of the Holy Grail*, *The Divine Comedy*, and (to a lesser degree) *Gawain and the Green Knight*, accord to prayer and liturgy central thematic importance.

(6) Sometimes the plot is conceived as a sort of liturgical journey in relation to time and self (*The Divine Comedy*; somewhat ambivalently, *The Canterbury Tales*. Other examples would be *Piers Plowman* and *Everyman*).

(7) Liturgy can be used to evoke many different feelings in the audience, such as sorrow for sin, pathos (as in Chaucer's The Prioress's Tale), and compassion, and joy.

(8) Some works contain liturgical scenes and references in fairly straightforward fashion, while others contextualize such elements in ways that make their interpretation highly problematic, as in *The Canterbury Tales*.

(9) Basic procedures for comic and satiric uses of the liturgy include: the setting of prayer in macaronic combination with, or in opposition to, strongly non-prayerful elements (e.g., farced "Our Fathers"; Chaucer's *Canterbury Tales*; Villon's poetry); the parodic inversion of the wording of liturgical prayer (the devils in *Mankind*); the representation of prayers as being said by stupid or contemptible "beasts" and the insertion of vulgarisms or obscenities into services (as in *The Romance of Renart*); the use of litany structures for non-

religious subject-matter (comically farced "Ave Marias," and *The Fifteen Joys of Marriage*).

But beyond all the extraordinary variety that we have seen in the literary handling of the liturgy in the Middle Ages, a few fundamental facts stand out. One of the most important bears on the relationship between vernacular literature, the liturgy, and the Bible. There is of course substantial overlap between Sacred Scripture and the liturgy, the latter being almost entirely composed of passages (sometimes amplified and explained) from the former.[181] But the Bible is at once expanded and contracted in the liturgy which has a particular focus in its selection: while the Bible is a vast and complex book, full of stories, moral precepts, and lore of all kinds, the liturgy is the Bible as prayer, *at* prayer. But the liturgy did not just pray the Bible and read it aloud, it also "performed" it, so to speak, infusing the sacred text with melody, drama,[182] emotional resonance and typological meaning.[183]

What we have seen in these pages is that a great many references that we might have thought of as being "to the Bible"[184] are, in fact, to the *liturgy*: it is largely *through* the liturgy[185] that medieval men and women

---

[181]See, for example, Pierre-Maire Gy, "La Bible dans la liturgie au Moyen" in *Le Moyen Age et la Bible*, ed. Pierre Riché and Guy Lobrichon (Paris, 1984), pp. 537–52; also J. A. Lamb, "The Place of the Bible in the Liturgy," in *The Cambridge History of the Bible, From the Beginnings to Jerome*, ed. Peter R. Ackroyd and C. F. Evans (Cambridge, 1970), pp. 563–86.

[182]See the classic work by O. B. Hardison, Jr., *Christian Rite and Christian Drama in the Middle Ages. Essays in the Origin and Early History of Modern Drama* (Baltimore, 1965).

[183]See, for example, Jean Daniélou, *The Bible and the Liturgy* (Notre Dame, Ind., 1956).

[184]The Reformation can, to a significant degree, be defined as that period when textual knowledge of, and direct quotations from, the Bible replaced intermediation by the liturgy. And yet!: even well beyond the Middle Ages, one often hears echoes of the liturgies—both Catholic and Protestant (e.g., Anglican)—in literary works.

[185]To some degree, as well, through sermons—and medieval sermons were typically explanations or discussions of the lectionary: the Bible readings for the day, in the liturgy.

knew, and poets "quoted," the Bible.[186] What they were echoing was, typically, particular prayers and supplications drawn from Sacred Scripture.

The liturgy gave to vernacular authors important, and often-repeated, words and formulas, themes and concepts. It also offered them the structures of the liturgical year with its strongly differentiated moments and themes, and other structures such as those of the Mass and Offices with their important opening and closing formulas, and the very shape of the liturgical ceremony, all of which could be reworked in many ways.

Finally, it is primarily the liturgy that taught medieval men and women about their religion—about themselves and the world, as well. The liturgy was at the affective religious core of medieval people. We see this clearly in medieval literature: men and women recited ritual prayers and heard particular chants sung from their earliest childhood. The words, the music, the gestures, and the theological meaning of the liturgy were at the very heart of their experience of the religious life and their knowledge of God.

Additional Bibliography

Brayer, Edith. "Catalogue des textes liturgiques et des petits genres religieux." In *Grundriss der Romanischen Literaturen des Mittelalters*, ed. Hans Robert Jauss, Vol. 6/1 (Heidelberg, 1968), pp. 3–21; vol. 6/2 (Heidelberg, 1970), pp. 19–53.

Dante Aligheri. *The Divine Comedy of Dante Alighieri*, 3 vols. *Inferno*, *Purgatorio*, *Paradiso* [dual-language editions]. Trans. and comments by John D. Sinclair. New York, 1939.

---

[186]This is remarkably true even of Dante. See, in *The Cambridge Companion to Dante,* ed. Jacoff: Peter S. Hawkins, "Dante and the Bible," pp. 120–35, esp. p. 123; Christopher Ryan, "The Theology of Dante," pp. 136–54, esp. p. 138; and Jeffrey T. Schnapp, "Introduction to *Purgatorio*," pp. 192–207, esp. p. 199.

Gellrich, Jesse M. "The Parody of Medieval Music in the Miller's Tale." *Journal of English and Germanic Philology* 73/2 (1974): 176–88.

Goldin, Frederick. *Lyrics of the Troubadours and Trouvères: An Anthology and a History*. Gloucester, Mass., 1983 (orig. Anchor, 1973).

Prier au Moyen Age: pratiques et expériences (V^e–XVe siècles): Textes traduits et commentés. Ed. Nicole Bériou, Jaques Berlioz and Jean Longère. Introduction by Nicole Bériou. Turnhout, 1991.

Wortley, John, ed. *Mosaic* 12/2 (Winter 1979) [special issue]: "Liturgy and Literature."

LITURGICAL DRAMA AND COMMUNITY DISCOURSE

THOMAS P. CAMPBELL

LIKE MANY OF THE SUBJECTS IN THIS VOLUME, the drama of the medieval Church can be understood as limited by its specific liturgical context, yet expansive in its broad cultural relationships. A wide variety of liturgical plays exists, centering primarily on the ecclesiastical seasons of Easter and Christmas. Like the liturgy, these plays combined words and music in a ritualistic and communal form to convey the major themes and activities inherent to particular feast days.

The origin of liturgical drama lies within the liturgy itself, yet its precise history is unclear. We know that within monastic communities of the ninth century there were a multitude of musical-textual additions to the liturgy; and particularly on festive occasions these additions grew in complexity. Liturgical plays appeared after the middle of the tenth century. It is a safe assumption that this liturgical drama first took form within monasteries, for the earliest plays, and indeed most liturgical plays, were wholly dependent upon the liturgy for their meaning and context. The audience, comprised of community members, also participated in the drama; the music and text were familiar; even the costumes were derived from monastic vestments.

The development of liturgical plays seems to have taken place independently of other dramatic or semi-dramatic activities on the European continent in the early Middle Ages. We have records of several such activities, including revisions of Roman drama, recitations of saints' Lives, and reconstructions of biblical events.[1] However, the heritage of classical drama was little understood; and many of these literary creations were unique to particular authors or locales.[2] There are tantalizing hints of biblical dramas—or at least what appear to be plays based on biblical themes—but nothing compares in depth, scope, and homogeneity with the Latin music-drama that emerged in the medieval Church. The texts of these plays were drawn primarily from the Scriptures, although they also used a number of liturgical passages as well as classical references. Their music, sung a cappella, was taken from chants and hymns of the liturgy, although a surprising quantity was newly composed. Their distribution was remarkable—for instance, over one thousand versions of the same Easter play existed in church communities throughout Europe, with striking similarities in text and music.[3]

---

[1]The best discussions of European Latin drama outside of the liturgical tradition still may be found in: E. K. Chambers, *The Medieval Stage*, 2 vols. (Oxford,1903), vol. 1; and Rosemary Woolf, *The English Mystery Plays* (Berkeley, 1972), chaps. 1–3; more recent discussion in C. Clifford Flanigan, "Medieval Latin Music-Drama," in *The Theatre of Medieval Europe: New Research in Early Drama*, ed. Eckehard Simon (Cambridge, 1991), pp. 21–41; and Peter Dronke, *Latin and Vernacular Poets of the Middle Ages* (Hampshire, 1991). On the recitation of saints' Lives see esp. E. Catherine Dunn, *The Gallican Saint's Life and the Late Roman Dramatic Tradition* (Washington, D.C., 1989). Peter Dronke's most recent edition, *Nine Medieval Latin Plays* (Cambridge, 1994), pp. xv–xxiv, contains interesting speculations about the tradition of biblical Latin drama before the appearance of liturgical plays.

[2]See especially Henry A. Kelly, *Ideas and forms of tragedy from Aristotle to the Middle Ages* (Cambridge, 1993), chaps. 1–3. Probably the best-known example of idiosyncratic drama based on the Roman tradition may be found in the work of the German nun, Hrosvitha. She created six moral plays based, in some degree, on the works of the Roman dramatist Terence. The most recent edition is *Rosvita. Dialoghi Drammatici*, ed. Ferruccio Bertini (Milan, 1986). For several points of view, see the volume, *Hrotsvit of Gandersheim, Rara Avis in Saxonia?: A collection of essays*, ed. Katharina M. Wilson (Ann Arbor, 1987).

[3]Some sense of the scope of these plays may be achieved by consulting the two most fulsome editions: Karl Young, *The Drama of the Medieval Church*, 2 vols. (Oxford, 1933); and

Within less than one hundred years after their origin, liturgical plays began to be written on many subjects, in varied locations and for different audiences. The vast majority remained closely linked to their monastic roots, confined to an intimate relationship among actors, audience, and setting. Some of the most spectacular used the vast spaces of Gothic cathedrals with the addition of elaborate costumes and props, before an audience of laity. Still others were written for (or read by) groups of scholars and may never have seen production in a church.

The earliest forms of liturgical plays are indistinguishable from liturgical chants, occurring in the form of **trope**s in the liturgical Offices and Mass.[4] A trope is composed as a verse unit of text and music that usually is

---

Walther Lipphardt, *Lateinische Osterfeiern und Osterspiele*, 5 vols. (Berlin and New York, 1975–81). Neither edition contains music; performing editions of several plays have been edited by Noah Greenberg and William L. Smoldon: *The play of Herod: A twelfth-century musical drama*, ed. Greenberg and Smoldon (New York, 1965); Officium pastorum *(The shepherds at the manger) an acting version of a 13th-century liturgical music-drama*, ed. Smoldon (London, 1967); Visitatio Sepulchri *(The Visit to the Sepulchre) an acting version of a 12th-century liturgical music-drama for Easter from the Fleury playbook*, ed. Smoldon (London 1964); *The Play of Daniel, a mediaeval liturgical drama*, ed. Smoldon (London, 1960); Peregrinus *(The stranger) an acting version of a 12th-century liturgical music-drama from Beauvais*, ed. Smoldon (London, 1965); Sponsus *(The bridegroom) an acting version of an 11th-century mystère founded on the Parable of the wise and foolish virgins*, ed. Smoldon (London, 1972); Greenberg's and Smoldon's editions of the Daniel and Herod plays, as originally performed by the New York Pro Musica, have been reissued as a compact disc, *The play of Daniel* [and] *The play of Herod* (Universal City, CA: MCA, 1991). A handy one-volume edition of the repertoire, with rhythmic musical transcription and somewhat free translation, may be found in Fletcher Collins, *Medieval Church Music-Dramas* (Charlottesville, 1976).

[4]The best recent discussion of troping is by Richard Crocker in *The New Oxford History of Music*, ed. Richard Crocker and David Hiley, vol. 2, *The Early Middle Ages to 1300* (Oxford, 1990), pp. 225 ff. See also the editions by Paul Evans, *The Early Trope Repertory of Saint Martial de Limoges* (Princeton, 1970); Alejandro Planchart, *The Repertory of Tropes at Winchester*, 2 vols. (Princeton, 1977); and *Corpus Troporum*, ed. Ritva Jonsson, et al., 5 vols. to date (Stockholm, 1975–).

combined with a specific liturgical chant. The words of a trope are often non-scriptural but are related in some way to the seasonal liturgy in which the trope appears. The trope music, too, is newly composed in "fully shaped, complete phrases" that bear some musical relation to the chants which they amplify.[5]

Every liturgical feast provided chants for troping. The celebrations of Easter were particularly suitable, since the services were longer and more elaborate. While there are many different kinds of Easter tropes, one of most complex—originally designed to cohere with the introit of the Easter Mass—was adapted also to the last antiphon of Easter Matins. Distinct from many tropes which consist of a single verse unit, it took the form of a dialogue. I cite the earliest known form of this trope, dated about 936, from the liturgy of St. Martial, Limoges (Paris, B.N., MS lat 1240, fol. 30v)[6]:

Trophi In Pasche

Psallite regi magno
devicto mortis imperio.
Quem queritis in sepulchro, o Christicole?
R[esponsio]:
Ihesum Nazarenum crucifixium, o celicole.
R[esponsio]:
Non est hic; surrexit sicut ipse dixit;
ite nunciate, quia surrexit.

Alleluia. Resurrexit Dominus.
Hodie resurrexit leo fortis, Christus, filius Dei.
Deo gracias, dicite eia!

[Tropes for Easter
Sing a psalm to the great king,

[5]Crocker, *New Oxford History*, p. 267.

[6]From Young, *Drama*, 1:210. A discussion of the trope, along with its music, may be found in the somewhat controversial book by William L. Smoldon, *The Music of the Medieval Church Dramas* (London, 1980), pp. 66–81.

to the mighty conqueror of death.
Whom do you seek in the sepulcher, O followers of Christ?
Jesus of Nazareth who was crucified, O heaven-dwellers.
He is not here; He has risen as He himself said;
Go, announce that He has arisen
Alleluia. The Lord is arisen.
Today is risen the mighty lion, Christ, God's Son.
Praise be to God, Say it indeed!]

The central dialogue, marked by the "*Responsio*" symbol, is troped itself by other verses, which usually can be found troping the Easter Mass Introit.[7] However, even in this earliest version, the ***Quem queritis*** dialogue is set off as a unit, marked by the signals of responsive singing and rounded off by the Alleluia. Although the music of the Limoges manuscript is difficult to decipher, its most notable characteristic, visible even in the somewhat loose notation of the manuscript, is a substantial uplift of notes for the words, *Non est hic*. Indeed, the higher notes even begin to encroach on the text above them.

The stability of this textual/musical form throughout the Middle Ages is quite remarkable. As the example illustrates, the *Quem queritis* trope occurs as simply one variant of the Easter introit, grouped with a large number of other tropes. Yet, with few exceptions, this trope functions as the core of all liturgical Easter plays, as well as the model for several other types of liturgical play.[8] Why was this particular form, among all the others, so conducive to drama?

To many scholars who have tackled the complex history of the *Quem queritis* trope, the answer lies in the essential dramatic nature of the dialogue. Karl Young—whose *The Drama of the Medieval Church* is the fundamental text in the field—speculated that the:

---

[7]Smoldon, *Music*, pp. 57–59.

[8]An especially good discussion is by Susan Rankin in *The New Oxford History of Music*, ed. Crocker and Hiley, 2:311–20; and see also, by the same author, *The Music of the Medieval Liturgical Drama in France and England*, 2 vols. (New York, 1989).

> dramatic potentialities of *Quem quaeritis* were realized . . . only when it was withdrawn from the Mass altogether, and was given a lodging-place in the Canonical Office. In this new position it achieved a generous amount of literary freedom, and developed into an authentic Easter play.[9]

Yet, there is little indication that the *Quem queritis* itself is conceived as "dramatic"—particularly when it was employed as a trope of the *Resurrexi* Introit, which seems to have been its original musical intention.[10]

Whether we agree with Young that "drama" was achieved by the transference of the trope from Mass to Matins, or with O. B. Hardison that the Mass itself provided the dramatic context, or with Timothy McGee that the trope was part of an intervening dramatic ceremony, we should probably not consider "drama" as inherent in the dialogue itself.[11] Rather, both music and text are directed toward one particular moment, reflected in the significant musical uplift and the surprising announcement: "*Non est hic*."

Contemporary tenth- and eleventh-century artistic renderings of the Resurrection reveal a strikingly similar attempt to point out the *absence* of the risen Christ. In this iconography, the angel wordlessly addresses the women at the tomb by pointing directly into the empty tomb, revealing the

---

[9]Young, *Drama*, 1:231.

[10]For a recent dissenting view see Rankin, *Music of the Medieval Liturgical Drama*, who points out that, "compared with tropes of the 10th- and early 11th-century Aquitanian repertory, *Quem queritis* is quite foreign to the Introit Resurrexi. . . . It seems unlikely, therefore, that *Quem queritis* was first written as a trope to the Easter Introit" (p. 22).

[11]Young, *Drama*, 1:223 ff.; O. B. Hardison, Jr., *Christian Rite and Christian Drama in the Middle Ages: essays in the origin and early history of modern drama* (Baltimore, 1965); and Timothy J. McGee, "The Liturgical Placement of the *Quem queritis* Dialogue," *Journal of the American Musicological Society* 29 (1976): 1–29. This is perhaps the central issue in any discussion of the origins of liturgical drama. For a brief but discerning overview see C. Clifford Flanigan, "Medieval Latin music-drama," in *The Theatre of Medieval Europe*, ed. Simon, pp. 21–41. More extensive discussions may be found in Helmut de Boor, Die Textgeschichte der lateinischen Osterfeiern (Tübingen, 1967); Johann Drumbl, *Quem Quaeritis. Teatro sacro dell'alto medioevo* (Rome, 1981); and C. Clifford Flanigan, "The Roman Rite and the Origins of the Liturgical Drama," *University of Toronto Quarterly* 43 (1974): 263–84.

graveclothes deprived of Christ's body.[12] Similarly, then, the revelation of Christ's resurrection is defined artistically by absence, rather than presence: He has risen because he is not here.

The close parallel between liturgical and artistic versions of the Resurrection scene in the post-Carolingian church is not necessarily an index of inherent dramatic potential. Later vernacular mystery playwrights dwelt very little on the scene at the tomb; of more significance to secular dramatists were the many appearances of Christ after his resurrection. They understood that a play's pious secular audience needed repeated demonstrations of the resurrected savior's actual presence among them. In contrast, ecclesiastical composers relied upon the context of the Easter liturgy and its participants to supply that demonstration. Thus, the drama of the *Quem queritis* arises from, and is dependent upon, the liturgy of Easter both musically—to extend the meaning of the introit, "*Resurrexi, et adhuc tecum*"—and contextually—to point to the liturgical meaning of the Resurrection. The Maries—in both the artistic and musical versions—are coming to the tomb with the expectation of finding Christ; but he is not there: that is the central reversal, the inherent dramatic peripetia, of the Easter liturgy.

A recent book by Pamela Sheingorn on the development of Easter sepulchers during the eleventh century cites a sepulcher at Gernrode upon which is depicted "one of the angels, pointing toward the grave with one hand, [who] holds in the other the staff of the Resurrection and a bandarole with the words . . . 'SURREXIT NON EST [HIC]. . . .'"[13] Similarly, other eleventh-century artistic renderings tied together text, tomb, and gesture. This correspondence not only confirms the close relationship between liturgy and art but also suggests that the plays which arose within the liturgical context had a similar iconographic function, "pointing out" the meaning of the Resurrection.

---

[12]A large number of these are collected in Gertrud Schiller, *Ikonographie der christlichen Kunst*, vol. 3, *Die Auferstehung und Erhöhung Christi* (Gütersloh, 1971), pp. 310–29.

[13]Pamela Sheingorn, *The Easter Sepulchre in England* (Kalamazoo, Mich., 1987), p. 17.

The depiction of the sepulcher in artistic renderings raises the question of staging in the early plays: how were they presented within the church? We can begin to address this issue by examining closely the very first version of a liturgical play, found in an English manuscript of the mid-tenth century—the ***Regularis Concordia***. Probably one of the best-known products of the Anglo-Saxon monastic revival, the *Regularis Concordia* was drafted at the Council of Winchester in about 973.[14] It prescribes a set of customs and observances to be followed by all of the monks and nuns in the English Church. Among the most interesting of these are the prescribed activities during Holy Week. On Good Friday, after the Adoration, the altar cross is "buried" in a representation of the sepulcher placed on or near the altar, "hung about with a curtain" [*quaedam assimilatio sepulchri uelamenque quoddam in gyro tensum*].[15]

On midnight of Easter Matins the cross is raised to its proper place on the altar. After the elevation, one of the monks is directed to "go stealthily to the place of the sepulcher, and sit there quietly, holding a palm in his hand." Three other brothers, vested in monastic capes, go toward the sepulcher carrying incense vessels "as though searching for something," as the text relates, "in imitation of the angel seated on the tomb and of the women coming with perfumes to anoint the body of Jesus."

> Dum tertia recitatur lectio, quattuor fratres induant se, quorum unus, alba indutus ac si ad aliud agendum, ingrediatur atque latenter sepulcri locum adeat ibique, manu tenens palmam, quietus sedeat. Dumque tertium percelebratur responsorium residui tres succedant, omnes quidem cappis induti, turibula cum incensu manibus gestantes, ac, pedetemptim ad similitudinem quaerentium quid, ueniant ante locum sepulcri. Aguntur enim haec ad imitationem angeli sedentis in

---

[14]Thomas Symons, "*Regularis Concordia*: History and Derivation," in *Tenth-Century Studies: Essays in Commemoration of the Millennium of the Council of Winchester and Regularis Concordia*, ed. David Parsons (London, 1975), p. 42.

[15]St. Aethelwold, *Regularis concordia Angliae nationis monachorum sanctimonialiumque*, ed. and trans. Thomas Symons (New York, 1953), p. 44. All subsequent citations in Latin, as well as translations from this text, will be indicated in parentheses by page number.

> monumento, atque mulierum cum aromatibus uenientium ut ungerent corpus Ihesu. Cum ergo ille residens tres, uelut erraneos ac aliquid quaerentes, uiderit sibi approximare, incipiat mediocri uoce dulcisone cantare Quem quaeritis? Quo decantato finetenus, respondeant hi tres, uno ore, Ihesum Nazarenum. Quibus ille: Non est hic. Surrexit sicut praedixerat. Ite, nuntiate quia surrexit a mortuis. Cuius iussionis uoce uertant se illi tres ad chorum, dicentes Alleluia. Resurrexit Dominus. Dicto hoc, rursus ille residens, uelut reuocans illos, dicat antiphonam: Venite et uidete locum. Haec uero dicens, surgat et erigat uelum ostendatque eis locum, cruce nudatuma sed tantum linteamina posita quibus crux inuoluta erat; quo uiso deponant turibula quae gesta uerant in eodem sepulcro, sumantque linteum et extendant contra clerum ac, ueluti ostendentes quod surrexerit Dominus et iam non sit illo inuolutus, hanc canant antiphonam: Surrexit Dominus de sepulcro, super ponantque linteum altari. (49–50)

As the text makes clear:

> When [the *Quem queritis*] has been said, [the angel] . . . shall rise and lift up the veil [of the sepulcher] and shall show them [*ostendat*] the place void of the cross and with only the linen in which the Cross had been wrapped. Seeing this the Maries shall lay down their thuribles in that same sepulcher and, taking the linen, shall hold it up before the clergy; and as though showing [*ostendentes*] that the Lord was risen and no longer wrapped in it, they shall sing this antiphon: "The Lord has arisen from the sepulcher." They shall then lay the linen upon the altar.

One immediately notes that the bare text of the *Quem queritis* has been surrounded by a number of symbolic actions, centered upon a representation of the sepulcher. I am particularly interested in the action indicated by the verb, *ostendere*, " to show, demonstrate, point out." This verb occurs in the rubrics of the play to indicate some object for particular attention—the abandoned tomb and the empty linens. In modern theatrical scholarship, the technical term, "ostension" designates the fragmentary visual elements of a production that are not completely shown—the ways in which the theater or film can suggest, "a complex reality by a characteristic detail: a crown for the King, for instance."[16] The term in its recent usage seems most

[16]Patricia Dorval, "Towards a Stylistics of the Modes of Ostension," *Theatre Research International* 18 (1993): 206.

indebted to the theory of discourse "relevance," in the 1986 book of that name by Dan Sperber and Deirdre Wilson. They define "ostensive behavior" within this context as "behavior which makes manifest an intention to make something manifest."[17]

Thus, in the text from *Regularis Concordia*, the *Quem Queritis* dialogue has been surrounded by actions which request attention to particular elements of the play. The actors point—make "ostensive motions"—toward key symbols of the Resurrection. For instance, the angel lifts the veil of the sepulcher to "*show* the place void of the cross and with only the linen in which the Cross had been wrapped." The women then hold up the linen "before the clergy, . . . *showing* that the Lord was risen and was no longer wrapped in it," placing the linen upon the altar. Ostensions can be more subtle: for instance, one participant wears only the white alb and carries a palm branch to manifest his role as angel; the Maries are dressed in copes and carry thuribles, or censers, as they approach the sepulcher. In even more sophisticated ways, the posture or demeanor of actors may indicate meaning: the Maries are instructed to "go . . . step by step, as though searching for something" and "wandering about as it were and seeking something"; the angel is "to sing softly and sweetly."

In this play, as in the iconographic representations of its subject, ostensive actions demonstrate meaning. Depictions of the Resurrection in medieval art often show the angel pointing to the empty grave or linens, in the same way we might imagine it being performed in the play. Within the liturgical drama, however, every gesture attains significance because of its liturgical context.

In the *Regularis Concordia*, the liturgical setting is the midnight Easter service. It is the first moment in which Christ's resurrection is celebrated, when the sorrow of Good Friday literally is transformed into the joy of Easter Sunday. The "actions" of the players specifically point to parallels

---

[17]Dan Sperber and Deirdre Wilson, *Relevance: Communication and Cognition* (Cambridge, Mass., 1986), p. 49.

between the altar cross, which has symbolized Christ, and the aftermath of Christ's resurrection. The linens which they discover and then display literally have enwrapped the cross since Good Friday, just as the historical grave cloths once enclosed Christ's body. The whole monastic community in fact "buried" the cross on Good Friday; and the sepulcher has been watched continuously by groups of monks throughout the weekend. The brethren depicting the three Maries, robed in copes and carrying incense vessels, are closely identified with the celebrants of the liturgical service.

Consequently, this moment of demonstration is the culmination of a whole series of liturgical activities engaged in by the entire community during Holy Week. The linens which are "pointed to" are altar cloths, which represent the wrappings of the cross and the burial clothes of Christ. And their display, their ostention, culminates in the communal celebration of Christ's triumph over death. Thus, the very next instruction reads, "When the antiphon (*Surrexit*) has finished, the prior, rejoicing in the triumph of our King in that He had conquered death and risen, shall give out the hymn *Te Deum Laudamus*, and thereupon all the bells shall peal." (50)

But the relevance of ostension can extend beyond the liturgy into the larger community and even, in some instances, the state itself. The play from *Regularis Concordia* is not just *an* Easter service; it is *the* Easter service for all of the "Monks and Nuns of the English nation." As the title, *Regularis Concordia* indicates, the book was drawn up by a council called by King Edgar to unify the English Church and State. The *Regularis* manuscript itself is prefaced with a drawing of a scribe presenting the Monastic Agreement to King Edgar and his bishops. The king and prelates—the document's authors—examine its contents, while the monk below looks pointedly up at them, girding himself protectively in its folds.

Not all liturgical dramas are so clearly divisible into layers of communal discourse—yet there are communities in which several distinct layers of drama were produced. One of the most striking of these is the Norman cathedral at Rouen. Here, in contrast to the private English monastic tradition, a public-spirited mode of presentation by the cathedral chapter developed an astounding variety of liturgical plays. A brief overview of these plays not only reveals the variety of liturgical plays available at a medieval cathedral but also indicates how the medium was altered in accordance to changes in community context.

The Easter ***Visitatio Sepulchri*** from this cathedral, like the English version from the *Regularis Concordia*, is presented in close proximity to the altar.[18] While it is a much more elaborate version (reflecting, in part, its composition in the thirteenth century), the Rouen *Visitatio* nonetheless features a sepulcher prepared near the main altar into which the cross has been laid on Good Friday. The cross having been raised and Matins having been chanted,[19] three canons—that is, clergy belonging to the cathedral chapter—have covered their heads with mantles [*amices*], and proceed through the choir toward the sepulcher, where they engage in the *Quem Queritis* dialogue with the angel. The angel points toward the sepulcher with his finger [*locum digito ostendens*] as in artistic renderings. The play then shifts to a scene involving Mary Magdalene and two angels within the sepulcher, addressing her with the familiar biblical words, *Mulier, quid ploras*? Again, the fact of Christ's resurrection is underlined by iconographic ostension: Mary Magdalene kisses the tomb; a canon representing the risen Christ appears beside the altar, shows her the cross which he carries [*crucem illi ostendens*] and speaks her name, at which point she falls to his feet. After Christ has disappeared, all three Maries bow to the altar [*lete inclinent ad altare*] and, turning to the choir, conclude the play by singing an affirmation of the Resurrection, *Alleluia, resurrexit Dominus, alleluia*.

Clearly, despite the addition of a scene between Mary Magdalene and Christ (the "Hortulanus" episode which marks this as a later elaboration of the Easter play), as well as graced by an appearance of the risen Christ, this

---

[18]For text see Young, *Drama*, 1:370–71. A transcription of the music from Paris, Bibl. Nat., MS lat. 904, with commentary, may be found in Rankin, *Music of the Medieval Liturgical Drama*, 2:65–68.

[19]While the *Depositio* from Rouen is described in the rubrics, the *Elevatio* is not. However, from an early (eleventh century) version of the liturgy of this cathedral we know that it was in use at that time. See Young, *Drama*, 2:135–36; 555.

version does not differ substantially in its staging from the earliest *Visitatio Sepulchri* examined above.[20] The Rouen *Visitatio* takes place in the environment of the main altar, and involves members of the choir, the canons, and the clergy. It features a number of specific demonstrations visible to, and probably only apprehended by, those in close proximity to the altar—such as the angel's finger pointing into the empty sepulcher, or Christ extending his Cross toward Mary Magdalene. Effectively, it is a monastic service transplanted into the vast cathedral; the drama is expanded, but the audience and the acting space are limited to participants in the Easter liturgy.

Similarly, the Rouen Christmas play entitled *Officium Pastorum*, or Service of the Shepherds, specifies that an elaborate manger is to be prepared "behind the main altar" containing figures of the Christ child and the Virgin Mary.[21] When the clerics singing the part of the shepherds approach the crib, two priests clad in long robes, or dalmatics—representing midwives—draw a curtain revealing the crib itself, indicating [*demonstrent*] the Christ child, then pointing [*ostendant*] to a statue of His mother, Mary. The cleric-shepherds even bow to the crib as they chant verses in honor of the Virgin; and then turn to the choir to sing the final verses confirming Christ's birth.

This Christmas play shows much indebtedness to the Easter *Visitatio*. The crib, like the sepulcher, is constructed near the altar; and the actions of shepherds and midwives closely resemble those of the Maries and angels. Indeed, the dialogue at the crib closely resembles that of the Easter play:

> Quem queritis in presepe, pastores, dicite?
> Salvautorem Christum Dominum, infantem pannis inuolutum, secondum sermonem angelicum.

---

[20]See de Boor, *Textgeschichte*, pp. 251, 327, who speculates that the Rouen *Visitatio* is the source of all Anglo-Norman plays which include a scene with Mary Magdalene, dating it at about the late eleventh century.

[21]Text in Young, *Drama*, 2:16–19. A full transcription with very helpful discussion may be found in John Stevens, *Words and Music in the Middle Ages: Song, narrative, dance, and drama, 1050–1350* (Cambridge, 1986), pp. 336–47.

> Adest hic paruulus cum Maria matre sua, de quo dudum uaticinando Ysayas dixerat propheta.
> [Whom do you seek in the manger, shepherds? Tell us.
> We seek the savior Christ the Lord as an infant wrapped in swaddling clothes, according to the words of the angel.
> Here is the little one with his mother Mary, of whom Isaiah had prophesied. . . .]

There are, however, some differences between the Christmas and Easter plays. The crib is certainly more "realistic," since it contains statues of the Virgin and Child; the ostensive actions center upon presence, not absence, of the infant Christ; and, most important, the music is newly composed for this particular play.[22] Yet, for all of its differences, the *Officium Pastorum* preserves the close-knit relationship among actors, setting, and audience that we have observed in the *Visitatio Sepulchri*. The actors are, in fact, the celebrants of the Christmas services in which the play is but a small component. We can see this clearly by the extension of the shepherds' activities beyond the play into the Christmas mass which follows. There, they sing the Mass introit, "rule the choir" by taking major parts in the regular liturgical chant, and receive the offertory.

Despite their expanded participation in the services, the shepherds were, like the Maries of the Easter play, less actors than celebrants. The cathedral at Rouen, newly built in the thirteenth century after a disastrous fire,[23] is huge, and the tiny manger constructed behind the altar would have been invisible to all but the celebrants and the choir. Indeed, even the procession of the shepherds through the great west door of the choir would have been unseen by the congregation. These two examples from Rouen suggest that even transplanted within cathedral settings, liturgical drama could remain

---

[22]See Stevens, *Words and Music*, p. 345; Smoldon, *Music*, pp. 341–44; and Rankin, *Music of the Medieval Liturgical Drama*, 1:178–81.

[23]Anne-Marie Carment-Lanfry, *La Cathédrale Notre-Dame de Rouen* (Rouen, 1977), pp. 27–29.

a private discourse, very much like the earliest Easter play.[24] However, there are other plays from this very cathedral that reveal a much keener awareness of the congregation, and explore the possibilities of constructing liturgical dramas which could be readily apprehended by a lay audience.

The ***Officium Regum Trium***, or Service of the Three Kings, begins before the Mass of Epiphany with the three kings processing from different directions to meet in front of the main altar, pointing up toward a brightly lighted chandelier, or *corona*, which represents the star of Bethlehem.[25] The kings, dressed in a rich array of ecclesiastical vestments to denote their station[26] process from the altar into the nave, toward the altar of the Holy Cross, where they see a *corona* suspended in front, probably over a representation of the creche, hidden by a curtain. Two canons, dressed as the midwives, pull aside a curtain to reveal the mother and child. The kings prostrate themselves in adoration and offer their gifts. Then the remaining members of the congregation come forward to offer *their* gifts to the newborn child, which are accepted by the canon-midwives.

While it is not clear whether the *corona* representing the star is carried in procession, or whether there are in fact two such chandeliers, the *Officium Regum Trium* clearly attempts to move the center of action away from the main altar and into the middle of the congregation. The construction of a creche with sculptured figures to be revealed to the audience at the appropriate time, as well as employment of lighted chandeliers to attract their

---

[24]Stevens, *Words and Music*, notes that the *Officium Pastorum* from Rouen "has little to offer of what we normally look for in a play; its force is derived from the larger 'drama' of which it is a small episode" and that it was enacted in a part of the church "where the congregation, if there was a congregaton, could not possibly have seen them" (p. 345).

[25]Text in Young, *Drama*, 2:43–45. For a transcription see Smoldon, *Music*, pp. 127–28, and discussion on pp. 344–46.

[26]The rubrics from Rouen specify that the kings are to be dressed in capes with ornate crowns [*cappis et coronis ornati*])—see Young, *Drama*, 2:436. Other Magi plays, such as those from Bensançon (Young, *Drama*, 2:38 and 434); and Limoges (2:34), describe several ornate accoutrements—derived from ecclesiastical vestments.

attention, underline this intention. While the ostensive actions are similar to those of the Easter and Christmas plays (the Magi process toward the star and point to it with their staffs; the midwives reveal the creche to the kings), the double offertory successfully fuses the historical adoration and the liturgical oblation into a larger communal, that is, congregational, act.

Other liturgical plays from the Rouen cathedral make even greater efforts to appeal to the congregation. A representation of the Journey to Emmaus, or the ***Peregrinus***, features a ***tabernaculum*** in the middle of the nave, a raised platform that represents the city of Emmaus, and contains a table with seats.[27] It begins with an elaborate procession during the Easter Vespers service, in which the choir, two canons playing the disciples, and the priest depicting Christ all process in grand fashion from the sacristy to the west door of the nave, halting at the *tabernaculum* before the congregation to present the drama. While the choir awaits, the canons representing the two disciples proceed slowly down the south aisle; meanwhile, the priest depicting Christ has entered quietly from the north door. He appears in their midst, but they fail to recognize him. Inviting him to join them on the *tabernaculum*, the disciples and Christ ascend the platform and take their seats. Christ breaks bread and suddenly disappears. The disciples, astonished [*quasi stupefacti*], lament their mistake and, turning toward the pulpit, address Mary Magdalene. A member of the choir, dressed in amice and dalmatic as Mary, testifies to Christ's resurrection by showing [*ostendat*] the empty grave cloths on either side of the pulpit, even throwing them down [*proiciat*] in front of the congregation. The disciples and Mary leave, and the choir completes its Vespers procession.

This play contains a number of spectacular elements, clearly intended for apprehension by a lay audience. It takes place in the middle of the nave. It is preceded by lengthy processions of the main characters through the

---

[27]The rubrics in Rouen, Bibl. de la Ville, MS 384 (Young, *Drama*, 2:693) read as follows: "Et ita cantantes ducant [Peregrini] eum usque ad tabernaculum, in medio nauis ecclesie, in similtudinem castelli Emaux preparatum. Quo cum ascenderint, et ad mensam ibi paratam sederint, et Dominus inter eos sedens panem eis fregerit. . . ."

congregation. Most importantly, it focuses the main action upon a specially built raised platform, presumably visible to all members of the congregation. Yet despite these many concessions to a lay audience—including the construction of a raised stage—the *Peregrinus* still remains solidly bound to the liturgy. Indeed, E. K. Chambers characterized the play as "a kind of dramatization of the procession itself";[28] and the rubrics seem to indicate that it is an optional activity during that time. The oldest Rouen text of this play, Bibliothèque de la Ville, MS 222, is indeed a processional, probably for use by a precentor. Finally, the play employs the same liturgical ostension of the grave linens seen in the earliest *Visitatio*—but sensationally displayed.

Even more spectacular in its concessions to a lay audience is the Rouen ***Processionis Asinorum*** (literally, the "Procession of the Asses") or Procession of the Prophets. It is the most elaborate of all liturgical dramas, featuring twenty-eight fully costumed prophets, a full-scale model furnace, and an actor impersonating a donkey. The costumes of the prophets differ markedly from the ecclesiastical vestments appearing in other plays. Moses, for instance, is depicted with his horns, carrying the tablets of the Law; Amos, Isaiah, Aaron, and Jeremiah are bearded, each with appropriate iconographic symbols; Daniel is a youth in a green tunic; Habbakuk is an old man, eating radishes and beating members of the audience with a long palm branch.[29] Each prophet is summoned by the choir and steps forward to deliver his prophecy in the middle of the nave; after he speaks[30] he is led to a position beside the furnace.

The solemn and formal recitation is broken by two dramatic scenes. In the first, two messengers of King Balak summon Balaam who, seated *super*

---

[28]Chambers, *Medieval Stage*, 2:38.

[29]For details see Fletcher Collins, *The production of medieval church music-drama* (Charlottesville, 1972), pp. 317–19.

[30]The rubric in each case is *dicat*. There is no version of the Rouen play with music; and, indeed, only two such Prophets' plays exist. Nevertheless, one must assume that it was sung, not spoken.

Asinam, is confronted by an Angel carrying a sword. The ass suddenly stops and refuses to budge, crying out despite Balaam's spurring. The angel calls upon Balaam to renounce his allegiance to Balak; and the call is underlined by the choir, who now ask for his prophecy. In the second scene, after the New Testament figures (Elizabeth, Simeon, St. John) have testified, King Nebuchadnezzar steps forward, pointing toward [*ostendens*] an idol. His soldiers display [*ostendant*] the idol, commanding the three youths Shadrach, Meshach, and Abednego to worship it, but they refuse. The king orders them to be led to the furnace and thrown in. The furnace, which has been the focal point of the production, since all speakers must stand in front of it to deliver their prophecy and must retire beside (or behind) it afterward, is set on fire [*accendatur*]. From inside the fiery structure, the boys praise God. The choir then directs King Nebuchadnezzar to prophesy. Gesturing toward the furnace [*fornacem ostendens*] he testifies to the presence of a fourth figure among the youths, all of them unburned.

We can appreciate the dramatic sensibility that could relieve the unremitting repetition of static prophecies with two lively spectacles. Appearing at the midpoint of the play, the Balaam episode injects a bit of humor in the braying of the unwilling donkey and the fruitless spurring of the reluctant prophet.[31] Even more compelling is the attempted sacrifice by King Nebuchadnezzar, utilizing the elaborate furnace constructed in the middle of the nave [*in medio nauis ecclesie*]. It not only involves a number of nonliturgical actions and actors but also calls for the structure to be set on fire. Whether the structure was actually kindled, or whether the fire was indicated by other means, is unclear. The fabric construction (cloth and rope; *lintheo et stupis constituta*), could easily have been set ablaze, providing a grand finale; but the logistical complications seem to argue otherwise.

---

[31]There is a demonstrable relationship of the Balaam play to the traditional "Feast of Fools" (or *asinaria festa*, as it was often called). A discussion of the feast with copious texts may be found in Chambers, *Medieval Stage*, 2:275–389. For a more recent discussion with specific reference to liturgical drama see Margot Fassler, "The Feast of Fools and *Danielis Ludus*: Popular Tradition in a Medieval Cathedral Play," in *Plainsong in the Age of Polyphony*, ed. Thomas Forrest Kelly (Cambridge, 1992), pp. 65–99.

Fascinated by these elaborate dramas of Rouen, historians of the theater have seen them as precursors for the later vernacular mystery plays. But the fact is that they were, and remained, closely bound to the services within the cathedral. They were called not dramas [***ludus***] but rather office [*officium*] or service [*ordo*]. These plays cohere closely to their liturgical setting, make use of primarily liturgical chants, and involve the actors in the services that follow. Every Rouen play is found only in wholly liturgical books, such as ordinaries, processionals, or antiphonals, as an extension of the services for that day. Thus, the *Peregrinus* occurs in the midst of the Easter Vespers procession; and the spectacular prophets' play, *Ordo Processionis Asinorum*, is appointed specifically as a substitute for the liturgical procession preceding the mass on the Feast of the Circumcision.

As capital of Normandy, Rouen was one of the richest cities in the Middle Ages; however, a long history of troubled relations between the commune and the cathedral probably mitigated cooperation between civic and ecclesiastical authorities. The archbishops maintained close control over the church's relations with the community, including the presentation of drama. Consequently, the plays from this cathedral were spectacular but privileged—extravagant examples of liturgical drama adapted to the needs of a prosperous congregation but rigidly controlled by Church authorities.[32]

But were all Latin musical plays intended for enactment within the confines of the medieval church? The specific examples cited above certainly support such a view. However simple or spectacular the staging, it is clear that the monastery or cathedral provided both communal setting and interpretive symbols. There are, however, a number of plays in this tradition which seem to contradict such a theory. A striking example is the fully developed Magi play. In contrast to the rather simple offertory ceremony of Rouen, other, more elaborate Magi plays seem to have developed

[32]See the arguments in Thomas P. Campbell, "Cathedral Chapter and Town Council: Cooperative Ceremony and Drama in Medieval Rouen," in *Medieval Drama on the Continent of Europe*, ed. Clifford Davidson and John H. Stroupe (Kalamazoo, Mich., 1993), pp. 100–13.

independently of the liturgical setting which produced the dramas we have so far examined. In contrast to the Easter plays, for instance, they are extraordinarily elaborate. Also, they develop a sophisticated and complex form quite early—a fragment of one such play in classical hexameters from the cathedral of Metz is dated about 1000.[33]

In order to appreciate more fully the distinctiveness of the Magi form, let me summarize briefly the contents of one, from the German monastery of Freising, dated about 1070. The play opens with an anthem to King Herod; Christ's birth, juxtaposed to Herod's reign, is then announced to the shepherds by an angelic choir. Immediately, the Magi meet, vowing to follow the star and inquiring where the newly born king might be found. The scene then shifts to Herod's court, where a messenger informs the tyrant of the Magi's coming and invites them to appear before him. Questioned closely, the Magi testify to the validity of their mission by interpreting the symbolic significance of their gifts. Herod, however, refuses to believe them and consults with his scribes; as soon as he hears the damning prophecy, he hurls the book from him and insults the Magi. The three kings depart, following the star; they meet successively with the shepherds, an angel, and the midwives, who finally reveal the Christ child. They worship, fall asleep, are warned to depart, and flee Herod's wrath. Meanwhile, Herod is informed of the Magi's deception and, waving a sword, vows to avenge it by killing all male children. I have neglected to mention many sophisticated poetic elements, such as classical hexameter verse, or dramatic elements, such as the crowded stage (a minimum of thirteen actors, not counting two choirs), and contrasting simultaneous scenes.

A more detailed account of the play's accomplishments may be found in Peter Dronke's recent edition.[34] Such a sophisticated and essentially self-contained play does not appear to stem from the ecclesiastical tradition which produced the *Visitatio Sepulchri* or the other plays—including the

---

[33]Young, *Drama*, 2:448.

[34]*Latin Plays*, pp. 24–51.

Officium Regem Trium—which we have examined above. The manuscripts in which several Magi plays are found, as Susan Rankin suggests, may indicate an origin quite separate from the liturgy.[35] Yet, as I have argued elsewhere, this does not exclude them from the canon of liturgical drama.[36] For the Christmas liturgy featured a large number of historical events: the birth of Christ; Holy Innocents (Dec. 28); the Purification (Jan. 1); and Epiphany (Jan. 6). Further, each of the events features a large case of historical figures acting within well-prescribed limits. It is interesting that almost all Magi plays, although dramatically sophisticated, include essentially the same events, the same characters, and the same textual/musical lines. Finally, all of the Christmas plays are focused quite narrowly upon the liturgical themes of prophecy and fulfillment—an activity which depends significantly upon participation of the entire community in which they are being presented. Even a play as sophisticated as the *Ludus Danielis*, from the cathedral school of Beauvais, may be said to be "liturgical" in this sense. For it appears within a manuscript of liturgical ceremonies at Beauvais for the feast of the Circumcision; its focus on the issues of true kingship, elevation of the lowly, and the power of prophecy are consistent with those of the Christmas season; and it ends not only with the prophecy of Daniel himself but also with an angel's announcement of Christ's birth.[37]

However, there are certain Latin plays to which liturgical connection may indeed be so slight as to be highly questionable. These are a group of plays—ranging from saints' miracles to depictions of the Passion—which I would call "academic drama." These plays fit within a group of criteria

---

[35]*New Oxford History*, p. 320.

[36]"Liturgy and Drama: Recent Approaches to Medieval Theatre," *Theatre Journal* 33 (1981): 289–301.

[37]A superb edition of the Beauvais *Daniel*, containing the entire manuscript of the services for the Christmas octave in which the play was enacted may be found in Wulf Arlt, *Ein Festoffizium des Mitterlalters aus Beauvais in seiner liturgischen und musikalischen Bedeutung* (Cologne, 1970).

which would seem to liberate them entirely from liturgical context. Thus, for instance, the famous Greater Passion Play, from the *Carmina Burana*,[38] is surrounded in the manuscript not with liturgical chants but with lyric poetry composed by students. The play itself features a large number of locales (called "*locus*" in the rubrics): the seashore, a tree, Simon's dwelling, a room for the Last Supper, and for Pilate, the Mount of Olives, a rope for hanging Judas, and the cross. Nowhere is church architecture mentioned. Finally, although the play uses liturgical music, it draws that music from a wide variety of liturgical services and books.[39]

But the most famous of all academic collections is the so-called Fleury Playbook. In contrast to the liturgical plays of Rouen, for instance, which are so tightly bound to particular church services, the ten Latin plays found in Orléans, MS 201, from the Benedictine monastery at Fleury, are gathered from separate sources and placed in a little booklet. Clearly, the peculiar status of the Fleury Playbook—inserted into a collection of sermons and hymns, without any relation to the rest of the miscellany—argues that it is primarily a *literary* phenomenon, whose relation to the liturgy is problematic at best.[40]

---

[38]For a complete edition of the *Carmina Burana* see *Carmina Burana*, ed. Bernard Bischoff, vol. 1, part 3 of *Die Trink- un Spielerlieder, die geistlichen Draman. Nachträge*, ed. Otto Schumann and Bernard Bischoff (Heidelberg, 1970). The text has been edited most recently in Dronke, *Medieval Latin Plays*, pp. 185–237.

[39]Thomas Binkley, "The Greater Passionplay in the *Carmina Burana*: An Introduction," *Alte Musik: Praxis und Reflexion*, ed. Peter Reidemeister and Veronika Gutmann (Wintertur, 1983), pp. 144–58.

[40]For a complete discussion of the Fleury Playbook, including photographic reproductions of the manuscript, see *The Fleury Playbook: Essays and Studies*, ed. Thomas P. Campbell and Clifford Davidson (Kalamazoo, Mich., 1985). The plays are edited in Young, *Drama*; references to particular plays in Young's book will be cited in parentheses by volume and page number. Musical editions of individual Fleury plays are numerous. All but one, in modern transcription with translation, may be found in Collins, *Medieval Church Music-Dramas*; a lavish edition of the Herod and Innocents plays is available edited by Noah

Of the ten plays in this anthology, only four—a *Visitatio Sepulchri*, two plays about the Three Kings (*Ordo ad Representandum Herodem*, *Ad Interfectionem Puerorum*), and a *Peregrinus*—seem to have overt liturgical connections. These four plays specifically mention church architecture or identify actors as *fratres*. On the other hand, the six other dramas do not refer to church architecture; instead they require separate construction of dramatic scenes. For instance, the Fleury *Filius Getronis*, another St. Nicholas play, calls for at least two elaborate sets, probably on raised platforms. The *Conversio Sancti Pauli* requires on one side seats [*sedes*] for the High Priest and Saul; on the other side seats for Judas and the High Priest of Damascus; and a bed in between for Ananias (2:219). These must also have been raised platforms or scaffolds, because the stage directions require Paul to escape from Damascus by being lowered "from a high place, as if from a wall" [*ab aliquo alto loco, quasi a muro*; 2:222]. Nor do these six plays refer to liturgical services (although they use liturgical chants). In one case at least, a Fleury play even seems to construct its own "liturgy."[41] A close examination of one representative play should demonstrate the literary nature of the collection as a whole.

The St. Nicholas play, *Tres Clerici*, concerns three traveling students who search for lodging in a foreign country. At an inn, they request hospitality from an old innkeeper and his wife. At first he refuses them, because he will gain nothing. However, the students appeal to his wife, flattering her that if she grants them hospitality God will give her a son. She persuades her husband to allow them shelter despite the lack of utility. After inviting them in, the husband remarks on the size of their wallets. His wife

---

Greenberg and William L. Smoldon, *The Play of Herod: A Twelfth-Century Musical Drama* (New York, 1965); more recent transcriptions of the *Visitatio* and *Peregrinus* may be found in Rankin, *Liturgical Drama*, 2:69–77, 155–60.

[41]In *Filius Getronis* the rubrics direct that bread and wine should be prepared in the "Church of St. Nicholas, unde Clerici et Pauperes reficiantur" (Young, 2:355)—"so that both clerics and the poor might refresh themselves." It is unclear whether the participants in this meal were drawn from the audience.

immediately responds that such money is theirs in exchange for death; and she counsels him to cast the youths into the grave for a life of wealth. St. Nicholas, disguised as a pilgrim, confronts the pair with their deed and restores the clerics to life.

In the manuscript, the play contains both music and text, plus interpolations indicating change of speaker. Each speaker is given a little box of rubrics, interrupting the musical/textual surface. The interruption is itself a kind of pointing, or ostention. Whereas the titles of such speakers as *Clericus* and *Nicholaus* are conditioned by the tale itself, the terms *Senex* and *Vetula* for the host and his wife seem unusual. Nowhere does the verse refer to them in these terms (they are called *Hospes* and *Coniunx*). I would suggest that these terms are used typologically: these are the original "old man" and "old woman"—Adam and Eve. In the "plot" of the Fleury play the old man is decidedly deferential to his wife—in acquiescing to house the clerics, in deciding to kill them, and in electing to receive St. Nicholas. Like Adam, the host is drawn to his wife's material needs, symbolized by her desire for riches. This is clearly a learned, perhaps Augustinian, interpretation of Adam's obedience to social compulsion rather than divine law, and reflects a fairly consistent treatment of the theme of the Two Cities throughout the Fleury plays.[42]

The insistent repetition of the same rhythmic musical verse, carried out eighteen times in the course of the play, raises the possibility of textual repetition as well. Indeed, the text is filled with repeated phrases which draw attention to certain key words: *hospitia* [hospitality]; *donare* [to give]; *morte* [death]; *carnes* [flesh]; and *peregrinus* [pilgrim]. Thus the paradigm of the Old Law vs. the New is carried out in the language of the play as well as its plot. The three clerks are slaughtered not for their knowledge but for their material possessions; the host and his wife, mistaking money for salvation, deliberately disobey the Mosaic injunction against murder. Nicholas' intervention, expressed through the food imagery of the Eucharist,

---

[42]For more complete discussion see Thomas P. Campbell, "Augustine's Concept of the Two Cities and the Fleury *Playbook*," in *The Fleury Playbook*, pp. 82–99.

confronts the killers with their carnal secret. Bringing the light of salvation, he restores the murdered clerics; but he cannot guarantee the same for the host and his wife who have, like Cain, murdered in cold blood.

A medieval audience of this play very well might have understood these many layers of meaning carried through the language, verse, and action. But it must have done so without a liturgical context to guide interpretation. The Nicholas plays may have been monastic in origin, if the attribution of the Playbook to the abbey at St. Benoît sur Loire is accurate;[43] but they were most certainly scholarly productions, intended for the refectory, not the church. As the patron saint of scholars, St. Nicholas would have patronized an audience familiar with liturgical exegesis, who would have been quite ready to comprehend the play's sophisticated literary and dramatic allusions. But it is equally likely that this play also was intended for a *reader*—one who would notice the text's own ostentions, just as we have here. There is no guarantee, after all, that a drama must be performed; and in a work as self-consciously literary as the Fleury Playbook, it may be possible to argue that we have a set of signals which can be interpreted by either an audience or a reader.

C. Clifford Flanigan wrote in the "The Fleury *Playbook*, Traditions of Medieval Latin Drama, and Modern Scholarship":

> The new literary history that the study of the Latin [liturgical] drama now demands must afford the place of eminence to readers and audiences, whose roles in determining the meaning of specific performances and written records of these performances was at least as crucial as that of the author or scribe. The attempt to determine the horizons of expectations out of which each drama grew, to which

[43]Solange Corbin, "Le Manuscrit 201 d'Orléans: drames liturgiques dits de Fleury," *Romania*, 74 (1953): 1–43, argued that the subject-matter and musical style of the manuscript belonged to another monastery, that of St. Lhomer-de-Blois. However, several scholars have subsequently rejected her argument. For a summary see Michel Huglo, "Analyse codicologique des drames liturgiques de Fleury," in *Calames et Cahiers: Mélanges de codicologie et de paléographie offerts à Léon Gilissen*, ed. Jacques Lemaire and Emile van Balberghe (Brussels, 1985), pp. 61–78.

> it was directed, and by which it was constantly in the process of transformation must be afforded the highest priority.[44]

In the preceding examples, I have attempted to suggest means by which such a history of liturgical drama can be attempted. That is, by focusing on the textual instructions and their communal setting, one can determine fairly precisely what *kind* of liturgical drama is being presented, and *how* that drama is intended to be received. Just because a drama is called "liturgical" does not mean that it is necessarily dependent upon the liturgy for its meaning. That may indeed supply a context for its presentation, but the play's meaning may extend far beyond the liturgical service itself. At the same time, liturgical presentation does not guarantee a cultic function. A liturgical play may be mere decoration, a spectacle to be observed but not absorbed by the participants in the service. Finally, a liturgical play may not be liturgical at all, and yet may depend upon a liturgical familiarity for its comprehension and significance. Clearly, liturgical plays were not static forms, unchanging in their history; rather, they were constantly being challenged by the shifting conditions of presentation and reception as represented by liturgical context and cultural understanding.

---

[44]In *The Fleury Playbook*, pp. 22–23.

MUSIC IN THE LITURGY

GABRIELA ILNITCHI

MUSIC WAS INHERENT IN THE CHRISTIAN LITURGICAL PRACTICE. It helped mediate between people and God; was a vehicle for words of worship, supplication, or revelation; and delivered the words of Scripture with a heightened rhetorical effectiveness. Almost no section of the various liturgical services was performed without some musical enhancement, be that a simple pitched recitation or virtuosic melodies. Liturgical music of the Middle Ages, commonly known as plainchant, features a wide range of styles and structures, and the manner in which it was performed was intimately connected with the function that it had in the unfolding of the liturgy. The various levels of musical expression contained in liturgical services as well as the complex set of relationships among liturgical action, text, music, and the categories of participants in the liturgical event constitute a complex and interactive set of factors that influence the liturgical substance. Much of what follows discusses the chants of the Roman liturgical practice, the most widely used in western Europe.

The Liturgical Year

Christian liturgical observance mainly follows four overlapping and highly interlinked cycles: the annual cycles of the liturgical seasons [*Temporale*] and of the feasts commemorating individual saints [*Sanctorale*], the weekly and the daily cycles of Mass and Divine Office. As an expression of the *Temporale*, the Christian liturgical year unfolds as a succession of feast days that recounts each year of the earthly life of Jesus Christ. Central to the liturgical structure of this yearly cycle are two dates, one fixed and the other variable, commemorating the birth and the resurrection of Christ, respectively: Christmas, falling on December 25, and Easter, falling on the first Sunday following the first full moon of the spring equinox.[1] The liturgical seasons are further delineated by the presence of preparatory penitential periods, Advent and Lent, that precede the Christmas and Easter festivals.

The liturgical year starts with Advent, the preparatory season for Christmas, adopted sometime before the pontificate of Gregory I (590–604). Although in the beginning the number of Sundays assigned to the Advent season varied somewhat, it became fixed at four and remained as such throughout the Middle Ages.

Lent, the period of forty days of fasting that precedes Easter, begins on Ash Wednesday. While Easter had been celebrated from the second century onwards, Lent came to be established only gradually, reaching its specific structure sometime around the seventh century. At its center was the Pascal *triduum* (Good Friday, Holy Saturday, and Easter Sunday in the fifth century, and Holy Thursday, Good Friday, and Holy Saturday after the fifth century). The liturgical entity of Holy Week [***hebdomana maior***] was established by the fifth century, with the two Sundays before Easter being named ***Dominica de Passione*** and ***Dominica in Palmis***, respectively. The Lenten period, or ***Quadragesima***, used to begin with the first Sunday of Lent and end on Holy Thursday; together with the Pascal *triduum* it constituted the six-week fast period. In the seventh century the fast days were calculated backwards from Easter Sunday itself; Lent consisted now of forty-three days and thirty-six fast days. One obtained forty days of fasting by adding the Wednesday (Ash Wednesday), the Thursday, Friday, and Saturday before the first Sunday in Lent.

---

[1]The point of departure in calculating the date of Easter was the Jewish Passover, observed during the night of 14–15 Nisan at the full moon of the first lunar month. The date of Easter is, therefore, different every year, and the entire liturgical year is essentially movable. The *termini paschales* are March 22 (the earliest possible date) and April 25 (the latest possible date).

The Easter season itself, Eastertide, extends for fifty days; it features Ascension Thursday, on the 40th day, and concludes with Pentecost Sunday, which celebrates the descent of the Holy Spirit upon the Apostles. The two fixed liturgical seasons thus devised around Easter Sunday, namely Lent and Eastertide, include fourteen Sundays in all (six Sundays of Lent, Easter Sunday, and seven Sundays after Easter). The first Sunday after Pentecost celebrates the Holy Trinity (Trinity Sunday) and the remaining Sundays, 22 to 27 depending on the date of Easter, conclude the liturgical year.

Concurrent to the cycle of feast days commemorating the events of Christ's life, the *Temporale*, is an annual cycle of feasts celebrating individual saints, the *Sanctorale*. Although the dates of the feasts celebrating individual saints are always fixed, the medieval *Sanctorale* calendar was far from being homogeneous. The main feasts and their dates were common throughout the Latin Christendom (St. Stephen on December 26, St. John the Baptist on June 24, and St. Andrew on November 30, for example). Feasts were added to the calendar in order to celebrate newly canonized saints, and some of these feasts (such as those honoring Thomas of Canterbury, Katherine of Alexandria, Elizabeth of Hungary, or Nicholas) became popular in the later Middle Ages. Moreover, various dioceses, individual monastic establishments, or churches celebrated saints who were venerated locally. Sometimes the cult of these originally local saints would spread to other areas of Europe (as in the case of St. Lambert of Liège): other times the cult would remain restricted to a single area or religious establishment (for example, St. Findani, patron saint of Rheinau monastery). These geographical and chronological distinctions among the various medieval *Sanctorale* often provide the strongest clues regarding the provenance or dating of medieval liturgical manuscripts.

The Liturgical Day

Two types of daily liturgical observance developed during the first three centuries of Christian worship: one that was centered around the ritual celebration of the Last Supper, which developed into what became known as the Mass, and the other centered on readings from Scripture, singing of psalms, and prayer, which become known as the Divine Office. As prescribed in the Rule of St. Benedict (c. 530), eight services constitute the daily Divine Office: the Night Office (variously known as Matins, Vigils, or Nocturns) followed by Lauds (at daybreak), and six other services performed between dawn and darkness: Prime, Terce, Sext, None (known as the Little Hours), Vespers (at sunset), and Compline (bedtime). The main Mass of the day usually came between Terce and Sext on Sundays and feasts, after Sext on ferial days.[2] The exact time during the day when a service was to be performed varied in conformity with the time of the year, and the length of the services depended on the solemnity of the feast.

The constituent elements of both the Mass and the Divine Office fulfill one of the following three functions: eulogistic (such as prayers and supplications), didactic (readings from Scripture that are chosen according to the feast or liturgical season), and lyric (the various chants framing the eulogistic and didactic elements).[3] The eulogistic and didactic components are not delivered *recto tono*; most of their text is sung upon a single pitch, known as the "reciting tone" [*tenor*], while melodic flourishes underscore the punctuation of the text. These melodic inflections, generally formulaic in character, observe a hierarchy of the grammatical divisions of the text corresponding to period, semicolon, comma, etc. Moreover, these recitation formulas manifest degrees of melodic elaboration that suit various liturgical occasions, and their musical sophistication depends on whether they are sung by the priest, celebrant, or deacon.

The majority of Mass and Office chants can be classified in two large categories: antiphonal and responsorial chants. The term *antiphona* designates a chant, usually short, that frames the recitation of a psalm or a

---

[2]The term ***feria*** denotes those days of the week with the exception of Saturday and Sunday on which no feast is celebrated.

[3]Michel Huglo, *Les Livres de chant liturgique* (Turnhout, 1988), p. 40.

canticle—a scriptural passage that has the form of a psalm but that does not come from the Psalter. In general these chants are performed by one or two cantors [***cantores***] or by a group of cantors [*schola cantorum*], while the psalms assigned to each day of the week are delivered by the choir. The responsorial chants consist of two main parts: a respond, usually performed by a small group of cantors, and a verse performed by one or two soloists and followed by a repeat of the final phrase of the respond [***presa***, ***repetendum***].[4] In addition, one encounters a third type of chant, the liturgical hymn; its metric or rhythmic poetic text is organized in stanzas, and each stanza is sung on the same melody. Each of these chants has a well defined musical form and fulfills a specific function in the liturgical action.

The Divine Office

A significant portion of the Divine Office was reserved for the reading of the Psalter. The 150 psalms were sung with antiphons and were distributed over the entire week; most of the first 100 psalms were performed during the Night Office, while the remaining 50 were performed during Vespers. Feasts from the *Temporale* or *Sanctorale* cycles would have had their proper psalms. In addition to psalms, all services except the four Little Hours contained canticles with antiphons, hymns, versicles with responses, prayers, lessons, and at least one responsory. While the psalms and their antiphons, the responsories, and the hymns changed every day according to the weekly cycle (Proper items), some material of the Office remained unchanged (Ordinary items), such as the canticles sung towards the end of Lauds, Vespers, and Compline: the *Benedictus* (Luke 1:68–79, the Song of Zacharias), the *Magnificat* (Luke 2:46–55, the Song of the Blessed Virgin Mary), and the *Nunc dimittis* (Luke 2:29–32, the Song of Simeon).

---

[4]This general description of antiphonal and responsorial chants generally corresponds to that offered by Aurelian of Réôme around the mid-ninth century; see *Aureliani reomensis musica disciplina*, ed. Lawrence A. Gushee (1975), p. 129.

The arrangement of the material in the Divine Office followed a fixed pattern referred to as the *cursus*. Two somewhat different cursus were observed during the Middle Ages: non-monastic churches such as cathedrals, collegiate, or parish churches followed the secular cursus ("Roman," "canonical"), while monastic establishments followed the monastic cursus.

Although the psalms constituted the focal point of the Office at large, the services varied somewhat in their liturgical structure, and their constituent chants manifested different degrees of musical sophistication. Lauds and Vespers had a similar structure, and some of the items for a given day could be sung at both services, such as the hymn or the psalm antiphons. Lauds and Vespers each began with versicles and responses followed by five psalms (in Lauds, the fourth is a lesser canticle) intoned with their respective antiphons. There followed a brief chapter, a hymn, a versicle and response, and then the major canticle (*Benedictus* at Lauds and *Magnificat* at Vespers) with its relatively long and elaborate antiphon.[5] The Little Hours each consisted of a hymn, three psalms with only one antiphon, a chapter with response, short responsory, and the usual series of versicles and responses and other prayers. Compline, the bedtime service, opened with versicles and responses as usual, followed by four psalms with only one antiphon, a hymn, a short reading with a short responsory, the versicle and response *Custodi nos* R. *Sub umbra* and the canticle *Nunc dimittis* with its antiphon; prayers and the *Benedicamus domino* concluded the service.[6]

The Night Office (Matins) started with versicles and responses: the first was usually *Deus in adiutorium meum intende* R. *Domine ad adiuvandum me festina* (the opening versicle for all the other Office services), followed by *Domine labia mea aperies* R. *Et os meum annuntiabit laudem tuam*. There followed the Invitatory psalm [Ps. 94, *Venite exultemus Dominum*] sung with its antiphon (the Invitatory antiphon), a hymn, and an additional

---

[5]Lauds and Vespers, both in monastic and secular use, included a short responsory after the reading; monastic Vespers contained only four psalms.

[6]Monastic Compline had only three psalms and they were sung without an antiphon; this service also lacked the *Nunc dimittis* (except during Easter when it was sung as a psalm).

versicle and response. This introductory material led to the first Nocturn: a group of psalms and their antiphons, lessons and responsories, and versicles and responses.

The number of Nocturns was variable and depended on the solemnity of the day: three on Sundays and feasts, and one on ferial days (two in monastic use). There were also different conventions regarding the number, order, and distribution of the psalms and antiphons, and lessons and responsories in the Nocturns. Unlike the order of the Lauds antiphons, which varied only slightly from one church to another, the order of the antiphons in the Night Office was often modified. This was due in part to the variation in the number of antiphons performed in each Nocturn as required by either the monastic or the secular cursus. For a festal Night Office, for example, the monastic cursus called for three Nocturns with thirteen antiphons (6+6+1), while the secular cursus called only for nine antiphons, equally distributed among the three Nocturns (3+3+3).

TABLE 1: Distribution of antiphons and responsories
in the Nocturns of the Night Office
(St. Vincent—22 Jan.)

Secular cursus*	Monastic cursus**
I Nocturn	I Nocturn
A_1 *Sanctus Vincentius* Ps. *Beatus vir*	A_1 *Sanctus Vincentius*
A_2 *Sanctitate quoque* Ps. *Quare fremuerunt*	A_2 *Sanctitate quoque*
A_3 *Valerius igitur* Ps. *Domine quid*	A_3 *Valerius igitur*
	A_4 *Tanto namque*
	A_5 *Levita Vincentius*
	A_6 *Iam tibi fili*
3 lessons	4 lessons
R_1 *Sacram presentis* V. *Per acto passionis*	R_1 *Sacram presentis*
R_2 *Sanctus Vincentius Christi* V. *Sanctitate quoque*	R_2 *Sanctus Vincentius Christi*
	R_3 *Sanctus martyr*
R_3 *Levita Vincentius* V. *Tibi enim*	R_4 *Levita Vincentius*

II Nocturn	II Nocturn
A_4 *Tanto namque* Ps. *Cum invocarem*	A_7 *Beatus Vincentius cuius*
A_5 *Levita Vincentius* Ps. *Verba mea*	A_8 *Nefarium enim*
A_6 *Iam tibi fili* Ps. *Domine dominus noster*	A_9 *Profitemur enim*
	A_{10} *In cuius nomine*
	A_{11} *Beatus Vincentius*
	A_{12} *Dixit sanctus*
3 lessons	4 lessons
R_4 *Ecce iam* V. *Insurge ergo*	R_5 *Ecce iam*
R_5 *Assumptus est* V. *Intrepitus*	R_6 *Assumptus est*
R_6 *Christe miles gloriosus* V. *Inter hec*	A_7 *Beatus dei athleta*
	R_8 *Vir inclitus*
III Nocturn	III Nocturn
A_7 *Beatus Vincentius cuius* Ps. *In domino confido*	A_{13} *Nisi granum*
A_8 *Nefarium enim* Ps. *Domine quis*	
A_9 *Profitemur enim* Ps. *Domine in virtute*	
3 lessons	4 lessons
R_7 *Beatus dei athleta* V. *Dantur ergo*	R_9 *Agnosce o Vincenti*
R_8 *Gloriosus dei amicus Vincentius* V. *Felici commercio*	R_{10} *Gloriosi domine*
R_9 *Agnosce o Vincenti* V. *Esto igitur*	R_{11} *Christe miles gloriosus*
	R_{12} *Gloriosus dei amicus Vincentius*

* Hereford usage; *The Hereford breviary, edited from the Rouen edition of 1505 with collation of manuscripts*, 3 vols., ed. Walter Howard Frere and Langton E. G. Brown (London, 1904–05).

** Fleury usage; *Consuetudines Floriacenses saeculi tertii decimi*, ed. D. Anselmus Davril (Siegburg, 1976).

Each Nocturn began with the intonation of psalms and their antiphons. A versicle and response followed by the Pater Noster separated the psalms from the lessons.[7] After each lesson came a versicle and a responsory. In secular use there would have been three lessons and therefore three responsories for each Nocturn. On Sundays and most feasts, the Night Office generally concluded with *Te Deum* and the closing formula *Benedicamus domino* V. *Deo gratias*.[8]

The Mass

The highlight of medieval liturgical daily celebrations, the Mass, acquired its more or less standardized form in the ninth and the tenth centuries and incorporated a large and varied body of prayers, Bible readings, and chants. Various levels of the clergy participated in the ceremony, which was performed at the main altar of the church. The resident priest, who in large monasteries and cathedrals was the abbot or local bishop, every day recited silently the canon or eucharistic prayer, and the three orations and Preface that changed daily; the book containing all these texts is called a sacramentary. In a cathedral, the subdeacon and the deacon chanted the two scriptural readings, the Epistle and the Gospel; the annual cycle of these readings appears in lectionaries (epistolaries) and evangeliaries. The *liber gradualis* originally contained only the antiphonal and responsorial Proper chants of the Mass that were performed by the *cantores* and the *schola cantorum*: introit, gradual, alleluia (tract), offertory, and communion. The Ordinary chants (Kyrie, Gloria, Credo, Sanctus, and Agnus Dei) appeared in collections of tropes or later as supplements to the gradual, and only in more recent times were assembled in books called *kyriale*.

---

[7]Not all the lessons were biblical. While the first Nocturn featured readings from the Old Testament (different books according to the season), the second and third Nocturns commonly had sermons, homilies, passages from the Gospel, or passages from a saint's *vita*.

[8]In monastic use *Te Deum* was followed by the hymn *Te decet laus*.

The Mass consisted of two sections: (1) the Fore-Mass, corresponding to the early Christian pre-Eucharistic service of the word, was open to those preparing for baptism (catechumens) as well as the baptized; and (2) the Eucharist, which was reserved in the early centuries for baptized Christians only, and which concentrated around the blessing and the partaking of the bread and wine.

Ceremonies of preparation preceded the beginning of the actual Mass. On Sundays, for example, these included the blessing and sprinkling of water and salt on the main altar of the church, prayers, versicles and responses, and the antiphon *Asperges me* with the psalm verse *Miserere mei*, more prayers and the recitation of Ps. 42. The Mass proper began with the intonation of the introit, a different one on each important feast of the year, which accompanied the entry of the priest and his attendants. Following the Kyrie and Gloria and concluding the introductory section of the Mass was the collect proper to the day, intoned by the priest.

There followed the scriptural readings, the Epistle and the Gospel, between which the gradual, alleluia, sequence, and tract were sung, in various combinations that depended upon the liturgical season. Among these four Proper items, the gradual was more or less a constant item, except for some days (the Saturday of Easter week, for example), when it was replaced by a second alleluia. The alleluia was not sung from Septuagesima to the end of Lent and on several other penitential days of the liturgical year, when it was replaced by the tract; the sequence was sung only on the highest feasts celebrated in a particular church. From the late eighth century, the Credo was sung following the Gospel reading.

The Eucharist section of the Mass began with the bringing of the gifts to the altar accompanied by the offertory chant that could last through the preparation of the altar and the prayers, including the prayer proper to the day, known as the secret. The chanting of the preface by the priest (at the beginning in dialogue with the congregation) led to the choral Sanctus that was in turn followed by the canon of the Mass (the set of prayers for the consecration of the bread and wine) and the chanting of the Paternoster [Lord's Prayer]. The choral Agnus Dei was chanted during a further set of

TABLE 2: The Mass
Invention of St. Stephen (3 Aug.)

PROPER*	ORDINARY	Prayers and lessons*
Introit: *Etenim sederunt* Ps. *Beati immaculati*		
	Gloria in excelsis deo	
	Kyrie eleison	
		Collect: *Omnipotens sempiterne deus*
		Epistle: *Submiserunt Iudei*
Gradual: *Sederunt principes*		
Alleluia: *Video celos apertos*		
Sequence: *Alma benigne*		
		Gospel: *Accesserunt ad dominum Ihesum*
		Homily
	Credo	
Offertory: *Posuisti*		
		Preface
	Sanctus	
		Canon of the Mass
		Pater noster
	Agnus dei	
Communion: *Video celos apertos*		
	Ite missa est	

*Fleury usage; *Consuetudines floriacenses*, ed. Davril.

prayers that were said while part of the bread was mixed with the wine. The last set of prayers was chanted while the priest consumed the bread and wine. Communion by persons other than the priest was customary only on one or two of the highest feasts of the church year and was accompanied by the communion chant (at any other time, the chant was sung during the clearing-up activities in the altar). The post-communion prayer intoned by the priest preceded the usual form of dismissal consisting of the words "Ite missa est" sung by the priest, to which the choir would answer with "Deo gratias."

Chants

Any discussion of a particular chant has to account not only for its liturgical function or mode of performance but also for some of its melodic characteristics. As far as the ratio between unit of text and melodic activity is concerned, one encounters three styles of textual setting: *syllabic*, *neumatic*, and *melismatic*. Syllabic setting customarily features only one pitch per syllable; chants characterized by a mostly syllabic setting sometimes feature two or three pitches per syllable (usually notated as a two- or three-pitch *neume*). In a *neumatic* setting, two- or three-pitch melodic gestures over one syllable are the norm. In a *melismatic* setting, a single syllable carries a large number of pitches that can sometimes form a melodic gesture of exceptional complexity. Although individual chants often feature a combination of two or of all three types of textual settings, the predominant one determines the overall style.

In terms of their melodic profile chants fall in one of the eight categories of classification known as the eight modes (*modus*, *tonus*, or *tropus*). By and large, the classification of a given chant in one of the eight modal categories is determined by the type of melodic formulas, range, recitation tone, and final note [*finalis*] featured by that chant. A hierarchical relationship among the pitches thus emerges, in which the *finalis* is followed in importance by the pitch of the reciting tone, the pitch around which the delivery of the chant centers. There were four possible *finales* that correspond to the modern pitches *D*, *E*, *F*, and *G*.[9] Chants ending on one of these finals were classified as *protus*, *deuterus*, *tritus*, or *tetrardus*. Each type could be divided into *authentus* [authentic, or "principal"] and *plagis* [plagal, or "subordinate"]. Chants in an authentic mode would feature a melodic range above the final and have the reciting tone a fifth above the final, while chants in a plagal mode would have a range that extends below the final and the reciting tone a third above the final.[10]

Office Chants: Antiphons

A staggering number of Office antiphons have come down to us from numerous medieval sources.[11] Most medieval antiphoners contain approximately 1500 antiphons each, and there is considerable variety among the sources; as a result the total number of antiphons used across Europe during the Middle Ages surpasses that of any other category in the chant repertory.

---

[9]Medieval theory recognized also the existence of the so-called co-finals, that is pitches on which chants ended that were related to the regular finals in respect to their interval surroundings: *D* resembles *a* in terms of their neighboring intervals (both have a tone, then a semitone below, and a tone and a semitone above), *E* resembles *b*, and *F* resembles *c*; see Dolores Pesce, *The Affinities and Medieval Transposition* (Bloomington, Ind., 1987).

[10]Except in mode 4, whose reciting tone is on *A* rather than *G*, and modes 3 and 8 whose reciting tones are on *C* rather than *B*. (The eight modes are numbered from 1 to 8 starting with the authentic on *D*—mode 1, the plagal on *D*—mode 2, and ending with the authentic on *G*—mode 7 and the plagal on *G*—mode 8.)

[11]The texts of the Office antiphons are edited in René-Jean Hesbert, *Corpus Antiphonalium Offici,* 6 vols. (Rome, 1963–79), esp. vol. 3. For facsimile reproductions of several medieval antiphoners see *Paléographie musicale*: vol. 9, *Antiphonaire monastique: XIIe siècle: Codex 601 de la bibliothèque capitulaire de Lucques* (Berne, 1974); vol. 12, *Antiphonaire monastique: XIIIe siècle: Codex F. 160 de la bibliothèque de la cathédrale de Worcester* (Berne, 1971); vol. 16, *Le Manuscrit de Mont-Renaud: Xe siècle: Graduel et antiphonaire de Noyon* (Solesmes, 1955); and 2e série, monumentale, 1, *Antiphonaire de l'office monastique transcrit par Hartker: Mss. Saint-Gall 390–391 (980–1011)* (Berne, 1970).

Most of these antiphons were coupled with the singing of the psalms and canticles in the Office, while some others were self-sufficient, non-psalmodic antiphons, sung in processions (processional antiphons) or as votive anthems, most often in the honor of the Virgin Mary (Marian antiphons).

The antiphons associated with psalmody are of three types: (a) ferial antiphons, performed during the offices of the ordinary days and Sundays of the year, when there is no feast; (b) the antiphons for the psalms at Matins, Lauds, and Vespers sung on days with a special liturgy (feast days); and (c) the antiphons for the *Magnificat* and *Benedictus*, the two canticles of Vespers and Lauds respectively.

Early antiphoners do not specify the number of times the antiphon was to be performed in the context of the recitation of the psalm. Descriptions of contemporary practice, however, appear in other sources. According to Amalar of Metz, for example, in the late eighth century the antiphon was repeated after each verse of the psalm. This practice of singing the antiphon at the beginning and the end of the psalm, as well as after every single verse, seems to have been typical during the early Middle Ages. It was maintained in the performance of the Invitatory psalm and its antiphon, sung at the beginning of Matins. For the other psalms, however, this time-consuming practice seems to have been abandoned in subsequent centuries. The performance of antiphons became restricted, therefore, to opening and closing each of the psalms they accompanied; the general performance formula had the antiphon rendered by the full choir, the psalm verses alternately by the two halves of the choir, and the closing antiphon again by the full choir.

The ferial antiphons have brief texts comprising a simple invocation or acclamation, not always grammatically self-contained, and drawn from the Psalter, specifically from the text of the psalms these antiphons accompany. Most of the melodies of the ferial antiphons are short, with a range restricted to a fourth or a fifth, and almost entirely syllabic.

The festal antiphons as well as the *Magnificat* and *Benedictus* antiphons for the *Temporale* have biblical texts drawn from the Office or Mass readings of the day, while those for the *Sanctorale* feature texts drawn from the

Acta martyrium, or the *vita* or Life of the saint read during the Office itself. While most antiphons have a relatively simple melodic style, with well-defined articulations and clear cadences, the canticle antiphons are generally longer and more elaborate musically, and the gospel canticles they accompany are sung to a more ornate psalm tone than those of the other office psalms and canticles.[12]

The eight psalm tones are characteristic of the antiphonal psalmody of the Office, and the choice of a particular psalm tone depends upon the mode that governs the framing antiphon. Most important in defining the mode of the antiphon is its final cadence; the last note of this cadence coincides with the modal *finalis*, which in turn determines the choice of psalm tone. All psalm tones have a similar configuration: melodic inflections occur at the beginning [*intonatio*], the mid-point [*mediatio*], and the end [*differentia, distinctio, varietas*] of the reciting tone.[13] The *differentia* is the most variable element in the psalm tone, for it has to provide a smooth passage from the end of the psalm to the incipit of the antiphon. Because even within a single mode antiphons can begin on any pitch, a variety of *differentiae* for each psalm tone were devised in order to prevent problematic transitions to the repetition of the antiphon. Moreover, because many antiphons share common opening and ending melodic formulas, lengthy lists of antiphons were compiled in medieval tonaries; these tonaries grouped the antiphons first according to the eight modes, and then, within each modal category, according to the psalm tone and *differentia* that they command.[14]

---

[12]Psalm tones are formulaic melodies to which the psalms distributed over the Office Hours of the week were sung. In addition to the psalm tones for antiphonal psalmody of the Office, there were series of psalm tones for the antiphonal psalmody of the Mass (introit verse and doxology, and communion verse) and for the Office canticles (*Magnificat* and *Benedictus*).

[13]Different texts can be adjusted to the same psalm tone; a second recitation tone (on the reciting tone) can be inserted, and melismas can be split or combined in order to accommodate differences in stress or textual articulation.

[14]A comprehensive discussion of medieval tonaries appears in Michel Huglo, *Les Tonaires: inventaire, analyse, comparaison* (Paris, 1971).

Among the non-psalmodic antiphons, the processional antiphons are required for days with special liturgies such as Palm Sunday and those of Holy Week, or for the Rogation days (Monday, Tuesday, and Wednesday before Ascension Day), among others. They are generally ornate chants, with lengthy melismas and stylistic features that suggest that the repertory as a whole contains chants of quite different origins. Some are from the Gallican liturgy, such as *Collegerunt pontifices* V. *Unus autem* and other Palm Sunday antiphons, while some others, such as *Ave gratia plena* and *Adorna thalamum suum* [Purification], were translated from Greek *kontakia* when the ceremony of the blessing of the candle was instituted in Rome by Sergius I (678–701).

During the twelfth and thirteenth centuries a proliferation of feasts that honored new saints paralleled a growing emphasis on the worship of the Virgin Mary. Votive chants that were not connected with psalm singing and that praised the Virgin Mary as mother and queen began to be performed during the Office, at the close of Compline. Devotional in character, many of these Marian antiphons were originally sung during the Office hours on various feasts of the Virgin, and some pieces feature texts of great antiquity. *Sub tuum praesidium*, for example, was part of the Ambrosian as well as the Roman liturgy, and its text can be traced back to a third-century Greek original. A large number of these chants, however, have texts drawn from the Song of Songs and were composed at the earliest in the ninth century. Perceived as "new" compositions, some of the most popular pieces were attributed to individual composers such as Hermann of Reichenau, but few of these medieval attributions can withstand critical scrutiny. Among the most important are the large scale Marian antiphons *Salve regina*, *Alma redemptoris mater*, *Ave regina*, and *Regina caeli*, which in Roman and Franciscan usage of the thirteenth century, for example, were performed one each for the four seasons of the liturgical year. The melodies of these antiphons are most often in a relatively ornate style that suits better their devotional function, and they clearly conform to modal requirements laid out in contemporaneous theoretical treatises: one-octave range, with each phrase begining and ending either on the final, the reciting tone, or on the third above the final, etc.[15]

Office Chants: Responsories

Responsorial chants of the Office are in most cases simple and quite short chants consisting of two parts—respond and verse—and involving alternation between solo singers and the full choir. The short responsories sung after the lessons of the Little Hours [***responsoria brevia***] are simple, mostly syllabic pieces, featuring melodic formulas that easily can be adapted to various texts. The repertory is relatively small, and single responsories tended to be used for whole liturgical seasons. Matins responsories, however, called also the Great Responsories or ***responsoria prolixa***, are long and ornate pieces, with intricate melodic shapes and often lengthy melismas. The medieval repertory is quite large.[16] Early notated antiphoners contain around 600 responsories each, while later sources may contain double that number. There is a core repertory that can be found in most medieval sources, but the correspondence between individual items and particular Nocturns varied a great deal. The general order of performance calls for a choral respond, a single solo psalm verse, and a choral *repetendum* [the second half of the

[15]Modal theory, fully developed by the late twelfth century, governs also the musical production of the rhymed Offices. These new Offices were composed to celebrate recently canonized saints or to replace less elaborate older Offices for the translation of relics or new dedications. The chants in the rhymed Offices followed the numerical order of the eight modes, and the antiphons in particular reflected rules of melodic composition (range, beginning, final cadence, and recitation tone) that strictly conformed to modal theory. For a searchable database of rhymed Offices see Andrew Hughes, *Late Medieval Liturgical Offices: Resources for Electronic Research*, *Texts* (Toronto, 1994) and *Sources and Chants* (Toronto, 1996).

[16]The texts of the responsories are edited in Hesbert, *Corpus Antiphonalium Officii*, vol. 4 (Rome, 1968) For the melodies see *Antiphonaire de Lucques*, *Antiphonaire de Worcester, Antiphonaire de Mont-Renaud*, and *Antiphonaire de Hartker*.

respond]. In the case of the last responsory of each Nocturn, this basic pattern was followed by the doxology [*Gloria patri*] as required by the Rule of St. Benedict, and then by the *repetendum*.[17]

The principal function of the Great Responsories is to underline the readings of the Night Office. Consequently, the texts of the responsories consist of verses drawn from the books of the Bible assigned for reading during the Night Office: from Genesis on the Sundays of Septuagesima, from the Prophets in Advent, the Book of Kings in July, the Books of Wisdom [*Libri Sapientiales*] in August, the psalms after Epiphany, etc. Although usually only one verse was selected for the respond, the choices that the medieval sources reflect differ widely, a fact that seems to suggest that originally the cantor may have selected the verses at will.

The respond melodies are highly neumatic, sometimes involve lengthy melismas, and often feature internal repetition of motifs. Introductory and cadential formulas and recitation passages reminiscent of the psalm tones are incorporated into much more elaborate melodies. The tones used in the responsory verses are more elaborate than those used in the antiphonal psalmody, though they exhibit similar structural characteristics: rising intonation (incipit formula), recitation tone, and cadential formula.

Respond melodies were composed in any of the eight modal categories. If statistical figures based on the repertory found in the earliest notated manuscripts are any indication, however, composers seem to have manifested a slight preference towards the framework provided by modes 7 and 8 (the authentic and the plagal on *G*). In Hartker's antiphoner almost half of all responsories are in the modes on *G*, extremely few in the modes on *F*, and the other half almost equally divided among the authentics and plagals on *D* and *E*.[18] Many of the responsories in the same mode often

---

[17]The practice could vary from church to church; for very important feasts the doxology was added to the first responsory of each Nocturn as well, and although normally only the first part of its text was sung, some sources extend the music over the entire text.

[18]See, for example, Leo Treitler, "'Centonate' Chant: Übles Flickwerk or *E pluribus unum*," *Journal of the American Musicological Society* 28 (1975): 1–23.

share significant amounts of material, a fact that makes it possible to group them in melodic families. As in the case of the Office antiphons, many responds within each modal category appear to be constructed from stock melodic phrases and formulaic patterns. They are to be seen not as compositions that utilize pre-existing material, however, but rather as pieces that reflect melodic conventions conditioned by modal framework and liturgical function.

The Proper Chants of the Mass

It is possible to distinguish among the proper chants of the Mass two basic types: antiphonal chants that are sung during some liturgical action (the introit, the offertory, and the communion chants), and responsorial chants set between the Epistle and Gospel readings (a gradual and a tract during Lent, two alleluias in Paschal time, a gradual and an alleluia throughout the rest of the year).

Almost two-thirds of the introits are drawn from the psalms, while the remaining ones, those for the most important feasts of the year, are essentially all from other books of the Bible. In earlier times, the introit could have a variable number of psalm verses in order to accommodate the length of time necessary for the entry of the clergy. The earliest manuscripts, however, transmit only one verse, and in some cases one additional verse called *versum ad repetendum*. The overall form of the introit can be, therefore, antiphon-psalm verse-doxology-[*ad repetendum*]-antiphon. Of the approximately 150 introit melodies found in the earliest written sources, almost two-thirds are equally distributed among the *protus* and the *deuterus* modes, while the rest are in the *G* and *F* modes (slightly less in the latter). Unlike the Office antiphons, the introits do not share significant amounts of melodic material among themselves. Within one modal category, however, the introit melodies may display some similarities in terms of their opening gestures and cadential formulas that suggest some compositional ground-rules.[19] The general melodic configuration of most of the introits, however, precludes any classification of the repertory according to melodic families.

The communion chants in the earliest sources are roughly as numerous as the introits (around 150), and like the introits they are transmitted with a psalm verse or verses that were dropped in the eleventh and twelfth centuries, after which only the antiphon remained. The texts of some 60 communion chants are from the psalms, while most of the remaining ones are from the Gospel of the day.[20] The modal tradition for many communion chants was rather unstable, but when the sources agree they feature almost half of the pieces in modes on *D* and *G*, slightly fewer in the modes on *F*, and even fewer in the modes on *E*. The communions in the *deuterus* modes have several sections that end with the same type of cadence, which provides a melodic rhyme relatively rare in the other modes. The style of the communion melodies varies greatly. Communions with Gospel texts resemble the style of the office antiphons and are usually syllabic; some of the psalmic communions can display lengthy melismas, or be mainly syllabic with relatively short melismas, and may also survive as office responsories.

The offertory, like the introit and the communion, accompanies a liturgical action, and it has often been supposed to have consisted of an antiphon with as many psalm verses as were necessary to accompany the bringing of the gifts to the altar. The melodies that survive in the earliest sources, however, are nothing like those of the office antiphons. Composed in a virtuoso musical style, they are highly melismatic, cover wide ranges and change registers quite frequently, and involve melodic intervals rather unusual in the chant repertoire, such as the octave and the seventh. The first part of the

---

[19]This particular aspect of the introit melodies is discussed in Helmut Hucke, "Gregorianische Fragen," *Musikforschung* 41 (1988): 304–30.

[20]Among the psalmic communions, the most famous group is that of the weekday communions of Lent which are derived in sequence from Psalms 1–26, probably a result of a single liturgical revision. Also derived from psalms in numerical order are the offertories of the Sundays after Pentecost.

chant, sometimes labeled in medieval sources as "antiphon," is followed by two or three verses with freely composed and elaborate melodies; each verse is followed by a refrain that is usually the end of the "antiphon" (as in the office responsories), although it sometimes can be a repetition of the opening phrase. Changes in tonality often occur within the melodies of both "antiphon" and verse, as well as between them, and this makes it often impossible to distinguish between authentic and plagal modes.

Most offertory texts are taken from the psalms; about a dozen pieces follow the text distribution characteristic of antiphonal psalmody—the verses feature the first verses of the psalm, while the "antiphon" uses a verse from elsewhere in the psalm. Over twenty offertories, however, display a selection of texts that resembles responsorial psalmody—both the "antiphon" and the verses select verses from later in the psalm.

The tract is yet another chant of the Mass that is sung by a soloist (or a small group of soloists) throughout. It consists of several verses intoned in succession with no return to a respond or a refrain, a practice called "direct psalmody." All the tracts fall under only two modal categories: mode 8 and mode 2, the plagals on *G* and *D*, respectively. The tracts in mode 8 have generally up to five verses, move in a fairly restricted melodic range, and seldom feature internal melismas. Among the mode 2 tracts, some can have 11 (*Eripe me*) or even 13 verses (*Qui habitat*) and can display melodic strategies that, although well within the modal boundaries, are nevertheless quite varied.

The graduals, called in some of the early sources of the Roman rite "responsorium grad(u)ale," are responsorial chants that were sung like the Great Responsories of the Divine Office, but with a repeat of the complete respond after the verse.[21] There is evidence that in the Frankish rite of the ninth century the full respond was performed by the soloist and repeated by

---

[21]For a detailed treatment of the gradual chant see Helmut Hucke, "Das Responsorium," in *Gattungen der Musik in Einzeldarstellungen: Gedenkschrift Leo Schrade*, ed. Wulf Arlt et al. (Bern, 1973), pp. 144–91.

the choir.[22] Later sources suggest that the soloist intoned only the opening of the respond, and that the rest was sung by the choir, which sometimes also sang the last word or two of the verse. Most of the graduals contained in the earliest Frankish sources can be classified in melodic families. The closest unified group consists of those pieces assigned to mode 2, which includes *Iustus ut palma*.[23] The chants in this group have both the respond and the verse arranged in four sections (the first and the third sections of the respond are practically identical in all the graduals in this family), and each section concludes with a long melisma. The accommodation of different texts to the basic melody is achieved after the fashion of the psalm tones. The second group consists of those pieces assigned to mode 5.[24] Both the responds and especially the verses in this category use standard melodic formulas and melismas that fulfill a specific function such as the cadence of the introductory or concluding phrases, end melismas, etc. The third family is that of the graduals assigned to mode 3, which have a standard melody consisting of four phrases, each concluding with a long melisma.[25]

The alleluia, which follows the gradual in the celebration of the Mass, is also a responsorial chant in which the first part (the melody over the word

---

[22]Amalar of Metz, *Ordinis missae expositio* I.6, in *Amalarii episcopi opera liturgica omnia*, ed. Jean-Michael Hanssens, 3 vols. (Rome, 1948–50), 3:302.

[23]More than 200 facsimiles of this chant appear in *Le Répons-graduel Justus ut palma réproduit en fac-similé d'après plus de deux cents manuscrits d'origines diverses du IXe au XVIIe siècle*, vols. 2–3 of *Paléographie musicale* (Solesmes, 1889).

[24]More than half of the graduals contained in the earliest Frankish sources were assigned to the modes on *F* (a proportion found in no other chant genre); almost two-fifths and most of the non-psalmodic pieces belong to mode 5.

[25]The graduals in modes 2, 5, and 3 are categorized as psalmodic, improvisational, and standard melody chants; see Helmut Hucke, "Gradual (i)," *The New Grove Dictionary of Music and Musicians*, ed. Stanley Sadie (London, 1980).

alleluia) constitutes a choral respond that is repeated after the verse.[26] There can be one or more verses, and they are sung by a soloist or a group of soloists. The respond can be further divided into two segments: the setting of the word *alleluia* and the ending melisma, which is called the ***jubilus***. By and large, the early manuscripts suggest the following manner of performance: *alleluia* +jubilus (*cantor*)—*alleluia* +jubilus (choir)+verse (*cantor*)—*alleluia* +jubilus (choir).

One criterion that modern scholars used to develop a stylistic chronology of the alleluias is the presence or absence of repeat structures in the melismas on the jubilus on *-ia*. The absence of repeats is generally assumed to define the earlier layer of chant (eighth-century or possibly earlier); conversely, their presence would indicate a ninth-century (or later) origin. Many of the melismas found in these younger chants display an AAB structure; some of the longer ones, however, can manifest a much more complex pattern of repeats as in *All. Veni sponsa Christi*.[27] Not only could alleluia texts be sung on the same melody but also the same text can be found with different melodies; both procedures are found in the older as well as in the younger layers and represent a compositional technique common to hymns and later sequences rather than to any other chant genre. The older nucleus of alleluias was expanded in the eleventh century and continued to be enlarged throughout the Middle Ages. These new or old verses with new or old melodies were assigned mainly to the proper feast of either the *Sanctorale* or the major *Temporale* festivals; many have freely composed non-biblical texts and favor the modes on *E* and *F*.

From the ninth century onwards, at Mass on feast days the alleluia was followed by a sequence. On the important feasts, therefore, the alleluia

---

[26]The alleluias are catalogued in Karl-Heinz Schlager, *Thematischer Katalog der ältesten Alleluia-Melodien aus Handschriften des 10. und 11. Jahrhunderts, ausgenommen das ambrosianische, alt-römische, und alt-spanische Repertoire* (Munich, 1965).

[27]For an analysis of the structure and patterns of repetition manifest in this chant see David Hiley, *Western Plainchant: A Handbook* (Oxford, 1993), p. 135.

would be performed according to a different pattern: alleluia-verse-sequence. Many sequence melodies that belong to the ninth-and tenth-century layers were sung in different areas with different texts. Most of them were local compositions and only about thirty melodies were known in both the East- and West-Frankish traditions. Most of these compositions have a parallel-verse structure (paired versicles), where each line of music is sung twice with different text, and feature a syllabic text setting throughout that rarely involves repeated notes. Many melodies are problematic in respect to their modal classification, which may suggest a non-Gregorian origin and the influence of secular music.[28]

The Ordinary Chants of the Mass

Performed in the early centuries by the entire congregation, the ordinary chants have texts that, although they remain the same throughout the liturgical year, are set to different melodies. Moreover, for all the ordinary chants except the Credo, there are a large number of tropes with texts that contain references to specific feasts that strengthen the "proper" aspect of the chant.[29] The earliest sources for the ordinary chant melodies are from the tenth century, later than those for most other chants, and almost all manuscripts are intended for the trained *schola* and soloists. The five sections have different histories and entered the liturgy at different points in time.

---

[28]For example the sequence "Planctus cigni"; see Bruno Stäblein, "Die Schwanenklage. Zum Problem Lai-Planctus-Sequenz," in *Festschrift Karl Gustav Fellerer zum sechzigsten Geburtstag am 7. Juli 1962*, ed. Heinrich Hüschen (Regensburg, 1962), pp. 491–501.

[29]Tropes are types of compositions that are added to a pre-existing chant. These additions can be: melisma, a musical phrase without text ("meloform" trope); a text added to pre-existing music ("melogene" trope); or a segment that consists of both new text and new music ("logogene" trope). An important part of the research on tropes is published in the various volumes of *Corpus troporum*, Studia Latina Stockholmiensia (Stockholm, 1975–).

The position of the Kyrie after the introit is specified in early eighth-century sources, and by the end of the century the number of petitions was fixed at nine:

Kyrie eleison ("Lord have mercy")—three times;
Christe eleison ("Christ have mercy")—three times;
Kyrie eleison ("Lord have mercy")—three times.

Many of the early sources contain Kyrie chants both in melismatic form with Greek text, and in syllabic form with individual Latin texts, acclamatory in nature and without strong syntactic cohesion. The various Kyrie chants are often identified by the incipit of the Latin text used with a given melody, such as *Kyrie fons bonitatis* or *Kyrie lux et origo*.

The text of *Gloria in excelsis Deo*, sung immediately after the Kyrie, is a non-biblical hymn of praise, an aggregate of phrases of various dates and origins that form sections: praise to God the Father, Christological petitions, and Trinitarian conclusion. Introduced by Pope Symmachus (489–514) into the Mass and found in the usual liturgical position after the Kyrie in eighth-century sources, the *Gloria* is omitted in Advent and between Septuagesima and Easter.

Originally intoned by the congregation, the *Gloria* was later sung by the clergy. More than fifty melodies were provided during the Middle Ages. By and large, they fall into two categories. One type consists of a highly ornate recitation with a central pitch and cadential melismas. The chief example for this type is the so-called Gloria A that is found, most frequently troped, in manuscripts from the ninth and the tenth centuries.[30] The second type covers the majority of the *Gloria* melodies. These *Gloria*s feature a more regular structure, and although they lack melismas they are not entirely syllabic; a melodic segment consisting of two or three phrases is used repeatedly during the chant and adapted to suit verses of different length.

The **Nicene Creed** [*Credo in unum Deum patrem omnipotentem*], originally part of the baptismal rites, was introduced in the Frankish-Roman

---

[30]For a transcription of the troped Gloria A melody with prosula see Hiley, *Western Plainchant*, pp. 228–30 (ex. II.23.15).

liturgy (after the gospel) in the aftermath of the Council of Aachen (798) in the Latin translation made by Paulinus of Aquileia. During the Middle Ages it seems sometimes to have been recited by the congregation, sometimes sung by the clergy. The earliest notated sources come from the eleventh century. They transmit variants of a syllabic chant known as Credo I that was rarely troped and has recitation tones on *G* and *a*.

The two ordinary chants most closely associated with the eucharistic section of the Mass are the *Sanctus* and the *Agnus Dei*. The *Sanctus* is one of the oldest acclamations to make its way into the liturgical service. It was probably added to the eucharistic prayer sometime between the first and the fifth centuries, and the same text appears in the Byzantine and Eastern liturgies as well. The earliest sources to contain *Sanctus* melodies originated in the tenth century, and the patterns of distribution indicate that only a few melodies were widely disseminated, while the great majority were known only locally. The *Sanctus* consists of five main statements: "Sanctus . . . ," "Pleni . . . ," "Hosanna . . . ," "Benedictus . . . ," and "Hosanna . . ." The settings are often elaborate and display a high degree of melodic repetition. The second "Hosanna," for example, often is set to the same melody as the first, and sometimes material from the first statement reappears in later verses.

The *Agnus Dei* is one of the most recent acclamations of the Mass. It was introduced probably in the seventh century by pope Sergius (687–701) as a *confractorium* (a chant that accompanies the breaking of the bread and is sung by both clergy and congregation), and most of the melodies were composed between the eleventh and the sixteenth centuries. Many *Agnus* melodies have a tripartite structure, with the verse "Agnus Dei qui tollis peccata mundi miserere nobis" to be sung three times, either with the same or slightly varied melodic settings (an AAA or AA'A form), or having the first repeated verse set to a different melody (an ABA form). Often the settings of *Agnus Dei* and *miserere nobis* have similar ranges, while the remaining text will develop in a slightly higher range, giving thus an ABA shape to the melody of the verse itself.

Conclusion

The composition of liturgical music was an ongoing activity throughout the Middle Ages and happened at an increased pace during the tenth to the twelfth centuries. Consequently, the musical style of an individual chant could be altered to suit different esthetic requirements, but only within parameters well established by the text it carried, the liturgical function it fulfilled, and the performance practice it expressed. Chants by now were mostly performed by trained singers; by augmenting their melismatic content, by textual or/and melodic troping, and later by adding polyphony, chants were continuously embellished and as such heightened the eulogistic dimension of Christian worship.

GREGORIUS PRESUL COMPOSUIT HUNC LIBELLUM MUSICAE ARTIS

JAMES W. MCKINNON†

IN THE EARLY MIDDLE AGES Gregorian chant was no mere ornament to the liturgy; it *was* the liturgy. Every word of a church service was sung: at Mass the celebrating priest chanted his prayers, as did the subdeacon the epistle and the deacon the gospel. The attending clergy and congregation sang from memory the simple tunes of the Ordinary, that is, those acclamations such as the *Sanctus* and *Agnus dei* that were the same at every Mass. A skilled chorus—made up of monks in a monastery, nuns in a convent, or clerical canons in a cathedral—sang the more elaborate melodies of the Proper, those chants that were different each day. The Mass Proper thus comprised a vast repertory that it was necessary to commit to writing in chant books, at first only with the texts but eventually with musical notation as well. In addition to the Mass, church men and women of the time also sang the Office, a series of eight services that occupied much of the day from dawn to dusk; it is hardly an exaggeration to say that for them the singing of Gregorian chant was their life's work. The present essay introduces the reader to Gregorian chant by examining the medieval legend that attributes its creation to Pope Gregory the Great (590–604).

GREGORIUS PRESUL COMPOSUIT HUNC LIBELLUM MUSICAE ARTIS [Pope Gregory compiled this little book of the art of music]. Thus reads a key portion of a short preface written in uncials at the beginning of several early medieval chant manuscripts.[1] The text continues, SCOLAE CANTORUM PER CIRCULUM ANNI. Thus Gregory (we must assume for the moment that the intended Gregory is the first pope of that name, Gregory the Great) arranged a book for the Roman *scola cantorum*, a book that contained chants for the *circulum anni*, that is, the annual cycle of the liturgical calendar. The very earliest of the manuscripts that have this brief preface, from the turn of the ninth century, are *libelli* [little books] in the true sense, not much more than pamphlets of about thirty folios that were usually bound together with more substantial books, for example, sacramentaries.[2] They were slight in size because they contained only the texts of the chant; chant manuscripts did not become fully notated until the end of the ninth century. A book that was to be notated was written with ample space between the lines of text so as to accommodate the neumes that were to be added by some musically expert scribe; it would be at least three or four times the length of an unnotated manuscript of the same content. The content of the earliest chant books comprised the five Proper chants of the Mass—the Introit, Gradual, Alleluia, Offertory, and Communion—for the *circulum anni*, beginning with the first Sunday of Advent and ending with the last Sunday after Pentecost. Such a book was at first called an "antiphoner" [*antiphonarius*], but in modern usage it is referred to by the slightly later term *gradual* [*graduale*] in order to avoid confusion with the book of Office chants, which was also called an antiphoner.[3]

Virtually all of the early chant books were northern in origin, several of them indeed closely associated with the Carolingian court. For reasons

---

[1]They are edited and discussed by Bruno Stäblein, "'Gregorius Praesul,' der Prolog zum römischen Antiphonale," in *Musik und Verlag: Karl Vötterle zum 65. Geburtstag*, ed. Richard Baum and Wolfgang Rehm (Kassel, 1968), pp. 537–61.

[2]They are edited by René-Jean Hesbert in his invaluable *Antiphonale Missarum Sextuplex* (Brussels, 1935).

[3]The book that is called a gradual can also be confused with the chant of the same name; here they will be distinguished by lower case for the former and upper for the latter.

not entirely known to us we have no Roman chant manuscripts, either notated or unnotated, until the later eleventh century.[4] It was, in any event, the northern clerics and monks who appear to have been most anxious to assert the authorship of Gregory for their chant books. The Gregorian gradual first came north, and with it members of the Roman schola cantorum, when Pope Stephen II made his momentous visit of 754 to the Frankish king Pipin III in order to seek protection for Rome from the Lombards. Stephen and his clerical entourage were in residence with Pipin at St. Denis for an extended period of time, and Pipin was so captivated by the Roman liturgy as it was sung by the schola (the *cantus romanus*) that he ordered it to be adopted throughout the entire Frankish domain, and at the same time ordered that the indigenous Gallican liturgy be abolished. Pipin died in 768, but his son Charlemagne (d. 814) and his grandson Louis the Pious (d. 840) saw to it that Pipin's ambitious project was brought to a satisfactory conclusion.

One can well imagine that it was no easy task for the Frankish canons and monks of the various northern ecclesiastical centers to assimilate the Roman chant. The Mass Proper amounted to more than 550 sophisticated chants (and the Office, not to be discussed in the present essay, comprised at least that many), and while the texts of the chants were written down, the melodies were not and had to be learned by ear and retained in memory. The precise manner in which this was accomplished and the degree of its success (that is, the extent to which the chant remained free of Frankish taint) is a

---

[4]These manuscripts open up a question of enormous importance in chant scholarship. They portray a chant that is virtually identical in text to the Gregorian and related to it musically. The musical difference between the two dialects of chant, however, is sufficiently great to raise the question of which—this Roman chant of the eleventh century, or the Frankish-Roman chant (the so-called Gregorian) of the ninth—is closer to the original Roman chant of the seventh and eighth centuries. There will be no reference to this question in the present text; for an early discussion of it that retains considerable value see Willi Apel, "The Central Problem of Gregorian Chant," *Journal of the American Musicological Society* 9 (1956): 118–27.

matter of considerable controversy among music historians.[5] For present purposes it is enough to know that by the end of the ninth century at the latest, there existed in notated manuscripts a unified Frankish-Roman chant, the superb body of ecclesiastical music known today as Gregorian chant.

The question to be considered in the present essay is not how *Roman* is the so-called Gregorian chant, but how *Gregorian*. Did Gregory I in fact compile the original gradual? The medieval savants of the ninth and succeeding centuries had no doubt on this score. In Rome, John the Deacon, writing his biography of Gregory during the 870s, stated that "the exceedingly diligent Gregory arranged an antiphoner of chants," adding, "he also founded the schola cantorum, which still sings in the holy church of Rome."[6] Meanwhile, in the North, the legend of Gregory's musical involvement grew to the point where he was looked upon as the inspired composer of the chant. The famous Carolingian portrait of Gregory that showed the Holy Spirit in the form of a dove on his shoulder, dictating a theological work into his ear, was adapted to musical purposes. In miniatures such as that at the beginning of the Hartker Antiphoner (Figure 1), the divine dove sings the chant melodies into Gregory's ear, while a scribe records them in neumatic notation.

The medieval belief that Gregory actually composed the chant that bears his name came to be questioned in the seventeenth and eighteenth centuries, but in the nineteenth, the great period of modern chant revival, Gregory still was credited with a key role in the creation of the chant. He was looked

---

[5]Among the principal figures in the controversy are: Helmut Hucke, "Toward a New Historical View of Gregorian Chant," *Journal of the American Musicological Society* 33 (1980): 437–67; Leo Treitler, "Homer and Gregory: The Transmission of Epic Poetry and Plainchant," *Musical Quarterly* 60 (1974): 333–72; Kenneth Levy, "Charlemagne's Archetype of Gregorian Chant," *Journal of the American Musicological Society* 40 (1987): 1–30; and David Hughes, "Evidence for the Traditional View of the Transmission of Gregorian Chant," *Journal of the American Musicological Society* 40 (1987): 377–404.

[6]*Antiphonarium . . . cantorum studiosissimus nimis utiliter compilavit; scholam quoque cantorum quae hactenus . . . in sancta Romana Ecclesia modulatur constituit* (S. Gregorii Magni vita 6; PL 75: 90).

Figure 1. The Holy Spirit Dictates the Chant to Gregory. (St. Gall, Stiftsbibliothek 390–391, *Hartker Antiphoner*, fol. 13).

upon as someone who personally supervised the members of the *schola cantorum* in their composition of the first chant books. Indeed the French Jesuit Lambilotte published in 1851 a hand-drawn reproduction of an early tenth-century gradual from St. Gall, in the belief that the manuscript was the original book of Mass Proper chants copied at Gregory's behest.[7] The Solesmes Benedictines who came to dominate chant scholarship for the later decades of the nineteenth century, and for much of the twentieth, were too paleographically sophisticated to make such a mistake. They published, under the series title *Paleographie musicale*, numerous important notated chant manuscripts in photographic facsimile.[8] They were fully aware that the earliest of these manuscripts were a contribution of northern cantors, but they continued to harbor the belief that the chant was created under Gregorian auspices and that it somehow maintained its Gregorian integrity through three centuries of oral transmission (including a trip across the Alps), until it was captured in the neumatic notation of late Carolingian scribes. Contemporary music historians, clerical and lay alike, have every variety of explanation for the fortunes of the chant during that period, but many of them seem unwilling to give up the last vestiges of the belief that Gregory was somehow responsible for the first *libellus musicae artis*.

One might best place the question in a new perspective by tracing the history of Mass Proper chants from the Early Christian period. There was no "little book of musical art" then, only the Psalter, and indeed the Psalter itself appears not to have been used as a chant book during the Eucharist with any regularity until the second half of the fourth century. The patristic literature of the time provides any number of references to the singing of a single psalm at two points during the Eucharist (hereafter Mass): at the distribution of communion and during the service of readings and discourse that preceded the Eucharist proper (hereafter Fore-Mass). The communion psalm was generally the same psalm, Psalm 33, which was chanted by a lector, and

---

[7]*Antiphonaire de saint Grégoire: Facsimile du manuscrit de Saint-Gall* (Paris, 1851).

[8]See Eugene Cardine and Richard Sherr, "Solesmes," *The New Grove Dictionary of Music and Musicians*, ed. Stanley Sadie, vol. 17 (London, 1980), pp. 452–54.

responded to by the congregation with the appropriate verse, "Taste and see that the Lord is good."[9] (The numbering of the Psalms used in this essay is that of the Greek and Latin tradition.) We might say, then, that this psalm, sung at every celebration of the Mass, was at first an item of the Ordinary rather than the Proper of the Mass, in the same sense that the *Sanctus* (also coming to be sung at this time) was a chant of the Ordinary.

The psalm sung during the Fore-Mass varied at each service, but this psalm, too, for reasons to be given presently, should be denied the status of a Mass Proper chant. Its origins are unknown to us, but the most plausible hypothesis is that it developed from the Old Testament readings of the Fore-Mass.[10] This is best studied in the sermons of St. Augustine, where he refers to the singing of a psalm in the service before the homily more than 150 times.[11] It is clear that this psalm was sung rather than simply read, indeed usually in the same responsorial fashion described above for the communion psalm; "The voice of the penitent is recognized," Augustine said, "in the words with which we respond to the singer: 'Hide thy face from my song, and blot out all my iniquities' [Ps. 50:11]."[12] But nevertheless Augustine spoke of this psalm as a reading; "We heard the Apostle," he said in another sermon, "we heard the Psalm, we heard the Gospel; all the divine readings sound together so that we place hope not in ourselves but in the Lord."[13] It seems, then, that the Old Testament reading, which must have included

---

[9]See James McKinnon, *Music in Early Christian Literature* (Cambridge, 1987).

[10]See James McKinnon, "The Fourth-Century Origins of the Gradual," *Early Music History* 7 (1987): 91–106.

[11]See James McKinnon, "Liturgical Psalmody in the Sermons of Saint Augustine," in *The Study of Medieval Chant: Paths and Bridges, East and West. In Honor of Kenneth Levy*, ed. Peter Jeffery (Rochester, N.Y.: Boydell, 2001).

[12]*Vox poenitentis agnoscitur in verbis quibus psallenti respondimus: Averte faciem tuam a peccatis meis, et omnes iniquitates meas dele* (Sermo 352; PL 39: 1549–50).

[13]*Apostolum audivimus, Psalmum audivimus, Evangelium audivimus; consonant omnes divinae lectiones ut spem non in nobis, sed in Domino colocemus* (Sermo 165: PL 38, 902).

readings from the Psalms upon occasion, was replaced by the singing of a psalm at every celebration of the Mass. This was done, apparently, in the latter decades of the fourth century, a period characterized by an unprecedented enthusiasm for the singing of psalms, for example, in extended psalmodic vigils held in the early morning hours before Saturday and Sunday Mass.[14]

The value of this hypothesis aside, it can be shown that the psalm sung during the Fore-Mass of Augustine's time, although functioning in the same place as the medieval Gradual and already displaying that chant's responsorial form, cannot be looked upon as a Proper chant. Proper chants are permanently assigned to specific dates in the liturgical calendar; they require, moreover, some sort of chant book to assure their maintenance from year to year. But it is clear that in Augustine's church the Gradual psalm was chosen from the Psalter on a day-to-day basis. "We had prepared for ourselves a short psalm," said Augustine, "which we had ordered to be sung by the lector, but as it seems, when the time came he was confused and read a different one";[15] and on another occasion, "We did not order the lector to sing this psalm, but he from his boyish heart, ordered what he thought would be useful for you to hear."[16] Another way to look at the question is to single out those places in Augustine's sermons where one can identify the liturgical occasion for which a particular Gradual psalm was sung and to compare that psalm with the text of the medieval Gradual for the same liturgical occasion. Some twenty-seven such instances occur in Augustine's

---

[14]See James McKinnon, "Desert Monasticism and the Later Fourth-Century Psalmodic Movement," *Music and Letters* 75 (1994): 505–11.

[15]*Psalmum nobis brevem preparavimus, quem mandaveramus cantari a lectore; sed ad horam, quantum videtur, perturbatus, alterum pro altero legit* (Enarratio in psalmum 138,1; Corpus Christianorum, Series Latina [hereafter CCL] 40, 1990).

[16]*Neque enim nos istum psalmum cantandum lectori imperavimus: sed quod ille censuit vobis esse utile ad audiendum, hoc cordi etiam puerili imperavit* (Sermo 352, PL 39: 1550).

sermons,[17] but for only three of them is there a coincidence with medieval textual choices. These are the singing of *Haec dies* (Ps. 117:24) on Easter, *Sicut cervus* (Ps. 42) at baptism, and *In omnem terram* (Ps. 18:5) on the feast of Sts. Peter and Paul. We do not know whether these exceptional texts were used both in Augustine's time and in Gregorian chant because of a continuous tradition, or because they were so obviously appropriate that they were chosen independently. But the fact that they are altogether exceptional (three instances from a possible twenty-seven) speaks against the existence of an early Christian *libellus musicae artis per circulum anni*.

The evidence relating to our subject is rare and scattered for the centuries that intervene between the time of Augustine and the appearance of the first chant books, but what there is of it suggests that the manner of singing at Mass changed at a barely perceptible rate. A passage from a sermon preached on Pentecost Sunday by St. Caesarius of Arles (d. 542) shows that he, like Augustine before him, conceived of the Fore-Mass as consisting of three scriptural readings—Epistle, Psalm, and Gospel: "Dear brethren, all that was read today is appropriate to the festival. The Psalm, *Redde mihi laetitiam salutaris tui*; the Gospel, *Venit spiritus veritatis*; and the writings of the Acts of the Apostles, *Repleti sunt omnes spiritu sancto*."[18] As for the question of continuity of psalmic assignment, one notes that *Redde mihi* (Ps. 50:14), presumably the refrain verse of the psalm sung that Pentecost Sunday in Arles, is a text not met with in the Pentecost Mass chants of any medieval Latin liturgy.

From Rome we have one relevant contemporary passage, a sentence from the biography of Pope Celestine I (422–32), that appears in the earlier sixth-century redaction of the *Liber Pontificalis*: "He [Celestine] decreed

---

[17]See McKinnon, "Liturgical Psalmody."

[18]*Hodie, fratres carissimi, omnia quae nobis lecta sunt cum festivitate conveniunt. Psalmus enim: redde mihi, inquit, laetitiam salutaris tui; evangelium autem: venit, inquid, spiritus veritatis; scriptura vero apostolicorum Actuum: Repleti sunt, inquid, omnes spiritu sancto* (Sermo 211.1, CCL 104, 837).

that the 150 Psalms of David be sung before the sacrifice, which had not been done before; only the Epistle of Paul the Apostle was recited and the Holy Gospel."[19] The passage has occasioned much discussion in liturgical and musicological literature, but for present purposes it is enough to note that a Roman cleric writing during the first half of the sixth century still looks upon the Fore-Mass as consisting of Epistle, Psalm, and Gospel.

We gain much the same impression from the single pronouncement that we have from Gregory I on music. He was disturbed that deacons (clerics of considerable authority in the Rome of his day) were serving as cantors at Mass and forbade them to do so:

> Wherefore I enjoin in the present decree that in this diocese the ministers of the holy altar ought not to sing, and should carry out only the task of Gospel reading at the ceremonies of the Mass; while the psalms and other readings, I would say, should be presented by the subdeacons or, if necessity demand, by those in lesser orders.[20]

Gregory cited the three essential liturgical items of the Fore-Mass: the Gospel (reserved to the deacon), and "the psalms and other readings" to be performed by those in lesser orders. One can hardly distinguish his language from that of Augustine.

It would seem to be a safe assumption that the chant book of Gregory's time was still the Psalter. It happens, in fact, that there exists a contemporary Psalter that was used as a chant book. Preserved in Paris, the manuscript is called the *Psautier de Saint Germain-des-Prés* because the Parisian

---

[19]*Hic constituit ut psalmi CL David ante sacrificium psalli, quod ante non fiebat, nisi tantum recitabatur epistola Pauli apostoli et sanctum evangelium, et sic missae celebrabantur* (*Le Liber Pontificalis*, ed. Louis Duchesne, vol. 1 [Paris, 1886], p. 89).

[20]*Qua de re presenti decreto constituo, ut in sede hac sacri altaris ministri cantare non debeant, solumque evangelicae lectionis officium inter missarum solemnia exsolvant: psalmos vero ac reliquas lectiones censeo per subdiaconos, vel si necessiatas exigit, per minores ordines exhiberi* (from *Gregorii I papae Registrvm epistolarvm: Monumenta Germaniae Historica, Epistolarvm I*, ed. Paul Ewald and Ludwig Hartman [Berlin, 1891], p. 363).

monastery of that name housed it before the French Revolution, but it is probably an Italian book, even if not Roman, copied in the later sixth century.[21] The Psalter has the letter *R* inscribed in gold leaf at certain verses of the Psalms, an indication, one assumes, that these verses were intended to be sung as psalm-responses. Seventy verses are so singled out, providing the opportunity to compare them with later chant texts. It turns out that only twenty-one of the seventy are used as Gregorian Graduals. When one considers that such verses were chosen not at random but because of some special quality of liturgical appositeness, as were also the later Gregorian texts, the comparatively small rate of coincidence between the two repertories strongly suggests a lack of continuity between them.

To return to Gregory's prohibition against singing by deacons, certain music historians have sought to construe it as evidence for Gregory's founding of the *schola cantorum*.[22] Since deacons could not sing at Mass, the argument goes, it was necessary for Gregory to establish a school of ecclesiastical singers. This is hardly a convincing line of thought; lectors had served as cantors since the fourth century, and there is no reason why they should not have continued to do so in Gregory's time. In point of fact there is no mention of the *schola cantorum* anywhere in the writings of Gregory. The first unequivocal reference to that organization comes from well into the second half of the seventh century, in the *Liber Pontificalis*' biography of Pope Sergius I (687–701), where we read of him, "because he was studious and competent in the task of chanting, he was handed over to the prior of the singers for education."[23] Sergius, a native of Syria, came to Rome during the reign of Pope Adeodatus (672–76) so that the earliest

---

[21]See Michel Huglo, "Le Réponse-Graduel de la messe: Évolution de la forme. Permanence de la fonction," *Schweizer Jahrbuch für Musikwissenschaft* 2 (1982): 53–77.

[22]See Helmut Hucke, "Zu enigen Problemen der Choralforschung," *Die Musikforschung* 11 (1958): 385–414, at p. 401.

[23]*Quia studiosus erat et capax in officio cantelenae, priori cantorum pro doctrina est traditus* (*Le Liber Pontificalis*, vol. 1, p. 371).

possible date of his entry into the *schola* would be 672.[24] Sometime in the mid-seventh century, then, would seem to be a fair guess for the time of the *schola*'s founding.

The issue of the *schola*'s existence is stressed here because it is crucial to an understanding of the origins of the so-called Gregorian chant. The arrival of the schola in Roman ecclesiastical history signals a paradigm shift in the nature of Christian ecclesiastical song, a shift from what one might call "lector chant" to "schola chant," that is, a shift from the solo chanting of psalms by a lector or cantor to the composition and maintenance of a large repertory of solo and choral chants by a group of expert musicians. Such a shift constitutes nothing less than a musical revolution, but before attempting to describe more precisely the nature of that revolution, it is necessary first to speculate briefly on the sort of historical circumstances that might favor the founding of an organization like the *schola cantorum*.

Its founding requires that a pope adopt the behavior of a patron of the arts. The Roman *schola cantorum* was the pope's personal choir, the choir of the Lateran Palace, as opposed to the monastic communities that sang the Office in the great basilicas of Rome (including St. Peter's of the Vatican and even St. John Lateran). It was quite analogous to the Renaissance popes' Cappella Sistina as opposed to St. Peter's Cappella Giulia. The *schola* would have to be housed, fed, and paid; valuable members of the Roman clergy would have to be freed of all other duties so that they could dedicate their entire lives to church music. This would require an ecclesiastical environment that was both sufficiently prosperous and sufficiently free from more pressing concerns to devote its resources and its imaginative energy to the cultivation of a splendid liturgical song.

Gregory's reign seems hardly to have been the appropriate time for such a commitment.[25] When he assumed the papacy in 590, the city of

---

[24]*Le Liber Pontificalis*, vol. 1, p. 371.

[25]The following two paragraphs about state of Italy and Rome in the sixth and seventh centuries are based on a number of studies including: Richard Krautheimer, *Rome: Profile*

Rome may have been in the worst condition of its long history. Italy was utterly devastated by the Gothic wars of 535–54, and in its weakened state it was not able to resist the Lombard invasion of 568. In Rome itself, natural disasters joined the ravages of war so that for more than half a century the city suffered nearly continuous famine, plague, flood, and seige. Its population, which is estimated to have been about 800,000 toward the end of the fourth century, shrunk to some 30,000 by mid-sixth century. It is true that it grew to about 90,000 by century's end, but this was because of an influx of refugees from the ruined and plundered countryside, who in turn contributed to the problems of the city.

It is part of Gregory's true greatness that he undertook heroic efforts, in spite of his wretched health, to return the city to some semblance of order. He saw that the hungry were fed and the sick tended to, he had the aqueduct system partially repaired, he restored civil procedures in the city, and he even supervised the preparation of military defenses against the ever threatening Lombards. It is little wonder that—contrary to the Gregorian legend—there is no evidence of special interest on his part for the liturgy, let alone evidence of partiality for ecclesiastical music. One might say, however, that his effort to restore health to the city was his long-range contribution to the cause of liturgical art. In any event the second half of the seventh century saw the increasing development of the circumstances that would favor the nurturing of the *schola cantorum* and its work. Rome was enriched by the restoration of the great papal agrarian properties of the South, and by an influx of pilgrims to a city that was more and more recognized as a Christian center of world stature. Constant political and theological tension with Constantinople had the dual effect of encouraging Italian nationalism in the peninsula as a whole, and the Roman conviction that the papacy was the true repository of Apostolic truth. Such a papacy

---

of a City, 312–308 (Princeton, 1980); Peter Llewellyn, *Rome in the Dark Ages* (London, 1970); and Thomas F. X. Nobel, *The Republic of St. Peter: The Birth of the Papal State* (Philadelphia, 1984), pp. 680–825.

deserved the sort of ecclesiastical music that only a group like the *schola cantorum* could provide.

These background considerations aside, one must further reflect upon the enormity of the task involved in the above-mentioned paradigm shift from lector to schola chant. The Roman Proper of the Mass comprised more than 550 sophisticated chants—about 150 Introits, 100 Graduals, 50 Alleluias, 95 Offertories, and 150 Communions.[26] It was thought at one time that these chants evolved steadily over the centuries from simple psalms, which, as they came to be chanted more elaborately, grew to be so long that they were reduced to single verses of the psalm. A more likely model, however, would seem to be that the chant was the product of a great burst of creative energy that lasted for only a limited period of time. Two of the more important arguments for such a view have already been suggested here: the lack of continuity between the early Christian liturgical assignments of psalms and medieval chant texts, and the circumstance that only a group like the *schola cantorum* could produce a large and stable body of church music.

Still, if the creation of the Mass Proper was not the result of centuries of evolution, it would seem to have been too large and complex an enterprise to have been accomplished in less than a generation or two. First of all, the *schola* would have had to develop the musical styles that are unique to the various genres of chant (Introits and Graduals, for example, have distinctly different musical profiles). One would imagine, too, that in the early stages of repertory accumulation there was no attempt to produce unique chants for each date in the calendar; perhaps there were instead lists of each genre from which the singers could choose appropriate chants on a day-to-day basis, in the same manner that psalms had been selected from the Psalter in Augustine's time. At some point, according to this imagined

---

[26]And about 20 Tracts, a chant that occasionally substituted for the Alleluia in times of penance; all discussion of the Tract is omitted here in the interest of avoiding needlessly complex exposition.

scenario, the ambitious plan was conceived to provide a set of Proper chants for virtually every date in the liturgical calendar—a true *libellus musicae artis per circulum anni*. The ideal would have been that every date in the temporal cycle would have its own chants; as for the sanctoral cycle, the more important saints would be given their own particular chants, while other categories of saints—martyrs, virgins, bishops, etc.—would share common sets. There existed recently completed models for such a project in the sacramentary, that is, the book of Proper Mass prayers recited by the celebrating priest, and in the Epistolary and Evangeliary, the books of Proper Epistles and Gospels. But certainly the creation of the sung Mass Proper was a far more formidable task; compare, for example, the composition of a single Gradual or Offertory with the writing of a collect or the selection of a Gospel.

Much insight into the process of creation can be gained from an analysis of the total Mass Proper, particularly its texts.[27] There is a wealth of internal evidence to be gained from this kind of investigation, evidence consisting especially in indications of large-scale compositional planning. The first feature of the process to be revealed in the course of such a study is that the *schola* worked more or less genre by genre rather than festival by festival, that is, they developed schemes for extended series of Introits, Graduals, etc., rather than working first on the chants for the first Sunday of Advent, then those of the second Sunday of Advent, etc. However, while the members of the *schola* appear to have worked genre by genre, they do not seem to have completed an entire annual cycle of given genre at one time. Rather, they divided the liturgical year into four distinct portions: the Advent-Christmas season, Lent, Paschaltime, and the Sundays after Pentecost. They approached these seasons in different ways and probably at different times.

[27]What follows is summarized from a number of the present author's works, most notably: "The Eighth-Century Frankish-Roman Communion Cycle," *Journal of the American Musicological Society* 40 (1992): 171–227; and "Properization: The Roman Mass," in *Cantus Planus*, Papers Read at the Sixth Meeting, Eger, Hungary, September 1993 (Budapest: Hungarian Academy of Sciences, 1995), pp. 25–34.

Lent, particularly its weekdays, seems to follow one mode of planning, and the festal seasons of Advent-Christmas and Paschaltime another. The weekday Lenten sequences consist in sequences of psalmic texts of little specific liturgical appropriateness, while the chants of the festal seasons are derived from colorful, liturgically appropriate texts, many of which are taken from other books of the Bible, particularly the Gospels. The chants of the Advent-Christmas season, moreover, clearly were composed before those of Paschaltime; its texts are selected meticulously and set out in coherent sequences (a phenomenon mirrored to some extent in musical characteristics), but there are signs of haste and compromise in the make-up of the Paschaltime chants (the last ten Communions of the period, for example, were borrowed from Office antiphons and responsories). The post-Pentecostal period figures as something of an afterthought to all this; many of its chants were borrowed from other seasons, with little seeming regard for liturgical appropriateness.

This last-cited imperfection in the Mass Proper, however, is confined almost exclusively to Graduals, Alleluias, and Offertories. The annual cycle of Introits and Communions appears to have been completed according to its ambitious plan. There are, as noted above, approximately 150 chants of each type, as opposed to some 100 Graduals and Offertories, and only 50 Alleluias. Virtually every date in the temporal cycle has its own Introit and Communion, chants that clearly are created to be appropriate to the date in question, and that, moreover, are not shared with other dates in the calendar. Graduals and Offertories, however, while they, too, have elegantly executed sequences of unique chants for the Advent-Christmas season, and complete if less interesting sequences for Lent, have hastily executed series of Paschaltime and post-Pentecostal chants, characterized by much borrowing from season to season. Alleluias create an even greater impression of incompleteness.[28] Of the approximately fifty Alleluias, only about fifteen appear to have been permanently assigned to festivals at the time the Roman

[28]On the early history of the Alleluia see James McKinnon, "Preface to the Study of the Alleluia," *Early Music History* 15 (1996): 215–51.

chant was transmitted north. The remaining thirty-five or so must have existed only in a list at the end of the Mass Proper *libellus*, to be chosen on a day-to-day basis. The probable reason for the radical incompleteness of the Alleluia cycle is that the genre became a part of the Mass Proper at a very late date—perhaps adopted from the Byzantine Alleluia during the reign of Pope Sergius I (687–701)—when much work had already been accomplished on the rest of the Mass Proper.

There are at least two other important chronological indications for portions of the Mass Proper. We know that the chants of the weekdays in Lent were in place before the reign of Pope Gregory II (715–31), who, the *Liber Pontificalis* tells us, ordered the Thursdays in Lent, previously days when the liturgy was not celebrated, to be included in the annual cycle.[29] We can observe from the manner in which chants were provided for these Thursdays that chants for the other days already had been assigned. Communions are particularly revealing in this respect; the texts of the weekday Lenten Communions are derived in order from Psalms 1 through 26, but there are gaps in the numerical sequence at each Thursday, gaps that came to be filled with Communions borrowed from the Sundays after Pentecost. The numerical series, then, was clearly in place before Gregory II's addition of the Thursdays to the calendar, sometime between 715 and 731.

The second chronological indication is both more relative and more difficult to summarize briefly. It has to do with the history of the season of Advent (a late entry into the Roman calendar, it should be noted),[30] and the circumstance that work on the festal cycles of chant—those of Advent-Christmas and Paschaltime—was begun with Advent.[31] A comparison of

---

[29]*Le Liber Pontificalis*, vol. 1, p. 402.

[30]On the history of Advent see especially Josef Jungmann, "Advent und Voradvent," *Zeitschrift für katholische Theologie* 61 (1937): 341–90; and Walter Croce, "Die Adventmessen des römischen Missale in ihrer geschichtlichen Entwicklung," *Zeitschrift für katholische Theologie* 74 (1952): 277–317.

[31]The following is summarized from McKinnon, "The Roman Advent Project."

how Advent is treated in the other liturgical books, that is, the sacramentaries and lectionaries, as opposed to the way it is treated in the chant books, reveals dramatic differences. In the sacramentaries and lectionaries the number of prayer sets and readings for the Sundays in Advent varies from as few as two to as many as six, and these are simply appended, as a seeming afterthought, to the list of Sundays after Pentecost. It is only in the chant books that Advent achieves its fixed number of four Sundays and its classic position at the beginning of the book, where it serves as a lyric prelude to Christmas. Advent as we know it, then, was a creation of the *schola cantorum*; it achieved its compelling place at the head of the church year as part of the grand project to create a *libellus musicae artis per circulum anni*. Now it turns out that the Roman sacramentaries and lectionaries of the mid-seventh century betray not a trace of this attractive liturgical development;[32] one can only conclude that the Advent chants were composed at earliest sometime in the second half of the seventh century—certainly long after the reign of Gregory I (590–604).

This brings us full circle to the GREGORIUS PRESUL preface of the early chant books. How could those responsible for it be so mistaken as to attribute the compilation of the gradual to Gregory? The close reader of this essay might reply, if only in jest, that perhaps they had in mind Gregory II, the pope who ordered that the Thursdays in Lent be included in the *circulum anni*. This may seem too pat a solution to be historically credible, but it appears in fact to stand up to close examination. Actually the idea is not a new one: the Belgian musicologist François-Auguste Gevaert advanced it already in 1890,[33] but his quasi-heresy met with powerful refutation at the hands of the great Benedictine liturgiologist Germain Morin,

---

[32]The manuscripts of these books are generally Frankish in origin and copied at a later date than the Roman books that one reconstructs from them; see James McKinnon, "Antoine Chavasse and the Dating of Early Chant," *Plainsong and Medieval Music* 1 (1992): 123–48.

[33]See his *Les Origines du chant liturgique de l'église latine: Étude d'histoire musicale* (Ghent, 1890).

and the matter remained thus settled for more than a half-century of Benedictine-dominated chant scholarship.[34] Part of the argument against Gregory II was that the descriptive words following Gregory's name in the preface (omitted above) could apply only to Gregory I: GREGORIUS PRESUL, MERITIS ET NOMINE DIGNUS, UNDE GENUS DUCIT, SUMMUM CONSCENDIT HONOREM [Gregory, the prelate, honorable in both name and deed; there (Rome) whence his family derived, he achieved the highest distinction]. Gregory I was both a native Roman and the scion of a distinguished family, the argument goes, but in point of fact, Gregory II was also from a distinguished family, and as for being a Roman, he was the only pope of Roman birth to interrupt the long series of Greek-speaking popes that extended from Agatho (678–81) to Zacharias (741–52).

Moreover, Gregory II was a far more prominent figure than Gregory I in the Roman clerical imagination of the later eighth century, the time that the preface was composed. Among other things, Gregory II was the pope who defied Constantinople by refusing to pay taxes on the Sicilian papal estates that fed Rome, and the pope who refused to accept the Byzantine position on iconoclasm. Gregory I, by contrast, was all but forgotten at the time, as his miniscule biography in the *Liber Pontificalis* suggests. He was forgotten with prejudice, one might say, because the Roman clergy of the early seventh century appear to have resented his arrogation of many clerical prerogatives and positions to monks, for whom he showed great partiality.[35]

Such speculations are confirmed by an acute observation about the GREGORIUS PRESUL prefaces made by the German chant scholar Bruno Stäblein.[36] It involves the oldest and the longest of the prefaces, that from the so-called Lucca Codex, an Italian chant book copied in the 780s. The

---

[34]See Peter Wagner, *Introduction to the Gregorian Melodies: A Handbook of Plainsong*, Part I [2nd ed.], trans. Agnes Orme and Edward G. P. Wyatt (London, 1901), p. 169.

[35]See Peter Llewellyn, "The Roman Church in the Seventh Century: The Legacy of Gregory I," *Journal of Ecclesiastical History* 25 (1974): 363–80.

[36]"Gregorius Praesul," pp. 552–53.

preface, which sings Gregory's praises for some thirty-two lines beyond the opening phrases given above, omits any mention of the single Gregorian achievement that remained well-known in Italy at the time, his authorship of influential books of moral theology. By contrast, the prefaces of a number of later northern books make it clear that they had Gregory I in mind by alluding to such writings; the Fleury preface, for example, seems to refer to the much-read hagiographical work, *The Dialogues*, with the words, *hic vitam scribens hominum moresque bonorum*, while the St.-Denis book appears to allude to Gregory's inspirational dove—*numerosa volumina. . . . afflatu finxit dictante superno*.[37] The most plausible explanation for this initially puzzling reversal is that the original Italian preface, while referring to Gregory II without making this explicit, was misinterpreted by Carolingian cantors as referring to Gregory I. But why ought the Carolingians to have done so? Did they have reason to assume that an unspecified Gregory must be Gregory I? It happens that they most certainly did. It was English scholars such as Alcuin of York who dominated the intellectual life of the Carolingian court, and while the memory of Gregory I was eclipsed in seventh- and eighth-century Rome, it was greatly cherished in England. He was remembered with gratitude as the pope who sent Augustine of Canterbury to convert England; the Venerable Bede mentions him on several occasions with admiration and affection.[38]

The original Gregory of the GREGORIUS PRESUL preface, then, appears to have been Gregory II. To make this assertion, however, is not the same thing as to maintain that he stood over the shoulders of the *schola cantorum* as they composed the Mass Proper, exercising a kind of papal micromanagement. An historian can claim no more than that some of the final

---

[37]"Gregorius Praesul," p. 545.

[38]The first biography of Gregory, moreover, is by an eighth-century English monk; see *The Earliest Life of Gregory the Great by an Anonymous Monk of Whitby*, ed. Bertram Colgrave (Lawrence, Kans., 1968). Interestingly enough, there is no mention of ecclesiastical music in this work.

work on the *libellus musicae artis per circulum anni* was probably carried out during his reign. And then later in the century some Roman cleric appears to have attributed the entire project to his active supervision. It remains, in any event, a curious historical circumstance indeed that the wrong Gregory is associated with that magnificent body of music we know today as Gregorian chant.

Additional Bibliography

General Works and Works of Reference

Apel, Willi. *Gregorian Chant.* Bloomington, 1958.

Crocker, Richard, and David Hiley, eds. *The New Oxford History of Music,* vol. 2, *The Early Middle Ages to 1300.* Oxford, 1990.

Hiley, David. *Western Plainchant: A Handbook.* Oxford, 1993.

Huglo, Michel. *Les Livres de chant liturgique.* Turnhout, 1988.

McKinnon, James. *Antiquity and the Middle Ages: From Ancient Greece to the 15th Century.* London, 1990.

van der Werf, Hendrik. *The Emergence of Gregorian Chant: A Comparative Study of Ambrosian, Roman, and Gregorian Chant,* 2 vols. Rochester, N.Y., 1983.

Special Studies

Jeffery, Peter. "The Introduction of Psalmody into the Roman Mass by Pope Celestine I (422–432)." *Archiv für Liturgiewissenschaft* 26 (1984): 147–65.

Martimort, Aime Georges. "Origine et signification de l'alléluia de la messe romaine." In *Kyriakon: Festschrift Johannes Quasten*, vol. 2. Ed. Patrick Granfield and Josef Jungmann. Münster in Westphalia, 1970. Pp. 811–34.

Nowacki, Edward. "The Gregorian Office Antiphons and the Comparative Method." *Journal of Musicology* 4 (1985): 243–75.

Treitler, Leo. "The 'Unwritten' and 'Written Transmission' of Medieval Chant and the Start-up of Musical Notation." *Journal of Musicology* 10 (1992): 131–91.

LITURGY AS SOCIAL PERFORMANCE: EXPANDING THE DEFINITIONS[1]

C. CLIFFORD FLANIGAN†, KATHLEEN ASHLEY,
AND PAMELA SHEINGORN

THE STUDY OF THE MEDIEVAL LITURGY has been, with a few notable exceptions, primarily an ecclesiastical subject, carried out most often by clerics or others with close connections to western liturgical churches. This is one reason that medieval liturgiology seldom has appeared in the secular university curriculum, apart from musicology, where attention is devoted almost exclusively to the musical as opposed to the verbal text. For most medievalists, in fact, liturgy is a "background" subject, one in which they are interested because it provides information necessary for the understanding of whatever they consider their "proper" subject matter. Furthermore, both the ecclesiastical and the secular study of the medieval liturgy are heavily laden with historical "data" in the narrowest sense of that term, focusing on manuscripts, paleographical issues, and "facts," often presented in a highly positivist manner.

Such studies are the indispensable base for medieval liturgiology, but by themselves they are unable to provide a point of departure that can

[1]C. Clifford Flanigan, who was commissioned to write an essay for this volume, had completed only an abstract before his untimely death. We have adapted that abstract to serve as the introduction to this paper and have carried on his project, using materials with which we are more familiar rather than those on rituals of baptism that he had intended to treat. We had many conversations with Cliff both on cultural theory and the Foy materials and had looked forward to working closely with him as one of our collaborators on the Foy project.

uncover the centrality of liturgical celebration in medieval culture. Nor can they provide a basis for making the study of the medieval ritual a subject that could occupy a central position in contemporary medieval studies. Theorizing liturgical history will enable it to assume its central position in our reading of medieval culture. Though a variety of theoretical perspectives can and should yield new understandings of the medieval liturgy, perhaps the most promising are those which grow out of cultural studies and ethnography. Indeed, these perspectives already have been invoked from time to time in handbooks of liturgical study, but all too often such evocations are discarded once one passes from introductory materials to the historical accounts that follow. Yet ethnography and cultural studies have much to contribute to a contemporary understanding of medieval ritual and its history.

At least since the time of Emile Durkheim, ethnology has emphasized the centrality of cultic practices to any understanding of a geographically or temporally alien culture. Functionalists have shown how rites, often with great subtlety, serve to perpetuate existing social organizations and gender and class differences,[2] while their more recent opponents, like Victor Turner, have qualified such claims in order to show how ritual is subversive as well as supportive of existing social structures.[3] Even more recent work has highlighted the use, rather than the production, of ritual performances and has stressed the importance of the ways that groups and individuals employ strategies and tactics to make rituals serve their own interests.[4] Seen

---

[2]See Maurice Bloch, *Ritual, History, and Power: Selected Papers in Anthropology* (London, 1989).

[3]See, among many other works, Victor Turner, *The Ritual Process: Structure and Anti-Structure* (Chicago, 1969; repr. Ithaca, 1977). See also Kathleen M. Ashley, "Introduction," in *Victor Turner and the Construction of Cultural Criticism: Between Literature and Anthropology*, ed. Kathleen M. Ashley (Bloomington, 1990), pp. ix–xxii.

[4]See, for examples, John Eade and Michael Sallnow, *Contesting the Sacred: The Anthropology of Christian Pilgrimage* (London, 1991); and Kathleen Ashley and Pamela

from these and similar perspectives, medieval liturgy, deeply embedded as it is in all manner of social "realities," becomes the arena of intense symbolic communication of the supposed and actual values of cultures and groups within them. When viewed through the optic of contemporary cultural theory, ritual practices (fully as material as they are spiritual) have much to teach us about ideology and the uses of power within specific social formations that existed at given moments in medieval history. Illuminated by such a contemporary concern, the study of the medieval liturgy will be of interest to all students of the Middle Ages as a central pole around which other subject matters and theoretical perspectives revolve in relationships that are at once centripetal and centrifugal.

In exploring these theoretical issues, and making our case for a reformulation of liturgy as social performance, we will draw our examples from the large body of surviving texts and artifacts from the saint's cult of the virgin martyr Foy.[5] Supposedly martyred in Agen in the Early Christian period, Foy's body was reportedly stolen in the ninth century by monks from the monastery at Conques, which has remained since then the center of her cult. Due to the fame of her miracles, Foy's cult spread across western Europe in the eleventh and twelfth centuries. From these multiple cult sites survives a wealth of monuments, artifacts, and texts that offers an unusually rich concentration of source materials for reconstructing the activities of the cult, including texts identified as "liturgical."[6]

Sheingorn, "An Unsentimental View of Ritual in the Middle Ages or, Sainte Foy was no Snow White," *Journal of Ritual Studies* 6 (1992): 63–85; see also arguments in our *Writing Faith: Text, Sign, and History in the Miracles of Sainte Foy* (Chicago, 1999).

[5]For an encyclopedic treatment of these texts and artifacts see A. Bouillet and L. Servières, *Sainte Foy, vierge & martyre* (Rodez, France, 1900). For a translation into English of the texts central to the cult see *The Book of Sainte Foy*, trans. and intro. Pamela Sheingorn (Philadelphia, 1995).

[6]These include the saint's *Passio*, *Translatio*, and the *Liber miraculorum sancte Fidis*, all translated into English in *Book of Sainte Foy,* trans. and intro. Sheingorn. Luca Robertini has published a new edition of the Latin text of the *Liber miraculorum* (*Liber Miraculorum*

Perhaps the most fundamental questions to be asked are what is "liturgy"? and what is excluded from the definition? Given its institutional basis in the Church, modern liturgical studies have been the preserve of scholars who identify with the point of view of the ritual specialist and have accepted the specialists' definitions of *liturgy*. A typical definition may be found in *The Concise Oxford Dictionary of the Christian Church*, where the word is defined in two ways as

> (1) all the prescribed services of the Church, as contrasted with private devotion; and (2) esp. in the E. Church, as a title for the Eucharist. In derived senses it is also used both of the written texts which order services and of the study of these.[7]

We might note a variety of ways in which this definition reinforces the authority of the ritual specialists, i.e., those whose job it is to conduct public services for the institutional Church. That authority is indicated by the term *prescribed*, and delimited with reference to texts that are "written." Thus, by implication, the ritual practices of those not in the employ of the institution or innovated rather than officially prescribed would not be considered liturgy. The acceptance of this definition within a Catholic context also has had the effect of excluding the laity, and especially women, as official liturgical practitioners. A further effect is that rituals innovated by lay practitioners have been marginalized through such terms as *para-liturgical.*

Sancte Fidis: edizione critica et commento (Spoleto, 1994), which supercedes A. Bouillet, *Liber miraculorum sancte Fidis* (Paris, 1897). Texts used in the liturgy of Sainte Foy are transcribed in Bouillet and Servières, *Sainte Foy*. There are translations into French of some liturgical pieces, as well as the version of the *Liber miraculorum* in the Sélestat manuscript (Bibliothèque Humaniste MS 22), in the *Annuaire des Amis de la Bibliothèque Humaniste de Sélestat* 44 (1994), which commemorates the 900th anniversary of the foundation of Sainte Foy's cult in Sélestat. Denis Grémont had apparently begun a study of the liturgy of Sainte Foy, but published only a preliminary article: "Le culte de Sainte Foy et de Sainte Mary Madeleine à Conques au XIe siècle d'après le manuscrit de la Chanson de Ste-Foi," *Revue du Rouergue* 23 (1969): 165–75.

[7]*The Concise Oxford Dictionary of the Christian Church*, 2nd ed., ed. Elizabeth A. Livingstone (Oxford, 1977), p. 306.

For medieval materials there has not been much explicit challenge to this definition or its implications, but here we will examine evidence from the surviving cult materials of Sainte Foy to support our arguments for expanding the definition of liturgy. In surveying the available data from this cult, it is striking to us how many ritual activities are performed by non-specialists, often lay people, and how unmarked the boundary is between "official" liturgical practice and what might be considered para-liturgical or even non-liturgical activities. Our best source for this kind of analysis is the *Liber miraculorum sancte Fidis* or *Book of Sainte Foy's Miracles*, an eleventh-century compilation of miracle stories centering on the Benedictine monastery of Conques. In the course of narrating Sainte Foy's miracles, these texts also provide ample and detailed information about ritual practices at her shrine.

The question of what constitutes a liturgical act is certainly raised by one of Foy's most typical miracles, the freeing of prisoners. We see in Book One, Chapter 31, of the *Book of Miracles* the explicit delineation of a protocol to be followed by any prisoner who has received his freedom through Foy's miraculous intervention.[8]

> One kind of miracle above others is specifically associated with Sainte Foy, for which she is best known and most highly renowned. This miracle is that she frees prisoners who cry aloud to her and orders the freed prisoners to hurry to Conques with their heavy fetters or chains to render their thanks to the Holy Savior.

The remainder of the chapter explicates the significance of these fetters, which were presented to the church of Foy and incorporated into iron doors and grills or left hanging from the ceilings as a material witness to the saint's power.[9] They even were shown on the tympanum over the main entrance to

---

[8]*Book of Sainte Foy*, trans. and intro. Sheingorn, p. 165. Subsequent citations to the *Book of Sainte Foy's Miracles* will be in the form 3.15 (Book Three, Chapter Fifteen).

[9]The narrator of the first two books of miracles, Bernard of Angers, reported in 1.31 that the miracle of freeing prisoners "kept happening with such great frequency that the immense quantity of the iron fetters they call 'bracelets' in the language of that district began to hold

the abbey church, where a carved scene representing the church's interior prominently features hanging fetters.

In the many chapters of the *Book of Miracles* that narrate episodes of the freeing of prisoners, this is exactly the protocol that is followed. For example, the monk-narrator of 3.15 tells how a prisoner who escaped with Sainte Foy's aid:

> soon carried his chains to the holy martyr's basilica and recounted to us the events I have recorded here. Then he completed a solemn vigil before the tomb of his glorious deliverer, devoutly and repeatedly offering heartfelt thanks to God and Sainte Foy.

The *Book of Miracles* provides evidence that the presentation of chains and fetters, delivering of thanks, and narrating of the miracle had a ritual quality. Prisoners might "carr[y] their chains wrapped around their necks to show their deep humility" and "make a great spectacle for all" as they entered the church (A.4); a gathering of the monks if not the general populace listened as the miracle was retold, and "all sang praises to God," while the freed prisoner offered his personal thanks to Sainte Foy (4.7). Obviously the freed prisoner protocol is more than just a spontaneous response to a miracle. It is presented in the *Book of Miracles* as a well known, reiterated set of actions to be followed at the saint's shrine in the presence of the monastic community every time Foy frees a prisoner. This obviously ritualized set of activities now is not considered "liturgical," but the *Book of Miracles* certainly suggests that we should see it as part of the expected "liturgical" response at a miracle-working saint's shrine. We conclude that liturgy during the Middle Ages was not seen as the unfolding of that which is rigidly scripted but as a flexible frame that could accommodate a wide range of human activities.

---

the monastery prisoner. Therefore the senior monks decided that this great mass of iron should be hammered out and converted into various kinds of doors by blacksmiths" (*Book of Sainte Foy*, trans. and intro. Sheingorn, p. 102).

The *Book of Miracles* itself, in 2.12, explicitly stages a kind of debate over what is properly liturgical. There an accepted distinction between lay, illiterate (i.e., non-latinate) pilgrims and clerics, who employ the sacred liturgical language of Latin, is dramatized and then exploded. The narrative also explores the difference between the written texts of the Psalms and Office and the pilgrims' oral "little peasant songs and other frivolities." In the cases of both the songs and the singers, the plot developments of the miracle story ask readers to question their definition of what is properly liturgical. The narrator first identifies with the clerical point of view—the narrow definition of liturgy—but is brought to expand that definition through the miraculous events:

> It has been a custom since the old days that pilgrims always keep vigils in Sainte Foy's church with candles and lights, while clerics and those who are literate chant Psalms and the Office of the Vigil [*clericis quidem litterarumque peritis psalmos ac vigilias decantantibus*]. But those who are illiterate relieve the weariness of the long night with little peasant songs and other frivolities [*cantlenis rusticis quam aliis nugis*]. This seemed to ruin utterly the solemn dignity and decency of the sacred vigil.

Any clear distinction between the official liturgy and lay celebration then is undercut by reference to an incident of the monastic past when the senior monks "forbade the unsuitable commotion made by the wild outcries of the peasants and their unruly singing," and barred the crowds of pilgrims from the monastery. However, in the middle of the night, "the bars of the doors were spontaneously unfastened. . . . Even the inner doors were unbarred, those that were usually kept closed in front of the shrine housing the relics in order to afford them the highest protection." The monks interpreted this as an authorizing miracle and "maintained that all these practices were valid and did not deserve censure" since they were not contrary to divine will. The miracle narrative thus rehearses a difference between monastic liturgical chant and unauthorized lay singing only to refute such a distinction; clearly a major part of its rhetorical project was to undermine the privileged status of the Latin liturgy controlled by the monks and to authorize lay and vernacular "liturgies."

In the miracle story just discussed, the liturgical context for this reformulation was the Office of Matins, which throughout the *Liber miraculorum* is one of the two most important temporal settings for the occurrence of miracles. The other especially fertile moment is Sainte Foy's feast day. The official definition of liturgy prescribes the daily and yearly order of services and thereby provides a temporal setting for highly significant events to take place, i.e., the miracles. The narratives of these miracles invite us to expand the definition of liturgy and to see lay activities as also "liturgical." As we have said, a high proportion of the miracles is triggered by the lay pilgrim coming into the presence of Sainte Foy's relics. These relics were housed in an elaborate golden reliquary-statue of the enthroned saint which stood at the high altar of the monastery church.[10] The miracle stories clearly indicate that the spot in front of the shrine was the appropriate place to petition for a miracle or to offer thanks to the saint. These rituals of petitioning and thanksgiving are integral parts of what we would consider the pilgrim liturgy at Conques. There is also a variety of especially appropriate times, the most frequently mentioned being while keeping a night vigil at the shrine and culminating at dawn, which was a particularly auspicious time for miracles to take place. Often the expectation was that the pilgrim would spend not just one but many nights at the foot of the altar, and the most auspicious day was that of the feast itself, which is mentioned in many narratives as the liturgically assigned date when miracles are more likely to happen.[11]

---

[10]See 1.32: "From the outside the basilica is made up of three forms by the division of the roofs, but on the inside these three forms are united across their width to shape the church into one body. And thus this trinity that fuses into unity seems to be a type of the highest and Holy Trinity, at least in my opinion. This right side was dedicated to Saint Peter the apostle, the left to Saint Mary, and the middle to the Holy Savior. But because the middle was in more frequent use due to the constant chanting of the Office, the precious relics of the holy martyr were moved there from the place where they had been kept." This is a description of the church at the monastery of Sainte Foy in the early eleventh century. The present church on the site was built during the later eleventh and early twelfth centuries.

[11]See, for example, 4.15, about William, a blind man hoping for a cure: "Since the feast day of

Other liturgical feast days also correlate with the performance of miracles. For example, in 2.1, Foy appears to the monk Gerbert on the night preceding the vigil of the feast of Saint Michael, which is on 29 September and thus near her own feast day of 6 October.

> For three whole months, [Gerbert] continued to keep vigil in the sanctuary through every single night, wearying everyone with his incessant outcries and scolding Sainte Foy quite insistently:
>
> O, Sainte Foy, Lady of Conques, why didn't you protect the eye you gave back to me after it had been torn out by the root? Why didn't you defend the wretched man whom you gained as a special servant because of your beneficial deed?
>
> He never stopped pressing her with persistent questions like these for the whole time until the feast of Saint Michael was at hand, and on that night preceding the vigil, behold! Sainte Foy appeared in a dream and seemed to speak to him: "To-morrow after vespers go with the procession of monks in front of the altar of Saint Michael, and there God will restore your eye to you."

The narrative comments that Gerbert listened to the divine vision and then:

> at the hour that [Foy] had commanded . . . he accompanied the procession into the chapel of Saint Michael. There, when they were singing an antiphon from the gospels in honor of the coming feast day, the heavenly Creator Whose wisdom finds nothing difficult deigned to make good the loss of that which He had made.

In this example, the official liturgical day, service, and text in honor of Saint Michael clearly are relevant to instigating the healing miracle, but just as relevant were Gerbert's own three-month vigil in the sanctuary at night and his "incessant outcries and scolding" prayers for relief. Numerous other miracles mention the noisy supplications of pilgrims before the shrine in the sanctuary, implying that they respond to a kind of ritual mandate. Should we not consider these prayers as part of the liturgical action?

---

this great virgin was drawing near, William himself went to Conques to keep the holy vigils."

A sequence of these para-liturgical actions that we would like to argue are in fact part of the medieval pilgrim's liturgy are specified in the very first miracle story, the foundational miracle of the cult (1.1). Foy tells the blind Guibert:

> ". . . if tomorrow, the vigil of my martyrdom, you go to Conques, purchase two candles, and place one in front of the altar of the Holy Savior and the other in front of the altar where the clay of my body is enshrined, you will have a proper reason to rejoice because your eyes will be wholly restored. . . ." He went to Conques, he related the vision to the monastic officials, he bought the candles, he placed them in front of the altars, and he kept the vigil near the most holy martyr's golden image. . . . But when they were singing the praises of matins he was awakened by the choir and the loud voices of those chanting the psalms, and it seemed to him that he could make out the shadowy forms of shining lamps and people moving about.

The very first miracle of the entire collection thus lays out a kind of miracle-seeker's protocol including the proper day (the vigil of Foy's feast day) the place (Conques), the purchase of candles for specific altars (Holy Savior's and Sainte Foy's), the report of the celestial vision to the monastic officials, and the keeping of night vigil near the martyr's golden reliquary, all of which are actions to be carried out by the *suppliant*, not the ritual specialist. Those actions culminate in a healing miracle during an official liturgical moment—the chanting of the psalms at Matins—so that the effect is of a seamless interweaving of both kinds of actions, lay and clerical, prescribed in visions and prescribed by texts.

Far from being the random occurrence of a miracle worked by the saint for an individual pilgrim who happens to be at her shrine, the story makes every effort to represent the event as one that is scripted by the saint at a "liturgical celebration, which, as usual, was public" [*publicam, ut fit, solemnitatem*]. It also emphasizes the necessity for the miracle recipient to take certain actions in order to elicit the act of healing. We are most definitely in a system of negotiated contracts whereby Sainte Foy expects effort before and reward after working a miracle.

The harmony of liturgical actions performed by clergy and laity is symbolized by the convergence of liturgical sites. The miracles that happened within the church were almost always located before Foy's shrine, which might have been seen as an alternative sacred location to the choir where the liturgical office was sung. However, the *Book of Miracles* explicitly demonstrates a lack of tension between the two liturgically laden sites when it notes that "because the middle [which was dedicated to the Holy Savior] was in more frequent use due to the constant chanting of the Office, the precious relics of the holy martyr were moved there from the place where they had been kept" (1.31). This rearrangement powerfully symbolizes the parity and compatibility of the liturgical Office and healing liturgies. Our reading of the *Book of Sainte Foy's Miracles* thus leads us to expand the traditional definition of liturgy to include actions now defined as "para-liturgical" because they are carried out by the laity.

Our texts also challenge any firm distinction between monastic celebrants and lay participants. A warrior from the Auvergne named Bernard, who was melancholy after losing all his hair, received a night vision from Foy, who told him:

> Do not delay to go confidently to the monastery at Conques. When you have arrived, make known to Abbot Girbert in my name that in my memory he should celebrate the divine mystery before the shrine of my body, while you stand on his left until the reading of the holy Gospel has been completed. After the offertory, when the abbot has washed his hands, collect that water. He should moisten your head, and after that you must go over to the right side of the altar (3.7).

Although here Abbot Girbert as ritual specialist is a necessary part of this liturgical action, Foy directs the bald warrior to carry out a complementary set of ritual actions ("while you stand on his left," "collect that water," "go over to the right side of the altar") that are not part of the prescribed liturgy and yet clearly are necessary to the miraculous restoration of Bernard's hair. Note that here Foy is very explicit that the liturgical celebration should take place "before the shrine of my body."

When Abbot Girbert is told about the vision "point by point," he,

> as is usually the case with spiritually advanced persons, immediately protested that he was not worthy of being involved in such a business. His resistance was finally overcome by their urgent pleas and he devoutly carried out everything he had been directed to do. The following night while Bernard was keeping vigil in holy prayers before the holy virgin's mortal remains, his scalp seemed to swell with little hairs, like the head of a newborn boy (3.7).

The warrior, a layman, is the relay between Sainte Foy and the abbot in explaining what actions must be interwoven with the scripted liturgy. The entire procedure thus includes both the traditional celebration of the Eucharist and innovative extensions, that is, the abbot's applying of the charged wash water to the warrior's head and the warrior's positioning of himself on the right side of the altar. As required by Foy, the liturgical performances of abbot Girbert and warrior Bernard result in a miracle the next night during Bernard's vigil at the saint's shrine, a location and ritual context that was, of course, not private but rather part of public worship.

The mandate to come to Foy's shrine did not cease with a miracle; rather, the beneficiary was expected to return, usually on a liturgically appropriate day such as Foy's feast day. The effect of this expectation was to construct a continuing lay liturgical community, not resident like the monks but commuters, who were ready witnesses for new miracles taking place at the shrine. The impression one gets from many of these stories is of miracles happening in the midst of noisy crowds of worshipers, and at times these groups of pilgrims appear almost indistinguishable from the monk-celebrants.

In one particularly disturbing miracle story (4.3), a five-year-old child who was abandoned by his parents suffered the putting out of his eyes by his father's enemies. The child became a beggar, living off donations from pilgrims to Foy's shrine, until one day "the inhabitants of Conques led him by the hand up to the holy virgin's altar. They eagerly requested of the highly renowned virgin that she deign to provide her customary mercy by granting a miracle for him." When his eyesight was restored:

> Everyone was filled with indescribable joy by this; the air rang mightily with their exuberant shouts; with their voices rivaling one another they made the whole

> basilica reverberate with declarations of praise. What more is there to say? The people gathered and no one of any sex or age stopped praising the holy virgin. No orator could find the words to describe their applause, their dancing. The boy was reciting the Psalmist's words, "My father and my mother have left me, but the Lord has taken me up,"[12] as the brothers carried him to the blessed virgin's holiest place. They nourished him with monastic support for the rest of his life, until death claimed what was owed, and his soul flew up to the heavenly kingdoms.[13]

In this striking text all distinction of age, sex, or occupation is erased as the whole community fuses to become liturgical celebrants in the sacred basilica. The boy himself recites the words of the psalm, thereby appropriating the task of the ritual specialist. The completeness of this transformation is signaled by the fact that he was supported by the monastery for the rest of his life.

Since women appear among these pilgrim-celebrants, extending the definition of liturgy to include this ritual would be a way of recognizing the evident participation of women in the central rituals of this High Medieval society. We notice how unmarked the boundary was between "official" liturgical practice and what is usually considered para-liturgical. For example, 3.22 relates the case of a man who had brought his paralyzed seven-year-old daughter to Conques for healing. While he was receiving the Eucharist during a Mass for the pilgrims, the little girl was miraculously cured. "When they saw this, the whole crowd standing there was filled with great joy. They sang praises to the most high God and the holy martyr, and rejoiced over such a great gift." The text sets no boundary between the Mass and the celebration of the miracle; rather, each of these interpenetrating rituals has a function—the Mass to assure the safe journey of the pilgrims and the celebration to thank God for the miracle.

The miracle texts have helped us to problematize the traditional definition of liturgical action. We turn now to the so-called *Chanson de Sainte*

---

[12]Ps. 26:10 (27:10).

[13]See also 4.1 for undifferentiated prayers to Foy and praises; an official burial service is woven together with popular mourning and celebration.

Foy, which raises the corollary question of what is a liturgical text.[14] Like the miracle stories, this Old Provençal poem was written in the eleventh century. Since it is one of the oldest extant texts in Romance vernacular, it most often has been considered from the point of view of philological history. However, Robert Clark has drawn attention to its anomalous traits; it is a "true generic hybrid" of liturgical and historical narrative genres.[15] As critics including J. W. B. Zaal have suggested on the basis of early medieval sources, readings from the Acts of the Apostles or narratives of saints' Lives were recommended reading during vigils of important feasts, and vernacular texts might even be read in church for a lay audience.[16] From his intensive codicological analysis of the manuscript context of the *Chanson*, Robert Clark argues that it was part of a manuscript produced at Conques for use on special feast days.[17]

---

[14]For a translation into English prose see "The Song of Sainte Foy," trans. Robert L. A. Clark in *The Book of Sainte Foy*, trans. and intro. Sheingorn, pp. 275–84. Clark relied upon two scholarly editions: Antoine Thomas, *La Chanson de sainte Foi d'Agen: Poème provençal du XIe siècle, édité d'après le manuscrit de Leide avec fac-similé, traduction, notes et glossaire* (1925; Paris, 1974); Ernest Hoepffner and Prosper Alfaric, *La Chanson de sainte Foy*, vol. 1, *Fac-similé du manuscrit et texte critique. Introduction et commentaire philologiques par Ernest Hoepffner*; vol. 2, *Traduction française et sources latines. Introduction et commentaire historiques par Prosper Alfaric* (Paris, 1926).

[15]Robert L. A. Clark, "Translating Saint Faith: Cult and Culture in the *Chanson de sainte Foy*," unpublished paper read at the Fourth Cardiff Conference on the Theory and Practice of Translation in the Middle Ages at Conques in France, July 26–29, 1993.

[16]Johannes Wilhelmus Bonaventura Zaal, *"A lei francesca" (Sainte Foy, v. 20): Etude sur les chansons de saints gallo-romanes du XIe siècle* (Leiden, 1962).

[17]The *Chanson* (which is untitled in the manuscript) is preserved in Leiden, Bibl. univ. MS Voss. lat. 0.60, which is only one of the four parts into which the original manuscript was dismembered. Denis Grémont reconstructed the contents, which included the *Passio*, *Translatio*, chapters from the *Book of Miracles*, an Office of Sainte Foy, the *Chanson*, and materials pertaining to the cult of Mary Magdalene. According to *Liber miraculorum sancte Fidis*, ed. Robertini (4–5), this manuscript was almost surely made at Conques. Frédéric de Gournay has suggested that the manuscript was made for a new Foy foundation at Morlaas in Béarn ("Relire la *Chanson de Sainte Foy*," *Annales du Midi* t. 107 [1995]: 397–98).

What is unusual of course is that the compendium of Latin liturgical texts includes the *Chanson de Sainte Foy*. For Clark, the employment of the vernacular does not preclude the use of this text in a variety of liturgical contexts, and he makes the argument that the poem's introduction "asserts both its clerical and its popular pedigree." Modern scholarship tends to assume that liturgical texts were in Latin before Vatican II; yet medieval practice suggests that the boundary between clerical Latin and lay vernacular texts was not so untraversable as we have thought. Perhaps the "little peasants' songs" were not so forbidden after all and, in any case, the miracle stories describe the monks intoning the praises of Foy and God in juxtaposition to pilgrims likewise singing Foy's praises (see 2.1; 1.33; 1.31; 3.23).

The examples we have given in this paper emphasize a lack of opposition between lay and clerical celebrants and the harmony of various kinds of liturgical practice. However, the discipline of cultural studies has alerted us to the technologies by which power is displayed, and we would argue that during the Middle Ages the social performance of the liturgy was one means by which social authority was constructed and maintained. The power to make the definitions and impose them on others becomes a means of displaying forms of social power. Although, as we have suggested, based on the miracle narratives, liturgical power was shared between laity and monks at Conques in the eleventh century, there were occasions on which liturgical acts were subjects of contestation between lay and monastic groups. The liturgical occasion itself might be a site for power struggles between and within many types of social groups.

Thus a castellan holding a warrior for ransom accepted the warrior's pledge that he would return to captivity and allowed him his freedom for Lent and Easter. The captive confronted his captor at the church of Sainte-Foy and "during the celebration of mass before the holy altar [the castellan] was humbly implored by the abbot and the monks and many of the faithful either to release the prisoner or to reduce his ransom" (4.7). The captive had chosen carefully the time and place for his plea, and we are reminded of the many ways in which ritual was wielded in the struggle to impose and maintain social order in the eleventh century.

For an example of contestation over the definition of liturgical events we turn to the town of Sélestat in the Alsace, where a priory of Sainte Foy was established in the late eleventh century.[18] The monks of Foy in Sélestat were considerably less powerful locally than were the monks in Conques, and their power struggles with both the town elites and the parish clergy were recurrent from the twelfth century on. For our purposes, what is most striking is that these power struggles were formulated as control over liturgical ritual. For example, in their founding documents, the monastery of Sainte Foy had been given and confirmed in its rights to provide burial sites for local townspeople and to administer the sacrament to the dying. At the end of the twelfth century, these clearly political and economic powers were contested by the local parish clergy, who presented their case to the bishop of Strasbourg; an arbitrated settlement was negotiated.[19]

Nevertheless, the relations among the monastery, parish church, and town magistrates remained conflicted. Between the thirteenth and fifteenth centuries the bourgeois of Sélestat built a new parish church very close to the priory church of Foy, and it became the site of elaborate liturgical celebrations, including numerous processions.[20] On August 14, 1401, there was an agreement between the magistracy and the rector of the parish church with regard to the liturgical feasts at which a High Mass would be sung: Christmas at the three Masses, Saint Stephen, Saint John, Holy Innocents, the octave of Christmas, all the feasts of the Holy Virgin, Palm Sunday, Maundy Thursday, Holy Saturday, Easter and the three following days, Ascension, the vigil of Pentecost, Pentecost and the three following days,

---

[18]See Kathleen Ashley and Pamela Sheingorn, "Le culte de Sainte Foy à Sélestat et à Conques: Étude comparative," *Annuaire des amis de la Bibliothèque Humaniste de Sélestat* 44 (1994): 77–83. See also Kathleen Ashley and Pamela Sheingorn, "*Discordia et lis*: Negotiating Power, Property, and Performance in Medieval Sélestat," *Journal of Medieval and Early Modern Studies* 26/3 (Fall 1996): 419–46.

[19]Paul Adam, *Histoire religieuse de Sélestat*, vol. 1: *Des origines à 1615* (Sélestat, 1967), p. 25.

[20]Ibid., p. 131.

feast of the Holy Trinity, Corpus Christi, Dedication of the Church, Saint John the Baptist, Saints Peter and Paul, Saint Mary Magdalene, Saint Laurence, Saint Michael, All Saints, Saint Martin, Saint Catherine, Conception of the Virgin, all the feasts of the Apostles, Saint Gregory, the Thursday of each Ember Days, and finally the two days when the rural chapter met at the church. Among these fifty-plus feast days, the feast of Sainte Foy is conspicuous by its absence. In 1489 a new official at the monastery, Jean de Monachis, tried to make Sainte Foy's feast day of October 6 an obligatory festival at least for the bourgeois. The magistracy protested to the bishop that they had never celebrated this feast; "it falls in the busiest season of the year and if we had to celebrate the feast then our poor commune would have a difficult time feeding itself." The clear implication of these two documents is that the cult of Sainte Foy commanded little social authority in Sélestat and its attempt to claim some such authority met with failure.

The use of liturgical activities to negotiate social power in Sélestat is strikingly demonstrated in the struggles to redefine a procession that customarily took place on Palm Sunday.[21] The whole parish went in procession to the Place Sainte Foy, where the monks of Sainte Foy and the parish clergy performed a ritual designed to mimic the flagellation of Christ. The prior of the monastery would prostrate himself, the curate or his vicar would hit the prior three times with a palm branch, saying each time, "I will strike the shepherd and the flock of sheep will be dispersed" [Mark 14:27, citing Zachariah 13:7], and then each of the two communities would return to its respective church to celebrate High Mass. This symbolic action identified the prior with Christ as he suffered his Passion and gave to the parish clergy the less desirable role of Christ's persecutors. Naturally the prior gained prestige by playing the part of Christ!

Eventually, in the early fifteenth century, parish church rectors objected to the power imbalance, vying for the right to be beaten on Palm Sunday.

---

[21]For a discussion of this incident, as well as references to primary sources, see Ashley and Sheingorn, "*Discordia et lis*."

As a result, on February 8, 1423, an agreement was signed that governed future processions. The parish procession would go, as in the past, to the church of Sainte-Foy, but the prior and the rector would take the role of Christ on Palm Sunday in alternate years. Symbolically, therefore, the parish and the monastic communities would maintain social equality, which was displayed, we note, in liturgical performance.

Traditional liturgiology, perhaps because it has defined the liturgy as a group of texts, has paid little attention to the larger social role of liturgical performance—with the obvious exception of those studying the music. Yet our medieval materials indicate clearly that the enactment of the sacred makes power structures visible. In Sélestat, this ritual of the Easter season functioned as a performance of the relative political power of the two ecclesiastical institutions and their relation to town government.

The study of church liturgy and social power by separate scholarly disciplines has diminished our understanding both of the role of liturgy and the symbolic subtlety of social dynamics. Likewise, a general twentieth-century conception of the sacred as cordoned off from either the secular or the material has impoverished severely our understanding of medieval religious culture. The Foy materials demand a reading that reintegrates the bodily into spiritual experience and acknowledges the validity of multiple performance registers. By that we mean to draw attention to the recurrent appearance of a grotesque mode in religious performance. In the miracle stories, for example, the amount of noise that accompanies prayer and petition as well as rejoicing and celebration is notable, as we saw above with Gerbert's loud three-month vigil. Yet in most cases the clamor is not represented as irrelevant to or disruptive of some sacred function, but rather essential to the liturgical act and the production of a miracle.

Modern sensibility demands, especially in a religious performance, not just one register of performance but a consistent, uninterrupted one. Yet our best descriptions of ritual experiences in the *Book of Miracles* reveal an amazing range of emotional response as well as (to us) incongruous juxtapositions of the gross and the sublime, the humorous and the serious.

Our modern understanding of religious experience has erased substantial registers of sensory and emotional response, so that we cannot recognize aspects of what would have been considered integral to a medieval liturgical moment. We might extend this point about the modern tendency to erect barriers between types of experience to textual genres as well; our modern definition of what a liturgical text must be may have blinded us to texts like the *Chanson de Sainte Foy* that, at least from the codicological evidence, had liturgical uses. Contemporary disciplinary boundaries have assigned texts dealing with heroic military activity to literary study and texts dealing with saints, martyrs, etc. to religious study. However, the *Chanson de Sainte Foy* is typical of many medieval narratives that combine those superficially incongruous subject matters. One might argue in fact that it is just this kind of combination that is most characteristic of medieval literature. It is our own contemporary categorization which demands that these two elements be separated.

As our final example of liturgical variation in mood and style we will examine a miracle story about a woman named Avigerna who had appropriated a ring promised to Sainte Foy, which then became stuck on her finger (1.22). Physicians were called in but, despite all their efforts, they were unable to reduce the swelling and alleviate her horrible suffering. For us this story typifies the incorporation of disparate modes and types of allusion: bodily and celestial; material and metaphysical; religious and military; playful and sober. Above all, there is a kind of deliberate rhetorical display in the juxtaposition of the grotesque and the elevated:

> They [Avigerna and her husband] made an open confession that they were guilty of wrongdoing and the feeble woman was led to the holy martyr's sacred reliquary. There she spent two nights keeping constant vigil; during the third, which was Sunday, the strength of the pain afflicted the suffering woman so grievously that the pitiable sound of her screams did not cease all night long. At last, when the monks were already intoning the praises of God at matins, divine mercy benevolently descended from the high-throned seat of the highest majesty. He did not allow such heavy crosses of punishment to vent their rage on human flesh any longer, nor did He wish the penitent's tears to reach the point of complete despair. For when the sorrowful woman happened to blow her nose, the ring flew off without hurting her fingers, just as if it had been hurled from the strongest siege engine, and gave a sharp crack on the pavement at a great distance. And for this reason there was a joyous celebration that Sunday, in which all the people of that

> region took part, because they saw that their compatriot and neighbor had been saved from grievous torment through the help of Sainte Foy.

This episode is presented by the *Book of Miracles* as a liturgy of healing, one which through its play of modes effects the social reintegration of the misguided woman. Despite its comic and grotesque elements, the action takes place in sacred space and is interwoven with official liturgical practice, so that the story implies synthesis of, not disjuncture between, "sacred" and "mundane." Were we to strip this narrative to the bare bones of its official liturgical components, excluding Avigerna's own ritual activities, we would surely create a cult of Sainte Foy and an experience of medieval liturgy sharply divergent from what we know of eleventh-century practice based on a reading of the *Book of Sainte Foy's Miracles*. Modern conceptions have not only cordoned off the sacred from secular concerns but also have isolated spirituality from its relations with the sensual and material realms. It seems relevant to us that during pilgrim rituals, as a visible sign that a migraine headache was being cured, "tears turned to blood, which flowed down in waves and lay in red clots on the ground" (4.15). We impoverish our understanding of medieval religious culture when we fail to include such material and bodily signs as integral parts of its rituals.

If we take an ethnographic and cultural approach, in which what has been called "liturgy" is viewed within the larger and more inclusive category of "ritual," then we can explore more fully how the liturgy could be the arena of intense communication of cultural values and negotiation of power within social formations at given historical moments. The thesis of this paper is that current working concepts about medieval liturgy need to be rethought. Liturgy needs to be understood as more than a script for church officials, a minutely detailed script whose complex development and difficult terminology too often cause our students to lose interest in the religious culture of the Middle Ages. To engage that interest and also to do justice to the historically complex realities of medieval liturgy, we need to begin viewing it as the cultural site for the most inclusive social and political as well as religious performance.

Glossary

Abboccamento. Initial marriage negotiations undertaken by the fathers or legal guardians of a couple in late medieval Rome.

Absolutio. A brief prayer typically used to mark the end or beginning of other liturgical ceremonies.

Acta martyrium. The corpus of texts that represent the narratives of the historical martyrs of the Christian Church.

Advent. The liturgical season which prepares for the **Christmas** feast.

Aedicula. A frame, as of a niche, formed by a pair of columns, piers or pilasters supporting a gable or **lintel**.

Agenda. Another name for the book called **Manuale** or **Rituale**.

Akathist Hymn. In the Orthodox **liturgy**, a hymn sung at a service dedicated to the **Theotokos** (the Blessed Virgin Mary as the mother of God) on Fridays in **Lent**.

Alleluia. A liturgical epithet of prayer from the Hebrew "Praise ye Yah."

Alma redemptoris mater. A popular Marian **antiphon**, "Gracious Mother of the Redeemer."

Ambo (pl. ambones). A raised platform from which the bishop reads the lesson and preaches; see **pulpit**.

Ambrosian. The name of the liturgical rite used in Italy, particularly Milan, before the dominance of the Roman rite and attributed to St. Ambrose.

Ambulatory. Passage around the **apse** of a **basilican** church.

Amen. A Hebrew word meaning "truly." Used at the conclusion of Christian prayers as a corporate assent.

Amulae. The jugs in which the wine brought by the faithful was held.

Anaphora. In the Orthodox liturgy, the offering of the **Eucharist**.

Annunciation. The observance on 25 March of the appearance of the angel Gabriel announcing to Mary that she would conceive and bear the son of God, Jesus Christ.

Antiphon. The alternating singing or chanting made by one side of the choir to the other; a verse sometimes sung before the recitation of the psalms or other liturgical hymns.

Antiphonary. A book (also known as "Antiphonale" or "Antiphonal") containing a collection of **antiphons**, often with the accompanying musical notation.

Apocryphal gospels. Accounts of the life of Christ composed after the canonical Gospels that depict aspects of his life before and after his resurrection. The majority of these gospels were composed between the first and third centuries.

Apostles' Creed. A public statement of faith usually attributed without evidence to the apostles. The title first appears in a letter of St. Ambrose (42.5) and was widely used in the **liturgy** of baptism (where the Nicene Creed was used in the **Mass**) from the eighth century.

Apse. A vaulted semicircular area facing the **nave** and housing the altar.

Aquamanilia. Jugs containing water used in the ritual washing of the celebrant's hands.
Arcade. A series of arches on pillars.
Architrave. A flat horizontal **lintel** spanning the tops of columns.
Arraglia. The third part of the marriage ceremony which included the vows and the bestowal of the ring that took place before a notary in the bride's home.
Aspergillum. A metal wand-like device with a handle and hollow head pierced with holes that held water used with the **situla** for sprinkling holy water.
Assumption. The **feast** that recognized the assumption of the Blessed Virgin Mary's body and soul; celebrated on the fifteenth of August.
Atrium (pl. atria). An open courtyard in the front of the church.
Axial. Situated on the axis; a central line bisecting a space.

Baldachin/Baldacchino. A freestanding or suspended canopy over an altar.
Baptisma. The Greek word meaning "immersion" from which we get the English "baptism."
Basilica. A longitudinal church with high central **nave** with **clerestory** windows, lower side aisles, and an **apse** beyond the **transept**.
Benedict of Aniane. Benedict (745?–821) was a reform minded Abbot who presented his program for reform of the Benedictines at the great council held in Aix la Chapelle in 847. He founded his first house near the Aniane River which soon became a model of monasticism and was promoted throughout the kingdom by Louis the Pious.
Benedictio. A brief verse recited or chanted in the second **nocturn** after the Lord's prayer.
Benedictus. A hymn of praise (**canticle**) frequently taken from the scripture (e.g., Luke 1:68-7) used in the **Divine Office**.
Biblia pauperum. The Latin term means "the Bible of the poor." Illustrated bibles which juxtaposed pictorial images of Old and New Testament figures in order to show the thematic relations between the types. Although there are examples from the early Middle Ages, the *Biblia pauperum* became quite popular after the invention of printing and woodblock prints.
Birth of the Virgin. Commemorated on the eighth of September, this **feast** appears to have been celebrated since the eighth century.
Breviary. A portable epitomized book devoted to the daily celebration of the **Divine Office**, originally developed by the mendicant orders.
Byzantine. A general term that refers to the culture, civilization and **liturgy** of the medieval Greek world based on its most influential city, ancient Byzantium. The Emperor Constantine transformed this port city on the Bosphorus and named it after himself, *Constantinopolis*.

Calix consecrationis (scyphus). An immense **chalice** holding the wine blessed by the pope or bishop before distribution by the celebrant.
Calix ministerialis. A **chalice** that contained the mixture of consecrated wine and water and to be given to the congregation on major **feasts** such as **Easter** Sunday.
Calix offerendae. A large **chalice** used to receive the wine offering of the community and offered in procession at the altar.
Calix sanctus. A small **chalice** used by an individual celebrant or small groups of communicants.

Campanarius. A participant in the performance of liturgical drama, like the ***Quem queritis***.

Campanile (pl. campanili). A large bell tower, sometimes detached from the building to which it belongs.

Canon of the Mass (Canon Missae). The most sacred part of the **Mass** during which the elements of bread and wine are consecrated into the body and blood of Christ. The elements of this ritual are fixed.

Canticle. From the Latin "canticulum" for a little song, a canticle is a song or hymn of praise based on the scripture and used in the **Divine Office**; see **Benedictus**. There are a total of ten canticles used in the **Liturgy**, seven taken from the Hebrew Bible and three from the Christian, e.g., **Nunc dimittis**.

Cantores. Principal singers who lead the **choir**s in liturgical singing.

Capital. The top of the column, frequently decorated under the **architrave** or **arcade**.

Capitella. Litanies composed of verses from the psalms.

Capitulum. A brief reading at the close of the hours of **Prime**, **None**, and **Vespers**. Originally a longer lesson that formed a significant part of the hour, as the hours of the Office were restructured the *capitulum* was abbreviated.

Capsa. A container to hold sacred objects, such as relics, and the Gospel Book.

Cardinal. The highest ranking church official chosen by the Pope.

Cathedra. The episcopal **throne**.

Cathedral. The church where the bishop celebrates the **liturgy** and has his residence.

Celtic/Irish. Terms that can refer to the **liturgy** and costume of the Irish Church, brought into compliance with Rome following the Synod of Whitby in 664.

Censer. The vessel that held the burning incense used in the censing of the altar and the eucharistic elements; also called the thurible or thuribulum.

Chalice. The cup-like vessel which contained the wine consecrated in the **Eucharist** liturgy.

Chancel. The eastern end of the church beyond the **crossing**.

Chi Rho. The first two Greek letters of the name Christ, often appearing on liturgical implements.

Choir. Area in front of the church reserved for clergy and singers; an organized group of singers.

Choir screen. A screen between the **choir** and the **nave** separating the clergy and the congregation.

Chord of the apse. The mid-point on the borderline of the **apse** space, often the location of an altar or a saint's shrine.

Chrismatory. A box in which the three vials of holy oils could be securely housed; see also **crismale**.

Christ in Majesty. A large image of Christ enthroned surrounded by symbols of the four **evangelists**, typically placed above the altar.

Christe eleison. The Greek words for "Christ, have mercy" enter the liturgy after the ***Kyrie eleison*** as a supplement and are in use in Rome according to Pope Gregory the Great at the end of the sixth century.

Christmas. The twenty-fifth of December has been observed as the **feast** of Christ's birth since at least the Philocalian Calendar (c. 336), evidence of **Roman** practice. Some suggest that the Christians chose this day to appropriate the festival of the birth of the Sun god *natalis solis invicti* of Mithraism. Three **Mass**es were traditionally celebrated.

Ciborium. A portable vessel (frequently silver or gold) reserved for holding the consecrated **host**; a **baldachin**.

Circumcision. The **feast** traditionally celebrated on 1 January, eight days after **Christmas,** commemorating the circumcision of Christ.

Cistercian. A reform movement begun within Benedictine monasticism by St. Robert, Abbot of Molesme at Cîteaux in the Diocese of Langres in 1098. The Cistercians wished to live the Rule of St. Benedict as literally as possible.

Clerestory. The upper story of the **nave** of a **basilica** set with windows.

Cluny. A reference to the reformed group of Benedictines who built the monastery at Cluny in Burgundy France. By the fifteenth century this house had approximately 900 dependencies. The **liturgy** at Cluny developed an elaborate ceremonial.

Collect. From the Latin verb "colligere" [to collect], these are brief petitioning prayers of the congregation spoken by the celebrant and addressed to God. They are typically offered after the "**Gloria**" before the lessons for the day.

Collecta (pl. collectae). Short prayers, often an invocation or petition traditionally found in the prayers in the celebration of the **Eucharist** before the lessons were read. In Rome the term was also used to designate a gathering of clergy and laity, particularly during **Lent**, before processing to the place where **Mass** was to be celebrated.

Commune sanctorum. A term meaning the "Common of the Saints"; lessons, **collect**s and chants designated for those **feast** days not set aside for a particular saint. The latter are celebrated on their specific feast day and called *Proprium sanctorum*.

Communicantes. The prayer in the **Canon of the Mass** which begins with this word and contains a memorial of certain especially revered saints, e.g., the Blessed Virgin and Perpetua and Felicitas.

Completuriae. Prayers used in the **secular** Office for the morning and evening hours celebrated in Spain.

Compline. The last hour of the day in the **Divine Office**, typically celebrated after sunset.

Conception of the Virgin. This **feast** for the eighth of December celebrates the idea that the Blessed Virgin Mary was free from all stain of original sin from her very conception by the grace of God. The feast has a complicated history and development. Commemorated in the Orthodox liturgy since the seventh century (Mary as *Theotokos*), it first appears in the West as early as the ninth century.

Conch. A half-dome covering the semicircular structure of the **apse**.

Confiteor. This prayer is a public confession of sins beginning "I confess to Almighty God to the Blessed Virgin Mary…." It is of considerable antiquity and appears in the west in the eighth century.

Consuetudines. A book which contained the rules and customs of a particular **diocese**, religious order or monastery.

Corona. Crown or wheel-shaped chandelier set with candle-lanterns.

Corporal. The square cloth (usually linen) on which was placed the bread and wine to be consecrated.

Corpus Christi. The feast celebrating Christ's kingship.

Crismale. A vessel that contained the holy oils used in anointings.

Crossing. The intersection of the **nave** and **transepts** of a church.

Curia. The administrative arm of a senior prelate's household, typically refers to the Papal curia.

Cursus. A term for the **Divine Office** used in the Middle Ages because of the daily patterned repetition of the services.

Dance of death. A representation in the plastic arts or in language of macabre skeletal figures threatening the end of the world. The tradition derives from the great fear that came from repeated occurrences of the Black Death in the fourteenth century.

Deacon. The clerical rank immediately below that of the priest. A related word (deaconess) referred to particular functions, typically ministry to poor, sick or women needing other help.

Deo Gratias. The Latin means "thanks be to God" was said at the end of the **Mass** after the priest said *Ite, Missa est* ["Go, the Mass is ended"].

Diaconia (pl. diaconiae). An early Christian church in Rome founded as a community welfare center, later serving as a parish church under the jurisdiction of a **cardinal**.

Diocese. An ancient administrative unit marking an area under the jurisdiction of a bishop; usually divided into parishes.

Disciplinati. Sometimes called flagellants, these were groups of lay penitents who wandered through the countryside singing hymns of praise to God and performing acts of penitential mortification, like self-mutilation.

Divine Office. The celebration of the psalms and other prayers seven times throughout the day; see individual hours: **Lauds**, **Prime**, **Terce**, **Sext**, **None**, **Vespers**, **Compline**, and **Matins**.

Dominica. The Latin for Lord's Day, i.e., **Sunday**.

Dominica de Passione. The fifth **Sunday** in Lent, called Passion Sunday.

Dominica in Palmis. See **Palm Sunday**.

Dominica Passionis. The fifth **Sunday** in **Lent**.

Dominicae Aestivales. The Sundays that follow **Pentecost** in Ordinary Time.

Doxology. The Greek term for a word of glory or a phrase of praise. In the church it typically can refer to one of four prayers in praise of the Trinity: the great doxology or the "Gloria"; the little doxology or the "Glory be to the Father…"; the words said at the conclusion of the **Canon** and, lastly, at the conclusion of certain of the canonical hours.

Dulia. The appropriate reverence and veneration to be given to the saints.

Duodecima. An evening hour in the **Divine Office** found in the **Gallican** liturgy of the first half of the sixth century.

Duplex. A reference to the solemnity of a feast; the second most solemn festival; see **totum duplex**, **semi-duplex**, and **simplex**.

Easter. The principal celebration of the Christian church celebrating the Resurrection of Christ.

Elevation. The raising of the **host** and **chalice** during the **Mass** immediately following the Consecration.

Ember Days. Four groups of three days given over to fast and abstinence, usually the Wednesdays, Fridays and Saturdays following the feasts of St. Lucy (13 Dec.), Ash Wednesday, **Pentecost** and the Exaltation of the Cross (14 Sept).

Enarxis. In the Orthodox **liturgy**, the beginning of the liturgy, including petitions, **antiphon**s and preparatory prayers.

Ephphatha. The words used in the Roman rite of baptism in which the celebrant pronounces the words "Ephphatha, that is be opened" and touches the ears and mouth of the candidate.

Epiclesis. In the Orthodox liturgy, the invocation that begins the celebration of the **Eucharist** liturgy.

Epiphany. The Greek word means to manifest. This **feast** observed on 6 January is celebrated in the Orthodox **liturgy** as a memorial of Christ's baptism. In the **Roman** rite, however, it has since the fourth century been an observance of Christ's appearance to the gentiles represented by the three Magi.

Epistle. The reading of a scriptural passage before the gospel. Although typically from the letters in the New Testament (hence "epistle"), in the early church there is evidence that readings could be taken from other biblical books, e.g., from Acts and the Old Testament.

Esonarthex. The interior part of the **narthex**.

Eucharist. The word refers to the transformed bread used in the **Mass** after it has been consecrated; from the Greek for "thanksgiving."

Euchologion. In the Orthodox **liturgy**, the book used to contain the text of the liturgies of Sts. Chrysostom, Basil and Liturgy of the Presanctified, in addition to parts of the **Divine Office** and prayers used in conferring the **sacrament**s. The euchologion contains what in the West was in the Missal, **Pontifical**, and Ritual.

Ewer. A utensil for holding holy water frequently made of glass or metal used to pour the water into the wine for the consecration.

Evangelists. The four Gospel authors, often represented by the symbols: Matthew, a winged man; Mark, a lion; Luke, a bull; and John, an eagle.

Exaltatio crucis. The **feast** of the Elevation of the Cross on 14 Sept. was celebrated to commemorate the recovery of the true cross by the Emperor Heraclius from the Persians and its exposition in Jerusalem in 629.

Exonarthex. An enclosed area immediately in front of the **facade**.

Facade. The exterior of the ecclesiastical building, frequently adorned with sculpture and painting.

Feast. A day set aside for special reverence, e.g., the Feast of St. Stephen, 26 December. Feasts can be moveable, like **Easter**, or immovable, like **Christmas**.

Feria. Days on which no significant **feast** day falls.

Fidanze. The second part of the marriage ceremony in late medieval Rome where the males from the two families draw up the marriage agreement, including dowry and set marriage dates.

Fistula. Metal straws used by the celebrant or communicant to empty the last of the consecrated wine from the **chalice**.

Flabellum (rhipidion, Gk.). A fan used to guard the **Eucharist** from pollution by flies, hair or other debris.

Gallican. The **liturgy** formerly celebrated in parts of France.

Gemellia. Shallow basins which received the water used in ritual washing.

Gloria. Also known as the "Greater Doxology" (see **Doxology**), the "Gloria" is a Christian hymn modeled on the psalms and sung after the **Kyrie**.

Gloria Patri. The lesser **doxology**; a brief prayer of praise to the Trinity.

Gradual. A set of **antiphon**s taken from the psalms sung immediately after the first Scriptural lesson. The name comes from the singing performed either on the altar steps (Latin *gradus* = step) or while ascending the **ambo**.

Grail. The vessel believed to have collected the blood from the body of the dying Christ (some thought it was also used by Christ at the Last Supper) and sent by Joseph of Arimathia.

Great "O's." Antiphons especially used during the **Advent** season, e.g., "O Eternal wisdom."

Guardian angel. An ancient idea common in paganism and Judaism that the Lord assigns to everyone an angel who looks out for our welfare and guards us from harm's way. The idea is present in the New Testament in Acts 12 and in Matthew 18:10.

Hebdomana maior. From the Greek for seven days, the phrase here refers to Holy Week.

Hierai akolouthiae. In the Orthodox **liturgy** the minor services such as the blessing of the waters on **Epiphany**.

Horae peculiares. The hours of the **Divine Office** introduced in Spain by Fructuosus of Braga in the mid-sixth century; not contained in the monastic rule written by Isidore of Seville, possibly intended for private observance.

Horologion. In the Orthodox **liturgy**, the liturgical book which contains the recurring parts of the **Divine Office**.

Hosanna. A Greek form of the Hebrew "Save, we beseech you." This greeting was given to Christ on his entry into Jerusalem on **Palm Sunday**.

Host. From the Latin *hostia*, a victim to be sacrificed and thus the bread that is consecrated in the **Eucharist**.

Hours of the Holy Cross. Sequence of seven short prayers honoring Christ's passion recited in tandem with the **Hours of the Virgin**.

Hours of the Holy Spirit. Sequence of seven short prayers honoring the attributes of the Holy spirit recited in tandem with the **Hours of the Virgin**.

Hours of the Virgin. Sequence of eight prayers in honor of the Blessed Virgin Mary recited, ideally, throughout the course of the day.

Hymnary. The book which contained the hymns used in the **Divine Office** arranged according to the liturgical year.

Icon. Images of God, the Blessed Virgin Mary and the saints often painted on wood and venerated in the Orthodox church. The flat two-dimensional image is indebted to **Byzantine** portraiture.

Improperia. See **Reproaches**.

In exitu Israel. This is an **antiphon** taken from Psalm 113 and used in **Mass**es and prayers for the dead from as early as the seventh century.

Incipit. The opening line of a reading.

Introibo. The opening words "I will enter" of the **Mass**, said by the celebrant at the foot of the altar.

Introit. The opening prayer of the **Mass.** Originally **antiphons**, psalms, and the lesser **doxology** chanted by the ***schola cantorum*** as the celebrant approached the altar.

Irish. See **Celtic/Irish**.

Ite missa est. Words announcing the ending of the **Mass**, "Go the Mass is ended."

Jubilus. The ending melisma of the setting for the alleluia respond.

Kantharos. A two-handled cup with a flaring lip, fluted bowl and tapering base. Some early medieval **chalice**s were based on this design.

Kyrie eleison. The Greek words for "Lord, have mercy" are recorded in pagan and Old Testament texts (Ps.6:3). They are recorded in the **liturgy** as early as the fourth century in Jerusalem and appear as the laity's response to the celebrant's petitions. Introduced into the beginning of the **Mass** proper in the late sixth century.

Kyrie rex splendens. A hymn of praise to the "Lord the resplendent King" sung in the last respond of the second **nocturn**.

Lady chapel. A chapel to the east of the main sanctuary, devoted to the Blessed Virgin Mary.

Laetare Sunday. The fourth Sunday in **Lent** which took its name from the words of the **Introit** for the day "Rejoice you with Jerusalem" (Is. 66:10). Some of the Lenten rigors were relaxed on this Sunday.

Lammas. Usually celebrated on 1 August when the consecrated **Eucharist** was made from the first of the wheat. The term "lammas" may derive from the early English words for loaf and **Mass**.

Latria. The appropriate reverence and veneration to be given to God.

Laude spirituali. The Latin term for spiritual songs typically sung in the vernacular languages.

Lauds. The early morning service of the **Divine Office**, usually requiring the recitation of six psalms and always Ps. 148–50 which contain frequent use of the word "laudate," hence the name.

Lectio divina. Reading from the scriptures or other pious texts, e.g., Patristic homilies, practiced first in the monastery.

Legenda sanctorum. The stories concerning the saints; sometimes collected in a volume.

Legitimae orationes. Obligatory hours of prayer first proscribed by Tertullian and based on practices mentioned in the Hebrew Bible.

Lent. The forty-day period of fasting and penitence initiated by Ash Wednesday and ending with **Easter**.

Letania maior. The great litany was celebrated on 25 April with the recitation of the **litany** during three days of penitential processions. Their introduction may have been an attempt to substitute the pagan robigalia festival (processions in the fields to beg the gods to protect the crops) on that day.

Liber sacramentorum. The liturgical volume used to assist the celebrant in the celebration of the **Mass**.

Lintel. The horizontal member supporting the **tympanum**.

Litany. A round of prayers that typically consist of a brief formula, e.g., "Blessed Mary Ever Virgin pray for us" with the particular personage changing every time but the end of the formula repeated. The clergy and the congregation take part alternately.

Lite. In the Orthodox **liturgy**, a procession of clergy and laity that walked to different "stations" where liturgies would be celebrated.

Liturgical comb. Used for the ritual combing of the hair so as to minimize the chance of pollution from hair or dandruff during the consecration; often made of ivory or bone.

Liturgy. The prayers and rituals of the worshiping church in all its different guises.

Lucernarium. An evening service in the **Gallican** rite of the **Divine Office**.

Ludus. The Latin word for dramatic presentation.

Maestà. A pictorial representation of the Virgin in Majesty surrounded by angels and supplicants.

Manuale. A book of small size (hence the name from the Latin for hand) delineating the appropriate way to administer the sacraments.

Mass. The word comes from a late Latin usage of *missio* based on the infinitive *mittere* "to send" and refers to the celebration of the sacrament of the Eucharist.

Matins. That hour of the **Divine Office** celebrated late at night, usually about 2 A.M.

Matutinaria. The chants used in the **secular** Office in Spain.

Mega Euchologion. The great prayer book of the Byzantine Greek church; see **Euchologion**.

Melismos. The icon of the infant Jesus depicted on the **paten**.

Menaia. In the Orthodox church, twelve liturgical books, one for each month, containing hymns and other texts for each **feast**-day of the month.

Mesonyktikon. In the Orthodox church, the prayer of the **Divine Office** celebrated at midnight.

Metropolitan. The title of a senior ecclesiastic, typically an archbishop ruling from a cathedral with a provincial jurisdiction.

Milanese. A term used to refer to the **liturgy** attributed to St. Ambrose celebrated in the archiepiscopal diocese of Milan and also called **Ambrosian**.

Miserere Psalm. A common designation of Psalm 50 taken from the initial word of the Latin "Miserere mei, Deus."

Missae. A term that designates groups of readings, orations, and psalmody; not to be confused with Missa, the **Mass**.

Monstrance. A substantial display case (often portable) typically made of metal with a crystal case at its center for the exhibition of the **host**.

Mosaic. Images made from glass cubes and stones set in a surface matrix.

Motet. A polyphonic vocal composition originating in the thirteenth century which combines two or three distinct melodies and texts. The lowest voice is always in Latin and based on a chant melody and its textual incipit. The higher, faster-moving, voices are often in the vernacular on topics ranging from sacred to secular.

Moveable feast. A **feast** which has no fixed date but moves as the calendar changes, e.g, **Easter** falls on the first **Sunday** after the first full moon after the vernal equinox.

Mozarabic. A term used to identify the liturgical forms used in Moorish Spain from the Arab conquest in 711 until their expulsion in 1492; a modification of the **Roman** rite.

Mysterion (pl. mysteria). In the Orthodox **liturgy** this term refers to the **sacraments**.

Narthex (pl. nartheces). The **vestibule** of a church, a transverse hall in front of the **nave**.

Natalis. A reference to the date in which a believer died as a martyr and whose birth into eternal life is celebrated on that day.

Nave. The central aisle of a church extending to the **transept**.

Navicula. A container used to hold the granular incense burned in the **thuribulum**.

Nicene Creed. The creedal formula agreed upon at the First Ecumenical Council of the Church in Nicaea in 325 attended by the Emperor Constantine and approximately 250 bishops.

Nobis quoque. The opening words in the **Canon of the Mass** of the prayer "nobis quoque peccatoribus" in which the celebrant prays that "we sinners also" can be admitted to the company of saints.

Nocturns. The prayers and readings said during **Matins**.

None. The ninth hour of the **Divine Office**, usually celebrated at 3 P.M.

Nunc dimittis. The hymn based on the gospel story of the **Annunciation** to Mary in Luke 2:29–32.

O intemerata. Prayer to the Blessed Virgin Mary.

Obsecro te. Prayer to the Blessed Virgin Mary.

Octonarium (pl. octonaria). The name given to one series of eight Sundays in ordinary time following **Pentecost**.

Odo of Cluny. Odo (878–942) was the second Abbot of Cluny and a monastic reformer. He undertook a number of sensitive diplomatic missions and was an accomplished author having written, among other things, twelve choral **antiphon**s in honor of St. Martin of Tours.

Office of the Dead. A liturgical service celebrated after the burial with the intention of reducing the deceased's time in purgatory; a service presented in a Book of Hours for private reading.

Officium Regum Trium. A liturgical representation on the **Epiphany** of the Magi processing from different areas of the church to the front altar where they gathered under a lighted chandelier representative of the star of Bethlehem.

Oikonomia. In the Byzantine Church this term refers to a judgment made based on the circumstances and needs of the parties involved, e.g, the legitimacy of a mixed marriage.

Oktoechos. In the Orthodox church, a book which contained the hymns in eight tones for the church year, except those of the **Lent**, **Easter**, and **Pentecost** seasons.

Olearea. Containers which held the three holy oils (that for catechumens, that for the sick, and the chrism, a mixture of oil and balsam used in the sacraments of baptism, confirmation and Holy Orders, and in other consecrations) blessed annually by the bishop on Maundy Thursday. See also **chrismatory** and **crismale**.

Opus Dei. The hours of the day devoted to community prayer.

Opus manum. The hours of the day dedicated to manual labor in Benedictine monasteries.

Orationes solemnes.

Ordinale. A book for the recitation of the **Divine Office** directing the celebrant to the variants in the ecclesiastical year.

Ordo (pl. ordines). A liturgical book with directions for the performance of particular liturgies.

Oremus. The Latin for "let us pray" used in a number of different moments in the **liturgy** where the laity is asked to join with the celebrant in prayer.

Orthros. In the Orthodox church a service celebrated by the priest at daybreak designed to introduce the people to the **Eucharist** liturgy and consecrate the day to the Lord.

Pall. The linen cloth which covers the **chalice**.

Palm Sunday. The Sunday in **Lent** immediately before **Easter** Sunday celebrating Jesus's triumphal entry into Jerusalem, introducing Holy Week.

Panegyreis. In the Orthodox **liturgy**, the **feast**s of the church apart from the Sundays.

Pantocrator. An icon depicting Christ in majesty frequently placed directly above the altar.

Pascha/Pesach. A term used to designate Passover and **Easter** Sunday.

Paschal lamb. A reference to Christ in the **Eucharist**.

Passio. The Latin for "passion"; usually refers to a saint's Life that narrates a saint's suffering.

Paten. Originally a dish to hold the bread for consecration, but by the eleventh century it had evolved into a small silver or gold plate which held the priest's **host** alone. Typically made from silver, they could be decorated and often had a slight depression in the middle of a diameter equal to that of the bowl of the **chalice**.

Pater noster. The Latin phrase for "Our Father," the first two words of the "Lord's Prayer."

Pax, pax brede, osculatorium. A small tablet used to transfer the kiss of peace enjoined by St. Peter (1 Pet. 5:14) on from the celebrant to other celebrants and the lay congregation.

Penitential Psalms. Psalms 6, 32, 38, 51, 102, 130 and 142. These seven psalms were recited at mournful liturgies, e.g., after Friday **Lauds** in **Lent**, and on Ash Wednesday.

Pentecost. The **feast** which celebrates the descent of the Holy Ghost on the Apostles fifty days after Christ's resurrection, possibly derived from the Jewish feast "of weeks" (see Exodus 34:22) .

Pentikostarion. In the Orthodox **liturgy**, the volume that contains the hymns for the fifty days between **Easter** and **Pentecost**.

Peregrinus. The Latin for pilgrim, the term can refer to the biblical story of Christ meeting the disciples on the road to Emmaus.

Pericope. The scriptural reading for the day.

Pietà. An image of the sorrowful Blessed Virgin Mary shown holding the dead body of her son in her lap.

Platytera. The name of the icon of the Blessed Virgin Mary, so named because she contained in her womb "the one whom the universe cannot contain." This icon was usually placed on the wall behind the altar.

Pomerium. The boundaries of a city; in particular, the sacred boundaries of ancient Rome.

Pontifical. A book with prayers and directions for services typically reserved for the bishop.

Portico or porticus. A covered arcaded walkway.

Precies maiores. The prayers that often concluded the hours of **Lauds** and **Vespers**.

Predella. The base of a large altarpiece, often painted or carved.

Presa/repetendum. The final phrase of the musical respond.

Presbyterium. The area in front of the altar reserved for the clergy, sometimes extending into the eastern part of the **nave**.

Prime. The hour of the **Divine Office** celebrated about 6 A.M.

Processionis Asinorum. A liturgical drama featuring twenty-eight prophets, an actor impersonating an ass, and a furnace. The prophets in elaborate costumes come forth into the middle of the **nave** and deliver their prophecies.

Proprium officii. The readings unique to the celebration of the **Divine Office** for a particular day.

Prothesis. In the Orthodox **liturgy**, the part of the liturgy where the celebrant prepares the gifts for the **Eucharist**.

Psallenda. The chants sung in the **secular** Office in Spain.

Psalterium currens. The monastic practice of reciting the requisite number of psalms at one hour and continuing the recitation at the next hour but with no plan to complete the Book of Psalms in a specific time.

Pulpit/pulpitum. An elevated structure reserved for reading scriptural lessons and preaching.

Purificatio/Purification of the Virgin in the Temple. The **feast** celebrated on 2 February to celebrate the purification of the Blessed Virgin Mary and the presentation of Christ in the Temple in Luke 2:21–39 forty days after his birth; also called Candlemas Day.

Pyx/pyxis. A box made to carry the consecrated **host**; came in many sizes and materials, but ivory and metals were the preferred materials.

Quadragesima. The first **Sunday** in **Lent** or a word that refers to the entire Lenten season.

Quadriporticus. The four colonnaded porticoes that envelope an **atrium**.

Quattuor tempora. Another term for **Ember days**.

Quem queritis. This Latin phrase "Whom do you seek?" formed the basis for dramatic presentations of the resurrection of Christ.

Red-letter day. An important **feast** and so marked in the liturgical calendars in red.

Regina caeli. The Marian hymn "Queen of Heaven" was composed in the twelfth century and was sung after **Compline** between **Easter** and **Pentecost**.

Regular clergy. A reference to any monastic clergy, or member of a religious order, e.g., Benedictine or Franciscan monks and nuns.

Regularis Concordia. This was a reform code (c. 970) designed to bring English Benedictine houses into some sort of uniformity. Influenced by the great St. Dunstan (c. 909–988) it was likely the work of St. Ethelwold (908–984)and was sanctioned by the Synod of Winchester.

Reproaches. The censures that the Crucified Christ addresses to his ungrateful people celebrated on Good Friday (in Latin *improperia*). Frequently chanted by a choir and with the characteristic refrain from Christ "My people what have you done to me / *Populé meus quid fecisti tibi*."

Requiem. The **Mass** for the dead.

Responsoria brevia. A short chant comprised of a respond and verse, usually sung after the Little Hours.

Responsoria prolixa. These are elaborate and often lengthy chants sung during **Matins**.

Retable. A sculptured or painted panel behind the altar.

Retrochoir. The area behind the **choir** in the eastern end of a Gothic church.

Rituale. The book which contains the prayers and formulae for the sacraments and various liturgical duties of the priest except the celebration of the **Mass** and the **Divine Office**.

Rogation days. The name comes from the Latin verb *rogare* [to ask] and refers to the days of prayer usually celebrated in the summer and associated with a supplication to protect the harvest, likely begun as an attempt to substitute for the pagan harvest ritual called Robigalia; see **Letania maior**.

Roman. The liturgical rites which emerged from Roman practice from the most ancient period of the church's history and with the growth of the importance of the papacy became the basis for all the western liturgies.

Rood. A cross or crucifix, often placed above the screen to the **choir**.

Sacrament/Sacramentum. A **liturgy** that confers on the petitioner through an external sign an interior grace conferred by God and established by Christ, e.g., Matrimony or Holy Orders.

Sacramentarium Gelasianum and Leonianum. Early sacramentaries that contain information on the celebration of parts of the **Mass** e.g., the Ordinary and martyr **feasts**, before the liturgical reforms instituted by Gregory the Great (540-604).

Salve regina. One of the four major Marian **antiphons**, the Latin "Hail Holy Queen" dates from the eleventh century and was frequently sung after the evening hour of **Compline**.

Salve sancta facies. A rhymed hymn in praise of the sacred image of Jesus.

Sanctorale. The festivals of the saints.

Sanctus. The words "Holy, Holy, Holy" meant to be an adaptation of the words of the cherubin in Isaiah (6:3). It announces the **Canon** and was frequently chanted accompanied by the ringing of a bell. Often called the "**Trisagion**" the prayer is found in the Jewish practice of the second century and was likely used in Rome in the early church.

Sarum. A term that refers to the **liturgy** celebrated in the diocese of Salisbury, hence Sarum **Use**; the cathedral of Salisbury; a modification of the **Roman** rite.

Schemá. The central prayer of the Hebrew people that begins "Hear O Israel" and affirms their belief in God's oneness and their special relation with him.

Schola cantorum. The papal **choir** in early Christian and medieval Rome; a choir that sings liturgical music.

Secular. A reference to clergy who do not belong to a religious order and who work in a more public fashion with laity. Secular clergy, unlike their monastic counterpart, do not live under a formal rule nor do they take formal vows of poverty and owe obedience to their bishops.

Semi-duplex. A **feast** that is not a solemn high feast.

Senatorium. The area in the right side of the **nave** beyond the **chancel** wings; reserved for the important male members of the congregation.

Septuagesima. The ninth **Sunday** before **Easter** and the third Sunday before **Lent**, heralding the coming of Lent. Purple vestments were worn from this time until Holy Week. The term Septuagesima meaning seventy days does not accurately reflect the number of days from this Sunday (sixty-four) but possibly arose by counting backwards from Quinquagesima Sunday which is exactly fifty days before **Easter**.

Septuagint. The most important Greek translation of the Hebrew Bible, traditionally attributed to the directive of Ptolemy Philadelphus (285–46 B.C.).

Sequence. A hymn which is sung between the gospel and the **gradual**.

Sequentionary. A song book with musical notation used in the **Mass** and the **Divine Office**.

Sexagesima. The term refers to the sixty days before **Easter** and is the second **Sunday** before **Lent** and the eighth before Easter.

Sext. The hour of the **Divine Office** celebrated about 9 A.M., sometimes called the second hour of the day.

Simplex. A simple **feast**; see **duplex**.

Situla. A small bucket used to hold holy water used in sprinkling the faithful and in other liturgical services like a **requiem**. The sprinkling was often done by using a sprig of a plant like a hyssop.

Soni. The chants used in the **secular** Office in Spain.

Speculum humanae salvationis. The "Mirror of Human Salvation" was a didactic treatise popular in the fifteenth century which made considerable use of woodblock prints.

Spolium (pl. spolia). In architecture, the reuse of ancient building materials.

Sponsus. An eleventh century play based on the biblical narrative of the wise and foolish virgins.

Stabat Mater. A hymn of the twelfth or thirteenth century recalling the sorrows of the Blessed Virgin Mary and attributed to many authors. Since the late Middle Ages it was used frequently to accompany the fourteen Stations of the Cross.

Stational Liturgy. Liturgical celebrations usually celebrated by the Pope in Rome at specified churches.

Stationes. The church or churches designated for the celebration of a papal **Mass** on a given Sunday or **feast** day in Rome.

Subdeacon. A member of the clergy but one who held the lowest of the three major orders (priest, **deacon**, and subdeacon) whose tasks often included chanting the Epistle and bringing the **chalice** and materials to the altar for consecration.

Subvenite. A prayer said at a **requiem**.

Suffragan. Any bishop in his capacity as subordinate to his archbishop.

Suffrages. Brief prayers of petition designed to help remedy the suffering of the souls in purgatory.

Sunday. From the Latin *dies solis*, a pre-Christian day dedicated to the Sun and retained in the Germanic languages as a reference to Christ, the Son of Righteousness (see Mal. 4:2); the Lord's Day.

Synaxis. In the Orthodox church, the term that referred to a gathering of the faithful for Bible reading, Communion and a meal.

Synthronon. A bench for the clergy that follows the curve of the **apse**, in the middle of which was the seat for the bishop.

Tabernaculum. A box-like receptacle (derived from the Latin "tent") which contains the Blessed Sacrament. It was placed in the middle and back of the altar and frequently is found on a side altar.

Te decet laus. A hymn of praise sung after the reading of the gospel in the hour of **Matins**.

Te Deum laudamus. An anonymous Latin hymn of praise to the Trinity, ascribed with little evidence since the ninth century to, among others, Sts. Ambrose, Augustine and Hilary. It was often sung following the fourth lesson in the third **nocturn** of **Matins**.

Temporale. Sundays that are not designated for particular **feasts**.

Terce. The hour of the **Divine Office** celebrated about 12 noon, sometimes called the third hour of the day.

Theotokos. A reference to the Blessed Virgin Mary as "God bearer."

Throne. The episcopal seat.

Thurible/thuribulum. See **censer.**

Titular churches. Early Roman churches identified by the name of the original holder of the title to a building, i.e., *titulus Clementis* (San Clemente).

Titulus (pl. tituli). The oldest places of Christian worship in Rome, later serving as a parish churches under a **cardinal**.

Totum duplex. The most solemn **feast** in the liturgical year; see **duplex**.

Trabeated. Built with horizontal **lintel**s, instead of arches.

Traductio. The final part of the marriage ceremony in which the bride leaves her parents' home, meets the groom at the church entrance, celebrates the nuptial **Mass** and returns to his home.

Transept. The transverse element separating the **nave** from the **apse** of a basilican church.

Très Riches Heures. A book of hours owned by Jean, duc de Berry, with sumptuous illuminations of the seasons and the signs of the zodiac for each month in the year.

Tribune. An arcaded gallery open to the **nave** of a church.

Triduum sacrum. The **liturgy** beginning on Holy Thursday and ending on Easter Sunday.

Triforium. In the interior elevation of a Gothic church, a passageway below the **clerestory** windows.

Trinia oratio. The introductory prayers for the **Matins** hour, typically consisting of seven penitential psalms and other brief prayers. The psalms were said in units of three and hence the name *Trinia Oratio*.

Triodion. A hymn book of "three odes" used in **Lent** and on **Easter** Sunday.

Triple-graded Calendars. Liturgical calendars with the holy days rubricated in gold, red, and black in order of their importance.

Trisagion. "Thrice Holy." The chant "Holy God, Holy and mighty, Holy and immortal, have mercy on us" was introduced from east and is part of the Roman liturgy for Good Friday.

Trope. A brief sung prayer often used to embellish specific seasonal liturgical ceremonies.

Trover. An Old French word (possibly derived from the Latin "tropare" [to compose verbal and musical pieces]) which is the etymological root on which the French "troubadour" and "trouvère" are based.

Trumeau. The central post of a portal supporting a **lintel** and **tympanum**.

Tympanum. The semicircular area between the **lintel** and the arch of a portal.

Use. A designation of the rites particular to a specific large diocese that modify the Roman Rite, e.g., the Sarum Use.

Venite. The opening Latin word of Psalm 94 "Venite exultemus domino" sung during the hour of **Matins**.

Vera icon. The Greek for "true image." The legend of St. Veronica's Veil describes a woman named Veronica (a pun on the Greek "true image") offering Christ her veil to wipe his face as he carried his cross to Calvary. In his gratitude the Lord left an impression of his face on her veil. A putative relic of the original Veil has been in Rome since the eighth century.

Vespers. The hour in the **Divine Office** usually celebrated at the end of the day and with the hour of **Lauds** the most solemn of the daily hours.

Vespertina. The chants used in the **secular** Office in Spain.

Vestibule. An entrance area.

Vexilla Regis procedunt. A hymn, composed by Venatius Fortunatus, in honor of the reception of a fragment of the True Cross. It was first sung 19 November 569 when at the request of St. Radegunde a relic of the cross was carried in procession from Tours, France to the monastery of the Holy Cross in Poitiers, France.

Visitatio Sepulchri. This is a liturgical play based on the visit of the women to Christ's Sepulchre.

Vita (pl. vitae). The Latin for life and typically applied to the biography of a saint or important figure.

Vitas Patrum. A collection of the Lives of the great monastic ascetics of the eastern deserts, e.g., Sts. Anthony, Hilarion, and Pachomius.

Westwork. A complex structure at the west end of a church consisting of a superimposed entrance, and often a **tribune** accessed by stair turrets.

Index of Medieval Manuscripts

Index of Biblical Citations

Christian Scriptures (New Testament)

Index of Modern Scholars

General Index